The Universities
and British
Industry
1850–1970

The Universities and British Industry 1850-1970

Michael Sanderson

School of Social Studies
University of East Anglia, Norwich

Routledge & Kegan Paul   London

First published 1972
by Routledge & Kegan Paul Ltd
Broadway House, 68–74 Carter Lane,
London EC4V 5EL
Printed in Great Britain by
Butler & Tanner Ltd
Frome and London
© Michael Sanderson 1972

ISBN 0 7100 7378 X

To my parents

Contents

Abbreviations

AEIC	Association for Education in Industry and Commerce
CAB	Cambridge Appointments Board confidential memoranda on visits to and interviews with firms 1919–39
CUR	Cambridge University Registry, the prefix to papers in Cambridge University archives
DNB	*Dictionary of National Biography*
EcHR	*Economic History Review*
HUC	Home Universities Conference
JC	*Journal of Careers*
JRIC	*Journal of the Royal Institute of Chemistry*
LCC	London County Council
OHMM	*Official History of the Ministry of Munitions*
RC	Royal Commission
UMIST	University of Manchester Institute of Science and Technology

Preface

This study arose from the considerable public concern in the 1960s about the universities, an important element in which was the relations of the universities with British industry. It was an issue that increasingly attracted the attention of various government reports, the CBI, the Committee of Vice-Chancellors, the Conference of the Universities of the UK, and the various professional bodies of industrial scientists and technologists. While this generated a considerable literature on the contemporary aspects of the problem, it remained relatively neglected by historians although considerable interest was beginning to be shown in other aspects of the history of higher education. Accordingly, it seemed a matter of interest and importance to consider the drawing together of the universities and industry in historical terms. Indeed, historically this phenomenon is one of quite recent origin in the long span of the history of British universities, covering scarcely more than the last hundred years. Throughout this relatively short time, industry has become highly dependent on the activities of universities, just as universities have to take account of the needs of industry in ways that would have seemed inconceivable in the mid-nineteenth century. Broadly stated, it is the purpose of this study to examine the pressures that brought the universities and industry so rapidly and closely together, how far the responses of the universities to the needs of industry changed the nature of higher education, and the various problems for both sides to which their involvement gave rise.

The research and writing of the study have been facilitated by the generosity of a number of bodies and individuals. In the early stages the Leverhulme Trust made an award which greatly helped with the costs of travel and for which I am most grateful. The bibliography indicates those librarians and archivists to whom I am indebted for assistance in my research, but I would like to thank especially Miss Heather Peek of Cambridge, Mrs J. Pingree of Imperial College and Mr Michael Cook of Liverpool. I must also thank the Librarian of the Marshall Library, Cambridge, for permission to use and to quote from Alfred Marshall's papers. Some individuals also made available private documentation. I am grateful to Professor Fisher Cassie, CBE, of Newcastle who allowed me to use his departmental record cards on past engineering students of the university. Mr R. N. Smart of St Andrews generously allowed me to use the typescripts he is preparing for a Biographical Register of Alumni of St Andrews, and Professor C. S. Whewell of Leeds made available the news-cuttings collections of the department of textile industries.

The co-operation of appointments offices in various universities has been of very great value. Mr E. A. Ovens of Sheffield, Mr J. K. Hudson of Durham, Mr A. G. Acaster of Edinburgh, and Miss Barbara Johnstone of Liverpool all made unpublished materials available. The University of Leeds Appointments Board allowed me to borrow their early MS. Register, and Mr J. G. W. Davies, OBE, gave me a complete set of the Cambridge Reports from 1899. Most important of all, however, I am particularly grateful to Mr W. P. Kirkman of the Cambridge Appointments Office for permission to use for the first time the confidential reports of the office on their visits to firms for the period 1919–39. Miss J. F. Holgate, also of Cambridge, allowed me to use the unpublished documents of the Cambridge University Women's Appointments Board.

I have also benefited from conversations with a number of people with special knowledge of certain university and industrial matters which their memory of the past was able to illuminate: Mr M. Parkin, Mr P. Stanley Briggs, Dr A. W. Chapman, Mr L. J. Lloyd, Dr A. Kent, Dr R. G. Cant and Professor A. L. Roberts were all kind enough to help in this way.

I am greatly indebted to Professor J. P. C. Roach of the University of Sheffield, Professor R. H. Campbell of the University of Stirling (formerly of the University of East Anglia), and Professor A. W. Coats of the University of Nottingham who all read substantial sections of earlier drafts of the typescript and helped with valuable criticism. Dr Roy McLeod of Sussex, Mr Michael Miller, and Mr Gerald Crompton of the University of East Anglia have also read and commented on certain parts and I am grateful to them all. I should also like to thank Mrs Margaret Richmond who typed the final typescript.

Finally the University of East Anglia provided generous study leave, secretarial help, project rooms and financial aid with travel which greatly facilitated this task and which I very much appreciate.

1
The Conditions of Involvement

'To take up the point which you have raised as to the necessity of bringing industries into touch with the Universities, I think we are there touching the root of the matter as regards industrial development.'[1]

For some six hundred years before the nineteenth century the universities of England and Scotland had fulfilled a variety of changing roles, none of which had much bearing upon industry. Throughout the Middle Ages they produced an élite skilled in canon law for the Church and the royal bureaucracy. In the sixteenth century they appealed to a gentry who saw attendance at the university as a mark of social advancement and who were willing to be turned into 'gentlemen who could be relied upon in a world constantly threatened, it was thought, by revolution'.[2] In the early and mid-seventeenth century the universities were the gateway to the professions, until the Restoration when London increasingly replaced them as the focus for medicine, law, insurance, and careers with the great trading companies. With internal reform in the early nineteenth century the universities once again became the school for gentlemen seeking to enter not only the traditional professions but also the City, banking, and perhaps most prestigiously the life of politics. But in all these changes and shifts of fashion it was never considered that the industrialist, as such, should stand beside the canon lawyer, the gentleman, or the cleric as the proper recipient and creation of a university education.

The reason for this disengagement for most of the period was the relatively slight development of industry itself. The expertise for the heavy industries of the sixteenth and seventeenth centuries, the coal, iron, and battery works, sugar boiling, alum and gunpowder, passed within an artisan class or was introduced by German miners. With

[1] Lord Haldane to G. A. Humphreys, RC *University Education in Wales*, Appendix to the First Report, Cd, 8507, 1917, pp. 193–4.
[2] Hugh Kearney, *Scholars and Gentlemen, Universities and Society in Pre-Industrial Britain 1500–1700*, p. 22.

1

textiles, quite the largest industry though still domestic in organization, skills were taught within the family and within the home. Even the most skilful of pre-industrial society professions, the master cathedral builders or ocean navigators, learnt their craft by long apprenticeship rather than as part of the formal educational process. In this pre-industrial society prior to the mid-eighteenth century this disengagement of industry from the universities is so unremarkable as to call for little comment, but more surprisingly it was to continue throughout the period of rapid industrialization of the later eighteenth and early nineteenth centuries. While the degree of 'science' in the Industrial Revolution is coming to be increasingly appreciated yet it is equally clear that the men of genius who created the industrialization—Telford, Brindley, George Stephenson, Gott, the Darbys, Boulton, Crompton, Arkwright, Wedgwood, Watt, and the rest—were not university men themselves and with the exception of the last owed almost nothing to them. In so far as science was fostered by institutions it was by the Dissenting academies and provincial scientific societies, like the Lunar Society of Birmingham, and the Literary and Philosophical Societies—notably that of Manchester. The ancient universities of Oxford and Cambridge on the other hand played virtually no part in this development. Furthermore, innovation came most commonly by the modification of existing technologies by experienced and observant men on the job unattached to any formal organization for the diffusion of science and still less involved with the universities. Cornish stationary pumping engines prompted the idea and working of the locomotive, the clock and watch makers of south Lancashire transmogrified into the cotton textile machine builders, the millwrights into contractors for shafting and gearing in the new factories, blacksmiths into spindle manufacturers, and so forth. With the Scottish universities the link was far closer. The particular prestige there of medicine and medical education and the subsequent development of chemistry as a university subject under the protection of materia medica had profoundly beneficial results for Scottish and, by migration, English industry.

University developments in England in the first half of the nineteenth century did little to bring that involvement closer. The foundation of the two original colleges of the University of London in the late 1820s might have been expected to produce an education more practically orientated than that of the ancient universities. Especially should this have been so with University College which was the creation of the Benthamite Utilitarian circle and notably Henry Brougham, the advocate of 'useful knowledge' and technical education. However, there were grave limitations on its usefulness before the mid century. Original intentions to have a chair of engineering at University College had to be abandoned because of resistance from natural philosophy, while their great chemist Thomas Graham deliberately avoided 'the temptations of technical chemistry' until his retirement in 1854. Perhaps the most significant development was engineering at King's in the 1840s under William Hoskin, the designer of the British Museum Reading Room. Of the other new foundation at Durham less need be said. It was intended as a specifically Anglican arts-oriented university with no interest in industrial science at all until the creation of its offshoot at Newcastle in the 1860s. The early days of London and Durham do little to alter the view that before the mid-nineteenth century the connections between the universities and industry in England were negligible.

As in the eighteenth century so in the early nineteenth the provision of higher scientific education took place outside the universities. The Royal Institution where Humphrey Davy and Michael Faraday lectured was perhaps the leading centre for science in England, rather than the universities. In the mid century the nearest equivalent to a university scientific education was provided by various colleges in London. The Royal College of Chemistry had been formed in 1845 under August Hofmann on the nomination of Liebig, thus injecting some of the excellence of German organic chemistry into English intellectual life. A few years later, in 1851, the Government School of Mines and Science Applied to the Arts was founded. These two provided the kind of education and catered for the kind of student who in the later part of the nineteenth century was to be the province of the civic universities.

But these institutions, enormously valuable as they were, did not obviate the need for an expanding civic universities movement for two reasons. First, even leaving industry out of account, an expansion was desirable solely on demographic grounds. The proportion of university men per population had been falling for a long time. In the early eighteenth century there had been 200 graduates per 5 million population and this had fallen to sixty-five in the decade 1855–65.[1] Within the nineteenth century with its enormous population rise the proportion of university entrants per million males aged between fifteen and twenty-five fell from 732 in 1821 to 541 by 1861.[2] On these grounds alone an expansion of university education was due in the mid century. Second, with the shift of predominance of population to the North new institutions were needed there due to the disincentive of the high costs of living away.[3] For this newly located population the London-based scientific institutions could do

[1] Charles Daubeny, *Communication to the Economic Sciences and Statistics Section of the British Association Meeting at Nottingham*, 1866.
[2] M. Greenwood, 'University Education, its Recent History and Function', *Journal of the Royal Statistical Society*, XCVIII, 1935.
[3] J. Percival, *The Connection of the Universities and the Great Towns*, and A. W. Ward, 'Is it Expedient to Increase the Number of Universities in England?', *Macmillan's Magazine*, November 1878, both stress the expense of living away from home as a motive for creating provincial universities.

little. The time was evidently ripe for the universities and industry to come together in a closer involvement, or indeed to create that involvement for the first time in their long history. It was observed, even in Scotland, in the late 1830s that 'our bankers, merchants, manufacturers, agriculturalists and civil engineers including railway engineers, lighthouse engineers, gas engineers and engineers of roads, harbours and bridges enter upon their respective professions without attending any lectures or going through any scientific system of instruction bearing directly on their pursuits.'[1] The writer added presciently, 'a change must therefore sooner or later take place in our universities'. It is the purpose of this chapter to consider the conditions that prompted that change and involvement with industry as a prelude to considering the development of the universities themselves up to the First World War.

Before this closer relationship could take place, some important and powerful assumptions had to be ignored or countered. The weight of the most articulate opinion concerning university education up to and in the mid-nineteenth century was firmly against the use of universities for vocational training as distinct from liberal education. Edward Copleston, the Provost of Oriel and the chief defender of the Oxford liberal education ideal in the early nineteenth century, while admitting the utility of 'those arts and studies which relate to the improvement of manufactures' firmly warded off the attacks of the *Edinburgh Review* by claiming that a university education should not relate to specific employments but should improve the individual by imbuing him with sound principles of policy and religion. Even William Whewell, the great mathematician of Trinity, did not believe that science was on a par with classics and mathematics as a mental discipline, and the possibility that science as a mass of observed information could be of any value to industry was not a consideration that entered his thinking.[2]

In the mid century, Newman, J. S. Mill, and Mark Pattison took their stance as the staunchest defenders of the traditional liberal education ideal. Newman pointed out that great discoveries in chemistry and electricity had not been made in the universities. On the contrary, for him the purpose of universities should be a liberal education which he defined as knowledge 'which stands on its own pretensions, which is independent of sequel, expects no complement, refuses to be informed (as it is called) by any end, or absorbed into any art'.[3] His rejection of education that is not 'independent of sequel' or 'absorbed into any art' at once seems to rule out the

---

[1] Anon, *St Andrews, As It Was and As It Is* (Cupar, 1838), pp. 170–1.
[2] Robert G. McPherson, *The Theory of Higher Education in Nineteenth Century England*, pp. 1–48.
[3] John Henry Newman, *Discourses on the Scope and Nature of University Education*, pp. 176–7, 196, 285–6.

notion of a university where training for industrial pursuits can take place; indeed such a purpose is not contemplated in his various comments on the positive function of the university. For Newman it was to produce 'a cultivated intellect, a delicate taste, a candid equitable, dispassionate mind, a noble and courteous bearing' in the individual, while in society at large it 'aims at raising the intellectual tone of society, at cultivating the public mind, at purifying the national taste, at supplying true principles to popular enthusiasm and fixed aims to popular aspiration, at giving enlargement and sobriety to the ideas of the age, at facilitating the exercise of political power and refining the intercourse of private life.' Whatever else a university ought to be doing, in Newman's view, the provision of science for industry was not among them. He accepts that 'experimentalists' and engineers may be included in the university, but the main purpose is liberal education and 'if a liberal education be good, it must necessarily be useful too'.

This liberal education view of the universities was given a more stringent statement by J. S. Mill in his famous Inaugural as Rector of St Andrews in 1867. He summed up prevalent feeling. 'There is a tolerably general agreement about what a university is not. It is not a place of professional education. Universities are not intended to teach the knowledge required to fit men for some special mode of gaining a livelihood. Their object is not to make skilful lawyers and physicians or engineers, but capable and cultivated human beings.' While he admits that engineering and 'the industrial arts' ought to be studied somewhere, the university in his view was not the place for this, on the curious grounds that 'these things are no part of what every generation owes to the next, as that on which its civilization and worth will principally depend'.[1] This was a strangely narrow and literary view of what constituted civilization so arbitrarily to exclude those feats of construction and engineering which were among the finest creations of the period. Had Mill been able to cross the Forth Bridge on his way to St Andrews for his Inaugural he would surely have been obliged to revise his views. Finally, the opinions of Mark Pattison, the Rector of Lincoln College, are worth considering for a continuation of Mill's attitudes through to the end of the 1870s. Indeed it is intriguing that Pattison's statement to the Social Science Congress in 1876 is so astonishingly an echo of Mill's words of 1867. For Pattison, 'It is no part of the proper business of a university to be a professional school. Universities are not to fit men for some special mode of gaining a livelihood; their object is not to teach law or divinity, banking or engineering, but to cultivate the mind and form the intelligence.'[2]

[1] J. S. Mill, *Inaugural Address delivered to the University of St. Andrews*, 1 Feb. 1867 (London, 1867).
[2] Cited John Sparrow, *Mark Pattison and the Idea of a University*, p. 140.

Such was the firm anti-vocational position which any movement to bring the universities and industry closer together would either have to refute or simply ignore. We need not exaggerate the importance of the old view. While its persistence kept Oxford and to a lesser extent Cambridge disengaged from industry until the 1900s it would be erroneous to suggest that these opinions presented any qualms to the men founding the technological civic universities, least of all to Josiah Mason, who specifically excluded literary subjects from his college at Birmingham. For them these arguments were not to be countered by reasoning but simply ignored. However they may have had an indirect and unfortunate effect in causing some over-reaction in colleges like Birmingham, Sheffield and Leeds which originally were more narrowly technical than Manchester and Liverpool.

But the anti-vocational liberal education position was subject to two changing pressures in the mid century. In the first place the attitudes to vocational subjects changed. The hostility to vocational education in the universities was associated with the fact that the traditionally dominant subjects—classics, pure mathematics and philosophy—were vocationally useless in any case. The defence of this 'useless' learning in arts too easily became an attack on useful learning when the sciences developed a subject matter both intellectually testing and practically applicable. However, with the advent of the Civil Service examinations and the creation of careers in the public service, especially in India, then higher education in classics became increasingly a vocational education and Pusey and Jowett in particular saw it as such.[1] If some shift towards the acceptability of vocational education could be made in the traditional arts subjects around which the liberal education defence had been woven then this made it easier to advance a similar argument for acceptance of the sciences. Second, there was a change in attitude to the sciences themselves. We have seen that Whewell, although an advocate of the sciences, did not regard them as providing the mental training of mathematics, and in the early part of the century there was much justification for this view. But with the publication of what became the great university textbooks in the sciences,[2] and the codification of a solid coherent mass of academically testing and teachable material, so this view became increasingly untenable.

The positive assertion of the rights of the sciences, and even industrial sciences, to be studied in the universities was made chiefly by Herbert Spencer and T. H. Huxley. Spencer was quite forthright in

[1] Charles C. Gillespie, 'English Ideas of the University in the Nineteenth Century' in Margaret Clapp (ed.), *The Modern University*.
[2] For example Roscoe's *Chemistry* in 1872, Thomson and Tait's *Elements of Natural Philosophy* in 1873, Clerk Maxwell's *Treatise on Electricity and Electromagnetism* in 1873.

claiming that knowledge could be graded in order of importance from that which was conducive to self preservation down to that which gratifies taste and feelings, a possible hit at Newman's 'delicate taste' as the object of university study. He deplored that there was too much stress on education for pure culture and leisure and that thereby the educational system 'neglected the plant for the sake of the flower'. Science in his view had prior claims to attention as part of that most valuable knowledge because it was necessary for self preservation, for maintaining life and health and it was in any case superior as an intellectual discipline to the arts. He also pointedly scotched the view that Mill was to repeat later, that culture and civilization did not embrace the industrial arts. For Spencer, 'that which we call civilization could never have arisen had it not been for Science'.[1] Huxley took up the themes on various occasions, especially when speaking at universities.[2] At Birmingham he supported the new scheme of education and even Mason's exclusion of literary subjects on grounds echoing Spencer, that the sciences were more useful than the classics, and for attaining 'culture' an exclusively scientific education was at least as useful as an exclusively literary one. It is interesting to see also how Huxley dealt with Mill's Inaugural. Rather than deliver a crushing refutation, he chose his own Inaugural as Rector at Aberdeen to quote verbatim a passage from Mill's speech but to insert his own words so as totally to reverse the meaning, substituting, for example 'science as an essential ingredient in education' for 'the ancient languages as our best literary education'. Of Mill, who had recently died, he spoke with respect but he made it clear by this curious exercise that he thought Mill's panegyric on the classics could be made with equal effect on the sciences. Huxley in his great advocacy of science in Victorian England was but the leading figure in a growing chorus of like minded propagandists, Sir Henry Roscoe, Lyon Playfair, the Duke of Devonshire, Bernhard Samuelson, Philip Magnus, R. B. Haldane, and others down to the outbreak of war. It was a measure of their influence that what they were saying rapidly became the banalities of almost any speech on university or industrial matters from the 1880s to the 1900s and now appears a kind of common-sense orthodoxy scarcely worth reiterating. Indeed it is now the old orthodoxy of the liberal education that needs a special defence, such as that made by John Sparrow in 1967 in his study on Pattison.

At the end of the century fresh weight was given to the new view of the functions of the university by an appeal to history. There had

---

[1] Herbert Spencer, 'What Knowledge is of Most Worth?' (1859) reprinted in F. A. Cavenagh, *Spencer on Education* (Cambridge, 1932).
[2] T. H. Huxley, *Science and Education*, collected works vol. III. See 'Science and Culture' (Address at Sir Josiah Mason's College, Birmingham, 1880) and 'Universities Actual and Ideal' (Rectorial Address at Aberdeen 1874).

been a hazy view implicit in the statements of Newman and Mill that the university had traditionally been concerned with culture and civilized values expressed in literary studies. The fact that the clientele of the universities had been well-to-do gentlemen, and that the serious work of learning a profession was largely followed in London when they had left the seats of learning, again fostered the view that the chief purpose of university life was not to train for a career but to develop less tangible faculties. This liberal education view had its historical supports neatly cut away by the great work of Hastings Rashdall on the medieval university. He pointed out that what Victorians understood by culture was unappreciated by the medieval intellect and that the medieval universities were essentially concerned with professional training for life's work, Salerno with medicine, Paris with theology, Bologna with law, and so forth. He concluded: 'we have been told that the great business of a University was considered to be liberal as distinct from professional education; we have seen that many Universities were almost exclusively occupied with professional education.'[1] Although his book was primarily a work of history Rashdall made it very clear that his conclusions had a particular relevance to his own day and to the search for a purpose for the new civic universities. He spoke, for example, at Birmingham and Liverpool repeating his view that 'the universities have been very largely places of professional education'. He urged the universities there 'to supply an education which will directly fit men for professional work' since manufacturing industry and commerce were as acceptable as objects of university study as medicine and law had been in former times.[2] Rashdall's influence was considerable and the appeal to historical tradition now became an important argument on the side of those seeking a justification of further involvement with industry and commerce.

The real factors underlying this change in attitude from the anti-vocational position stemmed from the fears of the retardation of growth and the increasing intensity of foreign competition in the British economy before the First World War. The thriving civic universities benefited from this stimulus which more than anything diminished the acceptability of the old liberal education view of the role of the universities in society. Our percentage change per decade in growth of industrial production was falling off markedly.[3]

[1] Hastings Rashdall, *The Universities of Europe in the Middle Ages*, vol. II, pt. II, pp. 707, 712–3.
[2] H. Rashdall, 'The Function of a University in a Commercial Centre', *Economic Review*, January 1902.
[3] H. W. Richardson, 'Retardation in Britain's Industrial Growth 1870–1913', *Scottish Journal of Political Economy*, XII, 1965.

1860s	33	1890s	**24**
1870s	23	1900s	9
1880s	16		

Moreover, our growth was comparing badly with that of our chief foreign competitors, the United States and Germany, and indeed with world progress in general (see Table 1).[1]

TABLE 1 *Annual rates of industrial growth*

	UK	Germany	USA	World
1860–80	2·4	2·7	4·3	3·2
1880–1900	1·7	5·3	4·5	4·0
1900–13	2·2	4·4	5·2	4·2

To a considerable extent this was scarcely surprising. It was inevitable that the superior resources of Germany and the United States should begin to be exploited, and starting from lower levels of production their rates of growth were bound to be higher. Similarly, we could not expect to continue indefinitely making the vast bulk of the world's iron and steel and cotton goods. But the coincidence of the onset of foreign competition with what was believed to be a long term world depression from the seventies to the nineties made contemporaries look upon Britain's changed position as in some way a reflection of her own weaknesses and defects. These fears had much of their origin in the traumatic experience of the 1867 Paris Exhibition. At the Great Exhibition of 1851 in London, Great Britain was awarded the palm of excellence in nearly all of the one hundred or so departments. At the 1867 Exhibition in Paris she won in only ten of the ninety departments. A professor of engineering recalled the event in suitably melodramatic terms: 'this defeat awakened England to the startling fact that the industrial sceptre was slipping from her grasp and she saw the result—her ships decaying in her harbours and the hammer falling from the hand of starving workmen.'[2] In the forefront were supposed weaknesses of technology or entrepreneurship and the panacea for some was tariffs and an end to free trade, and for others more technical and scientific education.

Changes in industrial structure also created a greater need for

[1] Surendra J. Patel, 'Rates of Industrial Growth in the Last Century 1860–1958', *Economic Development and Cultural Change*, IX, no. 3, April 1961.
[2] G. F. Armstrong, *A Lecture on the Progress of Higher Technical Instruction at Home and Abroad in Relation to the Education of Engineers* (Edinburgh, 1885) p. 6. He seems to be citing another unknown author.

higher education. If we consider those industries which were expanding and contracting in employment between 1881 and 1901, Professor Ashworth's approximate calculation suggests the following:[1]

Expanding industries with estimated amount of expansion in employment

Metals (a), engineering (b) and ship-building (c)	370,000
Mines (d) and quarries	202,000
Public utilities (e)	165,000
Paper (e), printing, and allied trades	97,000
Food (e), drink (f), and tobacco	93,000
Chemical (e) and allied trades	48,000

Contracting industries with estimated amount of contraction in employment

Textiles (g)	295,000
Clothing (g)	114,000
Miscellaneous	31,000
Leather (h), canvas, india rubber	3,000

What is interesting about this division and spread of industries from our point of view is that the rising expanding industries tended to require a higher scientific training at the top end of their labour force and this was reflected in the fact that most of their subject matter came to be dealt with by the universities in this period. With the contracting industries this was either positively not the case or was so to a much lesser extent. We can see this by considering the universities catering for the industries concerned as indicated by the alphabetical key.

(a) Metallurgy, notably Sheffield, Birmingham, Imperial College.
(b) Universally a university subject, even including Oxford by 1914.
(c) Marine engineering and naval architecture, based on university departments of high prestige, Glasgow, Newcastle, Liverpool.
(d) Mining, almost a surfeit of university departments, but notably Birmingham, Leeds, Glasgow, Newcastle.
(e) The chemical-based industries, dealt with in all universities. Some electrical engineering element in public utilities, notably London, Manchester, Liverpool.
(f) Beer, a specialized aspect of chemistry, dealt with at the brewing department at Birmingham University.

[1] William Ashworth, 'Changes in Industrial Structure 1870–1914', *Yorkshire Bulletin of Economic and Social Research*, May 1965.

(g) A subject largely neglected by the universities,[1] with the notable exception of the department at Leeds for the woollen and worsted industry and the faculty of technology at Manchester for cotton.

(h) A specialized subject dealt with at Leeds only.

It is accordingly a fair conclusion that in the changes in industrial structure in these years the expanding industries were those that required and achieved a supply of personnel and expertise from the universities and whose subject matter was scientifically interesting enough to become a part of university learning and study. Conversely, the health of these rising industries would have been seriously jeopardized had this university linkage not been forthcoming— a marked contrast to the preceding textile and clothing industries.

The closer involvement of the universities with these rising industries reflects a watershed in the sources of their technology. Around the middle of the century we find innovation in a range of industries passing from men outside universities to those either working in universities or who had benefited from university training. In thermodynamics Watt, George Stephenson, Trevithick, and Joule gave way to Rankine (Glasgow) and Parsons (Cambridge). In steel Darby, Cort, and Bessemer gave way to Gilchrist Thomas (Birkbeck College) and Sir William Siemens (Magdeburg). In metallurgy Professor Arnold of Sheffield was the direct heir of the non-university pioneers, Sorby and Hadfield, of the same city. In hydraulics George Rennie gave way to Osborne Reynolds (Manchester). In textiles the craftsmen Hargreaves and Crompton gave way to C. F. Cross and E. J. Bevan (Manchester) before the next advance could be made with synthetic fibre, changing the direction of innovation in textiles from mechanical engineering to chemistry. Finally, in electricity the great figure of Faraday was followed by a succession of university men: Wheatstone (King's College, London), Clerk Maxwell (Cambridge), Kelvin (Glasgow), Fleming (University College, London), with Swan as an unusual case by the end of the century as an electrical inventor not sprung from a university environment. And yet Swan was very closely involved with universities in his manhood as Vice-President of the Senate of University College, London, and for many years a member of the council and committee of management.[2] Even Ackroyd Stuart, the oil engine pioneer, needed to consult Nottingham University College about his work although

---

[1] Oscar S. Hall, 'Education and the Textile Industry', *Journal of the Manchester School of Technology Textile Society*, 1914, argued that textiles had been neglected in higher education and advocated more faculties of textiles in universities.

[2] M. E. S. and K. R. S., *Sir Joseph Wilson Swan, FRS: a Memoir* (London, 1923), p. 123.

he was not a university man himself.[1] The brewing industry was a further example of technology passing into the sphere of science. It has been suggested that 'little in the way of chemical knowledge was applied to brewing before the 1860s' whereas thereafter 'the emphasis which now came to be placed upon scientific analysis favoured those firms which were able to afford to employ scientifically trained brewers housed in laboratories' and these eventually became university graduates from Birmingham's brewing department established in 1900.[2] If there was a symbolic pivot in this transition it was the career of Sir Henry Bessemer. A non-university man himself, he was increasingly forced by the middle of the century to rely on people like Dr Henry, Dr Percy and earlier Dr Ure for scientific knowledge, of which his own lack of higher education had left him ignorant.[3] Bessemer's experience showed that it was becoming increasingly difficult to pursue the career of inventor independent of university expertise.

In some cases technologies passed into the sphere of university science because they ran against bottlenecks whose resolution depended on a more theoretical knowledge of adjacent disciplines. For example, in railway civil engineering, structures of greater size than experience had formerly dealt with came to be required—'the experimental side of the large subject of the strength of materials had been partially dealt with whilst the analytical side was weak and therein lay the hindrance to progress'—until Rankine's work on applied mechanics.[4] The same forced involvement was seen in the relationship between power generation and strengths of materials in the 1890s. The 1890s and 1900s were a notable period of exploding boilers and snapping shafts as the vast increase in power capable of being generated by the mechanical engineer outstripped the strengths of steel that could be provided by the metallurgist. This in turn called forth the various high speed hardened steels of manganese and vanadium compounds, a good deal of work in which was done by Arnold at Sheffield University, at the request of exasperated industrialists.

Moreover, from the mid part of the century many discoveries of industrial importance were arising from pure science and the industrialist had either to be trained in science himself or employ graduates who were. This was especially the case with the chemical and dye

[1] J. Jewkes, D. Sawers, and R. Stillerman, *The Sources of Invention* (London, 1962), p. 63.
[2] E. M. Sigsworth, 'Science and the Brewing Industry 1850–1900', *EcHR*, April 1965. Professor Sigsworth stresses that the impact of science on the industry was limited, but this does not alter the fact that much scientific research was done and a new highly educated kind of personnel needed, as he points out.
[3] Sir Henry Bessemer, *An Autobiography* (London, 1905), pp. 172, 179.
[4] W. Blackadder, 'Engineering in the University', *Aberdeen University Review*, XVII, 1929–30, pp. 12–13.

developments. Perkin's aniline mauve, Peter Griess's discovery of the azo dyes, the reds, browns and oranges, Faraday's discovery of benzene and the subsequent development of benzene compounds for drugs, Kelvin's work on electric cables and Fleming's on the valve, merely to take a few examples, were all products of high scientific intelligence and training. Consequently it required, if not the spark of insight that made the original invention, then an advanced routine higher education, to produce men who could use these inventions in industry. At this level the gadgeteer and the shrewdly observant man on the job had far less of a role to play as an inventor or even as a technical manager than he had in the late eighteenth and early nineteenth centuries. Contemporaries were well aware of this. Lowthian Bell, in conversation with Sir James Kay Shuttleworth, pointed out the watershed between the age of cotton inventions and the 1870s: 'I can quite understand that a man daily watching the action of a shuttle may raise himself to the position of an inventor; but if an improvement is to be suggested by a distinct knowledge of the chemical properties of a body . . . you will find that very few improvements indeed have emanated from uneducated men in recent times.'[1] The process was thus cumulative; as innovation became more scientific so universities were needed for the production of the rank and file scientists to manage the scientific industries. In turn the technologies of those industries were yet further developed by the research carried on by the universities themselves.

With the chemist and the electrical scientist this was evident, but there was also something of a watershed in the attitude to the education of the engineer in which the university came to play a more important role. The traditional mode of engineering training had been through apprenticeship in the workshops of some noted mechanical engineer, the offices of the Westminster civil engineers, the naval dockyards which were vital for the training of marine engineers and architects,[2] or later the workshops of the great railway companies, notably Swindon. But in the 1860s, judging by the advice given to one professor on the education of his son, some university education was thought desirable for a future engineer.[3] There were

[1] 1872 XXV RC *Scientific Instruction and the Advancement of Science* (Devonshire), Q. 9170.
[2] In 1918 eleven of the knighted naval architects and engineers had started as dockyard apprentices under the Admiralty Dockyard scheme. A. E. Berriman, 'The Engineering Pupillage and the Engineering Trade Apprenticeship' in papers of the Engineering Training Organization, 1917–20.
[3] Forbes MSS. University of St Andrews Archives. Collection of letters to J. D. Forbes and to Kelvin on behalf of Forbes from C. Heap, G. Deacon, J. T. Harrison, C. G. and W. Airy, Fleeming Jenkin, 1 July 1865–10 May 1867, on the question of the engineering education of Forbes's son. Jenkin was the exception, ironical in the light of the fact that he was shortly to become the first Professor of Engineering at Edinburgh and a defender of the role of the university in engineering education.

two distinct traditions, the English stress upon apprenticeship outside the university, and the continental which believed it possible to give virtually the whole of engineering education within colleges such as those in Zurich, Stuttgart, and Karlsruhe. Fleeming Jenkin, in his Inaugural as the first Professor of Engineering at Edinburgh, advocated a middle way—university followed by apprenticeship work—to replace the traditional training of engineers which had largely ignored the science of the universities. This wise and clear statement in 1868[1] set the pattern of the British approach to higher engineering training to this day. As engineers and academics repeated this new orthodoxy, so with the acceptance of engineering was forged one of the firmest links binding the universities and industry. With Jenkin's Edinburgh Inaugural in 1868, the advent of Sir Alexander Kennedy to University College, London, in 1874 and James Stuart to the new engineering chair at Cambridge in 1875, the late 1860s and early 1870s appeared a watershed in this regard.

This changing technology also caused some reappraisal in economic thinking which in turn resulted in greater importance being attributed to higher education. The comparative cost arguments for free trade as expounded by Adam Smith had been incontrovertible when expressed in terms of eighteenth-century commodities such as coal and wine. In these circumstances the climate and natural resources of a country were paramount in determining what it should produce and export. But in the nineteenth century many industries arose in which the possession of raw materials was of less importance than the technology with which they were worked—cottons, chemicals, the engineering industries, and notably electrical engineering. Indeed, two of the most successful nineteenth-century industries, the English cotton and German dyestuffs, were both based on imported raw materials. In these circumstances it was more often the level of training and science that was the limiting factor in a country's capacity to develop the new industries. For some this seemed to remove the validity of the free trade arguments. Since no country could have a natural advantage in, say, the electrical industry by virtue of its natural endowments, and since all countries could develop such an industry by attention to education and research, then tariffs could be meaningful to protect such an infant industry if they were reinforced by a programme of scientific education.[2] For

---

[1] Fleeming Jenkin, *A Lecture on the Education of Civil and Mechanical Engineers* (Edinburgh, 1868). See also T. Hudson Beare, *The Education of an Engineer* (Edinburgh, 1901), and Archibald Barr, *Address to Glasgow University Engineering Society* (Manchester, 1892).

[2] The theme that Britain could no longer rely on 'natural advantages' and had accordingly to develop scientific university education was a common one in university speeches. See Principal Randall's address at the Inauguration of Liverpool University, *Liverpool Mercury*, 16 January 1882; also Professor

those advocates of science like Lyon Playfair who still accepted free trade, technical education was equally imperative to enable British industry to withstand an onslaught of exports from scientifically advanced countries such as came with the 'Made in Germany' scare of the 1880s and the American 'invasion' of the late 1890s.[1]

From the 1870s there was a growing consciousness that certain areas of industry were technically or commercially backward or subject to severe foreign competition, and the recognition of these further prompted concern about the links of higher education and industry. In the steel industry our production was surpassed by the United States in 1886 and by Germany in 1893, and on the eve of the war we had become the world's largest importer of steel.[2] While much of this may be accepted as inevitable or attributed to tariffs or location or insufficient specialization, some authors are inclined to admit technological backwardness as part of the explanation. Burn[3] stresses that the advances in technical processes in the 1880s and 1890s came from outside Britain. Moreover, with the rise of the poor ore Cleveland field even more science was required than for the North West[4] and the changeover to open hearth basic steel production was hindered by the limited technical knowledge of those trying to use it.[5] In the coal industry, although we were not damaged by foreign competition, our industry was markedly less efficient than that of the Americans, with one-fifth of American coal being machine cut and only one-fiftieth of the British. Moreover, from 1880 our productivity in coal mining declined markedly and 'by comparison with this earlier period the years between 1880 and 1914 have less to show in terms of technological achievement'.[6] In the electrical industry there was considerable encroachment of foreign plant in the 1890s such that by 1898 one-third of generators in traction power houses were American. We were slow to recognize

---

William Tilden, *An Address chiefly upon the Subject of Technical Education* (Birmingham, 1882).

[1] Wemyss Reid, *Memoirs and Correspondence of Lyon Playfair* (London, 1899), p. 370. Playfair, among the advocates of scientific university education, was particularly interested in relating these views to his views on trade.

[2] P. L. Payne, 'Iron and Steel Manufactures' in D. H. Aldcroft, *The Development of British Industry and Foreign Competition 1875–1914* (London, 1968).

[3] D. L. Burn, *The Economic History of Steelmaking 1867–1939* (Cambridge, 1961), pp. 200–18.

[4] Alan Birch, *The Economic History of the British Iron and Steel Industry* (London, 1969), p. 172.

[5] W. A. Sinclair, 'The Growth of the British Steel Industry in the late Nineteenth Century', *Scottish Journal of Political Economy*, VI, 1959, p. 43.

[6] A. J. Taylor, 'The Coal Industry' in Aldcroft op. cit., and 'Labour Productivity and Technological Innovation in the British Coal Industry 1850–1914', *EcHR*, 2nd series, XIV, no. 1, 1961.

the importance of polyphase alternating current and we were not making large plant for power stations; consequently much of this had to be imported from Germany. Indeed much of British factory electrification was done by the German AEG.[1] In chemicals we clung far too long to the Leblanc process rather than adopt the Solvay as did our foreign competitors, and we virtually abandoned dyestuffs manufacture to the Germans. While we remained sound on heavy inorganic chemicals we failed to develop new lines of import replacing chemicals and our export surplus as a proportion of total exports declined sharply from the 1880s to the war.[2] Finally, in engineering our former supremacy in light machine tools passed to the Americans from the 1850s while we began to adopt their methods only from the 1890s.[3]

While these examples were but instances in an economy that was immensely strong and technically very advanced, any change from the unusual supremacy that Britain had enjoyed before 1870 appeared as a reprehensible decline and served to focus attention further on education. Accordingly the entrepreneur was blamed, his own educational background and his negligent attitude to higher education and science in the prosecution of his business.[4] While there are too many exceptions for this to be totally credible as a general explanation of retardation[5] there are also many disturbing examples of the neglect of higher education which, being publicized, were further spurs to a closer involvement of industry and the universities. The most blatant case of damage being done to industry through lack of a yet adequate university system was that of the loss of the coal-tar dye industry. W. H. Perkin recalled the circumstances in which his father abandoned the industry in 1874:[6]

inquiries were made at many of the British universities in the hope of discovering young men trained in the methods of organic chemistry, but in vain. At that time organic chemistry was scarcely recognized in the older universities and the newer universities . . . had not come into existence . . . I am strongly of the opinion

[1] I. C. R. Byatt, 'Electrical Products' in Aldcroft op. cit.
[2] H. W. Richardson, 'Chemicals' in Aldcroft op. cit.
[3] D. Burn, 'The Genesis of American Engineering Competition 1850–1870', *Economic History*, II, no. 6, January 1931. S. B. Saul, 'The Machine Tool Industry in Britain to 1914', *Business History*, X, no. 1, 1968. S. B. Saul, 'The American Impact on British Industry 1895–1914', *Business History*, III, no. 1, 1960–1.
[4] D. H. Aldcroft, 'The Entrepreneur in the British Economy 1870–1914', *EcHR*, 2nd series, XVII, no. 1, 1964.
[5] Charles Wilson, 'Economy and Society in Late Victorian Britain', *EcHR*, 2nd series, XVIII, no. 1, 1965.
[6] W. H. Perkin, 'Research Work at the University', *Manchester University Magazine*, December 1908.

that the manufacture of organic products during the important years 1870–80 was, owing to the neglect of organic chemistry by our universities, placed in a very difficult and practically impossible position.

While this was a particularly bad example of the failure of the university–industry link from the universities' side, more common was the failure of industry to employ men of higher scientific education. The great Royal Commissions of the Duke of Devonshire and Bernhard Samuelson in the 1870s and 1880s seized on these as further examples of where our backwardness could be attributed to and eradicated by education. In the early 1870s Sir William Armstrong deplored that 'there is almost a total absence of such (scientific) knowledge amongst persons who are engaged in manufactures, mines, agriculture and so on', and Professor Carey Foster of London complained that few manufacturing establishments except telegraph companies 'consider that there is any advantage in having in their service persons with a thorough knowledge of physics'.[1] In the next decade some surprising admissions were made by scientific industries and firms about their lack of employment of scientifically trained personnel. Lowthian Bell, himself a graduate and a keen advocate of technical education, considered that in the majority of iron works there were no scientifically trained men, but considered that 'before long' scientific education would be the prerequisite of such management.[2] James Kitson asserted that he did not know an ironmaster with an 'understanding of the elements of chemistry'.[3] Indeed Dr Erickson finds that for the period 1875–95 only 7 per cent of steel manufacturers had had any technical training at university or technical college.[4] In the china trade Wedgwood's confessed no use for a chemist, or indeed any research, on the grounds that it would take time and be 'a great nuisance', a curious observation from a firm whose founder had used Joseph Priestley for his chemical work. Indeed only Minton's in the trade did have a chemist.[5] It was revelations like these that prompted the icy conclusion to Samuelson's second report: 'The Englishman . . . has yet to learn that an extended and systematic education up to and including the methods of original research is now a necessary preliminary to the fullest development of industry.'[6]

[1] 1872 XXV RC *Scientific Instruction and the Advancement of Science* (Devonshire), Sir William Armstrong Q. 9204–5, and Carey Foster, Q. 7793.
[2] 1884 XXXI RC *Technical Instruction* (Samuelson), Lowthian Bell, Q. 287.
[3] D. L. Burn, *The Economic History of Steelmaking*, op. cit., p. 11. See pp. 11–12 for various instances of the neglect of scientific education.
[4] Charlotte Erickson, *British Industrialists, Stee land Hosiery 1850–1950* (Cambridge, 1959), p. 42.
[5] 1884 XXXI (Samuelson), Godfrey Wedgwood, Q. 920–1004.
[6] 1882 XXIX (Samuelson), p. 525.

The lack in Britain of a scientific graduate managerial class had forced British industry into a number of substitutions to fill in this gap. Most prominent was the use of German or Swiss chemists who were ubiquitous in British industry in the later part of the nineteenth century. The copper masters of south Wales had to get their chemists from Germany in the 1880s,[1] and German chemists were called upon to solve the biochemical problems of the nascent English canning industry before the war.[2] Read Holliday, the Yorkshire dyestuffs firm, used mostly Germans,[3] so did Morton's of Carlisle from 1909.[4] The English dye industry, such as it was, was highly dependent on Germans. Its leading chemists working in Britain—Martius, Caro, and Witt—were German. The best native firm, Levinstein's had been founded by a German émigré in 1864 and its chief innovator after Perkin, Peter Griess, the inventor of the azo dyes and the chemist of Allsopp's brewery, was also a German.[5] In chemicals, Ferdinand Hurter (the head of research at United Alkali in 1891) was from Heidelberg and his assistant from Zurich.[6] Crosfield's used German chemists until 1909[7] and Muspratt's had a Dr Jurisch from Berlin to start their laboratory in 1870.[8] In paper, Dickinson's had two German doctors as chemists within the firm in the late 1880s and another as outside consultant.[9] In short it was noted in 1919 that 'twenty years ago the research chemist qualified for industrial work could scarcely be obtained from English laboratories. He had to be imported from Germany'.[10] Less usually they were also imported for engineering. For example, when W. H. Allen originally established his great engineering works in Lambeth his first draughtsman was Gisbert Kapp from Zurich,[11] later a distinguished professor at Birmingham, and when David Brown started making gears German

[1] RC *Higher Education in Wales* (Aberdare), 1881, O. Roberts, Q. 8059.
[2] B. W. Holman, 'The British Canning Industry', *Progress and the Scientific Worker*, July–September 1933.
[3] D. S. L. Cardwell, 'The Development of Scientific Research in Modern Universities, a Comparative Study of Motives and Opportunities' in A. C. Crombie, *Scientific Change* (London, 1963), p. 673.
[4] *Fifty Years of Sundour 1906–1956* (report of an address by Sir James Morton, 1929, kindly loaned by the firm), pp. 14–15.
[5] See J. J. Beer, *The Emergence of the German Dye Industry* (Urbana, 1959), for this whole matter.
[6] D. W. F. Hardie, *A History of the Chemical Industry in Widnes* (ICI, 1950) pp. 175–6.
[7] A. E. Musson, *Enterprise in Soap and Chemicals, Joseph Crosfield and Sons, Limited, 1815–1965* (Manchester, 1966), pp. 146–7.
[8] E. K. Muspratt, *My Life and Work* (London, 1917), p. 149.
[9] Joan Evans, *The Endless Web, John Dickinson and Co. Ltd. 1804–1954* (London, 1955), pp. 138, 145.
[10] R. Blair, 'The Relation of Science to Industry and Commerce', *Nature*, 15 September 1910.
[11] H. Norman G. Allen, 'Ex Opera et Industria', Presidential Address to the Institution of Mechanical Engineers, 1965.

specialists had to be brought over to instruct the men in cutting bevel gears.[1]

The native Englishman seeking a chemical education before the rise of the civic universities had to resort to a variety of different ways of scraping an education. One way was to go to Germany to study at one of the great centres, with Liebig at Giessen or Bunsen at Heidelberg, as did the Muspratt sons Edmund and Sheridan. Virtually all the English professors of chemistry of the later part of the century had undergone this experience. Self-teaching was sometimes necessary. Edmund Muspratt taught himself assaying on his return from Germany,[2] and Walter Weldon, who worked for Gambles and discovered a new way of making bleaching powder with a greater yield of chlorine in the 1860s, was self taught in chemistry having begun life as a journalist.[3] Lectures might be attended. Henry Deacon, the only major pioneer figure in the chemical industry of the Mersey basin who was English educated,[4] went to Faraday's at the Royal Institution; John Barlow, one of the sons of one of the partners of John Dickinson, went to chemistry lectures at the Pharmaceutical Society in 1860; and John Evans, another young designated entrant to the firm, picked up some part-time lectures at University College, London, and in the United States in the 1870s.[5] These straws in the wind were indicative that there was emerging a class of people who, requiring a formal higher education in science, were having to resort to substitutes—journeys abroad, part-time lectures, self-teaching—when what ought to have been available to them in England was a formal full scientific degree course in a university. Their early careers were evidence that the time was ripe for such university expansion if the total reliance on Germany was ever to be outgrown.

There were also some rather curious managerial appointments being made at the end of the century indicative, like the German chemists and the substitute higher education of English chemists, that for lack of a native British graduate class alternatives had to be resorted to. At Shell, for example, in the 1890s heads of departments were merely promoted clerks, 'untravelled men whose experience was limited to ledgers and formal correspondence'.[6] Similarly, at Dickinson's in 1903 they appointed as export manager 'a young clerk . . . with half a dozen clerks under him as young as himself'.[7] When Marconi wanted a manager for his new firm he chose Godfrey

---

[1] Desmond Donnelly, *David Brown, the Story of a Family Business 1860–1960* (London, 1960), p. 32.
[2] Muspratt, op. cit., p. 91.
[3] Hardie, op. cit., p. 67.
[4] Ludwig Mond, Muspratt, Hurter, and Henry Brunner were all German- and Swiss-educated.
[5] Joan Evans, op. cit., pp. 113, 118.
[6] Robert Henriques, *Sir Robert Waley Cohen*, p. 85.
[7] Joan Evans, op. cit., p. 164.

Isaacs whose university education was continental not British, and who had 'no obvious qualifications for the post'.[1] Elsewhere in the electrical industry the management was foreign; American-dominated at English Electric, British Westinghouse and British Thomson Houston,[2] and German at Siemens.[3] Similarly, in the steel industry one of the reasons for the foundation of the Iron and Steel Institute in 1869 was the lack of training that forced British firms to look abroad for managers.[4]

In these last three paragraphs we have been indicating what were pathological signs of an industrial economy growing and innovating without a commensurate increase in the higher education sufficient to produce the scientists and managers to run it, hence these shifts and substitutes. It was this unsatisfactory condition that helped to give urgency to the movement to create universities and to link them to industry which by now clearly needed them.

Research within the firm, rising expecially in the 1890s, provided another important motive for industry to draw closer to the universities. This attention by British firms to research was part of the attempt to catch up with the Germans and was stimulated by the enormous research laboratories of the German chemical firms, BASF, Bayer, rising in the 1880s after the German Patent Act of 1876 and then at a phenomenal rate from the mid 1890s to the outbreak of war.[5] Moreover this rather spectacular activity with research teams of hundreds paid commercially. Of 166 companies in the German chemical industry in 1907, sixty-five paid dividends of over 10 per cent and high dividends went with the employment of large numbers of scientific experts.[6] Likewise in engineering English observers were familiar with the well-publicized laboratories of Krupp, of the Pennsylvania Railroad Company and of GEC at Schenectady. Accordingly one began to find the development of laboratories and research within British firms opening up in turn a field of activity for the science graduate. Nobel's at Ardeer in 1871, United Alkali in 1891, Burroughs Wellcome in 1894, the Cambridge Scientific Instrument Company in 1895, Ilford in 1898, Crosfield's in the 1890s and British Westinghouse just after 1899 were early starters. In the next decade or so they were followed by Rudge Whitworth (1901), the Calico Printers' Association (1902), Firth Brown (1908), Laurence Scott and the

[1] Frances Donaldson, *The Marconi Scandal* (London, 1962), p. 12.
[2] S. B. Saul, 'The American Impact', op. cit.
[3] J. D. Scott, *Siemens Brothers 1858–1958* (London, 1958).
[4] T. H. Burnham and G. O. Hoskins, *Iron and Steel in Britain 1870–1930* (London, 1943), p. 38.
[5] J. J. Beer, op. cit., Chapter VIII, 'The Rise of the Industrial Research Laboratory'.
[6] W. E. S. Turner, 'Scientific Research, Does it Pay in Business?', *Sheffield Telegraph*, 2 and 6 April 1909. Turner was the later Professor of Glass Technology at Sheffield.

Clayton Aniline Company in the 1900s and W. H. Allen in 1911. It is worth stressing this because the impression is sometimes given that virtually no research was undertaken in British industry before the war.[1]

Firms dealing with chemicals and metals tended to have laboratories to deal with routine testing, analysis and sampling of materials sent to them by suppliers and also for the examination of defects as reported by customers or arising during production. These activities imperceptibly began to merge into innovatory research preparing the way for the great expansion of this activity in the 1920s. Accordingly the firm had to turn increasingly to the universities for staff to man the laboratories. As early as 1899 all the research staff of United Alkali were graduates.[2] Graduates took over research at Crosfield's from 1907,[3] at Nobel's at Ardeer from 1909,[4] at Laurence Scott from 1910,[5] for example frequently replacing non-graduate predecessors. From the university side we can trace nine firms including only two mentioned above which took Manchester graduates specifically for research in the period 1896–1904.[6] Even Harry Brearley, perhaps the best known of this new breed of industrial researcher as the inventor of stainless steel, although not a graduate himself, attended courses at Sheffield University and had private tuition from a lecturer there.[7] It was clear that even before the war the developing field of industrial research was a further reason for industry and the universities to draw closer together.

Behind all these concerns to develop universities and improve the state of industrial science lay the fear of the menace of Germany, her education, technology, and commercial rivalry. She had been the supplier of our chemists and the resort of those seeking a chemical education, a standing reproach to our failure to develop our own universities. Matthew Arnold sounded an early admonitory note in the mid century before the civic universities had risen. By then he claimed that in Germany as a whole there was one matriculated student per 2,600 of the population compared with one per 5,800 in England. 'It is science that we have most need to borrow from the

---

[1] Sir James Dewar's evidence to the LCC Technical Education Board Subcommittee on the Application of Science to Industry, 1902, p. 19. S. H. Higgins, on the other hand, thought 'In English works a good deal of research is carried out . . .': *The Dyeing Industry* (Manchester, 1919, 3rd edition of his book first published in 1907), p. 79. (His comment was made in the 1900s.)
[2] Cited in *Statement of the Needs of the University* (Cambridge, 1899), p. 32.
[3] Musson, op. cit., p. 148.
[4] F. D. Miles, *A History of Research in the Nobel Division of I.C.I.* (ICI, 1955), p. 51.
[5] T. J. Barfield, *Scott built a Dynamo* (Norwich, n.d.), p. 28.
[6] Calculated from Reports of Manchester University, 1896–1904.
[7] Harry Brearley, *Knotted String, The Autobiography of a Steelmaker* (London, 1941).

German universities', he warned, and deplored that in England the middle business classes not only lacked the social standing of the professions but also the intellectual training in science necessary for their work. Accordingly, 'in every part of the world their [German and Swiss] men of business trained in those schools are beating the English', and he concluded by advocating presciently the formation of eight or ten provincial universities in Britain to remedy this defect.[1] Thereafter the leading protagonists of higher education expansion and technical education were all profoundly influenced by the German example[2]—Norman Lockyer and *Nature*, A. J. Mundella, Henry Roscoe, Magnus, and perhaps most of all Haldane[3] who was chiefly instrumental in the creation of Imperial College in 1907 as the English counterpart to Werner von Siemens' Physical Technical Institute at Charlottenburg, the greatest bogy of them all whose very name had become, as Arthur Shadwell put it, 'a regular Abracadabra'.

Shadwell's phrase well caught the atmosphere of childlike wonder and often irrational fear with which we regarded German higher education in those pre-1914 days. But some of this feeling was ill-founded and based upon misconceptions. In the first place, while the excellence of German chemistry was undeniable, yet beyond that the universities had many of the most conservative features of arts bias, class exclusiveness and disengagement from industry that Prussophiles despaired of in Oxford and Cambridge.[4] It was not only the university, however, that Prussophiles admired but especially the technical high schools which were in effect technological universities, indeed asserting this status in the 1900s by awarding doctorates in engineering. These had grown up from the mid 1820s and had developed specialisms—Stuttgart in engineering, Chemnitz in textiles Freiberg in mining—relating to the industries of their areas.[5] And yet for all the praise that was lavished on such institutions by such as Haldane we probably exaggerated their qualitative superiority. Sir William Siemens, who had a better right to an opinion than most on this matter, thought that the German Technical High Schools were not to be followed; they taught too much practice which their students mistook for unchanging principles; and in his view Cambridge, Owens College and King's College, London, were far better

[1] Matthew Arnold, *Schools and Universities on the Continent* (1865–7), ed. R. H. Super (Michigan, 1964).
[2] George Haines, 'The German Influence upon Scientific Instruction in England 1867–87', *Victorian Studies*, I, no. 3, March 1958.
[3] R. B. Haldane, 'Great Britain and Germany, a Study in Education' (1901), in *Education and Empire* (London, 1902).
[4] Fritz K. Ringer, 'Higher Education in Germany in the Nineteenth Century', *Journal of Contemporary History*, II, no. 3, 1967, is a good corrective.
[5] L. F. Haber, *The Chemical Industry during the Nineteenth Century* (Oxford, 1958), chapter 5, 'The New Schools of Science'.

places of higher scientific education.[1] By the 1900s whatever advantages Germany may have had in possessing these institutions seems almost totally to have vanished. The Cambridge's physics and mechanical sciences were superior to anything in Germany, so was Sheffield University's metallurgy and Birmingham's metallurgy and mining, as the Germans themselves recognized.[2] This optimistic view was amply confirmed by S. H. Higgins who was one of the best technically informed critical visitors to German industry and education in the 1900s. He found that stories of German superiority were totally exaggerated and had given 'an entirely wrong impression' to Englishmen at home.[3] Even Charlottenburg, he thought, 'suffers by comparison' with Manchester, and they had no dyeing schools as good as Manchester or Leeds. Whatever the truth of the matter, it was first the justified and then the possibly irrational fear of German education that was a most powerful sustained influence bringing together the universities and industry in Britain in these years.

On one level, however, there was no denying German superiority, and this was their capacity to turn out sheer numbers. As regards chemists in 1890 there were twice as many academic chemists in Germany as in Britain, 101 : 51, a clear German supremacy even when it is borne in mind that the British population was about three-quarters that of Germany.[4] The discrepancy became more marked at the post-graduate level. Around 1904–5 four hundred chemists received doctorates or post-graduate diplomas in Germany, whereas in Britain in 1908 there were not three hundred students of all faculties of applied science taking fourth year courses in British universities and technical colleges.[5] As regards chemists actually engaged in research there was no doubt of the superiority of the Germans. At the BASF works at Ludwigshafen in 1904 they had 195 qualified chemists and 101 engineers,[6] whereas the flow of chemists into British industry was, according to Blair, 'quite insignificant' compared with Germany. This reflected in research publications, 'some six times as many papers on chemistry were published in Germany in 1866 as in Britain and this highly unfavourable ratio was maintained until the end of the century, in 1899 some two-thirds of the world's chemical research came from Germany'.[7] As regards scientific staff in the universities we had 287 in mathematics, science, and engineering compared with 452 in Germany in 1892, again dis-

---

[1] 1884 XXXI (Samuelson), Sir William Siemens, QQ. 1415-33.
[2] Arthur Shadwell, *Industrial Efficiency, A Comparative Study of Industria Life in England, Germany and America*, vol. II, chapter XVII, pp. 434-7.
[3] Higgins, op. cit., pp. 81, 86 et seq.
[4] Cardwell, in Crombie, op. cit., p. 670.
[5] Blair, op. cit.
[6] J. J. Beer, op. cit., pp. 134-5.
[7] Cardwell, op. cit., p. 669.

proportionately low compared with the balance of our populations.[1]
As regards engineers, we were also backward compared with
Germany and especially the United States. In Germany the six
leading technical high schools contained 7,130 engineering students
compared with 1,433 in British universities.[2] Shadwell gives a figure
of 14,130 engineering students for the United States for 1906,[3] or
roughly ten times as many as in Great Britain, although the American
population was only about twice that of Britain in 1890. This could
be seen in another way. Hudson Beare estimated that the annual
output of highly educated American engineers was about one thous-
and a year whereas the British output was about two hundred,[4] giving
America five times the production of engineers with only just over
twice the population of Britain. By any criterion as a major industrial power our quantitative lag in producing scientists for industry
was plain compared with the capability of our chief competitors.

Thus far the assumptions of the discussion have been those of contemporaries, and have been namely that it was necessary to create
universities as providers of high scientific education to keep pace with
trade competitors. But the connection between higher education and
industrial competitiveness was not always so close as the Victorians
sometimes thought. In the first place it has been argued that there
was a certain inevitability about the decline of one of Britain's major
basic industries that any attention to education or science could do
little to influence. Given that Germany and the United States could
assemble the materials for steel-making as cheaply as we could and
given tariffs and their larger markets, then slight relative differences
in the quality or cost of producing steel or of the levels of higher
scientific education became irrelevant.[5] It is also interesting to
note that Lowthian Bell, although a keen advocate of technical education, in his evidence to the Samuelson commission had to admit he
was 'landed in a difficulty', as he put it, when he tried to argue any
connection between educational levels and the relative healths of
steel industries.[6]

Second, many of those industries that most effectively held their
own against the challenge of foreign competition owed relatively
little to the universities. This was the case with those defending

---

[1] Bertram C. Windle, *The Modern University* (Birmingham, 1892).
[2] T. Hudson Beare, *The Education of an Engineer* (Edinburgh, 1901).
[3] Shadwell op. cit., p. 439.
[4] *Report of the Committee on Education and Research in Aeronautics*, 1920,
Cmd. 554. Note on p. 6.
[5] Peter Temin, 'The Relative Decline of the British Steel Industry 1880–1913'
in H. Rosovsky, *Industrialisation in Two Systems* (New York, 1966).
[6] 1884 XXXI (Samuelson), Q. 280. P. W. Musgrave, in *Technical Change, The
Labour Force and Education, a Study of the British and German Steel
Industries 1860–1964* (London, 1967), argues the importance of education, but
for this industry we find Temin's argument the more convincing.

themselves against the American 'invasion' of the 1890s and the turn of the century. It was true of bicycles where 'the deliberate employment of technically educated, managerial personnel was the exception rather than the rule'.[1] The same was the case with the highly successful shoe industry where BUSMC machinery maintained technical parity between producers.[2] On the other hand, there could be drawbacks in industries based on engineering which concentrated too much on technical personnel and ignored the scientifically trained graduate. For example, in the motor car industry which employed few graduates 'the industry was quite unable to release itself from the traditional ways of engineering' and was too dominated by the mechanic as opposed to the engineer.[3] But in spite of the 'inevitability' of the decline of the steel industry and the successful retaliation of industries like bicycles and shoes, the weight of other evidence suggests that technical change and trade competition required the graduate and were powerful forces moving the universities and industry together.

As well as changing technology increasing the need of industry for the graduate and drawing him there, the changing scale of organization also played its part. This was put succinctly in 1912:[4]

> there has been a great development of the businesses conducted by a limited company and the size of those companies is increasing very much and so there is more difficulty in finding men for their top posts . . . that might be one reason why there is a change of feeling with regard to the use of the more highly educated man, that the system of promotion from the office boy of 16 has rather broken down in some of these large concerns.

Rather surprisingly, Mr Waterfield of the Oxford University Appointments Office, to whom this suggestion was put, admitted that he had not considered that argument before, but his counterpart, H. A. Roberts at Cambridge, was quite certain that this was so. 'The explanation of the employment of the graduate in commerce may be put in a very few words. It arises from the tendency to the formation of great organizations and the use of capital in the mass.'[5] Frank Taylor of the Linotype and Machinery Company also appealed

[1] A. E. Harrison, 'The Competitiveness of the British Cycle Industry 1890–1914', *EcHR*, 2nd series, XXII, no. 2, 1969. Mr Harrison gives some interesting examples of graduates in the industry who were exceptional.
[2] Roy A. Church, 'The Effect of the American Export Invasion on the British Boot and Shoe Industry 1885–1914', *Journal of Economic History*, June 1968.
[3] S. B. Saul, 'The Motor Industry in Britain to 1914', *Business History*, V, no. 1, 1962.
[4] 1913 XVIII RC *Civil Service*, Appendix to the Third Report, Minutes of Evidence, Q. 18829.
[5] H. A. Roberts, 'Education in Science as a Preparation for Industrial Work', *Journal of the Royal Society of Arts*, 1 March 1912, p. 424.

for graduates on the grounds that the modern corporation conducts enterprise 'on so large a scale' that it needs university men,[1] and Haldane likewise saw it as a function of the universities 'to provide the kind of education that would impart qualities' necessary for 'the control of great business organizations'.[2]

The process of the formation of the very large firm in British industry had gone much less far than in the United States, partly because the creation here of legal arrangements permitting the formation of joint stock companies with limited liability in the mid century 1844–62, did not coincide with a period of rapid formation of urban markets. Nevertheless, a spell of cheap money beginning in 1894 led to a surge of formations of limited companies during 1893–7, followed in the next four years by an 'enormous burst' of very large amalgamations in textiles, brewing, iron and steel, cement, wallpaper, and tobacco, the first two accounting for most of the very large firms. But the merger movement made comparatively little headway in steel where reorganizations tended to be vertical integrations of steel and engineering and shipbuilding, as with Vickers, John Brown's and Cammell Laird's in the 1890s. Thus by 1905 a number of very large firms with capitals of £2 million and over had come into being.[3]

The very large firm was attractive to the graduate partly because of the range of opportunity for advancement the size of its structure offered, but also because it might be expected to avoid the understandably nepotistic characteristics of family firms. This is not to make a criticism of the family firm arrangement for many very good firms like Bibby's, Cadbury's, W. H. Allen's and a host of leather-producing and using firms sent their sons to the university generation after generation even if they were the only graduates the firm employed. There was little point in the graduate without family connections seeking to make his way in such an organization. As a recent study of Winchester schoolboys has observed, 'the less formal recruitment and promotion system of private business accommodated greater opportunities for nepotism than did public service bureaucracy'.[4] Moreover, these authors considered that nepotism was becoming a more important factor in success than formerly. In these circumstances it is not surprising that graduates with only their professional qualification behind them sought firms where management was divorced from ownership and whose scale and impersonality gave them the characteristics and attractions of the Civil Service.

---

[1] Frank H. Taylor, *The Need of Educated Men in Industrial Affairs.*
[2] R. B. Haldane, *Universities and National Life.*
[3] P. L. Payne, 'The Emergence of the Large Scale Company in Great Britain 1870–1914', *EcHR*, 2nd series, XX, no. 3, 1967.
[4] T. J. H. Bishop and Rupert Wilkinson, *Winchester and the Public School Elite* (London, 1967), pp. 188–9.

How significant was this, and was it the large firms that the early graduates entered? Taking Professor Payne's list of the leading fifty-two firms in 1905 we find that they provide the percentages of employment for graduates entering industry; shown in Table 2. Where the figures are most consistently comparable at Birmingham and Sheffield it would seem that the very large firm became more important in the total pattern of employment in the 1900s to the war. This indeed is the period in which these large units were being formed in any case. Moreover, just below the very largest firms with their capitalization of around £2 million and above were the other stalwart graduate employers which recur from university to university— British Westinghouse, BTH, Levinstein, Tate's sugar, Crosfield, Kynoch, Rowntree, Pilkington, Hadfield, C. A. Parsons, and Mather and Platt, all either household names in their own right or well recognized as backbone firms of the capital goods industries.

TABLE 2 *Percentages of graduates entering industry recruited by the leading 52 firms of 1905*

	1900–4	*1904–9*	*1910–13*
Birmingham[1]	0	11·1	17·6
	1898–1906	*1904–9*	
Manchester chemists[2]	11·5	7·7	
	1900–12	*1913–14*	
Sheffield[3]	3·7	28·6	

[1] Calculated from University of Birmingham Register of Graduates (1932 edition) names A–J inclusive.
[2] Calculated from Reports of Manchester University Department of Chemistry.
[3] Calculated from lists in *Floreamus*.

There were two other factors pulling university men into industry, especially from the 1890s, namely the scholarship system and most important of all the revival of business activity. From 1891 a scheme worked out by Lyon Playfair was operated to use the finances of the Commissioners of the Exhibition of 1851 for science scholarships. Students who had finished their first degrees could hold scholarships for work in laboratories in universities or other institutions on branches of science 'the extension of which is especially important for our national industries'.[1] This orientation of advanced study towards industry bore fruit and between 1891 and 1906, 262 scholarships were awarded, of whose holders seventy-six were working in manu-

[1] Wemyss Reid, *Memoirs and Correspondence of Lyon Playfair* (London, 1899), p. 443.

facturing firms or public departments, and of the 112 chemistry scholars, fifty had been or were working in industrial chemistry.[1]

The final element pulling the graduate into industry was the marked recovery of business after the Great Depression from the 1870s to the early 1890s. The quickening pace of the industrial economy was undeniable. Hoffman's index of industrial production moved forward thirty points in the seventeen years 1896–1913 whereas it had taken twenty-seven years after 1869 to make an advance of the same magnitude.[2] Moreover, Hoffman's index underestimates the importance of miscellaneous consumer industries that were thriving in these years and the growth in the period of the 1890s and after was probably even faster than this index would indicate.[3] The revival of industry and what must have been a rising level of profitability after the doldrums of the depression were important factors drawing the graduate into this new occupation. Evidence that this was so in the cases of Oxford, Birmingham, Newcastle, and Bristol is considered more fully in later chapters.[4]

Thus far we have been considering various factors explaining why it was necessary for the universities, their graduates and industry to draw closer largely in terms of the 'pull' that industry could exert over the graduate. But there were two other factors 'pushing', so to speak, first the graduate and then the universities in the direction of industry; namely, the fear of overcrowding in the professions and the financial dependence of the universities.

There had been a considerable expansion of middle-class education in the two or three decades before 1870 followed by the growth of the civic universities from the 1870s. Yet the increase of middle-class traditional liberal professional employment did not match this extension of middle-class education. The three major professions—Church, law and medicine—increased only modestly compared with the expansion of the new scientific professions and the business-clerk class, while there was a more rapid development of lower middle-class than upper professional occupations from the 1870s to 1914.[5]

---

[1] R. Blair, 'The Relation of Science to Industry and Commerce', *Nature*, 15 September 1910.
[2] B. R. Mitchell and P. Deane, *Abstract of British Historical Statistics* (Cambridge, 1962), p. 271. The index referred to excludes building.
[3] Charles Wilson, 'Economy and Society in the Late Victorian Britain', *EcHR*, 2nd series, XVIII, no. 1, 1965, makes this point. See also Janet Blackman and Eric Sigsworth, 'The Home Boom of the 1890s', *Yorkshire Bulletin of Economic and Social Research*, May 1965.
[4] For Oxford in chapter 2 and for the civic universities in chapter 4.
[5] F. Musgrove, 'Middle Class Education and Employment in the Nineteenth Century', *EcHR*, 2nd series, XII, no. 1, 1959–60. Professor H. Perkin, however, convincingly indicates that Musgrove over-estimated the expansion and also contests the view that the professions were overcrowded. *EcHR*, 2nd series XIV, no. 1, 1961.

Moreover, commercial occupations grew faster than professional ones, for example:[1]

	1871	*Thousands*	1911
Professional occupations	204		413
Commercial occupations	212		739

To a considerable extent the overspill of those who would otherwise have gone into professions was able to find a new outlet in the Civil Service and the overseas Empire, but at home widening opportunities in business and industry beckoned. Sir Herbert Morgan, on the eve of the war, saw the problem clearly and urged graduates to get into industry rather than embark on a career 'struggling in the overcrowded ranks of some learned profession'.[2] Whatever the intrinsic attractions of business and industry as a career, the graduate found himself pushed to consider them by these non-industrial factors.

Finally there were also 'push' factors operating on some universities, forcing them into a closer liaison with industry. For most universities this did not apply since the civic universities began with industrial money, had always been dependent on it and throughout this time were closely orientated to industry as will be seen. However, the most striking case of reorientation to industry forced on by financial considerations was that of Cambridge. At the turn of the century Cambridge was in dire need of finance, especially for its scientific departments.[3] Apart from substantial help from Rothschild's, it drew next to nothing from industrial firms who were noted for their massive support of the civic universities.[4] The Chancellor, the Duke of Devonshire, saw clearly why this was. 'In the long run the old universities must respond to national wants or they will dwindle and become insignificant. Hence the opinions of great capitalist and commercial men are of importance.'[5] A secret meeting was held at which Cambridge's failure to tap the benefits of links with industry was freely discussed and most speakers agreed to make a 'new departure' to 'gain the confidence' of business.[6] Just as overcrowding in the professions pushed the graduate in the direction of industry so did a weak financial position do the same for Cambridge.

[1] B. R. Mitchell and P. Deane op. cit., p. 60.
[2] H. E. Morgan, *The Dignity of Business* (London, 1914), p. 10.
[3] *Statement of the Needs of the University, Pt II Scientific Departments*, (Cambridge University Association, 1899).
[4] 'Benefactions to the University to December 1902' in Papers of Sir George Darwin 1897–1904, Cambridge University Archives.
[5] Letter, Duke of Devonshire to the Vice-Chancellor, 12 May 1903, in ibid.
[6] MS. Report of a Conference convened by His Grace the Chancellor in the Combination Room of Trinity College, Saturday, 13 June 1903, in Darwin's Papers, op. cit.

In this introductory chapter we have been considering those factors that made it necessary and possible for industry and the universities to become more closely involved with each other. An attack had been made on the literary view of a liberal education. The unease of declining growth over a period when the sources of technology were passing from men of empirical genius to higher education, reflected in the changing attitude to engineering education in the 1860s, and the unease over signs of technical backwardness in certain industrial sectors, prompted a greater concern for science and education. It was also evident that we were relying too much on substitutes, on German chemists or on sending our own men to German universities, or on promotion from the ranks of clerks. These and the haphazard ways in which industrialists who stayed at home had to scrape a scientific education, were all indicative that the time was ripe by the 1860s and 1870s for the creation of a system of English universities orientated to industry. Most formally the rise of research in the 1890s and 1900s and the use of British as opposed to German graduates were most obvious aspects of this need. Over all these considerations of technology brooded the example of Germany and her education, which, justified or not, generated a fear and envy that was to be a powerful stimulus to our own integration of industry and education. In the 1890s and 1900s the rise of the large company and also the rapid revival of business activity were powerful forces drawing the graduate into the firm while the overcrowding of the professions created a surplus more willing to consider this relatively new graduate career. Finally, financial difficulties and a feeling of isolation pushed universities not hitherto involved with industry more in that direction as a condition of vitality if not survival.

With these general considerations of the forces underlying the closer involvement of the universities and industry before 1914, we should turn now to a consideration of the universities themselves, beginning with the most disengaged of all, Oxford and Cambridge.

2
Oxford, Cambridge and Industry 1850-1914

'That the ancient universities are keeping the Nation back there cannot be a doubt.'[1]

In 1899 Lord Rothschild stood in the Senate House at Cambridge and, part in whimsy but much in earnest, told a few home truths to the assembled dons seeking both his money and his moral support.[2]

> He was afraid that there was a hazy notion abroad that the University of Cambridge, like the sister University of Oxford was composed of an aggregation of Colleges where the Master and Fellows had taken monastic vows; where they were far removed from the world; where they spent their time in more or less abstruse studies; where the undergraduates usually followed their example, but if they were not so disposed were educated as athletes or gladiators.

This other-worldy image, though not totally justified, was one which Cambridge in particular was trying to shake off around the turn of the century as part of a long process of adjustment to the new demands on higher education posed by the commercial world. Traditionally Oxford and Cambridge were the natural resort for the complete education of the Anglican gentleman and the normal prerequisite for preferment in Church and public life. But this traditional purpose meant that at least in the mid century they were peculiarly unsuitable places for the education necessary to meet the henceforth increasing demands of industry and business life.[3] Both universities were faced with the problem of whether to take account of these new industrial

[1] H. E. Armstrong, 'The Place that Chemistry must take in Public Esteem', Address to Manchester University Chemical Society, 1906.
[2] The Cambridge Appointments Association, Report of a Meeting held 4 November 1899.
[3] J. P. C. Roach, 'The Victorian Universities and the National Intelligensia', *Victorian Studies*, December 1959.

developments in their own educational provision. Cambridge tried to do so with some success, but Oxford scarcely at all. Thus, before we can consider the necessity for the rise of the provincial universities with their creation of a radically different tradition, it is necessary to focus first of all on the ways in which the ancient universities sought with limited success to meet the new challenges up to the First World War and the reasons for their limitations.

What gradually reformed features made Oxford and Cambridge unsuitable as universities educating men for industry? In the first place there was the problem of religion, for Dissenters were not allowed to matriculate at Oxford until 1854 or to graduate at Cambridge until 1856. Considering the strong Nonconformist element among the northern and Midland manufacturing families this alone would prevent their sons from gaining any worthwhile qualifications at the universities even if they had wished it. They went instead to London or to Scotland. But even after 1856 anomalies remained, for Dissenters were excluded from fellowships and a number of crises arose in the 1860s at Trinity College, Cambridge, when the college was prevented from electing Nonconformist senior wranglers to fellowships although they urgently wished to do so. This also was finally reformed by the University Test Act of 1871. Henceforth this important barrier between Oxford and Cambridge and many business families of the North was removed and in a wider way it removed a brake on the teaching efficiency of the universities by allowing the free election to fellowships of the most talented, irrespective of religion.[1]

Another restriction on the quality of teachers at the ancient universities was that they had to be celibate and in Holy Orders. The deleterious effects of this scarcely need stressing. It meant that able young teachers had to leave when they married, unless they had professorships. It also gave an inward-looking character to the teaching body; ageing bachelor clergymen with little outside contact were hardly the ideal mentors for young potential businessmen, and they were unlikely to direct their charges towards careers in an industrial world of which they knew nothing and which they probably despised. It also led to the invidious position of bachelors remaining in college with no incentives to exertion, waiting for the deaths of colleagues so that they could take over college livings in the country, leave the university and marry. Raving eccentricity if not moral collapse was too often the fate of those left behind[2] and the Oxford Royal Commission found tutors often 'inferior men'.[3] At Oxford

[1] Leslie Stephen, *Life of Henry Fawcett* (London, 1885), p. 235. D. A. Winstanley, *Later Victorian Cambridge*, pp. 36–90.
[2] Sir Charles Oman, *Memories of Victorian Oxford* (London, 1941), pp. 193–4.
[3] *Report of Her Majesty's Commissioners appointed to inquire into . . . the University and Colleges of Oxford*, 1852, p. 30.

these requirements were relaxed after the Act of 1877[1] though they remained in Queen's, for example, until 1902.[2] In Cambridge they were abolished by statute in 1882,[3] and it led to the possibility of the introduction of a new type of secular don in touch with the world of affairs.

Third there were the barriers of cost. Even the prudent student at Oxford in 1850 would find his expenses for the course exceeding £300[4] and these high costs prevented the admission of a larger class. This was a good deal due to the inefficiency with which the colleges were run and the extravagance of their own expenses and charges. To some extent this was modified in 1868 when Oxford colleges allowed undergraduates to live cheaply in lodgings.[5] In such circumstances scholarships were clearly of crucial importance for those with their own way to make in the world. But here a fourth barrier existed since at Oxford there were no scholarships for proficiency in the physical sciences—precisely those subjects leading to careers most attractive for the careerist of humble origins without the connections necessary for a smooth entry and successful career in Church, law, and politics.[6] This still remained a deficiency at Oxford until the end of the century. In 1896, for example, only ten out of twenty-one colleges offered scholarships for science, and not more than forty out of five hundred scholarships were for these subjects.[7] Furthermore, the candidates for science scholarships were of 'low average merit' in any case, and this merely reinforced the vicious circle. The colleges were unwilling to increase scholarships provision for fear of giving awards to academically poor candidates, and because there were so few awards the best candidates went to Cambridge. Cambridge had no trouble in this regard;[8] it offered ample science scholarships and received good applicants. But Oxford differed from Cambridge in two specific ways that affected this question. Oxford scholarships were won before coming up to the university, and thus whether or not there was a flow of able candidates relied too heavily on the education in the schools. This in itself was an unpromising feature since Oxford more than Cambridge drew its candidates from the

[1] C. E. Mallet, *A History of the University of Oxford*, vol. III, 'Modern Oxford', p. 348.
[2] R. H. Hodgkin, *Six Centuries of an Oxford College*, p. 187.
[3] J. P. C. Roach, 'The University of Cambridge' in *Victoria County History of Cambridgeshire*, vol. III (Oxford, 1959), p. 265.
[4] RC *Oxford* (1852), p. 31.
[5] W. R. Ward, *Victorian Oxford*, p. 269.
[6] RC *Oxford* (1852), p. 113.
[7] 'The Position of Science at Oxford', *Nature*, 9 July 1895. Ray Lankester, while disclaiming authorship of the article, said he heartily agreed with it. Ibid. 30 July 1896.
[8] *Report of Her Majesty's Commissioners . . . University of Cambridge*, 1852, p. 144. Evidence of Rev. H. Arlett.

public schools where, with striking exceptions like Rugby and Oundle, science teaching was not good. At Cambridge, on the other hand, scholarships could be won after a year's residence, thus giving time for able men with a poor school science background to change over and prove their worth in the new field. Many Oxford science men had not studied science at school, but unlike Cambridge men they were unlikely to win the benefits of a scholarship from this position.[1] Furthermore, the entrance examination system at Oxford was also heavily weighted against science. Science had no part in university entrance examinations except in a few college matriculation examinations which 'in only a few cases give it a bare recognition'. In effect matriculation and responsions were prohibitive for 'modern' side boys and relatively easy for the classic. For students who on entering Oxford subsequently changed over to science, Greek remained a fifth barrier at Oxford, as at Cambridge. An unsuccessful move was made at Oxford in 1904 to remove compulsory Greek from responsions for mathematicians and natural scientists,[2] consequently Oxford did not abolish compulsory Greek until 1920, a year after Cambridge. In the meantime it continued to get badly prepared, poor applicants for its science scholarships.

Even worse than the entrance and scholarships positions was that of the provision of science fellowships. In 1900 Sir Ray Lankester calculated that of 250 fellowships over which the colleges had discretion—where they were not tied to subjects by statutes—only twelve were in sciences, and of nineteen heads of houses 'not one of these posts is or has been for the last seventy years given to a student of the Natural Sciences'.[3] As Oxford differed from Cambridge over its management of scholarships so it did over fellowships also. Cambridge colleges tended to give fellowships to their own scholars irrespective of subject whereas at Oxford fellowships were thrown open to the whole university, the college having decided beforehand on the subject. Since most Oxford fellows were literae humaniores or modern history men they tended to choose yet another of their own kind, whereas in Cambridge colleges such was the even balance of mathematics with arts that a greater chance was given to the newer scientific subjects. Lankester had calculated discretionary fellowships but taking all fellowships, both where the college had a free choice and where the subject was assigned by statute, the breakdown was as follows:

[1] Maurice Davidson, *Memoirs of a Golden Age* (Oxford, 1958), p. 20.
[2] List of Voting, Bodleian Library G. A. Oxon. b. 141 (195). Thomas Case, *The Uses of Greek to Students of Mathematical and Natural Sciences*, 1904. Case was the President of Corpus Christi College Oxford and on the Committee for the Preservation of Greek.
[3] Various correspondence on Oxford and Science by Lankester, J. K. Fotheringham, and others in *The Saturday Review*, 13 March, 14 April, 28 April, 5 May 1900.

Literae humaniores	*Modern history*	*Natural science*	*Others (maths, mod. lang., law, theology, etc.)*	*Total*
136	43	32	86	297

Whichever figures were taken, the inferior status of science as regards fellowships was clear.

In a sense these institutional barriers, like the fellowships, scholarships, and Greek issue, were but symptoms of the more deep seated fact that the ancient universities, especially Oxford, did not believe in education for industry. The pervasive belief in 'liberal', non-vocational education voiced most powerfully by Mill and Pattison, as we saw in the previous chapter, was the real inhibitor. Had there been a change in ideology these administrative matters could more easily have been dealt with. Similarly, strong leadership, such as that given by Sir John Burdon Sanderson at Oxford and Michael Foster at Cambridge for medical science, might have done more to break these barriers had there been comparable figures on the side of the industrial sciences.

Gradual reform, however, did take place in the direction of creating scientific education of potential use for industry. At Cambridge the natural Sciences Tripos had already been started in 1848 and intercollegiate science lecturing began in the 1870s, a procedure reversed in the 1880s when the university was able to centralize much of this work. As regards laboratories the sciences had a part of the New Museums Building in the 1860s until the great Cavendish Laboratory was built in the early 1870s. At the same time college laboratories supplemented the provision, notably St John's and Sidney Sussex in the 1850s.[1] The university science blocks had spurts of building: chemistry in 1888 and 1909, physics in 1873 and 1895 and engineering 1879–84, 1894, 1900, 1903, and 1912. The sheer physical impact of science and even technology on Cambridge was becoming evident.

At Oxford in the generation before 1850 dedicated men like Charles Daubeny, William Buckland, and Henry Wentworth Acland had pursued their interests in chemistry and geology and taught the few declining students who cared to listen.[2] Daubeny had great beliefs that chemistry could be made both part of a liberal education and useful for 'the processes of trade',[3] and in 1848 had

[1] Edward Miller, *Portrait of a College, a History of the College of St. John the Evangelist in Cambridge*, p. 85, and C. W. Scott Giles, *Sidney Sussex College, a Short History*, p. 97.
[2] J. B. Atlay, *Sir Henry Wentworth Acland, Bart., a Memoir*, p. 132.
[3] C. G. B. Daubeny, *Can Physical Science obtain a Home in an English University?* (Oxford, 1853) and *On the Importance of the Study of Chemistry as a Branch of Education for all Classes* (London, 1855) for his views.

his own laboratory built at Magdalen thus beginning the important tradition of Oxford college laboratories.[1] Following Magdalen, Balliol started its laboratory in 1855, Christ Church in 1866, Queen's in 1900, and Jesus in 1907. Even more important was Daubeny and Acland's successful attempt to make science an examinable subject, and as a result the School of Natural Science was created in 1850 and the first examinations held in 1853. Serious obstacles remained. In the first place only those who had previously obtained honours in classics or mathematics were allowed to present themselves for honours in natural sciences and, second, colleges were still not disposed to take into account distinctions in science in electing to fellowships, with the consequence that undergraduates whose ambitions lay in academic life had no incentive to pursue scientific subjects. Christ Church, under the reforming ordinance of 1858, had junior studentships compulsorily set aside for science, though, and the science teaching was among the most successful of this college's activities in the later nineteenth century.[2] The third drawback was that there were as yet no university laboratories. This was rectified by the building of the museum in 1860 with laboratories, followed by the Clarendon for physics in 1870, and a chemical department in 1877–9. Changes in the examination structure also seemed to help the sciences. Up to 1863 scientists had to take responsions, moderations and the final school of classics in addition to their scientific work, but from 1863 only moderations and religious knowledge were required, and after 1886 only responsions in Latin and Greek. In the 1890s more practical work was required in the scientific examinations.[3]

Most important were those reforms striking at the very root of the problem both at Oxford and Cambridge. The heart of the matter was the tension of vested interest between the colleges and the university. The colleges were rich and autonomous and the university relatively poor. Yet if science was ever to gain a foothold it would require vast expenditure on laboratories, equipment and staff; a kind of expenditure that it would be uneconomic for a college to make even if it were so disposed. This was also linked with another tension, that of the professors and the tutors. The professors, as professors, were poorly paid and the Oxford Commission considered their salaries 'not such as to command the services of the ablest men'. If professorial salaries were to be raised this would have to be done by the university, since they were university appointments, but using money raised from the colleges. Thus the three antagonisms ran

[1] R. T. Gunther, *A History of the Daubeny Laboratory, Magdalen College Oxford* (Oxford, 1904).
[2] E. G. W. Bill and J. F. A. Mason, *Christ Church and Reform 1850–1867*, pp. 46–7, 73, 185.
[3] F. Sherwood Taylor, 'The Teaching of Science at Oxford in the Nineteenth Century', *Annals of Science*, VIII, no. 1, 28 March 1952.

together—colleges *v.* university, tutors *v.* professoriate, arts *v.* science. The colleges had a profound vested interest in arts subjects because they were cheaper and gave no reason to the university to call upon them to give up revenues to endow sciences and science professors. Moreover, the onset of agricultural depression in the early 1870s, and the decline of rents and land values, much reduced the capacity of colleges, whose income largely came from this source, to bear these extra calls on their resources. It was the further commission in the early 1870s that tackled this impasse and, by the Oxford and Cambridge Act of 1877, obliged the colleges at both universities to support science. Consequently, at Oxford Queen's had to increase its endowment for the Sedleian chair of natural philosophy, Magdalen had to take on the chairs of chemistry, pure mathematics, and mineralogy; St John's, mechanics and civil engineering; and New College, the Wykeham professorship of physics founded in 1900.[1]

But these advances were far from sufficient for some contemporaries. In particular the whole Oxford approach to science came in for a swingeing attack from Professor John Perry, later of Imperial College, speaking at Oxford in 1903.[2] He accused Oxford not only of neglecting science, which was indisputable, but for neglecting research even in those subjects it professed to teach, and this had created a dangerously unscientific, anti-intellectual and anti-research atmosphere in Oxford. Then he focused his attack sharply on Oxford's failure to achieve a link with industry. This, he said, was especially dangerous for the country at large because Oxford was taking middle-class boys who ought to be succeeding their fathers in industrial management; 'their factories are so badly managed . . . They are what I call unskilled workmen, that is unskilled owners of works and it is Oxford which is to blame for their unskilfullness . . . she has always ostentatiously held herself aloof from manufacturers and commerce.' These were not merely the fulminations of a radical with a fashionable technological axe to grind for they were echoed by the Royal Commission of 1922 which looked back on pre-war Oxford science with what must be the last word in blasting criticism.[3] Its science teachers were 'too few', their accommodation 'insufficient', their equipment 'incomplete', their students 'lamentably small', and the 'output of work was less than should be expected from a university possessing such great opportunities'. There is no point in withholding the judgement that all this reflects the gravest discredit on that generation of Oxford men entrusted with a great tradition which they allowed through their own negligence, shortsightedness and college self-interest to fall into such disrepute.

[1] C. E. Mallett, op. cit., pp. 349–51.
[2] John Perry, 'Oxford and Science', *Nature*, 31 December 1903.
[3] *Report of the Royal Commission on Oxford and Cambridge*, Cmd. 1588, 1922, p. 114.

In the light of these deficiencies in the ancient universities, especially Oxford, and the attempts at reform, we may now turn to consider the actual achievements and industrial involvements of the two universities in their research and teaching interests.

The actual achievements of Oxford science and their relation to industrial development in the years before the First World War were remarkably disappointing. In spite of the work of Daubeny in the mid century his successors did not build a worthy tradition on the foundations that he had laid. His successor, Sir Benjamin Brodie, made one significant industrial contribution through his method for purifying graphite,[1] but after 1862 he did no significant work and indeed argued that the rise of manufactures was positively a danger to scientific investigation because the high salaries that industry could offer were diverting talent.[2] His successor, William Odling, was a disaster for Oxford chemistry. Holding the chair for forty years, from 1872 to 1912, he 'thought it rather derogatory to the dignity of a professor to appear in the laboratory'[3] and he 'did not consider that active research was part of his professorial duties'.[4] Thus for over a generation up to the war this virtually dead hand lay over Oxford research. That there was not total stagnation was due to the college laboratories which emerged as more vital if less adequate centres. Practically the only example of this work having any direct industrial application was that of Vernon Harcourt at Christ Church on the removal of sulphur from coal gas, the Pentane lamp and the chloroform inhaler. But it was only the war that really gave Oxford chemistry a practical turn, and only the building of the Dyson Perrins laboratories in 1916 that began a significant research school. An ex-student of pre-1914 Oxford chemistry, F. W. Gilbertson, a Swansea steelmaster, saw clearly what was lacking and regretted 'the enormous advantage which might have accrued if we had been in touch with the practical industries'.[5] Oxford physics was even worse. Professor Clifton, who held the chair for fifty years until 1915, was 'entirely opposed to research'. There were no facilities for research, not even electric power in the Clarendon, and scarcely anything had been done for years.[6] The main development

---

[1] *D.N.B.* Sir Benjamin Brodie.
[2] 1872 XXV RC *Scientific Instruction* (Devonshire) QQ. 3587 and 3642 et seq., especially his replies to questioning by T. H. Huxley.
[3] Sir Harold Hartley, 'The University of Oxford School of Chemistry', *Journal of the Royal Institute of Chemistry*, vol. 79, 1955, pt. I, p. 123.
[4] E. J. Bowen and H. Hartley (eds), *Chemistry at Oxford*.
[5] RC *University Education in Wales* (Haldane), Cd. 8699, 1917, F. W. Gilbertson, Q. 10156, p. 275.
[6] Earl of Birkenhead, *The Prof. in Two Worlds*, pp. 89–90. Ronald W. Clark, *Tizard*, p. 51; see also pp. 10 and 12 for Tizard's hostile reaction as an undergraduate to Odling and the feebleness of Oxford science.

on the physical side was the building of the electrical laboratory in 1910 by the Drapers' Company, but the work there was not evidently concerned with technical problems of electrical engineering.[1] As regards geology, there was likewise no close involvement with industry.[2]

Quite the most direct and important way in which Oxford sought to make itself relevant to industry, however, was through the setting up of the engineering chair and department. Oxford was late in doing this and until 1907 was probably the only first-rate university in the world without an engineering professorship. From 1905, however, the university had had an engineering and mining subjects committee which offered a diploma enabling the holder to take a Birmingham B.SC. degree in two years. For this work college laboratories at Trinity and Christ Church were used, but compared with the major technological universities of the North it was rather unworthy and the outside experts advising on the course urged that a proper professorship was needed.[3] Their advice was heeded: C. F. Jenkin became the first Oxford engineering professor in 1908.[4] Jenkin had an almost ideal background for the task. The son of Fleeming Jenkin, the great pioneer of Scottish university engineering, he was educated at Edinburgh and Cambridge and then experienced a wide range of industrial work with Nettlefold's Steel Works and Siemens before his accession to the chair. He also had decided, if orthodox, views on engineering education, taking the usual English university position that he would teach the science and theory of engineering and the practical side would still have to be learnt through apprenticeship.[5]

The new professor put life into Oxford's new discipline. The students went surveying in the vacation at Blaenau Festiniog, they visited GWR Swindon while Siemens and Westinghouse helped them with samples. The numbers of students rose to around thirty a year, mostly public school boys,[6] and when the first honours examination was held in 1910 two were entered, one of whom gained a 'first' going then as their first pupil to the Midland Railway Company's works at Derby. In 1912 the course was reshaped to cover a very wide

[1] C. N. Hinshelwood, 'Laboratories and Research in Natural Science', *Oxford University Handbook* (Oxford, 1939).
[2] Lady Prestwich, *The Life and Letters of Sir Joseph Prestwich* (Edinburgh, 1899), chapters IX and X. He did, however, show some interest in the artesian well of the brewery firm of Meux and Company in the Tottenham Court Road.
[3] T. Herbert Warren, Letter of Appeal . . . for Assistance in Starting a Professorship of Scientific Engineering, n.d., *c.* 1905–6. Warren was the Vice-Chancellor.
[4] Engineering and Mining Subjects Committee Reports 1905–13, *passim*.
[5] Charles Frewen Jenkin, *Engineering Science, an Inaugural Lecture* (Oxford, 1908).
[6] *Engineering Science, University of Oxford* (Oxford, 1909) and *Board of Education Reports 1911/12, 1912/13, 1913/14*, Cd. 7008, 1913; Cd. 7614, 1914; Cd. 8137, 1915 contain reports on Oxford University Engineering.

range of subjects including turbines, sanitary engineering, lubrication, and refrigeration as well as the normal civil subjects. They also purported to undertake mining education although this seemed difficult to justify.[1] Necessarily the research record of the nascent department was not particularly striking. Jenkin did some work on the thermal properties of carbonic acid, but their laboratory was completed only in 1914 and his best work on metal fatigue, corrosion and aircraft construction was done during the war and the 1920s. Though scarcely at this time a major department in national terms, it was Oxford's most significant gesture to the world of industry outside. If then, Oxford science was poor and its connections with and contributions to industry negligible, what of Cambridge? We have seen that Cambridge education was much more science orientated and that mathematics in her case held the same prestige as Greats at Oxford, also that her scholarship and fellowship policy concerning science was not an impediment. Now we may focus on five major areas—physics, chemistry, engineering, the changes in mathematics, and mining—to consider both their vitality and their relevance, if any, to contemporary industrial development.

The Cavendish Laboratory rose within this time to a peerless position in British physics, crowned with the three Nobel prizes of its successive heads, Rayleigh, Thomson, and Rutherford in 1904, 1906, and 1908 respectively. But much, though not all, of the work was necessarily of so fundamental and abstract a nature as to be of little direct relevance to manufacturers in that generation; nor indeed did the researchers particularly intend that it should be. Clerk Maxwell, the first Cavendish Professor in 1873, did little original research at Cambridge, being chiefly engaged in the editing of the papers of Henry Cavendish, but he did set the early tradition of work in electricity, determining electrical constants and testing the accuracy of Ohm's law before his early death in 1879.[2] His successor Rayleigh was likewise only in the chair a short time, until 1884. During his time at Cambridge he did much useful work, following Clerk Maxwell in redetermining electrical constants, the ohm, the ampere, and the volt. Although this clearly had considerable ultimate value for the electrical industry, Rayleigh himself had no particular contact with electrical firms nor was he then especially interested in practical applications.[3] Long after he had left Cambridge, he did become more involved in matters like explosives, gas, mines, and aeronautics, but his work at the Cavendish was more strictly pure in approach. His successor Sir Joseph Thomson, however, was quick

[1] Hebdomadal Council Papers, Oxford University Archives, no. 99, p. 127; no. 95, p. 35. Letters of 24 April and 26 May 1913.
[2] *A History of the Cavendish Laboratory 1871–1910* (London, 1910), *passim*.
[3] R. J. Strutt, *John William Strutt, Third Baron Rayleigh*, p. 242. His son contrasts him with his friend Kelvin.

to point out that Rayleigh's Cavendish work on electrical units did have incalculable commercial benefits for the electrical industry although this was not its motivating spirit.[1]

J. J. Thomson succeeded Rayleigh in 1884 and remained Cavendish Professor for the rest of our period. It would be true to say that owing to his background Thomson was more interested in industrial matters than Rayleigh. Born in Manchester, he was originally destined for an engineering career, though his mother's poverty forced him to switch from engineering to try to enter Cambridge via mathematics and physics. In the 1880s and early 1890s the bulk of Cavendish work remained in electricity and magnetism and traditional fields, then from the mid 1890s came a marked development. Thomson found that passing X-rays through gas made the gas a much more effective conductor. Further, he discovered that atoms were not indivisible but that negatively charged particles or electrons could be torn from them by great electrical force, and he also discovered the first isotope, that of neon. Finally, it will be recalled that Rutherford was already working on radio-activity and analysis of radiations in the Cavendish in 1902. It is almost an impertinence to ask the relevance of all this to industry, for it was clear that this basic research had moved far from such concerns. Whereas physics through the development of electricity had moved into close relevance with industry and engineering, most strikingly in the person of Kelvin at Glasgow, now these Cambridge developments of the subject, the investigation of the fundamental nature of matter, were moving the subject away again.

There were, however, certainly links between the Cavendish and practical industry before the First World War. Of 225 research workers in the Cavendish up to 1901, a few went into industry—an engineer in Greece, two consulting engineers, a manufacturer of machine tools, and a chemical manufacturer.[2] To these may be added J. C. McConnel of the Manchester spinning firm though his industrial work had no relation to his physics interests,[3] and R. S. Willow who became the head of research at Tootal Broadhurst and who had been a pupil of Thomson's at the Cavendish.[4] Perhaps the most important of the ex-Cavendish men moving into industry was Sir Horace Darwin who founded his Cambridge Scientific Instrument Company in 1881 chiefly to supply scientific apparatus for academic laboratory purposes.[5] But the vast majority of those working in the laboratory were destined for academic careers. More curious,

[1] Sir J. J. Thomson, *Recollections and Reflections*, p. 113.
[2] *History of the Cavendish*, p. 324 ff. List of Workers.
[3] Ibid., p. 83.
[4] Sir J. J. Thomson, op. cit., p. 26.
[5] *75 Years of Successful Endeavour, 1881–1956* (Cambridge Scientific Instrument Company, 1956?).

there was a distinct flow not so much of students but of laboratory superintendents into industry in the 1880s and 1890s one to an engineering firm in India, another who became head of research for GEC, and, best known, W. G. Pye who left to start his scientific instrument business, an offshoot of which became Pye radio.[1] While most of the Cavendish research was not of direct use in industry, the one striking exception in the 1890s was H. L. Callendar's high temperature thermometer which enabled steel-makers and brewers to measure furnace and vat heats.[2] But the Cavendish work cannot be considered as if it were that of a technical institute. What it was beginning to do through the fundamental work of Thomson and Rutherford was of incomparably greater importance than any other contemporary university or industrial development in the country, if not in the world.

Cambridge chemistry had little contact with industry and what relations there were, with one brilliant exception, were surrounded with controversy. From 1861 the Natural Sciences Tripos, which had started in 1848, was opened to undergraduates. A student did not now need to have already graduated before starting sciences and it thus became possible to gain the B.A. with science subjects. In the same year the new professor, George Liveing, was appointed who was perhaps the first man to teach practical laboratory chemistry in the university. Though important as a reformer and developer of the teaching side, his own work was almost entirely confined to spectroscopy and there is no trace of interest in or activity for industrial firms.[3]

From an industrial point of view a much more interesting figure was Sir James Dewar, the other professor of chemistry in this period. Dewar's Cambridge career well highlights the defects of the university at this time. In the first place he was disappointed by the facilities for research, and he spent most of his time at the Royal Institution rather than in Cambridge. Second, the acrimonious disputes he encountered about the use of staff and facilities when he tried to do some industrial chemical research in Cambridge throw a curious light on Cambridge attitudes to applied work.[4] Dewar was one of the greatest industrial chemists of the period. He is best known for his liquefaction of oxygen and hydrogen and the impetus this gave to the industrial use of liquefied air. He invented the Dewar's or vacuum flask for preserving cold and heat and was a co-inventor of cordite

[1] Sir J. J. Thomson, op. cit., p. 116.
[2] Ibid., p. 133.
[3] W. H. Mills, 'The University of Cambridge School of Chemistry', *JRIC*, LXXVII, 1953.
[4] Cambridge University Archives CUR 39.20 (Jacksonian Professor); various papers on the Dewar case, 1892, fol. 50 ff. Dewar had been doing analysis for Gilbey's port and Edison's filaments among other things; his dismissal of an assistant who claimed this was not university work led to unpleasantness.

with Sir Frederick Abel.[1] Further, he seemed to keep in touch with industrialists and industrial developments. For example, it was he who brought Pechiney's method of producing chlorine direct from magnesium chloride to the attention of Liverpool chemical manufacturers, pointing out the threat to their Leblanc based industry.[2] Finally, he was also a father of antipyretic medicine, that is those drugs that lower the temperature of the body, showing firstly that quinoline could be obtained from aniline, and secondly the action of certain pyridine salts in the curing of fevers.[3] In sheer practical results for human benefit through technology and medicine Dewar was one of the most prolific chemists of the time, and it is to Cambridge's reflected credit that he held the Jacksonian chair though a matter for regret that he felt ill at ease there.

We cannot leave Cambridge chemistry without pointing out the one brilliant example of its collaboration with a firm. This arose out of Shell's trouble with Borneo oil. Samples were sent to Dr H. O. Jones at Cambridge in 1901. He discovered 350 pure chemical substances in the distillate of crude petroleum, finding it suitable for motor spirit and rich in toluol for TNT. This was perhaps the first time that a scientific chemical analysis had been made of a petroleum distillate, and this early commercial contact with Cambridge chemistry reaped hugely disproportionate commercial gains. Significantly, this approach was made by a man who was one of the first Cambridge scientific graduates to enter industry.[4]

The new and rising department of engineering more than any other linked Cambridge with industry, a specialized chair of mechanism and engineering being created in 1875 and filled by James Stuart. Stuart, coming from a Scottish manufacturing background, had been third wrangler in 1866 and already had a reputation for his work in the Extension movement.[5] The project met opposition chiefly on the grounds, apart from expense, that engineering training required practical experience in commercial workshops for which no college education could pretend to be a substitute.[6] However, Stuart had some experience of Crewe workshops and, largely with his own finance, he embarked on his scheme. Perhaps sensitive of the suspicions of real engineers, he tended to stress—possibly to overstress—the practical and training workshop side of the course. It was clear that he was starting to turn out a new type of pupil. Of his seven students

[1] Henry E. Armstrong, *James Dewar, 1842–1923*.
[2] D. W. F. Hardie, *A History of the Chemical Industry in Widnes* (ICI, 1950), pp. 141–2.
[3] Thomas Carnelley, *The True Place of Chemistry in the University Curriculum*, p. 20.
[4] Robert Henriques, *Sir Robert Waley Cohen*, p. 92.
[5] T. J. N. Hilken, *Engineering at Cambridge University 1783–1965*. James Stuart, *Reminiscences*.
[6] Robert Phelps in *Cambridge Chronicle*, 30 October 1875.

in 1877, four intended to take up engineering as a career, and of his eighteen in 1878–9, six intended to become engineers and another five to follow allied professions. One found, for example, his future brother-in-law going to Cambridge to study engineering with Stuart and then spending a year in the Great Eastern Railway works at Stratford in 1888 before entering his family firm of Colman's in Norwich.[1] It was a new type of educational-career pattern for men of that social class.

Stuart, ever of practical bent, built up the workshop side and by 1890 Osborne Reynolds of Manchester thought the workshops admirable and better at handicrafts than his own course, indeed better in workshop training than most businesses.[2] However, this workshop was to cause much bad blood. In the first place, since Stuart had sunk so much of his own money into it, he wanted the university to take it off his hands for a suitable sum, which it did after some bad feeling which probably affected Stuart's other moves to get a Mechanical Science Tripos. His concern to have a practical workshop and laboratory was surely right and fits squarely into a common movement of the time. For example, engineering laboratories were started at University College, London, in 1878, at Mason College in 1882, at Bristol in 1883, at Firth College in 1885, and at Leeds in 1886, then before the end of the decade at Manchester, Liverpool, Dundee, and Edinburgh. In this context Stuart's work was original but not outlandish. However, there remained suspicion in Cambridge that Stuart's work was too practical. This reflected in the rejection of Stuart's attempts to get a separate Mechanical Sciences Tripos. It ran into flat opposition from J. J. Thomson (who it was easily forgotten was an ex-engineering pupil of Osborne Reynolds) who objected to the slant of the examination on these grounds. Stuart was by now losing interest. He resigned in 1889 and embarked on a political career, having already been elected an MP a few years before.

His successor, James Alfred Ewing, was likewise a Scot but steeped in the great Scottish scientific engineering tradition of Rankine, Tait, and Jenkin who were all his mentors, and he had been associated with Jenkin and Kelvin in their cable work. At this crucial time for Cambridge engineering it was thought that the electors 'would probably choose a man best fitted for developing the scientific side of engineering rather than one to carry on the present system in which most of the time was spent in teaching the men the use of tools in the existing workshops'.[3] Ewing was already an FRS, and this seemed to give a guarantee of Cambridge engineering's future academic respectability. But ironically, not only was Ewing more scientific than

---

[1] Laura E. Stuart, *In Memoriam Alan Cozens-Hardy Colman* (Norwich, 1898). The authoress was James Stuart's wife and the subject her brother.
[2] *Cambridge University Reporter*, 4 June 1890.
[3] A. W. Ewing, *The Man of Room 40, the Life of Sir Alfred Ewing*, p. 94.

Stuart, he also seemed to do a great deal more practical commercial work for industry—carrying on indeed the tradition of Glasgow and Edinburgh engineering professorships. He was a close friend of Sir Charles Parsons (an ex-Cambridge graduate) and did turbine testing for him at Newcastle and also for various city turbine driven electricity stations. He was also consulted on vibration caused by underground railways. His research work covered metallurgy, the structure and grain of metals under stress, and further commercial work followed from that—'the patent for his hysteresis tester . . . was largely used by people who were making transformers . . . Reports on samples of iron and steel sent from various firms were getting more numerous and more international. Even Fried: Krupp of Essen sent steel rings for ballistic testing. . . .'[1]

Not only did Ewing bring Cambridge engineering much more into contact with industry through science rather than crafts, he also succeeded where Stuart had failed in gaining acceptance for the new Mechanical Sciences Tripos. The new papers were to be in mathematics, mechanics, and strength of materials, theory of structures, the principles of mechanism, heat and heat engines, and electricity.[2] It passed 'with so little opposition and so much favour'. The immediate effect was marked. In the first year of the examination, 1894, seventy-four undergraduates read engineering, or 2·68 per cent of the university; by 1903 when Ewing left there were 226 or 8·34 per cent of the university.[3] Ewing, however, had one colossal secret failure that was no fault of his, but throws light on remaining defects in the university that still impeded the development of technology. He revealed in exasperation at a secret meeting that he had been privately offered a gift of £100,000 for a school of naval architecture at Cambridge, but when the would-be donor found that the students would have to qualify in Greek the offer was withdrawn in disgust. 'A scheme which if carried out would have been of great national importance was thereby frustrated'[4] and compulsory Greek was not removed until 1919. Ewing resigned in 1903 to become Director of Naval Education. His successor, Bertram Hopkinson, had strong links with industry, being the son of a manager of Chance's in Birmingham, who later became a professor at London University and a consulting engineer. Hopkinson himself worked as a consultant engineer, especially on municipal tramway construction, before entering academic life, and he was married into the Siemens family.

[1] Ibid., p. 113.
[2] CUR 28.17 Mechanical Sciences Tripos. Item 5 and 5a, Report of the Syndicate appointed to take into Consideration the Establishment of an Honours Examination in Mechanical Science, 23 May 1892.
[3] Hilken, op. cit., p. 122.
[4] Cambridge University Archives, Correspondence and Documents from the Papers of Sir George H. Darwin, notes of Ewing's speech at the Chancellors' meeting, 13 June 1903.

He was killed during the war in a flying accident while in charge of the test piloting at Martlesham Heath, but in the engineering department that he and Ewing left behind, Cambridge had by 1914 its firmest bond with scientific industry in the early twentieth century.

Mathematics was truly the queen of the sciences at Cambridge and the very backbone of much of her other intellectual developments— in mathematical philosophy, engineering, economics, and physics. What is of interest to us is the way in which the Mathematical Tripos was modified because of the practical needs of those subjects requiring applied mathematics and the arguments that arose over this extended movement. The problem arose in the 1860s when it came to be felt that more attention should be given by the Mathematical Tripos to some physical subjects like heat, electricity, and magnetism,[1] 'by reason of their great practical importance in relation to manufactures, telegraphy and navigation . . .'[2]. And so, partly on industrial grounds, mathematics embraced these physical subjects with technological applications.

But this reform was not enough, for in spite of it numbers taking the Mathematical Tripos fell from 107 a year during 1882–6 to sixty-seven a year during 1902–6. This was the background to further attempts at reform in 1900 and 1906–7. In 1900 it had been proposed to cut down the range of alternative subjects, but an opponent of the scheme pointed out that this was self defeating since people were now studying mathematics not to become mathematicians but as preludes to other careers: '. . . an Engineer or the taking up of business and commercial pursuits'.[3] If these physical subjects were cut the drain would be even greater. The force of this argument was seen and the move defeated by 151 to 130. The issue arose yet again, however, in 1906–7.[4] Here the move was to make Part I of the Tripos easier, recognizing that it was catering for potential physicists and engineers rather than pure mathematicians, and to keep Part II for the specialists. *The Times* urged the mathematicians that they should be 'prepared to accommodate its training to the demands made by such science', and naturally support for the change came from the engineers Hopkinson and Inglis, the physicists represented by Thomson, and the economist Alfred Marshall. The resistance was waged predictably by Routh, the backbone of the highest level of Tripos teaching, and less predictably by Lord Kelvin who feared any diluting of specialist mathematics even for the benefit of physics, but the reformers finally won in February 1907.

[1] First Report of the Syndicate . . . on the Examination . . . Mathematica Tripos, 25 February 1868, CUR 26.6(1), Mathematical Tripos.
[2] William Walton, *Examination for the Mathematical Tripos* (flysheet in CUR Mathematical Tripos 28.6(1) Item 46 i).
[3] CUR 28.6(2) flysheet, W. H. Besant, 8 February 1900.
[4] CUR 28.6(2) Various papers, flysheets, 20 October 1906, 22 October 1906, *The Times*, 20 and 22 October 1906.

The principles involved here were vastly more important than merely a trivial piece of university politics. The basic issue was whether this very high-quality but abstract study of mathematics developed at Cambridge over a century could adapt itself to the needs of those new mathematics-using sciences and arts which it had spawned, and whose very practitioners were themselves schooled in the old Tripos. It is one of the successful adjustments in this period that in the 1860s and 1907 modifications were made so that Cambridge mathematics filtered, via its physics and engineering and chemistry and economics, into industrial life rather than remaining altogether detached in its own expertise. One major professor bestrides Cambridge mathematics for the whole of this period, the Lucasian Professor of Mathematics, Sir George Stokes.[1] It is partly due to his own personality and willingness to involve himself in industrial matters that Cambridge mathematics remained in touch. Although primarily a mathematician, his bent was towards natural philosophy, indeed to physics of a more applied kind than was being pursued by the pure physicists of the Cavendish. For example, he wrote a study on railway bridges and their loading and took part in the Board of Trade investigation on wind pressure on bridges after the Tay Bridge disaster. He did work for the Madras Harbour Commission, and on the effect of boat speeds for the building of the Panama Canal. Lighthouse illumination, the lubrication of machinery, and the manufacture of glass were yet more matters on which he was consulted or was interested. It was plain, then, that the central figure of Cambridge mathematics from 1849 to the 1900s was highly sympathetic to the claims of industry on his subject. It is ironic indeed that there is more evidence of industrial involvement for the professor of mathematics than there is for the professor of chemistry.

As part of this increasing involvement with industry, Cambridge also undertook an excursion, that proved temporary, into mining education, although none of the work of the professors of geology and mineralogy showed much evidence of concern with industry.[2] However, in 1903 the Coal Mines Regulation Act (1887) Amendment Act was passed by which the five years' work for a colliery manager's certificate could be shortened to three years for men with diplomas from a university or college. The Appointments Office had received enquiries as to whether Cambridge men were qualified, and suggested a joint course with Imperial College,[3] while a scheme of instruction was devised which the Home Office approved in 1905. Students had

---

[1] Sir Joseph Larmor (ed.), *Memoir and Correspondence of the late Sir George Gabriel Stokes*, 2 vols.

[2] CUR 39.23 Mineralogy, including *Cambridge Review*, 30 April 1926, obituary of Prof. W. J. Lewis. CUR 39.17.2, Geology.

[3] Cambridge Papers Series, Anderson Room, Cambridge University Library DC/6950. Letter, H. A. Roberts to the Vice-Chancellor, 27 November 1903.

to gain practical experience. For example, one student took courses at Redruth, Roudny, for gold, Minera for lead, and Leanerch for coal, getting testimonials from each to help on his way to South Africa.[1] The course from 1905 was yet another way in which Cambridge sought to make itself more relevant to industrial needs.

It was evident that whereas Oxford almost totally failed to relate its studies and research to the new industrial demands, Cambridge on the other hand did so with a fair degree of success, though properly keeping in mind her main purposes of pure research. The crucial test, however, is whether these two systems really did turn out graduates who found their way into industry and commerce, thus bringing the benefits of the education of the ancient universities to serve the economy.

First, it is worth considering the social origins of Oxford and Cambridge students of the time to see to what extent they came from families in business and industry. The Anderson and Schnaper figures[2] for Oxford for the period 1752–1886 show only 0·1 per cent of students coming from business homes, considerably below the comparable figure for Cambridge. Thus purely on grounds of family background we might expect to find slight connection with industry in the career choice of Oxford graduates, up to about 1890. This low proportion of business backgrounds is a shade surprising in the light of recent evidence on Winchester College which shows a considerable increase in businessmen among parents sending children to the school, which had in any case a close connection with Oxford.[3] But the implication is that although more businessmen's sons went to public schools they returned to the business before going to university and did not yet begin to affect the social structure of higher education as they had of public school secondary education.

The social origins of Cambridge undergraduates were different. Taking the Anderson and Schnaper figures, 9·4 per cent of Cambridge students had fathers to do with business in the period 1752–1886, a considerable increase on the Oxford figure.[4] While it may be thought that their time span is too vast to draw conclusions for the post-1850 period, they are careful to note that there were no decisive changes in trend, 'no conspicuous alteration in the representation of the minor groups was revealed'. This can be associated with a much

[1] CUR 128. Mining Engineering. Report of the Council of the Senate on Mining Engineering, 22 February 1904, and Collection of Testimonials for student L. Melville, 1910.
[2] C. A. Anderson and Miriam Schnaper, *School and Society in England, Social Backgrounds of Oxford and Cambridge Students*, p. 6.
[3] T. J. H. Bishop and R. Wilkinson, *Winchester and the Public School Elite* (London, 1967), show a fairly sharp rise in business family backgrounds from the 1850s with nearly half the school being of this origin by the 1910s.
[4] C. A. Anderson and Miriam Schnaper, op. cit., pp. 6–7.

cruder figure which is, however, useful as an international comparison between Oxford and Cambridge and leading universities in other countries at the time. The combined Oxford and Cambridge percentage of students from business backgrounds was 4 per cent for the period 1870–86, well below the 46 per cent for Harvard, the 15 per cent for Halle in 1877–81, and astonishingly below the 22 per cent for Russian universities for the 1880s.[1] It makes clear the paradoxical point that in the most industrialized country in the world in the 1870s and early 1880s, sons of businessmen made up a much smaller proportion of the ancient university population than in her industrial rivals, Germany and the United States. This was but one facet of the situation against which the provincial universities were to react.

More precise figures for our period are provided by Jenkins and Caradog Jones who found that the social distribution of fathers of Cambridge students for 1850–9 was as follows, in percentages:[2]

Administration	3	*Medicine*	10
Banking	3	*Teaching*	4
Business	12	*Miscellaneous*	9
Church	31	*Landowning*	19
Law	9		

This 12 per cent is a slight rise over the Anderson and Schnaper figure of 9 per cent but obviously low compared with the Church which still held its traditional commanding lead.

At the college level, St John's intake of sons of middle-class commercial and industrial families became more numerous in 1842, while the intake of 1881 had a yet broader social catchment than the 1840s with still more sons of businessmen.[3] This was true of Cambridge as a whole, though at St John's, as in the rest of Cambridge, the majority of students were the sons of professional men. The most detailed college evidence is that for Sidney Sussex. Here Rothblatt's figures indicate that sons of businessmen as percentages of the total college student body were[4]

1850–9	*1860–9*	*1870–9*	*1880–9*	*1890–9*	*1900–14*
15	10	18	17	9	19

[1] C. Arnold Anderson, 'The Social Composition of University Student Bodies, the Recruitment of Nineteenth Century Elites in Four Nations: an Historical Study', *Year Book of Education*, 1959, section V, chapter V.
[2] Hester Jenkins and D. Caradog Jones, 'The Social Class of Cambridge University Alumni of the Eighteenth and Nineteenth Centuries', *British Journal of Sociology*, I, 1950.
[3] Edward Miller, op. cit., p. 92.
[4] Sheldon Rothblatt, *The Revolution of the Dons, Cambridge and Society in Victorian England*, appendix IIA. Calculated from background of Sidney Sussex students, 1843–1914.

It was evident that as regards family connections with industry, Oxford students very rarely had these links, but Cambridge undergraduates more frequently did so though only to a modest extent. Did this reflect itself in the pattern of Oxford and Cambridge graduates taking up careers in business and industry?

There is ample evidence of the future careers of Oxford graduates. The Schnaper and Anderson figures for occupations of students for the university as a whole from 1752 to 1886 show that the vast bulk, 64·2 per cent, became clergymen and all other occupations are very slight indeed by comparison. Law took 8·7 per cent, about 5 per cent took up an academic career, and the rest are negligible.[1] In particular only 0·6 per cent went into business. If only 0·1 per cent came from business families and only 0·6 per cent became businessmen themselves, the divorce of Oxford from the business and industrial world seems as complete as could be. It was virtually a training college for the clergy and little else.

However the evidence for careers of Oxford men is fuller than that for Cambridge and it is possible to analyse rather closely the shifting position of the increasing absorption of Oxford students into the industrial and commercial world through four colleges in particular. (See Table 3).[2]

The diversification of business careers away from traditional stockbroking and banking came for Brasenose in the 1870s and for Balliol in the 1880s. In these decades of diversification, shipping, breweries, railways, mines, and electrical engineering enter into the range of careers of such men. For both Brasenose and Balliol there was a slight decline in going into business in the 1890s which may reflect the later stages of the Great Depression before the revival of the 1900s. It is also interesting to note that peak swings to business at Brasenose and Balliol both occurred with men who graduated and came onto the labour market at the end of the 1870s and very early 1880s and at the end of the 1880s respectively, in time to benefit from minor upswings in the business cycle within the depression itself. In the 1900s large industries and firms, notably oil and manufacturing chemists, emerged as employers taking several graduates at a time even from the same college. These graduates now sought employment as professional scientists, going into large firms with which they had no connection rather than as younger sons going back into family firms as was common in the 1880s. In the 1900s, for example, only about one-seventh of industrial entrants from Balliol were going into their family firms. In spite of these changes, and evidently larger proportions going into business and industry in the 1900s compared

---

[1] C. A. Anderson and Miriam Schnaper, op. cit., p. 6.
[2] Calculated from *Brasenose College Register 1509–1909*; *A Register of the Alumni of Keble College Oxford 1870–1925*; *The Balliol College Register 1833–1933*; *Merton College Register 1900–1964*.

TABLE 3 *Percentage of graduates entering business and industry*

Matriculation dates	Brasenose	Keble	Balliol	Merton
1850–3	0			
1853–5			1·4	
1860–3	3·3			
1863–5			4·2	
1865–8	6·3			
1870–3	12·0	2·6		
1873–5			4·8	
1875–8	15·5			
1880–3	4·9	1·2		
1883–5			10·1	
1885–8	13·3			
1890–3	8·2	1·7		
1893–5			7·8	
1895–8	4			
19C0–3	10	1·7		
1903–5			9·5	
1901–10				8

with the pre–1870s, it will be borne in mind that the figures are still quite small and the vast bulk even of Balliol's output was clergymen and school masters. With Merton and Keble this was even more overwhelmingly the case.

The cause of this relatively small proportion taking up careers in business and industry lies partly in the defects in science that we have considered, but also in a more intangible, pervasive attitude that business was not seen by dons or presented by them to undergraduates as a suitable ambition. This shows itself in a number of ways. For example, in that classic of Oxford life and mythology *Tom Brown at Oxford*, whenever the subject of business and trade arose in the conversations between Tom and his friend Hardy it was strongly criticized.[1] Hardy despised Carthage as a trading nation and feared that England was going the same way ('I think that successful trade is our rock ahead. The devil who holds new markets and twenty per cent profits in his gift is the devil England has most to fear from') while Tom became a kind of anti-capitalist radical. At the end of the period another striking literary example depicted an undergraduate whose father wished him to follow on in the family business around 1912, being persuaded by his senior tutor, Prendergast, to think instead of India and the Civil Service. This was not pure fiction since

[1] Thomas Hughes, *Tom Brown at Oxford*; see pp. 100–1, 395, 501, for their anti-business conversations.

Prendergast was based on Sidney Ball,[1] a noted St John's tutor of the day. None of the Oxford professors giving evidence to the Devonshire Commission regarded the production of men for industry as a purpose of their activities.[2] At the college level, especially Balliol under Jowett and Strachan Davidson, powerful encouragement and tradition turned the thoughts of the ablest to the Civil Service and India and certainly not to industry and commerce.[3]

As at Cambridge, it was partly to encourage and increase the flow to business that Oxford began an Appointments Committee.[4] This had started in 1892 under R. W. Raper, a fellow of Trinity who had informally been acting as a link between headmasters and undergraduates for teaching posts. However, in 1898 a turning point in their functions came with the chairmanship of the Rev. M. B. Furse. He was widely travelled, had visited the United States, and generally had far more contact with the non-academic world than other dons of the time. He seems to have filled the same kind of role at Oxford as that of A. E. Shipley at Cambridge. Of Furse it was noted: 'perhaps the first attempt was made to include business appointments in the scope of the Committee when Furse wrote to the Chairman of the North Eastern Railway . . . as a result of this one undergraduate was found a place in a railway.' The Appointments Committee having failed, unlike Cambridge, to obtain official recognition from the university, the new chairman, J. Tracey, appealed again to the Vice-Chancellor on the grounds that 'the increasing numbers of men requiring business appointments made it necessary that contact should be made with great business companies, especially railways'. In the business world the committee found support from C. P. Scott, R. D. Holt of Lamport and Holt, and a representative of Sir Douglas Fox, the engineer, was induced to join the committee.

What success did this organization have in inducing undergraduates to enter industry and business and in finding openings for them? The records of the Appointments Committee provide an overall view of the future careers of Oxford graduates in the years just before the First World War. They are shown in Table 4.[5]

[1] Oona H. Ball, *Sidney Ball* (Oxford, 1923), pp. 80–2. The novel concerned was *My Father's Son* by W. W. Penn, 1912.
[2] 1872 XXV RC *Scientific Instruction* (Devonshire). Evidence of Acland, QQ. 2890, 2950; Clifton, QQ. 3005, 3042; Price, Q. 3422.
[3] For this attitude, see E. Abbot and L. Campbell, *Life and Letters of Benjamin Jowett*, 2 vols (London, 1897). J. M. Mackail, *James Leigh Strachan Davidson* (Oxford, 1925), p. 81. Sir John Lloyd (ed.), *Sir Harry Reichel, 1856–1931*, 'Oxford Reminiscences' by Reichel, p. 49. H. W. C. Davis, *A History of Balliol College Oxford*, p. 231.
[4] F. B. Hunt and C. E. Escritt, 'Historical Notes on the Oxford University Appointments Committee' 1951 (an unpublished typescript in the Bodleian Library, 2632, c. 17).
[5] Calculated from *Annual Reports of Oxford University Appointments Committee 1906–1914*.

TABLE 4   *Careers of Oxford graduates*

	1906	1907	1908	1909	1910	1911	1912	1913	1914
In business	6	7	5	8	8	14	14	22	9
With chartered companies (Rhodesia, Borneo)	0	0	0	1	5	1	16	4	4
Secretarial	0	0	5	2	10	10	7	9	8
School-masters, permanent	36	29	32	21	26	18	15	17	18
Civil servants	0	4	20	13	16	21	17	26	21
Total, excluding temporary tutors	82	54	89	65	97	100	97	112	93
Business as % of total	7·3	13	5·6	12·3	8·2	14	14·4	19·6	9·7

The figures show a steady increase of numbers from 1908 to 1913 and an increase in proportion from 1910 to 1913, although overall it appears somewhat erratic and generally rather low. In appearing before the Royal Commission on the Civil Service in 1912, the Secretary of the Oxford Appointments Committee[1] was brought up sharp by some persistent questioning by Philip Snowden who suggested gently if firmly that in spite of all this contemporary talk about the movement of graduates into industry it was simply not a significant trend at Oxford. It was a cold douche of realism, though a shade unfair, to direct it at one of the few men actively trying to improve the situation.

Let us now turn to Cambridge. First, Anderson and Schnaper found that for the period 1752 to 1886 only 3·9 per cent of Cambridge students went into business. In fact, over half the total output went into the Church and three-quarters of the graduates went into either the Church, law, or academic life. Thus, however few businessmen's sons Cambridge took, it turned out markedly fewer of those sons as business men. Half of those businessmen's sons with known careers went into the Church[2] and conformed exactly in proportion to the career choices of all other Cambridge graduates. The rest spread in small numbers over academic, legal, government life, and

[1] 1913 XVIII RC *Civil Service*. Evidence of N. Waterfield, QQ. 18743–18758.
[2] C. A. Anderson and Miriam Schnaper, op. cit., p. 8.

so forth. Cambridge was already playing her role as a powerful engine diverting ability away from business and into the professions, a characteristic that was to continue at least up to the Second World War.

The Jenkins and Caradog Jones figures for occupations of graduates reveal the following distribution for 1850 to 1899 in percentages:

Administration	6	*Medicine*	7
Bank	2	*Teaching*	12
Business	5	*Miscellaneous*	9
Church	38	*Landowning*	7
Law	14		

Again, fewer sons went into business than came from business backgrounds. Although the Church took fewer in the later nineteenth century than in the first half, yet it was still quite the largest employer and was a leading gainer along with public school teaching in the redistribution of occupations between fathers and sons. As before, Cambridge was acting as a channel away from business rather than into it. It is true that this 5 per cent represented an advance, but since it is an advance over a corresponding figure of nought for 1800 to 1849, this is scarcely saying very much.

The Jenkins and Caradog Jones figures, however, mask a considerable improvement in the situation right at the end of the nineteenth century. At Jesus College, of the undergraduates from the 1850s to the 1880s only about 1·4 per cent went into occupations having anything to do with business and industry, these consisting of engineers and stockbrokers in about equal proportions. Half the graduates went into Holy Orders as clergy or schoolmasters. However, in the period 1885 to 1900, whereas Holy Orders had declined to 30 per cent, business and industry had risen to nearly 15 per cent including 4 per cent in mining.[1] For another unspecified college H. A. Roberts found that proportions entering commercial life rose sharply from 3·3 per cent in 1865–70 to 11·5 per cent in 1885–90 and to 21 per cent in 1900–1. He also considered that in the 1900s 58 per cent of Cambridge chemists went into careers in industry and only 'a few of these' would be in their fathers' business.[2] Similarly 24 per cent of the pass men of 1903–7 went into business and engineering, again confirming the view of a marked improvement in channelling into business careers around 1900 and up to the war.[3]

---

[1] A. F. Gray and F. Brittain, *A History of Jesus College, Cambridge*, pp. 177, 190.
[2] H. A. Roberts, 'Education in Science as a Preparation for Industrial Life', *Journal of the Royal Society of Arts*, 1 March 1912, p. 426. Roberts was Secretary of the Cambridge University Appointments Board.
[3] J. P. C. Roach, 'The University of Cambridge' in *Victoria County History of Cambridgeshire*, vol. III (Oxford, 1959), p. 288.

Some of the credit for this trend was due to the formation of the Cambridge Appointments Association which was born out of the anxiety Cambridge felt around the turn of the century about its lack of connection with industry. W. H. Shaw, the leading advocate of the scheme within the university, put forward his plans in the summer of 1899 on the grounds that 'there is reason to think that many openings would be available for capable men . . . in Banks or other business houses, in Metallurgical and other industries requiring a knowledge of Chemistry . . . and in the various branches of Engineering'.[1] This led to a large meeting in the Senate House in November of the same year attended by interested representatives of industry and commerce including, Lord Rothschild, G. S. Gibb, the General Manager of the North Eastern Railway Company, W. H. Allen of the Queen's Engineering Works at Bedford, Sir Andrew Noble, and in particular Nathaniel Cohen.[2] Of the business leaders outside the university, Cohen was perhaps the most important in getting the new project started. He himself was a well-known figure in the City, through his stockbroking and foreign banking firm, and it was said of him that 'he was the first to conceive the twin ideas that the world of business needed university graduates and that university graduates needed business careers'.[3] Fittingly enough he was the father of Sir Robert Waley Cohen, one of the first Cambridge graduates to enter industry and the first to enter what became Shell, of which he was to become the head. Sir Robert also served with him on the Appointments Association until Nathaniel's death in 1913, but the son's services to industry and the universities continued long after as will be seen subsequently. His immediate importance was in publicizing the idea among his friends and especially the London Chamber of Commerce, a very valuable use of his influence to which Shaw paid tribute. Within the university, apart from Shaw himself, one of the leading protagonists for the association was Sir Arthur Shipley, the later Master of Christ's. Sir John Benn, the publisher, who knew Shipley at Cambridge, considered that

> Sir Arthur Shipley did more than anyone at Cambridge to bring the University into closer touch with the outside world. As a young don he had been impressed by the 'blank wall' which seemed to confront many undergraduates in their choice of career whereas in the United States enlightened businessmen were beginning to invite the co-operation of the universities in commercial affairs.

[1] CUR 48. Appointments Association, flysheet by W. H. Shaw, 'A Proposed Appointments Association', June 1899.
[2] The Cambridge Appointments Association, Report of a Meeting held on 4 November 1899.
[3] Robert Henriques, op. cit., p. 30.

Hence his early support for the foundation of the Appointments Association.[1]

The next step was to turn the newly formed association into an Appointments Board as a formal part of the university and financed by it. Moves in this direction came two years after its initiation in November 1901. Then a report noted that Oxford, Edinburgh, and Aberdeen already had boards, and moreover various firms wrote letters of support urging this step, notably the British North Borneo Company, the British South Africa Company, Sir W. G. Armstrong and Guinness.[2] This was discussed shortly after with general support. The later secretary of the board, looking back, recalled that there was some early opposition to the idea on the grounds that a strong appointments board may react on studies and push them in a technical direction. The secretary admitted that this may well be so; if some subjects were useless or badly mixed then employers would let the university know through the Appointments Board and the university then had the choice of adjusting accordingly. Expressed in moderate and matter-of-fact language it was nevertheless a revolutionary idea that firms should have a means of exerting this kind of pressure, however indirect and even desirable.[3] Conservatives could be forgiven for thinking that here was the thin end of a wedge of sinister potential. But the mood of the discussion of 1902 for setting up the board was sanguine and urgent, coloured by the university's failure to get industrial finance. The Rev. G. B. Finch of Queens' complained that 'during the last two or three years the response from the great industries of the country to the financial appeal from the University had been very poor nor did the leaders of industry send their sons here to be taught . . .'. When the Appointments Association had been set up 'representatives of large industries . . . came down here and almost implored it to wake up and show some practical interest in those industries for which they could do so much'.[4] It was now the purpose of the board to change this, both by encouraging undergraduates to think in terms of industrial careers and by urging on firms their usefulness as employers.

The new official status granted to the board was certainly a stimulus. Up to the end of 1901 they had established links with twenty firms who were taking Cambridge graduates, but in 1902 they added forty-eight more.[5] In their short existence as an association before becoming the board they had secured twenty-nine appointments as

[1] Sir John Benn, *Tradesman's Entrance* (London, 1935), p. 37.
[2] Report of the Appointment Association Syndicate, 19 November 1901.
[3] *Congress of the Universities of the Empire 1912* (London, 1912) 'Action of Universities in Relation to the After Careers of their Students', H. A. Roberts, p. 230.
[4] Discussion of the *Reports*, 30 January 1902. CUR 48, fol. 10.
[5] Report of the Appointments Board for the Year ended 21 December 1902.

well as persuading several manufacturers to reduce their premiums for Cambridge graduates.[1] In 1902 they obtained sixteen industrial and technical posts for their men and three railway appointments, and in 1903 fifteen industrial and technical posts, twelve engineering appointments, and four secretaryships. Thereafter they did not, unfortunately, specify types of appointments in detail but it was clear that their recognition as a board had led not only to a sharp increase in interested firms but also in industrial posts obtained. Also it led to more college assistance. In 1902 only nine colleges had been helping them with funds. By 1908 all were doing so, and its annual budget in 1912 was around £1,200.

The new board went from strength to strength up to the First World War. It started specialist advisory committees for the North of England and for London. By 1912 their industrial advisers included Sir William Mather for engineering, Mr Brooksbank for Yorkshire industry, Nathaniel Cohen for the City, Robert Waley Cohen, then Director of the Asiatic Petroleum Company (later part of Shell), the Managing Director of John Brown's, and representatives of Leeds and Birmingham industry. It could not be said that their advice did not cover a wide range of industry and regions or that they failed to tap the experience of those even at the highest levels. In 1914 Roberts sketched the chief fields into which Cambridge men were going through his office.[2] The first advance had been chiefly in employing the graduate in commerce as distinct from industry, and here it had been Eastern firms dealing in jute, oil, and grain. There was no explanation for this but it is not difficult to imagine that for the Cambridge man who would have reservations about going to work in a Lancashire cotton mill, work in the East for an imperial firm would have some of the glamour of a career in the Indian Civil Service. But industry was not far behind. Roberts noted, 'I know quite a number of young Cambridge men who are occupying responsible, though as yet junior positions in the management of factories.'

The flow of Cambridge graduates through the board may be considered in more detail from such figures as are available. The annual reports ceased to give a detailed breakdown of occupations for our purposes after 1903 but pieces of information fill the gap. In 1911 they reported that since 1907 they had supplied fifty-two firms or industrial organizations with men for the administrative side of business and twenty firms with scientific assistants other than engineering graduates.[3] Already several firms were becoming accustomed to taking numbers of Cambridge men year by year, some had nine, six, or four, but outstanding was one 'eastern house' with no

[1] Report of the Appointments Association Syndicate, 19 November 1901.
[2] H. A. Roberts, *Careers for University Men*.
[3] Second Quinquennial Report of the Appointments Board, 24 October 1911.

fewer than thirty-two Cambridge graduates. This unspecified firm must have been the Asiatic Petroleum Company, the body in which Shell and Deterding's Royal Dutch joined for marketing purposes in 1903. The reason for this was simply that Robert Waley Cohen had been the first Cambridge graduate to join Marcus Samuel at Shell, and Waley Cohen was filling up the firm with Cambridge talent. He told the Royal Commission on the Civil Service in 1912 that he had forty-one Cambridge men with him,[1] and he was also beginning to employ Cambridge geologists whereas formerly he had had to rely on the Swiss. It is interesting to note that just as Shell was building a special relationship with Cambridge so too was Sir Alfred Mond. Like Shell he had started using Zurich Polytechnic men but turned over to 'Oxford and Cambridge men who have taken high degrees' and these were his 'most successful young men'.[2]

In 1912 Roberts said that he had filled 420 posts among 213 firms.[3] There is a discrepancy with the report which cites 315 posts here but this scarcely matters; the really interesting point is that he thought 33 per cent of these went into manufacturing, 38 per cent into merchanting of all sorts, and 29 per cent into miscellaneous occupations. It was clear that about 70 per cent of the students passing through their office were destined for industry and business though this is far from saying that 70 per cent of Cambridge graduates found careers there since the bulk of clergy and schoolmasters would still be finding their feet by other routes. But this does not detract from the fact that the board had vastly increased its activities in the decade of its existence, and in establishing links with these firms was channelling Cambridge men, of the order of two to three hundred a year, directly into the economy. It was this that was totally new compared with the 1880s and 1890s.

There remains one point to stress about the kind of graduates that industry and business took from Cambridge, and presumably from Oxford also. From the civic universities industry demanded scientists and technologists, men with specific skills that could be directly applied to production or research. Accordingly in most universities the graduate entering industry was virtually synonymous with the scientist, and it was not until the 1950s and its shortage of technological manpower that there was much concern for the arts graduate in industry. At Cambridge before 1914, however, industry recruited arts graduates from the beginning. For example, Roberts found that the degrees taken by over fifty Cambridge men employed

---

[1] RC *Civil Service, the Employment of University Graduates in Business.*
Evidence of R. Waley Cohen, QQ. 21527–30 and 21575. This was a pamphlet published in 1918 giving extracts from the commission evidence of 1912.
[2] RC *University Education in Wales* (Haldane), Cd. 8699, 1917. Evidence of Sir Alfred Mond, QQ. 5207–8.
[3] Ibid., QQ. 21361; 21365.

in business by five or six organizations in the 1900s were eight in mathematics, eight in natural sciences and five in engineering—say twenty-one in sciences—but thirty-four in arts subjects including nineteen in classics.[1] Similarly, of the forty-one Cambridge men taken by Waley Cohen, fifteen were classics men and he had only two engineers and three natural scientists.[2] Roberts thought that employers were taking men with the highest degrees they could get almost irrespective of subject and that they believed that there was a strong connection between high academic ability and business success. This attitude to the employment of graduates from the ancient universities seemed to be a clear reflection and imitation of the Civil Service. The truly first-class mind, strongly motivated to success and tempered by Latin and Greek was being regarded as suitable for administration in industry as well as for the administration of government. Large employers were thus willing to take arts graduates from the ancient universities as they were not from the civic colleges. This meant that the backwardness in industrial science of the ancient universities did not necessarily imply so complete a rift with industry as such a defect would have entailed in other institutions. But this did not remove the real sense of dangerous isolation felt at Cambridge at the turn of the century nor does it excuse the scientific backwardness of Oxford. There were of course specific attempts at both universities to create a form of arts education in economics specially suitable for graduates entering industry. This matter is so important that it is discussed in a later chapter.

In conclusion we have seen in the case of Oxford a failure or unwillingness to adjust to new industrial needs, but a much greater degree of success on the part of Cambridge. While both were hampered by archaic features of religious exclusion and celibacy, which both reformed, Oxford unlike Cambridge was unwilling to strike at one of the roots of the matter in the provision of scientific scholarships and fellowships even at the end of the nineteenth century. Although both, with the rebalancing of power from the colleges to the university, considerably increased scientific personnel and building, the Cambridge performance in using both was vastly superior to that of Oxford. Much of this depended on the fortune of personalities. Cambridge had Stokes, Clerk Maxwell, Thomson and Rutherford, Ewing and Dewar. Oxford had Odling and Clifton. Oxford's main *rapprochement* with industry through engineering was quite lively with Jenkin, though development here was bedevilled by the lack of laboratory provision until 1914. Although Cambridge science was of

---

[1] H. A. Roberts, 'Education in Science as a Preparation for Industrial Work', op. cit.
[2] RC *Civil Service, the Employment of University Graduates in Business*, op. cit., Q. 21373.

world class much of it was disengaged from industrial purposes, notably its best work in physics and the chemistry of Liveing. But there seemed a greater urgency for reform in Cambridge than in Oxford, possibly occasioned by the former's anxieties about finance around 1900. Certainly their attitude to mathematics reform shows a greater foresight and open-mindedness than one associates with Oxford at this time, though both were conservative in their attitude to Greek for scientists. As regards the output of their graduates to business and industry, Oxford's contribution was well below that of Cambridge, and with both before the 1900s it was orientated towards commerce, often overseas, rather than manufacturing industry at home. However, the setting up of appointments boards gave a fillip to both universities though the Cambridge one seemed to be vastly more active and certainly far more in touch with influential businessmen than that at Oxford. Its performance in moving graduates into business from the 1900s was impressive. However, there is evidence for both universities that they tended to move sons of businessmen away from a business career, in Oxford this being reinforced in some colleges by a strong public service or professional ethic. The very valuable reforming and outgoing work of both universities in movements like examinations for secondary schools, the education of women, and the movements of university extension in the 1870s and 1900s should not be forgotten. But this outgoingness did not embrace at the same time or with the same enthusiasm an involvement with industry. In any case, many of their most active attempts to get this involvement came long after the provincial colleges had risen by exploiting it. Thus it can be seen why, if industry needed university graduates in its changing employment structure and university research for its innovation, it could not rely upon the ancient universities to provide sufficient of either. For this reason a new form of higher education had to be created in the North and the Midlands, relying from the first upon active industrial participation and untrammelled by traditions and regulations suited to a training college for the clergy. The example of the success of this alternative tradition was perhaps the most important influence aiding change in Oxford and Cambridge after 1900, just as the defects of the ancient universities before the 1890s had been a powerful stimulus to the creation of the civic universities themselves.

3
The Civic Universities
1850-1914—I

'. . . in places where the movement towards universities is taking place most rapidly it is in the main moving on the lines of professional and industrial science and on the lines of business training; and the greatest part of the direct contribution of the new universities appears to be devoted to such aims.'[1]

Since from the third quarter of the nineteenth century there was an increasing need for industry to be served by the universities, and since Oxford and Cambridge were not meeting this need until the 1900s, it was evident that a new style of higher education had to be created in the civic colleges of the new industrial cities. This chapter deals with the ways in which the colleges were created by industrial support and their resulting contributions to industry. The next deals with the output of students to industry, the consequential problems of excessive technology and interference from industry, and finally the special case of the University of London.

Although the active interest and support of business was a precondition for the setting up of most of the civic universities after 1850, there were considerable local variations in the nature of this support. Sometimes it was a clear case of the members of one local industry providing the money and expecting some return in the form of science for that industry; sometimes it was but one or two individual families in firms that could expect little tangible return to their own trades. On occasion it was national industrial support from outside the city concerned or sometimes a purely civic movement with no evident business initiative. It will be necessary therefore to examine something of the movements concerned to highlight these characteristics.

Manchester, the first of the civic universities, began with the large endowments of one businessman founder-benefactor and, after

[1] Professor Forsyth. MS. Notes of a Meeting held at Trinity College, Cambridge, 13 June 1903, in Sir George Darwin's Papers (Cambridge University Archives).

61

initial indifference from the manufacturing classes, it flourished on sustained financial support which was especially intense in the 1870s and after 1900. When John Owens died in 1846 he left £100,000 for the setting up of a college to teach such learning and sciences as were usual in universities.[1] Although a successful businessman himself, he made no particular statement that the college should especially serve industry, as was to be commonplace with most future civic universities after the late 1860s. The early trustees of the will were mostly men representing Manchester and Lancashire trade; George Faulkner, the fine spinner; Samuel Alcock, the calico manufacturer; Alderman Watkins, the drysalter; Mark Philips, merchant; Alderman Kay and J. B. Smith, cotton merchants; and Richard Cobden, print manufacturer.[2] And yet in spite of this early munificence and business interest the college did not attract the support of the industrial community for some years. This was largely because, having no precedents to follow, it tried to adopt the liberal arts education of the ancient universities rather than matching its education to the needs of the city. Indeed Owens's statement of intentions —not orientated to industry as Firth's at Sheffield and Mason's at Birmingham were to be—had much to do with this. The vital factor in reviving the college from its moribund state was the vision of Henry Roscoe, the Professor of Chemistry and one of the first English scientific professors to see the importance of relating the universities to industry. In 1866 he persuaded Thomas Ashton, the cotton manufacturer, and like himself an ex-Heidelberg student, to become interested in the college. Upon Ashton's being won over, £200,000 was raised by subscriptions which enabled the college to move from its old site in Quay Street to Oxford Road where it opened in 1873.[3] As with the Leeds and Birmingham movements, the coincidence of the early stages with the economic boom 1868–73 was profoundly beneficial in enabling the capital to be raised. The occupations of those providing subscriptions of between £300 and £1,000 for the move were[4]

27 cotton merchants, manufacturers
 4 engineers
 4 calico printers
 3 gentry
 1 tea dealer, publisher, wire manufacturer, blockmaker, banker, drysalter, card manufacturer, warehouseman

[1] B. W. Clapp, *John Owens, Manchester Merchant* (Manchester, 1965), chapter XI.
[2] Joseph Thompson, *The Owens College, its Foundation and Growth*, chapter III *passim*.
[3] Edward Fiddes, *Chapters in the History of Owens College and of Manchester University 1851–1914*.
[4] Calculated from Subscription List in 1872 XXV RC *Scientific Instruction* (Devonshire), p. 484 collated with *Post Office Directory, 1873*.

and the first life governors included seventeen men in business and four in the professions.[1]

From this point the public interest became intense, stimulated by parallel movements now beginning in other northern cities and the foreign competition that all experienced and feared. Gifts from industry for industrial purposes began to flow. In 1866 the engineers of the city, including Whitworth, William Fairburn, and the locomotive builder Charles Beyer, raised £10,000 for a chair of engineering. In the 1870s the college raised £131,000 in gifts of £10,000 and over for science subjects[2] and Beyer himself gave £108,000 over the years and at his death. In the Great Depression of the 1880s these massive donations ceased though now the college was a fully fledged university as part of the Victoria federation from 1881. With the lifting of the depression in the late 1890s the possibility of lavish munificence recurred. Between 1903 and 1913, for instance, the university received an average of £30,000 a session in gifts and legacies in that time of prosperous trade. Manchester was in fact quite the best endowed of all the modern universities, due to the support it was able to receive from the local business community.[3] Manchester had a wide hinterland to tap and a varied range of exceedingly prosperous industries, including cotton textiles which was almost giddily affluent before the war. Also engineering and chemicals both had considerable confidence in the university because of the work of its engineering and chemistry professors, Osborne Reynolds and Henry Roscoe. Manchester was thus doubly and unusually fortunate in having an opulent founder and a regular flow of financial support from the local industrial class which it served.

Liverpool, Manchester's first partner in the federal Victoria University, is a particularly good example of an immensely wealthy city whose university movement sprang neither from one individual industrialist nor particularly from the industrialists as a body. However, once started, it attracted support from them second only to that of Manchester. They were conscious of Owens college developments of the 1870s, the extension lectures movement, and what the mayor described as 'a sort of wave passing over the country in favour of the establishment of colleges for higher education in the various northern commercial and manufacturing towns'. Accordingly town meetings were held in 1877 and 1878 determining on the necessity of forming a university college in Liverpool. With the winning of the support of the Rathbones in trade and the Muspratts

---

[1] 1872 XXV, op. cit., p. 491.

[2] H. B. Charlton, *Portrait of a University 1851–1951*, appendix III.

[3] RC *University Education in Wales* (Haldane), Cd. 8993, 1918. Evidence of Sir Harry Reichel, Q. 14251. He noted that within a two mile radius of either Manchester or Liverpool there were at least a dozen businessmen who could each provide £20,000 for a university chair.

in the chemical industry the success of the movement was assured. By the time of incorporation in 1881 they had raised £100,000 and by the time they joined the Victoria University in 1883 they had raised another £30,000.[1]

It was the good fortune of Liverpool that it should have among its business class a reasonably wide range of individuals and industries—notably in shipping, chemistry, and the food trades—willing and able to raise the kind of money that gave such a powerful initial impetus to the movement in the absence of a founding benefactor. No other civic university had so short a period of tutelage to the London degree before, through Victoria, being able to control its own qualifications. Chairs, each endowed to the value of £10,000, were forthcoming; the shipowners raised their own fund for the chair of mathematics, and the traders and manufacturers similarly had their own for the laboratories, while Muspratt and Gaskell, Deacon and Company provided the funds for equipment. In this manufacturers' list we find the prominent chemical and food-chemical firms of the city and Mersey basin—Gambles, Gossage, Bibby, Walker, Tate, Jacob, and a score of others.[2]

After Liverpool became part of the Victoria federation the flow of beneficence continued unchecked. By 1886 the public of Liverpool had given £150,000 and the corporation £20,000 for the college.[3] In 1888 Sir Henry Tate gave £16,000 for the library,[4] and in the following year the engineering laboratories were built at a cost of £15,000 to Sir Andrew Walker, brewer of the local ale and donor of the Walker Art Gallery.[5] In the 1890s followed Sir John Brunner's £10,000 in 1891[6] and the chemical laboratories by Gossage in 1894. All this placed Liverpool in a powerful position to break away from Victoria in 1903 as a separate university. With renewed pride in this new independent institution and with an even more thriving trade, lavish gifts flowed to the university from industry up to the war. Sir William Hartley, the local jam manufacturer, gave £13,000 for botany and then a complete wireless station in 1911;[7] in 1910 Lever gave the proceeds of his libel action against the *Daily Mail*;[8] in 1906 Edmund Muspratt built and equipped the new chemistry labora-

[1] E. K. Muspratt, *My Life and Work* (London, 1917). J. C. Brown, *The First Page of the History of University College, Liverpool. University College and the University of Liverpool* (Liverpool, 1907). *Liverpool Daily Post*, 25 May 1878, and Newscuttings Books of the university for these early developments.
[2] University College Liverpool Donations List 1883.
[3] *Liverpool Mercury*, 26 May 1886.
[4] MS. Letter 23 October 1888, Harry Tate to Lord Derby, in File Misc. Hist. I. in the Liverpool University Registry.
[5] *Liverpool Mercury*, 9 September 1886.
[6] MS. Letter, Sir John Brunner to Robert Gladstone, 5 May 1891.
[7] Arthur S. Peake, *The Life of Sir William Hartley* (London, 1926), p. 211.
[8] *Journal of Commerce*, 7 March 1910.

tories,[1] and finally in an extraordinary spurt of philanthropy to cap all former donations the shipowners T. Fenwick Harrison, J. W. Hughes, and Heath Harrison gave between them £35,000 for new engineering laboratories and a further £4,000 for their extension.[2] This very close and generous involvement of the local business community with the university made it the second best endowed of all civic universities by 1914.

Why then was Liverpool University so especially fortunate in its industrial support? What were the motives of its supporters? Most obviously it was because the city and hinterland depended on a wide variety of highly science-conscious industries stemming from chemistry and engineering. That Muspratt, Brunner, Gossage, and the rest should support the sciences, and especially chemistry, is unremarkable. Similarly the greatest gifts, those for the Harrison Hughes laboratories of engineering, were made with strong commercial considerations in mind. When the foundation stone was laid the donors observed that 'as shipowners who use three hundred thousand tons of coal a year they see the advantages to be derived from the internal combustion engine so far as ships are concerned . . .'.[3] Hence the laboratories were to be especially strong in their work on such projects as engines and oil and gas for marine propulsion. Harrison indeed referred to his gift as an 'investment'.

And yet as with all these institutions there were cross-currents of motives other than the directly simple one. For example, Sir Andrew Walker was always suspected of using his philanthropy as a means of social advancement to a knighthood and baronetcy. It cannot have escaped notice that Tate, Hartley, Walker, and Brunner were all knighted, and in these days of low taxation and the accumulation of vast fortunes, spectacular philanthropy was but one attribute expected of the successful knightly businessman. Hartley's donations sprang not from such considerations nor even from an expectation of much scientific return to his own industry, but from deep religious conviction of which systematic philanthropy had long been a part.[4] This variety of industry and variety of motive was important for Liverpool in giving it a good range of arts, science and medical subjects. Alfred Booth, for example, financed classical history, Brunner Egyptology and archaeology, and the Rathbones English literature.[5] Thus there was not that narrowness imposed on the university by the nature of its support, as was most evident, for example, at Sheffield.

[1] *Liverpool Courier*, 13 July 1907.
[2] *Liverpool Daily Post and Mercury*, 24 October 1910.
[3] *Nature*, 27 October 1910, and *Liverpool Daily Post and Mercury*, 24 October 1910.
[4] Peake, op, cit., p. 212.
[5] A paper on the Unitarian influence in the support of the college indicates that a good deal of business support went to non-business subjects. See the file of unpublished papers Misc. Hist I. in the Liverpool University Registry.

Leeds was the third partner of the Victoria University trio, but was less happily placed than the other two as a vulnerable poor relation. Leeds University began as a reaction to the fears of foreign competition engendered by the visit of certain Leeds businessmen to the Exhibition of 1867 and their apprehension that the French were outstripping them in the quality of their textiles.[1] The proposals of the Nusseys in textiles and James Kitson, the locomotive engineer, led to the formation of the Yorkshire College of Science 'to provide instruction in such sciences and arts as are applicable or ancillary to the manufacturing, mining, engineering and agricultural industries of the county of Yorkshire'.[2] The scheme gained some early financial support from Sir Andrew Fairburn, the engineer; the Duke of Devonshire; Sir Titus Salt; Messrs Beckett and Company, the bankers; the Low Moor Iron Company and Hargreave and Nussey, each of whom gave £1,000. Yet in spite of this support 'they did not as a whole get on very prosperously', and although the canvassing covered the years of the boom of the late 1860s and early 1870s they raised only a modest £20,000 by 1874, which compared ill with the other major civic universities of the North and Midlands.[3] The Duke of Devonshire attributed this apathy to the great results that had hitherto been achieved in industry without scientific training but relying on practical skill; clearly this attitude was still strong in Yorkshire in the 1870s.[4] It could also be argued that the modesty of the support owed something to the position of Leeds within the West Riding. For whereas Manchester was a metropolitan city dominating the surrounding area, Leeds did not bear this same character within its own region which contained several other fiercely independent towns, notably Bradford.[5] Bradford was highly aware of the importance of technical education but was spending its money on its own institutions.[6] Moreover, Bradford was actually improving its trade at the expense of Leeds in the 1880s with the fashion change from woollens to worsteds.[7] However, one authority points out that Leeds did gain support not only from the city but also the West Riding.[8] Finally, one of the most prominent local businessmen admitted that their university movement was not flourishing in the 1880s because of the relative depression of trade. Sir Edward Baines

[1] G. H. and A. Nussey, *A Technical Institution for Leeds and District* (Leeds, 1867). Thomas Nussey wrote the report on woollen fabrics at the Paris Exhibition of that year.
[2] Cited A. N. Shimmin, *The University of Leeds, the First Half Century*, p. 13.
[3] Yorkshire College of Science, Report of the Inauguration 1875.
[4] Ibid. Speech of the Duke of Devonshire, p. 33.
[5] Asa Briggs, *Victorian Cities* (London, 1963), p. 149.
[6] 1886 XXI RC *Depression of Trade and Industry*, H. Mitchell, Q. 3969.
[7] Ibid., C. E. Bousefield, Q. 6367.
[8] E. J. Brown, *The Private Donor in the History of the University of Leeds*,

observed, 'we cannot get such donations as they get at Manchester and at Birmingham; we are a quieter, slower town and our neighbourhood is quieter',[1] a remarkably modest observation for a Yorkshireman to make *vis-à-vis* his Lancashire counterpart.

If anything injected life into the college it was not so much local financial support as that from the Clothworkers' Company. Obadiah Nussey drew the attention of the company to the slow financial progress of the college and they agreed to provide £10,000 for the textile department and £500 a year for a professor. Indeed from this time forward education became a major interest of the company and the Yorkshire College its most favoured institution.[2] Gift followed gift until by 1912 the Clothworkers had spent a total of £160,000 on the university, far and away the most important element in its finance and to some extent compensating for the lack of one wealthy original founder. The other major outside supporter was the Association of Civil and Mechanical Engineers who provided £9,000 out of £10,000 for the engineering buildings of 1886. For Leeds, then, this outside money was vital, probably more important than for any other civic university of the time and reflecting no great credit on Leeds and the surrounding county.

There was, of course, fairly substantial giving by the Kitsons, the Tetleys, Sir John Barran, Fairburn, the Becketts, and the Luptons, but it was not until after the war that Leeds received really massive six-figure gifts from Frank Parkinson and Lord Brotherton that shaped much of the physical form of the university as it is today. The relative weakness of Leeds made it a highly vulnerable partner of the Victoria federation. Formerly[3] it had been protected by the prestige of the federal form, gaining something of the reflected glory of Manchester and Liverpool. When these two senior partners chose to go their own way as independent universities, Leeds was fearful that students would no longer choose to come to a University of Leeds with markedly poorer finances and facilities, whereas formerly they had been willing to come to a Yorkshire College to take Vic-

---

p. 5. This useful study, by concentrating understandably on positive achievement and by not being comparative, presents a rather optimistic view of Leeds's position.

[1] 1884 XXI RC *Technical Instruction* (Samuelson), Q. 541.

[2] Thomas Girtin, *The Golden Ram, a Narrative History of the Clothworkers' Company 1582–1958* (London, 1958), pp. 235 et seq., 268.

[3] See *The Case against the Proposed disruption of the Victoria University* (Manchester, 1902) and the opposing and far better argued *Case for the Establishment of the Independent Universities of Manchester, Liverpool and Yorkshire* (Manchester, 1902). The latter was brutally frank about Leeds, saying that the dissolution would force it to stand on its own feet and raise its own finances as a proper university. It also noted darkly that weak institutions could exist within a federal system which would not survive as separate universities. It was significant that Leeds alone of the three partners opposed the dissolution of the Victoria federation.

toria degrees. Tactically, however, Leeds was shrewd enough to make a niche for itself by achieving excellence in one or two industrial specialisms like textiles and leather rather than spreading its resources too thinly. Accordingly it could rely on a flow of students for these activities and in this manner there may be some connection between Leeds's financial limitations and its tendency to the rather narrow technological specialism that its senior partners eschewed.

Its Yorkshire neighbour, Sheffield, was the most direct case of industrial initiative and support for specifically, even narrowly, industrial purposes.[1] Three institutions merged to form the Sheffield University College of 1897; Firth College, the Technical School, and the Medical School. Firth College had been opened in 1879 by Mark Firth, the great steelmaster who had been active in bringing the Cambridge extension lectures to the city. Determining that this should lead to a permanent institution, scientific chairs were endowed and Firth himself gave £25,000 for the college while seven out of the eighteen signatories of the deed were local industrialists. The greatest value of the institution was in providing tuition for part-time evening students working in Sheffield industry. Scarcely had Firth College opened than the Royal Commission on Technical Instruction began to meet and publish in the early 1880s and this so impressed Sir Frederick Mappin that he sought to raise funds for another technical school of his own.[2] He secured the backing of Sir Henry Stephenson, the typefounder, Cammell's, the Cutlers Company, and the City and Guilds of London. Thus clearly the initiative and financial support for these institutions came directly from industry for industrial purposes. And yet in spite of Mappin's efforts 'industrial support was curiously lacking' and 'what is clear is that in 1884 Sheffield industry did not want a Technical School enough to pay for it'.[3] Possibly Mappin's heavy paternalism in regarding the school as virtually a branch of his own works dissuaded other employers as did the depression of the decade. In the more buoyant 1900s when the possibilities of a charter were imminent then large sums did come forward—£7,000 from Mappin and £10,000 each from Stephenson and Edgar Allen, the chemical manufacturer. Sheffield was thus a case of intense interest by three or four large entrepreneurs whose motives were plainly the expectation of some return in terms of scientific manpower, but it did not become a broadly based opulent movement and the college remained one of the smallest and worst endowed up to 1914.

Birmingham, like Sheffield and Manchester, began with the

[1] A. W. Chapman, *The Story of a Modern University: the History of the University of Sheffield.*
[2] *History of the University of Sheffield to the time of its coming of Age*, 31 May 1926, p. 5 (pamphlet in Sheffield University Library, PAM Q. 378.4274).
[3] A. W. Chapman, op. cit., p. 39.

actions of an individual businessman, Josiah Mason, the largest maker of pen nibs in the world and the first to apply electro-plating to gilding and silvering.[1] An innovating scientific entrepreneur himself, he thus appreciated as well as Firth and more than Owens the potential importance of higher scientific education for industry. The foundation deed of the college made this plain, for he founded the college 'being deeply convinced from his long and varied experience . . . in different branches of manufacture of the necessity and benefit through systematic scientific instruction specially adapted to the practical mechanical and industrial pursuits of the Midland district . . .'.[2] He made it plain that the college was for science in the benefit of industry and indeed he held a low view of arts subjects which he excluded. He met the £60,000 costs of the building, and the total amount of his foundation including the site and endowment came to £200,000, the college opening finally in 1880. The time was opportune for the city had done well in the great boom of the early 1870s and 'Birmingham was ready for a period of civic spending'.[3] Moreover, in spite of the exhaustion of its traditional raw materials of coal and iron stone, the city was about to experience a diversification of its industry up to the war. This provided a healthy range of industries from whose support the university was to benefit—Cadbury's at Bournville from 1879, Dunlop's in the 1890s, GEC in the 1900s and a score of light engineering and chemical based firms and industries. The 1870s also began a period of redevelopment in the city with the new Council House, Mason's College, the Library, and School of Art succeeding each other closely. The university movement thus benefited from this varied and scientific character of industry at a time of enormous civic pride embodied in the person of Joseph Chamberlain. Mason's College had been founded during his mayoralty and he played the central money-raising role in converting the college into the first independent civic university.

As in the case of Owens College, Manchester, no particular financial support was forthcoming immediately after Mason's initial gift. But when schemes for a Midland federal university were abandoned and Chamberlain started his campaign in 1897 for a charter, the money flowing in from business was astonishing and fortuitously coincided with the revival of trade after the depression. Chamberlain aimed initially for a quarter of a million. The pre-charter appeal was characterized by really massive gifts.[4] Charles Holcroft gave

[1] J. T. Bunce, *Josiah Mason, a Biography*.
[2] Deed of Foundation of Josiah Mason's Scientific College, 12 December 1870.
[3] Asa Briggs, *History of Birmingham, Borough and City 1865–1938* (Oxford, 1952), p. 71.
[4] G. H. Morley MS. Recollections 1880–1924, in Box 1966/i/2/41, Birmingham University Library, is useful on the donations; also Julian Amery, *Life of Joseph Chamberlain*, vol. IV, 1901–3, chapter 84, on the pre-charter finance.

£20,000; Sir George Kenrick, the Chairman of the Buildings Committee, a further £20,000 over the years;[1] an anonymous donor, £50,000; Andrew Carnegie, £50,000; and Lord Strathcona a further large sum. The Birmingham and Midland Counties Wholesale Brewers' Association gave £28,000 for the School of Brewing in the university. By the time of the granting of the charter Chamberlain had raised £330,000, markedly more than his target of £250,000. Then he asked for yet another quarter of a million and still the lavish contributions flowed in, £50,000 from Sir James Chance of the glass firm for engineering in 1900, £20,000 from John Feeney for metallurgy, and the Edgbaston site from Lord Calthorpe. Chamberlain had raised 'direct endowments amounting to £450,000 as well as an annual income equivalent at that time to the interest on another £200,000',[2] and Birmingham was the third best endowed of the large city civic universities.

Bristol is an example of backward finance inhibiting development until the most spectacular leap forward from the end of the 1900s to the 1920s. The college rose from proposals in 1873 and the early support was clearly industrial, the three original secretaries being a corn merchant, W. Proctor Baker; Lewis Fry, the son of Joseph, the Quaker chocolate manufacturer; and W. L. Carpenter, the partner in a soap firm.[3] And yet attempts to raise money from the mercantile community proved disappointing, only £23,285 being raised in two and half years before its opening in 1876—a sum which in Liverpool and Birmingham would be regarded merely a respectable individual donation. There were a variety of reasons for the modesty of the response. In the first place the Principal, Alfred Marshall, attributed it to the 'depression of trade' which made it an inopportune time to be starting colleges.[4] Although it was an unfavourable time to appeal for funds they had to do so or close down altogether. Mrs Marshall[5] attributed the apathy of the monied classes to the fact that

> Bristol was a rich city but unlike the northern towns which had
> become rich suddenly and were unaccustomed to spending,
> Bristol had for many generations been the home of the well-to-

[1] R. A. Church, *Kenricks in Hardware, A Family Business 1791–1966* (Newton Abbot, 1969), p. 227.

[2] Julian Amery, op. cit., p. 219.

[3] Basil Cottle and J. W. Sherborne, *The Life of a University*. W. H. G. Armytage, *Civic Universities*, p. 223.

[4] *Report of the Committee . . . Higher Education in Wales* (Aberdare), C. 3047, 1881, Q. 18201. It is interesting to note that Marshall's much quoted denial of the existence of the Great Depression was made only a few years later. When he was at Bristol he was well aware of it and that it was hampering his work as a college principal. The Clerk of the Clothworkers' Company also agreed. Q. 8249.

[5] Mary Paley Marshall, *What I Remember*, p. 25.

do who understood how to turn their wealth to pleasant account and so had less margin to spare for gifts to education.

Third, Marshall himself was not in good health. He temperamentally found the raising of money from businessmen highly distasteful and seemed to make little impact on the business community—unlike scientists like Roscoe in Manchester, Lodge in Birmingham, or Viriamu Jones in Sheffield. Furthermore, Marshall was frankly, if secretly, unsympathetic to the civic universities movement. He had only left Cambridge to get married and he returned as soon as he could, for Cambridge to him was the 'model of unattainable perfection'.[1] But even after Marshall's departure the financial troubles of the college continued. The city was declining from its former commercial prominence and was in a hiatus before its upswing in the 1900s with the building of the Avonmouth Dock in 1904 and the rise of tobacco, chocolate and paper to their great importance. The Professor of Chemistry considered gloomily that 'the pause in development had doubtless affected the fortunes of the college . . .'.[2]

In 1904 Bristol was the worst endowed of all the colleges, with the exception of Nottingham. And yet almost overnight the whole picture changed. As the economy of the city prospered and as the other major cities of the country obtained charters for their universities in the 1900s, so Bristol felt that it had to follow suit. Having starved and neglected the college for decades, the city now blandly claimed that it had a wide range of industries 'which greatly need persons who have completed their training in a modern university',[3] a suspiciously belated discovery. But these claims had to be supported with cash and the most important element here was the volte-face performed by the Wills family. As late as 1905 W. H. Wills had written privately, 'for myself I am not in love with this idea of local Universities I would have preferred to develop Oxford and Cambridge, I fear making degrees too cheap and too local.'[4] And then within a short time the Wills family began a tradition of sustained lavish philanthropy to the college and university scarcely without parallel in Britain (see Table 5). Accordingly the endowment fund of the university was rapidly boosted from a feeble £5,000 in 1904 to £203,000 by the time of the reception of the charter in 1909. In this case a long period of industrial apathy combined with a somewhat declining economy kept the local college weak until revival in

[1] MS. Autobiography of Morris Travers (Bristol University Archives DM 389).
[2] Ibid. When Travers arrived as Professor of Chemistry, the College was so poor that it purchased only two chemical journals; the rest Travers bought from his own pocket.
[3] *Petition of the Citizens of the City of Bristol*, 5 August 1908 (pamphlet in Bristol University Library P. Bristol University II).
[4] Letter, W. H. Wills to W. J. Arrowsmith, 25 January 1905, in the Arrowsmith Collection of Letters, Bristol University Archives DM 219.

the 1900s. Yet we can scarcely believe that this revival was prompted by an urgent demand for graduates in tobacco factories in spite of the terms of the petition. Rather it was a most extraordinary case of family, even more than civic, pride detached from rational economic calculation.

Newcastle grew out of a number of abortive attempts to develop a technological education based on Durham University. There had been proposals for a mining college in the new university as early as 1836[1] but this proved fruitless for lack of funds, as did further schemes in 1858[2] and 1865. The root trouble was that Newcastle businessmen who were potentially interested in an institution for the teaching of science, and especially mining, were frankly unenthusiastic about a college located in Durham and under the control of a university which was clerical, Anglican, and arts-orientated. Accordingly, if such a scheme was to stand any hope of success it had to be situated in Newcastle itself. When a committee was formed for a science college in Newcastle there appeared to be no shortage of industrial support. Members of the committee included four chemical manufacturers, four mining engineers, two civil engineers, engine works proprietors and glass manufacturers and one iron manufacturer, a shipbuilder, and a shipowner.[3] Moreover, the Newcastle venture was not a purely local one but represented mining interests throughout the country. The original committee had been appointed by a meeting held in London, followed by another in Manchester, and the proposed title of the institution was 'British College of Practical Mining and Manufacturing Science'. A representative of Wigan mining interests, for example, sat with local figures such as the engineer, Armstrong, Lowthian Bell, the iron-master, and Nicholas Wood of the North of England Institute of Mining Engineers. Thus, unlike most other civic university movements it was not one confined to the city or region but in its initial stages was a national mining industry project as much as a civic concern.[4]

And yet nothing much seemed to happen. Lowthian Bell, who kept on insisting that the coal owners really were keen on education in spite of the continued failure of such schemes, was told dryly by a sceptical questioner that 'the natural and well-known laws of supply and demand do not appear to prevail in this particular line of

---

[1] 'Proposals for a Mining College in the University of Durham 19 December 1836', Thorp MSS., University of Durham, vol. IV, folio 658.
[2] RC *University of Durham*, Cmd. 4815, 1935. See also folios 443, 448, 451 of the Thorp MSS. op. cit.
[3] Report of the Provisional Committee of the Newcastle upon Tyne College of Practical Science for the Year ending September 1852.
[4] *Prospectus of a College of Practical Mining and Manufacturing Science proposed to be established at Newcastle upon Tyne* (Newcastle 1855), and 'Establishment of a Mining College and District Schools 23 July 1857', Thorp MSS. vol. V, folio 677.

TABLE 5   *The connection of the Wills family with the University of Bristol*[1]

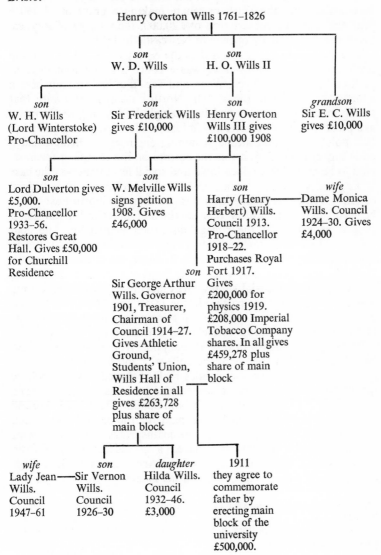

Henry Overton Wills 1761–1826

| *son*
W. D. Wills | *son*
H. O. Wills II |

| *son*
W. H. Wills
(Lord Winterstoke)
Pro-Chancellor | *son*
Sir Frederick Wills
gives £10,000 | *son*
Henry Overton
Wills III gives
£100,000 1908 | *grandson*
Sir E. C. Wills
gives £10,000 |

| *son*
Lord Dulverton gives
£5,000.
Pro-Chancellor
1933–56.
Restores Great
Hall. Gives £50,000
for Churchill
Residence | *son*
W. Melville Wills
signs petition
1908. Gives
£46,000 | *son*
Harry (Henry————Dame Monica
Herbert) Wills.
Council 1913.
Pro-Chancellor
1918–22.
Purchases Royal
Fort 1917. | *wife*
Wills. Council
1924–30. Gives
£4,000 |

son Gives
£200,000 for
physics 1919.
£208,000 Imperial
Tobacco Company
shares. In all gives
£459,278 plus
share of main
block

Sir George Arthur
Wills. Governor
1901, Treasurer,
Chairman of
Council 1914–27.
Gives Athletic
Ground,
Students' Union,
Wills Hall of
Residence in all
gives £263,728
plus share of
main block

| *wife*
Lady Jean————Sir Vernon
Wills.
Council
1947–61 | *son*
Sir Vernon
Wills.
Council
1926–30 | *daughter*
Hilda Wills.
Council
1932–46.
£3,000 | 1911
they agree to
commemorate
father by
erecting main
block of the
university
£500,000. |

[1] Worked out from details in 'George Arthur and Herbert Henry Wills and other members of the Wills family' in Tyndall Papers (Bristol University Archives DM 362/86).

life . . .'.[1] After another abysmal failure to teach practical science at Durham in the 1860s it became clear that the only solution was for Durham to throw its support and finance behind the project for Newcastle. With the Durham senate making a grant of £1,250 a year and a public subscription of £20,000, the College of Physical Science was eventually opened in Newcastle in 1871.

The immediate impetus was thus the repeated failures in Durham itself. Also by the 1870s there was a concern about foreign competition being felt on Tyne, Wear, and Tees that had scarcely been a spur in the 1850s and 1860s.[2] The North East was well aware that young men of the region had increasingly been going to Germany as a preparation for business and industrial life.[3] Moreover, Lowthian Bell pointed out that although mining engineers in Britain had a good higher education, it was the custom on the continent for overmen to be of a higher educational and social level than was the case in England since this was a step towards becoming a fully fledged engineer. Now that competition was pressing, the North East would be well advised to follow this continental practice.[4] Even so, it cannot be said that the college flourished financially. The coal owners raised an endowment for a chair of mining in 1880; but in spite of the support of Armstrong, J. T. Merz, the engineer, Thomas Hodgkin, the banker, and notably Mr Boyd of Learnside, the mining engineer, entrepreneurial support was lacking. It was noted during William Garnett's principalship in the 1880s and 1890s that 'at that time the attitude of the heads of the principal engineering and ship-building firms was hostile to technical education and the work had to be carried through with very little support from those who should have been the best friends of the college',[5] and 'comparatively few people in Newcastle in the eighties really believed that the college would be of any particular use to the business and engineering community',[6] in spite of its new site and building from 1886. Around the turn of the century Bell, who paid for the central tower, and G. B. Hunter of Swan Hunter, were mainsprings in the movement to raise funds.[7] In 1904 it received a considerable boost from £50,000 raised by the admirers of Lord Armstrong and the college was renamed Armstrong College in his memory.[8] But even so this

---

[1] Minutes of Evidence before the Durham University Commissioners, 1862, Q. 1742.
[2] Arthur G. Lane, 'The History of Armstrong College', Address to the Union Society, 11 October 1907.
[3] Minutes of Evidence before the Durham University Commissioners, 1862. Evidence of Rev. J. Cundill, Q. 480.
[4] Ibid. Evidence of Nicholas Wood and Lowthian Bell.
[5] B. M. Allen, *William Garnett, a Memoir*, p. 39.
[6] C. E. Whiting, *The University of Durham, 1832–1932*, p. 203.
[7] Report of the Durham College of Science, Newcastle, 1903–4.
[8] RC *University of Durham*, Cmd. 4815, 1935.

compares modestly with the £40,000 raised by three individuals for the Harrison Hughes laboratories at Liverpool only a few years later. Newcastle was thus an example of rather grudging support from industries which had traditionally relied on apprentice training in engineering. In spite of Bell's assertions, it was clear that most of them were not inclined to change, nor did it seem to have generated that cumulative imitative character that led to one massive gift following another as at Liverpool and Birmingham. Consequently Newcastle before 1914 was among the worst-endowed of the civic universities and the worst-endowed of those not still tied to the London external degree.

There remained the four university colleges which did not achieve independent status before 1914. By far the best-provided of these, due to its industrial links, was Reading. This began as a university extension outpost of Oxford and as early as 1893 they began their department of agriculture on which the reputation of the college was to be based. The college owed its development almost entirely to one family, the Palmers of the local biscuit firm. They gave building land in 1898, £10,000 in 1903, cleared off the debts in 1904 and 1908–10, helped to raise £15,750 in 1907, transferred a house as a common room in 1911 and finally in the same year gave £150,000 —certainly one of the very largest gifts from industry to a university before the war. Indeed, as a prominent business family intimately connected with the creation of a university, they are paralleled only by the Wills and then Boot in the 1920s. Yet the Palmers were not doing this out of any particular expectation that it would serve their firm or industry. Principal Childs who had most to do with them in the raising of this money noted of G. W. Palmer that 'helping education was to him a form of philanthropy', his chief motive was 'affection' for the college and 'it did not occur to him to impose conditions upon his gifts or to require some return for them in way of advantage to industry'.[1] The result of this was the astonishing position that Reading in 1913 was the third best-endowed university in England, surpassed only by Manchester and Liverpool.

The other university colleges fared far less well. At Nottingham a nucleus of local personalities interested in education had formed to consider rebuilding the mechanics institute, holding an industrial exhibition, and running university extension lectures, and their interests subsequently turned to the idea of creating a college.[2] The leading figures were chiefly professional men, solicitors, clergy, and

---

[1] W. M. Childs, *Making a University, an Account of the University Movement at Reading*, p. 144.
[2] A. C. Wood, *A History of the University College, Nottingham, 1881–1948*. Edith M. Beckett, *The University College of Nottingham* (Nottingham, 1928). Roy Church, *Economic and Social Change in a Midland Town, Victorian Nottingham 1815–1900* (London, 1966), chapter XIV.

a medical practitioner. With this social composition it is unlikely that the movement would have succeeded, but Nottingham was fortunate in arousing the interest of some local industrialists, notably Louis Heymann, a lace-curtain manufacturer, and Edward Gold-schmidt, a silk merchant and brewer. The third and probably most important was the anonymous donor of £10,000 to start the venture, now thought to be Louis Heymann's son William. The sum was given to force the hand of the town council to build a complex of buildings for the extension lectures, the public library and museum, which was opened in 1881 as the university college. With the start of engineering in 1883, support came from the Drapers' Company and F. C. Cooper, yet another hosiery manufacturer. Yet Nottingham, in spite of some industrial support, probably got the worst of both worlds in its relations with local industry. In the first place it was the college most dominated by its local town council on which the industrialists sat. Its finances were very largely dependent on the rates and this made it very vulnerable in times of rate-cutting economy drives as in 1887. It was also academically vulnerable in that it was kept very much a limited technical college with too much elementary work. This gave it a dubious reputation with the Board of Education which in turn affected its share of government grants for universities when they became available from 1889. Businessmen took an interest in the college by serving on the town council but the drawbacks of this were twofold. First, since the council was looking after the institution, this seemed to remove the incentive for private giving. Second, Nottingham, unlike Birming-ham, was not able to obtain the interest and service of its ablest and richest capitalists on the council and so their beneficial influence was not brought to bear on the college through local government.[1] Accordingly, 'the wealthy section of the citizenry have not shown that disposition to aid university education in Nottingham which has been evinced in other great cities of this country'.[2] Part of the trouble also arose from the nature of the industry of the town. Hosiery tended to be an industry of small family units, and Notting-ham a city of small masters rather than many large manufacturers in a wide range of diversified science based industries. Moreover, it was an industry suffering somewhat in the depression of the 1880s and 1890s when the college was trying to grow. All this engendered a certain scepticism, unwillingness, and inability to give generously to the college, and the control of the council seemed to remove the necessity, since the business classes could exert control in that fashion by using ratepayers' money. Nottingham was the worst-endowed of all university colleges and this peculiar situation, before the magnifi-

---

[1] Asa Briggs, *Victorian Cities* (London, 1963), p. 237, makes this comparison between Birmingham and Nottingham.
[2] A. C. Wood, op. cit., p. 60.

cent donations of Lord Trent in the 1920s, goes far to explain why Nottingham was in no position to obtain a charter before 1914.

Finally, there were the two rather struggling colleges of the southwest coast. Southampton began with commercial support of a dubious kind.[1] The initial finance had come from Henry Robinson Hartley, an eccentric recluse of a wine merchanting family, but his intentions were nebulous and it was only gradually that teaching became the chief purpose of the institution after its opening in 1862. One cannot claim that Hartley had any intention by his bequest to train up young men for industry and commerce; it did not excite the support of businessmen in the town and remained dependent on local rates. It was boundary extensions and increased rate revenue that enabled them to make the improvements prior to becoming a university college supported with government funds in 1902. But it remained throughout this time an object of suspicion in the eyes of the Board of Education and the advisory committee administering the grant, largely because of its lack of local support. Like Bristol before 1900 and Exeter, the college was weak because of the relative weakness of the economies of parent cities whose resurgence lay in the future. The college at Exeter arose as a School of Art after the Great Exhibition and then as the Royal Albert Memorial College in 1865 following the death of the Prince Consort.[2] It housed the normal range of Victorian after-school educational endeavour, technical education, evening classes and Cambridge extension lectures. Like Nottingham, it was very much a local authority-supported institution financed by the rates, for Exeter—which for much of the nineteenth century was in a state of economic decline—lacked a wealthy industrial class either in a position to be munificent to the college or indeed needful of any higher scientific personnel it might have provided. The chief supporters were a woollen draper, an optician, a bank manager, and an ironmonger, but only A. H. Willey, the head of the largest engineering firm in the West and an enthusiastic supporter of technical education, remotely approached the position of the great entrepreneur university supporters of the North. In this context the connection of the college with industry was only tenuous.

This consideration of the salient characteristics of the various movements in so far as they were concerned with industry prompts various observations of a wider nature. First, we should get some overall picture of the relative financial success of the movements in terms of the value of their buildings and equipment in 1904 or 1905 and their endowment income on the eve of the war. This is shown

[1] A. Temple Patterson, *The University of Southampton. The Hartley Bequest* (1858), a pamphlet of letters about the proposed use of the bequest.
[2] H. Lloyd Parry, *History of the Royal Albert Memorial University College, Exeter* (1911?). Robert Newton, *Victorian Exeter 1837–1914* (Leicester, 1968).

in Table 6 in ranking order of endowments. That Birmingham does not appear higher than it does in spite of its vast gifts is largely due to the fact that this university tended to spend on building, indeed at Edgbaston it must have had the best range of buildings of any civic university by 1914, a genuine 'campus' which was unusual for the time. Principal Oliver Lodge noted this as an aspect of their policy though he was not altogether happy with it.[1] It was evident that without massive support from industry no university movement stood much chance of successful development. The case of Leicester is an interesting negative example of this. Like Nottingham, it was chiefly an initiative by professional people, clergy and doctors, but

TABLE 6   *University endowment incomes*

	Value of buildings and equipment 1904 or 1905[1] (£s)	*Endowment income 1913*[2] (£s)
Manchester	400,000	23,255
Liverpool	310,000	14,374
Reading	?	9,715
Birmingham	300,000	8,579
Leeds	296,000	7,874
Bristol	60,000	5,208
Sheffield	197,000	4,835
Newcastle	150,000	3,154
Southampton	?	527
Nottingham	120,000	400

[1] Morris W. Travers, *A Contribution to the Study of the University Problem setting forth the need for the Establishment of a University in Bristol.*
[2] 1914-16 XIX *Reports from Universities and University Colleges*, 1913–14, Cd. 8137, 1915.

as it failed to secure the support of Leicester industry nothing was done until the 1920s.[2] The importance of industrial support is not diminished by the fact that the early phases of many movements had nothing to do with industry at all. For example, medical education or a pre-existent medical school was an important element in civic higher education at Leeds, Birmingham, Newcastle, and Sheffield, and a medical school was often merged with technical education to form the resultant university or university college. The medical side to this movement was of some importance to our concern because

[1] Sir Oliver Lodge, *Past Years, an Autobiography*, p. 318.
[2] Jack Simmons, *New University*, chapter 2.

however sceptical a local community may be about the value of technical and business training such scepticism could not attach to medical education. Medical schools thus often provided a stable element, ensuring the continuity of a college until the final formation of a full university. The rush to secure charters as independent universities on the part of the colleges had less to do with industry than with medical education as each college realized that if a neighbour secured the right to grant medical degrees then the bulk of its student body would migrate to its rival. It was medical education considerations which drove Liverpool into the Victoria federation[1] and which prompted Birmingham to seek a charter.[2] Once Birmingham had made her move this forced all her potential rivals to try to follow suit. The second non-industrial thread in the movement was the influence of the university extension lectures run from Cambridge and Oxford. The example set by these and the need to provide lecture halls was often an element in the decision to try to create a civic university, as at Liverpool, Exeter, Reading, Nottingham, and Sheffield. But granted these non-industrial elements, without the support of industry and the conviction in the business community that a local university was of some value, no movement could succeed.

Much of this was bound up inevitably, if not totally, with the enormous pride of the Victorian city. For cities over 300,000 in population in the 1900s it became a matter of civic disgrace not to have a university if for no other reason than that it was the proper embellishment and symbol of their status as a city. The relative populations of the cities with universities and colleges in 1901 were:

Liverpool	704,000	Leeds	429,000
Manchester	645,000	Sheffield	409,000
Birmingham	523,000	Bristol	339,000

All these gained independent charters. Clearly Bristol with its rather low endowments and considerably lower population was rather lucky and must have owed its inclusion to the last-minute heroic efforts of the Wills. But it is significant that Bristol's main motive for wanting a university was that Liverpool had one and as a west coast sea port of some pretensions they sought one also.[3] Below the chartered universities came the colleges taking the degrees of London or Durham:

Newcastle	247,000	Reading	81,000
Nottingham	240,000	Exeter	47,000
Southampton	105,000		

[1] Flysheet, March 1883, in Senate Minutes of Liverpool University.
[2] *Discussion on the Advantages that would result from the establishment of a Midland University*, 24 February 1884 (pamphlet reprinted from the *Proceedings of the Birmingham Philosophical Society*, Birmingham University Library Collection 1965/viii/6/8).
[3] Francis Gotch, 'Bristol and West of England University' reprinted from *Bristol Times and Mirror*, 2 October 1907.

It is also of interest to note that the leading towns in the 200,000 population range that one might have expected to form university colleges but which did not do so were Hull, Leicester, Salford, and Stoke, though all have in some manner done so since. It is probably fair to say that competition between the Victorian cities themselves was a more important dynamic in urging them to form universities than any fear of competition they might all have felt collectively from the Germans.

Most of the universities were the product of a genuinely civic movement. Leeds and Newcastle, in its early days, were less usual in having an important pan-industry element, with national support from textiles and mining being more important than civic support across a range of interests. For Leeds indeed it substituted for relatively weak local response. Furthermore, a sustained civic movement was a greater insurance of success than the benefactions of some individual founder. Indeed, to have one benefactor-founder was often a very dubious advantage for many colleges, leading to a period of total lack of interest on the part of other potential supporters. The poor state of Owens College until 1870, the perpetually feeble state of Southampton, the lack of financial support for Mason's College until the campaign for the charter, and the failure to support Mappin in Sheffield for fear of his excessive paternalism were all examples of this. The most successful movements were those where support was excited in a wide range of firms and industries, as in Manchester, Birmingham, and Liverpool, with no obvious single financial supporter on whom the college was dependent. If the civic movement was merely channelled into the routine forms of local government then this was little better than a kiss of death as the anaemic early history of Nottingham, Southampton, and Exeter indicated.

If the strength of these movements depended on the local business community so too the movements had to ride with them the booms and depressions of business fortunes. It was a most fortunate coincidence that many colleges were involved in collecting over the time of the 1868–73 boom or in its immediate aftermath when there was money available. This was so at Manchester, Birmingham, Durham, and Leeds. But reciprocally the effect of the depression of the 1880s was evident in the slackening of very large gifts to Manchester and the relative poverty of Nottingham and Bristol. Others like Exeter, Southampton, and Bristol again were doubly unfortunate in trying to start university movements in imitation of the others at a time when their cities' economies were in a dull state awaiting a revival—in all three cases attendant on transport changes—in the 1900s and then the inter-war years. Finally, in virtually all cases industry seemed to be supporting the successful universities with some expectation of return, most blatantly in Sheffield, Leeds, and Newcastle. Yet Bristol and most obviously Reading remain as cases where there was little connection between the enormous amounts of what was put in by certain firms and families and what they could possibly hope to get out in commercial terms. Behind all, there was an unmistakable air of sheer romanticism about the whole movement, not least in its architecture.[1] In part their derivative harking back to ancient styles was a means of clothing in respectability institutions which felt themselves to be self-consciously new and craving status. But in part it was also a kind of secular religiosity, the architectural expression of family and civic pride, the ideals of learning or the belief in material progress through science, in the forms that had symbolized the highest ideals of the past and which were frankly intended to evoke the glorification of the 'city' of some past medieval or Renaissance age. To observe these exterior forms of the old colleges is to appreciate that they could not have been conceived by their founders totally as the product of Victorian rational economic calculation.

In order to attract this industrial support, virtually all the colleges made at one time or another very clear statements that their purpose was to serve industry. At the outset of Owens College the Principal justified their study of the sciences on the grounds that 'your provision for the highest investigations of pure mathematics is your provision for actual and future engineering, surveying, statistics, time keeping, navigation.'[2] At Firth College, Sheffield, the Rev. J. Percival drew a sharp distinction between the old universities traditionally educating for the professions and the new ideal that a college like Sheffield had to follow, deliberately eschewing the old liberal education. 'The first object of a college in the centre of a great industrial population was that it should lay hold of the life of the industrial part of the people; that its education should start from the midst of their daily occupations, teaching them things which would help them in these occupations . . . (applause).'[3] Leeds too was particularly explicit about its industrial aims. It was stated that the purpose of the new Yorkshire College of Science 'is intended to supply an urgent and recognized want, viz., instruction in the sciences which are applicable to the Industrial Arts'.[4] At Birmingham,

[1] For example, the flamboyant Gothic of the Oxford Road entrance arch to Owens, the Siennese campanile at Birmingham, the Tudor Firth Hall at Sheffield, the Italianate Byzantine entrance hall of Walker's engineering laboratories at Liverpool, the English perpendicular of the Wills Tower at Bristol.
[2] A. J. Scott, 'On University Education', *Introductory Lectures on the Opening of Owens College Manchester* (Manchester, 1852). The other inaugural lectures by his professors of mathematics, chemistry, and languages elaborated this.
[3] J. Percival, *Firth College and its Future Work*.
[4] *Report of the Committee Appointed to Investigate . . . the Best Means to be Adopted for the Establishment of a Yorkshire College of Science* (Leeds, 1872).

Joseph Chamberlain likewise defined the purposes of his new university in similar terms: 'we desire to systematize and develop the special training which is required by men in business and those who either as principals or as managers and foremen will be called upon to conduct the great industrial undertakings,'[1] a view echoed by his principal who called for more education to help industry, 'for it is on such strenuous home industry of director, of manager, of foreman or artisan and of salesman that our Empire is established.'[2]

Chamberlain in the letter just cited claimed that the new form of university could do for commerce and manufactures what the old universities traditionally had done for the older professions of law and medicine. The theme raised by the historical writings of Canon Rashdall, that the universities had always engaged in professional training, was a powerful influence on those who sought to justify the new civic universities on industrial grounds. At Bristol, for instance, Sir Isambard Owen deplored the cult of 'useless knowledge', and welcomed that what he termed 'bread and butter studies' were becoming accepted in universities.[3] Owen was influenced by Rashdall to whom he referred with approbation. His chancellor, Haldane was also foremost in urging Bristol 'to be able to minister to the wants of the manufacturers'.[4] Similarly at Liverpool J. M. Mackay took up Rashdall's point to refute the idea that universities had ever existed merely for a cultivated public, asserting on the contrary that they were seats of the professions, including the engineer and chemist.[5] In short, almost all the new civic universities and colleges, with the possible exception of Reading, made it abundantly plain that one of their main purposes, if not their sole *raison d'être*, was training and research for industry.

It was surprising how outsiders could mistake this even at the time. Sir John Seeley, for example, speaking at Birmingham in 1887 in what is regarded as one of the seminal speeches of the movement, claimed that the new higher education was 'a demand for knowledge, not for training', in which he was patently wrong.[6] If any proof were needed of this it was the scramble for charters in the

[1] Letter, Joseph Chamberlain to ? 11 December 1899. Chamberlain Papers University of Birmingham JD 12/1/1/25 and 23 May 1900 JC 12/1/1/27.
[2] Sir Oliver Lodge, 'A Modern University' (Reprint from *Nature* 21 and 28 June 1900). See also W. Crosskey, 'A Plea for a Midland University', 10 February 1889, for similar views.
[3] Sir Isambard Owen, *The Significance of a University*.
[4] R. B. Haldane, 'A University for the West of England, Address at the Colston Society Bristol', 5 February 1902. Alfred Marshall's Inaugural at Bristol was equally explicit about the scientific education of businessmen. MS. 'Some Aspects of Modern Industrial Life', October 1877, Box 6 Marshall MSS.
[6] J. M. Mackay, *A New University*, and *A University for Liverpool* (Liverpool, 1901). *A Miscellany presented to John Macdonald Mackay*, p. 359.
[5] J. R. Seeley, *A Midland University*.

1900s as each institution saw plainly that without the capacity to grant hard paper qualifications its students would desert. Another good example of airy advice from outside that was disregarded was that of Gladstone to the young university college at Nottingham. At the opening in 1881 he told them in what spirit to study science: 'not the physical forces which could be harnessed to improve machinery, new chemical combinations, cheaper manufactures, but rather the rich enjoyment ... of all that physical world and the beauty and the glory with which it had pleased the Almighty to invest His visible creation'. The town council, who must have listened to and applauded this rhetorical flight with polite incredulity, made it clear that this was not their view. For them 'the teaching of the college should be very largely if not chiefly directed to those branches of knowledge which are capable of practical application in the various industrial pursuits'.[1]

If then the civic universities made their intentions so plain and their claims so bold, how did they fulfil them by serving industry through their teaching and study of industrial sciences? Any consideration of this question should begin with chemistry and the central figure of Sir Henry Roscoe, the most important of the early professors of the civic universities who brought the universities into contact with industry, and one of the first professor-industrial consultants in England in the nineteenth century.[2] A scion of the Liverpool Roscoes and a graduate of University College, London, and Heidelberg, he became Professor of Chemistry at Owens in 1857. He was clear in his own mind that the college could only be successful by gaining the confidence and the financial support of local industry. His letter books[3] display a remarkable range of industrial advisory work, bringing the benefits of chemistry to the firms around Manchester which in the 1870s was the largest centre of chemical manufacture in Britain, producing £1 million worth a year within a radius of twenty miles. He did much work in checking chemical nuisances for the local Board of Health, particularly those of the dreaded horseboilers, but went far beyond his negative investigatory capacities in advising chemical firms about the recovery of waste by-products, the avoidance of the loss of gases, and the layout of factories.[4] He tested cloth and its chemical qualities,[5] advised Charles Macintosh on his rubber solution,[6] did much analysis of water for steam boilers, and it was he who determined on

---

[1] A. C. Wood, op. cit., pp. 19–20.
[2] Sir Henry Roscoe, *Life and Experiences of Sir Henry Enfield Roscoe.*
[3] MS. Letter Books of Sir Henry Roscoe 1866–78; 1878–83. Manchester University Library MSS. CH R107, 108.
[4] Reports 24 January 1874 and 2 July 1872, for example, as typical of many.
[5] Messrs W. Calvert and Sons, 26 May 1873.
[6] 11 November 1878.

Thirlmere as the source of Manchester's water supply.[1] His consultancy went widely outside Lancashire. He advised Middlesbrough chemical manufacturers on the adoption of the Gay Lussac Tower[2] and Durham on coking coal, and made early spectroscopic studies in Sheffield on the changing chemical composition of steel in the Bessemer converter.[3] These are but examples of the hundreds of pieces of work recorded in his voluminous letters, and the deliberate policy of close involvement with industry paid the dividends he sought. He reflected after thirty years that 'there were I believe few engaged in that district in any large way of business in which chemistry plays a part who did not show their appreciation of the value of scientific education by sending their sons or their managers to learn chemistry at Owens College.'[4]

What he taught them when they arrived in his lecture room was orientated to their needs. He talked of the economic effects of coal, explosions and coal gas and bleaching, but he was also careful that his teaching did not become merely practical and technical.[5] He ensured that his pupils gained a thorough theoretical knowledge of the subject as a whole and it is also worth observing that the whole level of even his first year lectures seems remarkably advanced. Beyond his activities as a chemist, Roscoe was also most important in the civic university movement generally. At Kelvin's prompting he was a leading instigator of the schemes to turn Owens College into a university; he served on the governing bodies of Liverpool and Sheffield and as academic adviser to Dundee, while as Vice-Chancellor of London he was a figure behind the creation of Imperial College. In industry he was a founder, with Ludwig Mond and Edmund Muspratt, of the Society of the Chemical Industry. It is quite impossible to do justice to or to exaggerate the importance of Roscoe as the new model of the English industrially orientated scientific professor, as a conceiver of the idea of a civic university serving local industry, and as a founder of modern chemical education in this country.

While Manchester was the premier centre for chemistry in the provinces and also, with Roscoe's colleague Schorlemmer, the pioneer in England of German-style organic chemistry, other centres were able to achieve a limited excellence by specializing in separate industrial technologies. At Bristol, for example, Nierenstein's work on the biochemistry of cheese ripening after 1909 did much for the

---

[1] Report on Thirlmere Water Supply, 4 March 1878.
[2] 19 February 1875.
[3] *Floreamus*, March 1901, pp. 263–4, and *Life*, p. 132.
[4] Sir Henry Roscoe, op. cit., p. 103.
[5] Sir Henry Roscoe's MS. Lecture Notes 1857–8, MSS. CH R106. He told the Devonshire Commission, 'I deprecate altogether the idea of teaching . . . the arts of manufactures themselves'. 1872 XXV RC *Scientific Instruction* (Devonshire), Q. 7367.

local Cheddar industry, while J. W. MacBain's work on the colloid chemistry of soap in conjunction with Ernest Walls, a director of Levers, was not only of national importance for the soap industry but led to Leverhulme's benevolent interest in Bristol University.[1] A special forte of Birmingham was the chemistry of fermentation, and building on these fermentation biochemistry interests the brewers in 1900 established the British School of Malting and Brewing in the university. Beyond that, Birmingham was not eager to have too great a specialization in chemistry, largely because the industries of the city were so diverse—chocolate, explosives, rubber, for example—and since it would be impossible to cater for the techniques of any one it was better to give a thorough grounding for all.[2] This principle, also followed by Roscoe, was a further feature preventing these embryonic universities from sinking into trade schools.

The University of Leeds was particularly excellent in cornering three specialized fields of industrial chemistry in which it achieved some eminence. Leeds catered uniquely for the chemistry of leather. After long experience with his family firm and as a works chemist in the North East, Henry Procter, the first man to study the chemistry of leather scientifically in an industrial context, took charge of the new department of the leather industries at Yorkshire College in 1891.[3] At once close relations with firms were established. The department was used for analysis and investigations for the trade, with manufacturers coming into the university to experiment with new machinery in tanning and dyeing, while Procter himself visited the factories to advise on new processes.[4] His work paid off in the greatly improved quality and control of tanning materials and in the manufacture of chrome leather and especially of box calf which owed much to Procter's work. Even at the remedial level of detecting foreign techniques and advising manufacturers how to copy them, Procter's work was a valuable service to the British leather industry whose shoe section in the late 1890s was successfully fighting off a determined invasion from the Americans.[5] Leeds also served the scientific needs of the gas industry.[6] In 1907 their department of

[1] W. E. Garner, 'The School of Chemistry in the University of Bristol', *JRIC*, January 1954.
[2] Henry L. Heathcote, 'The University Training of Industrial Chemists', *Journal of the Society of the Chemical Industry*, 27 February 1909.
[3] 'Henry Richardson Procter 1848–1927' (pamphlet in the files of the Procter Leather Department at Leeds University) MS. Letter, Henry Procter to Arthur Smithells, 5 March 1890, on his early career, in the same section.
[4] Yorkshire College, Application to the . . . Company of Skinners, n.d., *c* 1896. Report 1899–1900 and MS. Letter, H. Breakbane to Procter, 9 May 1898. Report 1902–3.
[5] Reports of the Work of the Department of Leather Industries, *passim* 1903–13.
[6] The Department of Gas Engineering, Fuel and Metallurgy at the University of Leeds 1907. *The Gas World*, 20 December 1924. Department of Coal Gas and Fuel Industries, Report of the Livesey Professor 1912–13.

coal gas and fuel industries had been established as the first of its kind in any British university and in the following year the Institution of Gas Engineers induced the industry to endow a chair to commemorate Sir George Livesey, the Chairman of the South Metropolitan Gas Company. In conjunction with the industry, important work was done on the design of gas fires, gaseous explosions, and the carbonization of coal, much of their research being carried out in industrial conditions.

The third specialized area of chemistry in which Leeds excelled was tinctorial chemistry as applied to textiles. The department here began in 1874, watched over by a committee of local manufacturers headed by Obadiah Nussey.[1] With the works of the Professors J. and R. Beaumont, father and son, the industry began to be set on a scientific footing with the beginning of the photomicroscopy of fibres from 1905, and the standardization of colour gradings for blends of weaves in the 1900s.[2] Their stress on research carried over to benefit individual firms. We find seventeen firms having research done on their behalf between 1903 and 1905, and their students went out to dye firms such as Levinstein's and Read Holliday. The value of this department to local industry was considerable and well appreciated at the time.[3]

> When one compares the character of the trade of Leeds and the district of two decades ago with what it is at the present day and considers that many of the most important mills in the locality are supervised by Yorkshire College men, it becomes evident that the instruction imparted in that institution has in no small degree benefited the weaving industries of the city and neighbourhood. There has been a complete change in the classes and styles of fabrics made in the district since the textile departments of the college commenced work. Some years ago Leeds was noted for its production of plain textures: now fancy fabrics both of woollen and worsted materials in very extensive varieties are made in the neighbourhood.

This last was a most important factor in staving off French competition in the woollen and worsted trade with the change in fashion towards fancier materials.[4]

In these connections of university chemistry departments and

[1] *The Yorkshire College, Leeds* (London, 1895), reprinted from *The Record of Technical and Secondary Education*, October 1895.

[2] Reports of the Textile Industries Department, 1903–11 *passim*.

[3] *Yorkshire Daily Post*, 19 September 1894, cited Thomas Girtin, *The Golden Ram, a Narrative History of the Clothworkers' Company 1582–1958* (London, 1958), p. 20.

[4] E. M. Sigsworth and J. M. Blackman, 'The Woollen and Worsted Industries' in D. H. Aldcroft (ed.), *The Development of British Industry and Foreign Competition 1875–1914* (London, 1968). Professor Sigsworth, however,

industry there was one curious gap. If any civic university before 1914 ought to have had a most prominent industrial chemistry department one would have expected it to be Liverpool, a university cradled in the very centre of the British alkali industry and bolstered by Lever, Muspratt, Brunner, and the rest. And yet although it doubtless performed invaluable work in training chemists for the works, it does not seem to emerge as a significant research centre before 1914. Partly this may be due to the fact that the first Grant Professor came originally from the medical school and his interests were medical and public analytical rather than industrial. Second, it may have been less necessary since the great chemical works of this region had a longer tradition of research within the firm than any other sector of British industry. What they required from the university was usable graduates rather than research into their own technologies.[1]

Scarcely any industry had more university attention lavished on it than mining. Newcastle formed the first centre, one of the chief motives for the formation of the college having been the need for a national mining centre outside London. From here came as students many of the leading mining engineers in Britain, including Sir Richard Redmayne and Lord Cadman, successively professors at Birmingham. Before the 1920s, however, one has the impression that Newcastle's teaching in this field was more important than its research, though some original work was done on the electrical resistance of coal and steel wires for mining ropes.[2] In the teaching and production of graduates its achievement was more considerable. Of the students attending the college between 1871 and 1881 and whose occupations were known eighty-nine had by 1885 become mining engineers, including four owners, three assistant government inspectors, and the Chief Inspector of Mines in New Zealand.[3] Birmingham with little doubt was the most important of the English mining departments having started in 1902 under Sir Richard Redmayne. The emphasis tended to be on mineral mining, reflecting Redmayne's own South African interests, though he had also worked extensively in Durham and Northumberland. He built the underground model mine at the university and installed the first ore dressing laboratory in a British university. His course was highly science orientated but he never let himself get out of touch with

---

considers that technical education was not of much significance in Yorkshire's retaliatory capacity at this time. However, this evidence of the 1890s suggests that it was thought to be playing an important role.

[1] See *Liverpool Daily Post*, 21 March 1888, for a lecture on the recovery of sulphur from alkali waste which suggests the department was making itself useful.

[2] Annual Reports of Durham College of Science 1895–1903 and Armstrong College, 1904–5, et seq.

[3] William Garnett in the *Durham University Journal*, 23 May 1885, p. 122.

practice, acting as a consultant to the Duke of Sutherland's mines in Staffordshire, serving as a director of the Blaina colliery in South Wales, and returning to South Africa for further work during his tenure of the chair.[1] When Redmayne left to become the Chief Inspector of Mines in 1908 his place was taken by John Cadman whose interests lay in petroleum. It was he who advised the cabinet to purchase the Anglo-Persian oil shares in 1912, and accordingly he was able to diversify the mining interests of the department yet further from coal, a trend in keeping with the fact that Birmingham's local resources of coal were in decline. Leeds gave instruction in mining from 1877, supported by the Drapers' Company—a suitable complement to its later work on fuel economy and gas. Manchester ran a course dealing with the Lancashire and Cumberland fields from 1905 and Nottingham began in 1911, responsive to the rapid development of the Nottingham coalfield.

In the vital field of metallurgy, Sheffield necessarily had pride of place. The first principal, Viriamu Jones 'almost immediately conceived the hope of creating in Sheffield the greatest metallurgical school in England'.[2] This was apposite because the founder of modern metallography, Henry Sorby, was the first chairman of the Technical Committee of the university and a benefactor.[3] His examination of the crystal structure of metals, especially steel, at high magnifications attracted much, if belated, attention in the 1880s, and Sorby was instrumental in the formation of the Technical School which became part of the University College on its formation in 1897. From 1889 Dr Oliver Arnold, a friend of Sorby's and in many ways his heir, took over the department. From his surviving correspondence from 1904 it is possible to see something of his enormous contributions to the scientific health of the surrounding iron and steel industry.

Around the turn of the century he was undertaking important researches on high speed steels which he communicated in secrecy to a dozen leading Sheffield firms,[4] and he did much work on fractures and exploding boiler plates, using the microscopic techniques developed by Sorby. He was also important in the development of new forms of steel, notably vanadium steel for motor car parts[5] and the motor car steel made by Vickers in 1905.[6] In 1908 his department became the centre for a manufacturers' commission on

[1] Sir Richard Redmayne, *Men, Mines and Memories*. R. A. S. Redmayne, *The Mining Department of the University of Birmingham*.
[2] K. V. Jones, *The Life of John Viriamu Jones*, p. 57.
[3] Cecil H. Desch, 'The Services of Henry Clifton Sorby to Metallurgy', Sorby Lecture, 1912.
[4] Letter, 11 February 1909, to Colonel Hughes. The collections of Arnold's letters are kept at Sheffield University.
[5] 14 August 1907 to E. R. von der Osten.
[6] 14 August 1905 to E. R. Grainger.

electrical steels[1] and in that capacity he sent a deputation to Sweden to investigate the Kjellin furnace which he warned Sheffield may prove a serious competitor.[2] In 1911 he worked on stainless steel[3] and on a phospho-magnetic steel for BTH for whom he did much consultancy work,[4] while throughout this time, 1909–13, he was also acting as consultant to Simpson and Oviatt's attempt to find the direct steel process from iron sand.[5] Finally, he was the inventor of the alternating stress machine which came to be an important research tool for advanced mechanical engineers, Rolls Royce being one of the first users. So important was Arnold's work for Sheffield and so intimately did he know its work processes, many of which he had devised or improved, that he even became something of a security risk. For example in 1913 he complained, 'I am very much handicapped since the community here object to my writing a genuine book which might assist their American and German competitors.'[6] This very limitation was a profound compliment to the value of his work, most of which was too important to publish.

The other major metallurgical centre was Birmingham University which established a lectureship specifically in the subject in 1886, two years after Sheffield's. On the new Edgbaston site in 1904 they claimed that their metallurgy facilities were the 'largest and best equipped in the world' and this was capped by the Feeney £20,000 bequest to endow the chair. Whereas Arnold's work had been chiefly on high quality steels, the Birmingham work was more related to iron and brass. In particular they studied the influence of silicon on cast iron and laid the foundation of scientific iron founding, devised methods for determining the hardness of metals, and examined the microstructure of cast iron and brass and the effects of gases on metals.[7] All this was clearly of relevance to the pump and dynamo casting, cartridge, and other manufacturers making the myriad iron and alloy materials for which the city was noted. Although Arnold does not in his correspondence seem to have had much to do with the Birmingham department[8] the two universities

[1] 16 December 1908.
[2] First and Second Reports to the Steel Research Committee, 1907–10. Sheffield crucible steel was still considered the best. Arnold was generally dubious of electrical steels.
[3] 2 November 1917 to Sir George Kenrick refers back to this. Harry Brearley, the inventor of stainless steel, did not seem to like Arnold, see Harry Brearley, *Knotted String* (London, 1941), p. 145.
[4] 2 June 1911.
[5] 19 December 1917 to Dr Bowman.
[6] 9 May 1913 to R. A. Gregory. It will be evident that Arnold's position in relation to academic freedom was an involved one. This will be considered later.
[7] *The University of Birmingham and the Study of Metals* (c. 1920).
[8] Save a complimentary reference, 17 January 1913, accepting Birmingham as the only peer of his own department.

seem to have divided the metallurgical field sensibly between them, each relating to its own city.

Engineering was taught in most of the colleges, like chemistry, as a basic technological subject. Pre-eminent in mechanical engineering in the provinces was Manchester under Osborne Reynolds.[1] Engineering was always strong in Manchester due in large part to the continued interest of Whitworth, Fairburn, Beyer, and Mather among the leading engineering firms of the district. They were fortunate in their first professor, Osborne Reynolds, who attained an international reputation as a founding father of the science of flowing fluids.[2] He worked on the screw propeller, then vastly improved the design of the centrifugal pumps and turbines in the 1870s, a design that was taken up by Mather and Platt as the chief form of colliery pump in the later nineteenth century.[3] Finally, his work on lubrication made possible the development of the modern thrust bearing: 'it is hardly too much to say that the development of the modern high speed liner or battleship or of the modern low head large hydraulic turbine would not have been practicable had such bearings not been available.'[4] Just as Roscoe was the most important industrial chemist working in a civic university before 1900, so Osborne Reynolds was the most important English civic university professor of engineering, and Manchester was supremely fortunate in having the services of both.

Bristol engineering was flourishing on the eve of the war after a wretched period of poverty and lack of research.[5] But in the 1900s the faculty which was in the Merchant Venturers' Technical College successfully set itself out to be of service to local industry. It noted: 'it is especially incumbent on an engineering faculty to be of service to industry in general and more particularly to those engaged in engineering undertakings in the district in which the University is situated.' From then until the war they did work in the department for twenty local firms and it is of particular interest that they were an unusual example of a university department active in motor car engineering, largely due to Professor Morgan, formerly of Daimler's.[6]

[1] A. H. Gibson, *Osborne Reynolds and his Work in Hydraulics and Hydrodynamics.*
[2] It is interesting to note that Reynold's work was highly regarded in Russia in the inter-war years and was still relevant for the construction of the Dnieper dam in the first Five Year Plan. See J. G. Crowther *Science in Soviet Russia* (London, 1930) and *Soviet Science* (London, 1936) p. 209. By coincidence Egiazarov, the Russian consultant to the dam, had also worked in Manchester and was well aware of Reynold's work.
[3] Loris Emerson Mather, *Sir William Mather* (London, 1925), p. 16.
[4] A. H. Gibson, op. cit., p. 19.
[5] 'MS. Notes on the History of Engineering in University College Bristol' in Tyndall Papers, Bristol University Archives DM/363/14.
[6] MS. Minutes and Reports of the University of Bristol Faculty of Engineering, 1911 and *passim*.

Southampton, too, showed early signs of its later forte. The Advisory Committee, who usually looked on Southampton coolly, conceded 'the staff in civil and mechanical engineering seem to have a thorough contact with the engineering activities of the district',[1] and the students were certainly brought into contact with industry,[2] their most notable student of the period being Lanchester, later the motor car designer.[3]

Shipbuilding and naval architecture as specialized forms of engineering were dealt with in particular at Newcastle, initially as part of engineering from 1891 and then as a separate chair from 1907 under a former manager of Laird's of Birkenhead.[4] The initial moves to create the chair of engineering and naval architecture arose from the close contact of Principal William Garnett and the North-East Coast Institution of Engineers and Shipbuilders in 1886. It was by an interesting coincidence that Garnett knew Sir Charles Parsons, both at Cambridge and in Newcastle, and indeed Garnett worked with Parsons on the use of turbines for electrical generation for the Jubilee celebrations of Queen Victoria for which Sir William Armstrong had been the honorary electrical engineer. These matters are important for they indicate that Garnett was *persona grata* with the leading scientific industrialists of the North East who would be receptive to his ideas.[5] From the calling of the meeting of the Institution by Garnett in 1886 resulted the chair of engineering and naval architecture with an advisory panel including inevitably Armstrong and Parsons. The new professor, R. L. Weighton, began by making very plain his usefulness to his backers. He built an experimental quadruple expansion engine with their assistance and 'established a world wide reputation for his researches into the economy of steam engines by that long series of original investigations that are still referred to as "the Newcastle trials" '.[6] Work was done on the strengths of boiler plates and outside firms were able to come into the department to use its equipment as reciprocally Swan

---

[1] 1910 LXXII *Advisory Committee on Grants to University Colleges. Report on Hartley University College.*

[2] MS. Proceedings of Hartley University Scientific Society, 1904–13; notes of visits to pitch, acid, dye, cycle works, brewery, docks, ships, etc.

[3] 'Lanchester's Memoir of the Hartley Institute', in the University Collection *c* LF 782.2, for the ludicrous episode where his father was tricked into thinking that they taught practical engineering by having a stove pipe passed off as a driving shaft. This was in the early 1880s and well illustrates the shifty poverty in which the early colleges had to struggle. Things were much improved by the 1900s.

[4] Typescript 'Statement by Professor Burrill' and MS. note by J. H. Alexander 15 May 1929, on naval architecture at Newcastle. I am grateful to the department for making these available to me.

[5] B. M. Allen, *William Garnett, a Memoir*, p. 40.

[6] 'History of the Engineering Department of King's College' in *The Stephenson Building*, 1951.

Hunter and Wigham Richardson allowed students to make tests on their vessels.[1] The *rapport* between the department and the local shipbuilding firms was thus very close. The other major university centre for this discipline was inevitably Liverpool with its chair of naval architecture, founded in 1903 by Alexander Elder and greatly supplemented by the Harrison Hughes laboratories opened in 1912 for work on internal combustion marine propulsion engines.

The various colleges of London University were quite the most important centres of electrical engineering education in England before 1914, but in the provinces Liverpool had the leading place, largely due to the work of Sir Oliver Lodge in the 1880s and 1890s. Much of his work and teaching had industrial application[2] and he himself was closely involved with industry.[3] He was, for example, scientific adviser to the Eastern Telegraph Company and to the Electric Power Storage Company, doing work for them on batteries in his own laboratory. He also worked on the electrification of dust, 'now the foundation for a large scheme of dust and fume deposition in smelting and other factories', which his son Lionel developed on a manufacturing scale. He developed a loudspeaker and 'a very infantile kind of radio telegraphy' while his patent for selective tuning was bought by Marconi in 1897. Finally, Lodge plugs developed as a family concern from Lodge's electrical work. Lodge, by his capacity for multiple invention in the electrical field and especially by his capacity to relate this to practical industrial use and even to enter commercially into its exploitation, was the nearest English equivalent to the greater figure of Kelvin. Finally, it will be remembered that after Lodge's departure, Liverpool became the first British university with its own wireless station, given by Hartley in 1911.

Electrical engineering was closely associated with developments in the teaching of physics in the universities. In the 1890s and 1900s one found teachers of physics like Lodge at Liverpool, Poynting at Birmingham, Silvanus Thompson at Bristol, Ambrose Fleming at Nottingham, and then London choosing electricity as their main field of interest within physics. In this situation there was a close involvement between physics and industrial application as there was with physicists in the older thermodynamic tradition. Physicists assumed they were useful to industry, as did chemists. For example, Sir Arthur Schuster at Manchester in the 1890s wrote to firms asking them to advise him on the composition of his course, on the assumption that the bulk of his students would eventually

---

[1] Reports of the Durham College of Science and Armstrong College, 1896–7, 1909–10, 1911–12.

[2] 1884 XXIX RC *Technical Instruction* (Samuelson), p. 451, he 'pointed out the importance attaching to courses of electricity as applied to industrial purposes'.

[3] Sir Oliver Lodge, *Past Years, an Autobiography*, pp. 159–248.

become employees in industry.[1] But by the late 1900s we find the beginnings of the disengagement of physics from industrial application taking place in the provinces and following the lead of Cambridge. With J. J. Thomson's work at the Cavendish on nuclear physics so the discipline began to detach itself from industry. At Manchester this was most marked on the eve of the war with that remarkable galaxy of talent including Rutherford, Niels Bohr, Geiger, Chadwick, Moseley—all (with the tragic exception of the last) to become major international figures in the field, but with not the slightest interest in the local concerns of Manchester industry with its steam boilers and electric dynamos.[2] The same happened at Leeds with the advent of Sir William Bragg in 1909 and his work on the X-ray analysis of crystal structures. It was a parting of the ways from the industrially orientated physics-cum-engineering of men like Osborne Reynolds and the great electricians. Perhaps the parting was most dramatically symbolized in 1884 when J. J. Thomson defeated his old teacher Reynolds for the Cavendish chair at Cambridge. Ironically, it was Reynolds, the ex-fellow of Queens', who represented what was best in orthodox civic university industrially orientated engineering physics, but Thomson, the ex-Manchester engineering apprentice, who was to point the way to a new physics disengaged from industry. This was to become more of a problem in the universities in the inter-war years.

The contributions of the civic universities to industry, even in their early days, were thus remarkable and of considerable importance. They were now becoming a leading source of innovation for industry as Oxford and Cambridge never hitherto had been. The thrust bearing lubrication, colliery pumps, vanadium steels, chrome leather, gas fires, sparking plugs, and radio tuning all owed much to the work of their professors while products like cheese, soap, beer, and the quadruple expansion engine were all considerably improved by their work. Even more important than the spectacular innovation was the more routine but vital improvement of the practice of firms such as Roscoe was able to effect for the chemical using and producing industries around Manchester, Arnold for Sheffield metallurgy, and the Beaumonts for Yorkshire textiles. The importance of this is further enhanced when it is appreciated that there were no state centres for industrial research, save possibly the NPL, no research associations, and that research within the firm was in its

---

[1] *Annual Reports of Owens College, Manchester, 1891, 1892.*
[2] J. B. Birks, *Rutherford at Manchester*, p. 40. E. N. de C. Andreade who was also there notes that the researchers were 'eagerly engaging themselves in obtaining results that seemed remote from any possible practical application'. What might have worried industrial employers more was the admitted fact that the teaching course for ordinary undergraduates was shaky and left 'wide gaps in our knowledge of some important sections of classical physics'. Ibid., p. 68.

infancy in the 1890s and 1900s. The civic universities were thus proportionately more important in this regard than possibly ever again. Moreover, by their willingness to undertake testing for firms and by allowing firms to use university equipment, they introduced and raised scientific standards within the firm that often in turn induced them to begin their own testing and research departments using the graduates they had now grown to trust.[1] Having considered the closeness of the linkages between the formation of the civic universities and industry and the early contributions of the new colleges, we may now turn to consider the output of students, their social background and reception into industry, some of the dangers to the universities of this industrial involvement, and finally the special case of London University.

[1] For example Manchester chemistry department from about 1900 began to refuse to undertake chemical analyses for firms on the grounds that most ought now to be able to do them for themselves, forcing the laggards to provide their own facilities and presumably to employ Manchester graduates to man them. Likewise Arnold did some tests for Rolls Royce with his own stress alternator and this induced the firm to buy one of their own.

4
The Civic Universities
1850-1914—II

'He gets degrees in making jam
At Liverpool and Birmingham'.[1]

Having seen something of the industrial initiative and support in the formation of the universities and their response in the development of industrial technologies, we may now consider the students. First, Tables 7 and 8 give some idea of the size of the student body in the civic universities at this time.

The figures indicate a number of features about the increasing contribution of the civic universities. First, the growth in student numbers was most impressive over the late 1880s and early 1890s, with increases of 1,068 in seven years 1880-8 and 1,150 in five years 1888-93. The growth in the 1890s was not so great as that of the 1880s although this decade was one of marked increase in civic university graduates entering industry, as will be seen. However, more important in the 1890s than the increase in student numbers was the changing quality of work being done. The taking of degrees more than doubled between the first and second halves of the 1890s as the colleges were preparing for university status. In the 1900s numbers grew more quickly once again largely due to very large expansions in the three major civic universities of Manchester, Liverpool and Birmingham. Considering degree pupils only, it is probably fair to say from these figures that the graduate output of the provincial civic universities in the late 1880s and early 1890s was of the order of 100 a year (467 divided by 5 = 93); in the 1890s it was of the order of 200 a year (1,110 divided by 5 = 222), and in the 1910s was of the order of 500-600 a year (1,699 divided by 3 = 566), excluding medical people.

Let us focus more closely on the types of students whom the new civic universities served in these years. They were not university

[1] Oxford Broadsheet, 'Why I Vote Non Placet', *c.* 1914 (Bodleian G. A. Oxon b. 141.307).

TABLE 7 *Day students, excluding medicals*

	1880	1888	1893[1]	1900[2]	1913[3]
Manchester	392	389	600	528	799
Birmingham	159	449	409	474	695
Leeds	219	251	400	498	504
Liverpool		315(1887)	313	409	560
Newcastle		48	482	502	342
Bristol		154	195	153	375
Nottingham		232	431	432	198
Sheffield			158	338	303
Reading					397
Southampton					125
Total	770	1,838	2,988	3,334	4,298

[1] 1894 LXVI *Reports from Universities and University Colleges.*
[2] 1900 XX, ibid.
[3] 1914–16 XIX ibid. The 1880 and 1888 figures are calculated from the respective reports of the colleges. The Birmingham 1880 figure is calculated as a trebling of the known intake figure for that year. The Leeds 1880 figure includes medicals who cannot be distinguished. The Liverpool 1887 figure is from Ramsay Muir, *The University of Liverpool, its present State* (Liverpool, 1907).

TABLE 8 *Students who graduated with degrees*

	1889–93	1895–9
Manchester	262	491
Liverpool	66	205
Birmingham	57	60
Leeds	39	168
Nottingham	15	28
Bristol	12	32
Newcastle	11	111
Sheffield	5	15
	467	1,110

students in any modern sense: young people studying full-time by day for three years for a degree qualification. Rather they were a motley mixture of young ladies attending afternoon lectures on Renaissance Art, foremen from the steelworks or laboratory assistants from the dyeworks taking night classes in chemistry, possibly for a City and Guilds examination, schoolboys getting up some science before taking an Oxford or Cambridge scholarship, intending school-teachers in training, and the hard core of the dedicated studying for a London external degree.

How far then were the civic universities catering for the type of student whose background, studies and career were likely to be useful to industry? At Manchester it was assumed at the outset that 'a large proportion of the students will probably consist of sons of merchants or others engaged in the commercial pursuits of the district',[1] and so indeed it proved. A former student recalling early days at Quay Street remembered that 'businessmen of course preponderated in numbers'.[2] In the early 1870s Principal Greenwood estimated that of the day students two-fifths were of the 'higher mercantile class', one-third were professional, and the rest, say four-fifteenths, lower mercantile and artisan. On the other hand, in the evening classes (about a third of the size of day classes at Owens in 1870) five-sixths of the students were of the working class.[3] Roscoe before the same commission indicated some of the occupations of his chemistry evening class—manufacturing chemist, sugar refiner, metal broker, soap maker, calico printer, dyer, and so forth,[4] and the sixty pupils in his chemical laboratory included thirteen chemical manufacturers, four drysalters, two calico printers, two dyers, two glass makers and one manufacturing chemist, one metal broker, one paper maker, and one potter.[5] Working men, from Platt's for example, did go to Owens College[6] but such students did not intend to remain foremen and working men. As Sir Joseph Lee pointed out, 'the students at Owens College generally expect to be something a little better.'.[7]

This pattern was also evident at Leeds where 'generally the students attending the day classes are the sons of manufacturers, managers and designers, but the evening classes are chiefly attended

---

[1] *The Owens College, Substance of the Report . . . on the General Character and Plan of the College* (Manchester, 1850).
[2] Henry Brierley, *Memories of Quay Street and the Owens College* (privately printed, 1921). This referred to the early 1860s.
[3] 1872 XXV RC *Scientific Instruction* (Devonshire), J. G. Greenwood. QQ. 7288–94.
[4] Ibid., p. 499. Table submitted by Roscoe.
[5] Ibid., p. 498.
[6] Ibid., QQ. 1933–4.
[7] 1886 XXIII RC *Depression of Trade and Industry*. Evidence of Sir Joseph Lee of Tootal Broadhurst, Lee and Company. Q. 8140.

by artisans'.[1] In textiles most of the day students were the sons of masters and entered their fathers' works on leaving college.[2] In the leather department likewise in the 1890s more than half the students were relatives of employers already in the industry,[3] and of fifteen students going into leather firms around 1911, thirteen were going into their fathers' firms.[4] At Liverpool it was noted that 'nearly all the female students belonged to the higher ranks of society, while the male students had nearly all been engaged in business or had left some public school to further prosecute their education'.[5] Similarly at Bristol the women day students were 'daughters of the best families in the town' whereas the men students were socially somewhat below them. Moreover, the bulk of male evening students were engaged in business during the day.[6]

For Birmingham we may examine the social background of the students in detail. The usual general claims were made. It was said that it was the college 'to which the sons of the Midland manufacturer and mine owner . . . will naturally come' and that 'of the male students the majority are the sons of manufacturers in Birmingham and neighbouring towns'.[7] The social class of fathers of students for the intake of 1893 may be presented in the following rough spectrum of occupational grading.[8]

1 *Professional* (99)
   3 accountants, 2 army, 4 auctioneers, 1 almoner, 1 bailiff, 1 factor, 6 agents, 1 art director, 1 town clerk, 1 bank manager, 1 consulting brewer, 8 clergy, 5 government inspectors, 7 civil engineers, 3 doctors, 1 dentist, 15 managers, 1 organist, 4 professors, 1 physician, 9 solicitors, 16 schoolmasters, 3 surveyors, 4 surgeons.

2 *Manufacturers and merchants in large or expensive trades* (45)
   1 basket manufacturer, 1 cycle manufacturer, 11 builders, 2 chandelier makers, 4 manufacturing chemists, 1 contractor, 3 paper makers, 1 flour merchant, 1 diamond merchant, 1 farmer, 1 hat manufacturer, 1 iron founder, 3 iron masters, 1 iron merchant, 10 'manufacturers', 2 safety-pin manufacturers, 1 wine merchant.

[1] 'The Yorkshire College, Leeds' (London, 1895) reprinted from *The Record o Technical and Secondary Education*, October 1895.
[2] Report . . . Department of Textile Industries, 1888–9.
[3] Report . . . Department of Leather, 1895–6.
[4] University of Leeds Leather Department Appeal, 1911.
[5] *Liverpool Daily Post*, 12 May 1882.
[6] 1881 XXXIII *Report . . . Higher Education in Wales* (Aberdare) C. 3047, 1881. Alfred Marshall. QQ. 18165, 18186.
[7] Charles Lapworth, *The Mason College and Technical Education*, p. 18, and 1884 XXIX RC *Technical Instruction* (Samuelson), p. 402.
[8] MS. Register of Students in the Faculties of Arts and Sciences 1892–3, 1893–4.

3 *Trades and special skills* (56)
 1 butcher, 2 booksellers, 3 blacksmiths, 3 bakers, 1 cabinet maker, 2 confectioners, 7 grocers, 2 clothiers, 2 china gilders, 7 drapers, 1 decorator, 1 engraver, 1 goldsmith, 1 goldbeater, 7 jewellers, 1 mountmaker, 2 millers, 1 pawnbroker, 1 photographer, 1 silversmith, 1 tea dealer, 2 tailors, 1 tobacconist, 1 tool maker, 2 watch makers, 1 beer dealer, 1 boiler inspector.

4 *Semi-professional white collar literacy-using occupations* (35)
 3 bookkeepers, 16 clerks, 8 commercial travellers, 3 cashiers, 1 journalist, 1 printer's reader, 2 secretaries, 1 verger.

5 *Probable artisans* (35)
 1 engine driver, 14 engineers, 3 foremen, 1 gardener, 1 grazier, 2 gas engineers, 2 wire drawers, 2 joiners, 1 mechanic, 1 machinist, 1 miner, 1 metal worker, 1 packer, 1 quarryman, 2 turners, 1 weigher.

Two characteristics of this intake of Birmingham students in the 1890s become evident. First, the college was drawing its students from family backgrounds in industry and trade. Of these 270 students only seventy at a generous estimate could be said to have nothing to do with industry or trade. Secondly, there did seem somewhat of a predominance of upper middle-class among those students drawn from industrial and commercial backgrounds. Leaving categories 3 and 4 aside as a dubious middle ground, we would estimate sixty-one as coming from a middle- and upper middle-class industrial and commercial background and thirty-five from a working-class industrial and commercial background. Possibly one or two individuals could be moved from one group to another but this does not affect the general picture, which is in any case in accord with the impressionistic comments made earlier. Birmingham did draw its students from industry and commerce and within that area from the upper middle-classes more than from the working-class.

At Southampton, on the other hand, the class balance seemed to be the other way, with 118 of what they called the middle-classes and 395 of the 'industrial classes', the bulk of whom were clerks, engineers and fitters, pupil teachers, carpenters and plumbers.[1] This goes some way to account for the backwardness of the college which, unlike Birmingham, was clearly not tapping a large well-to-do business-class clientele. Finally, as another example of relative failure before 1914, there were at least two complaints from Nottingham that they were not attracting the sons of the manufacturing class of the city. Samuel Morley, referring to Nottingham, considered that 'the sons of the well-to-do and successful tradesmen and manu-

---

[1] Application of the Hartley Council for a Grant from the Corporation, 1891

facturers are not sent to our universities',[1] and the former Professor of Chemistry at Nottingham, remembering his experience there, also thought that 'it is very difficult to induce the proprietors and managers of works to give their sons a thorough training . . .', though the best students were the sons of managers when they could get them.[2]

If we suggest that the civic universities were further relating themselves to industry by drawing their clientele from the industrial classes, it is worth adding a comment about the professoriate. How far did they themselves come from this background and how far could they bring industrial experience to their work? First, certain posts required prior industrial experience as a matter of necessity. We do not know of a professor of mining who had not practical experience. So stringent were the qualifications for this profession—the only one whose conditions were laid down by Act of Parliament—that a purely theoretical professor of mining was inconceivable.[3] The same applied in engineering because of the English stress upon post-college apprenticeship training, especially in marine engineering. Chemistry is the most interesting case, sitting as it does around the middle of the spectrum. It was quite usual for professors of chemistry to have had prior industrial experience. For example, of five applicants for the chair of chemistry at Birmingham, three had had industrial experience; the only two who had not were Scottish which is surprising.[4] On the other hand it was not at all usual for professors of mathematics and physics to have had experience of this kind. None of the seven Birmingham applicants in this category had had it although it was common for such academics to have close contact with industry while holding their chairs.

Having studied the social and industrial background of the students, we may now consider what proportions went into industrial careers on graduating (see Table 9). The fairly clear pattern of rise in the 1870s, fall in the 1880s, rise in the 1890s, and sharp rise from 1910 to 1913 is consistent with the movement of the industrial economy and is also consistent between universities. However, the

[1] Samuel Morley speaking in *Report of a Public Meeting held at Bristol to promote the Establishment of a College of Science and Literature for the West of England and South Wales* (Bristol, 1874), p. 41.
[2] Frank Clowes in evidence to *LCC Technical Education Board Subcommittee on the Application of Science to Industry*, 1902, p. 19.
[3] Cf. Letter, 13 December 1904, in Letter Books of the Dean of the Faculty of Science, University of Birmingham. When the President of the National Association of Colliery Managers offered to nominate an advisory member of the department he was told this was quite unnecessary since the professor, lecturer, and external examiner were all colliery managers or surveyors. It would have required a colliery manager of some temerity to presume to 'advise' Professor Redmayne who was very shortly to become Chief Inspector of Mines.
[4] Testimonials of the applicants for the first professorships, Birmingham University. In the University Collection, 1965/viii/4/1–.

TABLE 9   *Percentage of students entering industry*

	1860-9	1870-9	1880-9	1890-9	1900-4	1905-9	1910-13
Birmingham[1]					8·64	25·2	31·6
Newcastle[2]				36·3	58·3 (1900-5)	46·2 (1906-9)	55·5
Manchester chemists[3]				47·3 (1896-1900)		32·6	
Manchester physicists[4]			33·4	48·3	21·2 (1900-6)		
Bristol[5]		12·5	5·3	17·9	30·4 (1900-9)		

[1] Calculated from University of Birmingham Register of Graduates (1932 edition) names A–J inclusive.
[2] Calculated from *King's (Newcastle) Old Students' Association Year Book, 1938.*
[3] Calculated from Reports of Manchester University Department of Chemistry, 1896–1909.
[4] Calculated from register in *The Physical Laboratories of the University of Manchester, a Record of 25 years work* (Manchester, 1906).
[5] Calculated from lists in *Nonesuch.*

1900s is a complicated decade. For both Newcastle graduates and Manchester chemists and physicists it seems to be a decade in which industry was less attractive than formerly, whereas for Bristol and Birmingham graduates it was a decade of upward trend. Broken into blocks of years, there seems to be clearer evidence that the latter part of the decade was less buoyant. The first part of the decade, 1899–1903, was fairly stagnant in industrial growth. There was a sharp boom in the middle of the decade, then a recession in 1908 and 1909 before a sharp and consistent pre-war boom. The low Birmingham figure for 1900–4 and the fall back for Manchester physicists between 1900 and 1906 reflect the former period while the figures for Manchester chemists and Newcastle reflect the recession of 1908–9. It is also probable that the building up of the state secondary school system after the Act of 1902 diverted young graduates into school-teaching who would not have contemplated a career in elementary schools in the 1890s. However, just as the preceding depression generated an unease and a change in attitude in favour of improving industrial efficiency through higher education, so the succeeding boom created the jobs, the optimism and the profits that enabled firms to give practical effect to these good intentions.

*   *   *

This close involvement of the universities with industry, both in the nature of their early support, in the subjects of their teaching and research, and the background of their students, brought them face to face with two problems that menaced their position as independent institutions of higher learning. The first was that of the dangers of lay interference and control, and the second that of the excessive domination of science and technology in the range of their activities. At Liverpool, for example, there was some friction between the academic staff and the lay council of the university about the latter's control. Sir John Brunner made no secret of his view 'that the finances should be in the hands of men of business. You may depend upon it that in order to give confidence to men of business it will be necessary to give power to those who hold the purse.'[1] His close collaborator and successor as chairman of the council, James Alsop, was as firmly determined to maintain business control as Brunner had been, and held that 'when a University came it should be no place for one sided government . . . but the city itself serving it and its great businessmen sharing in its government.'[2] In view of the tens of thousands given by the business interests of the city for the university it is difficult to see the Brunner–Alsop line as unreasonable. Alsop himself was a keen advocate of close links between the universities and industry, and as a solicitor having many businessmen and firms among his friends and clients he was closely identified with and sympathetic to their position. This did not, however, go unchallenged and Professor Mackay became the leading protagonist on the Liverpool faculty for the view that the total power in the university should be vested in the academic staff—the 'one sided government' deplored by Alsop. However, although this remained a smouldering issue there was little hope that Mackay could get his way. A certain amount of unpleasantness also arose at Sheffield about Arnold's work in metallurgy. He was complaining in 1909 of demands by certain industrialists 'that the scientific lecturers of the University should be compelled by the Council to make such lectures always subservient to the trade interests', and Arnold rejected 'this attempt of a limited number of manufacturers to dictate to its professors'.[3] Arnold was also troubled by the question of the secrecy of his academic work which was imposed by its commercial importance. For example, he was being accused by Firth's of using public university money to carry out secret investigations and for passing secret information to one firm, Jonas and Colver. Such was the nature of much of Arnold's consultancy work

[1] Sir John Brunner, *The Need of a University for Liverpool* (Liverpool, 1901), p. 20.
[2] *The Life of James W. Alsop by his Wife* (Liverpool, 1926), especially pp. 77–8.
[3] MS. Letters O. Arnold to Colonel Hughes, 11 February 1909, and to Sir Charles Eliot, 15 February 1909.

that questions of academic freedom and the free access to knowledge which should be made public became rather blurred at Sheffield. However, he dug his heels in over another matter and refused to let his department be used for commercial advertising.

Sir Oliver Lodge, when at Liverpool, ran into similar difficulties. When working for the Electric Power Storage Company he published some of his work, 'thereby', as he reflected afterwards, 'giving away some of the secrets in an injudicious manner'.[1] Here again the burdens of work for an outside commercial body were beginning to impose inhibitions on the free dissemination of knowledge which might otherwise have been regarded as the duty of a university. Because of its financial weakness, Bristol also was somewhat over-eager to accommodate any business interests willing to help the college. For example, firms becoming annual subscribers could virtually buy their way onto the governing body.[2] This caused a good deal of friction at the end of the period when a row blew up in 1913 about Bristol's being too free in granting honorary degrees to the merchants and industrialists on their governing body.[3] However, although these were straws in the wind we are not inclined to over-stress them. So much did the universities owe to the business communities of their respective cities that these occasional naïveties of over-pushing businessmen or lapses by academics scarcely seem to provide evidence of the debauching of the universities by their involvement with industry. Certainly on the most important issue, that between Mackay and Brunner and Alsop at Liverpool, it is the former's position that appears in retrospect the less reasonable. Interference was probably most marked and dangerous in the field of economics teaching, as will be seen in a later chapter.

However, a more serious issue was the tendency in some universities to an excessive technological specialization. This was the serious portent behind the mocking Oxford jingle at the head of this chapter. It was an early dilemma faced by Principal Scott of Owens in the 1850s. He was quite firm that 'the empirical formulas of engine making, navigation, dyeing or printing were not to be substituted for science and for scientific cultivation of the mind', although he observed sardonically that the industrialists of Manchester expected the college to be 'a living substitute for patent lists, commercial circulars and engine makers' working manuals . . .'.[4] By insisting on a balanced range of sciences and arts subjects Owens condemned itself to slow growth until the 1870s. But this rather dismal period of

[1] Sir Oliver Lodge, *Past Years, an Autobiography*, p. 179.
[2] Articles of Association of the University College Bristol 1876.
[3] Wilhelm Dibelius, *England* (London, 1930), translated M. A. Hamilton, book IV, chapter III, p. 442, draws attention to this point.
[4] Principal Scott's Statement at a Meeting, 20 May 1856 (in Manchester Central Library).

Owens College was in fact one of profound importance for the civic universities movement generally, for it meant that when the Victoria federation was formed Manchester was in a powerful position to force frankly philistine institutions like Sheffield and Leeds to widen their range of disciplines or suffer rejection from the advantages Victoria could bestow.

Some colleges openly wanted to concentrate almost exclusively on the technological sciences. At Leeds, Sir Andrew Fairburn strongly held the view that the college should confine itself to industrial science, first, because the arts were of no practical use and, second, because he feared that if the college became too arts inclined then this would dissuade manual workers from attendance. On the other hand, his Vice-Chancellor, Sir Nathan Bodington, was quite clear that Leeds would have to develop arts subjects if they were ever to achieve university status.[1] That Bodington was right was brought home forcibly to Leeds when their initial application to join Victoria was rejected and their reception delayed until 1887 because of their lack of arts degree work. Sheffield too was rejected from Victoria for the same reason in 1898 although it was not to know that the federation was on the point of breaking up. Mason's College, Birmingham, like Leeds, had a deliberate technological bias imposed by the views of its founder who likewise suspected the arts as useless subjects. E. A. Sonnenschein had the foresight to realize that if Birmingham were to become a university it would have to develop a greater balance between arts and sciences. It was to the credit of Sir George Kenrick, the ironware industrialist and great benefactor of the college, that he backed Sonnenschein's views,[2] though even in the 1900s Principal Lodge found that 'the arts professors were only admitted on suffrance'.[3] In some colleges the arts were squeezed out, if not by design then by the excessive pressure of scientific work. At Newcastle, for example, it was deplored that the arts classes were deserted because all the time was taken up with laboratory work.[4]

There were, however, three forces other than the sanctions of Victoria which forced the colleges away from excessive technical specialism, namely the University of London, the government grant, and teacher training. As regards the first, some subjects in literature and classics were necessary for London external degrees even in science. Thus colleges had to teach them, if not out of any conviction

[1] W. H. Draper, *Sir Nathan Bodington*, p. 140.
[2] E. J. Somerset, *The Birth of a University, a Passage in the Life of E. A. Sonnenschein* (Oxford, 1934).
[3] Sir Oliver Lodge, op. cit., p. 318.
[4] Letter, A. S. Farrar to the Provost of Dundee, 31 January 1875, in W. Knight *Early Chapters in the History of the University of St. Andrews and Dundee*, p. 59.

of their value then at least for the science students' degree work.[1] From 1889, the state began to give grants of public money to English universities, this came to be administered by an advisory committee that after the war became the UGC. Now this body was highly suspicious of institutions claiming to be university colleges when they were little more than local technical colleges, and it insisted that a fair range of subjects to degree level should be a criterion for the bestowal of a grant. In particular they cast a suspicious eye on Birmingham and Southampton which they insisted should extend and strengthen their arts side as a condition of grant. Since this body came to wield a vastly increasing amount of money so the beneficial pressures that it could exert commensurately increased.[2] Third, the demands for arts subjects by students intending to be teachers had a counterbalancing effect.

Manchester (with its excellent historical studies under Ward and Tout and philosophy under Alexander) and Liverpool[3] were the civic universities that most successfully aimed at a broad balance of arts and sciences in the tradition of English universities. But between them and the attempts of the other colleges to stress the technologies, even to the exclusion of arts, lay a serious clash between the English and German approach to higher education. The Germans, as we have seen, were developing their universities which excluded engineering and their technical high schools which included little but technology, thus creating a sharply divided dual form of higher education. This pattern received much rather indiscriminate praise, chiefly from Germanophile politicians of science rather than scientists themselves. On the other hand, the great German pioneer of physical chemistry, Ostwald, held that English universities were better than German ones for their mixing of technical and liberal subjects, 'and so the technical student found his work liberalized by contact with men who were not primarily thinking of the technical applications of their subjects'.[4] This view also was held by Sir William Siemens. The civic colleges might easily have become English versions of the German technical high schools had not these other pressures prevented them. Accordingly England gained a

[1] W. H. Draper, op. cit., p. 90.
[2] The government grant rose from £2,000 in 1887/8 and 1888/9 (to Manchester only) to £36,000 in 1901/2, to £115,000 in 1905/6, to £123,000 in 1910/11, to £170,000 in 1914. 1914–16 XIX *Reports from Universities and University Colleges*, 1913–14, 1915 Cd. 8137. Table 7.
[3] Liverpool University was very sensitive about this. See Sir Alfred Dale's defence, *Liverpool Daily Post and Mercury*, 21 March 1914, that Liverpool was a genuine university and not merely a technical school as a grossly unfair critic had suggested.
[4] Wilhelm Ostwald cited in 'The Proposed Bristol University, the Experience of Liverpool', *Western Daily Press*, October 1907. This also incidentally reflects the ambition of Bristol to follow Liverpool as a motive for creating its university.

widely dispersed pattern of genuine universities in the first decade of the twentieth century. The recent creation of technological universities in the 1960s is accordingly less fraught with danger in that they now overlay their smaller pattern on a broader liberal structure well rooted for half a century.

So far in these two chapters we have been considering the new civic universities in the provinces. But the greatest modern civic university of all was that of London, although its origins dated from the early nineteenth century rather than from the provincial movements of the 1870s and 1880s. Yet London University was also undergoing important changes in relation to industry from the 1880s to the war, and accordingly it should be considered not by itself but in conjunction with the provincial movement.

Unlike most other universities in Britain 'The University of London' raises problems of definition that should be cleared at the outset. The University of London strictly speaking was an examining body set up in 1836 to examine the pupils of University and King's Colleges and other places approved by the Privy Council. In 1858 a new charter dispensed with the requirement of attendance at an approved institution and for most of the nineteenth century the university was merely an examining body open to all comers and as such, through its external degree, played a vital role in enabling the civic colleges to transform themselves gradually into universities in their own right. Proposals to start a teaching university of London were examined by the Selborne Commission of 1888–9 and the Gresham or Cowper Commission of 1891–4, resulting in the University of London Act of 1898. Following this, University College became incorporated into the university in 1905 and King's in 1908. In 1907 Imperial College was formed by royal charter out of the Royal College of Science, the Royal School of Mines and the Central Technical College of the City and Guilds. Also from 1907 the East London (Queen Mary) College became a school of the university. By 1914 the university consisted of three incorporated colleges, University, King's, and the King's College for Women, thirty-one schools including Imperial, East London, Bedford, Westfield, Royal Holloway, and LSE, and twenty-five other institutions dealing with agriculture, medicine, theology, and teacher training. It also comprised thirty more institutions having recognized teachers, including Goldsmith's and Birkbeck.[1] Clearly we cannot consider here each

---

[1] For the constitutional developments see Sir Douglas Logan, 'Haldane and the University of London' (Haldane Memorial Lecture, 1960). Percy Dunsheath and Margaret Miller, *Convocation in the University of London, the First Hundred Years* (London, 1958), and T. L. Humberstone, *University Reform in London* (London, 1926). *Yearbook of the Universities of the Empire, 1914* (London, 1914), p. 242.

of these sixty-four institutions, most of which were in any case irrelevant for our theme. It is intended to focus on University, King's, Imperial, and East London Colleges as being the heartland of the university and those most engaged in scientific activities relevant to industry.

The contribution of London University to industrial science from the 1880s to the war was much greater than that of any other British university and merits special attention. Especially was this so in chemistry. Of particular relevance to London industry was the work of Sir Herbert Jackson at King's College. He took a keen interest in industrial technology and ran courses on laundry chemistry, alkalis, soaps, and starches for the National Laundry Association.[1] The value of his academic work was vividly brought home to the trade when he analysed an imported German laundry product and showed the launderers how to make it for themselves at a third of the price. In the 1900s he continued his practical industrial work on bleaches and detergents, and also on the deteriorating stonework of Canterbury cathedral for which he acted as a consultant.[2]

Better known than the King's school of chemistry was that of University College, particularly during the professorship of Sir William Ramsay. Before his arrival in 1887, the chemical studies of the college were closely related to industry with A. W. Williamson's involvement with his own industrial projects, the 'Williamson steam boiler' for ships, the Landore Steel Company, and his chemical works at Willesden. His contemporary at the college in the 1870s and 1880s, Charles Graham, was a central figure in the development of brewing science and had a 'large consulting practice for brewers' while also giving courses on bread making, soap, glass, and cement for London manufacturers.[3] The advent of Ramsay thus changed the character of University College chemistry from that of a technical college to high science. And yet while his name is chiefly associated with his pure research on the inert gases in the 1890s, both this and his other work was far from divorced from practical industry. Indeed, before starting academic life he had contemplated setting up as a chemical manufacturer and kept in close touch with such developments in London. For instance he worked out ways of recovering radium from pitchblende in Cornwall, and when the British Radium Corporation started a factory in London he acted as consultant to it. He co-operated with a chemical manufacturer on the treatment of the newly discovered thorianite to yield barium and

[1] *LCC Technical Education Board Report on the Application of Science to Industry*, 1902. Evidence of Professor Jackson, p. 35.
[2] King's College, London, Annual Reports, 1904, 1905, 1907, and D. H. Hey, 'Schools of Chemistry—King's College, London', *Journal of the Royal Institute of Chemistry*, June 1955.
[3] J. S. Rose, 'Chemical Studies at University College, London' (University of London, Ph.D., 1955), p. 654.

radium on a fairly large scale,[1] and was also an early interested visitor brought by Cross to look at his viscose spinning at Kew, the beginnings of what became Courtauld's.[2] It was symbolic that in 1904 Ramsay not only won the Nobel prize but was also President of the Society of the Chemical Industry in recognition of his scientific services to industry. Indeed his colleague Collie was at pains to point out that even his most famous inert gas work, though at first sight irrelevant, was of considerable importance: 'millions of electric lamps are filled with Ramsay's argon, and great airships filled with Ramsay's helium float over the continent of North America'.[3]

Imperial College chemistry had two particular industrial linkages before the war—gas and dyestuffs. The college was one of the first centres in 1912 to start chemical engineering education and all the staff had close industrial links.[4] More important in the immediate context of the attempt to improve the technology of a British industry over-dominated by the Germans, was the college's pre-war work in dyestuffs. Since 1904 G. T. Morgan and Frances Micklethwait had been working on coal-tar dyes, 'with the result that industrial applications of these substances have been patented with a view to their use by English manufacturers', and they also worked on sulphide dyes with Read Holliday and Sons of Huddersfield.[5] Here Imperial College was really fulfilling its function of anti-German retaliation in the field of scientific industry.

It is, however, perhaps chiefly in electrical engineering that London's contribution excelled. There had been a long and striking tradition of involvement in this field, stretching from Charles Wheatstone at King's and his 'bridge' and dynamo, through Clerk Maxwell's electromagnetic theory of light, to Grylls Adams' demonstration there in 1881 of electric light in a lecture room. The engineering students at King's doubled in the early 1880s and in 1890 Lady Siemens gave £6,000 for an electrical laboratory in memory of her husband, Sir William. At University College there were new engineering and electrical laboratories from 1893, further reinforced by a fund raised for electrical engineering in 1896.[6] All this set the stage for a decade or so, up to 1904, remarkable for the contri-

---

[1] Sir William Tilden, *Sir William Ramsay, KCB, FRS*, pp. 169–70.
[2] E. J. Beer, *The Beginning of Rayon* (Paignton, 1962), p. 113, entry for 15 October 1901. (This is a reprint of the diary of Mr Beer who was working for the Viscose Spinning Syndicate at Kew.)
[3] *University College, London, Centenary Addresses*. J. Norman Collie, 'A Century of Chemistry at University College', p. 26.
[4] 'History of the Department of Chemical Engineering and Chemica Technology, 1912–39', unpublished typescript in Imperial College Archives.
[5] Imperial College Annual Report, 1911.
[6] 'An Account of the New Engineering and Electrical Laboratories in University College, London', *Engineering*, 26 May 1893. H. Hale Bellot, *University College, London, 1826–1926* (London, 1929).

butions of the London colleges to the new electrical science and engineering.

At King's in the new Siemens Laboratory, W. J. Hopkinson and Grylls Adams developed techniques which had profound effects for electrical transmission, especially in the 1920s. The first was the theory of running alternators in parallel, which although arousing initial scepticism became the normal practice in power stations throughout the world. The second was the three wire transmission system, a 'tremendously important invention which is at the root of the present grid system'.[1] Hopkinson helped to make King's the largest school of engineering in the country until his death in the Alps in 1899. Marconi was in touch with King's, 'and Mr Evans and Mr Shawcross of the Electrical Department were concerned with some experimental demonstrations conducted by Marconi there'.[2]

Marconi ultimately, however, had far more to do with Sir Ambrose Fleming and University College. Fleming, who had been working for the Edison Electric Light Company before his appointment to the chair in 1884, maintained his industrial contacts while at the college. He did a great deal of consultancy work for municipal lighting systems, advised Edison Swan in legal matters, and acted as consultant to Ferranti's over their equipment for London power supply.[3] Within his laboratories also, as well as training the new generation of pre-war electrical engineers, he undertook research relevant to industry. He demonstrated how wasteful of energy were the large scale transformers with sheet iron cores which were in common use around 1890;[4] in conjunction with the Edison Swan lamp factory he devised the standard lamp for comparing standards of light which was adopted by the NPL, while his unpatented voltmeter was already being widely used in the trade. However, perhaps his most important piece of industrial consultancy was for Marconi from 1899. Fleming played a vital part in Marconi's Atlantic signalling by setting up the station site at Poldhu. Fleming noted, 'the plans for the first building were drawn by me on my lecture table at University College London'.[5]

Fleming is best known for his invention in 1904 of the thermionic valve, made for him by Edison Swan but quickly adopted under prior agreements by Marconi, the vital link for the reception of wireless waves. Scarcely less important was Fleming's continued

---

[1] *Daily News*, 5 May 1929.
[2] W. O. Skeat, *King's College, London, Engineering Society, 1847–1957* (London, 1957), p. 31.
[3] Sir Ambrose Fleming, *Memoirs of a Scientific Life*, pp. 110–12.
[4] *University College, London, Centenary Addresses*. J. A. Fleming, 'A Hundred Years of Electrical Engineering', p. 18 and *passim*.
[5] Sir Ambrose Fleming, op. cit., p. 122.

training of engineers for the industry he was creating. In 1909 University College divided engineering off as a separate faculty in recognition of the specialized advances being made, and Fleming's courses were packed out with students—'many of them are engineers sent by the General Post Office, Telephone Companies and Cable Companies . . .'. As a relevant touch of showmanship he established a telegraphic wireless link between his Pender Laboratory and the Siemens Laboratory at King's in 1910, a fitting symbol of the dual role both colleges had played in the scientific development of the electrical industry in England.[1]

Apart from electricity, the contributions of the university to other engineering and allied fields were also considerable. It is well appreciated that Sir Alexander Kennedy at University College virtually created engineering as a modern university subject in England, especially the laboratory training of students, of whom the most famous industrially was Sebastian de Ferranti. Kennedy's own work dealt with strengths of materials in riveted structures, marine engines and boilers,[2] and this interest in the strength of materials was taken up in a more sophisticated manner on the eve of the war by two other University College workers, Coker and Filon. They collaborated from 1909 on means of photoelastic testing for stress in engineering components, a technique of considerable long term importance used in the First World War though largely neglected by industry in the inter-war years.[3] Imperial College likewise branched out into new areas of engineering before the war, notably in aeronautics. The Women's Aerial League had founded a scholarship in aeronautics at the college and an aviation school was formed as a memorial to C. S. Rolls.[4] By 1910 the department was already playing a vital research role, undertaking 'confidential work of importance to the National Defense . . . for the Government'.[5] The East London College also started aeronautics from 1909.[6] Secondly, Imperial College dealt with the engineering problems of the early motor car and an optical indicator was devised in 1911 'which will

[1] University College Reports, 1909–1911.
[2] E. G. Coker, 'Engineering at University College, London' (unpublished typescript BD1 COK in the college collections, 1925); also 1884 XXXI RC *Technical Instruction* (Samuelson). Evidence of A. B. W. Kennedy, QQ. 1995–2033, and Obituary of Sir Alexander Kennedy in *Minutes of the Proceedings of the Institution of Civil Engineers*, vol. 227, 1928–9, pt. I, pp. 269–75.
[3] *Photoelasticity at University College, London, Jubilee Commemoration of the Work of E. G. Coker and L. N. G. Filon, 1909–1937* (London, 1959).
[4] Imperial College Report 1910, and Aeronautics Committee, 1909–1913. File, 1928, 'Aerial League Educational Proposals', 1910 (Imperial College Archives).
[5] File, 1928, op. cit. Letter, Richard Glazebrook to Mr Gow, 28 October 1910
[6] George Godwin, *Queen Mary College, an Adventure in Education* (London, 1939).

probably be largely used in future in connexion with the petrol engine industry'.[1] Finally, their geology very shrewdly diversified from 1911 to train men for the developing oil-fields.

We have considered this in some detail because London University's record of industrial scientific achievement before the First World War was the most distinguished of any of the universities. It was a good mixture of work of immediate practical use, like Graham's on beer, Jackson's laundry and stone work, the dyestuffs and radium extraction, and also research whose value was to become more fully appreciated in the future, like Hopkinson's on electrical transmission, Coker and Filon on photoelasticity, and the work of Fleming. A good deal of work was in conjunction with firms, for example Jackson's, Ramsay's radium research, Imperial College's dyes and TB drug work, while Fleming had close connection with Marconi and Swan—who was also Vice-President of University College. In the 1890s Fleming observed that nearly all the professors of engineering in the university were consulting practical engineers, 'and it is the same way with many other technical subjects such as chemistry . . . they have connection with outside work by being advisers of chemical works . . .'.[2] Moreover, the reception of this work by industry, with the exception of the photoelasticity and Hopkinson's ideas, was quite rapid, not to say eager. Some of their work was deliberate and successful retaliation against German industry, notably the dyes and drugs of Imperial College and Jackson's synthesizing of German cleansing agents. Finally, while British science and industry is sometimes accused of 'over-commitment' to old basic industry technologies in this period, it was to London's credit that the oil, aeronautics and petrol engine work was a fruitful and forward looking widening of interest as the predominant electrical innovations of the 1890s appeared to slacken after 1904. The contribution of London University was excellent and lends no weight to exaggerated views that British industrial science was weak or backward and her higher education out of touch with industry.

Next, what of London's output of students? How far were they orientated towards industry? It is unfortunate that apart from Imperial College the other parts of the university with which we are concerned did not publish lists of future occupations of their students, and it is necessary to piece together a picture from scattered information. University College recorded some of their graduates' occupations in the 1890s: engineers to British Thomson Houston and Birkenhead as well as to electric lighting in Holland and South Africa, chemists to an alkali works and the Great Northern Railway,

---

[1] Imperial College Report, 1911. The advanced course on the thermodynamics of the petrol motor was very popular.
[2] 1897 XXXIV *Report of the Commissioners . . . University of London* Cowper). Q. 15145.

clearly reflecting the research interests of the college in that decade.[1] The 1911–12 report likewise provides a rare glimpse of a few of their alumni. Two went to Crosfield's, the Warrington soap and chemical firm, one to Levinstein's, the great Manchester dye company, and another two stayed with London firms in photography and metals.[2] This was probably not untypical. Sir William Ramsay said that 'the majority' of his pupils 'are likely to enter chemical works' at the turn of the century,[3] and looking back on his students in 1910 he thought the balance was 60 per cent into industry, 25 per cent into teaching, and 15 per cent married women.[4] Thus the great bulk of the output was to industry.

As regards the engineers, at University College Professor Kennedy noted that 90 per cent of his pupils were going to be working engineers aiming for the MICE.[5] At King's College likewise the engineering students aimed to become 'superior employers or managers' in engineering. Grylls Adams observed that 'the greater number of those who are connected with the engineering department go out into engineering works. I think that there are no less than six of my old pupils working under Dr. Siemens . . . seven or eight have entered Easton and Anderson works. Many are to be found working with the principal engineers in Westminster.'[6] At the East London College the connection with industry seemed equally close though at a lower level. The Great Eastern Railway Company used the engineering department of the college for part of their training since the science there was of a high standard.[7] From this evidence, expert if necessarily impressionistic and fragmentary, it would seem that there was a very close connection between the output of engineers and chemists at these three colleges and their reception into industry. Fortunately we can make this more precise by a closer consideration of the component parts of Imperial College for the period 1907–14.

The formation of Imperial College joined together the Royal School of Mines, the Royal College of Science, and the City and Guilds College. By considering the London graduate output of each of these in turn we may obtain a clearer picture of the liaison. We

---

[1] 1897 LXX and 1899 XXI *Reports from University Colleges to the Board o Education.*
[2] University College, London, Report to Senate, 1911–12. (These are kept in the Records Office of the College.)
[3] *LCC Technical Education Board Report on the Application of Science to Industry,* 1902, p. 23.
[4] R. Blair, 'The Relation of Science to Industry and Commerce', *Nature,* 15 September 1910, citing Ramsay. Blair was the Education Officer of the LCC.
[5] 1884 XXXI RC *Technical Instruction* (Samuelson). Q. 2032.
[6] Ibid. Q. 2699.
[7] 1910 LXXII *Advisory Committee on Grants to University Colleges, Report on East London College,* p. 12.

may consider first of all eighteen students from the School of Mines who gained London B.SC. degrees between 1907 and 1914.[1] Of these the vast majority went to work overseas, two to South Africa, two to Australia, two to Spain, and one each to Alaska, Rhodesia, Russia, Rangoon, Italy, South America, and West Africa. Only five remained in Britain and two of those were teachers. Interestingly, only one went into coal mining in Britain. It was commonly said in the nine-teenth century that the School of Mines was not providing a useful education for the British coal industry. In practice this scarcely mattered for the school chiefly served metalliferous mining in the Empire rather than British industry directly. Turning to those students graduating between 1907 and 1914 in science other than mining and engineering, the connection with industry was less direct. Of these ninety-seven, only twenty-one could be said to be using their sciences in industrial firms, whereas forty-seven took up some level of teaching.[2] Unfortunately, with this list we are told the final occupation and not the first, consequently it is not meaningful to analyse the firms into which they moved since many were creations of the inter-war years.

From the City and Guilds part of Imperial College, 131 students graduating B.SC. in the university from 1907 took up work before the outbreak of war.[3] The chief absorbers of graduates from the City and Guilds College in these years were the Woolwich Arsenal which took seven of them; Western Electric, also in Woolwich, with four; Siemens in Woolwich, Stafford, and Berlin was the largest single employer with eight; various parts of Vickers took three, as did British Thomson Houston, whereas W. H. Allen of Bedford and Huntley and Palmers took two each. Eleven went into railway com-panies and six into public works departments in Egypt and India, while fourteen became pupils with engineers, frequently prominent civil engineers in London itself. If we consider the location of these scientists, 113 served the British economy, nine the Empire which is surprisingly low, and nine went overseas other than to the Empire. If we focus on those staying in Britain we can see how far they were serving distinctively London industry or Britain as a whole. Of locatable destinations London itself was predominant in providing work for graduates of the college, thirty-one of whom stayed to work in the vicinity. The Midlands took eleven, the North East seven, Lancashire and Yorkshire four each, and Scotland and South Wales three each.

[1] Calculated from Margaret Reeks, *The Royal School of Mines, Register of Old Students, 1851–1920* (London, 1920).
[2] Calculated from *Register of Old Students and Staff of the Royal College of Science* (Royal College of Science Association, 1951).
[3] Calculated from John Walker, *Register of Students of the City and Guilds College, 1884–1936* (London, 1936).

We can make a cruder assessment of the types of work taken up by students of the college by considering the members of the Students' Association with the important proviso that the majority of those would not be graduates but were associates of the college before it became part of Imperial College. However, taking all these in 1909 the following were the leading activities in percentage proportions:[1]

Railways	15·3	Cellulose industries	5·7
Consultants	12·8	Telephones and telegraphs	5·3
Teaching	10·7	Draughtsmen	5·3
Electricity supply	7·5	Dynamos and motors	4·6

In short, virtually the whole of the Imperial College mining output went into industry but abroad rather than in Britain, and to a great extent to the Empire. Only about one-fifth of the chemists seemed to be using their chemistry in firms, which seemed a dangerous gap, and a contrast with the 60 per cent entering industry among Ramsay's chemistry students at University College. On the other hand, the engineers went overwhelmingly into industry, but British industry rather than Imperial, in contradistinction to the miners. Moreover, within Britain they served the specifically London engineering economy and benefited by continuing their training with London-based engineers.

So far we have been considering the good features of the University of London *vis-à-vis* industry, but there are four main defects in the relationship which were not entirely the fault of the university; namely the failure to cover certain areas of industrial study, the limitations on the quantity of their student output, the relative lack of support from industry, and failure of industry effectively to absorb its output. First, there were some curious curricular gaps that ignored certain key London industries.[2] In particular the university neglected the vital advancing field of electro-chemistry which had transformed the commercial production of copper and aluminium, and yet 'London offers no means and no opportunities for instruction and research in the subject'. Also the chemical-using trades—leather, rubber, clothing—found no help although London had more of such local industries than any other British city. Most scandalous was the fact that although London was a major gas producer it was notoriously casual about its by-products: 'practically all the skilled and remunerative treatment of coal tar products is left to Germany, to which country we export what is virtually a raw material of a most valuable trade'. As regards the sea, although London was a great

---

[1] Calculated from *Central Technical College Old Students' Association List of Members, 1909* (Woking, 1909).
[2] *The Times*, 4 and 8 June 1901, 'The Organisation of University Education in the Metropolis'. One suspects that these were written by Sidney Webb; compare his *London Education*.

port the university had no school of nautical astronomy and navigation or marine engineering and architecture. Finally, although
biochemistry and its importance for brewing, sewage, and food
preservation had been appreciated for half a century, in London
'there is no institution teaching it'. What was worse, even in a subject
they did teach well, like chemistry, industry did not regard the content
sufficiently directed to their needs. Sir William Ramsay admitted
that in the 1880s a London B.SC. in chemistry was 'anything but a
recommendation' to manufacturers, and when asked in 1910, 'what
is the value for practical purposes in the market of a London University B.SC. in chemistry?' he replied, 'Nothing'[1]. It was a problem
not really overcome until the rise of chemical engineering at University and King's Colleges in the 1920s transforming chemistry for
analysis and research into chemistry for production management.

Second, even in those sciences covered, though the quality was
good, the output was far too low for much of the period. *The Times*
correspondent in 1901 calculated that 'the total number of science
students of undergraduate status in the whole six millions of people
apparently does not reach one thousand'—that was 600–700 in the
Royal College of Science, King's, University, Bedford, and Holloway Colleges, and 200–300 in the Polytechnics and City and Guilds
Colleges. On this assessment this would give an annual output of
about 300, which may be thought on the low side as the scientific
output of the major city in the world when we bear in mind that the
staff alone of Charlottenburg in 1906 was 402 and that the two leading German dye firms between them employed 293 chemists in
1900.[2] Sir Joseph Swan put it another way. In London there were
2,000 students of technical education working for a university degree
and lower qualifications, but in Berlin 5,000. By this standard, given
that the ratios of the population of the UK and Germany in 1900
were 38 million to 50 million, it is evident that there was an undesirable discrepancy, but one that Imperial College as the English
Charlottenburg was intended to eliminate. The ten years before the
war did see aconsiderable improvement on this situation which was
criticized at the turn of the century.

The limitation of numbers was partly caused by the third defect,
namely the relative lack of support from industry. It meant that
the endowments were too low and in consequence fees were too
high.[3] Also laboratory facilities were not all that they ought to have

[1] 1910 XXIII RC *University Education in London* (Haldane), Cmd. 5166.
Evidence of Sir William Ramsay. QQ. 2256–7.
[2] *LCC Technical Education Board Report on the Application of Science to
Industry*, 1902, op. cit., referring to Badische Aniline Works and
Farbenfabriken Bayer and Company.
[3] Evidence of J. W. Swan, Principal Rucker and J. D. Cormack to the *LCC
Technical Education Board Committee*, 1902, op. cit., and J. D. Cormack,
'Technical Education in the University of London', *Engineering*, 31 October 1902.

been.[1] The financial neglect of industry and its dangers were often deplored. Charles Graham, whose courses were well supported by the London brewers, found that when appealed to for a fund 'I do not think that the brewers as such were contributors at all', and he attributed this to their lack of patriotism.[2] This was not an isolated case. The point was put bluntly in 1907—'it is almost impossible to secure money in the metropolis for the applied science section of those colleges which are closely allied with the London University . . . the London University does not seem to have been able to keep so closely in touch with the large works of the metropolis'—and in this the city contrasted badly with the civic universities of the North.[3] This feature was also reflected in the board of Imperial College which, although containing eminent scientists, did not contain practical workshop industrialists—a sharp contrast with the board of the Manchester University faculty of technology.[4]

Just how unfortunate London University was in this respect can be seen by considering the income structures of the colleges[5] in Table 10.

Imperial College had quite the most lavish industrial support. The £100,000 from Wernher, Beit and Company, Beit's own gift of £50,000, and Sir Ernest Cassel's £10,000, as well as that of Maxi-

TABLE 10   *Percentage of income, 1914*

	Fees	Endowments	Donations and subscriptions	Local authorities	Parliamentary grant
University College	40·1	15·7	2·8	9·3	29·8
King's	42·6	1·6	2·1	12·6	37·3
Bedford	53·0	6·6	0·3	5·3	33·9
LSE	34·2	2·2	4·4	27·4	30·6
East London	14·4	35·0	10·0	5·9	32·9
England total	28·1	14·8	3·0	16·0	34·0

[1] Sir Ambrose Fleming's evidence to the Technical Education Board and to the Cowper Commission, 1894, XX. Q. 15192.
[2] 1884 XXXII RC *Technical Instruction* (Samuelson). Q. 1536.
[3] 'Engineering Notes', *Daily Telegraph*, 25 February 1907.
[4] *The Times*, 17 July 1907, letter from Charles Rowley who was on the Manchester Board.
[5] 1914–16 XIX *Reports of Universities to the Board of Education*, table 1a.

milian Michaelis, and the £50,000 plus £87,000 for engineering from the Goldsmiths all saved it from the dismal financial history of King's.[1] And yet we cannot see this convincingly as reflecting the interest of British industry. Wernher, Beit, Cassel, and Michaelis were all financiers and bankers in South African gold and diamonds and all—curiously for an institution intended as a retaliation to Germany—of German origin. We do not see in them that close connection of indigenous British industry financing the training of its future experts that is most evident in the cases of Leeds, Sheffield, and Manchester, for example.

If industry could be criticized for not contributing to the university as much as it ought to have done, was it also at fault in not absorbing its students? There was disturbing evidence that fault lay with the employers who were unwilling to take on more graduates. Sir William Ramsay lamented that although the university could continue to turn out excellent chemists yet 'the demand for such men is not keeping up with the supply. Manufacturers are not as yet sufficiently alive to the necessity for employing chemists'.[2] The same was feared for engineers. It was pointed out that there were only about 10,000 jobs in engineering in England in the £500–£1,500 bracket, with replacement needs of about 300 a year, and yet Imperial College alone was aiming to turn out 200–300 engineers and this could only lead to gross over-production. What industry was willing to absorb in ever-increasing amounts was 'dial watchers at 25/- a week', not graduates.[3] The experience of the newly formed Appointments Board confirmed this for they soon found themselves operating in the context of a vastly increased output of graduates creating an excessive supply for the rather restricted demand from industry, even in the thriving years up to the war. In 1909, 'the supply of candidates with chemical and engineering qualifications exceeds the demand for persons holding such qualifications', and in 1910 chemists and engineers are still having 'great difficulty' in getting into works.[4] By 1912 matters picked up and they were being approached more by firms though they left the Royal Commission on the Civil Service in no doubt that there were still too many graduates in engineering, chemistry and physics, though too few in mining and metallurgy.[5] The university was meeting the constraint of a lack of ability or willingness of industry greatly to expand its absorptive capacity commensurate with the rise in the number of London graduates in the 1900s. The blame for this was put squarely

[1] *The Royal Charter of the Imperial College of Science and Technology 1907–57* (London, 1957). Imperial College Annual Report, 1913.
[2] *LCC Technical Education Board*, op. cit., p. 23.
[3] *The Engineer*, 2 August 1907, letter from 'B.Sc.'.
[4] University of London Appointments Board Reports, 1909–1914; *University of London Appointments Board, its Aims and Work* (London, 1914).
[5] 1913 XVIII RC *Civil Service*, Statement, 18 December 1912.

with industry which had lost the dye trade and looked likely to lose the electricals as well due to its casual attitude to research and its tardiness in employing the graduate in that expanding role.[1] And yet there was plenty of evidence that the employment of men with university education could pay off considerably in terms of cost and time saving. Sir Alfred Keogh cited two such cases, one of a London graduate halving the oil costs of a textile firm and of another turning his employers from producing shale for road making to the more lucrative trade of winning oil from the shale.[2] Again, Sir Alexander Gibb in his youth astonished his non-university fellow engineering pupils by the ease and speed with which he performed exercises by using the mathematics he studied at University College and of which they were ignorant.[3] The knowledge and the talent were there if industry would only use it.

A number of salient points emerge from this consideration of the rise of the civic universities in the later nineteenth century. It is quite evident that the various movements owed what success they enjoyed to the initiatives and financial support of the business classes. Movements that failed to secure this, like Nottingham or Southampton, were for the time doomed to limited activity, or like Leicester were stillborn. The most fertile conditions of success were usually a wide range of diversified industries such as were found notably in Liverpool and Birmingham. Manchester was slightly unusual in having large support from the cotton industry although this was one with relatively little expectations from higher education. Sheffield and Newcastle, as cities committed to a greater specialization of industry, did not seem so successful as those colleges where a wider range of chemical and engineering technologies formed the basis of a parent city's economy. The question of size was also important, large populations being a factor of success in the provinces whereas London, on the other hand, was too large to generate a cohesive movement of loyal support to its own university, which suffered in comparison with those of the great northern cities. Because of the importance of this business support for the life and death of movements so the movements themselves had to accept a pace of development dictated by the booms and depressions of business activity. Accordingly starts were often stimulated and helped

---

[1] See a spate of letters in *The Times* throughout March 1906 under the heading 'Science and the Industries' by Silvanus Thompson, Ivan Levinstein, Sir Joseph Lawrence, and a Times Correspondent (A. G. Green?). The moves to form Imperial College coincided with the jubilee of Perkins's great aniline dye discovery, the conjunction of the two was made the occasion of much self-criticism in scientific industrial circles.
[2] 1911 XX (Haldane), Cmd. 5528. Alfred Keogh, Q. 4575.
[3] Godfrey Harrison, *Alexander Gibb, the Story of an Engineer* (London, 1950), p. 31. The incident was in the 1890s.

by the boom of the late 1860s and early 1870s, there was some holding back of support in the 1880s, but a further marked advance in the 1900s with the business recovery coinciding with the attempts to secure charters and to build up the newly chartered independent universities.

We have stressed the scientific contributions of the civic universities which became leading centres of scientific advance in almost all areas of industry, such as mining, metallurgy, leather, engineering and naval architecture, the chemistries of soap, beer, dyes and, perhaps most of all, electrical engineering. The role they played in this respect *vis-à-vis* industry was relatively more important in the nineteenth century than at any time since, for before the advent of research within the firm and the industrial research association the universities were more uniquely the fount of new expertise. The civic universities served industry not only through their more spectacular research but more pervasively through their output of students to industry. The students of the civic universities did tend to come from industrial and commercial backgrounds and more from the middle- and upper-classes than from the working-class, though Sheffield was, and was longer than most to remain, especially noted for its education for the lower ranks of industry. There was a sharp upturn of the output of students to industry in the recovery of trade from the late 1890s, and especially just prior to the war, and a rising tendency to go into the large firm.

This close involvement with industry did lead to some friction and fears of encroachment, notably over issues like lay control by businessmen and the inhibition on publication that some academics felt to exist and which some businessmen thought necessary. While we recognize this we do not regard it as a serious danger. Certainly it was nothing like so serious as the danger that would have arisen from the withdrawal of business interest and support. More important in our view was the way in which many of these institutions which might have remained merely large technical colleges were moulded to become genuine multidisciplinary universities by the pressures of Victoria, the London external degree and the government grant. England was saved from the dual form of higher education such as existed in Germany and which many politicians of science wished Britain to emulate. It thus preserved the mutually beneficial linkages of science and technologies in the same institution, prevented the creation of non-technological 'universities' which would rapidly have become chiefly narrow arts teacher training colleges, and so avoided a situation whereby a 'second rate' stigma would have attached to centres dealing purely with the technologies.

In the special case of London, the university was reformed and brought even closer to industry with the formation of Imperial College and the reception as a school of the East London College.

The contributions of London University to British industry were outstanding and greater than those of any other British university, including inert gas, radium extraction, the voltmeter, the thermionic valve, techniques in photoelastic testing, engine instrumentation and electrical transmission, and various important if less spectacular improvements in soaps, beer, dyestuffs, and others. Much of the work was in conjunction with firms, rapidly received into industry, and much was retaliating against German dominance in certain technical fields. The drawbacks of the London connection with industry were certain curricular gaps, notably the neglect of chemistry for local London industry, a relatively low output of students, the lack of finance from industry for the university which kept endowments low and fees high and the resistance of industry to absorbing graduates. If any balance of blame is to be apportioned for the defects of the London connection it lies considerably more with industry than with the university itself.

The vitality of the English civic universities movement thus owed much to its intimate connections and interrelations with industry. In Manchester, Birmingham, and Liverpool the generosity of the business community to their universities was amply repaid by the work of the colleges. In Leeds, Newcastle, Sheffield, and above all London, where the universities were not supported as they ought to have been, the value of the colleges to industry far outweighed what they received from it. This interrelatedness as a condition of vitality in the English civic universities may be even better appreciated as we turn to consider the parallel Welsh movement as one disengaged from industry and made shallower and less effective by that isolation.

5
The Welsh Universities
Movement 1850-1914

*'As it is now, there is very little connection between the
University and the industrial minds . . .'*[1]

Broadly contemporary with the rise of the civic universities in England there was the parallel creation of a university system in Wales.
Welsh consciousness of their own culture, scarcely less fervent than
that of the Scots, had been rekindled and kept alive by such institutions as the Cymmrodorion Society from the eighteenth century and
the revival of the eisteddfod from 1819. More pervasively, the power
of religion in Dissenting chapel and Sunday school both contributed
to a sense of cohesiveness and identity and inculcated a certain
respect for intellectual values and literary learning. The retention of
their national language yet further served to confirm their cultural
unity and distinctiveness. Yet, unlike the Scots, the Welsh had never
developed a tradition of higher education, nor had they produced
without it great men of science and learning as had Scotland. The
concern to create a university movement was thus in part an attempt
to redress the imbalance between the Scots and the Irish and themselves. It was an end to the acceptance not only of exclusion from
English universities because of the tests against Dissenters, but of
dependence on the Scottish universities which were otherwise their
main source of higher education. Such rejection by the one nation
and dependence on the other was a double humiliation which Wales,
growing richer and more powerful as a result of industrialization,
had no need to tolerate by the third quarter of the nineteenth century.
Industrially, too, Wales was developing an economy which needed
leadership from men with scientific university education. In the north
the years from the 1850s to the 1880s saw the great expansion of the

---

[1] H. S. Thomas of Richard Thomas and Company, quoted in RC *University
Education in Wales* (Haldane), Cd. 8699, 1917 (henceforth cited as Haldane).
Q. 10082, p. 266. Richard Thomas and Company was the largest producer
of tinplate in Wales and the second largest producer in the world.

slate and stone quarrying industry on the western part of the coast-line for which mining education would have been an asset, while in the north east towards Cheshire were the chemical industries of Queensferry and Flint, the iron of Shotton, bricks, paper, and pottery—all potentially science based industries. In south Wales the massive export of coal replaced steel as the major industry, in turn stimulating the local transport industries. Also peculiar to the area was a wide range of metallurgical industry, notably tinplate, at a peak in 1891, copper, most thriving in the 1860s, and nickel, notably at the Mond Works at Clydach from 1902 and which grew to become the largest in the world.[1] Although Wales was predominantly an agricultural country and much of its land poor grazing, yet there was enough varied industry the demands of which ought to have created a university movement closely related to the commercial life of the homeland and serving it by the production of expertise in mining, chemicals, and metallurgy. And yet what is remarkable is the lack of contribution of the Welsh universities to Welsh industry and the reciprocal lack of support they received from it. The Welsh university colleges are thus of interest to us here as a pathological example of the dangers of disengagement between the universities and industry. In the next section we will consider the motives behind the setting up of the various movements. The third section will consider the research and other servicing contributions and interests of the colleges in relation to Welsh industries, and in the final section attention will be focused on the output to industry of the students from the colleges, how far they stayed in Wales, and which industries did and did not absorb them.

Industrial motives played virtually no part in the early proposals for university education in Wales in the 1850s.[2] In the 1860s, however, Dr Thomas Nicholas, a Nonconformist minister, couched his arguments for a university for Wales in unmistakably industrial terms not found in his predecessors. He envisaged collegiate institutions 'properly adapted to the scientific and practical wants of its chief centres of manufacture',[3] and stressing the sciences, 'matters which directly concern the great industries of the Principality'.[4] Nicholas's activity revived the movement started under Hugh Owen, but these new claims to be valuable to industry were later to cause trouble.

---

[1] W. E. Minchinton, 'Industrial South Wales 1750-1914' in *Industrial South Wales 1750-1914, Essays in Welsh Economic History* (London, 1969).
[2] Cf. B. T. Williams, *The Desirableness of a University Education for Wales.* Evidence of Williams to *Report of the Committee . . . Intermediate and Higher Education in Wales* (Aberdare), C. 3047, 1881, Q. 7363, and evidence of Hugh Owen, Q. 307.
[3] Thomas Nicholas, *Middle and High Schools and a University for Wales.*
[4] W. C. Davies and W.L. Jones, *The University of Wales*, p. 74, citing Nicholas.

There were three very odd features about this movement and its claims to form a university serving Welsh industry. First, the supporting personnel were all professional men with no trace of active participation by industrialists. Second, most of its main meetings were held in London, where most of the members lived and worked; and third, and most bizarre, they proposed to establish their institution in Aberystwyth, a town not only lacking industry itself but located most remotely from the industries of north and south Wales.

However the college began by the purchase of the Castle Hotel, Aberystwyth, in 1867. The early finance was a disaster. The hotel had cost £10,000, but throughout the 1860s they totally failed to raise anything like this purchase price and it became clear that the movement elicited no response whatever from Welsh industrialists or even landowners.[1] At this point expatriate Welsh in Lancashire stepped in to provide the funds to enable the college to open, which it did belatedly in 1872, but still with a deficit of £7,700. In the 1870s not only did industry continue to withhold its support from attempts to raise an endowment fund, but even those industrialists who had helped at the outset grew disillusioned with the project. They had blatantly been given the impression by Nicholas's pamphlet that the college was to be valuable for industry, but now they found that it was drifting into being yet another training college for teachers and clergy. David Davies of Llandinan, the coal owner and leading subscriber, expressed his frank dismay and concluded, 'I would sooner my money was in the bottom of the sea.'[2] It was yet further evidence of the serious rifts between the college and the industrialists of Wales, without whose support they languished. Accordingly 'from its inception the movement had hanging over it a cloud of penury'.[3]

During the 1880s the whole position became much firmer, when from 1882 the college was given a government grant of £4,000 a year and granted a charter in 1889. Further government aid came in 1894 when Aberystwyth was given the first government grant for building, £10,000 for a central block. Yet more came from private sources in 1904 with £20,000 from the estate of Edward Davies, the former treasurer of the college, which was used for fine chemical laboratories opened in 1907 and then among the best in Britain.[4] It was evident that, probably chiefly because of its location, Aberystwyth

---

[1] *Report of the Committee . . . Intermediate and Higher Education in Wales* (Aberdare) (henceforth cited as Aberdare), Hugh Owen's evidence; and W. E. Davies, *Sir Hugh Owen, his Life and Work* (National Eisteddfod Association, 1885), p. 111, for these troubles.

[2] T. I. Ellis (ed.), *Thomas Charles Edward's Letters, National Library of Wales Journal*, Supplement, series III, no. 3, 1952. Letters from John Griffiths, 18 June 1873; J. F. Roberts, 20 September 1873; and David Davies, 29 March 1876.

[3] *University College of Wales, Aberystwyth, an Outline History, 1872–1947*, p. 16.

[4] I. Morgan, ed., *The College by the Sea*.

college obtained very little support indeed from industry apart from one or two individuals like David Davies, and even he was disillusioned by the results. The main support came from large numbers of comparatively poor people whose collective efforts could raise little,[1] and more important larger amounts from expatriate Welsh in south Lancashire and London. It is possible to express this balance fairly exactly by analysing the list of all subscribers from 1863 to 1881 and their locations.[2]

	Wales	Liverpool	Manchester	Rest of England
Raised	£12,575	£3,347	£4,429	£11,420
Average donation	£48	£58	£87	£173

Not only did England raise more for the college at Aberystwyth than the Welsh did—at least those in Wales—but the individual donations from Manchester, Liverpool and London were considerably higher than those from the principality. This feature of the Welsh university movement depending on Welshmen in English industry and commerce was also found at Bangor. But the real turning point came with the steady and sizeable financial aid of the state, and it was this that enabled the effective rise of the college in the 1880s, not the industrialists whose lack of support had kept it weak in the 1860s and 1870s. The Treasurer summed up the position clearly for the Haldane Commission in 1916 as he admitted that the local area had not been able to support the college generously for 'they are agricultural counties with no big industries'.[3] There was in fact a basic incompatibility between the claims with which Nicholas had started the movement and the choice of such a location.

The college set up at Bangor in 1884 displays a similar disengagement from Welsh industry, both in the motivations behind its starting and in its initial and subsequent support. It arose out of a recommendation of Lord Aberdare's committee of 1881 which proposed colleges for north and south Wales in addition to Aberystwyth. Industrial considerations played no part in siting the North Wales College at Bangor.[4] Had such criteria been considered a location further east along the coast would have commended itself,[5] but

[1] W. C. Davies and W. L. Jones, op. cit., p. 102, claims that 5,000 people each gave 2s. 6d.
[2] Calculated from *List of Subscribers, 1869–1881*, University College of Wales, Aberystwyth.
[3] Haldane, Cd. 8507, 1917, D. C. Roberts, Q. 1820.
[4] 'The University College of North Wales', MS. in Lloyd Papers 231 in University College of North Wales, Bangor; *The North Wales College, History of the College Movement . . . and the Claims of Bangor*. The *Claim* was printed in various forms. The original forms are in the Belmont MSS. in the college, but industrial arguments figure in none of the versions.
[5] *The Claims of Rhyl* (Rhyl, 1882); see also *The Claims of Wrexham* (1882 or 1883).

the new college was built in the least industrial area of the coastline. At the various speeches of the opening ceremony itself it was highly significant that no Welsh speaker ever referred to industry or trade as a motive for the movement or as a theme of the college's future work.[1]

Where, then, did the financial support come from, and was the college, in spite of all its apparent aloofness from industry, able to tap that source of wealth? What saved Bangor from much of the early struggles of Aberystwyth was an annual government grant of £4,000 from the beginning, but they still needed local finance from an area that looked unpromising as a potential provider of it. As with Aberystwyth, they did receive an astonishing amount of support from the lower classes, and the Penrhyn and Dinorwic quarry workers raised over £1,250 for the opening of the college.[2] The support of the working quarrymen and other humble people is a feature that markedly distinguishes the Welsh universities movement from that in England. It is possible to analyse closely the social composition of support from the surviving list of one of the districts. This was as follows, taking leading supporting groups.[3]

farmers	28	blacksmiths	6
farm labourers	23	carters	6
labourers	15	slate workers	5
joiners	11	masons	5
woodmen and		millers	5
gamekeepers	9	clerks	4
gardeners	6	school-teachers	4

In all, 252 people (including wives and daughters, etc.) raised £171, and there were only twelve donations over £1. This was at once the strength and weakness of the movement—enormous good will widely felt but chiefly by people who were totally unable to support their sentiments with hard cash. Their motives were probably twofold. The founding of scholarships by the quarrymen suggests that they were concerned that at least one or two of their sons should escape from their life of toil via the college, probably into the ministry or teaching. For the rest there was undoubtedly the feeling that book learning and culture was desirable and worth both acquiring and supporting even at some cost, a view fostered by chapel and eisteddfod and probably a more distinctively Welsh attitude at this

---

[1] *Opening of the University College of North Wales* (Bangor, 1884). A. J. Mundella, the Nottingham hosier, was a significant—non Welsh—exception.
[2] Haldane, Cd. 8507. Evidence of Professor J. E. Lloyd, p. 187. See also Belmont Papers 67 (iii), letter E. Williams to J. H. Lewis, 27 June 1883, and letter Ed. Folkes to Hy. Lewis, 28 June 1883, for the quarry collections. These MSS. are in the Library of the University College at Bangor.
[3] Calculated from Subscription List, North Wales College, Bangor District, Lower Llandegai and Llanllechid, sometime 1884 or 1885 (in the college collections).

social level than an English one. It was largely due to this evidence of genuine local support that Bangor was selected as the location of the college. As one of the subscribers to the list noted sometime later, the college at Bangor 'owes its existence to the deep seated belief of the Welsh peasant and craftsman and shopkeeper in education'.[1]

And yet on none of the lists do we find really generous donations from an élite of industrial or commercial magnates. Quite the largest was the £1,000 of Lord Penrhyn, the leading slate quarry owner, but in the whole list of promises there are only four other sums of £100 or over.[2] The local firms, especially in slate, were either not contributing at all or contributing sums of derisory smallness. The slate industry of the region was highly concentrated into virtually two firms, the Penrhyn quarry under the Pennant family, and the Dinorwic quarry; thus a wide catchment area of varied local industrial support was not available. Slate profits had soared in the 1870s and it is estimated that Dinorwic's profits were already £90,000 a year in the 1860s. But after the mid 1880s, as the college was rising, the Penrhyn quarry went into a decline due to competition and labour troubles, which left the college in the unfortunate position of being linked to a local monopolist firm in an industry that was declining.[3] The failure to set up a mining department in the college seemed further evidence of the unwillingness of the chief industry to provide the money even for a project that would have benefited it. Similarly, one of their best industrial scientific departments, electrical engineering, relied for financial support outside Wales, from the Drapers' Company in London. For the lack of a rich entrepreneurial stratum in Bangor itself, it was the south Lancashire cities and their business classes who stepped into the breach.

In 1885 leading Liverpool businessmen with Welsh or educational connections pledged themselves to support the college, which resulted in the raising of £8,579 in Liverpool itself and £485 in Bootle.[4] The largest subscriber was William Rathbone, indeed the largest single subscriber either in Wales or outside. Furthermore, due to his influence he was able to interest Sir Henry Tate, of the sugar firm, and Tate in the 1885 list gave £1,000 and another £1,000 after his death. The Manchester support came chiefly from Dr Thomas Evans, a prosperous Manchester physician who left the whole of his fortune of £47,000 to the college. Bangor, like Aberystwyth, was

---

[1] W. C. Davies and W. L. Jones, op. cit., p. 160. Cadwaladr Davies gave the comparatively large sum of £10 in the early 1880s; he was Secretary of the College.
[2] North Wales College, Bangor District, List of Promises (1884?).
[3] A. H. Dodd, *A History of Caernarvonshire, 1284–1900* (Caernarvonshire Historical Society, 1968), pp. 254–5.
[4] University College of North Wales, Open Letter about the Meeting by Cadwaladr Davies, 1 January 1885; and Liverpool, Birkenhead, and Bootle Subscription Lists.

relying on small sums from the not so well-to-do in the locality and also on the fortunes of expatriate Welsh and other well-wishers in south Lancashire. The one area was being called upon to redress the balance of the other. In these ways they sought to substitute for what was really lacking, a local Welsh very wealthy and interested commercial class that genuinely believed the colleges could provide any service for their own activities.

Even if Aberystwyth and Bangor reveal little of either industrial motivation or local Welsh industrial support in their founding we should expect much more of both for the University College of South Wales at Cardiff. This, like Bangor, was set up after the Aberdare Report which recommended a college for the south of the principality. Certainly the early motivation for locating the college in Cardiff was firmly industrial. The corporation urged that Cardiff be chosen on the grounds that the college could 'provide for the wants of a large commercial, manufacturing and mining population . . .'.[1] Also the money initially seemed to be forthcoming since the city was able to raise £7,250 in 1882, and on these grounds Cardiff was chosen as the site of the new college rather than its rival Swansea. Moreover, when the college started in 1883 they had a scientific principal, John Viriamu Jones, an electrical physicist, already of the stature to serve with Kelvin on the Standards Committee of 1880. This in itself was in sharp contrast to the principals of the other Welsh colleges before the war, all of whom were classicists or theologians with no industrial or scientific background at all.

Yet in spite of this apparently more favourable beginning, not even this college seemed to be able to tap the financial resources of south Wales industry. Cardiff was generous with the land for the site and Lord Bute, the great coal owner, gave the site for the college in Cathays Park in 1887. And yet although Cardiff itself was generous from the beginning two things went wrong. Initially they were unable to arouse the support of the hinterland.[2] Swansea handed over the sums it had raised while trying to secure the college for itself, but there was no successful appeal to the lower classes of south Wales for financial support in the way that was such a marked feature of the Bangor and Aberystwyth movements. Second, after the start there were continued disappointments about the lack of response to appeals. For example, in the 1880s appeals for chairs in mining and engineering were made but met with nothing like adequate response. As supplementary support in the Bangor and Aberystwyth cases came from south Lancashire, so for Cardiff it came from London with the Drapers' Company providing a £1,000 donation and, more importantly, £3,000 a year for maintenance.

[1] University College for South Wales and Monmouthshire, *Memorial of the Cardiff Corporation*, 13 February 1882.
[2] W. C. Davies and W. L. Jones, op. cit., p. 142.

The same happened in the 1890s over the new site when, although the corporation gave them part of the Cathays Park site and the government provided £20,000 and the Drapers £10,000, yet local support could raise only another £20,000. 'The merchant princes of Cardiff failed as a body to respond to this challenge as readily and as liberally as Principal Jones had expected.'[1]

The sorry story of mining education at Cardiff was an extreme example of this apparent disengagement of support.[2] The Principal had been trying to get coal company finance for a large mining department. He aimed to raise £50,000 and obtained promises for £35,000, only £9,000 of which materialized. But then the coal owners began to demand what seemed excessive control over the department, and on the college's being unwilling to allow this the coal owners set up their own college at Treforest which virtually killed off mining education in the university until the inter-war years. What is instructive here is that whereas the college had been able to raise only £9,000 for its proposed mining department, yet when the owners set up their own college they spent £250,000 on it, and thirty firms representing more than half the output of south Wales supported it. The money was there in abundance, and one industry alone could spend on one project as much as the university was able to raise for all its activities from all sources in thirty years before the war.[3]

In short, the Cardiff college was conscious that it was none too well treated; indeed financially it did not do as well as Bangor, which is as surprising as it was reprehensible. The endowment incomes of the Welsh colleges on the eve of the war were[4]

	£
Aberystwyth	573
Bangor	2,020
Cardiff	1,603

which is curious when one compares what was a heavily industrialized area with one almost entirely lacking in industry. Clearly local support of the lower classes and support from south Lancashire were making Bangor more prosperous than Cardiff in spite of the latter's vastly richer potential catchment area. To put Cardiff into context with some English cases, in 1919[5]

[1] W. C. Davies and W. L. Jones, p. 151.
[2] Haldane, Cd. 8507. Evidence of Hugh Ingledew, Q. 637, et seq., on this issue.
[3] Ibid., evidence of D. J. A. Brown, the Registrar. He noted that the total sum subscribed to the college since its foundation was £209,883 including the Treasury grant for building. This compares badly with what was spent on Treforest alone.
[4] Sir D. Emrys Evans, *The University of Wales, A Historical Sketch*, p. 65.
[5] A. H. Trow, *Inaugural Address* on his succession to the principalship at Cardiff.

Cardiff had 23 professorships but only 1 fully endowed
Bristol had 26 professorships but only 8 fully endowed
Liverpool had 56 professorships but only 36 fully endowed

or, to carry it through a little later to the inter-war years, in 1930–1 the endowment income of Cardiff was about £4,000, while the endowment incomes of Bristol and Liverpool were £30,000 and £36,000. By any standards there was some disengagement here. Why was it that a university in a major and thriving industrial centre should have received by English standards such comparatively little support in spite of its avowed intentions to relate itself to industry?

First, the college was not producing in its research output and teaching either useful information, techniques, or the kind of students required by south Wales industry, and certain leading industries in south Wales, notably tinplate, were not graduate employers in any case. While these matters will be considered more fully in the next sections, there are two other specific factors inhibiting the flow of money from Welsh industry to Cardiff. First was the lack of a large middle-class element in south Wales such as was found in larger British cities. Furthermore, even though it was admitted that many Welsh firms were very wealthy, there were two difficulties here which explained why this wealth was not easily tapped. In the first place the founders of large concerns in south Wales industry tended to move out of the district. One did not find a large number of people who had made their money in the area staying in the vicinity of Cardiff as one found such similar people still living in Sheffield and Bristol. In the second place, much of the ownership was no longer in the hands of approachable individuals, even if living afar off; it lay rather with the shareholders of limited companies, who by their elusiveness and diffusion were less easy to tap for large donations.[1] Admittedly there were large generous supporters like Bute, Tredegar, the Cory Company, Lewis Davies, the Ocean Coal Company, and Sir Alfred Thomas, among others, but in general financial support was patently lacking.

The second broad reason for the aloofness of south Wales industry from the college lay in suspicions about the constitutional position of the institution. Before 1893 when the federal University of Wales was formed the colleges prepared for London degrees. Ironically, as it turned out, one of the chief arguments of the leading protagonist for a University of Wales, the Principal of Cardiff, was that such an arrangement would be better for industrial training.[2] Clearly, dependence on London could not be indefinite, but Jones was wrong

[1] *Report of the Committee on the University of Wales and its Constituent Colleges*, Cd. 4572, 1909. (Sir Thomas Raleigh's Committee, henceforth cited as Raleigh). Evidence of Lewis Williams and Hurry Riches.
[2] J. Viriamu Jones, *Prifysgol Cymru*, pp. 15–16.

in thinking south Wales businessmen would prefer the federal concept of a University of Wales as an alternative. It fixed in their minds an unfortunate if slightly irrational notion. As Hugh Ingledew told the Haldane Commission, 'the ordinary businessman . . . looks upon the University College at Cardiff as a local part of an institution in north Wales for the training of divinity students . . .'.[1] The situation might have been eased if Aberystwyth's title had been changed from that of the University College of Wales which implied a certain metropolitan status over the colleges of north and south Wales. The only solution which would have resolved this suspicion would have been the creation of an independent university at Cardiff, but this would have made no sense of the position of the other two colleges, indeed it was an eventuality they both feared. In a sense, Cardiff was a victim of the University of Wales concept just as Dundee was a victim of the concept of the dual University of St Andrews and in both cases the business classes reacted with apathy.

The real pity of the lack of private endowment finance was the fact that it could not redress an already existing imbalance *vis-à-vis* England in government and municipal finance. In 1911, for example, Wales was receiving less government grant per student than England.[2]

	Students	Treasury grant £	Grant per student £
England	5,505	158,777	28·8
Wales	1,222	27,122	22·1

However, broken down among the colleges, the disparity in its implications for industry was more disturbing.

	Students	Treasury grant £	Grant per student £
Aberystwyth	448	9,000	20·3
Bangor	295	10,000	33·8
Cardiff	479	8,122	17·0

Bangor was not only the best endowed but the best government financed and its output like Aberystwyth was predominantly teachers and clergy, as we shall see. Cardiff, potentially the most significant for industry, was less well endowed than Bangor and had the lowest government finance of any. Finally, there was another imbalance

[1] Haldane, Cd. 8507, Hugh Ingledew, Q. 660. See also T. I. Ellis, *The Development of Higher Education in Wales*, p. 131, for the deadening effects of this.
[2] Principal's Statement to the Court of Governors on State Assistance to Universities, October, 1911. University College of South Wales and Monmouthshire, Cardiff.

or anomaly that Principal Griffiths experienced at Cardiff concerning his abortive mining department. He had found that whereas the Board of Agriculture gave generous capital grants for setting up agricultural departments, yet he had been unable to obtain a similar grant from the Board of Education for setting up mining. As an anomaly it further reinforced the driving of the Welsh colleges' specialisms away from industry to agriculture, it reinforced the backward position of Cardiff in government finance in relation to the other colleges, and it made even more serious the inability of this college to tap private coal owners' money for mining education.[1]

Further, the Welsh colleges complained that they were much less municipally financed than their English counterparts. The Nottingham town council provided £7,380 and Sheffield £6,000 a year for their respective universities while the Lancashire universities received £1,000–£2,000 apiece. Aberystwyth, on the other hand, got a mere £30 for scholarships and £400 for building a hall. Bangor argued that the town could afford to support the college handsomely since they shrewdly calculated that all the college residents were worth £12,000–£15,000 a year to the town's commerce.[2] It was also the burden of Principal Griffiths' statement, cited earlier, that Wales was getting much less local authority aid, itself a reflection of the lack of wealth of the locality where the colleges were situated and in two cases the result itself of the lack of industry. Thus poor local industrial support could damage the finances of the colleges both directly and indirectly, and central government finance could not redress it.

What services in teaching and research specialisms did the Welsh colleges provide for local industry? With Aberystwyth it was virtually negligible. Apart from some extra lectures on the technology of woollen manufacture there is no trace of any contribution to industry before the 1900s.[3] Before the Haldane Commission the claim was made that from 1906 'an increasing number of departments mainly but not exclusively in the Faculty of Science has pursued a policy of organized co-operative research on the problems of the region around the College'.[4] One suspects either that this claim was an exaggeration prompted by a desire to put on a good face to the commission or that it referred almost exclusively to agriculture, for there is no trace of this activity in the college's own report on

---

[1] Raleigh, Cd. 4572, 1909. Evidence of E. H. Griffiths, pp. 79–80.
[2] 'Memorandum to the Town Council of Bangor, December 1901', Belmont MSS/67. University College of North Wales, Bangor.
[3] Principal's Reports *passim*. The reference to woollen technology was 1892/3. The report of 1896/7 which reviewed the first twenty-five years' work also made no reference to industry.
[4] Haldane, Cd. 8507, p. 288.

the period.[1] In applied mathematics there was some work on electricity, but very little; in physics some on the coagulation of copper, but again very little work was being done. Geology had been created a separate department in 1909 and intended to start a survey of north Cardiganshire metal mining, 'of great economic importance', but had not done so yet. As regards chemistry, that department only started doing any sort of research from 1901, with proper laboratories only from 1907, but before the war their research was insignificant.[2] The only important area of *rapprochement* between the college and industry was with fishing. In 1912 the government had made a grant to the zoology department for a study of the local mussel industry and the lobsters and crabs of Cardigan Bay, as well as local salmon and trout problems arising from the pollution of rivers by lead.[3] Outside Wales they also did work on the lobster hatcheries on the Beaulieu river in Hampshire. In short, the contribution of the college at Aberystwyth to Welsh industry apart from fisheries was virtually nil. Its real strength wisely lay in agricultural education and research and this alignment and disengagement from industry was exactly what we should expect in this predominantly farming area of central Wales.[4]

Bangor in its location seemed as unpromising as Aberystwyth for a college expecting to develop any potential links with industry. Indeed before the war they totally failed to make themselves useful to the one industry near to them, the slate quarries. The whole story was most unsatisfactory.[5] In 1900, a meeting had been held at Blaenau Ffestiniog which resulted in a delegation to ask the college to set up a mining department. The court received the suggestion favourably and called a conference 'of representatives of the Quarry, Mining and Metallurgical industries of North Wales'. Although in principle everyone agreed with the proposal, nothing whatever was done, and when the 1902 Education Act put heavy pressures on the finances of local authorities then the mining scheme was dropped as one that could no longer be afforded.[6] At the time of the Haldane

[1] University College of Wales, Aberystwyth, Quinquennial Report 1908–1913.
[2] T. Campbell James and C. W. Davies, 'Schools of Chemistry in Great Britain and Ireland—XXVII The University College of Wales, Aberystwyth', *JRIC*, October, 1956.
[3] Report on Investigations towards the Improvement of Fisheries and Cardigan Bay and its Rivers (Aberystwyth, 1913); also Quinquennial Report, 1908–1913.
[4] It was noted of Principal Roberts, 1891–1919, that 'in his own mind the Principal thought of the physical sciences . . . as studies ancillary to agriculture'. David Williams, *Thomas Francis Roberts, 1860–1919*, p. 33.
[5] University College of North Wales, Bangor. Minutes of the Court, 18 April, 24 October 1900; 17 April, 23 October 1901.
[6] Raleigh, Cd. 4572, 1909. Evidence of Sir Harry Reichel, Q. 322. Reichel also asserted against sceptical questioning that the slate industry really needed university trained labour and expertise.

report this project was still being discussed as one which ought to be implemented sometime in the future, but even if a mining department might have been rather ambitious, Bangor yet more surprisingly in view of its location did not even have a chair of geology.[1]

Perhaps the most successful liaison, as at Aberystwyth, was with the fishing industries.[2] In 1892, the Professor of Zoology at the college acquired the marine biological station on Puffin Island and started the scientific study of the sea fisheries of the north Wales coast. The fishery collection that he formed was 'largely made use of by fishermen', but in 1900 the station was abandoned chiefly because of its distance from the college and the failure to raise funds to build one nearer at hand. However, local lectures for fishermen on spawning and migration and the development and feeding of fishes were well attended in the early 1900s. As regards the research of the department, their greatest achievement was the work on the Conway mussel fishery in 1893, which the studies of the college helped to save from extinction. Also on the Conway, they undertook several years' work on the sparling fishery in the early 1900s, and in the Menai Straits improved the mussel and oyster cultivation. Bearing in mind the work of St Andrews, Dundee, Liverpool, and Aberystwyth, this was further evidence that the fishing industry was one that unobtrusively enjoyed one of the most fruitful links with university work at the turn of the century. Bangor's other forte was forestry in which it was unique in Wales in possessing a department from 1904. From 1906 the Denbighshire County Council gave them fifty acres for research and they quickly began to act in an advisory capacity to afforested estates throughout north Wales and thence into Cheshire and Shropshire before the war. Indeed, most of the department's time was spent on this consultancy activity. They were highly conscious of the industrial significance of their work and indeed noted that 'practically all research in forestry bears directly upon industry'.[3]

The other industrial contributions of the college were minor and fragmentary. Its chemistry was not prominent for industry, partly because, as they boasted in 1911, they had the worst facilities in Britain and partly because the professor throughout most of this time had wisely related the subject to agriculture and not to industry.[4] More important for industry from the research side was the work of the mathematics department which from 1910 focused much of its activity on aeronautics, not only studying the theoretical aspects

[1] Haldane, Cd. 8993, 1918. Evidence of Reichel, Q. 14240.
[2] Haldane, Cd. 8993, p. 181–2, and Reports of Heads of Departments, University College of North Wales, Bangor, 1904/5, 1905/6, 1911/12.
[3] Haldane, Cd. 8699, p. 80, and QQ. 6420–6458, and Reports of Heads of Departments 1908/9 and 1912/13.
[4] Harry Reichel, 'In Memoriam J. J. Dobbie', *Magazine of the University College of North Wales*, June, 1925.

of stability but actually building and flying a 'flying machine' in 1911.[1] Apart from that the only other feature of note about Bangor was that it was one of the three selected universities in Britain—the others being Cambridge and Newcastle—where holders of Surveyors Institution Scholarships attended.[2] But, like Aberystwyth, its chief forte was agriculture, the first school in any university college in Britain. Although Bangor seemed to have slightly more relevance to industry than Aberystwyth, in spite of their essentially non-industrial surroundings, one cannot contemplate this project before the war without some sense of waste. At the eastern end of the coastline, in the region of Flint[3], there were engineering, chemical, paper, pottery, corrugated iron, and lead mining industries all in operation before the war, which were receiving no benefits from higher education at all and which, more than the slate quarries, were in considerable need of it whether they realized it or not. It is difficult to avoid the conclusion that in hindsight to recreate another Aberystwyth-type college in north Wales was a pity and some location further east than Bangor might have resulted in more varied industrial benefits for the Welsh economy.

However, if we seek industrial linkages we should surely expect to find them in Cardiff if not in the other two. Disengagements from industry in Bangor and Aberystwyth which were orientated towards agriculture were not particularly serious, but similar features existed also in south Wales which were a much graver matter for the competitive health of Welsh industry. Serious defects were evident in the coal mining and tinplate industries and in the departments of the college at Cardiff that should have been servicing them with science. The situation in mining was little short of a scandal, in which both university and industrial sides were both to blame. When the mining department had started in 1891 its head, Sir William Galloway, remained far too busy with his practice as a working engineer to trouble with building up the work of his new department. Consequently what should have been a scientific centre for the south Wales coalfield 'did not prove a complete success', as the historians of the college euphemistically put it.[4] The coal owners, seeking to provide themselves with what the university would not provide for them, set up their rival college at Treforest in 1912 to the detriment of the mining department at Cardiff, which on the eve of the war had only one student.[5] The college was much to blame. Although the south

---

[1] Reports of Heads of Departments 1909/10 and 1910/11.
[2] University College of North Wales, Principal's Review of the Work and Growth of the College, July 1905.
[3] Haldane, Cd. 8993, 1918, QQ. 11492–5.
[4] A. H. Trow and D. J. A. Brown, *The University College of South Wales and Monmouthshire, 1883–1933, a Short History of the College*, pp. 52–3.
[5] Haldane, Cd. 8507. Evidence of Hugh Ingledew on this question.

Wales mines were the most dangerous in Britain,[1] there is no trace of the college doing valuable research that would have helped problems such as these, thereby demonstrating the potential use of a university department.[2] Indeed the professor of geology told Haldane that the college would never get the standing that it should unless it turned out original work 'partly in relation to the industries of the area'.[3] The seriousness of the failure of mining education at Cardiff is further emphasized when it is appreciated that the college served an area producing a larger output of coal than any other field in Britain. The coalfield served by Cardiff University College produced 53 million tons a year, and that served by Newcastle 52 million tons, with the other fields served by universities each producing only half as much.[4] It was ironic and pitiful for south Wales that the largest field should have been so badly served by its educational facilities.

Metallurgy was little better. It was continually complaining that it had far too little accommodation and facilities and that it had scarcely any students. We do not find that the department made any research contribution to the metallurgical industries. But in any case it would seem that the tinplate industry cared scarcely anything for research at all with the exception of Thomas's.[5] If the industry had this attitude to science and research it is little wonder that the metallurgical department, which like coal mining should have been at least as good as at an English civic university like Sheffield or Newcastle, made so little impact. This will become more evident when we consider the attitudes to the output of students for these industries. Chemistry was of slight importance, with little research and no significant development.[6] The engineering department was largely ignored[7] by local industry and the Powell Duffryn Steam Coal Company, an employer of 14,000, pointedly said before the war

[1] Of the twenty-seven principal colliery disasters, 1890–1914, thirteen took place in south Wales, and 1,467 south Wales miners were killed in them compared with 1,115 in all the rest of Britain. R. Page Arnot, *The Miners: Years of Struggle* (London, 1953), p. 24. Galloway was one of the most prominent mining engineers and author of the coal dust theory of colliery explosions, though not a good professor.
[2] Principal's Reports, 1897–1914 yield no evidence; also Mr D. Davies, the Treasurer of Aberystwyth, deplored it as 'an extraordinary thing that with a big coalfield like South Wales . . . hardly anything has been done in the way of mining research . . .'. This was in 1909. Raleigh, Cd. 4572, p. 538.
[3] Haldane, Cd. 8507, 1917. Evidence of T. F. Sibley, Q. 896.
[4] 'University Provision for Mining Instruction in Britain, 1914'. Document in a file of the Joint Advisory Committee of the RTC and University, Glasgow, in Principal's Papers (uncatalogued) in the Archives of Glasgow University.
[5] Haldane, Cd. 8699, 1917. Evidence of T. J. Williams, Q. 5256.
[6] N. M. Cullinane, 'University College of South Wales and Monmouth, Cardiff, Chemistry Department', *JRIC*, October 1955.
[7] See the gloomy evidence of Professor F. Bacon, Haldane, Cd. 8507, Q. 972, et seq.

that if it had electrical problems with its pits it consulted Germans from Berlin, not the Welsh colleges.[1] In addition to a rather hostile industrial milieu which it had to face, Cardiff partly brought its weaknesses upon itself. The root cause now seems to be an absurd over-diversification of activities in the early stages of the college. In 1904 there were twenty-three different departments, none distinguished, all short of funds and space, and this lack of realism about how much could be done lay behind the failure to develop limited areas of excellence that would have won over a sceptical industry before 1914.

Considering the record of the Welsh colleges before 1914 it must be admitted to be poor—vastly inferior to the Scottish universities in the same period, and even taking all three together inferior to most single English civic universities. There can be no doubt of this. The evidence of internal reports is fairly full. Also the Welsh universities received some of the most thorough government investigation with three large committees or commissions of inquiry in these years. And yet neither in all this nor in the necessarily laudatory official histories is there any but the slightest evidence of developments coming from the colleges which materially assisted Welsh industry, or still less revolutionized it.

If the other services of the colleges to industry were negligible, what of their output of students to industry and commerce? In the case of Aberystwyth it was evident that at least up to about 1,900 students going into industry and business had been a small proportion of the total output of the college since its beginning. The Principal gave a breakdown for the first twenty-five years of the college as follows:[2]

	No.	%		No.	%
Teachers	400	45·4	Farmers	22	2·5
Ministers of religion	222	25·3	Journalists	12	1·4
Medical doctors	82	9·3	Barristers	10	1·1
'Have entered different walks of business life'	59	6·7	Engineers	6	0·69
Solicitors	33	3·75	Civil Service	4	0·4
Music teachers	25	2·9	MPs	3	0·3

Thus about 7 per cent could be said to have gone into industry and trade, which is fairly respectable and considerably better, for example, than St Andrews or Aberdeen, to take two comparable universities. However, wherever these people went it was evident that they were not serving the industrial economy of Wales in the

[1] Haldane, Cd. 8699, evidence of Joseph Shaw, Q. 10117.
[2] Principal's Report, 1896/7.

south. F. W. Rudler, the Professor of Natural Science there in the 1870s, said that he had been anxious to get students from the mining and metallurgical area of Glamorganshire who would have benefited from his mineralogy and chemistry, but 'very few agreed to it, I had only two or three'.[1]

His successor found only one student from the industrial regions of south Wales, and he was a medical student. Indeed most of the advanced scientists were destined for medical and not industrial careers.[2] By the war, however, this had certainly changed and an interesting trend had emerged. From about 1910 almost all the honours chemists produced by the college went into industry,[3] but the professor indicated precisely where they had gone.[4]

Ironhurst Peat Company, Dumfries-shire	Brotherton and Sons, Leeds (2)
South Metropolitan Gas Company, London	Nobel's (2), Ardeer
Cotton Powder Company, Faversham	Baldwin's Steel Works, Swansea

Almost all their industrial chemists were taking up posts outside Wales. Thus, although the science department had been more successful in adding training for industry to its predominant training for medicine from the 1890s, yet this played no part in benefiting the Welsh economy.

In the case of Bangor the output of known students in the twenty years before 1909 was as follows:[5]

	No.	%		No.	%
Teachers	774	59	'Trade and commerce'	16	1·2
Clergy and Ministers	210	16	Law	10	0·77
Agriculture	179	13·7	Chemists and analysts	9	0·61
Electrical Engineers	35	2·68	Mechanical engineers	6	0·46
Medicine	34	2·6	Army	3	0·23
Architects, surveyors, estate agents	25	1·9			

[1] Aberdare, C. 3047, 1881. Q. 7111.
[2] Ibid. Professor T. S. Humpidge, Q. 9945.
[3] Haldane, Cd. 8507. Q. 2183.
[4] Ibid., p. 295.
[5] Raleigh, Cd. 4572, 1909, pp. 226–7.

Thus just under 5 per cent of the output could be said to have anything to do with industry or business compared with Aberystwyth's
7 per cent. It is also interesting to note that at Aberystwyth clergy
and teachers made up 70 per cent of the output and at Bangor 75
per cent. This great output to teaching is partly a reflection of the
prestige of cultural occupations in Wales and also a reflection of the
disparity of remuneration. For example, it was complained that
industrial chemists in Wales were very poorly paid before the war,
with £120 per annum for a laboratory chemist and £130 for a works
chemist.[1] On the other hand, it was noted by Bangor that salaries
for teachers were high and attractive, even for those who were
tempted by them to start teaching before completing a degree.[2]
Bangor and Aberystwyth were roughly similar in outputs though
Bangor was slightly more disoriented from industry.

How does this relate to the social background of the students at
each college? We have full evidence on the social class background
of Aberystwyth students[3] for 1909 and on those of Bangor[4] for
1906/7.

	Professional non-industrial		Industrial and commercial		Agricultural		Working-class	
	No.	%	No.	%	No.	%	No.	%
Aberystwyth	55	34·8	44	27·9	23	14·5	36	22·9
Bangor	64	21	91	30	50	16·4	99	32·6

Bangor was clearly somewhat more plebeian in tone than Aberystwyth whose predominant class was professional, but both have
about equal proportions of parents in industry and trade. Both
colleges were doing exactly what the Scottish universities and Oxford
and Cambridge were doing, namely taking students from business
backgrounds and turning them into young professional people
divorced from industry and commerce.

Bangor had one special connection in training students for industry and one glaring defect. It was particularly good in feeding
students into the electrical industry via its physics department, as
the above figures show. It was noted of their electrical engineering
course in 1906 that 'all the students of this department who have
completed the course have proceeded to electrical supply stations or
manufacturing works',[5] and every year students went to jobs with

[1] Haldane, Cd. 8699. Q. 7600.
[2] University College of North Wales, Bangor, Reports of Heads of Departments,
1904/5.
[3] Raleigh, Q. 659–60.
[4] Haldane, Appendix to First Report, p. 187. We have, however, recounted
engineers and chemists in the industrial and commercial classes leaving
as professionals only those without industrial connections.
[5] Reports of Heads of Departments, 1905/6 and *passim*.

BTH as well as less regularly to Siemens, Marconi, and others. Professor Andrew Gray, as Professor of Physics from 1884 to 1899, devised a course to train managers and foremen in local electricity work and this was taken up by men from the local electric lighting works.[1] But if the linkage with the local electricity industry was good there remained the perennial problem of their neglect of the local quarrying industry that nagged consciences up to the war.[2] Principal Reichel said in defence that Bangor's problem in relation to their main local industry had been the fact that mining and quarrying of this nature involved a good deal of mechanical engineering and Bangor was not otherwise a mechanical engineering centre—'that always created a certain hesitation in our dealings with the subject'.[3] It remained one of the worst disengagements between a university and its local industry before the war.

As regards the output of the University College of South Wales at Cardiff, while there are no overall figures it is possible to calculate exactly what happened to two of the most important groups, engineers and mining students, and the relevance of their future careers for the Welsh economy. They may be presented in this manner.[4]

	Making a career wholly in Wales		Having a career partly away from Wales but moving back to Wales		Starting a career in Wales but moving away and not returning		Making a career totally outside Wales	
	No.	%	No.	%	No.	%	No.	%
Engineers	23	20·35	12	10·6	19	16·8	59	52
Mining students	40	48·8	5	6	14	17	23	28

It is evident that the local mining industry provided a much stronger outlet for the mining students than the Welsh engineering industry did for its engineers. Nearly 70 per cent of the engineers ended up in careers outside Wales, while over half of the miners ended up in careers within Wales. Whatever the suspicions of the coal owners that induced them to set up their own institutions at Treforest, and

---

[1] Ibid., 1907/8, and Harry Reichel, 'In Memoriam Andrew Gray', *Magazine of the University College of North Wales*, June 1926, p. 111.
[2] Haldane, Cd. 8507, 1918. G. A. Humphreys, Q. 3334–8.
[3] Haldane, Cd. 8993, 1918. Harry Reichel, Q. 14260.
[4] Calculated from lists of students in Engineering and Mining in *Calendar oj the University College of South Wales and Monmouthshire, 1913–14*, pp. 536–58. Sir Joseph Thomson also noted that 'a comparatively small number of university students pass into the local industries [of South Wales]', *Natural Science in Education* (Sir Joseph Thomson's Committee), 1918, p. 86.

however backward the college was in mining research, yet its output of students for the Welsh industry was fairly good. With engineering there was much less local pull for local reasons. Hurry Riches, the President of the Institute of Mechanical Engineers and a member of the Court of Governors of the college at Cardiff, explained that in Cardiff there was not a class of manufacturers interested in employing engineers as in Manchester and Birmingham. Also with few exceptions, including himself, what engineers there were were engaged in repairing work, using a floating body of men inter-mittently. They did not need 'officers' of university level for their sort of engineering; all they wanted were a few foremen and these they got 'without much trouble', usually from the North of England, Yorkshire and Tyneside. In short, the firms were not interested in having a permanent body of men properly trained like the artisan élites of Crewe and Horwich railway workshops.[1] In any case the Professor of Engineering admitted that the qualifications of the college had 'hardly any professional value outside the college' and that, even worse, his students were 'not equipped, in the best sense of the term, for industrial purposes'.[2]

If this was the case, where then did those Welsh engineers making a career in Wales go?

Railways	22	Dowlais steel works	2
Collieries	5	Representatives of Eng-	
Local government engin-		lish firms in Wales	2
eering	4	Copper mine	1
South Wales Electricity		Gas Company	1
Distribution Company	4	Tube works	1
Consultants	3	Boiler works	1
Ebbw Vale steel works	3	Motor cars	1
Iron works	2	Engine works	1
GEC	1	GPO	1
'Electrical engineer'	1		

Riches's point was justified by the facts, the vast bulk of Cardiff college engineers were going into the railways, especially Taff Vale, the chief coal carrier, if only for a short time. The collieries, local government engineering, and electricity distribution took some, but there was evidently no tradition of a wide range of firms taking them beyond that. Hence their exodus is not surprising.

Yet even the connection with the coal industry which appeared

---

[1] Raleigh, Cd. 4572, 1909. Evidence of Hurry Riches *passim.* Sir Edward Nichol a few years later made the same point with regard to Cardiff shipyards that they were chiefly for repair. They had no shipbuilding industry which absorbed graduates like the North of England. Haldane, Cd. 8993, 1918, Q. 11593.

[2] Ibid., Professor A. C. Elliott, Q. 1056.

much better did not escape criticism. The Professor of Engineering observed of coal owners that 'their method of dealing with university graduates is to have nothing to do with them'.[1] If we consider the lists of mining students in more detail we may discover that forty-four different collieries in south Wales were taking Cardiff students, which seems a fair number, but it is presumably small in proportion to the total collieries in the area. However, we find that it was most common for such collieries to employ only one such university man, and even large employers like the Ocean Coal Company at Treorchy, the Cambrian Colliery at Clydach Vale, and the Ebbw Vale Company took no more than three or four in all in the whole of the period before the war, which seems rather fewer than it would have been advantageous for them to absorb. For instance, it was claimed that there were about 4,000 agents and overlookers in the collieries and steelworks of south Wales, even at the end of the 1880s, who needed advanced scientific education.[2] In the light of this the college output of mining and engineering students who made a career in Wales was a very small proportion of this large required stock of managerial labour.

At least the railways and the collieries and, to a lesser extent steel, firms were absorbing Cardiff college men, but with the other main south Wales industry, tinplate, it was not so at all. Hubert Spence Thomas of Richard Thomas and Company said that 'there is not more than one person engaged in the industry who has had a university scientific education, and I am not aware of anyone in the trade who holds a degree in Science'.[3] The local MP agreed that 'there are no trained chemists to my knowledge in any tinplate works',[4] in spite of the fact that the industry very much lent itself to a scientific treatment with its problems of the oxidization of tin, annealing, and the problems of breakages. What scientists Swansea employed traditionally came from the continent, especially Germany.[5] This lack of involvement between the tinplate industry and the local university is hardly surprising for a number of reasons. First, the industry consisted of a large number of small employers, frequently sprung from the ranks of shopkeepers, this being financially an easy trade to enter. They had little appreciation of the university world or how to use graduates. In the words of their historian, they 'brought with them not a spirit of enterprise but the outlook of the small property owner'. Second, it was an industry which, astonishingly, had experienced no technical change from the beginning of the

[1] Haldane, Cd. 8507, Professor F. Bacon, Q. 972.
[2] K. V. Jones, *The Life of John Viriamu Jones*, p. 173.
[3] Haldane, Cd. 8699. Statement of H. S. Thomas, p. 263.
[4] Ibid., T. J. Williams, MP, Q. 5257.
[5] Aberdare, C. 3047. Evidence of Lewis Williams, Q. 17876, and R. Martin, QQ. 14676–8.

eighteenth century, and not until 1919 was there any research in the south Wales tinplate industry, with the setting up of the Swansea University College. In short, from the point of view of entrepreneurship and technical change there was scarcely a worse industry in Britain as a potential graduate employer, though as contemporary American examples showed they could well have done with some new scientific blood.[1] When Mond Nickel started up in 1902 this was no help to the Welsh colleges either, because Sir Alfred Mond established a particular link, not with the local colleges before the war, but with Cambridge.[2]

With regard to the output of Cardiff chemists, no full figures exist, but expert evidence for this field is also far from encouraging. The University of Wales Appointments Board was created in 1912 and the Secretary said that he had had 'no difficulty' in placing chemists in works. 'Some went to explosives factories, others to peat factories, tar and ammonia distilleries, dye works, etc.'[3] But it soon transpired that this was no exception to the common theme of disengagement, for almost all these placings were 'not in Wales but in Scotland and England'. Only during the war did Welsh employers become interested in Welsh chemists. In fact in Wales, on the eve of the war, there was a glut of university graduates who could not find work in an apathetic industry, hence the exodus of engineers and of chemists out of the principality to other parts of Britain.[4] When the Secretary published his first report his placements had a predictable ring:[5]

Teaching 94
Works chemists 8
Engineering 7
Works physicists 2

In short, across the range of industries in this region there was 'a tendency to regard men with pure science training as not being very efficient commercially or in the industries. Unfortunately that view is very strongly held throughout Wales . . . men with scientific degrees are not looked upon favourably . . .'.[6] And more than one observer noted that attitudes of apathy or hostility towards graduates

[1] W. E. Minchinton 'The Tinplate Maker and Technical Change', *Explorations in Entrepreneurial History*, VII, 1957. Professor Minchinton's *The British Tinplate Industry* (Oxford, 1957) significantly and legitimately contains no reference to Cardiff University College.
[2] Haldane, Cd. 8699, Sir Alfred Mond, QQ. 5207–8.
[3] Haldane, Cd. 8699, Silyn Roberts, Q. 7595.
[4] *The Appointments Board for Wales, What it is and What it Does* (Cardiff, 1913).
[5] First Annual Report of the University of Wales Appointments Board ,1914.
[6] Haldane, Cd. 8699, George Knox, Q. 6056.

persisted in Wales up to the war. Such attitudes had vanished from the Midlands and Manchester some ten or so years earlier.[1]

It will have become apparent that there was a considerable network of factors all militating against the close liaison of the Welsh colleges and Welsh industry and that neither side of the partnership was blameless.

If we consider how far the situation may be attributable to the colleges and their founders, the chief factor was probably that of location. By siting the colleges at Aberystwyth and Bangor they not only divorced them from industry in south and north-east Wales but from the financial aid that industry could provide, from the scientific stimulus that industrial demands would occasion, and also from the wealthy municipal finance which was only to be found in industrial areas. The location also turned specific subjects, quite understandably, away from industry to agriculture, as at Bangor, or kept them poor, as at Aberystwyth. Second, the federal solution meant that Cardiff, although potentially the richest of the three, was retarded because of the suspicions of local industry about the functions of the University of Wales as a whole, and their lack of proprietorial civic pride in their own university. Third, although the principals of the three colleges were first-rate men, only one of them, Viriamu Jones, was a scientist and he in a field not calculated to appeal to the needs of south Wales. Their classics and theology backgrounds were certainly no help to the rest in trying to convince businessmen that their institutions could be useful to them. Fourth, there were certain tactical mistakes. Cardiff, for example, was obviously trying to do far too much rather thinly instead of developing centres of excellence in ways that would attract the attention of industry in certain specialized fields. Also Aberystwyth was clearly at fault in seeming almost deliberately to contradict in its practice its early claims to be relevant to industry, by allowing itself to drift into becoming yet another teacher and clergy training college. Also, by not starting engineering when it was expected to do so it antagonized even those business elements who would have been prepared to help it. Similarly the failure of Bangor even to develop geology lent itself too easily to an interpretation by local industrial interests that it had little interest in them. It is very much a question of chicken and egg, but it was a duty of these pioneering universities not to wait until there was a proved demand but to go ahead with certain developments to prove that they were useful and to create their own demand. This was the case with fishery education and forestry, to take successful Welsh examples.

[1] Evidence of Knox and Bacon, op. cit. Both felt this keenly and suggested that the attitudes of Welsh industry to graduates were 'ten years' behind those of the North of England.

Yet if part of the blame lay with the colleges much also lay with Welsh industry. The nature of financial support for the Welsh colleges is certainly bizarre, with these large sums for Aberystwyth and Bangor coming from a genuinely democratic support that could ill afford it and vast injections of money coming from outside Wales altogether, especially south Lancashire. Welsh industry was simply not supporting the university movement as well as it might have done. Some of the reasons for this arise from peculiarities of industrial structure. In north Wales the college was faced with an industry beginning a period of decline from the 1880s under two or three virtually monopolistic quarries and families who were little better than lukewarm about the college. A vicious circle set in; they did not give enough money for a geology department and without a geology department the college was of negligible use and this gave further reason for withholding support. In the south there were various reasons special to each industry. Marine engineering used floating poorish labour and was not engaged in building so much as repairing. The tinplate industry, contrary to the quarries, was split up into a vast number of small units, heedless of technical change, and with scarcely any firms large or scientific enough to make it worth their considering using graduates. The coal owners failed to understand that they could not interfere with a chartered university college and diverted all their support into a new institution of their own that they could control, stultifying what should have been the main department serving them. Bedevilling much of Welsh industry was the problem of absentee ownership, such that there was a lack of a local wealthy class willing to subscribe to local projects, a situation different from the Sheffield or Bristol context.

That industry valued the graduate so little in Wales set up its own chain reaction. It underpaid him and he sought instead a career in the expanding secondary school system or in English industry. Hence what engineers and chemists were produced migrated. In turn, since so much of the output was lost to Welsh industry, this was yet a further reason for Welsh industrialists to withhold support. We could not, on the other hand, claim in the defence of the industries that they were not supporting the colleges because they could not afford to do so. Tinplate was doing very well until the 1890s, coal throughout the whole of this time and nickel in the 1900s; indeed their very success may have been a further factor reinforcing their lack of appreciation of the necessity of graduates. If they were successful without them then there was no need for a change and less for the extra expense involved. When they ceased to be successful then they could not afford graduates on their cut profits; any excuse would do for inactivity. It may be that it was exactly Wales's good fortune that kept her some ten or so years behind the North of England and the Midlands in her attitude to universities and their role in industry. The superb quality of her steam coal, unrivalled for value in quality and price in coaling stations throughout the world, gave her easy captive markets up to the war that depended very little on her scientific education or her innovation. The same might equally be said of slate in the north. At the very root of the disengagement was the tendency of the two northern colleges to regard themselves as agencies not for industrial but for Welsh cultural and religious regeneration. The Welsh universities movement was essentially a cultural rather than an economic movement in contrast with the English civic universities movement. The penalty for this disengagement was not paid at the time but in the inter-war years in the relative failure of the Welsh to develop the 'new' industries to absorb the unemployment of the old, and in such specific instances as the lamentably slow reception of the strip mill in the tinplate industry, delayed until 1939. In the meantime the industrialists made profits they did not disburse, the colleges produced clergymen and school-teachers, and what scientists were eventually educated by the system for the most part migrated to England, to serve an industry both more varied in its opportunities and appreciative in its rewards.

6

The Scottish Universities 1850-1914

'*Scotland is exceedingly well off in respect to educational facilities and is holding its own in respect to foreign competition better than England.*'[1]

'*The four Scottish Universities . . . in the main owing to their sluggishness and want of ideas of their governors, [are] of little use from the point of view of the application of science to industry . . .*'.[2]

During the nineteenth century Scotland possessed a university system quite distinct from that of England both in its fundamental assumptions and in its administrative arrangements. Its salient characteristics were two-fold; namely an attempt to provide higher education for a large proportion of the population with the intelligence to benefit, and to make that education broad and multi-disciplinary even at the expense of specialist knowledge. These features gave Scottish higher education a distinctive stamp, particularly in the period from the mid-eighteenth century through to the 1890s. Thereafter, following the Act of 1889, the ordinances under the Act in 1892, and further adjustments in the 1900s, the Scottish universities were brought more into line with English assumptions of restrictive entry and specialist study.

The traditional Scottish system had seemed justified by its past achievements. In the late eighteenth century many of the science based innovations for the Industrial Revolution in Britain were of Scottish origin. The well-known scientific advances of Joseph Black in his introduction of Turkey Red dye and his discovery of latent heat, Watt's steam engine, Roebuck's sulphuric acid, James Keir's

[1] J. W. Swan, in Report of the LCC Technical Education Board Sub-Committee on the Application of Science to Industry, 1902, p. 14.
[2] R. B. Haldane, 'Great Britain and Germany, a Study in Education' (an address at Liverpool, October 1901) in *Education and Empire* (London, 1902) pp. 33–4.

caustic alkali, were all the products of men who had taught, studied, or worked in the Scottish universities at a time when those of England stagnated.[1] At a lower level there was the tradition of the Scots mechanic, the McConells, Kennedys, Cannans, Napiers, Nasmyths, and others who were the backbone of the engineering industry in England itself. At another level again the cultural flowering of the arts and social sciences in Scotland with Sir Walter Scott, Adam Smith, David Hume, and others further betokened the vitality of Scottish intellectual life in this period. This is well known but its familiarity never dims the wonder that it was all produced by a nation of a mere one and a half million people. This may have been mere genetic good fortune, but more commonly it is attributed to the virtues of a superior education system. It was, however, not to last. One Scottish historian goes so far as to write of the 'paralysis of intellectual life associated with Victorian Scotland',[2] and although this is too sweeping and its chronology is misleading there was a tailing off towards the end of the nineteenth century.[3] This whole period 1850–1914 in Scottish university history was one of a slow coming to terms with the recognition that in the changed and more scientific technology of industry after the mid century, the broad democratic university education that had served hitherto was no longer sufficient to train Scotland's own scientists. First, we will consider the features of the 'democratic' system and its defects, and how it was reformed. Then the industrial content of teaching and research in the universities will be examined, and the support or lack of it accorded by industry to Glasgow and Dundee as the main industrial university centres. Finally we shall consider the actual output of the Scottish universities to industry and commerce and how far such an education was a feature of the business élite by 1900.

The fundamental problems facing the Scottish universities arose from the dilemma between retaining the traditional virtues of the old type of arts degree or of introducing new subjects, and particularly allowing specialization in those subjects to produce an industrial scientific and managerial class for the Scottish economy. The arts curriculum of the early nineteenth century consisted of combinations of classics and sciences but with a specifically Scottish emphasis on philosophy.[4] The stress upon philosophy distinguished the Scottish

[1] A. and N. Clow, *The Chemical Revolution* (London, 1952), for an exhaustive study of the Scottish scientific contribution and its cultural milieu.
[2] G. E. Davie, *The Democratic Intellect, Scotland and her Universities in the Nineteenth Century*, p. 3.
[3] A. G. Clement and R. H. S. Robertson, *Scotland's Scientific Heritage*, indicates the decline in Scotland's capacity to produce scientific innovators by the later part of the nineteenth century.
[4] Alexander Morgan, *Scottish University Studies*, pp. 75, 80. David Murray, *Memories of the Old College of Glasgow*, pp. 81–2 for the curricular details of

curricula from Cambridge and their inclusion of sciences distinguished them from Oxford, but the spirit of the whole education was more fundamentally different than the details of its parts. The Scottish concern was for a broadly based, mixed arts and sciences education to create a roundly educated youth, but at the sacrifice of that specialist expertise that the ancient English universities could give in mathematics or classics. This kind of approach was particularly suitable for the occupations of the students it was aiming to produce. These were to a great extent clergy and schoolmasters, or people with no particular profession to follow but who wished to satisfy a general desire for culture. David Murray remembered that:[1]

> The Arts curriculum of that day was intended for culture only, not as providing something which was to have commercial value; the idea that any of its subjects could be made the foundation of industrial training in science as now understood and that the students could specialize in such a subject had not then been contemplated.

The other Scottish virtue was that, unlike the English universities of the time, they took their students from a wide social range including the lower as well as the middle-classes. At the end of the eighteenth century nearly a half of those students coming from an industrial and commercial background were of the working-class, and even in the 1830s, although there had been a slight fall, it was still as high as one-third.[2] The fundamental cause of this basic difference from England was that Scotland had far more university provision in relation to its population. In 1801, England and Wales had but two universities for a population of 8·8 million and Scotland four (or five if the two universities at Aberdeen be counted) universities for a population of 1·6 million. In 1850, England and Wales had four universities for a population of 17·9 million and Scotland four for 2·8 million. In the 1880s, Scotland had one university per million inhabitants while England had one per 6 million.[3] Thus the Scottish universities provided opportunities, as the English did not to anything like the same extent, for the 'lad o' pairts' from a humble cottage to tramp to the local university and, well provendered with

---

Aberdeen, Edinburgh, and Glasgow. These were chiefly combinations of Latin, Greek, Mathematics, Natural Philosophy, Moral Philosophy, Logic, and Rhetoric.

[1] David Murray, op. cit., pp. 120, 306–7.
[2] W. M. Mathew, 'The Origins and Occupations of Glasgow Students 1740–1839', *Past and Present*, April 1966.
[3] University College, Dundee, Opening Ceremony and Professor Stuart's Address (Dundee, 1883), p. 18.

herrings and oatmeal, to stay out the course there, returning to his native village for farm work in the summer.[1]

This was also made possible by another peculiarity of Scottish universities, namely the low age of intake. That students could enter the Scottish universities at the age of about fifteen without an entrance examination made it quite possible for the intelligent boy from an obscure village school to enter higher education. Indeed, since it was not uncommon for Scottish schoolmasters to have been to university themselves, even without graduating, this would be presented by them to their pupils as a realistic aim. But it was an aim that could be fulfilled from what we would call an all-age primary school. No necessity to go through 'secondary' education acted as a restrictive barrier preventing the lower classes from proceeding to university. Since the professors derived much of their income from modest class fees they accordingly had a vested interest in welcoming such entrants to swell their large lecture classes. Furthermore, the lower classes found no great barrier of cost in attending lectures as would have been the case in England. The Science and Art Department subsidized Scottish universities in the early 1870s at the rate of about £3,100 a year, providing 150 to 160 free places,[2] and in the next decade it was noted that 'access to the courses is cheap and untrammelled'.[3] Finally, after this education nearly half of the students went into the ministry, 44·7 per cent from Glasgow taking this path.[4] Here evidently lay a prestigious career, aspirations to which lay within the horizons of the lower class lad with a university education.

Such then were the salient features of what the Scots regarded as the virtues of their 'democratic' higher education in contradistinction to the Oxford and Cambridge pattern. It entailed taking large numbers of students, many from poor homes, accepting them without examination at the age of fifteen from all-age schools, teaching them in large professorial lectures and giving them a broadly based mixed arts and sciences curriculum in which philosophy figured prominently, and then sending the vast bulk back as clergy to the parishes, or such similar ones, whence they came. There is a great deal which is attractive about this nexus of attitudes, but within Scotland itself this system of higher education became subject to criticism as its deficiencies for a scientific industrial society became increasingly evident.

[1] University of Glasgow Library, Papers of G. G. Ramsay. Item Bh 19-y31, 'Occupations of Students in Arts 1890'. See also 1878 XXXII RC . . .
Universities of Scotland. Evidence of Professor Swan, Q. 1570, for 'labouring men' at St Andrews.
[2] 1872 XXV RC . . . *Scientific Instruction* (Devonshire), evidence of Henry Cole, Q. 245.
[3] 1884 XXIX RC . . . *Technical Instruction* (Samuelson), Glasgow University, p. 491.
[4] W. M. Mathew, op. cit.

In particular the standard of mathematics was too low to support the advancing sciences. For example, up to the mid century natural philosophy had been taught at Aberdeen as little more than a popular diversion, but when from 1845 Professor David Thomson tried to teach it as a quantitative science he found that the numerical skills of his pupils were not sufficient to enable them to understand his courses[1] and Lord Kelvin found the same at Glasgow in the 1850s.[2] Partly this arose from the fact that students were studying such a range of arts and science subjects that they could not specialize sufficiently to build a firm mathematical base for the science teaching, and partly it was the result of the peculiar Scottish attitude to mathematics which differed from that of Cambridge. Mathematics in Scottish universities was regarded as being part of a liberal education rather than as a technical skill to be acquired as a tool for other applications. Thus great stress was laid upon the historical approach, considering the mathematics of the Greeks, and upon the philosophical approach, considering such abstract questions as the definition of a straight line or whether points exist in space. By linking mathematics to philosophy as the root subject of the Scottish arts degree the Scottish universities fell increasingly behind Cambridge in the level of expertise they could impart to their students. As Dr Davie has observed, Scottish university mathematics was 'practically unfruitful and may be regarded as a dead end, irrelevant to modern problems and developments'.[3]

This defect in mathematics meant that leading Scottish scientists of the later nineteenth century had to go to Cambridge after studying in a Scottish university in order to remedy the gaps in their earlier education. David Thomson of Aberdeen went at the end of the 1830s, Kelvin in 1841, P. G. Tait in 1848, Clerk Maxwell after finishing at Edinburgh in 1850, D'Arcy Thompson in 1860, like his father before him. And none of them troubled to take a Scottish degree first; for them the Cambridge Mathematical Tripos was the only examination and qualification of any value. This steady exodus of Scotland's best scientists deserting the universities of their homeland was a severe indictment that for the education of the highest levels of scientific talent the Scottish university system was inadequate. When these men returned to Scotland and schooled their successors, England in turn benefited from an influx of Scottish talent—Clerk Maxwell, James Stuart, Alfred Ewing, Frewen Jenkin —much of which it had helped to educate and which in the fields of physics and engineering greatly enriched her own intellectual and industrial life. But it was Cambridge mathematics that lit the fire.

---

[1] W. L. Low, *David Thomson, Professor of Natural Philosophy in the University of Aberdeen* (Aberdeen, 1894), p. 51.
[2] James Coutts, *A History of the University of Glasgow*, p. 386.
[3] G. E. Davie, op. cit., p. 150.

The majority of the Scottish professoriate had obtained their essential education outside Scotland[1] and, far from diminishing, this tendency to complete a Scottish higher education in England actually increased after 1880.[2]

Two other virtues of the democratic character of Scottish education also militated against science, namely the schools and the teaching methods in the universities. One of the root defects lay in the schools that fed pupils at an early age into higher education. For example, Benjamin Jowett observed in 1862 that 'the Scottish universities labour under a great disadvantage from the deficiency of a superior class of schools in Scotland.'[3] Even where there were such schools in the larger towns their teaching of science was poor or non-existent. At Stirling and Falkirk burgh schools, for example, there was no science provision until the 1870s.[4] In Ayrshire, academies had arisen as a distinctive form of secondary education in which science was to play a prominent part, but they too reverted back to classical grammar schools in the nineteenth century.[5] At Edinburgh likewise the high schools had a severely classical tradition with a narrow concentration on Latin,[6] and this situation lasted into the late nineteenth century.[7] On balance the west coast schools supplying Glasgow University were even worse than those supplying Edinburgh and Aberdeen,[8] and Professor Purdie well summed it up that 'as regards science teaching in schools in Scotland . . . its condition is deplorable'.[9] Similarly, what was seen as a virtue in the teaching methods at the university level, namely the large professorial lecture, became criticized as particularly unsuitable for the sciences. For arts subjects not involving practical manipulation it had proved its worth but it was patently less successful for scientific demonstration.[10]

From the 1870s these defects in the Scottish system were subjected to an onslaught of criticism from those wishing to bring it into line

[1] Patrick Geddes, 'Scottish University Needs and Aims', *Dundee Advertiser*, 1 July 1890.
[2] D. B. Horn, *A Short History of the University of Edinburgh, 1556–1889*, p. 194.
[3] *Durham University Commission*, 1862. Evidence of Benjamin Jowett, Q. 1904, p. 94.
[4] A. Bain, *Education in Stirlingshire* (London, 1965), p. 238.
[5] William Boyd, *Education in Ayrshire* (London, 1961), pp. 112, 157.
[6] Alexander Law, *Education in Edinburgh in the Eighteenth Century* (London, 1965).
[7] J. M. D. Meiklejohn, *Life and Letters of William Ballantyne Hodgson* (Edinburgh, 1883), p. 280.
[8] 1874 XXII RC . . . *Scientific Instruction* (Devonshire). Evidence of Professor John Young, QQ. 9585–91.
[9] T. Purdie, *The Relations of Science to University Teaching in Scotland*, p. 10.
[10] James Finlayson, *Plea for a Reform of the University Teaching in Scotland* (Glasgow, 1890), p. 19.

with the demands of an industrial society. First, it was pointed out that only a minority of students were graduating in the 1870s,[1] because the Scottish degree system, based on the assumption that many students wished to become clergy and schoolmasters, was unsuitable for 'an increasing class to whose future career parts of it have little relation'.[2] The result was 'an intense disgust with a great deal of the work on the part of the students' who left without graduating.[3] The root of the matter was that the Scottish universities were not providing high level specialized science teaching as an education suitable for industry, for 'the sons of our manufacturers and young men in general who are to be engaged in industrial pursuits of all kinds'.[4] The Scottish universities were urged 'to provide the general training for the equipment of the leaders of industry',[5] and to build up the whole scientific industrial side of their activities in the way that the English civic universities had done.

From the 1850s to the outbreak of war, in response to this ground swell of criticism, there was a long period of adjustment in Scottish universities, the effect of which was to make more possible the education of an industrial technocratic class. The turning point of the mid century was the Act of 1858,[6] which established a commission that laid down the uniform four years' curriculum for the M.A. The M.A. was to consist of English, Latin, Greek, mathematics, natural philosophy, logic, moral philosophy; after which, most importantly, it was possible to specialize in honours in one of four departments of grouped subjects including mathematics with natural philosophy as one and natural science including chemistry or geology as another.[7] This was in some ways a compromise, for there had been strong moves in the first Scottish Universities Commission of 1826–30 to attack the liberal democratic Scottish concept and replace it with Anglicized specialism. The 1858 Act and the commissioners, by introducing honours, made some specialization possible but not to the extent that the Anglophiles desired. From the point of view of training for industry this seemed to be an improvement in that the scientist was now allowed more time for his specialism. However,

[1] W. R. Kerkless, *Scottish University Reform* (Glasgow, 1884), p. 10.
[2] 1878 XXXII RC . . . *Universities of Scotland*, p. 25.
[3] Henry Dyer, *A Modern University, with Special Reference to the Requirements of Science.*
[4] T. Purdie, op. cit.
[5] Alexander Darroch, *The Place and Function of Scottish Universities in our Educational System.*
[6] 21 and 22 Vict. Cap. 83 1858. *An Act to make Provision for the Better Government and Discipline of the Universities of Scotland.* (It also united the modern university of Aberdeen and gave Edinburgh University independence of the city, among many other things.)
[7] Alexander Morgan, op. cit., p. 81.

in reality the situation was not so advantageous as it might appear. At Glasgow, for example, which should most have benefited in this direction, only seven people obtained honours in natural sciences in the whole period 1864–93.[1] If there had been any expectations that this would produce the scientific expert for industry they were disappointed, for the old Scots tradition had reasserted itself through the preferences of its students. At Edinburgh University likewise the 1861 ordinance provided for graduation with honours in natural science or mathematics and natural philosophy, but only forty-one people took the option of graduating with honours in natural science in 1861–92,[2] and one suspects that the majority of those were intending to become doctors.[3] Natural science still had no place in the ordinary curriculum which remained much the same as before. For example, at Aberdeen in the 1860s it was Greek, Latin, and English for the first year; Mathematics, Greek, and Latin for the second; natural philosophy (but *not* natural science), mathematics and logic for the third, and moral philosophy and natural history for the fourth year.[4] The last year's courses are of some interest, for the commissioners under the 1858 Act empowered the courts of each of the universities to introduce a branch of natural science into the ordinary curriculum. Aberdeen chose natural history and St Andrews, chemistry, but Glasgow and Edinburgh took no action[5] to introduce science. Otherwise the ordinary curricula remained much the same in each of the four universities.

It was evident that in spite of the introduction of the possibility of specialist science honours these were not really developing, save in the case of Edinburgh medical students, and certainly the problem of providing the scientist for industry was not being met at all. In the 1870s this problem was debated once again by the Royal Commission of 1878, and before it certain grievances about factors impeding the value of the universities to industry were aired. Some witnesses argued that the old B.A. which had been abolished by the 1858 commissioners ought to be restored since it had been useful for students going into industrial and commercial life.[6] More typically

---

[1] James Coutts, op. cit., p. 437.
[2] A. Logan Turner, *History of the University of Edinburgh, 1883–1933*, p. 170.
[3] D. B. Horn, op. cit., p. 180, notes the medical students as the chief growing category 1860s–1880s. The Professor of Chemistry, Crum Brown, noted that in his class there were 125 medicals to fifty-four non-medicals. 1874 XXII RC . . . *Scientific Instruction* (Devonshire), Q. 9345. This was an average for the last ten years.
[4] John Malcolm Bullock, *A History of the University of Aberdeen 1495–1895*, pp. 199–200.
[5] 1878 XXXII RC . . . *Universities of Scotland*, p. 24, was critical of this inertia.
[6] 1878 XXXIII RC . . . *Universities of Scotland*. Evidence of Professors Black and Geddes, QQ. 6366 and 5307.

the Glasgow scientists expressed their dislike of the irksomeness of an excessive amount of arts that was preventing the widening of the scope of their science teaching. Kelvin in particular thought that far too much attention was being paid to logic and Greek and frankly wanted to borrow some of their time for his own sciences,[1] though he still believed in the fundamental virtues of the Scottish system which ensured 'attainment in a variety of subjects'.

The third important issue raised was that of the entrance examination. It was part of the Scottish democratic tradition of university education that people handicapped by their prior education were not excluded by the operation of an entrance examination. On the other hand it was recognized that the raising of standards within the university entailed the abandoning of a good deal of elementary teaching that was properly the province of the school. But without an entrance examination it was impossible to avoid elementary teaching since one could not guarantee the level of attainment, especially in the crucial subject of mathematics, for more genuinely university work. The introduction of an examination or the retention of free entry was thus fundamental to the whole generalist versus élitist and specialist issue. Kelvin did not want such an examination and this was the view of the Commission as a whole, partly on the grounds that in Scotland it was a tradition for people from business to enter university in later life and they did not want to discourage this. Thus the 1878 Commission wished to retain the free entry, they did not recommend the revival of the old B.A., but perhaps most important they took heed of the Glasgow evidence and expressed a concern that degrees in science should be started. This was the most important positive result of the commission in its potential effects for industry.

In the 1870s one accordingly found the introduction of the B.SC. degree, partly in response to the Commission's suggestions. The Glasgow B.SC. was first conferred in 1873, and at St Andrews the degree was started in 1876 and a special science committee established which was part of St Andrews' general recovery from the late 1870s.[2] Equally important new scientific chairs were founded to cater for the teaching for the hons. M.A. and the B.SC. At Edinburgh the engineering chair had been founded in 1868 followed by that of geology and mining in 1871. At Glasgow the chair of naval architecture was founded in 1883 and the compulsory arts content for the

---

[1] 1878 XXXIV RC . . . *Universities of Scotland.* Evidence of Sir William Thomson, Q. 10123, et seq. (Throughout this study Professor Sir William Thomson is usually referred to as Kelvin although he did not assume the title of Lord Kelvin until 1892. However, it is by this title that he is best known to history and it avoids confusion with a number of other Professor Thom(p)sons who were active in Scotland at the same time.)

[2] R. G. Cant, *The University of St. Andrews, a Short History*, p. 120.

engineering degree was cut.[1] All this was desirable from the point of view of creating a new industrially orientated graduate, but a much sharper turning point came in 1889 and the 1890s.

In 1889 came the second major Act of the period.[2] The commissioners under the Act found the existing curricula of Scottish universities far too rigid, indeed from 1861 the curricula of the four Scottish universities had been virtually uniform.[3] Thus the commissioners were concerned to allow a greater range of options in order to enable the student to attain a greater depth of study, and 'a salient feature of the new Arts course is the large infusion of Science which is admitted'.[4] They also initiated preliminary examinations, allowed women into Scottish universities, and rectified the scandal of excessively large professorial classes.

The commissioners devised the new arts degree regulations which included chemistry as one of the alternative subjects.[5] But, more important from our point of view, they created regulations for degrees in science allowing flexible combinations of chemistry, mathematics, geology, natural philosophy as well as the life sciences.[6] Indeed they were regarded as going too far in their reaction against the rigidity of the former system into one of extreme flexibility.[7] Following the science degree ordinance, faculties of science were set up in Glasgow, Aberdeen and Edinburgh in 1893, with St Andrews following suit in 1897. This had some further stimulating effect. Glasgow started a B.SC. for engineering in 1893 and a mining chair in 1907 while St Andrews engaged in considerable science laboratory building in the late 1890s and 1900s. In 1907 and 1908 came further curricular revisions allowing yet more specialization than before. At Aberdeen, 'the general principle in the new Arts curriculum of 1908 was more specialization of study and a concentration upon a smaller range of subjects'.[8] At Glasgow the seven subjects were cut down to five or six and only two were required at honours level. In short, it was a further move in the direction of greater allowed

---

[1] Glasgow University Archives items 4776, 4600, 4781, 'Students Memorial', 11 November 1873, and J. B. Neilson (ed.), *Fortuna Domus* (Glasgow, 1952), 'Engineering' by James Small, p. 350.
[2] 52 and 53 Vict. Cap. 55, 1889. *An Act for the Better Administration and Endowment of the Universities of Scotland.*
[3] Alexander Morgan, op. cit., p. 86.
[4] 1900 XXV *General Report of the Commissioners under the Universities (Scotland) Act, 1889.* Cd. 276. (The Command number is misprinted as 176 on the document itself.)
[5] Ordinance 11, General No. 6, 3 February 1892.
[6] Ordinance 12, General No. 7, 3 February 1892.
[7] John Malcolm Bullock, op. cit., p. 207. He worked out that it was possible to graduate in arts in 617 different ways by ringing the changes on possible combinations.
[8] W. Douglas Simpson, *The Fusion of 1860 . . . a History of the United University of Aberdeen, 1860–1960*, p. 34.

specialization though within a wider range of subjects than was possible before 1892.

The commissioners of 1889, because of the ordinances of 1892 and the subsequent changes they set in train, are regarded in some circles to this day as the final wreckers of the old Scottish higher education system in the name of Anglicization. They attacked its open democratic character by abolishing unrestricted entry and starting the matriculation examinations. In doing that they changed the peculiar nature of the Scottish school-university linkage by forcing up the school-leaving age by two years. They suppressed the general with honours degree, leaving the general degree for school-masters and clergy, but created parallel courses in which it was possible to begin specializing from the start in imitation of English-style honours. And all this was urged on by men like Huxley and Playfair, deliberately intending for technical education and industrial efficiency reasons to bring Scottish higher education into line with England. Counter to that, it may be argued that what they were doing was necessary if Scotland was ever to produce her own pure scientists of the highest quality and industrial scientists in the new electrical and chemical technologies. Certainly it was not the old Scottish system that had produced Kelvin or Tait or Clerk Maxwell or Fleeming Jenkin and this was the greatest indictment against it. For an eighteenth-century land of ministers and schoolmasters the old general degree was sufficient, but not for the later nineteenth century. Hence the necessity for the painful path of adjustment from 1858 to 1908 that we have been analysing.

We have been considering the defects of the Scottish education system for the production of scientists for industry and the measures taken to reform that deficiency. Implicit in this is the assumption that it was scientific education that industry needed, and this assumption merits some defence. It could be argued that this rather general broad-based education was more suitable for the businessman than specialist expertise in science, and that defects in science were no necessary drawback to the provision of an adequate higher education for industry. It is true that this general education is what many businessmen of Glasgow and Dundee received because it was the only one available, though that is not to say that it was the most desirable form of university education for their future careers, and still less that it remained so as the nineteenth century drew towards its close. The stress laid here upon the necessity for more specialist higher level science as a component of a university education for industry is defended by four arguments.

First, Scottish universities were somewhat behind England in devising a form of arts education based on economics particularly suitable for the businessman. Courses orientating the arts subjects towards business existed on a far smaller scale in Scotland than

England before 1914 and this placed an even greater importance on the sciences for industrial training. Second, it is very difficult to imagine what the man educated in rhetoric, classics and philosophy could bring to the affairs of the shipyard, ironworks, or engineering shop beyond personal qualities that would have little to do with his actual subjects of study. It is also difficult to see that a smattering of science plus these arts subjects was necessarily more fitting for work in such industries than the pursuance of mathematics, physics, and chemistry to a higher level than was possible under the old Scottish degree. It was certainly not the belief of the 1878 Royal Commission, of Dyer, Purdie, Haldane, Playfair, or Huxley that the old Scottish education was a suitable one for industry, hence their concern to reform it in the direction of science for that reason. Third, there is the negative evidence that this traditional general university education simply did not produce in practice an entrepreneurial class markedly successful in facing competition. Their historian, after some long consideration, concludes that 'Scottish entrepreneurs were inadequate in their response'.[1] Moreover, whatever criticisms may be levelled at the English entrepreneur, he was at least developing the newer industries of electricals, aeroplanes, synthetic fibres, photography—many of which had close links with university science, in ways that the Scottish entrepreneur and the Scottish universities conspicuously failed to do before 1914. Fourth, many of the most active and successful Scottish entrepreneurs of the period were men of high technical expertise in their own industries— 'Paraffin' Young, William Beardmore (educated at South Kensington), John Elder ('great scientific knowledge'), William Arrol ('high quality of technical ability'), John Inglis, W. M. Neilson, and most obviously Kelvin himself. It was not Kelvin's study of rhetoric, classics and philosophy that made him a businessman in the electrical industry but his physics and Cambridge mathematics. Indeed Kelvin himself wanted to cut down some of the time spent on the arts in the Glasgow course to allow more specialization in the sciences. It may well have been true that in the 1840s the old curriculum provided a rounded education for businessmen more suitable than that obtainable in England, but this had ceased to be adequate by the end of the century. Hence the concern of contemporaries for the reform of science in Scottish higher education for the health of industry, and hence the stress laid upon that aspect here.

If such was the changing framework within which scientific teaching and research was carried on in Scottish universities, we should now turn to consider more closely the potential industrial relevance and

[1] T. J. Byres, 'Entrepreneurship in the Scottish Heavy Industries 1870–1900' in P. L. Payne (ed.), *Studies in Scottish Business History* (London, 1967). The references to individuals are also taken from Byres.

content of this science and the linkages between the research and teaching and Scottish and British industry.

As regards the actual content of the science teaching in Scottish universities, there is considerable evidence that industrial relevance was taken into account, but chiefly in the physical sciences rather than in chemistry. If we consider first natural philosophy, or physics with some applied element, the seminal professor of this subject in Scotland was in many ways J. D. Forbes of Edinburgh, the teacher of Tait, Clerk Maxwell, and MacQuorn Rankine. He dealt with topics such as boiler safety plugs, tubular bridges, locomotives, and the steam engine, and used his collection of instruments to demonstrate these matters.[1] This brand of physics was clearly destined to direct the minds of his students to the application of theory to practical engineering. At Aberdeen in the 1870s natural philosophy dealt with pulleys and gearing, ballistics, and the inevitable steam engine, with a great deal of mechanics.[2] The lectures of P. G. Tait at Edinburgh, although dealing with the steam engine and electricity, were not particularly orientated towards industry, reflecting Tait's own position as one of the least industrially orientated of the Scottish natural philosophers.[3] Conversely, Tait's close friend and counterpart at Glasgow, Lord Kelvin, dealt considerably with industrial matters in his own lectures. There was a treatment of the chemistry of batteries, reflecting his abortive venture for a battery company, and Swan's lamp was dealt with, Kelvin being a consultant to Swan. He dealt with the mathematics of fluids in motion and related this to Froude's work on hull design at the testing tank at Torquay, thus showing the relevance of higher physics and mathematics for potential naval architects in Scottish shipbuilding yards.[4]

In geology Sir Archibald Geikie at Edinburgh made it clear that 'during the course opportunity will be taken to point out the industrial value of Minerals . . .', and he dealt with mining, coal and minerals, gold and petroleum, as well as the engineering of tunnelling and cuttings.[5] His course would have been of great value to men entering the industry and some of his pupils were already mining

[1] Papers of J. D. Forbes in the University of St Andrews. Examination Book 1859–60 and Catalogue of Instruments. J. C. Shairp, P. G. Tait, and A. Adams-Reilly, *Life and Letters of J. D. Forbes* (London, 1873). Forbes's own research interests were glaciers and climate.
[2] MS. Notes taken by P. F. Anderson of Natural Philosophy Lectures at the University of Aberdeen (Professor David Thomson's), 1870–1. In Aberdeen University Library.
[3] MS. Natural Philosophy Lectures of P. G. Tait. Notes taken by A. D. Sloan, 1881–2, 2 vols., Edinburgh University Library MS. Collections Dc. 5.98–99.
[4] MS. Notes by J. McCallum on Natural Philosophy Lectures at Glasgow University *c*. 1880. Glasgow University MSS. 1–c. 13.
[5] Archibald Geikie's MS. Lectures on Geology, Edinburgh University, 1871–2. Edinburgh University Library MS. Gen. 694.

engineers.[1] In chemistry there was something of a transition. Lyon Playfair, the professor at Edinburgh in the 1850s and 1860s, was a noted advocate of technical education for industry. Although disclaiming in his lectures, 'I do not generally enter into the several manufactures . . .', as a keen advocate of the application of science to industry he did in fact do so. He dealt with boiler explosions, mine fires and their extinguishing, the lead chamber process, coal gas and fuels, and even demonstrated cloth dyeing.[2] The potential industrial entrant would have picked up much of value from such teaching. By severe contrast his successor, Crum Brown, seemed to swing Edinburgh chemistry away from industry. Crum Brown was an important channel through whom Kekulé's benzene ring hydrocarbon chemistry entered Britain. Indeed it was he who devised much of the now familiar graphical notation of writing such formulae. But his lectures contain scarcely any references to industry[3] though ironically he dealt with industrial matters more in his lectures to medical students.[4]

In short there is a good deal of evidence from teaching material that the content of natural philosophy courses took considerable account of industrial practice. Forbes, Thomson, and Kelvin in physics and Geikie in geology all related their teaching towards industry. In chemistry, at least at Edinburgh, there was a marked shift from industrially relevant material with Playfair to the excessively abstract Crum Brown. This reflects a point to emerge later that the research contributions to industry in Scotland in this period were more significant on the natural philosophy based side than on that of chemistry, a reversal of the eighteenth-century position.

If then much of the science teaching did take account of industrial needs and conditions, how far did the Scottish scientific professoriate involve itself with industry and commerce through its research, advisory, and other work? There was a prevalent criticism that Scottish universities were poor on research especially in relation to industry,[5] a defect it was one intention of the Carnegie Trust, established in 1901, to remedy.[6] Were these complaints correct in

---

[1] 1874 XXII RC . . . *Scientific Instruction* (Devonshire). Evidence of Archibald Geikie, Q. 9493.

[2] Lyon Playfair's MS. Chemistry Lectures, 1858–69. Edinburgh University MSS. DK. 5.3.

[3] A. Crum Brown's MS. Chemistry Lectures, 1884. Edinburgh University MSS. Gen. 47 D.

[4] 'Alisma', *Reminiscences of a Student's Life at Edinburgh in the Seventies* (Edinburgh, 1918), pp. 58–9. See also J. S. Flett, MS. Account of Student Days at Edinburgh, 1886–1894. Edinburgh University MSS. Dc. 6.116.116.

[5] University of Glasgow, General Council Business Committee Report, 24 April 1887. J. G. MacGregor, *Research in the Scottish Universities*.

[6] James Robb, *The Carnegie Trust for the Universities of Scotland* (Edinburgh, 1927).

suggesting there was a lack of research, and do historians overlook too much in speaking of intellectual stagnation in this period of Scottish university history? We may consider in turn the broad areas of engagement with industry of physics and engineering, chemistry and natural history.

The greatest contributions of the Scottish universities to industry came from physics and engineering and the interconnecting relationships of many of the professors and ex-professors in those subjects. One of the first links in the chain was Lewis Gordon, the first holder of the Glasgow chair of engineering, which, founded in 1840, was the first in Britain. Gordon was a civil engineer in Glasgow and during his period as professor from 1840 to 1855 he continued his practice, thus wedding his departmental academic work firmly to industry.[1] For example, he decided on Loch Katrine as Glasgow's water supply, then serving as the engineer to the subsequent Glasgow Loch Katrine Water Company, and did much mining, railway, and bridge work in both Scotland and England. His fame chiefly rested, however, on his wire rope invention leading to the formation of the famous cable making firm at Gateshead, which manufactured the first Atlantic cable laid by that later Glasgow professor, Sir William Thomson.

Gordon's successor, MacQuorn Rankine, brought Glasgow University to the service of the great shipbuilding industry of the Clyde.[2] His contribution to industrial science was four-fold. First, he played a vital role with Kelvin in the resurrection of Carnot's thermodynamics, and its application to the steam engine technology used by marine engineers, notably James Napier. Second, he created with William Froude the modern science of hydrodynamics. His researches on fluid motion were of profound significance for hull design and he acted as consultant to Napier's and to John Elder, the inventor of the compound engine, over problems of ship construction. Third, in more traditional civil engineering fields, Rankine's methods of curve laying in railway tracks, of calculating earth pressures and stresses in masonry, long survived his death. Finally he performed the signal service of codifying knowledge and practice for teaching purposes in his important treatises on the steam engine, civil engineering, shipbuilding, and millwork, yet further adding strength to the claim to be regarded as virtually the founding father of engineering as a British university subject. Edinburgh likewise had an early if abortive attempt at starting a similar chair of technology that was intended to have very immediate industrial application. Providing rather practical teaching in matters such as sugar,

[1] Thomas Constable, *Memoir of Lewis D. B. Gordon*. J. B. Neilson (ed.), *Fortuna Domus* (Glasgow, 1952), James Small, 'Engineering'.
[2] W. J. MacQuorn Rankine, *Miscellaneous Scientific Papers* (London, 1881) incl. 'Memoir' by P. G. Tait. Sir James Henderson, *MacQuorn Rankine*.

paper, and leather, and attracting the industrial classes, the chief legacy of its short life was the creation of a Scottish Industrial Museum still existing in Edinburgh.[1]

The central core of engineering personnel associated with industry among Scottish university teachers was that connection centred around Sir William Thomson, Lord Kelvin, who succeeded to the moribund chair of natural philosophy in Glasgow in 1846.[2] Beginning with work on thermodynamics, he moved, however, to develop his theory of electrical oscillations in 1853 which formed the basis of subsequent wireless telegraphy technology. This brought Kelvin into the first of his many connections with industry, the laying of the Atlantic cable. Kelvin acted as a director and consulting inventor to the enterprise, which was eventually successful in 1865–6. Kelvin was knighted in the latter year. Thereafter he undertook much other international cable work, notably the French Atlantic cable and that to India via the Red Sea. He also served as a consultant on ship design[3] and invented the compass to resist deviation from iron ships, and also sounding devices, forming his own company to manufacture these.[4] The rise of the domestic electrical industry gave a further boost to Kelvin's activities and led to his most fruitful patenting period of 1881–96. For example, he invented the zig-zig winding for alternators used by Ferranti in 1881, acted as consultant to Swan, to C. H. Stearn who devised the vacuum glass bulb for Swan,[5] and to British Westinghouse, and was Vice-Chairman of Kodak.

Kelvin was one of the very ablest men produced by Britain in modern times and it would be too much to attribute virtues to any educational system or to stress its links with industry solely on the evidence of his own activities. But what is more remarkable is that he was a part of a wider circle of Scottish entrepreneur-professors doing similar work, often in conjunction with him. Kelvin was connected with the first Professor of Engineering at Glasgow, Lewis Gordon, whose firm produced half the cable for the Atlantic crossing. One of Gordon's employees was Fleeming Jenkin, the first Edinburgh

---

[1] 'In Memoriam Professor George Wilson', *Good Words*, 1860. J. A. Wilson, *Memoir of George Wilson*. George Wilson, *What is Technology?* (Edinburgh, 1855). George Wilson, *The Industrial Museum of Scotland in its Relation to Commercial Enterprise* (Edinburgh, 1858) for this episode which ended with Wilson's death in 1859.
[2] Silvanus P. Thompson, *The Life of William Thomson, Baron Kelvin of Largs*.
[3] MS. Collections of Lord Kelvin's Papers, Natural Philosophy Department, University of Glasgow. Letters, 13 December 1886 and 11 January 1905 with A. Denny and William Froude.
[4] A fine collection of these instruments is still to be seen in the Physics Laboratories at Glasgow University. The firm after various changes became the Kelvin Hughes division of Smiths Industries in 1965.
[5] MS. Letter, C. H. Stearn to Thomson.

Professor of Engineering, and he, being introduced to Kelvin by Gordon, eventually formed a partnership with him for the French Atlantic cable. They also had other partnerships as consulting electricians.[1] Another of Kelvin's close friends and academic collaborators was P. G. Tait,[2] Professor of Natural Philosophy at Edinburgh, who did work on lighthouses and fog signals but was chiefly important for the development of the calculus which was a basis for Clerk Maxwell's work on electricity, itself a fundamental theoretical rock of the late Victorian electrical industry. One final figure fits into this circle, Alfred Ewing, the first Professor of Engineering at Dundee, and a pupil of Rankine, Tait, and Jenkin.[3] He worked with Kelvin and Jenkin on one of their cable enterprises in South America while still a student, and in his own right devised a new form of revolving dynamo core to cut down loss of energy in generation. This connection of Gordon, Kelvin, Jenkin, Tait, and Ewing as teachers, pupils, and business partners embracing both university science and practical activity and entrepreneurship in the electrical industry was one of the strongest areas of close contact of the universities and British industry in the nineteenth century. It was a tribute to the Scottish universities at this time that there was nothing comparable in England.

Apart from these, the chief orthodox fortes of Scottish university engineering lay in shipbuilding with Elgar and Biles at Glasgow, both in close touch with industry,[4] the former destined to become the director of H.M. Dockyards and the latter coming from the Clydebank yard. Dundee also served the local Caledon and Gourlay yards though largely with routine testing rather than innovatory research until A. H. Gibson's work there on wave resistance.[5] Although much of this was merely developing the technology of an old basic industry rather than looking forward, one curious departure within naval architecture was at Glasgow with Percy Pilcher's work in developing and flying the first glider in Britain in 1895.[6] Unfortunately this proved abortive. Pilcher died in 1899, and Scotland failed to develop aeroplanes as a new industry in the inter-war years.

[1] *The Papers of Fleeming Jenkin* (London, 1887), 2 vols. 'Memoir' by R. L. Stevenson and 'Notes on the Contributions of Fleeming Jenkin to Electrical and Engineering Science' by Sir William Thomson. Robert Louis Stevenson had been a pupil of Jenkin's. See also Jenkin's evidence 1878 XXXIV RC . . . *Universities of Scotland*.
[2] C. G. Knott, *The Life and Scientific Work of Peter Guthrie Tait*.
[3] A. W. Ewing, *The Man of Room 40, the Life of Sir Alfred Ewing*. L. F. Bates, *Sir Alfred Ewing, a Pioneer in Physics and Engineering*.
[4] *The University of Glasgow, its Position and Wants* (Glasgow, 1900), J. H. Biles, 'The Chair of Naval Architecture'.
[5] Principal's Reports, 1910–11.
[6] R. H. Campbell, *Scotland since 1707* (Oxford, 1965), p. 246.

By contrast Scottish chemistry in the later nineteenth century seemed less vital in its industrial links. Indeed both Aberdeen and Dundee Universities were examples of actually diminishing involvement with industry in this field. At Aberdeen there were many linkages of a minor sort in water softening, photography, and launderies until the brief tenure of Thomas Carnelley from 1888 to 1890 raised chemistry at Aberdeen to a more academic and less patchily technological level. Science degrees were started in 1889 and the curriculum made of direct relevance to industry, dealing with coal gas, bleaching, explosives, coal-tar dyes, and so forth. From 1890, however, its chemistry swung away from these concerns with F. R. Japp who worked on benzene and whose research 'concerned itself at no point with problems of everyday experience or of immediate industrial importance.'

Dundee experienced a similar transition from a host of small applied interests of benefit to the firms of the city to a more abstract and less obviously applied chemistry in the 1890s. For example, in the 1880s Dundee under Carnelley undertook teaching in bleaching and dyeing, assisted by local firms,[1] culminating in the opening of the museum and new dye house in 1889. Carnelley claimed frankly that 'my aim has been to make our chemical instruction useful, chiefly to the manufacturing industries of the town and district . . .'[2] His successor, Percy Frankland, shared Carnelley's interest in dyes and even started tuition in fermentation, baking, and brewing. But with the advent in 1894 of Sir James Walker, one of Britain's first great physical chemists and the first British pupil of Ostwald, a certain austerity set in. Although Walker himself was an ex-jute industry apprentice, this kind of applied work was moved to a separate technical institute and he made Dundee a centre of the new physical chemistry with studies in the hydrolysis of salts. As at Aberdeen, so at Dundee a university chemistry department of formerly close applied connections with local industry was diverted from this in the 1890s into the mainstream of German-influenced theoretical chemistry of no immediate application.[3]

If Aberdeen and Dundee were examples of chemistry departments changing their interests away from industry, the other departments were examples of almost total disengagement. Neither St Andrews under Purdie nor Edinburgh under Playfair, Crum Brown, and Sir James Walker showed any signs of being important in research for industry prior to 1914, though the first was important in stereo-

---

[1] See especially Principal's Reports, 1887–8, 1888–9, 1889–90, 1890–91.
[2] Thomas Carnelley, *Introductory Lecture on the Occasion of the Opening of the New Dye House and Technical Museum of the Chemical Department of University College, Dundee*, p. 5.
[3] N. V. Sidgwick, *The Chemistry Department, University College, Dundee, 1883–1950*.

chemistry and carbohydrate chemistry and the latter in hydrocarbon and physical chemistry.[1] Glasgow by even sharper contrast was in a state of almost total disaster. Whereas chemical teaching there had seemed to relate to chemical manufactures just before the mid century,[2] from the 1850s to the 1870s, under Thomas Anderson, attention focused more on agriculture. Then from 1874 to 1915 the department lay under the dead hand of John Ferguson who did no research but devoted himself to historical bibliography. Frederick Soddy, its most distinguished member, was then doing his best work on uranium decay and the concept of the isotope, but he and Ferguson detested each other and Soddy left for Aberdeen *en route* for Oxford. Glasgow chemistry was thus isolated not only from industry but even from the mainstream of chemical research of any kind in the forty years before the war.[3]

In contrast with chemistry, one of the most successful linkages of Scottish university science with its home industry was that of biology with the fisheries. From 1884 Professor Macintosh of St Andrews laid the foundation of modern British marine biology with his work on the food fishes, culminating in the building of the Gatty Laboratory, partly supported by the university and the Board of Fisheries.[4] Macintosh was not alone for his successor, Sir D'Arcy Wentworth Thompson, was already working at Dundee from 1884, one of the very greatest of the late nineteenth- and early twentieth-century biologists.[5] Thompson made contact with the local whaling captains and established the department as a centre of expertise on Arctic marine biology,[6] notably in his work on seals. Nearer home, he was scientific expert to the Fishery Board for Scotland, touring fish markets and harbours and intervening in trawling disputes, while

[1] Sir James C. Irvine, *The Chair of Chemistry in the United College of St Salvator and St Leonard*. John Reed, 'The United College of St. Salvator and St. Leonards in the University of St. Andrews', *JRIC*, January 1953. Wemyss Reid, *Memoirs and Correspondence of Lyon Playfair* (London, 1899). E. L. Hirst and M. Ritchie, 'The University of Edinburgh', *JRIC*, November 1953. A. Logan Turner, op. cit.
[2] Sir William Thomson at *The Opening of the New Laboratories at the University College, North Wales, 1885* (Bangor, 1885), pamphlet in the collections of Bangor University College.
[3] Andrew Kent (ed.), *An Eighteenth Century Lectureship in Chemistry*, articles by R. Broom and A. Todd. J. B. Neilson (ed.), *Fortuna Domus* (Glasgow, 1952), J. W. Cook, 'Chemistry'. J. W. Cook, 'The University of Glasgow', *JRIC*, December 1953, for these dismal years. Though it may be said in Ferguson's defence that he did compile a fine collection of early alchemical literature.
[4] William Carmichael, *The Gatty Marine Laboratory . . . in the University of St. Andrews* (Dundee, 1896).
[5] Ruth D'Arcy Thompson, *D'Arcy Wentworth Thompson, the Scholar Naturalist, 1860–1948*.
[6] University College, Dundee, Principal's Reports, 1899–1900, for his connection with the whalers.

on his own waterfront his research helped the Tay sprat industry.[1] It was, however, at the international level that Sir D'Arcy's services were greatest to his native Scottish fisheries. Following the First International Conference for Oceanography in 1899, an International Council for the Exploration of the Sea was formed. Under this Thompson, as the leading British representative, did much work on tracking the migrations of fish in the North Sea and he collaborated with Liverpool University in plaice and plankton surveys.[2] Through Thompson's work Dundee became a major centre of world oceanography, serving the Scottish food fisheries of the North Sea.

What relevance, then, had these academic scientific achievements for the problems of the Scottish industrial economy in the later part of the nineteenth century? The pre-eminent industries in the country within this time changed from iron and cotton to steel and shipbuilding. As regards the iron and steel industry we can see no particular connection at all with the universities. There seems to have been no Scottish equivalent of the important work of the metallurgical department at Sheffield University *vis-à-vis* the English industry, and it is noted that the iron industry in Scotland was technically backward and that the Scottish ironmasters 'lacked technical ability'.[3] Whether this mattered very much in the iron trade is questionable. Carron Company, for example, faced difficulties in this period not because it was technically backward, but because its quality was too high to compete against inferior and cheaper grades and its technical improvements between 1876 and 1880 proved merely a 'white elephant'. Their better times before the war were the result of widening overseas market opportunities rather than technical innovations.[4] But in any case, a company like this could look for little help to the Scottish universities. On the shipbuilding side relations were closer and the universities certainly played an important role with the work of Rankine, Kelvin, Biles in Glasgow, and Gibson in Dundee, while shipbuilding firms were an important element in the support of those respective universities as we shall see.

As regards the chemical industry, there was rather more disengagement than there ought to have been in the light of Scotland's eighteenth-century tradition of close university-industry involvement in this field, and also in view of the importance of this industry in the Scottish economy. One theme emerges as common to a number of universities. In the 1880s and 1890s very practical chemistry had been taught at Dundee and Aberdeen which specifically served local

[1] Ibid., 1908–9.
[2] MS. Papers of Sir D'Arcy Wentworth Thompson, St Andrews University Library. MS. 19920–73. Correspondence with James Johnstone of the Liverpool University Department of Oceanography, 1906.
[3] R. H. Campbell, op. cit., p. 240.
[4] R. H. Campbell, *Carron Company* (Edinburgh, 1961), part III, 1874–1914.

industry. But in the 1890s both departments swung away from this admittedly limited approach and focused their attention instead on German-influenced theoretical chemistry (as Edinburgh had earlier changed in the 1870s). In consequence they jettisoned much of their practical industrial work. In Glasgow and St Andrews, on the other hand, the professor was either inactive, as in the former case, or had no interest in industry anyway and no tradition of local service to it. Haldane criticized Scottish chemistry, drawing the inevitable comparison with Germany. In Germany, he said, 'you come out proficient in chemistry, not as it is taught in the Scottish universities, but in special departments of chemistry as applied to varying phases of practical industry'.[1] The chemistry of Japp, Walker, and Crum Brown, to which in effect he was referring, though excellent, was too abstract and disengaged, though the proper rejoinder to Haldane would have been that this new non-technological chemistry was essentially German in its origin, stemming from Ostwald and Kekulé. It is an interesting negative point that up to 1909 virtually all the chemically trained staff of Nobel's explosives works at Ardeer came not from the Scottish universities but from the Andersonian College in Glasgow. Indeed, in 1909 'only one member of the factory staff was a university graduate'.[2] This, in what was the most scientific chemical works in Scotland, suggested that the chemistry departments of the Scottish universities were not yet producing suitable chemistry graduates.

Of the purely native Scottish industries besides shipbuilding it was fisheries that most benefited from the university work of Dundee and St Andrews, though the disengagement we have noted from Aberdeen is curious. But quite clearly the most brilliant industrial work of the Scottish universities did not serve specifically Scottish industry. The electrical and engineering work of Kelvin and his group was of British and world importance and seemed to have no particular repercussions in giving Scotland itself a leading electrical industry. Indeed, it is highly significant that Kelvin's cables were usually constructed in England, at Millwall, the Isle of Dogs, Birkenhead, or Gateshead. Again we remember that Lewis Gordon, though a Scottish professor, started his own cable company in England. In short, the very best Scottish academic talent was nourishing not Scottish industry but British or even specifically English industry.

Finally, Scotland did not seem to develop specialisms of powerful significance in single industries like Leeds's leather and fuel technology or Birmingham's brewing—nor even in the electrical field

---

[1] R. B. Haldane, 'Universities and the Schools in Scotland' in *Education and Empire* (London, 1902), pp. 49–50.
[2] F. D. Miles, *A History of Research in the Nobel Division of I.C.I.* (ICI, 1955), p. 51.

was it an innovator in wireless like University College, London. We have already seen the institutional reasons for this. Being well provided with universities it did not, with the exception of Dundee, need to develop civic universities on the English pattern. At the same time the older ones, though in industrial towns, were bound by the old arts curriculum into which such outlandish new subjects could not easily fit. This was a pity, especially because it did not give the steel industry a specialist centre of training and research. One may say that this period, particularly after 1870, saw a shift in which physics replaced chemistry as the leading Scottish industrially-orientated science. The great Scottish scientific achievements of the Industrial Revolution had been chiefly chemical; thereafter Scottish chemistry seemed to abandon its close links with local technologies while physics, and especially the physics of electrical engineering and shipbuilding, took pride of place in the contributions of the Scottish universities to industry. If we seek sharp turning points there are three interesting coincidences. In 1866, Sir William Thomson was knighted on the completion of the Atlantic cable. In the same year Rankine published his major treatise on shipbuilding; and two years later, in 1868, Crum Brown succeeded Playfair in the chair of chemistry at Edinburgh. These were the three hinges that marked the beginning of the ascendancy of physics and engineering and the beginning of the disengagement of chemistry from industry in Scotland.

If such were the chief areas in which the universities served Scottish industry and where they were disengaged from it, let us now consider the reverse side of the picture. To what extent did the industries and firms of Scotland actually care for and succour the native universities?

How enthusiastic was Scottish industry in supporting its own universities? There are certain obvious difficulties in such a question. The response will vary between depressions and good times and particularly between industries. But looking specifically at Glasgow and Dundee as the leading industrial city universities, what was the precise nature of the linkage between them and the support of local firms and industries?

One crucial testing point was the financial support for Glasgow's move from the city to the outskirts on Gilmorehill. The appeal began in unfortunate circumstances since local industry regarded itself as depressed.[1] However, the university did secure the active participation of industrialists in canvassing committees. For example, in

---

[1] Report from the Committee on Subscriptions (1867 or 1868?), Glasgow University Archives F/NCB/F 5705. See also letters, Peter Coats, 31 December 1868, W. R. Copland, 20 April 1868, referring to depression as a reason for not yet subscribing.

one 'ward', of which record survives, of ten men on the committee the occupations of eight were known, and they were: foundry, boiler works, spinning company, iron founder, engineer, paint manufacturer, contractor, and banker.[1] If they had consisted predominantly of clergy and professional men the university would have had good reason to be apprehensive. But the link with industry seemed to have been well forged and this paid off in the success of the campaign. They aimed to raise £120,000 from industry and local subscriptions. By 1871, they had raised £114,216[2] of this and by 1876 £159,705,[3] which was regarded as a considerable success; indeed, the university was congratulated by the Royal Commissioners of 1878 on their achievement.[4]

We may analyse where the first £100,000 or so came from in the first waves of donations, and in particular how representative such giving was of various industries within the city. We worked out the

TABLE 11   *Donations to Glasgow University*

Occupation and industry	Numbers of firms (either as individuals or firms) contributing to the appeal by 8 October 1867	Amount given in £s	Total no. of firms in Glasgow	Proportion of firms contributing	Ranking by sums given
Calico printers	7	6,250	36	1:4	4
Cotton spinners	8	2,450	42	1:5	6
Carpet manufacturers	3	375	17	1:5	8
Chemists	7	7,100	63	1:9	3
Dyers	7	4,000	69	1:9	5
Shipbuilders	2	2,000	24	1:12	7
Ironmasters and founders	8	11,600	103	1:12	1
Coalmasters	5	8,500	139	1:28	2

[1] Names written in pen on a canvassing circular, the 16th Ward Canvassing Committee, Glasgow University Archives, F/NCB/F 6061. No date, almost certainly 1868.
[2] Printed Circular Appeal 1870 or 1871 in Glasgow University Archives, F/NCB/F 6427.
[3] J. D. Mackie, *The University of Glasgow, 1451–1951*, p. 285.
[4] 1878 XXXII RC . . . *Universities of Scotland*, p. 130.

occupations of the individuals and firms on the list[1] and then calculated what proportion of the total number of firms in that occupation had contributed to make some comparison between industries. Where a number of individuals from the same firm contributed then this was still counted as one firm. The figures are given in Table 11.

As regards proportions of an industry supporting the appeal, calico printers and cotton spinners came out best. This is somewhat curious since the universities did not normally benefit textile industries and Glasgow had no textile department as had Leeds. If they expected to benefit it must have been through the chemistry department, and this makes all the more reprehensible the long research stagnation of Glasgow chemistry under Ferguson. But the textile firms, with the striking exception of J. and P. Coats, gave only modest sums and their totals are not particularly large. In the heavy industries, shipbuilding, iron, and coal, much smaller proportions of the potential catchment responded but on a more massive scale, with the highest aggregate totals from the last two. In iron and coal one found a few firms of very large resources willing to give large sums to the university in the hope of benefiting from its technology. In textiles there were fewer firms and of smaller scale, but more of moderate prosperity who could give moderate sums, and there was less mass apathy among them than among the myriad iron and coal firms that did not respond. If we consider now the appeal of 1902 the nature of known support by occupations is as follows:

Coal company	1	(J. S. Dixon, Bent Colliery Company)
Shipowners	5	(Dunlop, Bell, Cayzer, Henderson, Burns)
Carpet manufacturer	1	(J. S. Templeton)
Calico printer	1	(Andrew Stewart?)
Chemicals	2	(Sir Charles Tennant; Hurlet and Campsie Alum Company)
Iron merchants	2	(Jas. Napier; Napier and Macintyre)
Shipbuilders	2	(John Brown's; Fairfield's)
Locomotive engineers	1	(Dübs and Company)
Integrated coal, iron, chemicals	1	(William Baird's) 4 items of gifts
Dyer	1	(J. and W. Campbell)
East India Merchant	1	(D. S. Cargill)
Warehousemen and manufacturers	3	(Arthur; Mann, Byers and Company; Steward and McDonald)
Timber merchant	1	(Jas. Kennedy)
Shipbuilders requisites	1	(John Inglis)
Cotton textiles	1	(Houldsworth's)

[1] Calculated from list in *Glasgow Herald*, 8 October 1867, (Glasgow University Archives, F/NCB/F 5822) collated with *Glasgow Post Office Directory*, 1867–8.

It is immediately apparent that there are fewer names on the list[1] but that the whole level of donations was vastly higher than that of 1868. J. S. Dixon's benefaction alone was £10,000 and Templeton's and Dunlop's £5,000 each, whereas the bulk of items were £1,000 each. Dixon's was a lectureship in mining, later raised by further gift to a professorship in 1907. But in spite of his individual gesture the mining industry in general did not seem to support him, a reflection of the 1868 position with this industry—large sums but few firms. The largest block of support came from firms to do with shipping, either in building or owning, both sides of which stood to gain from the work of the new naval architecture department which they had established in 1883. It is also noteworthy that as Mrs Elder had been a leading figure in the financial support of the new department, so Charles Randolph, of the shipbuilding family associated with Elder's, together with the Marquess of Bute, the coalowner, gave much of the money for finishing off the new Gilmorehill buildings. The relative position of the shipbuilding and shipping interest was much more important in the 1902 than the 1868 appeal.

Textiles of various branches form a group of seven though they stood to gain little from the university's work. The paucity of support from the chemical companies compared with their relative position in 1868 probably reflects their disillusion with the inactivity of the Professor of Chemistry and his department. Indeed the chief industrial academic chemical links in Glasgow were to be found not at the university but at the technical college with Professor Henderson who mercifully took over the university department in the inter-war years.[2]

At the time of this appeal there is evidence of the too slight involvement of certain groups with the university. The usual complaint was made that Glasgow merchants' sons were not sent to Glasgow University. 'Who for the most part attend the Arts classes there [in Glasgow] . . . are they as a rule the sons of Glasgow merchants who prepare themselves by academic training for business life? No.'[3] Shipbuilders were still not so unanimously behind Glasgow University, although they were an important element of support as the university had a right to expect. John Inglis noted that 'a majority of those engaged in those industries are not yet convinced that the adoption of scientific methods in naval construction has any ad-

---

[1] 'The Extension and Better Equipment of the University of Glasgow, November 1902', Glasgow University Archives, UBE 17560, collated with *Glasgow Post Office Directory*, 1902–3. Although this list is not complete it accounts for about £55,000 of the £73,000 raised in response to the £100,000 appeal.
[2] Sir Ian Heilbron, *The Life and Work of George Gerald Henderson*.
[3] W. Knight, *Early Chapters in the History of the University of St. Andrews and Dundee*, p. 38.

vantage over what is generally known as rule of thumb . . .'[1] In short, although the appeal of 1902 was a fair success in terms of sums raised, it indicated that the industrial and commercial community of Glasgow as a whole had not warmed to the university in the last generation of the nineteenth century. Very large sums were coming from too few people, and even in shipping, where support was most obvious and most was to be gained, the mass of the industry stood aloof. The small number of firms, as opposed to amounts given, from the coal industry in both years was little short of a scandal compared with the textile industry which had potentially less to gain

Dundee is a specially interesting case as the only new university college founded in Scotland within this period, and one more than any other except Glasgow dependent on an industrial milieu.[2] The college was virtually the sole creation of the Baxter family, the large local flax, jute, and hemp importing and manufacturing company.[3] Mary Anne Baxter, a sister of Sir David, gave £140,000 in 1880 and 1883 and a further £10,000 for chemical laboratories. She remained in the background, and the moving spirit was her relative J. B. Baxter who had been one of the advocates of a college in the 1870s and who gave £20,000 to supplement Miss Baxter's gifts.[4] It may be noted that this early endowment was £110,000 more than Firth's gift for Firth College and £65,000 more than Owens for Owens College. Financially it was an astonishingly brilliant start, and in this most direct way, of which Reading is perhaps the only other example, Dundee was the creation almost solely of one business family in the local dominant industry. And yet curiously there was virtually no trace that they were doing this to provide the technological training and research for Dundee industry.[5]

Did the business community of Dundee, besides the Baxters, support the new college? The occupational composition of the large committee set up to bring the college into being may be analysed as follows. It contained eight clergy, five lawyers, twenty-three spinners and manufacturers of flax, jute, or tow in fourteen firms, four engineers, machine makers, or iron founders, eight 'merchants' of unspeci-

[1] John Inglis, 'The Application of Systematic Experiment in Naval Architecture' in *Glasgow University, its Position and Wants* (Glasgow, 1900), p. 60. See also J. M. Reid, *James Lithgow, Master of Work* (London, 1963), for a good instance of scepticism of college trained men on the part of a prominent Glasgow shipbuilder.
[2] W. Knight, op. cit.
[3] William Kidd, *Dundee Past and Present* (Dundee, 1909), 'The Industrial and Commercial Enterprise of the Baxters', pp. 94–100.
[4] *Dundee Advertiser*, 23 December 1880. 'Proposed Collegiate Institution for Dundee' refers to the initial £125,000 gift. This was raised to £160,000 in 1883.
[5] J. B. Baxter rather gave the impression, on the contrary, that the college would counteract the materialism of business. See his evidence 1878 XXXII RC . . . *Universities of Scotland*, QQ. 11105–16.

fic trades, four professional people in financial occupations, and various individuals: architect, brewer, tanner, builder, fishing-tackle manufacturer, painter, two newspaper proprietors, and a confectioner (Keiller's, the marmalade firm). On this reckoning, the involvement of the textile firms of the city appeared very close, but what proportion of Dundee textile and engineering firms supported the college in this way at its outset? For textile firms it was fourteen firms out of sixty-eight in the city, according to the Dundee *Directory* for 1880–1, that is 20 per cent or 1 : 5; and for engineering and iron founders four out of twenty-two or 18 per cent or 1 : 5. These figures compare very well with those for Glasgow given earlier and suggest a quite healthy movement at the outset.

But this did not last. By the 1890s there were a number of complaints that the business community did not value or support the college.[1] Why was there this apparent long-term disengagement of business interest after so brilliant a start? First, in 1890 Dundee formally became united with St Andrews, finally ending any hopes for a separate university college for the city. This removed a good deal of possessive pride from businessmen who could no longer feel that they were supporting their own civic university. Second, whereas the textile firms had originally rallied round, they did not seem to benefit from the college. The college did work briefly in dyeing chemistry, but as this was moved out to a technical college and as physical chemistry predominated, the main research connections with industry were removed. Consequently in the 1900s and the years up to the war, numbers of governors (local subscribers of £5 per annum) fell off from 105 in 1904 to eighty-one in 1914 and continued to slump through the inter-war years.[2] Starting with considerably more money than most other civic universities, and a brilliant staff—five of its early professors were knighted—the subsequent history of Dundee up to the war, through failure to maintain and develop a promising relationship with industrial backing, is one of the sadder themes of Scottish university history.

Considering Glasgow and Dundee as test cases of business support, the situation they reveal is not one to arouse unqualified satisfaction. They certainly gained more industrial support than Oxford or Cambridge in this time but both seemed to experience a tailing off of interest after an initial spurt. The financing of the move to Gilmorehill was very creditable, and the early support for Dundee,

[1] *Dundee Advertiser*, 10 February 1891 and 2 July 1891. Dundee University possesses one of the very best collections of newspaper cuttings concerning its own history of any British university. Newspaper references are usually to their cuttings books. University College, Dundee, an Appeal for the Improvement of Equipment (Dundee, 1901), p. 22. Ruth D'Arcy Thompson, op. cit., p. 125, for such evidence.
[2] *Dundee Courier and Advertiser*, 5 March 1938, for the statistics of Governors which were causing concern at the time.

both financial and moral, excellent. But the Scottish universities did not benefit from a parallel wave of enthusiasm such as in England attended the granting of full university charters to the civic colleges in the 1900s. It may be that the Scottish business community was not really obtaining what it wanted or needed from these institutions in terms of research or personnel. There are some curious misalignments between areas of Scottish industry that supported universities and areas that benefited. For example, the textile and jute industries of both cities were prominent supporters in the early days although they got little out of the universities. The iron and coal industries gave most money to Glasgow in the 1860s although they benefited little until the setting up of the chair of mining in 1907. The three shipbuilding firms of Dundee all supported the college in various ways but got little return. Conversely, there was virtually no industrial support coming from those areas where Scottish university research was most valuable, namely electrical engineering and fishery firms. On the other hand there were expected alignments. The westcoast shipbuilding and shipping industries stood much to gain from Glasgow and were an important element of support. Likewise the chemical firms soon realized that they had little to gain and were clearly withholding their support in 1902—regrettable if understandable. Let us turn now to consider what these firms and industries were getting from the universities in terms of personnel.

If such was the nature of what the universities were doing for industry in terms of teaching and research and what the industries were doing for the universities in terms of support, the final and crucial question is the nature and level of the output of Scottish university students going into industry and commerce.

St Andrews is easily dismissed since this had a negligible role in providing graduates for such occupations. Of St Andrews students with surnames beginning A and B in the period 1850–1900 the output to industry and commerce was in the proportion of 1 : 120 or markedly less than 1 per cent, and this was consistent for both letters.[1] St Andrews served as an educational centre for Dundee business families, and their sons tended to return to manage Dundee industry though scarcely using with benefit what they had learned at the university. Indeed there was only infrequently any relationship between what was studied at the university and the subsequent career. It is also interesting to note that of the forty-three first class degrees awarded by St Andrews betwen 1907 and 1912 only one was gained by a student from a business background.[2] This may further

---

[1] Calculated from unpublished typescripts being compiled by Mr R. N. Smart of the University of St Andrews for a Biographical Register of Alumni. I am grateful to Mr Smart for being allowed to use some of his files.
[2] 1913 XVIII RC . . . *Civil Service*, appendix XXXIX, St Andrews.

suggest that such families did not encourage their offspring, even if they went to the university, to take the St Andrews degree too seriously.

For Glasgow University we may expect a much closer relation between student careers and business and industrial life. Numbers of graduates going into occupations in business, commerce, or industry as a proportion of those with B.A., M.A., or B.SC. degrees were as shown in Table 12.[1] These figures are capable of further

TABLE 12   *Careers of Glasgow graduates*

	(a) *Glasgow graduates going into industry, commerce, or business*	(b) *Total* M.A., B.A. *and* B.SC. *degrees awarded*	(a) *as a percentage of* (b)
1850s	5	260	1·92
1860s	8	296	2·7
1870–4	7	206	3·4
1875–9	22	280	7·85
1880–4	30	490	6·12
1885–9	51	597	8·5
1890–6	58	705	8·22

refinement. It is especially interesting to know whether this output of industrial and business graduates was for the benefit of the Scottish economy or more commonly for the English or imperial economy. The role of Scotland at this time as an exporter of educated talent is well appreciated.

Table 13 shows where the Glasgow graduates listed in Table 12 found employment. Not only was there a fair movement away to England, but there was an even more marked feature of Glasgow graduates taking work in the Empire, if only for a part of their careers; since the mid 1870s at least to the end of the century it was usually about a half. This was no necessary loss to the British or even the Scottish economy for by their work as engineers and railway men they presumably further stimulated the demand for British goods, or as planters and miners they increased that cheap stock of food and raw materials on which the metropolitan economy and its work peopled thrived. The benefits of Glasgow University to the economy were thus rather more indirect in form than those of the English northern civic universities with their more direct link with local indigenous industry.

In what fields, then, did those graduates of purely Scottish ex-

[1] Calculated from *A Roll of the Graduates of the University of Glasgow, 1727–1897.*

TABLE 13   *Employment of Glasgow graduates*

	England	The Empire	Other places	Total outside Scotland	Total no. of graduates
1850s	2	—	—	2	5
1860s	2	—	Portugal 1	3	8
1870–4	1	Australia 1		2	7
1875–9	1	Australia 4 Canada 1 India 1 Malaya 1	Spain 1 Japan 1	10	22
1880–4	—	Australia 1 Canada 1 India 1 Africa 1	South America 1 USA 1	6	30
1885–9	6	Australia 2 Canada 2 India 1 Africa 1 South Africa 6	USA 2 South America 2 China 1 Persia 1	24	51
1890s	8	Australia 4 Canada 1 India 3 South Africa 1 Ireland 1	USA 3 South America 5 Japan 1	27	58

perience serve the Scottish economy and is there a change in direction here? Table 14 gives us some indications.

In the early decades, graduates went chiefly into the merchanting side. From the 1870s, however, manufacturing predominated through the rise of the various forms of engineer, especially in the 1880s, and with the electrical engineer coming into his own in the 1890s. At the same time a range of new commercial activities arose in the 1880s and 1890s such that, whereas graduates were less frequently merchants in their own right than before, they now more commonly acted as agents and brokers of various specialities. In short, the Glasgow output shows a steadily increasing movement of graduates to commerce and industry from the 1850s but within that from the 1870s about half sought some experience outside Scotland and overseas. However, of those who served the distinctively Scottish economy at home there was a marked move from merchanting into engineering

TABLE 14   *Careers followed in Scotland by Glasgow graduates*

	1850s	1860s	1870s	1880s	1890s
Merchant	2	5	5	2	1
'Manufacturer'	1	—	—	1	1
Clerk	—	1	—	3	1
Engineer	—	—	4	6	11
Civil engineer	—	1	1	8	5
Railway engineer	—	—	1	5	1
Marine engineer	—	—	—	4	4
Mining engineer	—	—	—	5	1
Electrical engineer	—	—	—	1	3
Shipbuilder	—	—	—	1	2
Shipowner	—	—	—	2	—
Chemist	—	—	1	4	2
Soapmaker	—	—	—	1	—
Iron founder	—	—	—	1	—
Ironmaster	—	—	—	1	—
Iron merchant	—	—	—	1	—
Steel manufacturer	—	—	—	1	—
Boiler maker	—	—	—	2	—
Coalmaster	—	—	—	1	—
Biscuit manufacturer	—	—	—	1	—
Carpet manufacturer	—	—	—	1	—
Shipbroker	—	—	1	1	—
Stockbroker	—	—	—	3	2
Commercial agent	—	—	—	1	1
Assurance	—	—	—	1	—
Factory inspector	—	1	—	—	—
Publisher	—	—	3	—	—

and manufacturing from the 1880s, accompanied with new middle-man brokerage functions in commerce from the same decade.

For the University of Aberdeen, D. I. Mackay found that the proportion of men graduates entering industry and commerce from 1860 to 1955 was 6·8 per cent, and of women 1·3 per cent.[1] Of their principal places of work betwen 1861 and 1911, 37–48 per cent stayed in Scotland, 27–37 per cent went to other parts of Britain, and 19–26 per cent went abroad. We may penetrate beyond these figures in two ways. First, we may gain some idea of the proportions of students entering business and industry from the class records of all students and not merely the graduates.[2] Taking sample classes at the end of each decade the picture shown in Table 15 emerges.

[1] D. I. Mackay, *Geographical Mobility and the Brain Drain*, pp. 81–2, 110.
[2] Calculated from A. Shewan and John Duguid, *Meminisse Juvat* (the class of 1866–70) (Aberdeen, 1905); Records of the Arts Class of 1876–80 (Aberdeen,

TABLE 15   *Careers of Aberdeen students*

Class	Entering commercial or industrial life			Not doing so	Percentage serving British economy	Percentage serving Imperial economy
	In Scotland or rest of Britain	Empire	Elsewhere			
1866–70	10	8	2	107	7·9	6·3
1876–80	4	—	—	96	4	—
1886–90	9	5	—	100	7·9	4·4
1895–9	1	—	—	69	1·45	—
1909–						
1912/13	2	—	—	84	2·38	—

Men serving the home economy included the usual engineers, paper makers, jute manufacturers, and an electrical engineer who had worked with Kelvin and Jenkin on cables. But the only one worthy of note was Mr Clegg of the Phoenix Foundry, London, 'where he has been instrumental in bringing aluminium and its alloys before engineers and consumers in this country'.The few imperialists were in Canadian lumber and mining, South African gold and diamonds, and West Indian sugar.

The above figures were for all students whether graduating or not, but we may also consider more closely those occupations chosen by Aberdeen graduates entering business and industry, using the roll (See Table 16).[1]

Although there is some increase in going into commerce and industry it is very slight indeed because the overall levels are extremely low, especially in the nineteenth century. There is nothing particularly interesting about final careers save the considerable rise of the chemist in the 1890s and 1900s. This seems to have been perhaps Aberdeen's main contribution to the economy. There is curiously little connection with fisheries, also reflected negatively in the research interests of the university. These figures represent people going into industry and business, including the Empire. If purely those staying in Britain are taken it alters the figures very slightly for the 1880s and 1890s to 1·27 and 0·9. The output of Aberdeen graduates, like that of St Andrews, was negligible as a proportion of its total output. Over

1907); Records of the Arts Class of 1886–90 (Aberdeen, 1924); Records of the Arts Class of 1895–99 (Aberdeen, 1900); Records of the Arts Class of 1909–1912/13 (Aberdeen, 1959).
[1] *Roll of Graduates of the University of Aberdeen, 1901–25 with Supplement. 1860–1910*, ed. Theodore Watt.

TABLE 16   *Aberdeen graduates entering business and industry*

	1860s	1870s	1880s	1890s
Stock or share broker	1	—	1	—
Finance	—	—	—	—
Insurance	—	—	—	—
Accountant	—	—	—	1
Land agency	—	—	1	—
Civil engineer	—	1	—	—
Railways	—	1	1	1
Mining	—	—	1	2
Engineer	—	—	1	1
Electrical engineer	—	—	—	2
Distilling	—	—	3	—
Brewing	—	—	1	—
Food industry (milk, baking, chocolate)	—	—	—	1
Fisheries	—	—	—	—
Tea	—	—	1	—
Rubber	—	—	—	—
Oil	—	—	—	—
Chemicals	—	—	2	7
Textiles	—	—	—	—
Clothier	—	—	—	—
Merchant	—	—	1	2
Combs	—	—	1	—
Publishing and newspapers	—	—	—	2
Factory inspection	—	—	—	—
Total	1	2	14	19
Estimated percentages entering industry and business	0·5	0·4	1·78	1·6

three-quarters of the output of Aberdeen students went into two professions, medicine and teaching; the output to business was marginal. That the arts class figures are higher than those of the graduate roll indicates that business entrants probably did not trouble to complete their degrees, or that non-graduates from the universities were rather more likely to enter business. Thus taking graduate evidence only in considering the proportions of Scottish students going into business will give an underestimate, but the arts class figures show that it is not a degree of underestimate that would change the general conclusion that the proportion was low.

Aberdeen University also acted as a channel diverting the children of business families away from business and into professions.

Calculating from the roll the occupations of fathers of fifty-four graduates who went into business and industry between 1901 and 1914 we find that twenty-nine of them were themselves in occupations we would classify as 'business'. But calculating from surnames A what happened to all the children of all seventeen fathers in business we find that not one went himself into business between 1901 and 1914. They all became teachers, doctors, and clergy as was typical of the Aberdeen output. It suggests a net loss to business in the inter-generation succession of occupations when the offspring had received a pre-1914 Aberdeen University education. This point can also be supported by the evidence of the arts class. It will be recalled that of

TABLE 17   *University education of Scots-born Glasgow businessmen*

Education	Birth dates					
	pre-1839	1840–9	1850–9	1860–9	1870–9	Total (67)
Had been to Glasgow University	3	3	5	2	1	14
Other Scottish university or Andersonian	1	6	2	1	—	10
An English university	—	—	—	2	—	2
No university education	9	10	17	3	2	41

the arts class of 1909–1912/13 only 2·38 per cent took careers serving the British industrial and commercial economy. But from other data it is possible to calculate that 25·8 per cent of the parents of 727 arts class students were of a commercial background in 1908 to 1912, indicating a similar loss to industry in the change of occupations between fathers and children.[1] It is interesting in the light of this to note that the careers advice of the university at the time was highly orientated to education, medicine, agriculture, and so forth. The advice on business was slight and rather denigratory and may have aided this diversion.[2]

We may test this question of the output of the Scottish universities in another way by considering the impact that Scottish graduates

[1] 1913 XVIII RC . . . *Civil Service*, appendix XXXIX, Aberdeen.
[2] R. N. Gilchrist (ed.), *After Graduation What?* (Aberdeen, 1911). This was originally a series of articles in *Alma Mater*, 1904–6, the magazine of Aberdeen University.

made upon the business community of the two chief cities. Did in fact the leading business élites of Glasgow and Edinburgh at the end of the century contain a significant proportion of men who had experienced a Scottish university education, or were they men without experience of university life and work?

In the 1850s David Murray remembered that most of the prominent businessmen of Glasgow had attended the university.[1] How does this compare with 1900? Taking the leading businessmen of Glasgow in 1900 we can make an analysis of their connection or lack of it with Glasgow University (see Table 17).[2]

Of these sixty-seven Scots-born leading Glasgow businessmen in 1900, fourteen had been to Glasgow University and twenty-six in all, or 39 per cent, had received some university education though forty-one had not. Were these 39 per cent in fields where their university experience was needed? Taking select scientific occupations in the Glasgow economy:

of 5 shipbuilders and naval architects	5 had university or Andersonian education
of 3 engineers excluding shipbuilders	3 had university or Andersonian education
of 4 ironmasters and manufacturers	2 had university or Andersonian education
of 6 chemical, dye, manufacturers, exporters, or brokers	3 had university or Andersonian education

These figures suggest that those needing higher education had received it, though those for businessmen in the chemical industry have a somewhat sinister aspect. This, as well as the feebleness of Glasgow University chemistry, may partly explain why this industry did not tend to support the university in the 1902 appeal.

We may make a similar calculation forEdinburgh around 1900 (see Table 18).[3] Here twenty out of the seventy-eight received some university education. Taking select occupations groups, we find that ten out of twenty-two engineers had had a university education, as had one out of the three chemical manufacturers and both the iron and paper manufacturers listed, but those in brewing, distilling and leather had not. In the light of this, and bearing in mind that in Edinburgh thirteen, out of seventy-eight had been to Edinburgh University whereas in Glasgow fourteen out of sixty-seven had been to Glasgow University, we may say that university education was

---

[1] David Murray, *Memories of the Old College of Glasgow*, p. 466.
[2] Calculated from *Glasgow Contemporaries at the Dawn of the Twentieth Century* (Glasgow, c. 1900).
[3] Calculated from A. Eddington, *Edinburgh and the Lothians at the Opening of the Twentieth Century* (Brighton, 1904).

rather less important for the business élite of Edinburgh than it was for that of Glasgow, and this may reflect the difference between an industrial and a commercial city.

The contradictory views of Swan and Haldane with which this chapter began both contain elements of truth and falsehood, for the first was an off-the-cuff impression and the second a piece of propaganda exaggerated for effect. It was evident that the old arts degree arrangements were not suitable for producing the scientific specialist for industry, but that adjustments were made, especially after the setting up of the B.SC. in the 1870s, the new science degree in 1892, and then the greater degree of specialization allowed after 1907, all of which made the education of such a type more possible. We have suggested that for those who did receive science teaching there was a strong

TABLE 18   *University education of Scots-born Edinburgh businessmen*

| | Birth dates | | | | | |
Education	pre-1839	1840–9	1850–9	1860–9	1870–9	Total (78)
Had been to Edinburgh University	2	3	5	3	—	13
Other Scottish university or Andersonian or Heriot-Watt	—	1	4	1	—	6
An English university	—	—	—	1	—	1
No university education	13	19	14	10	2	58

element of industrially relevant content in some of the main lecture courses of the period, but more consistently in physics than in chemistry. This was also in accord with the changing research and consultative value of Scottish university subjects to industry. The areas of greatest value in this time were in physics and engineering, especially electrical and shipbuilding. Chemistry, however, which had previously been the university subject of chief value to Scottish industry, seemed to become disengaged from these immediate interests, in Edinburgh and Glasgow in the 1870s and at Dundee and Aberdeen in the 1890s, in many cases under the influence of various branches of German chemistry. In the 1890s and 1900s scientific fisheries studies joined electrical engineering as the other chief area of university-industry engagement.

One could not claim that Scottish industry was particularly keen on the support of its university institutions. While the early days of Glasgow at Gilmorehill and the start of Dundee reflected the interest of the business classes, there seemed a tailing off of interest in both centres in the 1900s, in contrast to the contemporary movement in England. Although money came in, it was in large amounts from individuals rather than as the result of wide support from a broad range of firms in the industries as a whole. Moreover, we have noted curious misalignments whereby the industries that stood most to benefit from university work did not support the universities, who relied often on firms and industries for whom they could expect to provide very little. Finally, the available figures for the output of students to industry and commerce, whether graduate or not, are moderate for Glasgow but not markedly different from those of an English civic university, while Aberdeen and St Andrews display almost Oxford-type characteristics in their low proportions and in the effects they were having in diverting children of business families into professions. However, taking purely the business élites of the two main cities, we find the proportion of ex-university men among those at the turn of the century fairly good. This suggests that even if a fair number of potential business entrants did not trouble to take degrees while at university, yet a fair proportion of those who achieved success in the business world had had some university education. A great deal of the output of Scottish universities taking up commercial careers did so outside Scotland in any case. If one considers the research contribution in comparison with the contribution of personnel to industry, it would appear that the former is far more impressive although innovation in Scotland was declining from the 1870s.

If there was one salient feature that distinguished Scottish higher education from English in this period it was the lack of a civic universities movement. From this viewpoint Scotland was almost unfortunate in being so well endowed with universities by 1850, for it meant that her problem was the slow adjustment of an old system in which there was too little variation between institutions. Scotland had not the necessity or the room to start up a completely new set with new subjects and attracting an intense local industrial loyalty. This largely accounts for her lack in universities of such specialisms as textiles, dyeing, leather and, most serious of all, iron and steel. In hindsight it is now well appreciated that one of the gravest mistakes of policy was not allowing Dundee to develop into an independent civic industrial university before 1914 like its English counterparts. Thus, whereas England began the period under consideration with two universities almost totally disengaged from industry, she was able to set up in stark contrast her civic colleges that all together provided a wide range of specialisms and linkages. Scotland began with hers more traditionally involved with industry and in 1850 it would be fair to say that the Scottish universities at that time were better than the English. But by 1900 this was no longer the case for the English system had developed into one of vastly greater variety than its Scottish counterpart as befitted both a larger and more technologically complex industrial economy. Starting afresh in the northern cities did more good for English universities than adjustment of an older structure did for the Scottish. Britain and the Empire, probably more than Scotland herself, had good cause to be grateful in these years for the export from Scotland of doctors and engineers of all kinds, for the electrical technology of Kelvin and his circle and for the reception of the chemistry of Kekulé and Ostwald. But more particularly the Scottish system performed a signal service to England in providing a working alternative to élitist specialism in non-technological subjects and in presenting the example of a country trying to give a broadly liberal higher education to a large proportion of its population. If the English universities became more democratic in intake and more broad in curriculum it was partly under the pressure of such Scots as Playfair and Haldane, for the presence of an alternative tradition over the Border was salutary both in showing what virtues might be adopted as well as a warning against the dangers attendant upon them.

7
The Arts of Commerce
1890-1914

*'What "Economics" may be or how they
affect Commerce, I do not altogether
understand.'*[1]

In so far as industry valued the universities before the First World
War, it was chiefly for their science and technology. However,
particularly from the 1890s to the eve of the war, a further element
in the closer involvement of the universities and industry was the
concern to fashion a new form of business education out of arts
subjects and the emergence of economics as a major independent
university discipline. As it emerged, so various academics sought to
define, reshape, and to orientate the subject towards business,
thereby creating a new entrée into the commercial world alongside
more obviously relevant technological studies. There was also a
further major change in the early 1900s as 'economics', once having
gained a foothold, then spawned 'commerce' as yet a fresh development, placing economics within a wider and more practical context
amid such subjects as accountancy, law, and languages. This chapter
examines the reasons why these developments came to be regarded as
necessary, how new types of professional economics became crystallized at LSE, Birmingham, and Cambridge which in turn influenced
the phasing of developments in the other universities, how the view of
the subject changed in the transference from 'economics' to 'commerce' in the 1900s and, finally, how the relevance of the output of
students from such courses to industry was as yet only modest.

Why then was more attention paid to higher commercial education
in these years? In the first place, there was a concern to reverse old
attitudes that business required no special talents or training.[2] G. S.
Gibb, the General Manager of the North Eastern Railway, for

[1] Letter, George H. Pope to Professor J. Wertheimer, 1911, in Wertheimer's
papers, University of Bristol Engineering Department Library. Pope was
Deputy Lieutenant of Gloucestershire and a local JP.
[2] Letter, G. B. Dibble to Alfred Marshall, 28 April 1902. Marshall Papers in
Marshall Library, Cambridge (Marshall 1.54). '. . . if there is a fool in the
family he will be asked to keep on the business.'

example, observed 'a growing desire . . . that the young men who enter business with the hope of reaching the higher posts of management, shall come with faculties trained by a thorough education and by studies of university rank'[1]—a view with which Charles Booth, the celebrated social researcher and Liverpool shipping magnate, agreed.[2] Similarly in Scotland it was noted that 'the employment by large commercial houses of promising university graduates at reasonable salaries is increasing and being encouraged . . .'.[3] The older attitudes were giving way to a recognition that even the non-technical businessman had to be given a higher education relevant to his future career.

This task was thrown on the universities because traditional forms of business training within the firm were ceasing to be effective. As an American visitor observed, 'The old system of training young men in the great business houses has almost completely disappeared . . . even in the old countries—England, France and Germany it has broken down like the apprenticeship system in the trades—and at present the only possible substitute for it seems to be the properly organized commercial school'.[4] Something of the haphazard and unsatisfactory nature of this in-service training can be seen in the experience of Desmond Young who left Oxford to go to Shell on the eve of the war. He was put to trivial clerical routine under the tutelage of an office boy but, getting nowhere at all with his 'training', he left in disillusion.[5] If even firms like Shell could not provide proper training for themselves, the implications were that the universities ought to do it for them before the graduates arrived in their employ.

In particular the rise of accountancy called for a specific academic training which many university commerce courses included in their curricula. The Limited Liability Acts from 1856 to 1862 demanded the proper keeping and publication of accounts and the drawing up of prospectuses in standard forms, all of which gave a greater importance to the trained accountant. Successive changes in legislation demanded yet more publicity. For example, the Companies' Act of 1879 introduced compulsory annual audit for all banking companies registered with limited liability, and that of 1900 made annual audits obligatory for all companies registered under the Companies' Act.[6] Company secretaries and accountants became more professionally

[1] Letter, G. S. Gibb to Alfred Marshall, 19 April 1902 (Marshall 1.58).
[2] Letter, Charles Booth to Alfred Marshall, 17 April 1902 (Marshall 1.51).
[3] Statement by Mr John Mann, Jnr., to the Committee on Educational Policy on the Faculty of Commerce, University of Glasgow, 10 April 1911.
[4] Edmund J. James, *The Education of Businessmen in Europe, a Report to the American Bankers Association*, p. xvii. James was a professor at the Wharton School, University of Pennsylvania.
[5] Desmond Young, *Try Anything Twice* (London, 1963), pp. 35–6.
[6] H. C. Edey and Prot Panitpakdi, 'British Company Accounting and the Law 1844–1900' in A. C. Littleton and B. S. Yamey, *Studies in the History of Accounting* (London, 1956).

self-conscious; the Corporation of Chartered Accountants was formed in Glasgow in 1854 and the Institute of Chartered Accountants in London in 1875 while the Chartered Institute of Secretaries was founded in 1891.[1] The development of this commercial expertise created problems for newly developing economics and commerce departments, some of whom, like Birmingham, espoused accountancy training with enthusiasm while others, like Cambridge, rejected it as too technically vocational.

Furthermore, cost accountancy became important for production management in the factory itself, especially in quantitatively exact scientific industries like machine tools and electricity. Thus one found before 1914 one of the chief firms interested in this kind of study was that of Hans Renold, the chain makers, and J. Slater Lewis in the electrical industry was one of the main influences through which the scientific management ideas of F. W. Taylor filtered into Britain. Cost accountancy as a technique then became most widely diffused through Edward Elbourne's *Factory Administration and Accounts* in 1914, following on such other pioneer works as Slater Lewis's own *Commercial Organization of Factories* and Garcke and Fell's *Factory Accounts* of 1887. Finally, in these years before 1914 railway economics enjoyed a marked rise in the United States and Russia as another area of economic organization that lent itself to exact accountancy analysis. Although Britain was backward in this in the 1890s[2] it became a specialist interest in some new departments, notably Newcastle.

Apart from these technical expertises, now developing as part of the equipment of the businessman, it was also believed that a study of economics would help the apparently deteriorating state of industrial relations.[3] Even though it may have been naïve to think that a university education in economics would have helped managers to curb labour militancy, it was more certain that the procedures and institutions of labour relations were becoming so complicated that a new type of manager, well versed in paper work and report-reading was called for. The Fair Wages Resolutions of 1891, the Brooklands Agreement of 1893, the Conciliation Act of 1896 and the Trade Boards of 1909, for example, all contributed to this bureaucratization of labour relations and in turn made it a possible subject of study.[4]

---

[1] L. Urwick and F. L. Brech, *The Making of Scientific Management*, vol. II, 'Management in British Industry' (London, 1957, reprint, 1959), p. 132.
[2] Letter, H. S. Foxwell to Alfred Marshall, 12 March 1893 (Marshall Misc. 2.9) deploring the neglect of railway economics in Britain.
[3] See J. M. D. Meiklejohn, *Life and Letters of William Ballantyne Hodgson* (Edinburgh, 1883), p. 168, and *Congress of the Universities of the Empire* (London, 1912): 'Action of the Universities in Relation to the After Careers of their Students', Sir George Gibb, p. 254, for such views.
[4] E. H. Phelps Brown, *The Growth of British Industrial Relations, 1906–1914* (London, 1960).

Furthermore, an interest in commercial subjects was aroused by the defects in our wider overseas trading position. This focused the attention of businessmen on such academic but practical economic questions as bi-metallism and the role of gold in the Depression, and the respective merits of protection and free trade. It also occasioned sharp comparisons with the attitudes of our chief business rivals to this area of higher education. In the United States, economics had risen in repute with the rapid growth of the economy itself from the 1870s, and by 1914 higher commercial education was to be found in the universities of Pennsylvania, Chicago, and California, as well as most notably at the Harvard Business School.[1] In Germany, the noted Handelshochschulen of Leipzig, Berlin, and Cologne played the same role for commerce as their technical high schools did for technology. But whereas it may be argued that English civic universities were the equivalent of the German Technische Hochschulen, yet it would be difficult to point to any part of the English education system in the 1890s as the counterpart of the German trade schools. There was no doubt that the example and threat of Germany and the United States were a powerful influence in inducing us to embark upon university commercial education just as they had been a spur to our technical education.[2]

And yet, while there were these increasingly good reasons why economics and higher commerce training were desirable, little was done until the 1890s when a barrage of propaganda began to urge the desirability of this form of education. Edmund James noted in 1893 that 'England is beginning to wake up to the necessity of this sort of education', but he forcefully pointed out our extraordinary backwardness in the field.[3] The next year, the British Association deplored that economics formed no part of any Civil Service or professional qualifications and they condemned 'the condition of economic studies at the universities and colleges as unsatisfactory'.[4] In 1898 and 1899, various London bodies took up the same theme. The London Chamber of Commerce held a conference at the Guildhall which favoured more high level commercial education,[5] and the London Technical Education Board Subcommittee on Commercial Education strongly publicized the view that Britain had fallen conspicuously behind in university level commercial education.[6] This

---

[1] Melvin T. Copeland, *And Mark an Era, the Story of the Harvard Business School* (Boston, 1958).
[2] The Oxford Diploma in Economics and Political Science, *c.* 1910. Oxon., c. 249 (Bodleian Library) cites this as a motive.
[3] Edmund J. James, op. cit., p. xx.
[4] *Report of the British Association for the Advancement of Science*, 1894, pp. 365–91: 'Methods of Economic Training in this and other Countries'.
[5] *The Times*, 9 July 1898: 'London Chamber of Commerce in the Guildhall'.
[6] *LCC Technical Education Board, Report of the Subcommittee on Commercial Education, 1899*. See also John A. Meelboom, *Commercial Education,*

clustering of propaganda in the late 1890s provided a conducive atmosphere in which LSE, the Birmingham University Faculty of Commerce, and the Cambridge Economics Tripos were to get under way.

Not all, however, shared this belief that economics was a desirable subject. For example, it was found that in 1899 of forty-two employers interviewed in London only three were in favour of higher commercial education; Brown Shipley and Company, the bankers, Joseph Barker, the milling engineer, and the London, Chatham and Dover Railway.[1] At Liverpool University it was admitted that commerce courses had had only limited success because the sons of the prosperous went to the older universities while business houses preferred school leavers. Commerce course 'are on the whole suited to those who have a fairly assured career before them.'[2]

Resistance to economics as a university subject useful for business and industry arose on six main grounds. Firstly, Sir Bernhard Samuelson, the steelmaster and great champion of technical education, did not have the same enthusiasm for commercial education, because unlike technical education 'there is not that pure science in commerce which there is in engineering.' Second, there was also some special suspicion of the accountant's over-intrusion into business decisions. Sir Joseph Lawrence was acidly droll about transport economists with a taste for accountancy, 'amiable critics who are always wanting to work out to the third decimal of a penny the ton mile cost of every ton of goods carried by the railways . . .'.[3] Alfred Mond, to take one entrepreneur, also liked to keep his accountants at arm's length.[4]

Third, university economists were regarded with scepticism as theorists with no practical experience of business affairs. Whereas it would have been inconceivable for a university to appoint a professor of engineering or mining who had not worked in industry, yet scarcely any professors of economics had done so. There were occasional exceptions, Smart and Scott in Glasgow and Kirkaldy in Birmingham all had been in business, but this was very unusual. This in itself was a change. Whereas economists prior to the 1890s had been predominantly men of affairs, bankers, and the like, the new professionalizing of economics and its reception into universities ironically made it

---

a Review and some Criticisms, which, by reprinting articles originally in *The Accountant* dealing with the two London conferences and reports, gave their views an influentially wide circulation.

[1] *LCC Technical Education Board, Subcommittee*, op. cit. The first of the three was the only one that actually took graduates. Montagu Norman, the future Governor of the Bank of England, was one of their most noted university entrants.

[2] John Montgomery, 'Ideals of a School for Commerce' in *A Miscellany presented to John Macdonald Mackay*, pp. 45–6.

[3] *The Times*, 6 March 1906. Letter from Sir Joseph Lawrence.

[4] Hector Bolitho, *Alfred Mond, First Lord Melchett* (London, 1933), p. 44.

less credible since its professorial practitioners rarely had much direct experience of what they professed. Accordingly, as one economics professor wrote to another, 'no one cares a straw for us, least of all our banking and commercial magnates'.[1] Fourth, it was a curious feature that the economics professors were almost all free traders, though Foxwell and the economic historians Ashley and Cunningham tended to protectionism. As the Conservatives espoused tariffs and marshalled business support behind them, the professors of economics were easily seen as a hostile body of opinion to be regarded with suspicion, especially after their letter of the fourteen professors to *The Times*, re-affirming the principles of free trade. It was no coincidence that Sir William Ashley, entrenched in Birmingham, was more of a historian than an economist, was a protectionist, and had better relations with the local business community than almost any of his colleagues. Fifth, as economics developed as a university subject under the influence of writers skilled in mathematics like Marshall and Edgeworth, so it developed in ways, and even in printed appearance, apparently remote from the comprehension of busy practical men of affairs. This worried Marshall considerably and posed him a dilemma, but it troubled Edgeworth not at all.

A final reason for scepticism was the amorphous nature of the subject itself and the fact that as it became more clearly defined and professionalized by the universities so it seemed to become less directly involved with business matters. Economics in the 1880s and early 1890s was in no condition to form the hard core of business training, partly because it was unclear exactly what the subject was about, or indeed that an economist was a distinctive professionally skilled sort of person. The academic economist was often merely a mutant from other forms—philosophy, history, law, journalism—and this necessarily entailed as many different views of economics as there were entrées into the subject. In the third quarter of the century this was not necessarily undesirable. It is noted that in the 1870s 'professor, banker and cabinet minister still approached the subject with, to a large extent, a common language and not too widely diverging standards'.[2] Indeed, the involvement of bankers and journalists discussing topical matters of the day gave the subject a strong relevance for trade concerns. However, the 1880s was a period of stagnation and hiatus caused by the early deaths of Cairnes, Bagehot, Jevons, and Fawcett. Consequently, while this decade saw the development of the American business schools and the concern about depression and German trade competition, the revival of economics as a business training subject in England did not come until the 1890s and the 1900s. Then, as Hutchison observes, after the

[1] Letter, H. S. Foxwell to Alfred Marshall, 23 May 1898 (Marshall, Misc. 2.11).
[2] T. W. Hutchison, *A Review of Economic Doctrines, 1870–1929*, p. 2.

1880s 'economic theory was to be rebuilt mainly by university economists, by men who specialised much more thoroughly than their mainly non-academic predecessors—financiers, journalists and civil servants'.[1]

Just as the subject of economics and its content had to be rethought after the late 1890s with the formation of the leading university 'schools', so too the economics profession began to take an embryo shape. In 1890, the same year as the publication of Marshall's *Principles of Economics*, the British Economic Association was formed which began publishing the *Economic Journal* the next year. After obtaining its Royal Charter in 1902, it became the Royal Economic Society. But, in spite of this cachet and prestige, they did not consolidate a truly professional position largely due to the 'prevailing disagreement about the nature and scope of economics'.[2] Between the formation of the society and the war there was a marked social change in membership that betokened the rise of the study as a university subject rather than an intellectual interest of businessmen. Members in business and banking declined as a proportion from 32 per cent down to 16 per cent between 1891 and 1915, while university teachers rose from 17 to 26 per cent within the same time.[3] One of the impulses bringing the society into being had been the need to break away from the Royal Statistical Society, which was 'too full of business men'. In the new organization, the role of businessmen considerably declined; but from the viewpoint of economics as a training for industry this decline in their membership was perhaps unfortunate.

The rise of the subject and its later extension into commerce courses waited upon the formation of three strong schools with clearly defined ideas about the role and content of the discipline. Thence, by imitation and in the light of their experience, other university schools could follow their example or could refashion their own alternative to avoid defects they discerned elsewhere. The influential pioneers were LSE, Sir William Ashley at Birmingham, and Alfred Marshall at Cambridge, and to these three we should now turn.

The London School of Economics was the first of these three pioneering institutions, having been started in 1895.[4] Yet in its

[1] T. W. Hutchison, op. cit., p. 30.
[2] A. W. Coats, 'The Origins and Early Development of the Royal Economic Society', *Economic Journal*, June 1968.
[3] A. W. Coats, 'The Social Composition of the Royal Economic Society and the beginnings of the British Economics "Profession" 1890–1915', *British Journal of Sociology*, March 1970. I am most grateful to Professor Coats for making this available in typescript.
[4] F. A. Hayek, 'The London School of Economics, 1895–1945', *Economica*, vol. XIII, 1946, Sir Sydney Caine, *The History of the Foundation of the London*

origins it was intended not so much as a business school as one for young potential politicians. It was said of Beatrice and Sidney Webb, in many ways the school's founders, that in the early 1890s 'their absorption was in government as a theory. They wanted to provide an institution where men and women could be educated in subjects relevant to such ambitions.'[1] The Webbs visualized a form of education that would enable students with Socialist political inclinations to move into central and local government and they took as their prototype not so much MIT which Sidney had visited in 1888 but L'Ecole des Sciences Politiques in Paris. It was the politician moving into Socialist government for whom they intended to cater rather than the businessman moving into capitalist industry. In 1894, they were given their opportunity through the bequest of Henry Hunt Hutchinson, who left £10,000 to five trustees under Sidney for the purposes of 'propaganda and other purposes of the said Society (the Fabians) and its Socialism' and 'advancing its objects in any way they deem desirable'. The money was thus used to establish the school.

The early financial support also indicated a certain disengagement from business and industry. This came from Charlotte Payne Townshend (later Mrs G. B. Shaw), Sir Hickman Bacon, a Lincolnshire farmer, Bertrand Russell, the Webbs themselves, and Passmore Edwards, a newspaper proprietor with a long interest in diffusing useful knowledge through mechanics' magazines and libraries. Most directly concerned with business were the Clothworkers' Company and Lord Rothschild, but one did not find that spread of support from firms who hoped to benefit from the kind of students the school was to produce, and in this it differed from the northern civic universities.

Why did it come about that this institution, political and Socialist in origin, acquired the character of a business school before the war? In the first place, the British Association report revealing the backward state of economics teaching in England was published in 1894, which must have had some influence on Webb, who was then formulating his plans. Second, the chief interests of the first director, W. A. S. Hewins, were essentially economic although he was later to plunge into political life over an economic issue. But probably more important than the 1894 report and Hewins's own predilections was the increasing support for the school from two City bodies. In the first place Sidney Webb was already Chairman of the London Technical Education Board. It so happened that the Science and Art Department regarded certain 'commercial' subjects as falling within

School of Economics and Political Science. Janet Beveridge, *An Epic of Clare Market, Birth and Early Days of the London School of Economics.*
[1] Janet Beveridge, op. cit., pp. 16, 18.

the sphere of technical education and these included, for example, banking and finance, commerce, commercial law, history, geography, and insurance. Thus the TEB was well within its rights in making grants to the new school, and Sidney as the chairman of both bodies was the last to demur. Second, the London Chamber of Commerce was favourably disposed towards the school. They had a Commercial Education Committee under Sir Albert Rollitt which was strongly in favour of the TEB's taking on responsibility for commercial subjects, and the formation of LSE seemed an ideal way of arranging this. In particular, they recommended railway economics as a study for the new school, and as a gesture of good will they lent it rooms for lectures 'with a view to encouraging an interest in the City on commercial questions by young men engaged in business during the day'.[1] It will be apparent from some of the wording of this statement that a modification had taken place in the purposes of the college. What had begun as a political school floated by money avowedly for the propagation of Socialist, anti-capitalist ideas was turning into a school for predominantly commercial subjects for young men entering business, with the hearty encouragement and financial support of the City. That this posed a strange dilemma was seen in a dispute that arose over the teaching of economics between Shaw and Webb. Shaw wanted specifically Socialist economics taught, whereas Webb saw that this blatant propaganda role was now impossible, and Hewins had to assure the Chamber of Commerce that the economics teaching would be nonpolitical.

The school thus settled down under Hewins as a respectable business college with an economics bias. They secured the lecturing services of Dean Cunningham, the eminent economic historian then at King's College, London, H. S. Foxwell of Cambridge and University College, while Sir Arthur Bowley became the first Professor of Statistics in any English university. Law was taught, geography by Sir Halford Mackinder, and railway economics by Sir William Acworth. They were thus particularly fortunate in their early teachers, many of whom rose to considerable eminence in later life. The nature of the courses will be readily inferred from the teachers' specialisms. It was the special aim of the school to study the 'concrete facts of industrial life', as Hewins put it, and this consisted of economic theory, economic history, statistics, with lectures on the state and industry, immigration, railway economics, commercial law, banking, rates, and the English Constitution, with the structure of modern business and economic terms added later.[2]

On the reconstitution of the University of London in 1898, LSE

[1] Janet Beveridge, op. cit., pp. 33–4.
[2] W. A. S. Hewins, 'The London School of Economics and Political Science' in 1898 XXIV *Special Reports on Educational Subjects*, C. 8743, p. 86.

became part of the university and undertook the bulk of the work
of the new University Faculty of Economics. This led most importantly to the creation of a new degree, the B.SC.(ECON.) in 1901,
probably the first British university degree of its kind specifically in
economics. This, in turn, was followed by further changes in
academic content with mathematics and biology as preliminary
subjects so to link economics with sciences rather than metaphysics
and what Beatrice called 'shoddy history'. The other main curricular
development of relevance to industry after 1900 was the formation
of the railway department. Although railway employees had already
been attending the school, the railway companies formalized this in
1904 and agreed to finance a railway department, which remained
a permanent feature of the school. Less permanent was the other
professional study of insurance, which had been started at about
the same time as the railway department, but which was discontinued
in 1907. Finally, of potential industrial relevance was the formation
of the School of Social Science and Administration in 1912–13.
Its relevance here is not its social service work, but the fact that it
became a centre for the training of women graduate factory welfare
workers. It was evident that in its transformation from a Socialist
political school, LSE had emerged as a leading centre for a whole range
of commercial subjects centred on economics and highly orientated
towards industrial needs. As such it served as an exemplar to other
universities in the 1900s, as did Birmingham to which we now turn.

The faculty of commerce at Birmingham University owed its
origins to the demands of the business community of the city.[1] Possibly influenced by the British Association report of 1894 and the
setting up of LSE in 1895, the Birmingham Chamber of Commerce
discussed the idea of a faculty of commerce for the university on
16 November 1898, and two days later Joseph Chamberlain put the
proposal to the Court of Governors of the then Mason College.
Financial help came from Carnegie and Lord Strathcona, while
Arthur Chamberlain led a deputation to the United States to examine
university education for business. Thus when the charter for the
university was secured in 1900 provision was made in it for a faculty
of commerce. That the university had been willing to take what was
for the time a bold step in claiming to teach commerce is partly
explained by its anxiety about its clientele. [Mason College had not
been attracting students of business families in the numbers they
hoped, and commerce education, like the charter and university
status, was a means of attracting the young industrialist on his way
into the firm.

In the city there was some plainly spoken scepticism from business-

[1] For its prehistory see 'John Adamson', *Birmingham University and Commerce*,
a collection of documents; B. M. D. Smith, *Education for Management, its
Conception and Implementation in the Faculty of Commerce at Birmingham*.

men whose reaction to the new faculty counted for much. When Professor Ashley was first appointed to take charge of the scheme he was challenged by a 'very successful' businessman who asked him bluntly, 'Can you point to any teaching in any text book of Economic Science that is practically useful in the management of a business?', and Ashley had to admit that the literature was a 'pretty complete blank' on that particular subject.[1] Likewise Sir Richard Redmayne, Ashley's distinguished mining colleague, recalled of Birmingham that 'especially sceptical was it of the appointment of a professor of economics. At first a high value was not set on the professoriate by the businessmen. . . .'[2] Ashley, who usually presented a sanguine picture of his activities, admitted to the Royal Commission on the Civil Service that 'the whole thing was regarded very sceptically by the business community'.[3]

It would clearly need an experienced and remarkable head of department, both to clarify the content of the subject and to sell it to the graduate employers of the Midlands. This the university got in Sir William Ashley. Ashley had originally graduated at Oxford in history though developing an increasing interest in political economy, partly under the personal influence of Arnold Toynbee. In 1888, he became Professor of Political Economy and Constitutional History at Toronto, where he remained until moving to the chair of economic history at Harvard in 1892. After nearly ten years' absence he was glad to return to England as the first Professor of Commerce at Birmingham. As one strongly influenced by American attitudes on the relation of higher education and business, he came hoping to create 'a university department which might help to produce intelligent and public spirited captains of industry'.[4]

What did Ashley think was the purpose and relevance of economics? He was concerned, he said, not with educating the rank and file of industrial workers, but with 'principals, directors, managers, secretaries, heads of departments, etc. [who] will ultimately guide the business activity of the country'.[5] There were various considerations that made it worth while to experiment with a new type of course. In the first place there was too much rule of thumb routine because boys entered offices at the age of sixteen. The accelerated

---

[1] William Ashley, 'The Enlargement of Economics', *Economic Journal*, 1908, p. 190.
[2] Richard Redmayne, *Men, Mines and Memories* (London, 1942), p. 54.
[3] 1913 XVIII *Royal Commission on the Civil Service*, appendix to the Third Report, Minutes of Evidence, 10 October 1912–13 December 1913, Q. 21271.
[4] Anne Ashley, *William James Ashley* (London, 1932), p. 88.
[5] W. J. Ashley, *The Faculty of Commerce in the University of Birmingham, its Purpose and Programme*. See W. J. Ashley, 'British Universities and Training for Commerce', reprinted as chapter 4 of *Commercial Education*, and also 'The Enlargement of Economics', op. cit., for his views.

speed of change, he argued, called for greater flexibility in managers due to the more rapid changes resulting from the application of science to manufacturing processes. Similarly, the extension of communications entailed a widening area of competition and more frequent transfers of markets. An awareness of these factors through the study of commerce would give this flexibility which pure technologists might lack. He believed commerce training could give more zest and stimulus to those third-generation entrepreneurs who were inheriting family businesses, especially since public school men tended to despise industry. His course for these well-to-do scions would counteract such ideas, a particularly relevant point since many of his pupils were from family firms they expected to inherit. Finally, business heads complained that they were unable to obtain the personnel they wanted; Ashley claimed he would supply them from those non-family firm men with their own way to make. He would teach a form of 'business economics' dealing with the realities of commercial and industrial activity rather than traditional economics of more use to the politician and Civil Servant.

How was his course constructed to serve these broadly stated purposes?[1] First, he laid considerable stress on foreign languages. Students were expected to matriculate with one already and then acquire another on the course, German, French, Spanish, or Italian. A speaking knowledge was aimed at, and in the final year foreign commercial correspondence was taught. At the same time the student was made familiar with foreign economic literature and technical and business periodicals. This was clearly a response to the unease of the 1890s about the German commercial traveller and his linguistic expertise. In his acceptance of commercial correspondence as a university subject, Ashley showed that he was willing to go much further than Marshall, for example, to cater for practical office needs. He was also revolutionary in making accountancy part of the course, and claimed that Birmingham was the first English university to appoint a professor of accounting (he preferred the American term to 'accountancy'), though Harvard, Michigan, and Wisconsin had already done so. Accounting was taken in each of the three years, and Ashley had been careful to consult a committee of the Birmingham and Midland Society of Chartered Accountants when devising the syllabus. All students studied commercial law, while those choosing a career in trade would take courses on the technique of trade, money and banking, and on transport. He was especially proud that although transport economics was studied as a matter of course in leading German and American universities Birmingham was the first to adopt it in England.

The commerce courses were the heart of the programme. In the

[1] W. J. Ashley, *The Faculty of Commerce*, op. cit., and 1914–16 XI rc *Civil Service*, W. Ashley, 10 July 1914, QQ. 43591–8, for his description of the course.

first year this was a matter of looking at various leading industrial countries from the point of view of structure and position of industry, population, resources, and so forth. In the third year this became more specialized, dealing with such topics as location of industry, limited companies, advertising, trade cycles, methods of remuneration, industrial relations, and like topics. Finally, there were courses on geography, public finance, modern history, logic and ethics, and economic analysis—this last reflecting Ashley's bias towards the practical and his self-confessed lack of aptitude for abstract theoretical economics.[1]

One of Ashley's particularly valuable innovations was a willingness to provide courses mixing economics and technology. For example, elementary engineering courses for economists were begun in 1904, and he noted in 1908[2] that

> the direction we find things are going is toward the association
> of a course mainly commercial with a considerable element
> of engineering. This is, I find, a welcome alternative in many
> cases to a purely engineering course, which occupies four
> years in turning out an engineering expert with much more
> technical knowledge than is wanted on the commercial and
> administrative sides of the big iron businesses.

Some firms requested almost tailor-made mixes of economics and technology for their needs; for example, metallurgy and commerce for the son of a Wolverhampton brewer,[3] while Muntz's Metal Company sent technology students for a year's commerce.[4] Ashley even devised a special course for jewellers, combining jewellery trade work and commerce.[5] This breaking down of subject barriers to combine the two basic managerial skills was particularly original for those times and indeed presaged calls in the 1960s for a form of technological economics.

We can obtain some insight into the content of part of the course through the records of his seminar between 1902 and 1908.[6] The topics covered ranged very widely over industry and commerce as the following classification of seminar papers indicates.

British industries and trade	22	Technical processes and	
Foreign industries and trade	17	commodities	6
Local industries and trade	9	Banking and insurance	5

---

[1] J. H. Muirhead in Anne Ashley, op. cit., p. 103, and Letter, Ashley to Sir Mathew Nathan, 17 January 1919.
[2] Letter, Ashley to R. Cary Gilson, 5 February 1908.
[3] Letter, 6 October 1908.
[4] Letter, Ashley to R. C. Porter, 7 November 1912.
[5] Allen Edwards, 'What Birmingham University is doing in the Interests of Higher Commercial Education', *Jeweller and Metalworker*, 15 June 1906.
[6] MS. Minute Books of Sir William Ashley's Commerce Seminar 1902–8, 2 vols.

Shipping and foreign trade	8	Transport	5
Social and labour questions	7	Agriculture	5
Economic literature	1		

As we may expect, the bulk of the interest was in British industries, and there was a healthy interest in a wide range of foreign industries and trades. Transport was rather under-discussed and most surprisingly there was very little on railways, which seemed at variance with his claims for transport economics. To read today, most of the papers are thin and superficial because the writers were inexperienced and the literature almost non-existent. But it was desirable that such potential entrants to industry should at least have been brought into contact with a range of issues and information that must have had some relevance for their later careers. Particularly was this so with the papers on foreign subjects which were usually given by foreign students speaking from first-hand experience.

Ashley ensured that his course kept in touch with the realities of business life in the Midlands through his own and his staff's close contacts with local industrialists. One of his lecturers, A. W. Kirkaldy, later professor at Nottingham and a close personal friend of Ashley, was himself a wealthy man with his own business, and the lecturer in accountancy, C. E. Martineau, held several directorships in local firms. Most important, the faculty had an advisory body of businessmen. For example, in 1906 it consisted of eight individuals who between them were managers, chairmen or directors of fourteen firms including BSA, W. and T. Avery, the Metropolitan Railway Carriage and Wagon Company, Docker Brothers, Tarmac, Lanchester Motor Company, Rudge Whitworth, and others, including Neville Chamberlain as a director of Elliot's Metal Company.[1] The personnel changed from time to time and other well-known names came and went; Cadbury, Keen, Tangye, Chance, and so on. There was also a Social Study Committee advising the faculty and two of them, George Cadbury and George Tangye, financed a series of lectures on the Poor Law.[2] Ashley was quite blatant in his proper intention to capture and retain the interest of local industry. Having finished a series of public lectures on British industries, he at once proposed another on colonial trade on the grounds that this would 'call the attention of the businessmen of the Midlands anew to the existence and work of the Faculty of Commerce'.[3] He had a shrewd awareness that such pioneering work in a relatively new institution could only achieve success not just by its inherent quality but by a watchful eye for publicity. In his sense of salesmanship he differed from Marshall, whose problem was rather an internal one, to change

---

[1] List in the 1906 edition of W. J. Ashley, *The Faculty of Commerce*, op. cit.
[2] Letter, Ashley to H. Morley, 2 May 1910.
[3] Letter, 25 June 1910.

Cambridge tradition and create an economics course in many ways more conservative than LSE or Birmingham but, like them, orientated towards business.

The study of economics at Cambridge long preceded Alfred Marshall and the creation of the Tripos, but to appreciate his attempts to relate the subject to the real world of business and industry it is necessary to consider the treatment of the discipline there before his advent. Marshall's predecessors in the chair, George Pryme[1] from 1828 to 1863 and Henry Fawcett[2] from 1863 to 1885, had many characteristics in common that gave a certain tradition to Cambridge economics which Marshall was to change. Both were mathematicians and wranglers, and both followed this with study in the law with the aim of practising at the bar. Both were keen university reformers and both became Members of Parliament as Liberals—indeed Fawcett's election to the chair was almost a political election in itself.[3] Also their non-academic careers outside Cambridge were far more important than anything they did as professors, Fawcett being a Paymaster General under Gladstone. Pryme had no evident connection with industry nor had his lectures.[4] Fawcett had slightly more connection with industry than Pryme. He had knowledge of Cornish tin mining and also some genuine contact with working men, but his interest was not generally in the field of industrial economics but in free trade, the Poor Law, savings banks, and co-operation. Both Pryme and Fawcett regarded their professorial work as purely part-time, travelling to Cambridge to give their lectures for part of the year.

The third major Cambridge economist prior to Marshall was Henry Sidgwick and, more even than those of Pryme and Fawcett, Sidgwick's economics and interests were divorced from a consideration of industry.[5] Most interesting from our viewpoint, he tried to explain why economists had not hitherto been concerned with industry itself. 'For more than a century the general interest taken in the analysis of the phenomena of industry has been mainly due to the connection of this analysis with the political movement towards greater industrial freedom.'[6] This explains much about Pryme, Fawcett, and Sidgwick himself. They were more interested

---

[1] Alicia Bayne, *Autobiographical Recollections of George Pryme Esq.* (Cambridge, 1870). 'Obituary of George Pryme' (Cambridge University Library, Cam. 869.23).
[2] Leslie Stephen, *Life of Henry Fawcett* (London, 1885).
[3] CUR 39.26. Professor of Political Economy. Items 16, 17, 18.
[4] George Pryme, *A Syllabus of a Course of Lectures on the Principles of Political Economy.*
[5] Arthur and Eleanor Mildred Sidgwick, *Henry Sidgwick, a Memoir* (London, 1906).
[6] Henry Sidgwick, *The Scope and Method of Economic Science, an Address to the Economic Science and Statistics Section of the British Association at Aberdeen.*

in the freeing of industry as a political movement than in industry itself. Hence their attention focused on the wider level of trade and commerce and the economy as a whole rather than on the lower level of the actual workings of industries and firms, which were in any case more difficult to research and less amenable to treatment in political terms.

Such, then, was the nature of Cambridge economics prior to Marshall. It was a subject whose relevance was seen very much in political terms, taught on a part-time basis by professors who were politicians themselves, away from Cambridge most of the year, in public affairs, but with virtually no concern with industry or business. It was scarcely surprising that it was such a struggle at the turn of the century for university departments to convince industry and commerce that university economics courses had any relevance as training for their work. This linking of economics to industry, so neglected in his predecessors, was Alfred Marshall's task.

Marshall, before being elected to the chair, had for some time been helping Fawcett and Sidgwick to establish economics at Cambridge. In 1875 he visited the United States and on his return lectured on American industry, the kind of industrial topic new to Cambridge interests. During the 1870s Marshall, like Sidgwick, lectured on political economy to the girls at Newnham, where he met his future wife and with whom in 1876 he began to write *The Economics of Industry*. It was clear that already from the mid-1870s Marshall was beginning to move Cambridge economics more in the direction of industrial economics than it had hitherto gone. He was also beginning to bring the subject to an audience much more involved with industry than the girls and the moral sciences students of Cambridge, for his *The Economics of Industry* was written for the university extension classes. On his marriage he moved to Bristol as principal of the new university college, where his economics classes were 'composed chiefly of young businessmen'.[1] This concern for the businessman as a student of economics was henceforth to influence his attitudes strongly and represented a further movement away from the tradition of Pryme, Fawcett, and Sidgwick. On Fawcett's death he returned to Cambridge as professor in 1885.

We have seen that Marshall's intellectual interests on the eve of his departure from Cambridge and during his absence had moved further from the prior non-industrial tradition. His consciousness of this was expressed in his Inaugural Lecture in 1885.[2] He deplored that academics had drifted into an attitude of indifference to wealth and its concerns. Then he made a plea that he was often to re-echo— that the university and economists should put themselves in touch

[1] J. M. Keynes, 'Alfred Marshall 1842–1924' in A. C. Pigou (ed.), *Memorials of Alfred Marshall* (London, 1925), p. 16.
[2] Alfred Marshall, *The Present Position of Economics* (London, 1885).

much more with the businessman and industry; '. . . if more university men looked upon their life here as preparing them for the higher posts of business what a change they might make in the tone of business.' Here for the first time was a Cambridge economist who was concerned about factories and entrepreneurs and who did not intend almost at once to leave for a Parliamentary seat. Indeed, Keynes called him 'the first great economist *pur sang* that there ever was . . .'.

He sought to effect this link in the early days of his professorship both through his visits to industrial establishments[1] and his contact with labour leaders. Marshall indeed gained such a knowledge of factory processes, techniques, and skills that he could guess correctly at workers' wages by watching them at work.[2] Furthermore, Marshall had a direct contact with working men and labour leaders that went beyond Fawcett's. Thomas Burt, the miners' leader, and Ben Tillet and Tom Mann, the dockers' leaders, were frequent weekend guests between 1885 and 1900 at Balliol Croft, Marshall's Cambridge home, and Marshall was a genuine sympathizer with the labour movement.[3] At the public level he was a member of the Royal Commission on Labour 1891–4 and gave evidence to the Industrial Remuneration Conference of 1885 as well as on gold and silver, Indian finance, taxation, and so forth.

If Marshall's approach in trying to bring economics more into touch with industry and commerce was original, so also was his introduction of mathematics into the discipline, and this posed him a serious dilemma. Marshall, second wrangler only to Rayleigh, was no mean mathematician, but his dilemma was that if he carried mathematical economics too far then he would lose the attention of businessmen whom he wished to read his work. Marshall felt obliged to compromise and to react against excessive mathematics, and in this way his concern to establish the relevance of economics to the entrepreneur and his fear of not being read by the industrialist outweighed his other inclination to follow his mathematical bent.[4]

By the 1890s Marshall had already moved economics much more towards industry and practical affairs, but his aims in this regard were crowned with the setting up of the Economics Tripos. Economics in the Cambridge examination structure was merely a subordinate part of the Moral Sciences[5] and Historical Triposes, and

---

[1] Mary Paley Marshall, *What I Remember*, p. 43.
[2] A. C. Pigou, op. cit., p. 85.
[3] Beatrice Webb on the other hand thought Marshall was rather out of touch: 'He seems to lack the human experience of everyday life'. Beatrice Webb, *My Apprenticeship* (Pelican ed., London, 1938), vol. II, p. 415.
[4] A. C. Pigou, op. cit., (Keynes), pp. 20–6. Hence in the *Principles* the mathematical parts tend to be kept to footnotes and the Mathematical Appendix.
[5] Letter, Alfred Marshall to J. M. Keynes, 16 August 1897 (Keynes 1.111), complaining that the heavily philosophical part I of the Moral Sciences Tripos

Marshall saw that economics had to have the dignity of a separate course and a separate examination.[1] This might have been argued on purely intellectual grounds, but Marshall considered it not only an academic matter but one of national urgency.[2] In the first place, extended communications had made every country more sensitive to the economic movements of its neighbours and these were phenomena that had to be understood. Furthermore, our old easily won predominance was with us no more. Hard pressed by trade rivals and in military danger in her far flung Empire, Britain had to look to her economy. Also, with the rise of the concern for social problems in the 1890s, there was need for graduates skilled in social economics who had studied working-class problems in a scientific spirit. As regards the needs of business, he thought that as there was an increase in the specialization of the work of subordinates, so there was diminished specialization in that of heads of businesses and directors of companies. Here was a field in which the broadly based non-technological graduate was needed. Furthermore, he argued that the study of economics tended to make students favour the worker's point of view. This in itself was desirable because when these same students came into management then they had some insight into both sides of the case. *The Times* welcomed Marshall's claims for the development of economics as a separate subject on the grounds that business needed managers so trained and with this blessing the campaign got under way.[3]

The Senate was asked to nominate a syndicate to enquire into the ways to enlarge the opportunities at Cambridge for the study of economics.[4] This syndicate reported and made some illuminating comments about the university's relations with business.[5] It will be remembered from chapter II that it was exactly at this time, around the turn of the century, that Cambridge was beginning to become anxious about its finances and its neglect by the business community. The economics debate, to Marshall's advantage, fell squarely in this time of self doubt. The syndicate pointed out that abroad the responsibilities of universities to study the economy were more clearly recognized, but that in this country we lacked provision for the subject. This was regretted in itself 'and incidentally it seems to

---

made it impossible to get a respectable school of economists in connection with that Tripos. The 'mathematical casuals' were 'almost the only men worth teaching economics at Cambridge'.

[1] Alfred Marshall, *A Plea for the Creation of a Curriculum in Economics and Associated Branches of Political Science.*
[2] Alfred Marshall, *The New Cambridge Curriculum in Economics . . . its Purpose and Plan.* Many of the arguments he used also in the *Plea* and elsewhere.
[3] *The Times*, 18 April 1902.
[4] CUR 28.1. 'Memorial to the Council of the Senate', 26 April 1902.
[5] Report of the Economics and Political Science Syndicate, 4 March 1903.

involve some risk of the alienation of English businessmen from the universities'. The younger universities were trying to remove this reproach of the neglect of business by setting up faculties of economics and commerce and they recommended that Cambridge should do so too. Such a course would serve not only those preparing to become professional academic economists but also 'those who are looking forward to a career in the higher branches of business or in public life', and this would be welcomed by businessmen who wished to send their sons to the older universities. Marshall confirmed that this was so, reprinting letters from various business heads heartily agreeing with the scheme. He obtained support from, among others, seven knighted leaders in shipping, iron, paper, gas, and electricity who lent their names to his cause, effectively scotching opposition and scepticism within Cambridge itself. It was a well won case, and in June the honours examination in economics was instituted and a Board of Economics and Politics was to be constituted.[1]

The plan of the curriculum included the British Constitution, political theories, economic history, law, the structure and problems of modern industry, wages and conditions of employment, money, credit and prices and international trade.[2] However, no provision in the course was made for accountancy. This was to lead to a controversy in 1905 as *The Times*, which had enthusiastically supported Marshall in 1902, cast doubt on the value of the scheme to businessmen because of the omission of this subject.[3] Marshall's problem was the degree to which economics should become practical technical training. He accepted law, but thought that if accountancy became book-keeping then it was not a university subject but a practical skill. Basically, it was a question of how far Marshall was really willing to go to help the businessman and still remain academically respectable. For a man of his intellectual background of Mathematical Tripos and moral sciences, that limit was reached with accountancy which he equated with book-keeping. Other protagonists of commerce crossed that boundary more willingly.[4]

If, however, we consider the 1911 curriculum under Pigou it must be admitted that it contained a wealth of material of great interest to anybody entering industry—structure and problems of modern industry, localization of industry, methods of production, joint

[1] *Cambridge University Reporter*, 14 May 1903, pp. 766 et seq., for the debate.
[2] Alfred Marshall, *The New Cambridge Curriculum in Economics*, op. cit.
[3] *The Times*, 18 November, 23 November, 11 December, 18 December, 26 December, 29 December 1905.
[4] Herbert E. Morgan, *The Dignity of Business, Thoughts and Theories on Business and Training for Business* (London, 1914). He urged on Cambridge a more thorough-going commerce course, considering even this expansion of economics had not gone far enough to meet industry's needs. Sir Herbert was variously with W. H. Smith's, Mac Fisheries, and Chairman of Smith's Crisps. He coined the famous World War I slogan 'Business as Usual'.

stock companies, trusts, cartels, fluctuations of demand in industries, marketing and transport, wages and conditions of labour, trade unions and employers' associations, industrial insurance, and government interference with industry.[1] Compared with Pryme's lectures in the 1850s, the Cambridge view of economics had become closely relevant to industry and almost all the credit for this was due to Marshall.

Having considered the three main schools it will be apparent that various interesting comparisons and contrasts arise in their different approaches and attitudes, both to the subject and their relations with business. Between Ashley and Marshall especially there were important points of difference. With the former an Oxford historian and the latter a Cambridge mathematician, it was indicative of the early stage at which economics stood as a discipline that its leading practitioners should have come from such contrary backgrounds. Marshall inclined to the development of theory and the use of mathematics; Ashley was disinterested in this approach but embraced in his view of the subject branches like accounting and railway economics which Marshall either ignored or was positively dubious about. Their totally different attitudes to accounting best illustrate this, with Ashley especially stressing it as vital and Marshall being drawn into public criticism because of his deliberate neglect of it. Their relations with the outside world were also quite different. Ashley seemed to revel in his contact with businessmen, chasing them for jobs, getting them to lecture and above all having them on advisory bodies to help him. Marshall, on the other hand had made very little impact on the local business community as principal at Bristol and the duty of courting them to help the university had been positively painful to him. Likewise at Cambridge, although he was always talking about the need to attract the support of the business community and genuinely tried to make his work readable by businessmen, yet he did not feel the need to have an advisory body for the Economics Tripos as Ashley had. Further, Ashley was a figure in public and political life of greater standing than Marshall, hence the former's knighthood, though Marshall did take part in various Royal Commissions. These considerable contradictions between the two men were especially apparent to Marshall himself, and when Marshall retired from the Cambridge chair and the question of his successor arose, Ashley was firmly ruled out. Sidney Webb wrote to Ashley, 'Marshall seems to have moved Heaven and earth to exclude you and Foxwell.'[2]

---

[1] *Report of the Special Board for Economics and Politics on the Regulations for the Economics Tripos*, 2 May 1911. Marshall retired in 1908 and was succeeded by A. C. Pigou.
[2] Letter, Sidney Webb to William Ashley, 16 December 1908 in Ashley's Correspondence, Birmingham University Library 1967/iii/24–25.

Ashley had much more in common with Hewins, although the latter had retired before Ashley's department really got into its stride. Both were deeply interested in political questions and both were keen imperialists and protectionists; indeed Hewins gave up his academic career to join Chamberlain's tariff campaign. In that sense both were part of the intellectual wing of the Birmingham reaction against Manchester school free trade economics and both knew the Chamberlains personally. In details of curriculum there was likewise greater similarity between the LSE and Birmingham approaches, though commerce as opposed to economics was built up more at LSE in the inter-war years. However, that both espoused transport economics heartily is one important point of similarity.

With these points of accord between Ashley and Hewins there were, conversely, important differences between Hewins and LSE and Marshall. Marshall certainly approved of the starting of the school; Beatrice Webb noted that Hewins had 'talked over' Marshall and others to get their support in 1895.[1] But later, Marshall came to suspect Hewins of seeking to belittle Cambridge. Beyond these irritations Marshall was also concerned about the direction that LSE was taking. He told Hewins that he had heard that LSE 'pays scant honour to the Scientific as distinguished from the technical aspects of economics', and he was very doubtful whether commercial law was a suitable subject.[2] If he thought that about Hewins in 1901 we may imagine how much more strongly he would feel it about Ashley after 1902. Furthermore, Marshall was also suspicious of Hewins's being 'dominantly historical', adequate for taking a course in conjunction with the Historical Tripos from which Marshall was trying to extricate himself, but 'after all, that is not Economics proper'.[3] Even worse, Marshall held that LSE was simply ruled by those members of the Fabian Society who could bother to attend meetings regularly and such people were not devoted to the truth as such, but rather to making people believe in the truth of their own doctrine.[4] The fact that Hewins was also a protectionist like Ashley added yet further fuel to Marshall's suspicions of their intellectual respectability. In fairness to Marshall's relative conservatism it will be remembered that he had had the task of moving Cambridge economics away from a long tradition. There were borders he was still unwilling to cross that Hewins and Ashley, who began with new departments and no inhibitions, felt less constraining. Such then

---

[1] Beatrice Webb, *Our Partnership*, 8 May 1895, p. 91.
[2] A. W. Coats, 'Alfred Marshall and the Early Development of the London School of Economics, some Unpublished Letters', *Economica*, vol. 34, November 1967, p. 414.
[3] Letter, Alfred Marshall to J. M. Keynes, 16 August 1897 (Keynes 1.111), referring to Hewins.
[4] Letter, Alfred Marshall to Sir William Ramsay, 21 April 1902 (Marshall 3.82).

were LSE, Birmingham, and Cambridge attempts to solve the problem of the economics graduate in industry. They served as pioneers and exemplars and ushered in a period of intense activity in this field among other universities in the 1900s to which we now turn.

The formation of LSE, the Birmingham commerce course, and the Economics Tripos were but the chief and most influential developments in a movement echoed in other universities in Britain in the late 1890s and 1900s. At Oxford, for example, the early 1900s saw a marked revival in the study of economics after a long period of ineffectiveness under the negative leadership of successive Drummond professors.[1] As in Cambridge, there were moves both to enhance the status of economics in Oxford and to bring it into line with contemporary business needs. Indeed the agitation of L. L. Price, the tutor at Balliol, came in the same year as Marshall's campaign for the Tripos. Price was concerned to disengage economics from its subordinate role in literae humaniores and modern history, and as a result of his efforts a diploma was set up in 1903. Price saw an increasing wish on the part of merchants to 'receive a training more useful for the careers for which they are destined',[2] while more Oxford students were choosing business careers for which the diploma would be useful. The success of the diploma soon led inevitably to demands that it should lead to the creation of a new school[3] which came about with the creation of PPE in 1921.

The early 1900s also saw similar developments in other universities. At University College, London, a permanent resident staff of four was established in 1903 for economics teaching.[4] At Manchester a chair of economics was created in 1898, certificate courses were given from 1900 and 'over a hundred business firms stated their approval of the scheme and promised to give due weight to the certificate in making appointments',[5] while they began commerce as a distinct subject in 1903. At Leeds a chair of economics was formed in 1902, supposedly 'adapted to the needs of students who proposed

---

[1] A. W. Coats, 'Sociological Aspects of British Economic Thought 1880–1930' *Journal of Political Economy*, vol. 75, October 1967. J. M. Keynes, 'Francis Ysidro Edgeworth' in *Essays in Biography* (ed.), Geoffrey Keynes (London 1933, reprint 1961). R. L. Hall, 'Economics at Oxford', *Oxford Magazine*, 27 January 1933.
[2] L. L. Price, *The Present Position of Economic Study at Oxford*.
[3] *Wanted—a New School at Oxford* (Oxford, 1909), and Report of the Committee on the Proposed Degree in Economics, 10 June 1915.
[4] University College London Reports, *passim*, 1900–1914. J. M. Keynes, 'Henry Somerton Foxwell', and C. E. Collet, 'Professor Foxwell and University College', *Economic Journal*, December 1936.
[5] P. J. Hartog, *The Owens College Manchester*, pp. 88–90. Edward Fiddes, *Chapters in the History of Owens College and of Manchester University, 1851–1914*, pp. 148, et seq.

to enter upon a commercial life',[1] and at Bristol University in 1907 H. B. Lees Smith became part-time professor of economics and then straightaway moved to create a distinct commerce course under the Bristol Chamber of Commerce.[2] Finally, Armstrong College, Newcastle, started its own department of economics in 1912.

The phasing of developments was remarkably similar in Scotland and Wales. In Wales, Cardiff began economics from 1906 and Bangor a lectureship in banking in 1902. However, the Glasgow case is most interesting in illustrating the bandwagon effect of change. Glasgow founded the Adam Smith chair of political economy in 1896 with an endowment from Andrew Stewart, a Glasgow ironmaster. Local business bodies acted as patrons and the two leaders of the department, William Smart and W. R. Scott, both 'served actively in business as directors of manufacturing concerns'. And yet even with so industrially orientated a department, the university was unwilling to proceed from 'economics' to 'commerce'.[3] A committee set up to investigate this in 1901 decided that there was no need for a new degree in commerce.[4] But by 1905, under the influence of English universities' experience, they had completely changed their minds and decided that a faculty of commerce was 'urgently needed' at Glasgow.[5] Few cases could better illustrate the very marked change in attitudes favouring the reception of economics and then commerce as university subjects in the decade 1895–1905. In England at least the creation of economics departments or their reform and reshaping was very markedly a feature of the 1900s. Given the broad pressures examined earlier, it was clear that imitation served to spread the form rapidly within a very few years.

The change from 'economics' to 'commerce' that some of these departments were making in the 1900s entailed a radical broadening of the curriculum and an even greater orientation towards business and industry. Traditional curricula like Oxford and University College, London, were not particularly directed towards these ends. At Oxford, for example, they dealt with economic history, the Austrian marginalists, and the theory of wages, and they admitted that their course differed from those 'in those newer seats of academic education which are located in manufacturing and commercial centres'.[6] University College, London, dealt with the theory of

[1] A. N. Shimmin, *The University of Leeds, the First Half Century*.
[2] 'Notes on the History of the Department of Economics, University of Bristol' (Bristol University Archives, D.M. 219). H. B. Lees Smith, *A Chair of Commerce in connection with the University of Bristol*.
[3] J. B. Neilson, *Fortuna Domus*; A. L. McFie, 'Political Economy'.
[4] University of Glasgow General Council Minutes: Joint Report . . . on Commercial Education, 18 March 1901.
[5] University of Glasgow General Council Minutes: Joint Report . . . on Commercial Education, 21 March 1905, and ibid. 16 October 1906.
[6] *The Oxford Diploma in Economics and Political Science* (1910).

value, public finance, statistics, law, economic geography, competition and combination, and Manchester before 1900 with economic history, international trade, the Poor Law, geography and law. Programmes like this provided a content fairly relevant to business interests, but nothing like so directly linked as they might have been. This was the point of the transition that many institutions made in the watershed of the 1900s, largely under the influence of Ashley. We can see this change in emphasis by considering the curricula of commerce courses.

In commerce courses there was a greater range and variety of accepted material.[1] In Manchester, which under Sir Sydney Chapman was one of the best of such departments, they included languages, even teaching Oriental languages for the Far Eastern and Egyptian trades of the city. They also ran courses in banking and accountancy and railway economics, taught by men actually engaged in those occupations. As Marshall had drawn the line at accountancy so Chapman resisted 'trying to invent a new business science or of teaching office technique on the lines of the "toy counting house"'.[2] This was a threshold not crossed in universities until Edinburgh's extraordinary activities in the 1930s. At Bristol, where Lees Smith was trying to create a chair of commerce out of economics, he too was proposing foreign languages, commercial geography, accountancy, law, transport, and even commercial correspondence, which few others would have cared to justify. At Leeds they offered B.COMM. and diplomas in commerce from 1902, likewise dealing with languages, geography, accounting, and law, in addition to economics; and a similar transition was discernible at Newcastle between 1912 and 1913.

In the wake of the English universities, Glasgow University followed with due caution, but with the enthusiasm of late conversion. They envisaged that there would be a strong core of arts subjects, but with the addition of accounting, insurance, public finance, and statistics, and it was suggested that an advisory committee of businessmen be formed.[3] Whereas the English creation of commerce courses was a feature of the 1900s, in Scotland they were started around the end of the war, partly because local Chambers of Commerce flush with war profits were able as well as willing to invest in such projects for the coming peace.[4]

---

[1] See the reports of various universities to the Joint Report . . . on Commercia Education, 16 October 1906, in the University of Glasgow General Council Minutes. These are an unexpected and valuable source on developments in economics teaching in English universities.
[2] Sir Sydney Chapman, 'Some Memories and Reflections' (an unpublished typescript MSS. EH. C.91 in Manchester University Library).
[3] Report of the Committee on Education Policy on the Faculty of Commerce, 10 April 1911.
[4] E.g. *Dundee Citizen*, 17 August 1918.

It was clear that this transition from economics to commerce courses, as universities sought to align themselves more with the needs of business, had involved a wider conception of the subject than that encompassed in traditional departments of economics. Perhaps potentially the most important of these new subjects, and one which certainly ought to have been prosecuted more, was modern languages. While we had made an effective retort to German technical education before 1914 the same could not be said for commercial languages, which in the overall economic struggle were quite as important. The advanced study of modern languages in England developed surprisingly late in the nineteenth century, and it was 1886 before Cambridge held its first examination in the Mediaeval and Modern Languages Tripos, though without even optional conversation until 1909, and 1903 before Oxford established her honour school.[1] Needless to say, the interests of these disciplines in relating themselves to the needs of exporters was nil.

However, by the turn of the century it had become evident that although the study of languages for literature and culture was eminently desirable in its own right, yet they ought also to be taught for commercial purposes. Lord Balfour, on being installed as Chancellor of St Andrews in 1901, made the rather unusual but percipient remark that universities would do more good for the British economy by teaching languages than by direct commerce teaching.[2] For lack of worthwhile training in universities at home, the sons of shrewd businessmen were sent to learn languages on the continent, as was Simon Marks in contrast with his friend and partner Israel Sieff, who went to Manchester University.[3] Liverpool University especially developed language teaching orientated towards business. Its chair of Spanish was founded in 1909 by Captain G. Gilmour, who was active in business in South America,[4] and the chair of Russian began in 1908 with the support of Sir William Mather, the exporter of textile machinery to Russia.[5] One of the lecturers in the department used to visit the Chamber of Commerce regularly to give trade intelligence to Liverpool merchants trading to Russia before the war.[6]

However, in spite of this the report of Sir Stanley Leathes' 1918 committee amply revealed our weakness in commercial languages prior to the war.[7] They criticized the paucity of provision for modern

[1] Sir Charles Firth, *Modern Languages at Oxford, 1724-1929.*
[2] Lord Balfour, *Dundee Advertiser,* 25 October 1901.
[3] Conversation of Lord Sieff and Kenneth Harris, *The Observer,* 30 June 1968.
[4] Sheaf of papers 'Modern Languages' in Misc. Histories II in Liverpool University Registry.
[5] Sarolea Papers 81/1, University of Edinburgh. A private typescript memoranda drawn up at the request of the Russian ambassador by Sir Bernard Pares and sent to Charles Sarolea.
[6] *Liverpool Courier,* 8 March 1910.
[7] 1918 IX *Report of the Committee . . . Position of Modern Languages in the Educational System of Great Britain* (Leathes), Cd. 9036.

languages in the universities. While French and German were fairly well catered for, there were only eleven teachers of Italian and, even more scandalous in view of the importance of the South American market, only seven teachers of Spanish. Even more astonishing was the fact that none of the Scottish universities had professors of even French or German. In spite of the improvement in the ten or fifteen years before 1918, in none of the British universities was the staff in modern languages 'even moderately sufficient', and their teaching of languages was unduly philological and antiquarian. They urged upon the universities 'an improved conception and scheme of studies; a larger and more adequately paid staff representing more aspects and more countries than have hitherto been represented in most centres'. Likewise, on the employers they urged 'that industrial and commercial organizations dealing with foreign countries should make a fuller and more adequate use of the supply of women of trained intelligence now proceeding from our Universities . . . with an adequate knowledge of foreign languages'. Clearly if these criticisms were applicable even after the slight improvements of the war, the whole language teaching position was very unsatisfactory as a weak link in our commercial education before 1914. It was one of the services of the commerce courses that they focused attention on the need for this skill in the complete equipment of the British businessman.

The involvement in business education by the universities did lead to traces of improper interference by business in university matters, since the study of economics bordered on political ideology and public affairs which made the colleges particularly vulnerable to this kind of pressure. The basic suspicion was that economics had something to do with Socialism and that this was fundamentally contradictory to the private enterprise capitalism of the business employers themselves. For example, at Bristol George Pope wrote to Professor Wertheimer of the faculty of engineering, 'I am very glad that you are taking precautions in regard to the proposed "Economic" lectures. To have Socialist doctrines preached in our college would be a scandal . . . it would be advantageous if we could appoint some lecturer who . . . should ordinarily preach our own creed. . . .'[1] At Nottingham University College likewise the Rev. J. E. Symes, the economics lecturer, came under severe public attack from the local business community and others in the 1880s for his Socialism and for lecturing on Henry George.[2] Finally, at LSE in

[1] Letter, George Pope to Professor J. Wertheimer, 25 February 1911, in Wertheimer's Correspondence, Bristol University Department of Engineering Library.
[2] A. W. Coats, 'J. E. Symes, Henry George and Academic Freedom in Nottingham during the 1880's,' *Renaissance and Modern Studies*, vol. VII, 1963.

1910, Sidney Webb made a speech supporting the railway workers' demands for higher pay, and as a result the railway companies threatened that either Webb should resign from the chairmanship of LSE or their £1,000 a year support for the school would be withdrawn. Sidney selflessly resigned.[1] We do not find that Ashley or Marshall had to face such pressure, but events at Bristol, Nottingham, and LSE, highlighted the hazards of close financial involvement of colleges and business and their implications for academic freedom, especially in economics teaching.

Did all these developments really produce students who actually went into industry and commerce before the war? At LSE, Hewins claimed that his students consisted of 'railway officials, young men and women engaged in business, bank managers and clerks . . .';[2] and Beatrice Webb confirmed that the 'successful classes are those giving purely technical instruction to professionals'. At the end of the decade Hewins, on being asked, 'Are the students at the school engaged in business?' replied, 'Yes, both as principals and clerks', and these made up the bulk of the students. The women students there were 'indexers, teachers, journalists, business women . . .'. Likewise the lecturer in commercial law found that his pupils 'come from various trades, but they are mainly engaged in commerce . . . a few owners of businesses and junior partners' with several graduates 'already engaged in commercial industries'.[3] In the early days of the college, then, the main body of students were certainly going into business and most were probably working there already. But with the starting of specific economics degrees the destination of graduates as opposed to these part-timers was rather different, for of those with first degrees from LSE between 1902 and 1920 only 13 per cent went into business. The great bulk went into teaching and research and into government posts. However, the value of LSE for business before the war chiefly lay in its courses for non-graduates. King's College, London, was also extremely important in this regard in running the annual, vastly attended Gilbart banking lectures which served the same purpose.

There was also a close connection between Ashley's student output from Birmingham and business. Indeed, finding commercial work was no problem for a large proportion of his pupils since 'perhaps half of our graduates have had businesses waiting for them'[4] and 'about half the students in the Faculty of Commerce have family

---

[1] Janet Beveridge, op. cit., p. 66.
[2] W. A. S. Hewins, 'The Teaching of Economics', *Journal of the Society of Arts*, 4 December 1896, p. 45.
[3] *LCC Technical Education Board . . . Commercial Education*, op. cit., 1899. Evidence of Hewins and Montague Barlow, pp. 1–2, 12–13.
[4] Letter, 1 August 1908.

business connections'.[1] For the rest, Ashley worked hard at placing able non-connected students in promising positions. We learn that 'very promising openings into business life have been found for such of our students as have already completed the whole curriculum in such concerns as the Rudge Whitworth Company, Averys, the Metropolitan Wagon Company and Pigotts',[2] while conversely firms like GKN and Leylands contacted him for students.[3] By and large, Ashley was successful in his placements. Between 1905 and 1914, sixty students had taken degrees from the faculty 'almost all of whom have subsequently entered business and some of whom have already reached positions of considerable importance'.[4]

From Armstrong College, likewise, there seemed to be a fairly direct flow of graduates into business. Of their six degree students before the war, four were going into business, all good class public school men.[5] Also they ran a course for railway employees, specifically paid for by the North Eastern Railway Company (whose chairman, Sir George Gibb, was a warm supporter of Marshall and Ashley). Thus the output of students at Newcastle could be said to be properly related to business callings. At Oxford the students taking the diploma in economics chose business as merely one of a wider spectrum of careers: 'the successful candidates have gone, some into business, some into political and some into administrative life, while others have followed a professional career or become teachers.'[6] Finally, there was some evidence at Leeds that students who had taken economics and commerce degrees had a propensity to choose business careers.[7] In the period 1890–9 six chose business careers and four did not, for 1900–9 the balance was thirteen to eight, and for 1910–19 twenty-eight to eight.

While the available evidence presented so far suggests that the courses were fairly successful in serving industry through their pupils' careers, there were certain exceptions. In south Wales, there was no demand for men with commercial qualifications and the Appointments Board had been unable to place any in business.[8] There seemed to be a similar disengagement resulting from the Manchester

---

[1] 1913 XVIII RC . . . *Civil Service*, Q. 21,271. For example Ashley's letters to Sir Lincoln Tangye and Sir George Gibb, 5 October 1912 and 11 January 1913, about their sons on the course.
[2] Letter, 6 December 1907.
[3] See letters, 5 February 1908, 10 June 1912, 11 June 1913.
[4] Letter, Ashley to Sir Albert Rollit, 29 November 1917.
[5] Report of the Department of Economics, Armstrong College, 1913–14.
[6] Reports for the Committee for Economics (Oxford Diploma) 1905/6, 1906/7, 1910/11, 1911/12.
[7] Calculated from MS Survey Register of Leeds Appointments Board. I am grateful to the board for allowing me to use this document.
[8] 1918 XIV RC *University Education in Wales* (Haldane), Cd. 8699. Evidence of R. R. Roberts, QQ. 7611 and 7614.

course, for of all nine traceable graduates in economics and commerce before 1903 only one went into business, he in charge of a piece goods department for a British firm in Shanghai. All the rest found careers in academic life with the exception of one lawyer.[1] The awareness of such still persisting disengagements prompted the energetic Sir Herbert Morgan[2] to ride his hobby-horse, resulting in a business appointments bureau established in London to feed university and public school men into commerce and to provide a flow of information between universities and firms.

We have seen that various long-term movements such as increasingly difficult trade competition, deteriorating industrial relations, the rise of forms of accountancy, and the insufficiency of traditional methods of training in increasingly large firms, all created pressures for an improved business and commercial, as opposed to scientific and technological, university education. After the hiatus of the 1880s economics began to become professionalized as a university subject, and the three leading centres of LSE, Birmingham, and Cambridge all within the same few years crystallized their views of its content and orientated it towards business. Under the influence of the common long-term pressures and specifically stimulated by the example of the three main schools, other universities rapidly reformed their teaching of economics, expanding departments, creating distinct examinations, and changing and widening the content of the courses. Most importantly, following Birmingham some centres made the transition from economics courses pure and simple to commerce courses, fitting economics into a context of languages, law, and other subjects, though our language teaching for commerce was a salient weakness in the educational system. Scotland lagged slightly behind these English developments, Glasgow as the leader deliberately waiting the outcome of Birmingham and Manchester experience. However, Wales made no progress at all in this field before the war, reflecting the backward state of university-industrial linkages in the principality.

Although there was some resistance on academic grounds from within universities and also some sinister signs of interference from business outside, the general outcome in the future careers of students was broadly satisfactory in that most economics and commerce students were channelled into business careers. However, in

[1] Calculated from the *Victoria University of Manchester, Register of Graduates up to 1 July 1908.*
[2] Herbert E. Morgan, 'The Dignity of Business', *Review of Reviews*, 1913, pp. 21, 123, 137, 270, 418. This was a series of articles with editorial comment and letters continuing throughout the year. It is not to be confused with Morgan's later book of the same name. The articles attracted considerable academic attention at the time.

some centres, notably London, the provision of non-graduate education for the working commercial classes of the City was probably a more important contribution than their degree work. Whatever the achievements of the rapidly clustered changes between 1895 and 1905, they were rather late compared with American developments in the same field from the 1880s. Ironically perhaps the chief benefits to the economy of these new forms of higher education came not so much from producing personnel to fight the trade war of the 1890s and 1900s but from producing the Civil Servants for the ministries in the subsequent world war. Their success in that was the chief vindication of the reform of university economics education from the 1890s.

8

The Universities and the War 1914-18

*'The problem of linking university work with the scientific
industries is being solved . . . with marked success, and is part
of the great and growing movement to which the War has given
a fresh stimulus.'*[1]

*'The War has brought the professor and the manufacturer
together with results which neither of them is likely to forget.'*[2]

In August 1914 a generation of intensifying economic rivalry between Britain and the new German empire gave way to a military
conflict which was to test the industrial and scientific strengths of
the two nations still more severely than the preceding period of
peaceful competition. Whereas the overall and long-term outcome
of the war was disastrous for the British economy its immediate
effect in stimulating industrial science was extremely beneficial.
Before the war the spur of trade competition was not in itself sufficient to force British industry to match the Germans in the espousing
of science or in the appreciation of the value of higher education.
In those times the penalties for such neglect in lost exports and trade
deficits had little effect on the standard of living in an economy where
the balance of payments was never remotely in jeopardy. But in war
the penalties when reflected in reduced military effectiveness were
direct, immediate, and mortal. The successful waging of this new
form of modern war depended as much upon chemistry and engineering applied to industry as upon the sheer size of fighting forces,
and the very development of these subjects under the heightened
demands of war further increased their importance. As H. A. L.
Fisher observed, this 'in a degree far higher than any other conflict
in the whole course of history, has been a battle of brains. It has

[1] Sir William Osler, *Science and War* (Oxford, 1915), p. 14.
[2] *Report of the Board of Education*, 1915–16, Cd. 8594, 1917, p. 70, 'University
Institutions in Relation to Industry and Commerce'.

214

been a war of chemists, of engineers, of physicists . . . whatever university you may choose to visit, you will find it to be the scene of delicate and recondite investigations, resulting here in a more deadly explosive, there in a stronger army boot, or again in some improvement to the fast advancing technique of aerial navigation.'[1] Their involvement in these activities as one of the few sources of scientific expertise enormously increased the significance and appreciation of the universities whose role in the war effort, especially from 1915, brought them into a much more central place in national life than they had hitherto enjoyed.

The universities had to be called upon because Britain entered the war with certain very serious gaps in her military technical capacity. For example, before the war we were dependent for magnetos on Stuttgart firms, notably Bosch,[2] and for much of our optical glass on Zeiss of Jena. The Germans derived their potash for glass manufacture from their own supplies at Stassfurt on which we were equally dependent, having done too little before 1915 in the recovery of potash chloride from the fumes of iron smelting furnaces. Third, our artificial dye industry was notoriously backward, such that even the colour for the army khaki and navy blue had to be imported from Germany. Moreover, the German development of the synthetic dye industry had provided them with a number of by-product technologies of more profound economic and military significance. For example, the Germans had a monopoly of Trypan blue manufacture, a substance which was both a dye and a cure for piroplasmosis, one of the chief cattle diseases.[3] Also the Germans found that photographic plates became sensitive to primary colours if bathed in solutions of dyestuffs, giving them an advantage in aerial photography. More important, the Germans had developed fine drugs as an adjunct of their coal-tar industry, giving rise to salicylic acid and its derivatives (aspirin), also phenacetin, antipyrene, and salvarsan. Finally, and most sinisterly, their explosives and lethal gas manufactures stemmed from the same technology. Picric acid and lyddite, the chief explosive before the adoption of TNT was manufactured by treating phenol separated from coal-tar with mixed nitric and sulphuric acids. Its successor, TNT, also depended on coal-tar toluene as one of its main constituents as its name indicates. Also the vast amounts of chlorine needed for the artificial indigo process prompted the Badische Anilin Company to develop its manufacture, and this led directly to the use of chlorine as an asphyxiating war gas by the Germans. Thus the coal-tar technology which the Germans

---

[1] *British Universities and the War* (London, 1917), introduction by H. A. L. Fisher, p. xiii.
[2] G. A. B. Dewar, *The Great Munition Feat, 1914–1918* (London, 1921).
[3] W. J. Pope, 'The National Importance of Chemistry', in A. C. Seward (ed.), *Science and the Nation, Essays by Cambridge Graduates.*

had chiefly developed through dyestuffs was at the very heart of the killing and curing of the war itself.

There were two other fundamental differences in the attitude to chemistry between us and the Germans that gave the latter an apparent advantage. Before the war the chief activities of the British chemical industry had been the production of sulphuric acid, carbonate of soda, and bleaching powder, whereas the Germans had developed much more the organic side. Thus the chemical industries of each country had diverged somewhat into different specialisms. With the war, however, it was the organic side that proved to be militarily the more important in the production of TNT, acetone, synthetic phenol, the bacteriological sugars, and so forth, and this required adjustment on our part.[1] Second, the chemical industries of the two countries, because of their different technologies, had radically different approaches to the supply of constituents whose strategic implications placed us in a vulnerable position.

This is best illustrated by considering the key roles of nitric and sulphuric acid. In the soap-boiling process, glycerine is produced as a by-product. This glycerine, being treated with a mixture of nitric and sulphuric acid, yields nitroglycerine, which is half the constituent of the explosive propellant cordite. Also, nitric acid and sulphuric acid mixtures were used for treating coal-tar benzene for the production of picric acid, the chief high explosive of the early stages of the war. Given the key role of these acids, the different modes of production used by the belligerents was a major consideration. We produced sulphuric acid from Spanish iron pyrites or from sulphur from Sicily or the United States. The Germans produced it from gypsum from Central European ores, over which they had control and which were inviolate from our interference. We produced nitric acid from Chile saltpetre by distilling crude sodium nitrate with sulphuric acid. The Germans, on the other hand, made theirs from ammonia made by direct combination of nitrogen and hydrogen, and they were experimenting with the nitrogen and hydrogen contained in the air. The implications of this were that, whereas our own chemical industry was dependent on natural constituents brought large distances by sea and dependent in turn on British naval supremacy but always vulnerable to German attack, the Germans themselves by their more sophisticated chemistry had achieved a security of explosives production based on self sufficiency.

In practice it may be argued that this vulnerability was not very great. From the defeat of von Spee's squadron in the South Atlantic in December 1914 we retained sea supremacy as far as surface ships were concerned. However, the real danger to British supplies lay

---

[1] Henry Louis, 'Presidential Address to the Society of the Chemical Industry', *Journal of the Society of the Chemical Industry*, vol. XXXVIII, July 1919. Henceforth cited as Louis.

not from surface raiders but from submarines, especially after the battle of Jutland in 1916 when the Germans gave priority to this form of sea power. This meant that the most dangerous time for British supplies was the spring of 1917 until the adoption of convoys from May 1917, which greatly reduced losses.[1] Thus, in spite of our naval superiority on the surface of the sea, we could not regard ourselves safe from a grave threat to imported supplies. Nor were we absolved from the effort by the employment of science to find substitutes for such imported raw chemicals which, even if they evaded attack, took up valuable cargo space better used for food.

In the early stages of the war there seemed to be little appreciation of the potential value of the universities for the war effort. H. A. L. Fisher noted that 'at the beginning of the War there was a most inadequate apprehension of the results which might be derived from the laboratories and brains of the universities',[2] and G. G. Henderson, the Professor of Chemistry at Glasgow and President of the Society of the Chemical Industry, used his presidential addresses in 1914 and 1915 to lambast the government for this neglect.[3] Some universities almost seemed to be written off as having little beyond their buildings to contribute to the war. For example, at Newcastle the army took over the metallurgy laboratory, the engineering laboratories were taken over and most of the time spent on the OTC, while virtually the whole of the college became the First Northern General Hospital, with the chemistry department as the linen store.[4] Southampton likewise gave over its new buildings for a hospital,[5] while Nottingham felt bitterly that 'no serious attempt was made in the war to use the specialized knowledge or training which university institutions could supply'.[6]

There was also a much worse short-sighted attitude to the personnel of universities. The most immediate effect of the war on the universities was a drastic diminution of numbers. Oxford fell from 3,097 in 1914 to 369, and there was a similar fall in staff. It was noted that 'there were but very few heads, professors or official fellows under sixty left'.[7] Manchester fell more slightly from 1,655 to 1,031, with a rise in medical students offsetting a decline in arts and even in technology. University College, London, fell from 2,200 to 1,000 as its buildings were chiefly given over to war work, and

[1] A. J. P. Taylor, *The First World War* (London, 1963), pp. 34, 109, 138.
[2] H. A. L. Fisher, *The Place of the University in National Life* (Oxford, 1919), p. 6.
[3] Sir Ian Heilbron, *The Life and Work of George Gerald Henderson*, p. 7.
[4] N. Atkinson, 'Armstrong College in the Great War', *The Northerner*, June 1932, and Armstrong College Principal's Reports, 1914–1918, *passim*.
[5] A. Temple Patterson, *The University of Southampton*, p. 138.
[6] A. C. Wood, *History of the University College, Nottingham, 1881–1948*, pp. 65–6.
[7] W. T. S. Stallybrass, 'Oxford in 1914–18', *Oxford*, winter 1939, p. 41.

Dundee suffered a similar proportionate reduction from 202 down to 122 in 1916. At Bangor the intermediate chemistry class of 1914–15 vanished and of thirty-seven students only two were expected to return; the rest had gone to fight or had dissipated to work, half-trained, at jobs well below their capacities. Accordingly the lack of research students in mathematics impeded Bangor's important aeronautical work in 1916.[1] The assumption underlying this prodigal dissipation of university talent in the volunteering period before conscription was clearly that the war was to be a short, sharp one and would not require the careful husbanding of scientific talent for developments that would take years rather than months. Still less did it indicate any prescience that relatively small numbers of university scientists working on armaments were to be vastly more effective than thousands engaged in routine fighting, or that for a long war the scientific officering of the industrial army was as important as that of the combatant troops. The same confusion was caused in the ranks of skilled artisan manpower by over-enthusiastic volunteering. Much of the responsibility for this rested on Lord Derby, who sadly admitted it to a university audience at the beginning of the second war. 'In looking back on the recruiting for which I was mainly responsible at the beginning of the last war I recognized that one of the greatest mistakes that I made was in not discriminating between the various recruits that came forward. I did not realize as I do now that many men went into the ranks who would have been infinitely more valuable owing to their qualifications in other branches of the services',[2] and he might have added, out of the services altogether. Thus it was that H. G. J. Moseley, Lord Rutherford's assistant, went out to Gallipoli to be killed in 1915 with incalculable loss to British physics.[3]

When conscription came in 1916, managed by Derby, the Board of Education granted exemption to 'students of technology' in their third and fourth years. And yet the position even of university scientists engaged on war work remained unclear. Either they were given a false medical exemption or even as late as 1917 they had to appear before military tribunals to be allowed to continue their work.[4] There was also some evidence of an equally casual attitude in the early days to university discoveries even of considerable military significance. Although the War Office in August 1914 circularized scientists asking for discoveries of military value to be reported

[1] University College of North Wales, Bangor. Reports of Heads of Departments, Chemistry, 1914–15; Mathematics, 1915–16.
[2] *Liverpool Daily Post*, 7 July 1941. Lord Derby speaking at Liverpool University.
[3] Arthur Marwick, *The Deluge, British Society and the First World War* (London, 1965, reprint 1967), p. 249.
[4] Selig Brodetsky, *Memoirs*, p. 85.

to them, yet they ignored Weizmann's new process for the manufacture of acetone. Accordingly this crucial discovery for cordite
manufacture and naval gunnery remained neglected until 1916.[1] One
of the last symbolic gestures of official slight regard for the universities came on 28 July 1915 when the Treasury attempted to impose
drastic economies on them which they successfully resisted. That
such cuts were contemplated was indicative of the persistence of the
old unappreciative attitude but that they were not made was also
indicative that the universities were beginning to show their worth
for the scientific waging of the war.[2]

This early attitude of casualness was at one with the approach to
the war economy as a whole in the early stages. It was assumed that
private firms would provide armaments as a commercial arrangement while state manufacture was confined to Woolwich, Enfield,
and Waltham Abbey. Not until March 1915 did the DOR regulation
empower the War Office and Admiralty to take possession of factories. The shell shortage of 1915 led to the creation of the Ministry
of Munitions under Lloyd George in May of that year and thence
to a much more directed style of economy that brought the universities into closer involvement with war industry. It is not difficult
to see why the universities had to be called upon to serve the war
effort. The staff of the Royal Arsenal simply could not cope with
the vast new demands made upon them, and it was difficult to obtain
civilian engineers to supplement them. In any case, in a situation in
which research within the firm was in its infancy, the great bulk of
scientific expertise remained within the universities. Bodies like the
Royal Society, the Admiralty, the British Association, and, soon,
the DSIR, all with their specialist sub-committees of university
scientists, had already been enrolling many of the most eminent
professors in the service of invention for the war, but it was the
beginning of the Ministry of Munitions in 1915 that marked a
watershed. With the advent of the ministry 'the knowledge and
equipment of the universities were utilized in many directions, as
well as in respect to the evolution of new equipment as in the development of processes, the study of methods of testing'.[3] The ministry
realized that without the services of the universities impossible
expense would have been incurred in the unnecessary establishing
and equipping of laboratories. The brilliant success of universities
and university teachers in dealing with the scientific problems posed
by the war bred both more problems and increasing official interest
until, by the end of the war, the universities were an absolutely indispensable part of the war-time industrial economy. Now we shall

[1] Chaim Weizmann, *Trial and Error* (London, 1949), p. 218.
[2] Annual Reports of Leeds and Manchester Universities for 1915 on this crisis.
[3] *Official History of the Ministry of Munitions* (henceforth cited as *OHMM*),
vol. IX, pt II, 'Design and Inspection', pp. 60 and 72.

examine some of the fields in which their contributions and achievements were vital for the scientific war effort.

At the outbreak of the war the explosives used were cordite for propellant and picric acid or lyddite for high explosive, but gradually, due to the highly unstable quality of picric acid, TNT was adopted in 1914 to replace the former. Then from 1915 and especially from 1917 amatol, a mixture of TNT and ammonium nitrate, was found to be more powerful than TNT alone. One of the first problems was the production of nitrogen compounds for the tri-nitro-toluene. Sir William Crookes had experimented before the war with obtaining nitrogen from the air, and this idea was taken up in Germany by Haber, who perfected the synthetic ammonia process. When the war started the Germans were thus self-sufficient in nitrogen, whereas our dependence on imports of saltpetre from Chile both placed our supplies in jeopardy and limited food cargo space. Consequently a Nitrogen Products Committee was set up in 1916 to institute research on the production of synthetic ammonia on the lines of the Haber process, and University College, London, became the leading academic centre for this work.[1] It was for this nitrogen fixing that the government built Billingham during the war, which was taken over by ICI in the 1920s.

The other constituent, the toluene, was obtained as a by-product of coal-tar in gas manufacture. Late in 1914 Lord Moulton's Committee on the Supply of High Explosives mobilized coke ovens and tar producers to produce toluol, and several universities became involved with this. Offers of service from university laboratories were accepted by the High Explosives Committee in December 1914 and 'the work of the universities gradually increased in amount and importance. In 1917 the system of arranging their researches was reorganized to admit fresh bodies and to establish systematic methods of allocating investigation, coordinating research and ensuring close touch with practicalities of manufacture.'[2] At Manchester, Professor Lapworth's gas-tar staff worked on the improvement of the washing of gas and the recovery and assessment of the benzene and toluene content, and the faculty of technology cut the process of recovery from three days to seventeen minutes.[3] At Bangor chemistry department the test was devised for the purity of toluol, which was then officially adopted by the Department of Explosive Supply.[4] The actual manufacture of TNT was, of course,

[1] 'University College London, History of the Faculty of Engineering' (typescript in the College Library, Box BD).
[2] *OHMM*, vol. X, pt IV, 'Gun Ammunition and Explosives'.
[3] Manchester University Report of Council, 1916; 'Report on the War Work of the Manchester College of Technology', 1920.
[4] University College of North Wales, Bangor. Report of the Department of Chemistry, 1917–18.

undertaken not by universities but private firms such as Nobel's and the Clayton Aniline Company or government factories such as those at Oldbury and Queensferry. However, of particular interest in the university connection was the government factory at Craigleith outside Edinburgh operated by the Professor of Chemistry at Edinburgh University, Sir James Walker, who organized the staff and students of his department to produce TNT there with record efficiency.[1]

If the universities did not manufacture the high explosive they were called upon to test it. When the National Filling Factories were set up, large quantities of propellant and high explosive had to be sent to them from various sources and the problem immediately arose of the consistency of these chemicals. From August 1915 the universities of Liverpool, Leeds, Manchester, and Birmingham tested the high explosive on a regional basis, which had an enormously beneficial effect on the explosives chemical industry generally, greatly tightening up pre-war laxness and imposing more rigorous standards of chemical consistency on their products.[2] Professor Dixon described how they operated at Manchester. 'We can collect samples in the morning and report the sentence on the explosive in the afternoon so that it may be dispatched if necessary the same evening. I visit the various works in our district at intervals to report on the processes employed and check the purity of the materials.'[3] Professor Percy Frankland and his staff in Birmingham organized the inspection and testing of high explosive in the Midland area and examined the coal-tars of gas works for toluene content[4] and the staff of Liverpool did the same for the vast area from Fleetwood to Bristol.

Such was the universities' concern with high explosive. But although they neither manufactured nor inspected propellant cordite, one university had a vital role in the technical change of its manufacture during the war. One of the essential chemicals necessary for the production of cordite was acetone, also needed for fabric dope for aircraft. The relatively small amounts of pure acetone that could be prepared by traditional methods from acetic acid were an important brake on armament production. Oxford University was working on the commercial preparation of acetone from alcohol,[5]

[1] *OHMM*, vol. X, pt IV, 'Gun Ammunition and Explosives', p. 57; and E. L. Hirst and M. Ritchie, 'The University of Edinburgh', *JRIC*, 1953.

[2] *OHMM*, vol. IX, pt II, 'Design and Inspection'.

[3] Manchester University Report of Council, 1915.

[4] Letters from P. F. Frankland, A. Parker, S. R. Carter, W. Wardlaw, in Sir William Ashley's Papers, Birmingham University Library, 1962/vii/8. In 1919 Ashley asked all the staff to write to him describing in detail their war work. The resulting collection of letters and memoranda, which he does not seem to have published, form one of the most complete records of a British university's contribution to the war effort. Henceforth in this chapter they will be referred to as Ashley Papers.

[5] Twenty-Eighth Annual Report of the Delegates of the University Museum (Oxford), Bodleian Library, Oxon., c. 249.

but the vital achievement was that of Chaim Weizmann working at Manchester University. Although he had discovered his process of fermenting starch in 1910–11 and had offered his findings to the War Office, they remained ignored until Dr Rintoul of Nobel's visited him, saw the importance of his work and brought it to the attention of the government. Weizmann was immediately given the task of setting up a pilot plant and soon the process was being carried out in converted distilleries throughout Britain. 'Without this solvent', Weizmann remarked, 'it would be necessary to make far reaching changes in naval guns.' He left Manchester to become a consulting chemist to the new Ministry of Munitions which was clearly more receptive than the War Office had been.[1]

The universities were also responsible for the equally unpleasant but less efficient lethal weapon of gas. On 22 April 1915 the Germans made their first gas attack, thus removing any moral scruples we may have had about developing forms that we already possessed. Our first laboratory experiments had been made before the German attack, chiefly at Imperial College, which had developed the lachrymatory ethyl iodoacetate SK (called after South Kensington).[2] This lachrymator SK was manufactured by the Cassel Cyanide Company of Glasgow under the direction of George Beilby of Glasgow University. Soon after the German attack, Professor Cadman of Birmingham University, who had been working on sulphuretted hydrogen with Chance and Hunt, was ordered to erect plant for its production in bulk and liquefying for use as a weapon. Neither this tear nor stink gas, however, was as bad as what was to come. In 1917 Sir James Irvine of the University of St Andrews analysed the German phosgene mustard gas, used by them for the first time in that year, and began to produce it in his own laboratory before it was put into commercial manufacture.[3] In turn, Irvine's method of production was superseded by work at Manchester and Cambridge Universities. Professor Pope of Cambridge showed how 'the disulphide could be made in what was practically a single stage operation by the direct action of sulphur chloride on ethylene',[4] and this was the method adopted by Nobels' at Ardeer, while Chance and Hunt also erected a plant for its manufacture under the supervision of Professor Richard Threlfall, formerly of the Cavendish and the inventor of the Threlfallite phosphor bomb. As a result of all this expertise our gas ironically proved superior to that of the Germans, who had

[1] University of Manchester Report of the Council, 1915, and Chaim Weizmann, op. cit., chapter 7, et seq., pp. 218–22. Weizmann is of course better known to world history as a Zionist leader (like his friend Brodetsky) and as the first President of Israel.
[2] OHMM, 'Chemical Warfare Supplies', vol. XI, pt II.
[3] The Citizen, 19 February 1921.
[4] F. D. Miles, A History of Research in the Nobel Division of I.C.I. (ICI, 1956), p. 79.

started on this deadly course. By the end of the war 'our process for the production of mustard gas gave us an output thirty times as great as had been obtained by the Germans at one thirtieth the cost'.[1] It is also interesting to note that the Chemical Advisory Committee of the Ministry of Munitions which supervised these factories and activities consisted of five professors, two FRSS, and two doctors with only two soldiers, while the Chemical Warfare Committee consisted of nine professors and three soldiers. It was a symbolic indication of the predominance of the university over the army when it came to this new kind of warfare, which was one less between soldiers than between professors and rival chemistry departments in the belligerent countries.

Just as the production of gas was a university activity so too was the problem of defence against it. The credit for this seems to be shared between various centres. B. Lambert of the Oxford chemistry department, while serving with the Royal Engineers, devised a box respirator with soda lime granules which became the origin of the British service gas mask.[2] This work was complemented by that of O. C. M. Davies of the University of Bristol, who had been working on the absorption of charcoal before the war, and it is claimed that 'he was largely responsible for the success of the absorbent in the British respirator'.[3] On the large scale the work of Birmingham was equally if not more important. After the first German gas attack Professor Cadman, the mining expert, was called in and he devised a respirator which he claimed was 'the first box respirator ever made'. Professor Frankland and he 'organized the first field experiments on a large scale with poison gas at Cannock Chase, the importance of which lead to the establishment of the Porton Chemical Warfare School'.[4] Imperial College was also prominent in this field, Professor Baker detecting the absorbent for phosgene and the college generally acting as a centre for anti-gas work under the Ministry of Munitions.[5]

Of more lasting beneficial effect in peace-time was the enormous development in drugs, which wiped out our pre-war backwardness and dependence on the Germans. Perhaps the chief centre for the production of drugs was Sir James Irvine's laboratories at St Andrews.[6] Arising out of their pre-war chemical interests in the bacteriological sugars, St Andrews was especially important for the production of three such drugs: dulcitol, inulin, and novocaine. Dulcitol was needed for the treatment of typhus and stocks had been rapidly exhausted in 1914, although we were able to borrow from

[1] Louis.
[2] E. J. Bowen, *Chemistry at Oxford* (Cambridge, 1966), p. 6.
[3] W. E. Garner, 'The University of Bristol', *JRIC*, January 1953.
[4] Ashley Papers. Letter of Sir John Cadman.
[5] G. A. B. Dewar, op. cit., p. 210.
[6] J. C. Irvine, 'The Work of St. Andrews University Chemical Laboratory during the War', *The Citizen*, 19 February 1921.

the United States until February 1915 when supplies once again ran out. This substance had formerly been produced from the sap of a plant grown in Turkey, which was now fighting with the Central Powers, and so St Andrews was called in to synthesize the product. By the end of 1916 so successful were they that the process was ready for transfer to factories, where it was carried on under the control of university graduates. The same laboratory also synthesized inulin from dahlia tubers, which were collected by Boy Scouts for miles around. These were used for inulin and fructose for combating meningitis in Salonika. The preparation of novocaine, the anaesthetic, was prepared in about forty different universities and colleges, but St Andrews was by far the most successful and eventually devised a means of producing the substance at half the cost in a fifth of the time of the German method of the Hochst factory. The development of drugs was quite a common university activity in these years. The Royal Holloway College chemistry department was devoted to this,[1] Birmingham made novocaine and then switched in autumn 1915 to the other anaesthetic, B-eucaine.[2] Reading also made B-eucaine.[3] Less usual, Bristol worked on anti-malarial drugs[4] and Leeds developed a new antiseptic hypochlorite. In this, as in many other respects, the war brought nothing but good in forcing British science to do what it had the ability but not the incentive to do before the war and to catch up the Germans in this now urgent field.

Another major chemical field where the universities played an important part in enabling British industry to eradicate a lag behind the Germans was that of glass. Before the war, Zeiss of Jena had reigned virtually supreme in the production of optical glass and British scientific glass users were heavily dependent on German and Bohemian products. The scientific instrument makers using the glass, moreover, had let the manufacture of small precision measuring instruments pass to the Americans.[5] Thus, when the Ministry of Munitions was established, Professor Cheshire of Imperial College, joined as an expert on glass matters, and in July 1915 a special branch was set up under him responsible for this industry. Three university centres emerged as especially interested in tackling the glass problem, Imperial College, King's College, London, and Sheffield.

Imperial College finally agreed to establish a technical optics department in 1916 and representatives of the industry—Adam Hilger, R. and J. Beck, and Chance's—undertook to advise it.[6] The

[1] M. J. Powell (ed.), *The Royal Holloway College, 1887–1937*, p. 36.
[2] Ashley Papers. 'Statement of Dr F. Challenger.'
[3] Henry Basset, 'The University of Reading', *JRIC*, July 1955.
[4] W. E. Garner, 'The University of Bristol' *JRIC*, January 1954.
[5] *OHMM*, vol. XI, pt III, 'Optical Munitions and Glassware', pp. 1–13.
[6] 'London County Council Report of the Education Committee, 26 July 1916, in File 131, Technical Optics, 1912–1918, Imperial College Archives.

Navy also welcomed the new development, since they had hitherto had to send their personnel to an unspecified private firm (probably Barr and Stroud?) for instruction in range finding.[1] The new department sought new sources of British sands for glass making to substitute for the pre-war supply areas of Belgium and Fontainebleau which war dangers and the high costs of shipping had rendered inaccessible.[2] At Imperial College itself they tested lens systems for giant land and submarine periscopes, designed a range finding submarine telescope,[3] and engaged in research on glass surfaces for gun sights.[4] Apart from its research work, Imperial College was also a most important centre for training for industry.[5] The other centre in London for this work was King's College, where Professor Herbert Jackson was working on the problem of fireclays to reduce the time allowed for the maturing of glassware pots and to reduce breakages.[6] He also discovered the batch mixtures necessary for several types of glass hitherto exclusive to Jena, and discovered three more.[7]

The third major centre was Sheffield University. On the outbreak of war a university scientific advisory committee was set up to deal with difficulties notified by local manufacturers. It was found that many of the requests came from glass firms and also other manufacturers enquiring about glassware. Consequently a department of glass manufacture was set up under W. E. S. Turner and an advisory committee to bring the department into touch with industry.[8] From 1916 the Glass Research Delegacy was formed to administer the funds that the new DSIR gave the department; also local glass firms subscribed to its upkeep as members. So successful was this university-based research that when a Glass Research Association was set up in 1919 it quickly became redundant and closed a few years later in 1925. Turner ran courses for glass manufacturers not only in Lancashire and Yorkshire but beyond, in London and Scotland,

[1] Board of Scientific Societies Report of Committee . . . on National Instruction in Technical Optics (Sir Arthur Schuster), 12 October 1916.
[2] *OHMM*, 'Optical Munitions', pp. 53–4; letter from P. Boswell, 29 April 1920, in a collection of papers 'War Work in Liverpool University' in Assistant Registrar's Office, Liverpool University; Report of Imperial College, 1917.
[3] An Agreement, 20 July 1917 (on war work of Alexander Conrady for W. Watson), in File 131, op. cit.
[4] Report of Imperial College, 1918.
[5] *OHMM*, 'Optical Munitions', p. 17.
[6] Ibid., pp. 57–80.
[7] *Report of the Committee of the Privy Council for Scientific and Industrial Research, 1916–17*, 1917, p. 24.
[8] W. E. S. Turner, 'The Department of Glass Technology, its Foundation and Work since 1915', *Transactions of the Society of Glass Technology*, vol. 21, 1937. A. W. Chapman, *The Story of a Modern University, the History of the University of Sheffield*. 'William Ernest Turner, 1881–1963', *Biographical Memoirs of Fellows of the Royal Society*, vol. 10, November 1964.

and overall he had dealings with 295 glass firms which he visited and advised in the course of the war.[1] On the research side the department was not so much concerned with optical glass, like the London colleges, as with bottle, lamp, and valve glass, one of its most important pieces of work being the curing of milkiness arising in glass from the use of substitute Russian potash that replaced traditional German supplies during the war.[2] The plate-glass industry, largely dominated by Pilkington's, did not seem to need this stimulus, but the war certainly gave a vivifying boost to the optical, bottle, lamp, and valve sides of the industry and the new expertise was largely created by the universities.

The final area of the chemical industry where the universities enabled British industry to catch up pre-war lags behind the Germans was that of dyestuffs. During the war the government gave financial aid of £1·7 million to the industry and supported the formation of British Dyes Ltd, which acquired Read Holliday, the prominent Yorkshire firm. Then, with the concern to create yet larger units, the British Dyestuffs Corporation was formed in 1918 by the absorption of Ivan Levinstein's by British Dyes.[3] At the governmental level, Lord Moulton's Chemical Trades Committee was set up to investigate dyes as well as explosives. Two universities formed the third part of this firm and government triangle, Leeds and Manchester. The Leeds department of tinctorial chemistry was placed at the disposal of Moulton's committee and Professor Green acted as adviser to it.[4] Similarly, the links with British Dyes were firmly forged as the department ran courses for their staff, while their industrial chemists were working in the university under the professor.[5] Manchester University also had close links with British Dyes as most of their research students in chemistry went there during the war; and Levinstein's, as a local Lancashire firm, also took a keen interest in the university as a leading absorber of Manchester chemists both before the war and after, when Blackley became the research establishment of the British Dyestuffs Corporation and then of ICI.[6]

If we turn from chemistry to physics and engineering we find that the universities played a scarcely less important part in the creation and development of new industries. Almost certainly the leading industry to which they contributed in this sphere was that of air-

[1] Typescript list of Glass Manufacturers, 1918 (one of Turner's papers in the offices of the Glass Department, Sheffield University).
[2] Conversations with M. Parkin, Esq., M.SC., AIC. Mr Parkin, formerly of the Sheffield Glass Department, was a colleague of Turner's from the early days.
[3] H. W. Richardson, 'The Development of the British Dyestuffs Industry before 1939', *Scottish Journal of Political Economy*, June 1962.
[4] Annual Reports of the University of Leeds, 1913–15, and Report of the Department of Textile Industries, 1915.
[5] Annual Report, 1916–17.
[6] Report of the Council, Manchester University, 1916.

craft. On the outbreak of the war, aeronautical science had already been placed on a fairly solid scientific footing. The method of propulsion and the problem of inherent stability had been solved, and the value of cambered surfaces for wing sections appreciated. To a considerable extent this was due to university work, notably that of Professor Bryan of Bangor, whose *Stability in Aviation* was already a pioneering classic in the field. Outside the universities the government had set up an aeronautical department as part of the NPL at Teddington in 1908. However, it was the war that gave an enormous stimulus to this industry and forced on the development of aircraft in a way inconceivable in peace-time. For example, comparing the output of the first ten months of the war with the last, the output of machines rose from 530 to 26,685, and of engines from 141 to 29,561.[1] Qualitatively too, the aircraft improved out of all recognition. The carriable bomb size increased from 20 lb. in 1914 to 3,000 lb. in 1918 due in turn to a reduction in gross weight per h.p. in the aircraft itself from 23 lb. per h.p. to 7 lb. Similarly, the ceiling rose from a normal 7,000 feet in 1914 (though de Havilland's height record of 1912 was 10,000 feet) to 25,000 feet in 1918. The war transformed the short-hopping kite-like 'flying machine' of the pre-war enthusiast into a craft like the Vickers Vimy, capable and ready, had not peace intervened in 1918, of delivering bomb attacks on Berlin itself.

In the early stages of the war both the Army and the Navy had their own air services until February 1917, when the Air Board was formed and this became the Air Ministry in January 1918. The aircraft for the services were produced by eight private firms working to government designs, the rest being produced at Farnborough, which chiefly engaged in experimental work. Innovation in the industry came not so much from the firms as from the Royal Aircraft Factory at Farnborough where many university men worked, from the National Physical Laboratory, and from certain universities themselves.[2]

The universities became involved in this partly through sending men to work at Farnborough or NPL and partly through work within the universities, particularly on structures, materials, and design. University academics were attracted to Farnborough and to its experimental department on accessories, photography, and bullets in Battersea Park. At Farnborough, Lindemann undertook his hazardous experiments on aircraft spinning as his later protagonist, Henry Tizard, was making high altitude tests at Martlesham.[3]

---

[1] *British Air Effort During the War*, Cmd. 100, 1919.
[2] *OHMM*, vol. XII, pt I, 'Aircraft', p. 114.
[3] The Earl of Birkenhead, *The Prof. in Two Worlds*, and Ronald W. Clark, *Tizard*. See also Constance Babbington Smith, *Testing Time* (London, 1961), chapter 5.

It was indeed an indication of the new style of this war that two Oxford physicists should have been among the originators of the profession of test pilot. This work was often dangerous,[1] and it was especially tragic that two Cambridge scientists, E. H. Busk and Keith Lucas, an FRS of Trinity College, were both killed during their work at Farnborough.[2] Farnborough scientists played an especially important part in the design of accessories. For example, Keith Lucas, before his death, invented the Lucas compass which counteracted the centrifugal effect of banking turns in deflecting the indicator.[3] Professor Hopkinson of Cambridge designed there the 336-lb. bomb as most suitable for the destruction of buildings.[4] James Gray of Glasgow University developed the gyroscopes and stabilizing devices for finding the true vertical in aeroplanes, and these were adopted for bombing in 1917,[5] while at the NPL Professor Chattock of Bristol devised the pressure gauge for wind tunnels.[6] As regards the airframes themselves, however, much of this work tended to be done within the universities, chiefly in London and Bristol.

Imperial College became perhaps the chief centre, largely because in 1916 Sir Basil Zaharoff, the armaments manufacturer, offered £25,000 to the government for a chair of aviation as a counterpart to one he had founded in Paris,[7] and in the following year it was recommended that Imperial College should be an institution dealing with the highest specialized demand for aeronautical engineering.[8] The Professor of Woods and Fibres worked on the materials of aircraft construction, which in the early days were chiefly wood spars and fabric covers, while on the metallurgical side Frewen Jenkin, the Professor of Engineering at Oxford, moved to Imperial College to work on the corrosion of aeroplane metal parts.[9] University College was also greatly concerned with problems of aircraft materials. The chemical laboratory there was the chief testing centre for all metallic components of aircraft construction, dealing chiefly with the development of dope and eradicating the deleterious effects on workers who became 'dopey'. With the loss or uncertainty of supply of linen

[1] Letter, Professor A. H. Gibson to Professor D'Arcy Thompson, 18 February 1917. Sir D'Arcy Thompson MSS., University of St. Andrews, DWT Corr. 989, referring to four killed and six injured in one week of crashes at Farnborough.
[2] Sir Richard Glazebrook, *Science and Industry, the Place of Cambridge in any Scheme for their Combination*, p. 5.
[3] *OHMM*, 'Aircraft', p. 3.
[4] *OHMM*, vol. XII, pt II, 'Aerial Bombs', p. 5.
[5] J. B. Neilson, *Fortuna Domus*, p. 330.
[6] W. E. Garner, 'Science and Technology in Bristol', *Discovery*, September 1955.
[7] Zaharoff Chair of Aviation, 1916–17. File 1120, Imperial College Archives.
[8] Draft Report of the Civil Aerial Transport Subcommittee relating to the Education of Engineers for Aeronautics Work, 1917, in Zaharoff File.
[9] Letter, A. H. D. Acland to Sir L. A. Selby Bigge, 21 December 1917 in File, op. cit., outlining activities of Imperial College war workers.

from Russia, Courtrai, or Ireland, they also worked on the substitu-
tion of Lancashire cotton as an aircraft building fabric.[1] Within the
same college similar structural work of more lasting theoretical
importance was in progress. Before the war, L. N. G. Filon and E. G.
Coker had developed photoelastic techniques of determining stress
in materials, and this was then applied to the wing spars of bi-planes,
the practical work being carried out in Coker's laboratory at
University College.[2] Although the first planes were made of timber,
research was also in progress to find suitable light alloys. This was
particularly urgent in 1917 and 1918, when supplies of timber were
proving inadequate (almost all aircraft timber was imported, especially spruce) particularly for the construction of new very large craft.
As a result of the work of Professor Lea of Birmingham 'standards
of specifications were drawn up for suitable light alloys to which all
manufacturers had to work and much work was done in various parts
of the country in teaching manufacturers to make and cast aluminium
alloys'. In close collaboration with manufacturing firms, experiments
were carried out and all-metal wings were then made to Lea's designs.[3]

The universities were even more important for their work on the
mathematics and physics of aerodynamic design. Dr N. A. V. Piercy
at Queen Mary College, London, worked for the Admiralty on wing
design, which 'resulted in the discovery of the best form of aeroplane wing, widely adopted at the time',[4] and at Oxford, despite
Jenkins's removal to Imperial College, the mathematical school was
able to help with problems of aerial flight and a school of military
aeronautics was formed there.[5] Finally, Bristol University also was
a significant centre for this work, focused on the important local
British and Colonial Aircraft Company. Selig Brodetsky was working there on the mathematics of aircraft structure and was joined
by G. H. Bryan from Bangor, the great pioneer of the discipline.
They then worked together in the later stages of the war on aeronautical mathematics for the aircraft factories.[6] The importance of
the mathematical work on aircraft structure cannot be exaggerated.
It resulted above all in our own aeroplanes being considerably more
stable than those of the Germans, an important factor in the development of aerial acrobatics and tactics. The stirring occasion on which
Albert Ball, vc, flew his sk 5 machine back to the lines, almost

[1] *OHMM*, 'Aircraft', pp. 117, 142.
[2] *Photoelasticity at University College, London . . . the Work of E. G. Coker
and L. N. G. Filon, 1909–37*, p. 6.
[3] Ashley Papers. 'War Service of Professor F. C. Lea' and 'Account of the
Personal War Work of Frank Raw'.
[4] G. Godwin, *Queen Mary College, An Adventure in Education*, pp. 154–5.
[5] 1922 X RC . . . *on Oxford and Cambridge Universities*, Cmd. 1588, p. 47.
W. T. S. Stallybrass, 'Oxford in 1914–18', *Oxford*, winter, 1939.
[6] Selig Brodetsky, *Memoirs*, p. 83, and H. I. Owen and H. I. Owen, *Sir
Isambard Owen, a Biography*, p. 92.

totally out of action and with the controls shot away, was a tribute not only to his own courage but to the subtlety of British mathematics and aerodynamic design.

Just as the universities played a vital part in the development of the aeroplane so inevitably they were to do so in certain electrical products needed for the war. The problem of the magneto was tackled and quickly overcome such that by the end of the war fourteen British firms were able to manufacture it, replacing the Stuttgart monopoly. To a great extent this seems to have been done by the firms themselves, especially BTH and ML Magneto Syndicate at Coventry. However, at the university level Bangor physics department made a special study of this, and their work was adopted in the practical design of magnetos.[1] No less urgent was the problem of wireless valves. While Dr Crippen had been arrested by wireless in 1910, this was no help to the troops on the Somme in 1916, not the least impediment to whose advance were the crates of carrier pigeons they had to carry for communications. Nor was it until 1917 that an efficient wireless telegraphy set was designed and demonstrated in the air, thus widening the scope of tactics by better air and ground co-ordination.[2] It was only to be expected that since the thermionic valve had been developed at University College, London, so, when the war came, the Admiralty belatedly applied for the expert assistance of Sir Ambrose Fleming and his staff for work on wireless apparatus.[3] The Royal Holloway College physics laboratory was devoted to the successful improvement of the valve, their improved type being adopted by the Navy.[4] Finally, the problem of wireless signalling to submarines was dealt with at Birmingham University, where T. F. Wall invented the apparatus for signalling by morse code to submerged vessels and was responsible for the complete mechanical and electrical design of the Apparatus which was adopted as the standard type by the Navy.[5]

One submarine electrical device of great military significance was the hydrophone for the detection of U-boats. The Admiralty Board of Invention and Research set up a sub-committee under Sir William Bragg to work on the problem, using microphones to detect undersea sounds. They even investigated schemes for using sea lions and seagulls to trace submarines.[6] However, another biological idea

[1] University College of North Wales, Bangor, Report of the Head of Physics Department, 1917–18.
[2] *British Air Effort During the War*, Cmd. 100, 1919, p. 11.
[3] University College Minutes, 29 June 1915, in University College, London, Record Office. The reports of the college yield almost no information about their World War I activities and their other records were destroyed by fire in 1930.
[4] M. J. Powell, *Royal Holloway College, 1887–1937*, p. 36.
[5] Ashley Papers. T. F. Wall.
[6] Sir Joseph J. Thomson, *Recollections and Reflections*, p. 209 ff.

bore more fruit, and from Professor Keith's studies on the hearing of whales resulted the device of a towing body based on the form of the porpoise, which was dragged behind ships to catch submarine sounds.[1] Manchester and Liverpool Universities co-operated on the Lancashire Anti-Submarine Committee which also co-operated with Bragg's group. Within Lancashire this was especially valuable in cementing the close connection of Manchester University and the firm of Metropolitan Vickers, with academics and the firm's employees working together, notably Miles Walker, formerly of British Westinghouse, who had moved onto the university staff. Bristol[2] and Birmingham[3] also worked on this problem, but the most successful seems to have been Queen Mary College, London. There Professor MacGregor Morris and A. F. Sykes carried out the work which had resulted in the directional hydrophone. Before this, while it had been possible to detect the presence of submarines by sound, it had not been possible to ascertain with accuracy their direction. But by experiments proceeding from a bucket of water, via the Peoples Palace swimming baths, Andelstree reservoir, and ending off the east coast of Scotland, they perfected the anti-submarine device used by the Royal Navy.[4]

Thus far we have focused chiefly on the innovative contributions of the universities to war industry, but many departments were more important in industrial training and even in actual manufacture than in research, though often these functions overlapped. Faced with the problem of the movement of orthodox labour into the Army, especially before conscription, means had to be found of quickly training dilutees and women, and often whole university departments were given over to this. Bristol, for example, undertook a good deal of this work, training 479 workers for the munitions industry, 142 mechanics for the RAF, and turning disabled officers into engineers.[5] Manchester trained 900 munitions workers in the summer of 1915[6] and Leeds 460 men between July 1915 and April 1916 for the Ministry of Munitions, then they switched to the training of women during 1916.[7] Liverpool faculty of engineering became a chief centre for training in the manufacture of shells, dealing with over 300 representatives of engineering firms who were able then to retrain their own men.[8] King's College, London, probably trained

[1] Sir Charles Parsons, Presidential Address to the British Association, 1919, pp. 3–23.
[2] Document headed 'War Work', File 17, 1919, in Archives of Bristol University Engineering Department.
[3] Ashley Papers. Letters H. B. Keene and Guy Barlow.
[4] G. Godwin, op. cit., p. 149.
[5] 'War Work', File 17, 1919, op. cit.
[6] 'Report on War Work, Manchester College of Technology', 1920.
[7] University of Leeds Annual Report, 1916.
[8] Sir Alfred Dale, 'Liverpool University's Contribution to Victory', *The Liverpool Courier*, 23 September 1919.

the most with 1,000–2,000 munitions workers and over 400 aero-nautical instructors passing through their laboratories.[1]

The use of university facilities for actual manufacture as opposed to training or research and development was more unusual and distinctly temporary. University College, London, manufactured time fuses[2] and Dundee was used for the production of shells for trench howitzers.[3] Both Cardiff[4] and Liverpool manufactured shell gauges. However, there are indications that the manufacturing phase in the use of university facilities was only a temporary one, particularly for the period 1915–16. At Manchester munitions were made from September 1915 until 'some months later' when they returned to scientific work. Similarly at Aberdeen anaesthetics were produced from summer 1915 to spring 1916, by which time the chemical industry had expanded sufficiently to take over the work.[5] At St Andrews they actually manufactured their own dulcitol until the end of 1916, when this too was transferred out to factories. Finally, Southampton manufactured shells in 1915, but with the overcoming of the shell crisis they too switched the laboratories back to other activities.[6] Using the universities for manufacture was clearly uneconomical and when the costs of factory production became markedly cheaper, presumably in 1916, such work generally was transferred out of the colleges. This was the reason given for Manchester's switch in policy over shell manufacture. The training in routine skills also seemed a somewhat uneconomical use of facilities, but we can see no neat pattern of a change from manufacture to training to research as the immediate crises of shortages were overcome. Manchester changed from production to training and Southampton from training to production. However, both were responses to the shell crisis that brought the Ministry of Munitions into being and to the loss of skilled labour in the pre-conscription and early conscription period in 1916.

We have just considered some of the ways in which the universities and their scientific expertise played a vital part in the developing technologies of several industries necessary for the war. But the interaction was reciprocal, and if the universities modernized and aided industry so, too, they did not remain unaffected by the war in ways relevant to our present theme. The war brought the woman graduate into close touch with industry for the first time and it also

[1] J. F. C. Hearnshaw, *The Centenary History of King's College, London*, p. 463.
[2] E. G. Coker, 'Engineering at University College, London'.
[3] Dundee University College Principal's Report, 1915–16.
[4] 1917 XII RC *University Education in Wales* (Haldane), Cmd. 8507, appendix to the First Report, appendix II, table VII, p. 279.
[5] A. B. Strathdee, 'The University of Aberdeen', *JRIC*, 1953.
[6] Temple Patterson, op. cit., p. 141.

modified the view of commercial education and its content. However, we shall say something on both these matters in later chapters. Here we want to draw attention to the impact on Wales, to the closer co-operation with firms, to the closer involvement with government through the advent of the DSIR. Finally in the next section the changing attitudes to career aspirations of would-be graduates brought about by the war will be considered.

We saw in the last chapter that Wales was about ten years behind England in its attitudes to the value of the universities for industry. However, during the war the universities came to be seen in a fresh light in the principality. The war contributions of the Welsh colleges had been surprisingly creditable. There was Bangor's magneto work, Professor Bryan's aeronautics, and the standard toluol test. Aberystwyth did routine work on drugs, and Cardiff in shell gauges. While not remarkable by English standards, it was for Wales, and especially Bangor, a more radical change, and favourably impressed those who with good cause had hitherto regarded the Welsh colleges as merely for the education of clergy and school-teachers. The Professor of Chemistry in Aberystwyth was able to note in 1916 that 'the lessons of the War are being rapidly learned' and he noted with satisfaction that the manufacturers and colliery proprietors in Wales were adding chemists to their staffs, whereas they had not done so before the war.[1] Witnesses before the Haldane Commission also observed that this was so. R. S. Roberts said that 'he noticed that there was a complete change in the point of view among them ["big employers of Cardiff"] with regard to the value of university education',[2] and the same was noted among forestry proprietors who, being faced with massive demands for timber and the denuding of Welsh forests, were turning much more to the departments at Bangor and Aberystwyth. The same astringent and beneficial effect was seen on St Andrews, which changed overnight from being by far the least industrially orientated of Scottish universities to the one with quite the most brilliant war record.

In Britain as a whole the war also introduced universities and individual firms to each other with often lasting results. For example, at Nobel's, Rintoul had been considering a scheme of using universities to carry out various researches, and the war prompted him to put this into action; 'a list of subjects was prepared and from it selections were made by each professor in consultation with the department. The work was then carried on under his control by his post-graduate students' financed by Nobel's.[3] And this was a firm

---

[1] Alexander Findlay, *The Training of Chemists a National Duty* (broadsheet in Aberystwyth University Library, LD 1155 (1) item 21).
[2] 1917 XII RC *University Education in Wales* (Haldane), Cd. 8699. QQ. 7615 and 7597.
[3] F. D. Miles, op. cit., p. 82.

that did not even employ graduates until 1907. At Manchester University close liaison was set up with British Dyes and Levinstein's, whose research chemists worked in the university laboratories. Similarly, their co-operation on the Lancashire Anti-Submarine Committee forged the link with Metro-Vickers, as important for Manchester University engineers in the inter-war years as the dyes link was for their chemists. The government also encouraged this closer *rapprochement* in engineering. Under the auspices of the Board of Education in 1917 a series of meetings was held between manufacturers in the engineering industry and professors of the subject on the better training of engineers.[1] Not that they were dissatisfied with the education as it then was; the discussion was rather intended to consider adjustments needed in the near future to meet industrial changes that the manufacturers could foresee more clearly than the professors. While all this may sound quite unremarkable at the present time, the bringing together of university teachers and businessmen was not always effected during the war without a certain friction and anti-university suspicion.[2] But friction or not, the fact that the universities were brought into close working contact with a variety of agencies, all concerned with industrial production in the most urgent circumstances, did them nothing but good.

The universities also benefited from the war in the acceptance undertaken by the government of a more direct responsibility for the state of industrial science embodied in the new Department of Scientific and Industrial Research. In May 1915 the Royal Society sent a deputation to the Presidents of the Boards of Trade and Education urging government assistance for scientific research. In July 1915 a committee of the Privy Council was set up for this purpose with an advisory body, the chairman being Sir William McCormick, already the chairman of the Advisory Committee on University Grants, the predecessor of the UGC. The committee began work in 1915 with a fund of £1 million to try to encourage firms to group together to form industrial research associations and to support 'research of special timeliness and promise'. This became the DSIR in 1916.[3] It is worth noting that during this first year of the committee, before it became the department, there was heavy academic and industrial pressure deploring that science had been too much neglected. The usual points were made about how our backwardness had placed us in a dangerous position for fighting the war, and

[1] *Report of the Board of Education*, 1916–17, Cd. 9045, 1918, p. 82.
[2] Letters, Professor A. H. Gibson to Professor Sir D'Arcy Thompson, 10 August, 26 December, 1917. D'Arcy Thompson MSS. University of St. Andrews, DWT Corr. 989, for private complaints of this at Farnborough and the Admiralty.
[3] *Report of the Committee of the Privy Council for Scientific and Industrial Research, 1915–16*, 1916, VIII, Cd. 8336. Sir Harry Melville, *The Department of Scientific and Industrial Research.*

twenty-five professors signed a memorandum to *The Times*,[1] while many others supported the resolutions of a meeting on the Neglect of Science, including J. J. Thomson and Alfred Marshall.[2] They wanted a ministry of science and industry to be created in recognition of government obligations towards science. Although this did not come about the early activities and formation of the DSIR were the product of this climate of opinion when, as Dewar put it, 'technology certainly became a cult in Great Britain between 1915 and 1919'.[3]

The DSIR was concerned with a wider field of science and industry than that purely concerning the universities. It was concerned with the NPL, the research associations and national research boards such as that for fuel, but in certain areas of its activities it had direct bearing on the universities and on their links with industry. In the first place, they wanted to encourage professional societies to use the facilities for research provided by the universities in a systematic way. They noted that the Institute of Chemists and the Society of Dyers and Colorists were forging such links, with the latter acting as a kind of middleman between manufacturers with problems and universities whose knowledge might be called upon to solve them.[4] Second, the department was most anxious to encourage the formation of research associations for industrial research. They deplored the fact that before the war research within individual firms had been so slight, partly due to the small scale of firms, and they saw this kind of combination as the answer to our backwardness in such research. This in turn led to the problem of the role of the universities in such an arrangement. They saw universities as helping smaller firms in their vicinity, but they also saw that it would be undesirable to start research associations straight away independent of universities since this would deplete the scarce scientific staff available. On the other hand, they recognized that in some powerful and large industries with complicated problems peculiar to themselves a university link may not be necessary.[5] However they welcomed, for example, the collaboration of Imperial College with the work of the Silk Association Research Committee as a good example of the former case.

The DSIR also had the power to give financial assistance for research, and here perhaps most directly the universities became involved with the new department. In the first year they helped work already in progress on laboratory glass at King's College, London,

---

[1] *The Times*, 2 February 1916, 'The Neglect of Science'.
[2] The Neglect of Science, Report of the Proceedings at a Conference 3 May 1916 (London, 1916).
[3] Dewar, op. cit., p. 268.
[4] DSIR Report, 1915–16, p. 17.
[5] Ibid., p. 35.

that on the corrosion of metals at Liverpool which was then transferred to Imperial College, and they helped to initiate the new work on glass technology at Sheffield, the degumming of silk at Imperial College, and tin and tungsten research at the Royal School of Mines.[1] In the following year, with £1 million at their disposal, the activities of the department expanded, and they gave £1,000 a year for five years for technical optics at Imperial College, work on hot deep mines was carried on in Oxford, and nine universities were testing various types of concrete made from local aggregates. It was also clear that the department was giving aid to special projects with a very close university–industry linkage. For example, they aided Manchester's study of the flow of steam through nozzles in conjunction with British Westinghouse, and that of Liverpool, the heating of buried cables in conjunction with the Institution of Electrical Engineers.[2] Towards the end of the war, much attention was paid by the DSIR to university experimentation on food storage, possibly spurred on by the fact that earlier in 1917, at a time of intense German U-boat activity, reserves of wheat fell to only one month's supply.[3] In June 1917 the Cold Storage and Ice Association urged the importance of the systematic investigation of the problems of cold storage, and this resulted in a Fruit and Vegetable Committee to investigate, in Cambridge and at Imperial College, the storage of food at low temperature.[4] By 1918 there were various committees for food, fish, meat, fruit and vegetables, and oils and fats. As regards the projected research associations, only three were in being by 1918—photography, scientific instruments, and wool, in the latter of which Leeds University had a strong interest. But already some thirty industries were engaged in the preliminary work for the establishment of such associations. By summer 1919 they had been quickly joined by boots and shoes, cotton, sugar, iron, motor cars, and cement.[5] Both directly, by its financial support for research within the universities, and indirectly, by arousing an interest in research in firms who would thereby need university men to prosecute it, the DSIR was to prove one of the greatest benefits to the universities arising out of the war.

The final benefit to the universities and the industrial economy arising out of the war was the way in which war-time service experience changed the career aspirations of potential university entrants in the direction of industry and industrial subjects. With this impressive development of science and technology during the war, new

[1] DSIR Report, 1915–16, appendix III.
[2] DSIR Report, 1916–17, Cd. 8718, 1917.
[3] A. J. P. Taylor, op. cit., p. 138.
[4] DSIR Report, 1917–18, Cd. 9144, 1918.
[5] Ibid., 1918–19, Cd. 320, 1919.

interests were aroused, aptitudes developed and skills acquired by men in the forces for whom contact with vehicles, aeroplanes, electrical components, and the mechanisms of guns became an everyday part of their lives. It may be expected that this abnormal exposure, far more abnormal before the advent of the common motor car and wireless set, might have suggested to the most intelligent and receptive of the troops new opportunities for the post-war years back in civilian life. This was well appreciated at the time. For example, the *Liverpool Daily Post* observed that 'a great eagerness is being displayed among men who, before the War were engaged in non-constructive work such as banking, insurance and various clerical duties to take up engineering as a profession . . . Most of them have decided on this step after serving in the Army.'[1] The same could be said of chemistry, of which a Liverpool careers pamphlet noted that 'the War opened the eyes of all to the national importance of chemistry. As a consequence after the Armistice a remarkable number of men determined upon chemistry as a profession.'[2] Fortunately it is possible to analyse in more detail the effect of the war in changing aspirations towards science and industry through the interview records in connection with the scheme for the higher education of servicemen.[3] After the war priority was given in university entrance to ex-servicemen, and special awards were set aside, distributed between the subjects with a weighting towards science and technology as follows[4]

arts	4,238	medicine and dentistry	2,732
pure science and mathematics	2,407	commerce	2,975
		miscellaneous	2,241
engineering and technology	6,491		

Applicants were interviewed concerning their pre-war occupations and the careers for which they wished to train after the war. The interview forms we deal with here were for men from the Midland area, but although they were kept in Birmingham University this does not mean that all the men entered that university, presumably they took what places they could get. However, what interests us here is not what happened to them in fact, which we cannot know, but how they thought their experience in the war had changed their job aspirations. This was to have profound implications for the pool of labour after the war.

[1] *Liverpool Daily Post*, 17 May 1919.
[2] *Careers for University Trained Men and Women* (Liverpool University, 1925), p. 7.
[3] Boxes 1970/iii/1–2, Birmingham University Archives. Registrar, Higher Education for Ex-Servicemen.
[4] *Report of the Board of Education*, 1918–19, Cd. 722, 1920.

First, we took men of commissioned rank and these can be presented as follows.

Post-war career aspirations of officers seeking university places

		No.	%
A	**Already in industry and business**		
	Men staying in the same business or industrial occupation	21	25·9
	Men staying in a business or industrial occupation but aiming at a higher level	9	11·1
B	**Moving into industry and business**		
	Men changing to a business or industrial occupation from one outside	16	19·7
	Former schoolboys choosing a first career and choosing industry and business	11	13·6
C	**Moving out of industry and business or rejecting it**		
	Men leaving business and industrial occupations for non-industrial occupations	2	2·5
	Former schoolboys choosing a first career and not choosing industry and business	1	1·2
D	**Already outside industry and business**		
	Men in non-industrial occupations returning to those occupations	18	22·2
	Men in non-industrial occupations returning to other non-industrial occupations	3	3·7

Given that in this sample about 37 per cent of officers were already in industrial jobs and 26 per cent were not, the very much greater discrepancy between the 33 per cent moving into industrial jobs compared with a 4 per cent seeking to leave them, suggests that the war had had some effect on changing aspirations as the contemporary comments observed. We may present men of non-commissioned rank in the same way.

Post-war career aspirations of NCOs and other ranks seeking university places

		No.	%
A	**Already in industry and business**		
	Men staying in the same business or industrial occupation	44	22·7
	Men staying in a business or industrial occupation but aiming at a higher level	51	26·3
B	**Moving into industry and business**		
	Men changing to a business or industrial occupation from one outside	33	17·0
	Former schoolboys choosing a first career and choosing industry and business	7	3·6

C   Moving out of industry and business or rejecting it
    Men leaving business and industrial occupations
        for non-industrial occupations   3   1·5
    Former schoolboys choosing a first career and not
        choosing industry and business   0   0
D   Already outside industry and business
    Men in non-industrial occupations returning to
        those occupations   52   26·8
    Men in non-industrial occupations returning to
        other non-industrial occupations   4   2·0

With the NCOs and other ranks there were more men already in industry than in the officer group, and accordingly proportionally fewer moving into it. However, the vast discrepancy between the 20 per cent moving into industry and the 1·5 per cent moving out confirms the feature indicated in the officer table. The most common drift in both groups was that of clerks seeking to escape from the poor pay and prospects of their pre-war life into engineering, and especially into automobile engineering. It is interesting to note that the largest single pre-war occupation of non-commissioned men was schoolteaching, and the fact that this was totally superseded by engineering in the first career choice of non-commissioned ex-schoolboys adds further weight to the argument that the war was changing career aspirations in the direction of industry. We have been suggesting, then, that one of the hidden effects of the war immediately upon the universities, and then through them upon industry and society at large, was to change the career aspirations and interests of many men away from common pre-war occupations like clerkship and school-teaching into industrial careers and especially into engineering. That this was the case, that the scheme catered for it, and the universities adjusted accordingly, was yet another benefit arising from the war.

The years of the First World War were in many ways most glorious ones for the British universities. Their contribution to the war effort by their industrial science was superlative and the prosecution of the war, let alone its winning, would have been quite impossible without their services. Their work was absolutely indispensable to national survival. As *The Times* noted, 'when the story of the scientific side of the War comes to be told in full, it will be found that our modern universities have woven themselves into the very fibre of our national life in a way which had never been open to them before',[1] and H. A. L. Fisher looking back at the end of the war noted that 'all over the country people have begun to realize that

[1] *The Times*, 9 February 1916, 'Science for War, the Work of the Modern Universities'.

the universities and technical colleges have stood for a good deal in the national equipment during these times of stress and strain.'[1] At a stroke the war forced many areas of British science and technology to wipe out its backwardness *vis-à-vis* the Germans and in many of these fields actually to attain a supremacy. For example, our manganese steel helmets were superior to those of the Germans in stopping power, our cloth for uniforms was tougher, our aeroplanes were more stable. Even in former areas of drastic backwardness we overhauled the enemy. After the crash programme of 1915 and 1916 our production of novocaine anaesthetic was better than the Germans' and our mustard gas much cheaper. Finally, even in glassware the Barr and Stroud range finder, the product of two entrepreneurial professors, was regarded as better than the Zeiss model. When forced by war, we had no difficulty whatever in proving to the Germans that we could match their own scientific products when circumstances obliged us to do so. Within a year or a year and a half we were making our own magnetos, dyes, and glassware, and what had appeared to be very serious defects on the eve of the war were shown to be illusory and speedily overcome.

This in itself was a tribute to the inherent soundness of our higher scientific education. Here, again, the pre-war complaints about our supposed backwardness compared with the technical high schools of Germany proved exaggerated. For all the prestige of Chemnitz, Stuttgart, Freiberg, and Charlottenburg, when it came to a scientific contest it was evident that Leeds, Manchester, Birmingham, and Imperial College were not a jot behind. Even the 'purity' of the ancient universities in England and Scotland was vindicated against pre-war carpers who condemned their irrelevance and urged them to get into closer touch with industry. While the technological activities of the civic universities played their vital role, some of the cleverest strokes came from scientists moving from their pure disciplines to consider with a fresh eye technological problems they would not normally have been involved with. For example Pope of Cambridge's phosgene, Keith Lucas's compass, the Oxford and Cambridge mathematics for aeronautics, were all the product of a high theoretical science nurtured away from the pressing concerns of industrial application, but which could be enormously effective and innovative when called upon to be so. A most vivid case of a rapid shift from 'pure' to applied was at St Andrews, where a professor with chemical interests not apparently industrial was able to use his research to create a virtually new drug industry. If any university justified itself during the war, however, it was surely Imperial College. This brain-child of Haldane, a direct copy of and challenge to Charlottenburg, became perhaps the most important single centre dealing

[1] H. A. L. Fisher, *The Place of the University in National Life*, p. 6.

with a wider range of problems than any other. Its formation in 1907 was prescient and just in time to ward off the threat from the country that was in many ways, through Haldane, its spiritual father.

In the use of the universities for innovation there seems to have been a variation of strategy differing between products. For example, some problems seem to have been dealt with on a very narrow front, with one or two specialized centres taking responsibility for them. This was the case with textiles and dyes at Leeds and Manchester, with glass in London and Sheffield, acetone in Manchester, the sugars in St Andrews, and the nitrate fixing at University College. Other problems seem to have been dealt with by a number of different centres, though yet without large numbers being involved. The hydrophone in London and Lancashire universities, aircraft structures at Bangor, Bristol, Oxford, Cambridge, and London, and explosives testing in Liverpool, Birmingham, Manchester, and Leeds. Yet others again seem to have been dealt with very commonly over a very wide front with almost all universities taking part. This was the case with the crash programme for novocaine, toluol and the concrete experiments under the DSIR which were widespread throughout the country. The first category was clearly using the specialisms and interests of old established centres, Procter's leather centre at Leeds for example, and in these cases little could be gained from duplicating effort and much lost by diffusing scarce technical workers. With the second category, apart from the explosives testing which was scattered for geographical convenience, there seems to have been the assumption that if a few centres worked on the problem then one would be likely to strike the solution or pull ahead of the others. This was especially the case with the hydrophone, where East London College developed the instrument with directional properties. Since this was a totally new product, devised by physicists new to the problem, there was less need to have one centre of scarce talent. There seemed less justification for the third policy of having vast numbers all doing the same thing, most rather inefficiently, and this was only justified by the urgent need for the production of novocaine in the early years of the war. After 1916 this kind of crash programme was dropped. In general it seems to be true that the most successful projects were those in which one or two centres were involved rather than those where activity was very widely diffused among a large number of universities.

The war was thus a period of enormous fruitfulness for scientific industry and for the universities who had made it possible. But for the economy as a whole it was a disaster for, by removing the comfortable cushion of invisible earnings that had permitted us the luxury of an adverse balance of trade in the nineteenth century, it brought near the dangers of an adverse balance of payments for the first time since the 1840s. The reduction of this supporting role played by finance placed the brunt of the burden on our capacity to maintain trade in efficiently produced industrial goods and hence placed an even greater importance upon science and technology and hence on the universities as the supporters of such 'new' industry. Sir Alfred Ewing,[1] looking to the end of the war, saw this clearly. After the war they would have to recreate the wealth destroyed and

> . . . it will be for the universities to bring science to bear on manufacture to see that no barriers are allowed to come between the laboratory and the workshop, to promote the nuptials of theory and practice . . . It rests partly with manufacturers and partly with the universities to see that this handicap to national prosperity is removed.

The war had given much new science to industry and great prestige and recognition to the universities, while a closer involvement between the partners had been forged. It remained to be seen how these benefits could be realized as they moved from war into a peace that in many ways was to prove as hazardous for both of them.

[1] Sir Alfred Ewing, 'The Universities and the New Era', 11 July 1916, reprinted in *An Engineer's Outlook* (London, 1933).

9

The Inter-war Years
1919-39—I

*'One of the many lessons of the Great War was that industry
needed all the help that science could give her. That help could
best be given through the universities by training experts and
conducting research'.*[1]

'Hyman Levy: *So you agree that universities, whatever else they
are doing are unconsciously playing their part in
assisting industrialists to carry on their business?*
'Julian Huxley: *Yes that is so. . . .'*[2]

In the inter-war years the university population of Great Britain
stood at around 40,000 in the early and mid 1920s, then rose steadily
from 1926 to 1932 to around 50,000 where it remained fairly constantly throughout the 1930s. In contrast to the relative stability of
the universities, in a hiatus between the great expansions of the
pre-1914 and post-1945 periods, the experience of industry was
necessarily far more volatile. Post-war boom gave way to severe
slump in 1920, followed in turn by a modest recovery in the later
1920s. This, although less marked than that of other major industrial
countries, was yet as powerful as the 1930s recovery in its beneficial
effects on graduate employment. The good times of the 1920s were
ended by depression initiated by the American crash of 1929 and the
crisis of 1931. Recovery followed, notably from 1933, though it was
interrupted by the milder recession of 1938. But the broad trends of
the moment of the economy masked wide divergences of fortune
between the declining basic old industries of the nineteenth century,
often located in the North of England, and the rising new industries
of the South, highly science-conscious and developing technologies
originating from the turn of the century. It is the purpose of the

[1] Pro-Chancellor Alsop of Liverpool University, *Liverpool Courier*,
29 November 1918.
[2] Conversation of Professor Hyman Levy and Julian Huxley in Julian Huxley,
Scientific Research and Social Needs (London, 1934), p. 22.

next two chapters to examine the interplay of the universities and industry in these conditions. This chapter will consider the new factors creating a greater need for graduates on the part of industry and industrial attitudes towards graduates. Then the contribution of the universities to industrial science and business education will be examined. The next chapter will deal quantitatively with the flow of manpower through the universities to industry, the intake from schools, the output to industry, and the universities' suspected role in deflecting graduates away from industry. Next, from the industrial side the areas and rates of absorption of graduates by firms and salary levels will be considered, and finally the reaction of university opinion against this increasing involvement of the universities and industry in the inter-war years. Both chapters accordingly should be regarded as one sequence.

We have examined earlier those various conditions creating the involvement of the universities and industry before 1914; however, some new elements were introduced into the situation in the inter-war years. First, many of the new industries of these years were scientifically very sophisticated. It was a period of the cumulative working out of developments in radio, aircraft, motor vehicles, synthetic fibres, dyes, and so forth, many of which had been virtually created by the needs of war and all of which called for a high degree of scientific and technical expertise.[1] Moreover, many old industries were forced into technical improvement under the spur of depression,[2] and some old industries so changed their techniques as to render the common distinction of 'old' and 'new' industries practically meaningless. Such examples were the application of X-ray analysis to textile fibres and the cold rolling of steel, or the altering of the chemical structure of cotton fibre to render it crease resistant.

While technical change was scarcely new, organized research became one of the leading sources of invention in the inter-war years and this by its very nature required graduate labour. Research became important in the 1920s for a variety of reasons.[3] First, the experience of the war had shown the possibility of universities, firms, and government departments being geared to the solution of specific research problems as a basis for production. Second, in chemical and particularly in mechanical processes, the new mass production conditions of manufacture made research as a distinct activity all the more necessary. Modification on the job became far

[1] R. S. Sayers, 'The Springs of Technical Progress in Britain, 1919–39', *Economic Journal*, June 1950. H. W. Richardson, 'The New Industries between the Wars', *Oxford Economic Papers*, vol. XIII, 1961.
[2] *Britain in Depression* (British Association, London, 1935), pp. 158–9, 257, 276, specifically noted technical improvement spurred on by depression in coal, steel, and shipbuilding.
[3] Michael Sanderson, 'Research and the Firm in British Industry 1919–39', *Science Studies*, April 1972, examines this more fully.

less possible when vast capitals had been sunk in plant for processes which scarcely allowed any possibility of interference when they were set in train. In these circumstances research in laboratory conditions beforehand became a vital adjunct to test the feasibility of large-scale manufacture.[1] Third, the research department became a useful nursery for introducing into the firm able graduates who may later move to management.[2]

The rapid formation of research departments by firms was a remarkable feature of the years at the end of the war and the early 1920s. Tootal's and Courtauld's began theirs in 1918, and among the electrical firms Metro-Vickers began their laboratory in 1917 and BTH had one by 1919, while the great GEC laboratories at Wembley and those of Siemens in Preston were opened in 1923. Apart from these, by 1922 Lever's, Boots, Kynoch's, Brown and Firth, Brunner Mond, Chance's, Adam Hilger, Nobel's, and Burroughs Wellcome, merely to select some of the main ones, were all undertaking research of first-rate importance.[3] Research within the firm rose markedly during the 1930s from 422 firms spending £1·7 million in 1930 to 566 firms spending £5·4 million in 1938.[4] At the same time research associations undertaking research for whole industries arose under the DSIR, creating yet further demand for the research scientist. Accordingly industry had to turn more to the graduate. The universities in turn, with the impossibility of travel to Germany during the war, had started their own PH.D. higher research degrees, at the same time providing the new type of advanced graduate for research.

It was not only the increasingly scientific character of industry in these years that created a demand for graduates; it was also felt by several eminent business leaders that management was becoming more difficult and called for better educated and more intelligent minds than before. Part of the difficulty arose from the severe depression of the period which increased the keenness of competition and the dangers of failure. But also the actual performance of the job seemed to many to be becoming more demanding. Sir Robert Waley Cohen of Shell thought that, compared with the past, industry now 'demands exact thought and power to analyse a difficult and complicated situation'.[5] Likewise Sir Kenneth Lee of Tootal's, perhaps the most dynamic figure in the cotton industry, held that higher management needed 'minds trained to appreciate reports on highly specialized and complex matters of production, merchanting and

---

[1] Hugh Quigley, 'Engineering in the Economic Development of Manchester', *The Woman Engineer*, March 1924.

[2] A. P. M. Fleming in *Daily Dispatch Industrial Survey*, 1936.

[3] A. P. M. Fleming and J. G. Pearce, *Research in Industry* (London, 1922).

[4] *Industry and Research, Report of the FBI Industrial Research Committee*, October 1943.

[5] Report of the Proceedings of the Fourth Congress of the Universities of the British Empire, 1931, 'The University Graduate in Commerce and Industry'.

finance and to give sound judgement thereon'.[1] The complexity was both technical and organizational. Not only was research more technical but so also was the management of production, and this called for a massive upgrading of jobs and higher demands on the labour required to fulfil them. R. H. Clayton addressing Manchester businessmen observed that, whereas formerly university men in industry were predominantly researchers, now they had invaded works control, 'the mass of graduates is at the present time employed in controlling works operations previously run by skilled artisans, who are, under the complexities of modern methods, now unable to fill these positions'.[2]

There were also complexities of an organizational kind. Through the process of rationalization and merger several industries became more concentrated, with larger firms and wider integrations that called for a greater degree of administrative ability at the top. This was certainly true in bricks, metal boxes, sugar, soap, steel tubes, and flour milling, for example.[3] T. M. Knox of the Oxford Appointments Board considered that 'the demand for graduates in business is perhaps contemporaneous with the amalgamation of firms into large units, and in fact demand arises in the main from such industrial combines'.[4] Similarly, the Liberal Industrial Inquiry of 1925, after commending a university education as necessary for the higher direction of industry, noted 'the present tendency towards the creation of large industrial units' as 'a particular reason for industry to select administrators of the broadest and most highly educated outlook'.[5] Another change in managerial organization resulting from increased scale was the tendency towards functionalism. In small firms the old style of manager dealt by himself with a wide range of technical and personnel issues, but increased scale had led to increased specialization of managerial functions and consequently greater expertise demanding in turn a higher level of education.[6] A. S. Rowntree, for example, observed that ' . . . today is the day of the specialized. The day of the all round manager is disappearing. Businesses, or at any rate the larger ones, are becoming functionalized.'[7] Both these characteristics of undertaking research and the

---

[1] Sir Kenneth Lee, cited in Sir David Milne Watson, 'University Men in Commerce and Industry', *Oxford*, winter, 1934.
[2] R. H. Clayton, 'Training Leaders for Industry', *Memoirs and Proceedings of the Manchester Literary and Philosophical Society*, vol. LXXII, 1937–8.
[3] Richard Evely and I. M. D. Little, *Concentration in British Industry* (Cambridge, 1960).
[4] T. M. Knox, 'Graduates in Business,' *Oxford Magazine*, 20 January 1938.
[5] *Britain's Industrial Future . . . Report of the Liberal Inquiry* (London, 1925).
[6] L. Urwick, *Management of Tomorrow* (London, 1933), p. 164, and especially pt 4, 'Training for Management'.
[7] The Association for Education in Industry and Commerce Report on Education for Management, May 1928, p. 5. See J. Dummelow, op. cit.,

formation of large units and bureaucratization were especially features of the rising new industries and both created an extra demand for graduates in these years.

Expertise, however, was not enough. It was felt in these difficult times that extra, less definable qualities were necessary, and that they were to be found in the university man, not so much for his skills, as for his wider culture. Sir Kenneth Lee considered 'a bigger outlook is necessary and that is more likely to be produced by a university education', the Liberal Inquiry referred to a 'wider outlook', Knox to a 'broader vision', and the UGC 1925 report to a 'breadth of outlook'. This was all somewhat broad and vague, but the cliché expressed an implied dissatisfaction with the narrowness of the technical college product and the ex-apprentice. There was a belief that the new ideal needed by industry was the graduate with horizons widened through social mixing, sport, the OTC, and travel— the NUS, for example, became very active in student travel in the 1930s. All this produced what came to be called the 'right type' in industrial and careers literature of the period, superseding the 'right stamp' and 'right calibre' metaphors of earlier periods.

There were, however, other less ethereal motives for looking to the graduate that were more important in these years than formerly. First, although the university population rose only modestly, the proportion of university students per head of the population rose fairly markedly from one per 1,146 to one per 929 between 1921 and 1939, a trend encouraged in the lower levels of society by the state scholarships and local authority awards for university entrants. Since intelligent boys were thus more likely to go to university in the inter-war years, firms had less likelihood of picking up the talented youth straight from school, and had instead to wait to catch him at a later stage as a university graduate. Indeed, the depressed state of the economy increased this probability of attending university for two reasons. In the first place, job opportunities and the very prospects of work were greater for the graduate than for even the skilled apprentice, since the former always had teaching as a possible alternative. Second, in depression, as several observers pointed out, a university education was often entered simply to bide time in the hope that conditions would improve.[1] In fact, this seemed to be the case, for it was over the years of depression that

---

p. 85, for a good specific example in the case of Metro-Vickers where in the 1920s some functions of foremen were centralized into a specialized rate fixing department dealing with the works as a whole.

[1] Edwin Deller, *Tendencies in University Education* (Oxford, 1933), University of London Institute of Education Studies and Reports, No. 3, p. 10. This was not an uncommon observation; see *University of Liverpool Society Chronicle*, July 1931, p. 8, and 'The Overproduction of Graduates', *The Weekend Review*, 2 July 1932.

the university population climbed from 40,000 to 50,000, whereas in more normal times of the twenties and thirties it was fairly constant. For these reasons firms had now more often to catch young talent at a higher level up the educational ladder.

A further reason why many of the most important firms in British industry turned to the graduate in these years of organizational growth and technical change was the problem of management succession. Part of the problem arose from the war itself. During this time recruitment had ceased in many firms and some of the younger workers who had gone to fight had been killed off, leaving in the post-war years an age structure in the firm divided more sharply than usual into older managers and youthful newcomers. As the older ones came to retire, so they cast an eye vainly over the ex-elementary school and still relatively young labour force or the equally ageing and even worse-educated old style foremen. Consequently, managements thought in terms of bringing in graduates and expecting them to rise to top management within a very short time. Many firms approached the Cambridge Appointments Board with this problem,[1] seeking Cambridge graduates as a solution. For example, at Tate and Lyle's process work in the 1920s had been managed by relatively uneducated men who had risen within the firm, and it was intended eventually to replace them with twenty or thirty graduates. Graduates were especially necessary for higher sales management. Pilkington's tried selling their luxury Vita glass through ordinary commercial travellers, without success, and then formed a special marketing board for Vita with a picked team of graduates in 1929. In this most pointed way they introduced graduates to sidestep the traditional labour on the sales side. Rural industries like Clark's also found that local labour was not throwing up the higher calibre personnel necessary for a national firm and turned to Cambridge graduates to fill in the gap. What the Cambridge Appointments Officer noted of Pilkington's was true of all —'they hope to get men who will fill all the higher posts in the firm. This move represents a quite definite break with previous policy. They are aiming for a higher type altogether.'

However, if many firms turned eagerly to the graduate, yet there

[1] For example, Burmah Oil, 1920; Ryland's of Warrington, 1925; **Gas Light and Coke Company**, 1925; Tate and Lyle, 1928; J. Dickinson, 1928, **Tootal's,** 1929; Pilkington's Vita, 1929; C. and J. Clark, 1929; Coast Lines, 1933; Pilkington's, 1933; Ocean Accident and Guarantee Corporation, 1933; Rio Tinto, 1933; Atlas Engraving Company, 1936; Norfolk Rush and Reed Industries, 1938; Longman's, 1938; London Passenger Transport Board, 1939. These are taken from a collection of several hundred private memoranda of the Cambridge Appointments Board. I am particularly grateful to the board for allowing me to use these documents. Since they were confidential the author will not be cited and on occasion the firm concerned will not be revealed. Henceforth they will be referred to as CAB Memoranda.

was still a body of opinion hostile to his reception into industry. Lord Leverhulme was perhaps the most eminent businessman noted for his scepticism about graduates. He believed that 'the Oxford graduate is not a patch on the "hard knocks" graduate',[1] the grounds of his resistance being that the knowledge of book-trained students was of less value than that of practical craftsmen.[2] That the universities did not teach useful practical knowledge was a prime grievance among businessmen who affected to despise graduates.[3] A second ground of scepticism was the view that universities led graduates to 'hold decided opinions without first giving them the sound knowledge on which those opinions should be based'.[4] A third argument, a curious reversal of the second, was that practical men of business made decisions subconsciously and a university training ruined this facility by replacing it with logical thought without common sense.[5] A fourth argument was that twenty-one, after completing a degree, was too old to start a business career,[6] while a fifth was that the irregular hours induced by university work ruined men for the discipline of business; both Leverhulme and Benn believed this. A sixth ground of suspicion of the graduate was more serious, namely the tradition of irresponsible hooliganism among students in the 1920s[7] and then the notorious 'King and Country' debate in 1933 evoking Churchill's condemnation of university students as 'callow ill-tutored youths'. All this cast doubt on the claims that universities were fit places to train the sober and reliable young men needed to run business concerns. But underlying many of these

[1] *Progress* (Lever's house magazine), October 1924, p. 206.
[2] Lord Leverhulme, 'Victims of Education', 1917, in *The Six Hour Day and other Industrial Questions* (London, 1918), pp. 221–30. His son noted of him that 'on the whole his prejudices were perhaps against the university man'; *Viscount Leverhulme by his Son* (London, 1927), p. 145. Lever's nephew, J. L. Tillotson, sought to overcome his uncle's prejudices against graduates; Charles Wilson, *A History of Unilever, a Study in Economic Growth and Social Change* (London, 1954), vol. I, p. 50.
[3] See Julian Hall, *Alma Mater, or the Future of Oxford and Cambridge* (London, 1928), p. 89, and Keith Briant, *Oxford Limited* (London, 1937), pp. 271–2, for a defence of universities against this attack. The former also included an attack specifically on Leverhulme.
[4] Anon, 'Business Careers for Undergraduates', *Oxford Magazine*, 30 January 1930, citing the views of Sir Ernest Benn the publisher.
[5] Lord Melchett, 'The Relation of the Universities and Industry', *The Universities Review*, October 1928, cited this argument with which he heartily disagreed.
[6] Sir David Milne Watson 'University Men in Commerce and Industry', *Oxford*, winter, 1934, cited this though he disagreed with it. However, Sir Robert MacAlpine and A. W. Gamage thought this was so. *Evening Standard*, 13 January 1927, 'Is the University Man a Failure in Business?'.
[7] For example, the Pussyfoot riot at King's, London, 1919; the riot in a theatre by undergraduate ex-servicemen of Liverpool University, 1920; the Phineas War, 1922, between University and King's Colleges, London; the Exeter statue-painting scandal of the early 1920s, and others.

arguments was a genuine fear that the university graduate, because of his scholastic success, 'pretends to a knowledge and authority which he cannot justify',[1] and this makes him unwilling to settle to the humdrum tasks of business life and, even worse, makes him impossible for others to work with. C. F. G. Masterman considered 'the class instinct of the undergraduate of Cambridge and Oxford makes him difficult and impossible in business and industry'.[2] This was best expressed in a student cartoon from Manchester University in 1924 which depicted an enthusiastic young graduate, hands in pockets, haranguing a dismayed managing director with the words 'moreover I'll soon put this moth eaten old works on its feet for you', to the consternation of his secretary and an ancestral portrait on the wall.[3] It was an amusing caricature, but underneath lay the serious unease that many conventional businessmen felt about graduates and their pretensions.

But whatever the grounds for suspicion against graduates in industry, some having sound foundations and others being merely bizarre, informed opinion tended to move more in their favour as the death of Leverhulme in 1927 removed the last great reactionary. The pro-graduate views of such business leaders as Waley Cohen, Melchett, Kenneth Lee, and David Milne Watson were also in accord with the facts. Industry moved more towards the universities and the universities were more than willing to meet it halfway. We should now turn to examine the universities' half of the link through their development of fields of teaching and research orientated to science in the service of industry.

The response from the universities in developing studies of industrial relevance was considerable, and we are here concerned to highlight specialities and fields which certain universities were particularly prominent in developing for the service of local and national industry.

Cambridge had an unequalled reputation in pure science and especially physics. On the other hand, the great achievements of the Cavendish Laboratory had little effect on industry at the time; indeed some argued that they were diverting attention from traditional industrial themes with positively harmful results for industry.[4] There was, however, no doubt of the importance of industrial back-

[1] Irvine Masson, 'University Training and Business Posts', *Durham University Journal*, March 1935, citing E. A. Eaton's Presidential Address to the Durham Union Society.
[2] C. F. G. Masterman, 'The Boy, Where Should He Go?', *Evening Standard*, 11 January 1927.
[3] 'George M', 'That Degree Feeling' (cartoon), *The Serpent* (Manchester University), 18 November 1924.
[4] A. W. Haslett, 'Scientific Careers, the next Thirty Years', *Journal of Careers* June 1937.

ing for the extension of Cambridge science in the inter-war years. Money came from the oil companies for chemistry in 1919, from Mond and Austin for physics, and Sir John Siddeley for aeronautics in the 1930s, and it was in this latter decade that the building expansion of Cambridge physics was most marked.[1] Of immediate industrial application, however, Cambridge was perhaps best known for its engineering school. The professor throughout this time, Sir Charles Inglis, had close contacts with industry as a consultant, especially in bridge and railway work,[2] while aeronautical engineering was a new post-war departure.[3] Low temperature research was another Cambridge forte which had important implications for the food preservation and refrigeration industries.[4] Oxford, by contrast, had little part to play in industrial science at this time. Lindemann revived the Clarendon Laboratory from its abysmal state, and he was on close personal terms with Lord Melchett and Sir Harry McGowan of ICI as well as Nuffield,[5] but, like Cambridge's science, Oxford's was pure rather than applied.[6] Indeed, Tizard, a staunch advocate of science at Oxford, did not consider it wise to develop a large school of applied work.[7] At the end of this period Lord Nuffield sought to link Oxford more closely to the industrial world with grants of money for Nuffield College and for physical chemistry in 1937, to bridge the 'gulf which at present exists between academic studies and practical affairs'. The part-time fellows of Nuffield especially were to enrich the university with the 'fruits of their practical experience . . . in industry or commerce'.[8] But for the most part Oxford did not claim to be a technological university and it would be irrelevant to criticize it for not doing what it did not set out to do.

Almost every conceivable science was studied at London University, but here we may isolate certain fields in which it played a special role. London was chiefly instrumental in meeting the shortage of chemical engineers in the inter-war years with the Ramsay Chemical Engineering Laboratory at University College powerfully supported by ICI, Lever's, and Shell. The new professor, E. C. Williams, formerly of the British Dyestuffs Corporation and National

---

[1] J. P. C. Roach, 'The University of Cambridge' in *Victoria County History of Cambridgeshire*, vol. III, 'The City and the University', pp. 295–9.

[2] T. J. N. Hilken, *Engineering at Cambridge University, 1783–1965*, p. 171.

[3] CUR 39.54. Professorship of Aeronautical Engineering. Items 1 and 11a.

[4] Ezer Griffith, 'Refrigeration Engineering', *Journal of Careers*, October 1937. Low Temperature Research at Cambridge was a joint DSIR and university project.

[5] The Earl of Birkenhead, *The Prof. in Two Worlds*, p. 101.

[6] C. N. Hinshelwood, 'Laboratories and Research in Natural Science', *Oxford University Handbook*, 1939.

[7] H. T. Tizard, 'The Needs of Oxford Science', *Oxford* (special number), February 1937.

[8] *The Times*, 13 October 1937.

Benzol, pointed out that such had been the development in plant that chemical expertise was becoming even more important for the engineers building the plant than for the industrial chemists who used it, hence the necessity for the fusion of the sciences.[1] Industry certainly regarded the department a success; its graduates were absorbed into industry even before they finished their courses, and as a result of research within the department a new industry was started in Coventry, the production of bi-metallic sheets of nickel and copper by electrolysis.[2] King's College, too, was noted for chemical engineering and also engaged in photochemistry as one of its main lines of research. In physics they made special studies in electricity, radio waves, and thermionic vacuum tubes, claiming that they proved excellent qualifications for men entering industry.[3] Imperial College naturally had a wide range of sciences, but it is worth drawing attention to its particular concern with aeronautics. Sir Basil Zaharoff had founded the chair there with Sir Richard Glazebrook as the first professor in 1919. Within the industry C. R. Fairey and Handley Page took a particular interest in the department, and Zaharoff expected Churchill to keep an eye on it.[4] With good fortune, in 1929 Henry Tizard, celebrated for his aeronautics work during the war, became Rector of Imperial College, further cementing the close links of the college with this new technology.[5] In one or two other areas the college also played an important part in British industrial science. Sir Patrick Linstead's work created the Monastral pigments marketed by ICI in the 1930s,[6] and it was also a leading centre for geophysics and chemical engineering —both areas in which output of graduates was short in the inter-war years.[7]

By virtue of their origins the civic universities of the North of England and the Midlands remained closely linked with local industry at several points. Manchester University science was first-rate; indeed that the university had the services of Rutherford, Bohr,

[1] E. C. Williams, *The Aims and Future Work of the Ramsay Memorial Laboratory of Chemical Engineering; University of London, University College Department of Chemical Engineering* (1931); H. Hale Bellot, *University College, London, 1826–1926* (London, 1929).
[2] University College London Report, 1937–8.
[3] H. W. Cromer, 'Industry and the Universities I—King's College, London', *JC*, September 1933. It is a pity that this series was not continued. Annual Reports of King's College, London, 1928–1939, *passim*.
[4] Zaharoff Chair of Aviation, 1918; 1919–23. File 1120, Imperial College Archives. Letter, Sir Basil Zaharoff to W. S. Churchill, 18 November 1919.
[5] Ronald W. Clark, *Tizard*, chapter 4.
[6] 'A History of the Chemistry Department at Imperial College' unpublished typescript in the college, 1963, p. 62.
[7] W. D. Wright, 'History of the Physics Department, Imperial College', p. 24, and 'History of the Department of Chemical Engineering and Chemical Technology 1912–39' in Imperial College Archives.

Robert Robinson, Alexander Todd, and Lawrence Bragg within these years indicates its very high importance.[1] On the other hand, the excellence of its physics had already swung this field away from the traditional local industrial interests to which it had related in the nineteenth century.[2] However, there were certain fields in which Manchester and its faculty of technology had valuable vitalizing effects on the new sectors of the Lancashire economy. The electrical industry in particular benefited. Sir Ambrose Fleming recommended Manchester for those seeking a degree in electro-communication engineering[3] and Metro-Vickers of Trafford Park sent its best people there for training. The university also had close links with the Chloride Electrical Storage Company, the largest battery makers in Europe, who drew most of their research staff from there, while the university was associated with the company's metallurgical research.[4] Indeed, metallurgy was one of the growth points of the university in the 1920s.[5] On the industrial chemistry side, Manchester had special facilities for dyestuffs research and close association with the British Dyestuffs Corporation (later ICI) research laboratory at Blackley.[6] Professor Robert Robinson had already worked there before he moved into academic life and Heilbron, who moved to Manchester from Liverpool, maintained the ICI link. Finally, in the 1930s Manchester was rare if not unique in Britain in providing university education for the paper and building industries.[7]

Of particular local maritime relevance, Liverpool University was already by 1920 one of the two main centres of marine engineering education in England, based on the Harrison Hughes laboratories. Also the university developed two specialisms of particular value for the port and its produce. J. Wemyss Anderson was a noted pioneer of refrigeration engineering, putting cold storage on a scientific footing, while Professor Percy Hilditch transformed the chemistry of fats in the twenties and thirties, vital for the West

[1] W. L. Bragg, 'The Physics Department', *Journal of the University of Manchester*, 1938.
[2] 'Put and Take', 'An Appeal', *The Serpent*, 31 January 1921, for such a complaint about the university's disengagement from local industry. This was the magazine of the Students' Union.
[3] Sir Ambrose Fleming, 'Electro-communication as a Career', *JC*, July–August 1930.
[4] 'The Chloride Electric Storage Co.', *JC*, July–August 1931.
[5] Description of the New Metallurgical Laboratories opened by Sir George Beilby, F.R.S. (Manchester, 1923).
[6] 'The British Dyestuffs Industry', *JC*, June 1926. Colin Campbell, 'The Chemistry Department', *Journal of the University of Manchester*, 1939.
[7] Manchester Municipal College of Technology Jubilee, 1902–1952 (this was the faculty of technology of the university). It is worth noting that the official history—H. B. Charlton, *Portrait of a University, 1851–1951*—is highly misleading in having virtually nothing on the inter-war years' science of the university.

Africa trade and the fat processing chemical industries of the hinter-land.[1] Finally, at the local level, the university was the main centre of oceanographic research on the English north-west coast, and in the 1920s it was the professor's stated policy to relate his work to the Irish Sea fishery and the Manx lobster hatcheries.[2] In service of the wider national economy, Liverpool was a major centre of electrical engineering. It had particularly close links with British Insulated Cables and the Automatic Telephone Company, while their Professor of Applied Electricity co-ordinated all experimental work in wireless throughout Britain for the Radio Research Board.[3] In chemistry, the department had very close links with ICI and Lever's who each year made large donations for research, while Sir Ian Heilbron, the Professor of Organic Chemistry, sat on the Organic Research Committee of ICI. It was a fitting and natural relationship with the chemical industry of the Mersey basin. They also helped to fill an important national shortage of scientific expertise by specializing in geology[4] and especially oil from 1919.[5]

In the Midlands, these were the decades of the striking rise of Nottingham University with the outstanding benefactions of Lord Trent. One of their first post-war actions was the establishment of a separate department of textiles in 1922, while the university also served the local coal mining industry, its department being supported by a levy on the coal owners. Sir Jesse Boot's gifts to the college began in 1920 and made possible the building of engineering laboratories between 1930 and 1934 catering for civil and mechanical engineering. Nottingham University, like the city, was thus a mixture of old basic and new industries in the inter-war years. Most of the university's money came from a new scientific industry though its own industrial contribution was chiefly to the old ones of coal and hosiery.[6] Leicester presents an interesting Midlands contrast. A more prosperous town, and more committed to light new industry than its neighbour, its firms were, however, smaller and less able or willing to support the university.[7] Accordingly, while the college developed a normal range of subjects, nothing emerged of special interest to industry.

---

[1] 'Thomas Percy Hilditch, 1886–1965', *Biographical Memoirs of Fellows of the Royal Society*, November 1966.
[2] Sir D'Arcy Thompson MSS. St Andrews University. Letter, Jas. Johnstone to D'A. T., 22 January 1920. '. . . it's rather useful that we should deal with the industry . . . So I say trawling be it. I'm sure it will be appreciated.' For the lobsters see Vice-Chancellor's Report, 1926.
[3] *Liverpool Courier*, 20 January 1920 and 4 June 1920.
[4] *The Jane Herdman Laboratories of Geology* (1929?).
[5] *Liverpool Daily Post*, 3 September 1919. See also 3 April 1919; the Liverpool Geological Society urged this course on the university because there were then only two schools of petroleum geology in the country.
[6] A. C. Wood, *A History of the University College, Nottingham, 1881–1948.*
[7] Jack Simmons, *New University*, p. 69.

Birmingham University on the other hand, a much older institution in the heartland of heavy industry, inevitably had much closer links. Here mining remained a particular strength under Sir John Cadman, the cabinet adviser on coal and petroleum and later Chairman of the Anglo-Persian Oil Company. In 1921 the Doncaster Coal Owners' Research Association was moved to the university under Cadman, so that during the inter-war years the mining research laboratory had a mixed university-industrial character. Its members worked on safety and illumination in hot and deep mines and on the Bergius process of hydrogenation of coal, turning it into thick oil under pressure.[1] They also had especially good facilities for coal dressing and preparation for marketing, and for ore crushing and dressing, as well as a working mine under the university grounds itself.[2] But beyond its orthodox mineral mining education, Birmingham was especially valuable in widening its activities into oil engineering, a more promising field in which university expertise and men were lacking.[3] In chemistry, Birmingham was foremost in the development of carbohydrate chemistry in the tradition of Irvine's school at St Andrews, and it was the first university to synthesize vitamin C in 1933.[4] Its brewing work continued and this moved into a £100,000 laboratory block in 1927 with other biological subjects, and was the chief centre for higher scientific biochemistry training in this industry.[5]

The Yorkshire universities were not to be outdone in serving the local economy.[6] At Leeds, mining and geology were important studies, with pioneering work on mapping the concealed east Midland coalfield and on rescue apparatus. Equally significant was the university's contribution to the woollen textile industry of Yorkshire. W. T. Astbury used X-ray techniques to reveal the molecular framework of wool, while the importance of the sulphur linkages in wool fibre and their breaking as a cause of shrinking was for the first time appreciated.[7] Leeds' unique specialism in leather remained strong,

[1] Reports on the Work of the Mining Research Laboratory, University of Birmingham, 1921-4.
[2] University of Birmingham Mining Department, Opening of the Coal Treating Laboratory, 25 November 1926, and Opening of the Ore Dressing Laboratory, 16 December 1931.
[3] Report on the Work of the Department of Oil Engineering and Refining, 1926-8.
[4] S. R. Carter and Maurice Stacey, 'The School of Chemistry in the University of Birmingham', *JRIC*, August 1954.
[5] E. W. Vincent and P. Hinton, *The University of Birmingham, its History and Significance*.
[6] A. N. Shimmin, *The University of Leeds, the First Half Century*.
[7] A. T. King, 'A University's Assistance to Industry', *Yorkshire Observer Trade Review*, 23 January 1937, and *Yorkshire Post*, 16 November 1937. I am grateful to Professor Whewell for being allowed access to the news-cuttings books of the department.

dealing with the protein chemistry of skins and the mineral tanning of leather.[1] Lines of research were also developed linking with the new industries, notably aeronautics through Professor Brodetsky, a war-time pioneer of aerodynamics. Sheffield University was somewhat less diversified in industrial research than Leeds though it had close links with local mining and metallurgy. The particular importance of the mining department was its pioneering work on the devising and testing of flameproof electrical equipment for mines; indeed, it was said that 'the extensive use of electrical plant in mines today has been largely rendered possible by the work carried out in the department'.[2] In metallurgy a new laboratory was built with money from Sir Robert Hadfield, the pioneer of manganese and hardened steels, and from 1934 attention was paid to the scientific aspects of metal foundries. In particular, they were pioneers of the cold working of steel, stamping, wire drawing, and cold rolling.[3] Finally, Sheffield was famous for its glass research that we have seen starting during the war under Professor Turner.[4] Their chief work was with container, tableware, and electrical glass, unlike the optics of the London colleges. The sheer change in physical appearance of the humble jam jar between the 1920s and the 1930s, for instance, was but one of the important ways in which this department was helping to change both industry and the amenities it provided. Finally, Hull, emerging as the third Yorkshire university in the late 1920s, shrewdly chose its own specialisms. Principal Morgan planned to link university science with fishing, through marine biology, and to the port, through seed crushing and oil extraction, while of more national importance they also did aeronautics work.[5]

The universities of the South and West more usually found their strengths in engineering, physics and the food industries than in the basic industry technologies of the North of England. From 1928 the college at Southampton was seeking to become an independent University of Wessex providing engineering training and research for a revivified port and city.[6] Internal combustion engineering became a special forte of the college under Wing Commander Professor

[1] *Department of Leather Industries Prospectus, University of Leeds, 1933.*
[2] *Sheffield Telegraph,* 4 November 1936. Reports on Research Work . . . Departments of Mining and Fuel Technology, 1928–1937.
[3] University of Sheffield, Reports of the Research Department for the Cold Working of Steel and other Ferrous Metals, 1932–1936.
[4] 'William Ernest Stephen Turner 1881–1963', *Biographical Memoirs of Fellows of the Royal Society,* vol. X, November 1964. A. W. Chapman, *The Story of a Modern University: the History of the University of Sheffield.* The glass museum within the department at Sheffield well illustrates the comment about jam jars, a tacit tribute to the department's work.
[5] A. E. Morgan, 'The Project of a University College at Hull', *The University Bulletin,* April 1927.
[6] University of Wessex, an Appeal to Southampton, 1928. 'The Trend of Engineering in the South', *Wessex,* June 1928.

T. R. Cave-Brown-Cave, especially in problems of high speed engines.[1] He began the work on the suppression of noise that has broadened into one of Southampton's well-known specialisms of the present time.[2] They had close links with local engineering firms Thornycroft's, Avro, and Supermarine Aviation, that were powerful prestige builders for the struggling University College.[3] Bristol University, too, was strong in engineering and maintained pre-war and war-time links with the local aircraft industry, though the chief forte of Bristol in the inter-war years, its physics based on the superb new Wills laboratories, had little immediate industrial significance.[4] On the chemistry side, Leverhulme endowed a chair of physical chemistry in 1919, whose first occupant, J. W. McBain, worked on the colloidal chemistry of soap[5] in the twenties. Less usual in character was Bristol's contribution to the food industry. First, from 1921 they supervised the Campden Research Station, which virtually created canning as a scientific industry in Britain from the mid 1920s.[6] Chivers, Hartley's, and the cws were among the business interests on the management committee. The other food industry connection of Bristol was with cider and perry manufacture. The Long Ashton station established in 1903 had been part of the university since 1912 and their scientific work developed cider into a national industry as well as creating non-alcoholic apple juice and blackcurrant juice as commercial drinks. Equally important, the discovery in 1924 of potash deficiency as a major cause of fruit failure revolutionized the efficiency of industrial fruit production in England.[7] By contrast, the other two universities of the South and West had little industrial significance at this time. Reading stands apart as being deliberately and wisely orientated towards agriculture and does not concern us.[8] Exeter, young and struggling, intended to become a centre of research for the economy of the far west[9] yet one finds very little evidence of this kind,[10] partly because

[1] T. R. Cave-Brown-Cave, 'Our Engineering Development' and 'Progress in Engineering', *Wessex*, June 1931 and June 1932.
[2] Unpublished memorandum by Cave-Brown-Cave, 'Investigations and Experimental Developments made between 1934 and 1939'.
[3] A. Temple Patterson, *The University of Southampton*.
[4] Basil Cottle and J. W. Sherborne, *The Life of a University*.
[5] W. E. Garner, 'Schools of Chemistry . . . the University of Bristol' *JRIC*, January 1954. Lever was persuaded to do this by Ernest Wells, an ex-Bristol student and a director of Lever's.
[6] *The Campden Research Station* (University of Bristol, 1937).
[7] *University of Bristol and the National Fruit and Cider Institute Jubilee Celebrations of the Long Ashton Research Station* (Bristol, 1953).
[8] W. M. Childs, *Making a University, an Account of the University Movement at Reading*.
[9] *Western Morning News and Mercury*, 17 June 1925.
[10] University College of the South West of England Annual Reports, *passim*. A possible exception was the work of E. C. Wray, formerly of ici Dyestuffs in the new Washington Singer chemistry laboratories.

mining technology was dealt with already at Camborne and marine engineering at the Plymouth Technical College, both of which were better sited for the practical aspects of this work.

Finally, by contrast, Armstrong College, Newcastle, still an off-shoot of Durham University, was firmly wedded to the basic industries of the North East.[1] Mining remained its particular strength, and in 1927 various miners' associations made grants for a new laboratory creating one of the finest mining schools in the country. They also did important work on coke for the Durham Coal-owners' Association. Its naval architecture department was somewhat stultified by depression though their staff designed the Channel train ferry,[2] and Professor Hawkes became one of the leading authorities on the diesel engine.[3] Electrical engineering being a prominent industry of Tyneside, the university also had a flourishing electrical engineering department which did research on insulators. But the studies of Armstrong and King's College in these years remained rather too committed to old declining industries and they seem to have done little to help the diversification of new scientific industry in the area.

This spread of interests and specialisms prompts comment on a number of points. First, the universities, by dealing with the various forms of engineering, including the newer forms of electrical and petroleum engineering, aviation, the chemistry of fats, dyes, and soaps, the food industries and nutrition, were certainly contributing to the change in industrial structure and the rise of 'new' industries. Second, there was plenty of evidence of close collaboration with industry and firms—the support of the coal owners and brewers for various departments, Manchester and Metro-Vickers and ICI Dye-stuffs, Sheffield and Hadfield's, Southampton and Supermarine, Bristol and Chivers, and many others referred to in the preceding pages, not to speak of others too numerous to mention. Third, almost all universities, with the exceptions of Cambridge, Oxford, Exeter, and Leicester, drew much of their strength through their service to local industry as well as national. The interests of local industrial needs and the civic universities were well matched.

But on the other hand, certain criticisms arise. In the first place there did seem to be a great deal of university expertise being lavished on the mining industry. Tizard and the UGC came to think so in the mid 1930s,[4] pointing out that there were ten university schools of mining and that this was probably too many, leading to duplication

[1] C. E. Whiting (ed.), *The University of Durham* (Durham, 1937), p. 57; see also his *The University of Durham, 1832–1932*.
[2] Armstrong College, Reports of the Standing Committee on Research, 1927–1938.
[3] 'History of the Engineering Department of King's College [Newcastle]' in pamphlet *The Stephenson Building*, 1951.
[4] UGC *Report for the Period, 1929/30–1934/35*, published, 1935. Tizard (speaking, 1934) cited, p. 40.

of effort. This compared with five in Germany, and yet while most of the senior positions in German collieries were occupied by university men, in Britain 'although there is a distinct tendency in this direction progress is slow'.[1] Certainly if anything was satisfactory about this worst of inter-war industries it was its improving technical performance and raised productivity, while the deep mining and electrification that lay behind it was made possible chiefly by the universities.[2] Yet all this expertise yielded but a sorry return in terms of employment, growth, or exports. One or two departments like Leeds and notably Birmingham diversified into oil engineering and also metal mining, which was starved of recruits, but this might have been done with fewer centres. Overall there ought to have been a much more radical shift away from coal mining education to these other forms whose shortages of manpower reflected in the highest salaries of any graduate industrial occupations in these years.

Second, of the new industries, aeronautical engineering seemed to become fashionable in perhaps too many places. Tizard, who often cast an astringent eye over the higher education-industrial scene in these years, thought that at the beginning of the period aero research was rather split up.[3] Similarly, the Air Ministry Committee on which he sat, while admitting that the subject might be taught in various places, insisted that research had to be concentrated at Farnborough and Imperial College.[4] In these circumstances, due to the vast costs involved, it seemed to doom most other centres to teaching without real practical research. To have minor university colleges like Southampton and Hull moving into the field might have seemed inappropriate, had not the energy and qualifications of Cave-Brown-Cave justified the former.

Third, it may be somewhat surprising that electrical engineering does not figure rather more prominently in the preceding paragraphs. It was a common university subject and there was no particular shortage of university electrical engineers, but the universities were not prominent as sources of innovation in the industry in the inter-war years as they had been in the 1890s and 1900s. Innovation moved from the university laboratory to the research laboratory of the firm, especially GEC at Wembley, Metro-Vickers, Siemens at Preston, and BTH, whence came, among much else, strip lighting, continuously evacuated valves, the first provincial broadcasting, the transistor, and the first talking cinematograph apparatus in Britain. It was said with regard to electro-technics just prior

[1] J. Crosland, 'Organisation of the Modern Colliery', *Leeds University Mining Society Journal*, September, 1933.
[2] W. H. B. Court, 'Problems of the British Coal Industry between the Wars', *EcHR*, vol. XV, 1945.
[3] Ronald W. Clark, *Tizard*, p. 65.
[4] 1920 IX *Report of the Air Ministry Committee on Education and Research in Aeronautics* (Glazebrook), Cmd. 554.

to 1939, that 'our research activity in those branches of science likely to affect engineering development at a reasonably early date was on the whole inadequate . . .'.[1] This was said at Manchester University, which did more than most in the electrical field. It was only the Second World War, this report thought, that had brought an intimate liaison of industry and university departments in this work. There also seemed to be a gap in the provision of education for metallurgists, with only Sheffield appearing really prominent, and it did lead to a serious shortage of men in this profession. Of the new industries it may be remarked that the universities seemed to do virtually nothing for the motor car industry, a less serious matter since this was a successful industry that arranged its own training and research outside the universities.

Fourth, how far were the universities creating fruitful cross-fertilizations of the sciences from which new industries might be expected to flourish? In one or two fields they were strikingly not doing so. Although chemical engineering was developed at some London colleges in the mid 1920s, not enough was done in this particular field. Also there seemed to be a positive disengagement between physics and engineering in some areas. The predominance of Cambridge theoretical physics, and its migration to most of the chairs in the country, swung the subject, notably at Bristol, Manchester, and Liverpool, away from a concern with matters of immediate potential relevance for engineering. At Cambridge it created a situation of engineers not much interested in research, and of physicists whose work was to have no practical effect on industrial engineering until the nuclear reactors of the 1950s. Perhaps the best example of successful cross-fertilization of physics and chemistry into a new technology, however, was the textile work at Leeds. Consequently chemistry was the predominant industrial science rather than physics, and this temporary disengagement of mainstream university physics from industrial concerns was an unusual interim in the span of industrial science from Watt to the present day.

Of Scotland and Wales there is much less to be said. They were in any case at this time less important than the English universities as suppliers of scientists and technologists. Table 19 puts this in perspective, giving scientists and technologists as a percentage of total students.[2] Scotland continued as before with her fortes of engineering and geology, for which very large sums were given to Edinburgh in the inter-war years. But what is interesting about Scotland is rather the negative question of why she should be so

[1] *Report on the Extension of Scientific Research in Manchester University, particularly in Relation to the Industries of its Area* (Manchester, 1944), p. 18. The quotation referred to electro-technics.
[2] Calculated from UGC Returns.

TABLE 19 *Full-time students and degrees obtained in science and technology as a percentage of total full-time students and degrees*

Scotland (students)			Wales (students)		England (degrees)		
	Science	Tech-nology	Science	Tech-nology		Science	Tech-nology
1920/1	7·4	17·9	26·3	9·9	1920/1 –3/4	22·9	13·0
1930/1	10·1	6·8	22·0	4·8	1928/9– 31/2	26·4	10·4
1938/9	11·4	8·9	20·1	6·6	1936/7– 8/9	25·9	10·6

much less to the forefront in industrial science in these years compared with the nineteenth century.

First, her real strengths in developing new sciences lay in agriculture, forestry, and nutrition, while the scientists of greatest value that she produced were of course medical doctors, who bulked larger in her total output than for Britain as a whole. Scotland also had a higher proportion of arts graduates than the other British countries, continuing to produce teachers and clergy as in former times. Why Scottish universities, which pioneered engineering and were far from averse to vocational training, should have been so backward in espousing technologies is intriguing. It probably stems from the very high prestige enjoyed by her purely technical institutions, the Royal Technical College at Glasgow and the Heriot-Watt College at Edinburgh. Since technologies were dealt with there, and textiles at Galashiels, there seemed less cause for Scottish universities to develop the kind of specialisms one finds, for example, in Leeds and Sheffield, especially since the Scottish tradition of the nineteenth century had been averse to specialism. Also it should be noted that, small as the Scottish technology percentage is, about half of that figure is accounted for by the Glasgow Technical College which was included in the UGC accounts although not technically a university. Thus, leaving that out of account, the Scottish technology figures would more fairly be nearer to the Welsh.

Second, where Scottish technology departments were strongest they were also most vulnerable. In mining and marine engineering and naval architecture, which were so especially suitable for the Scottish economy, there was a considerable slump of students, reflecting the slump in employment prospects in the industries to which they related. Nor do we find this matched by the development of departments and sciences relating to new home industries. This in turn must reflect the defects of the Scottish economy itself. We do not find any great motor car firm springing from there, nor was it the headquarters of any great electrical firm, in spite of the enormous scientific contribution of Kelvin and others to the technology of the industry. Astonishingly, even in 1935 no aircraft were made in Scotland,[1] and in spite of a fine literary and scenic heritage and the pioneer figure of John Grierson they did not develop an indigenous film industry as did Sweden at this time. Thus, as the 'new' scientific industries did not develop in Scotland so they did not react back on her universities, which continued with the same emphasis on engineering, chemistry, and shipbuilding and suffered through the depression accordingly.

Third, there was a personal element at work. It was a curious coincidence that the four professors of chemistry at Glasgow, Aberdeen, and Dundee all held their tenure for virtually the whole of the inter-war years, and Henderson at Glasgow had already done his best work at the Technical College before he arrived. The only Scottish professor of chemistry of national prominence of these years was Sir Robert Robinson who spent a fleeting couple of years at St Andrews on his way to Oxford. This was a marked change from the nineteenth century. Scotland's innovators per thousand per decade sank to 1·2, the lowest nadir in its history, in the period 1900–49, while her proportion of FRSs fell to half that of the nineteenth century.[2] Nor was she producing the entrepreneurs, the Nuffields, Michael Balcons, Geoffrey de Havillands, who enriched industry in these years and gave it new departures. This relative dearth of imaginative scientific and industrial talent for which migration must take some blame reacted adversely on the interconnection of the Scottish universities and industry.

Of Wales there is still less to say. We have seen that by tradition the various Welsh colleges were considerably divorced from industry, although the war brought a somewhat closer involvement. The technological education for the main industry, coal mining, was dealt with not in the universities but in the coal owners' own college at Treforest, and it was not until 1935 that Cardiff revived its own chair of mining. The other major developments were the opening of the Tatem laboratories for chemistry and physics, and also the building expansion for metallurgy, both at Cardiff, while along the coast the Swansea technical college became a university college. Otherwise there is little of interest about the Welsh universities in this period from our point of view. But unlike the Scottish universities they represent a slight improvement on their nineteenth-

[1] R. H. Campbell, *Scotland since 1707* (Oxford, 1965), p. 271.
[2] A. G. Clement and R. H. S. Robertson, *Scotland's Scientific Heritage*, p. 131 and *passim*, amply confirms and stresses the remarkable decline of Scottish scientific achievement in the twentieth century.

century position rather than a decline from some glorious former state. Both the Scottish and Welsh universities were now markedly less important in a consideration of our theme than the English.

However, considering all three countries together there is one final disturbing feature to be noted that is masked by a consideration of positive achievements, and this was the changing balance of arts, sciences, and technologies throughout the inter-war years (see Table 20).

TABLE 20 *Full-time students by faculty in British universities* (*percentage of total students*)

	Arts	Pure sciences	Technologies
1920/1–1924/5	39·8	17·0	13·5
1925/6–1929/30	52·3	16·9	9·3
1930/1–1934/5	49·9	16·9	8·9
1935/6–1938/9	46·5	16·3	9·7

It may be regarded as disturbing from the point of view of the university-industry linkage that the proportion of arts students should have risen so sharply, the bulk of whom must have been destined to be teachers who were going to experience difficulties in obtaining employment. The stability of the sciences is more pleasing though it is rather low, but the low proportion of students studying technology, and the consistent decline in that proportion down to the early 1930s, may be regarded as a weakness in the inter-war years' manpower situation. This was especially so when manifest in the shortages of oil mining engineers, geologists, metallurgists, and others we shall have cause to examine in the next chapter. There was however, one mitigating factor in that the first group of years contained the ex-servicemen who tended to be scientists and technologists, and their leaving the system is a part explanation of the fall. But that these mature science-educated men were replaced by arts students straight from school in the late 1920s and early 1930s offered little help to the economic recovery preceding the Second World War. However, some proportion of these arts men were studying a new range of economic and commercial subjects and having thus seen something of the technological contribution of the universities we may finish this chapter by considering how these 'commercial arts' we saw developing in the 1890s underwent further change in the inter-war years.

Apart from their contributions to technology, the universities continued trying to serve industry in the fields of economics and business

training. We have seen in an earlier chapter how this form
of university education became prominent in the 1890s and 1900s,
and we wish now to consider how it developed in the inter-war
years.

The immediate post-war years saw the extension and creation of
economics and commerce courses in universities continuing the trend
begun in the 1900s. At the 1921 Congress of the Universities of the
Empire, Ashley, his prestige further enhanced by his war work and
knighthood, yet again urged the necessity of university commercial
education.[1] After the war, Aberdeen and Edinburgh began Bachelor
of Commerce courses in 1919,[2] and by the same year Leeds, which
had started economics in 1902, had joined commerce to it and had
an advisory committee of businessmen.[3] By the time of the Balfour
Report in 1927, Reading, Nottingham, and Southampton had followed suit. These were the later workings out of the pre-war movement begun by Ashley at Birmingham. However, perhaps the most
important single change was at Oxford which, almost twenty years
after the Economics Tripos, came into line with Cambridge by
establishing the Honour School of PPE in 1921.[4]

In spite of these developments there were others who remained
unsatisfied at the state of economics and business training and who
sought to push on even further than Ashley in relating such education
to industry by the creation of studies in industrial or business
administration. The most lively advocate of this approach was
Dr James A. Bowie of Manchester. In 1918 a committee of prominent
industrialists in Manchester was instrumental in forming and financing the department of industrial administration in the College
of Technology (the faculty of technology of the university). Bowie
joined this is 1919 and became its director in 1926.[5] He was critical
of the Birmingham and other conventional programmes of commercial education, pointing out that foreign languages, geography, and
banking, although academically respectable and closer to business
interests than traditional arts subjects, were of little practical use to
factory managers. His course, by contrast, would be focused on
more immediately vocational matters including industrial finance,
costing, business statistics, the study of wages systems, and factory

[1] Second Congress of the Universities of the Empire (London, 1921), 'The
Universities and Training for Commerce and Industry'. Sir William Ashley's
contribution was also reprinted as chapter 4 of his book *Commercial Education*.
[2] W. Douglas Simpson, *The Fusion of 1860 . . . a History of the United
University of Aberdeen, 1860–1960*, p. 35.
[3] Department of Economics and Commerce Prospectus, 1919 (University of
Leeds).
[4] T. Henry Pearson, *A Plea for the Greater Recognition of Economics in Oxford*,
1920. Pearson was a Fellow of Pembroke. G. N. Clark, 'Social Studies at
Oxford', *The American Oxonian*, July, 1934.
[5] James A. Bowie, *Education for Business Management*.

law.[1] He was also the pioneer of the American case study method in Britain[2] and his Manchester department acted as secretary to fifteen firms engaged in management research, thereby keeping the academics in touch with business conditions.[3] This is what he claimed, though Abraham Flexner, who intensely disliked this kind of education, considered that his staff had no practical connection with industry, nor did local businessmen contribute anything to the course. In 1931, Bowie moved to Dundee to establish the Dundee School of Economics.

Industrial administration gained another strong foothold in England at the London School of Economics.[4] In 1929–30 the school was offered £5,000 a year for five years to establish a department of business administration for research and training. After discussion with a wide range of firms, the school accepted the idea in 1930. It is interesting to note that, as with the Manchester scheme, the initiative came from business rather than the university; this indeed was the best augury of success. The plan of study was more avowedly like the Manchester course, including accounting, business statistics, commercial law, marketing, finance, and factory organization and control. Several prominent firms had a right to nominate students to the course as a condition of their support, including giants like ICI, GEC, Imperial Tobacco and stores like Debenham's, Harrod's, Lewis's and Selfridge's. The course was also proving a success in attracting the attention of employers beyond those who sent their own selected students.[5] Evidently this 'industrial' or 'business administration' approach was itself more practical than 'commerce' or 'economics' and was proving attractive to employers.

Perhaps the most extreme development in practical business training in the universities was found surprisingly at Edinburgh University in the 1930s. They had started their B. COMM. in 1919, supported by the Edinburgh Chamber of Commerce, typical of the formation of many such courses at this time. However, from 1935 this development was given an unusual direction by the gift of £10,000 from J. Albert Thomson, a former president of the Scottish Motor Trade

[1] James A. Bowie, 'Industrial Management as a Career', *JC*, October 1928.
[2] L. Urwick (ed.), *The Golden Book of Management* (London, 1956 and 1963), pp. 259–262. Bowie is still revered as one of the few British pioneers of management training.
[3] James A. Bowie, 'The Manchester Experiment' in *Business and Science, the Collected Papers to the Department of Industrial Co-operation at the Centenary Meeting of the British Association* (ed.), R. J. Mackay.
[4] Lord Beveridge, *The London School of Economics and its Problems, 1919–1937* p. 86. Prospectus of the Department of Business Administration London School of Economics, 1931. 'Training Administrators for Industry and Commerce', *JC*, May 1929.
[5] CAB Memorandum, 28 May 1934, on a visit to LSE: 'he [Mr Menken of LSE] has a good many enquiries for men who have been through the course without being earmarked in advance'.

Association. This money was used to create the Jane Findlay Thomson Commercial Laboratory in the same year on the astonishing grounds that 'those who aspire to the higher positions in industry should have an intimate working knowledge of all up to date office machinery',[1] and the B. COMM. was revised to include this practical work.[2] They claimed this was a success and that industry was receptive to their graduates.[3] Indeed, in 1939 they considered that even more practical business procedure training was necessary and that all graduates ought to undertake some as a new kind of liberal education.[4] The reception of this essentially empirical office machine and procedure training into a university was all the more remarkable in that the Scottish universities had been cautious and even laggard over starting Ashley-type commerce economics. Now that Edinburgh had veered into this extreme it is difficult to avoid the view that they had moved beyond the pale of genuine university work. That this 'commercial laboratory' opened in 1935 and Keynes's *General Theory* was published in the following year most sharply indicates to what polarized extremes the divergent interpretations of 'economics' as a university subject had led.

Apart from economics and commerce, however, three other adjacent university subjects experienced considerable development in the inter-war years as managerial skills, notably modern languages, industrial psychology, and statistics. Just as we saw earlier that languages were held to be part of commercial education before 1914, so in the 1920s there were important new departures in this field. Sir Stanley Leathes's committee of 1918 had been highly critical of the state of modern languages teaching, and this report and the war especially stimulated some new development. For example, a charter was granted in 1916 to the School of Oriental Studies in the University of London, partly to match the Germans whose linguistic superiority before the war had facilitated their penetration of Far Eastern markets.[5] There was also a much greater concern for the teaching of Russian, especially as she became our ally during the war, and the London School of Slavonic Studies was established following the lines of Sir Bernard Pares's pioneering department at Liverpool. The Liverpool and London schools worked in cooperation and Liverpool was consulted about similar projected developments at Sheffield, Manchester, Nottingham, and Bristol. Pares noted that 'there is also a strong development of Russian

[1] *The Scotsman*, 2 April and 24 October 1935.
[2] W. T. Baxter, 'Careers for Graduates, Prospects offered by University Training', *The Scotsman*, 15 and 16 October 1936.
[3] William Oliver, 'The Bachelor of Commerce Degree as an Aid to Training for Business', *The Student* (Edinburgh University), 17 May 1938.
[4] Alastair Mackenzie, 'The Graduate in the Commercial World', *The Student*, 25 April 1939.
[5] 1917 XI *Report of the Board of Education*, 1915–16, Cd. 8594.

teaching in English Schools of Commerce',[1] and that 'the English interest [in Russian] is so largely economic'. The concern to expand language teaching for commerce apart from French and German was evident in a number of universities. At Leeds, departments of Spanish and Russian were begun in 1916; at Birmingham the Russian chair was founded in 1917 by the Chamber of Commerce; at Sheffield Russian was started in 1916 and Spanish in 1918 because Sheffield businessmen were established in the Russian steel industry and interested in the South American trade. It was unfortunate that the new Soviet régime's restrictive view of foreign trade rendered university attempts to widen the teaching of languages for commerce and industry somewhat less effective and relevant than they might otherwise have been.

Also arising from the later years of the war, but having fewer pre-war antecedents than the developments in languages teaching, was the involvement of universities in industrial psychology.[2] Although there had been little interest in British universities in the subject before 1914, it was the war that effectively created the study of industrial psychology in Britain. In 1915 Lloyd George set up the Health of Munitions Workers Committee and this began to study the psychological aspects of fatigue in industrial working. More important, their work led to the creation of two other bodies, the National Institute of Industrial Psychology in 1921 and the Industrial Fatigue Research Board, which were to develop its work in the inter-war years. At a stroke, the universities became deeply concerned with the study. Bernard Muscio of Cambridge published his pioneering lectures on industrial psychology in 1916, and this stimulated the future doyen on the subject, C. S. Myers, also of Cambridge, to turn his own attention to this field. He further aroused the interest of various firms, and as a result the National Institute of Industrial Psychology was formed in 1921 with the backing of Rowntree's, Cadbury's, Tootal's, Cammel Laird, and Harrison and Crosfield's, while Myers left Cambridge to become its director. The Cambridge psychology department ran the important summer school in industrial administration, and Cambridge remained preeminent in this field with the work of Sir Frederick Bartlett on fatigue, skills, and incentives. Industrial psychology is an interesting example of a subject of ill-defined limits separating itself from philosophy and the pure arts to become, like economics, its predecessor in the fission, a component of the new industrial administra-

---

[1] Sarolea Papers 81/1, University of Edinburgh. Typescript memorandum, Sir Bernard Pares to Charles Sarolea (Professor of French at Edinburgh), March 1916.
[2] L. S. Hearnshaw, *A Short History of British Psychology, 1840–1940* (London, 1964). L. Urwick and E. F. L. Brech, *The Making of Scientific Management* (London, 1959), vol. II, chapter XII.

tion idea of the 1920s and a new and important point of contact between the universities and industry.

The third special area of higher commercial training developing in the inter-war years was that of statistics. Hugh Quigley noted that in 1932 efficient statisticians were fewer than the posts available, and he noted a change in attitude in favour of the use of statisticians within the firm in recent years. He deplored that probably only about ninety firms in British industry used statisticians, but warned that foreign competitors in Germany, France, and the United States had 'evolved a technique in market research and product control which is rooted in economic analysis'.[1] The idea caught on in the thirties. For example, William Hollins approached the Cambridge Officer for 'an economist who can interpret statistics . . . they have quantities of machines and people to work them but no one really to interpret the results and apply them'.[2] Hollins's concern arose from part of their attempts to improve efficiency in the later 1930s. They began various statistical exercises and charts on costs and profits which was 'something of a novelty in British industry at the time',[3] and clearly needed statisticians to do it for them. On the university side, Oxford set up its Institute of Statistics in the mid 1930s,[4] and another major centre, Egon Pearson's department at University College, London, also began at the same time. Pearson was especially careful to establish contacts with industrial firms 'as the future of its work is most likely to be related to the application of statistical method in industry'.[5] In perspective, only forty-six men gained degrees in statistics between 1925 and 1939 in British universities, but presumably some firms were using pure mathematicians for this, of whom over 2,000 were produced.

These important developments were enthusiastic attempts by universities to cater for the careers of non-scientific graduates in industry. However, there were less encouraging features of this particular liaison, several of which were revealed by the Balfour Committee.[6] It was especially difficult to get qualified teachers in statistics and transport economics, and especially instructors with industrial experience. There was considerable and widespread doubt about the quantity and quality of students choosing such pro-

---

[1] Hugh Quigley, 'Where Trained Economists and Statisticians are Wanted', *JC*, March 1932. G. R. White, 'Openings for Statisticians in Industry and Research', *JC*, September 1935, also noted their increased use in the last ten years.

[2] CAB Memorandum, 25 May 1937.

[3] F. A. Wells, *Hollins and Viyella* (Newton Abbot, 1968), pp. 193–4.

[4] A. D. Lindsay, 'Social Studies in Oxford' *Oxford* (special number), February 1937.

[5] Report of University College London, 1934–5.

[6] *Committee on Industry and Trade*, 'Factors in Industrial and Commercial Efficiency' (Balfour), 1927, pp. 236–41.

grammes in commerce, and there was little co-operation with commercial interests in planning curricula. What must have been more disheartening were the rather cool and even hostile attitudes towards commerce courses from both industry and universities alike. Lord Leverhulme (II) had no belief in the value of university economics and commerce studies.[1] F. J. Marquis (Lord Woolton) deprecated the university study of commerce, preferring a broad liberal education,[2] and Milne Watson, though a backer of the LSE business administration course, thought that commerce courses could be of only limited use since 'the particular needs of any given commercial concern are too specialized to be served very materially by any general commerce course'.[3] These were far from isolated examples. In 1929, Harold Rostron of Tootal's undertook an enquiry for the AEIC that must have chilled the hearts of commercial education enthusiasts. The general view among their members (which included virtually all the significant firms of British industry) was[4]

that a degree in arts, science, mathematics, modern languages, etc. gives a man a wider training than that obtained with a degree in economics or commerce—which they regard as a more technical nature, and as such, is more rightly placed as a course of study to be followed after a general degree course in one of the former subjects . . .

Two years later the Goodenough Committee found the same position, that 'commercial faculties have not so far received any great encouragement from employers' and 'recruitment to commerce of men with commerce degrees was comparatively small'.[5] The same also seemed to be the case in Scotland at the end of the twenties.[6]

However, if this was the position around 1930 there is some evidence to suggest that more firms were becoming slightly more interested in graduates with economics and business degrees in the 1930s than they had been in the 1920s. This was an issue that the Cambridge Officer raised from time to time with the firms with whom he dealt, and from his memoranda (see Table 21) we can see the changing pattern of reception of the idea throughout this time.[7]

[1] Young Men in Industry and Commerce, A.E.I.C. Conference at Liverpool, June 1930, p. 5.
[2] Ibid., p. 15.
[3] Sir David Milne Watson, *Oxford*, winter, 1934, op. cit.
[4] Association for Education in Industry and Commerce Report on Education for Higher Positions in Commerce, October 1929, especially p. 20.
[5] *Final Report of the Committee on Education for Salesmanship* (Sir Francis Goodenough) (HMSO, 1931), p. 65.
[6] W. R. Scott, 'Report of the Special Committee on University Training in Industrial Administration', *Monthly Journal of the Glasgow Chamber of Commerce and Manufactures*, March 1929.
[7] CAB Memoranda for firms and dates concerned.

TABLE 21   *Firms' stated attitudes to graduates in economics and commerce*

Favourable	Opposed
Mather and Platt 1923	
Energen 1930	
Jantzen 1930	
United Steel 1932	
Lamson Paragon 1932	
Sir Alfred Read of Coast Lines 1933	Equitable Life 1933
Hudsons Bay Company 1935	Selfridge's 1935
New South Wales Bank 1936	
J. and P. Coats 1936	
Hollins 1937	

The mass of firms of course were not moved to express strong opinions one way or the other, but it is significant that there did seem to be a drift of opinion in industry moving slightly more in favour of the economics graduate in the 1930s that was not so discernible in the 1920s. And yet we should not exaggerate this for the bulk of firms as a whole. For example, Mr Locke of Rowntree's considered that the view 'common among business people and employers' was that if they had any belief in economics it was only as a study to follow practical business experience.[1] In the important Cambridge survey of 1937–8 it was found that although firms were actually more prepared to use arts men in administration than technical men, yet they did not want such arts men trained in commerce or even in the Cambridge Economics Tripos which they regarded as too theoretical.[2] Finally, in 1939 the Association of British Chambers of Commerce could offer only a gloomy conclusion to the period. The actual intake of commerce graduates by firms, it pointed out, was slight, probably 'well below 100', and in any case 'sporadic and exceptional'.[3] The Chambers of Commerce piously hoped that a larger proportion of graduates would be recruited into commerce, but even by 1939 opinion was against it.

[1] Eugen M. Chossudowsky, 'Graduate Employment in Industrial Management', *The Student*, 18 October 1938. This was a report of the main views expressed at the Universities Commerce Association Conference held at Leeds University, March 1938.
[2] *University Education and Business, a Report by a Committee appointed by the Cambridge University Appointments Board* (Cambridge, 1946). The survey was made in 1937–8 though not published until after the War. It was under the chairmanship of Sir Will Spens.
[3] The Association of British Chambers of Commerce Report on the Commercial Employment of Students with Degrees in Commerce, 11 January 1939.

Whatever the scepticism from business, advocates of commercial education faced some hostility from academic colleagues. The Principal of Armstrong College, for instance, frankly admitted that he really thought commerce in universities was 'a bit of eyewash'.[1] At Nottingham, Professor A. W. Kirkaldy, who held strong views that universities should train men for industrial life, ran a three-year commerce course as well as being closely involved with the local Chamber of Commerce. Even in so industrially orientated a university as Nottingham it was felt that 'what he was trying to do was not the proper function of an academic institution . . .', and when he retired in 1931 his chair was not filled.[2] At Oxford, likewise, T. M. Knox of the Appointments Office was publicly hostile to commerce and even economics education for industry as being useless.[3]

The output of men with first degrees in economics in the inter-war years was modest.[4]

Output of economists from British universities

1925–6	60	1932–3	127
1926–7	65	1933–4	126
1927–8	60	1934–5	106
1928–9	82	1935–6	106
1929–30	80	1936–7	99
1930–1	85	1937–8	102
1931–2	81	1938–9	115

It compares unfavourably with a reputed 16,000 students of industrial administration in Germany in 1929, and 80,000 in the United States.[5] By 1938–9, in spite of the expansion evident from the above figures, economics and the social sciences generally were still a markedly lagging sector of British university education, as Sir John Clapham's committee found (see Table 22).[6] By any criterion economic subjects seemed to be underdeveloped, and Clapham noted that his committee 'cannot regard as satisfactory' the situation revealed.

But what happened to graduates in economics and commerce, and did they filter into industrial posts or not? At the London School of Economics 13 per cent of graduates taking the B.sc. (Econ.) between 1902 and 1920 went into business, and 16·4 per cent between 1920 and 1932. On the other hand, almost 60 per cent of those taking the

[1] Report of Proceedings of the Second Congress of the Universities of the Empire, 1921, 'The Universities and Training for Commerce and Industry', Sir Theodore Morison.
[2] A. C. Wood, op. cit., p. 115.
[3] T. M. Knox, 'University Men and Appointments in Business', *Oxford*, summer 1934, p. 89.
[4] Calculated from UGC Returns.
[5] W. R. Scott, 'Report of the Special Committee', op. cit.
[6] 1945–6 XIV *Report of the Committee on the Provision for Social and Economic Research* (Sir John Clapham), Cmd. 6868.

TABLE 22   *Findings of Sir John Clapham's committee*

	Professors and readers	Expenditure (1938–9)
		£
Arts	463	1,084,873
Pure sciences	296	984,663
Social sciences	52	115,909

B.COMM. went into business between 1921 and 1932. The largest proportion of graduates in the 1920s went into teaching and research. Clearly whatever hopes there had been about the B.SC. Econ. as a feeder into industry were not well grounded, and it needed the new form of commerce education with the B.COMM. to make a really distinctive change from other arts subjects. With the espousing of business administration in 1930 so LSE courses became more directly related to business and so presumably did its graduates' careers.

What did LSE male graduates do and what sort of firms and industries thought it worth while to absorb men so educated? For the 1920s we can trace 145 graduates going into 102 firms, or 1·42 graduates per firm. It is interesting to note that the market for economics graduates was rather less specialized than that for engineers—the ratio for Liverpool engineers for the 1920s was 2·14 graduates per firm—but slightly more specialized than that for graduates in general —the Sheffield ratio was 1·27 graduates per firm.[1] But while there was a fairly healthy spread of takers for LSE graduates, some were especially keen and repeated employers. Those taking three or more were the Bank of England, Barclay's Bank, Candles Ltd, GWR, ICI, Sir William Crawford, Lever Brothers, Midland Bank, Henry Schroder's Bank, Westminster Bank. We can get some idea of what the graduates were used for in the firms by considering the relative incidence of job specification. The actual work is not always or usually indicated, but from those instances where it is we can obtain some rough idea of what economics graduates were used for. First in importance was statistics. This was quite the most commonly cited use, and bore out Quigley's pleas for more statisticians and the heavy demand for them. Next they were mostly commonly used as accountants, with nine specific cases. Then came various aspects of the sales and distribution side of the firm's work, with five in advertising, four in transport and distribution management, and four including commercial travellers and their organizers. It was in these fields rather than the management of technical production in which men

[1] The Liverpool and Sheffield evidence is considered more fully in Chapter 10.

with economics training were most sensibly used. Finally, the areas of business and industry taking most LSE graduates were communications, electricals and banking.

At other universities the fate of their economics students must have given some concern. At Southampton, for example, things seemed to be going wrong even in the buoyant late 1930s. In 1936 and 1937 they produced nine economists, seven of whom became elementary school teachers. They observed jadedly, 'it seems a pity that some more specialized kind of employment should not have been found for them'.[1] At Leeds, likewise, of twenty-three graduates in economics between 1919 and 1930 eleven went into some kind of teaching and only two into firms.[2] At Newcastle, of twenty-six graduates in commerce and economics between 1919 and 1938, only eleven at a generous estimate could be said to be engaged in administration and sales in industry, commerce, or banking. Here again, school-teaching and accountancy were the largest absorbers.[3] Of those for which we have figures, the Aberdeen commerce department seemed perhaps the most successful in feeding its students into business. Of the 117 graduates they produced between 1919 and 1933, forty-three went into business, twenty-one into accountancy, seven into banks, insurance, and telephones, three into the law, two into inland revenue, two into railways, two secretarial, and nineteen into teaching.[4] Although the Aberdeen figures are fairly creditable, the experience of the others suggests that the early claims of economists such as Ashley and Marshall that economics was going to prove especially suitable as a university training for industry proved, in the inter-war years, to be largely unfounded. The large numbers still going into teaching suggest that it had not proved itself as distinctively different from any other non-vocational arts subject as its pioneers would have wished.

But how did graduates in commerce and economic subjects fare in comparison with their arts fellows in job satisfaction, employment, and salaries? Only 65 per cent of Birmingham commerce graduates considered that their qualifications were relevant to their work compared with 82 per cent of arts graduates, 75 per cent of applied scientists, and 78 per cent of pure scientists. It was curious that the least practically orientated subjects were those whose practitioners found them most relevant to their everyday work, while those designed to relate most closely to industrial work proved to their practitioners to be less relevant. One suspects the higher figures

[1] Reports of the Secretary of the Appointments Board, University of Southampton, 1937–8, 1938–9.
[2] Calculated from *Leeds University Old Students' Year Book, 1930–31.*
[3] Calculated from *King's Old Students' Association Year Book, 1938.*
[4] D. J. B. Ritchie, 'The Graduate in Business, Scottish Graduates and Business Careers', *JC*, April 1935.

for arts are due to the fact that arts men were using their subjects by teaching them. However, the point at issue here is that not many fewer than half of commerce graduates did not really find their skills useful in the work they adopted. Commerce graduates were slightly less satisfied with their jobs than their colleagues. Sixty-two per cent were satisfied with their work compared with 64 per cent of applied scientists, 65 per cent of arts graduates, and 58 per cent of pure scientists. On the other hand, commerce graduates' salaries compared well with their scientific and arts colleagues' at various stages of their careers (see Table 23). Generally they compared well but it is

TABLE 23   *Salaries in 1938 of men graduates, University of Birmingham (in £s)*

Date of leaving university	Commerce	Arts	Applied science	Pure science
1937–8	150–200	150–250	150–200	200–250
1928–33	250–350	300–350	250–350	250–350
1923–8	350–400	300–350	350–450	350–400
1918–23	c. 600	450–500	700–800	400–450

worth noting that for those beginning a career in the 1930s with this qualification their salaries were slightly unfavourable. Those who began in the 1920s and persevered found their relative salary position improved *vis-à-vis* arts and pure science men.

In summary, the inter-war years saw considerable new developments in commercial higher education, notably the new concept of industrial administration and the rise of such ancillary subjects as languages, statistics, and industrial psychology; though in some cases these experiments proved so radical as to pass beyond what was acceptable as university education. Considerable resistance to graduates so trained persisted in the 1920s, though with some traces of a slightly more favourable drift of opinion in the 1930s. The social sciences remained under-represented and under-financed and their output of graduates was modest. Most, in any case, experienced little career choice different from those who had taken pure arts subjects since most still went into teaching. Commerce graduates were at risk in experiencing low job satisfaction, and in feeling that their training was irrelevant to their future occupations. On the other hand, they were quite well remunerated if they stuck to their posts.

There is not very much about all this that would have gladdened the hearts of Ashley and Marshall had they lived to see it. But the chief developments were not so much the forging of closer links between economics and commerce and industry but the building up of the whole intellectual level and standing of the subject itself in the 1930s. These theoretical accomplishments proved in the long run more important than the excessively practical activities into which Edinburgh had been sidetracked. There are indeed analogies with physics here. In both cases the intellectual developments of the subject by a few people were of vastly greater significance than any short-term immediate services to industry. As these developments came to be appreciated, thus enormously raising the prestige of the subjects, so accordingly there followed at a gap of a generation or so the expansion of the routine output of students to industry—the nuclear physicists of the 1950s and the economists in the 1960s, both of which would have been impossible without the scholarly developments of the 1930s. Thus while the development of closer connections between the universities and industry in economics and commerce subjects seemed to be modest in the inter-war years, the importance of the period lay in the creation of the intellectual seed corn for the post-war years.

In this chapter we have been considering the reasons why industry needed the graduate in the inter-war years and the technological and commercial spheres of interest of the universities. We should now turn to consider the more quantitative aspects of the flow of manpower through the educational system and the universities and the problems of its absorption into industry.

10
The Inter-war Years
1919-39—II

'*You do not have to go back beyond the memory of most of those present to arrive at a time when it was the rarest thing for a graduate to go into commerce or industry unless his father was already there, and the son followed him. There has been nothing less than a revolution in this respect. . . .*'[1]

The flow of educated talent through the universities and out into industry in the inter-war years was subject to various forces working either to benefit industry and the graduate or positively hindering them. In the first place, some element of inefficiency arose from the fact that a sizeable proportion of high intelligence was not entering universities due to inequalities in the school education system. In the early 1920s only 0·73 per cent of elementary school children reached the university,[2] while Kenneth Lindsay found in the mid 1920s that of the 550,000 children who left elementary schools each year only one in a thousand reached the university, or in London one in eight hundred.[3] Moving into the 1930s, the situation seemed to be scarcely better. Glass and Gray found for 1933–4 that only 0·596 per cent of an age group of elementary schoolboys reached university, whereas 20 per cent of an age group of non-elementary schoolboys did so.[4] Mrs Floud, in a study made in 1949 on the educational experience of the adult population, found likewise that of persons in status groups 5, 6, and 7 born before 1910 (and so presumably going to university, if ever, in the inter-war years) only 0·9 per cent got to university.[5] Put in another way, only half a per cent of children born

[1] Report of the Proceedings of the Fifth Quinquennial Congress of Universities of the British Empire, 1936, 'Careers for Students' O. V. Guy, Secretary of the Cambridge University Appointments Board, p. 101.
[2] G. S. M. Ellis, *The Poor Student and the University* (London, 1925), pp. 22 and 24.
[3] Kenneth Lindsay, *Social Progress and Educational Waste* (London, 1926).
[4] D. V. Glass and J. L. Gray, 'Opportunity and the Older Universities' in L. Hogben (ed.), *Political Arithmetic* (London, 1938).
[5] Jean Floud, 'The Educational Experience of the Adult Population of England and Wales as at July 1949' in D. Glass (ed.), *Social Mobility in Britain* (London, 1954, reprint 1963).

pre-1910 of skilled, semi-skilled, and unskilled manual workers succeeded in reaching the university.[1] At the end of the 1930s it was
pointed out that if the various classes were represented in the universities as they were in society at large, then the proportion of public
elementary school children in the university population should be
81·1 per cent and of the others 18·9 per cent, whereas the actual ratio
was 40 : 60. Professor Greenwood concluded that 'ex-public elementary schoolchildren have not quite half and others more than
three times their proper share of the university population' and a
'large number of children of ability fit to profit from higher education do not receive it'.[2]

There were several reasons for this markedly disproportionate
under-representation of the lower classes in higher education. In
the first place, few of such children were likely to enter secondary
schools as a starting point for university entrance. Mrs Floud found
that 4 per cent of the pre-1910 birth group of the three lowest status
groups went to secondary school, and Lindsay found that this was
5 per cent for Warrington and Oxfordshire in the 1920s. Even though
working-class chances of going to grammar schools rose slightly in
the 1930s, a second barrier was the manner of awarding scholarships
from school to university. Since 1919 state scholarships had been
awarded for students leaving secondary schools, but only 200 were
allocated, rising to 300 in 1931. However, with over 4,000 school
leavers competing for them the chances of winning one were slim,
and the successful tended to be public school boys going to Oxford
and Cambridge. The ordinary working-class student hoping to aspire
to the local civic university had more often to rely on a less satisfactory system, the local authority award. The local authorities had
been making an attempt to provide scholarships for worthy local
students since 1902, although they had no legal obligation to do so.
Consequently a haphazard system of anomalies had arisen with
great variations in the criteria on which awards were based and in
the value of the awards themselves.[3] It was evident as G. S. M. Ellis
remarked, that 'the possibility of getting educated has come to depend over much on accidents of birthplace and residence and the
exact position of the county or county borough boundary has assumed a fortuitous and unreasonable importance'.

Given then that only about 2 to 6 per cent of the lower classes
were getting to secondary schools and less that 1 per cent of them to
university, why should this matter to industry. It was serious because of a massive misallocation of intelligence between the resources

[1] Alan Little and John Westergaard, 'The Trend of Class Differentials in
Educational Opportunity in England and Wales', *British Journal of Sociology*,1964.
[2] Major Greenwood, 'The Social Distribution of University Education',
Journal of the Royal Statistical Society, vol. CII, pt III, 1939.
[3] Doreen Whiteley, *The Poor Student and the University* (London, 1933).

of the educational system in the 1930s. Gray and Moshinsky calculated that 73 per cent of the nation's children of high intelligence were trapped in elementary schools and central schools and destined to leave at fourteen or fifteen. 'Practically none of these has the opportunity of entry into the professions and the higher ranks of the business world enjoyed by those who have attended fee paying schools.' But what was almost equally undesirable was the fact that about 49 per cent of fee-paying pupils in grammar schools were not of the intelligence to benefit from a grammar school education. That the unintelligent well-to-do were cluttering the grammar schools and that three-quarters of the national stock of high intelligence was kept out, and thus kept out of the universities, and thus denied the opportunity to become graduates in industry, may be regarded not only as socially unjust but also economically bizarre. Fortunately, or unfortunately, with a depressed economy and the limited job opportunities of the inter-war years, the defects of the educational system could not have such retarding effects on industry as they might have had in a time of greater shortage of skilled graduates. Indeed the fact that this high intelligence went straight into industry created a good quality craftsman and foreman class on the shop floor. It was fortuitous that the 1944 Act, by re-aligning the school structure to relate to bands of intelligence rather than to social strata (though this is questioned), should have served to prepare for the full employment and shortages of highly educated labour that have been experienced since the war.

If the flow of ability into the universities left much to be desired, what was the flow of graduates out of the universities into industry? The calculable available figures are given in Table 24. Certain points emerge to which it is worth drawing attention at this stage. First, the figures are fairly high. It was believed in some quarters that the output was much lower than this. For example, the AUT considered that those 'who find congenial employment in industry' was 'small indeed' or 'negligible or if figures are given they are 1 or 2 per cent'.[1] We find these latter estimates quite incredible and can only suppose that an attempt was being made to quantify 'congenial' employment. Furthermore, any possible criticisms that could be levied against the figures in our table would be that they are underestimates of the output to industry. It could be argued that some graduates found employment in industry without going through the Appointments Board, thus making the figures based on such records too low. This would tend to cast further doubt on the low AUT estimates.

Second, the figures reflect the general trends of advance and recession in business as we may have expected with fairly high figures for

[1] Interim Report of the Committee on Universities and Industry, 11 October 1929, in AUT Files.

TABLE 24 *Percentage of graduates going into industry and business from various universities, 1919–39*

	1919	1920	1921	1922	1923	1924	1925	1926	1927	1928	1929	1930	1931	1932	1933	1934	1935	1936	1937	1938	1939
Oxford[1]	7·9	17·1	13·6	21	24·8	21·8	22·4	24·1	19·3	31·4	26·6	26·7	18·8	25·7	30·4	29·6	25	26·1	26·2	22·8	23·9
Cambridge[2]	46·7	42·3	32·1	48·5	43·7	48·3	42·6	37·4	42	42	51·7	41·1	40·3	37·2	46·1	41·9	40	43·1	46·4	40·6	37
London (King's)[3]												40·5									
Durham[4]													2·5	5·3	2·5	4·4		2·4	2·6		
Durham[5] (scientists)						6·6	7·7			9·1	3·7	4·3									
Birmingham[6]	←			32·3	→																
Liverpool[7]	←			52	→																
Sheffield[8]								18													
Leeds[9]										17·6	19	17·6	20·6	21·6	21·8	21·2	20·2	18	20·3	21·8	
Newcastle[10]	←		63·5	→										27·9							
Exeter[11]														6	10·5	7·4	17·2	15	7·3		
Glasgow[12]									50·5								12·3	10·6	9·1	15·4	12·7
Edinburgh[13] (excluding medicals)							13·3	11·4	9	8·9	10·1	8·7							13·3	11·9	9·8
University of Wales[14]						15·3	14·5		14·6	16·7		17·9	11	10	14·1	21·7	21	23	29	30	
Aberystwyth[15]											10·8									8·8	
Bangor[16]																				8·8	

[1] Reports of the Committee for Appointments, University of Oxford (Per G. A. Oxon 4° 178, Bodleian Library).
[2] Reports of the Cambridge University Appointments Board, 1919–39.
[3] King's College, London Annual Report, 1929/30 (the only one listing these statistics).
[4] Durham Colleges, the University of Durham. First Appointments obtained by Students leaving during the period 1929–38 (unpublished typescript in the University Archives, Newcastle).
[5] The University of Durham, Durham Division, Department of Science, Record of the Period October 1924–December 1934 (Durham University Library).
[6] Calculated from *Register of Graduates* to December 1931 (1932 ed.) names A–J inclusive.
[7] Calculated from *University of Liverpool Society Chronicle*.
[8] *Journal of Careers*, September 1926.
[9] Leeds University Appointments Board Report on the First Ten Years Work of the Board, December 1931, and Annual Reports, 1932–8.
[10] Calculated from *King's [Newcastle] Old Students' Association Year Book*, 1938.
[11] Reports of University College, Exeter, 1933–5.
[12] Glasgow University Appointments Committee Reports (typescripts in their offices in Glasgow).
[13] Reports of the Edinburgh University Appointments Secretary, 1924–39 (in the possession of A. G. Acaster, Esq.).
[14] University of Wales Appointments Boards Reports, 1919–39 (in Registry, Cardiff).
[15] Report of the Appointments Committee, University College, Aberystwyth, 14 February 1939.
[16] Calculated from *Omnibus*, November 1930, listing students leaving 1929.

the late 1920s and especially for 1929 before the crash. The slump is reflected in low figures for the early thirties, which then rise with recovery. High figures for the early 1920s reflect not so much good business conditions as the movement into jobs of the ex-serviceman generation which, as we have seen, was highly orientated towards science, technology and industry. However, what is interesting about the spread of figures is not their predictable response to business fortunes but the similarity between the 1920s and the 1930s. Percentages of output achieved in the good years of the late 1920s are about the same as, and not normally exceeded by, those during the recovery in the 1930s. An exception was the University of Wales (presumably Cardiff for the most part) for whom the 1930s were more significant than the 1920s in raising the level of graduate output to industry. We shall see also that there is little difference between the decades in the rates of absorption of graduates into firms.

Although we are unwilling to compare universities too closely, yet it does seem that the levels of the Scottish and of most of the Welsh output were rather below those of the English ancient and older civic universities. This is also in accord with the UGC figures cited earlier indicating that the output of students in technology and industrial pure science from Scottish and Welsh universities was lower than that of England, the particular virtues of the former being agriculture and medicine. Finally, the rather high figures for Cambridge may be noted, and the fact that the Oxford figures are at about the same level as those of Leeds. The old pre-1890s criticisms that the ancient English universities were out of touch with industry are much less relevant though not totally removed. Within a generation —say 1900 to 1930—Cambridge had joined the older civic universities as a major supplier for industry, a leap not achieved by Durham or the Scottish universities within this time.

One specialized form of output was that of the post-graduate, who merits some separate attention. The war, by stopping the traditional traffic of scholars to Germany and the United States for post-graduate education, prompted British universities to create their own PH.D.s as a more specialized training in research than the first degree should be. Did this have any implications for industry and did such new doctors embark on industrial careers? Full-time research students in British universities rose from 600 in 1920–1 to 2,624 in 1938–9, just over a quadrupling. On the other hand in certain areas vital for industry the expansion of research students was remarkably slight. Apart from chemical engineering, scarcely any showed a marked increase, and the increase in chemistry was almost entirely after 1934. However, the research student quickly came to be appreciated, especially with the rise of research within the firm in the 1920s. Lord Emmott's enquiry found that industrialists favoured an

extension of post-graduate education,[1] and a few years later Sir
Ernest Barker noted that firms were coming to prefer that scientists
going into industry should do some research first.[2]

It is possible to trace the future destinations of PH.D.s for one or
two universities to throw light on whether they did after all go into
industry. If we consider Newcastle PH.D.s for the 1920s and 1930s,
we find six out of ten in the 1920s and twelve out of twenty-three in
the 1930s (60 per cent; 52·5 per cent) did go into industry, a higher
proportion than for non-post-graduate degree students. While we
cannot know exactly what these men did within the firm, one out of
six for the 1920s and four out of the twelve for the 1930s were
specifically engaged in research. At King's College, London, 40·5 per
cent of first degree men of 1929/30 went into industry and 41·6 per

TABLE 25   *Branches of study in which advanced students were engaged*[3]

	Chemistry	Applied chemistry	Electrical engineering	Mechanical engineering	Metallurgy	Chemical engineering
1925–6	357	75	47	47	44	8
1938–9	510	54	49	47	42	60

cent of men with higher degrees, but we do not know exactly where
they went.[4] At Durham of the post-graduates of 1924–34, two out of
seven in the 1920s and four out of six in the 1930s went into industry.
Here too there was a greater tendency for research men to go into
industry than first degree men. Finally, for Scotland we have fairly
detailed evidence from St Andrews.[5] In the 1930s of seventy-five men
going into firms twenty had doctorates and they were absorbed as
shown on page 282. Of all St Andrews men doing research within
firms eleven out of the seventeen were doctors, indicating just how
far this aspect of the firm's work was coming to be post-graduate
activity by the 1930s, just as reciprocally it was the most important
element in the activities of post-graduates within the firm.

We may conclude, first, that PH.D. scientists had a slightly higher

[1] *Report of an Inquiry into the Relationship of Technical Education to other
forms of Education and to Industry and Commerce* (Lord Emmott) 1927. This
Report was by the Teachers in Technical Institutions with the collaboration of
the AUT, FBI, AEIC and others. (Copy in AUT Files, file 158.)
[2] Ernest Barker, 'Universities in Great Britain, their Position and their
Problems' in W. M. Kotschnig and E. Prys (ed.), *The University in a
Changing World*, p. 92.
[3] UGC Returns for subjects and dates concerned.
[4] King's College, London Annual Report, 1929/30.
[5] Calculated from *Alumnus Chronicle of the University of St. Andrews, passim,*
for 1930s.

Firm	Doctors	Doing Research within the firm
British Cyanides	1	1
British Xylonite	1	1
ICI	7	5
Kodak	2	1
Scottish Dyes	3	1
United States Steel Corporation	1	1
Jas. Williamson	1	1
Shell	1	–
Reyrolle	1	–
J. Mackay	1	–
Universal Grinding Wheel Company	1	–
	20	11

propensity to move into industry than men with first degrees, and this may reflect a growing preference for such men by firms, especially in chemistry where graduates found strong competition for such jobs. Second, as research became an increasing activity of firms within British industry, so post-graduates came to predominate in the labour force in this field. Third, certain major firms—Kodak, GEC, and ICI above all, seemed to be recurrent post-graduate employers. Indeed, with regard to ICI, Sir Frank Spicknell specifically told the Cambridge Appointments Officer in 1933 that he was keen on post-graduate chemists and that they had established beyond question the value of post-graduate training.[1]

Thus far we have shown the fairly creditable levels of output of graduates from universities to industry. But during these years there was some apprehension and evidence that universities were swaying graduates away from industry and into the professions. At Glasgow, for example, a motivational survey in 1937–8 revealed that of 165 arts men going in for teaching only five had fathers who were themselves teachers whereas eighty of their fathers 'were in industry' and another forty-one in selling and commerce.[2] This phenomenon was true of scientists also. Of 117 registering to read science in 1937, ninety-six wanted non-industrial careers, leaving only twenty-one potential industrial entrants at the outside. And yet the family

[1] CAB Memorandum. ICI, 20 December 1933.
[2] The Glasgow University Appointments Board Typescript Report, 1937–8 contained this important survey which does not seem to have been published.

background of these 117 scientists contained thirteen men in senior industrial posts, fifty-six in minor industrial posts, sixteen in commerce and ten in sales. Thus ninety-five sons of fathers in industry and commerce went to Glasgow University to study science and only twenty-one of those sons at the very most could have gone back to use their science in industry. Here again the university was diverting the second generation of industrial families away from those occupations. But could it be that there was really a net gain to industry, that industrial occupations were attracting the majority of their students from sons of fathers in non-industrial occupations? There is little evidence of this. In the Glasgow survey 60 per cent of engineering students were sons of fathers in industry, while at Newcastle in the 1930s the proportion was 67 per cent.[1] Engineering was not succeeding in drawing men from non-industrial backgrounds to counteract the seepage of industrial sons into teaching. There was probably an inter-generational net loss.

This trend was most strongly confirmed by a study of 2,295 Cambridge graduates in 1937–8.[2] This study found that scholars and exhibitioners and 'firsts' tended not to go into industry. Moreover, commerce was the occupation in which fewest sons followed their fathers. Of 651 sons of men in commerce leaving Cambridge in 1937 and 1938 only 22·7 per cent themselves went into commerce, lower than any other career choice. This was the occupation that suffered a loss whereas all the others, except Holy Orders to a negligible degree, gained in the redistribution of occupations between fathers and sons. It was clear that for whatever reason, going to Cambridge had turned many young men away from commerce and industry and into the professions. The report concluded that 'if the training or mental outlook given by the universities tends unduly to direct the minds of students towards non-industrial occupations, they will be robbing commerce and industry of many able men who in the past would have been recruited direct from school'. At Oxford, too, Sir Noel Hall recalled that when he expressed a wish to go into industry in the 1920s his tutor sought to dissuade him on the grounds that 'I had a moral duty not to seek personal gain but to carry out public service.'[3] In this way the university could become not a channel flowing talent into industry but one diverting it away.

*   *   *

[1] Calculated from record cards of Newcastle engineering department in the possession of Professor Fisher Cassie, CBE. I am grateful to Professor Cassie for access to these private documents.

[2] *University Education and Business, a Report by a Committee appointed by the Cambridge University Appointments Board.* Although the survey was made in 1937–8 it was not published until 1946. It was under the chairmanship of Sir Will Spens.

[3] Sir Noel Hall speaking at the Conference of Universities of the United Kingdom, 1962; 'Relations between the Universities and Industry', p. 47.

So far this chapter has been concerned with the question of how far the universities absorbed the nation's high intelligence and what proportion of it was redeployed out into industry in spite of diversion into the professions. Now we should move over to consider the other side of the linkage and the problems of the absorption of the graduate into the industries and firms of the inter-war years.

The 1920s and 1930s saw the creation of many fresh openings for graduates in the 'new' science-based, domestic market industries. Other opportunities arose in old industries which, changing their technologies and their attitudes, began to turn to this higher level of the educational system for their recruits. Among the new industries canning, for example, enjoyed a very rapid rise in the 1920s and the canning and fruit preservation firms began at once to take on chemists and agricultural graduates from Oxford, Cambridge, Reading, and Bristol.[1] Equally rapid was the rise of broadcasting and wireless industry. Of the latter it was said in 1932 that 'the key posts in the industry are mainly held by engineering graduates' while the Chief Engineer of the BBC, who held a Manchester degree himself, advised potential wireless engineers to go to university.[2] Scarcely any new industry had the allure of aircraft and aeronautical engineering, and there were close links between the firms and universities. Fairey, and Handley Page served on the advisory body of Imperial College, Supermarine worked closely with Southampton University, and de Havilland's, as well as taking graduates, ran their own technical school and encouraged their staff to take London external degrees.[3] It was not surprising in the light of the universities' contribution to the development of the industry during the war that they should be receptive graduate employers in peace-time. As Handley Page observed to Tizard, 'the opinion generally was that the industry is being fairly well supplied with people of higher education ... technical graduates as a rule take posts in connection with the aerodynamical or stress side of the aircraft works'.[4] By the end of the 1930s it was noted that all aircraft and component companies wishing to stay in business were virtually obliged to run their own research departments and this provided yet further openings for the graduate.[5] This in-

---

[1] Sir William Lobjoit, 'The Canning Industry' *JC*, July–August 1932. Lobjoit was Controller of Horticulture at the Ministry of Agriculture and Fisheries in the 1920s and chairman of his family firm of W. J. Lobjoit.

[2] 'The Wireless Industry', *JC*, June 1932, and P. P. Eckersley, 'The Future of Wireless Engineering', *JC*, December 1933.

[3] 'The de Havilland Aircraft Co.', *JC*, March 1927, and Sir Geoffrey de Havilland, *Sky Fever* (London, 1961).

[4] Letter, Handley Page to Tizard, 24 March 1931. Advisory Committee on Aeronautical Education, 1925–34, Imperial College Archives, File, 1921.

[5] Oliver Stewart, 'Specialised Opportunities in Aircraft Manufacture', *JC* March 1938.

dustry remained especially and unusually valuable as an absorber of pure mathematicians from the universities who were not otherwise widely used in industry.[1]

The film industry is of some interest as an essentially 'new' industry trying to break American domination and turning to the graduate to help it to do so. Although an industry of very varied and haphazard entry, some attempts were made to attract graduates even in the early 1920s. For example, in 1924 the Stoll Company at Cricklewood approached the Cambridge Appointments Board for 'men of culture' as actors, and the Appointments Officer, with some sense of humour, sent them one with what he termed a 'Biarritz manner'.[2] Similarly when Sir Michael Balcon began as a producer in 1920 he already had graduates on his staff. In the early 1930s, after the Cinematograph Act of 1927, there was a determined bid to create an indigenous British industry.[3] Balcon took over production at Gaumont British, starting an apprenticeship scheme which graduates took, and later he remembered that 'a number of promising young men came from the universities'.[4] In the thirties the Cambridge Board had dealings with the British and Dominion Film Corporation, Sir Alexander Korda, and Basil Dean, the founder of the Ealing Studies.[5] Oxford and Cambridge graduates moving into the film industry in the 1930s[6] came eventually to play an important part in the creation of a film industry both artistic, distinctively British and, equally important, commercially exportable.

Finally the dyestuffs industry proved to be a successful technically efficient new industry in the inter-war years, highly dependent on graduates in organic chemistry and normally requiring four-year trained graduates for control and research work. This latter was especially important for, whereas firms had formerly relied on university departments for their innovation, in the 1920s the new large units, especially the Dyestuffs Division of ICI, undertook their own research within the firm.[7]

[1] Report of Birmingham University Appointments Board, 1937–8.
[2] CAB Memorandum, 26 January 1924, on O. E. Taylor of the Stoll Company.
[3] Alfred Plummer, *New British Industries of the Twentieth Century* (London, 1937), 'Films and the Cinema'.
[4] 'The British Film Industry', *JC*, May 1933, and Sir Michael Balcon, *A Lifetime of Films* (London, 1969), p. 59.
[5] For example, CAB Memorandum, British and Dominion Film Company, 20 December 1933. CAB Memorandum headed *Daily Mail*, 3 April 1936, and Associated Talking Pictures, 3 April 1936.
[6] For example, Anthony Asquith, the documentary director Humphrey Jennings, Robert Hamer (*Kind Hearts and Coronets*), Robert Stephenson (*Mary Poppins*), Charles Crichton (*The Lavender Hill Mob*), Michael Redgrave, James Mason.
[7] 1930–1 XI *Report of the Dyestuffs Industry Development Committee*, 1930, Cmd. 3658.

It was characteristic of these new industries that they began to employ university men almost immediately, largely because many were heavily reliant upon academic science, which in turn had originally sprung from university research. On the other hand, there were traditional industries which spawned new developments in these years and also turned more to the universities. This was especially the case with various branches of engineering and the gas industry. Within construction, technical changes opened important specialisms in the early 1930s. Ventilation, acoustic, and hydraulic engineering, for example, began to absorb graduates and put yet a further demand on the diminishing mechanical engineers.[1] Changes in electrical power supply also created new openings for those with degree qualifications in the very extension of the electricity that was to be the basis of several new industries. While power stations would be fewer with the extension of the grid, yet more opportunities were opened up for graduates in load distribution and control, research and sales.[2] Just as with the grid extension the emphasis of work had shifted from power station to heavy transmission up to about 1935, so in the later 1930s it shifted again away from the extension of supply to the light current side, the development of appliances, and the commercial aspects of inducing the greater consumption of electricity.[3] Finally, in this transmutation of older industries the gas industry became a very important developing field for graduates in the inter-war years. Sir Ernest Smith remembered in 1930 that 'when I began my career it was *infra dig* for any university man to enter the [gas] industry'.[4] But all this changed in the inter-war years. Already in 1926 it was noted as an increasing tendency that gas works managers were taking degrees.[5] By 1931 the London gas companies would not take engineers without a B.SC., and it was said that 'this standard is slowly permeating the whole industry'.[6]

There were, on the other hand, certain crucial areas of disengagement between the graduate and industrial employment. These were of two kinds; first, those where industry was at fault in being negligent in using university men, or positively rejecting them and, second those areas where the universities were to blame for not producing sufficient of certain skills to meet the demands of industry. For

---

[1] J. W. Cooling, 'Prospects in Heating and Ventilation Engineering', *JC*, December 1932. A. M. Low, 'Acoustical Engineering', *JC*, April 1933. W. T. Halcrow, 'Hydraulic Engineering as a Profession', *JC*, March 1935.
[2] Standen Pearce, 'Power Station Engineering', *JC*, February 1933.
[3] Hugh Quigley, 'Are we training too many Electrical Engineers?', *JC*, June 1938.
[4] E. W. Smith, 'Scope for University and Public School Men in the Gas Industry', *JC*, March 1930.
[5] A. B. Searle, 'Fuel Technology as a Career', *JC*, November 1926.
[6] 'University Men in the Gas Industry', *JC*, July–August 1931; also noted in J. R. Willis Alexander, 'The Gas Industry as a Career', *JC*, January 1935.

either reason inefficiencies arose in the supply of highly skilled manpower.

In the first category may be placed wool textiles, leather, and motor cars. From some points of view wool textiles appeared to be a highly science-conscious industry, with its research association and the Leeds University department. Yet this approach did not permeate down to the firms, which were not absorbing highly educated scientists.[1] The leather industry was even more blameworthy. This too had a research association and an excellent university department also at Leeds. But the small scattered family firms of under two hundred employees that characterized the industry were scientifically backward; 'on the whole the industry does not utilise the scientist as much as it should and could'.[2] Consequently in the 1930s, in spite of our good quality in natural tanning, we remained behind the Germans and Americans in chrome salt tanning.[3]

The motor industry is a third which did not employ graduates as much as one might expect. This industry preferred to take school leavers and to give them a lengthy premium apprenticeship course of their own. Austin's and Ford's, for example, not only neglected graduates—they positively disliked them. Sir Herbert Austin stated bluntly that 'the University mind is a hindrance rather than a help',[4] and Sir Percival Perry of Ford's likewise made it clear that he did not want university men.[5] Similarly, William Morris, although a noted supporter of universities for medicine and social studies, had little appreciation of the potential value of university science for his industry.[6] Accordingly education for the industry, more than locomotive or marine engineering, was seen almost entirely in terms of apprenticeships and technical college training for school leavers.[7] Yet if certain firms remained aloof, some universities did engage in research in automobile engine problems, notably Liverpool, Sheffield, and Bristol; and a few firms began to consider graduates

---

[1] 'Careers in the Wool Textile Industry', *JC*, July–August 1934, made this criticism. Other evidence suggests that of forty-two leading West Riding manufacturers only one was employing a Leeds graduate in the 1920s: *Leeds University Old Students' Association Year Book*, 1930–1, collated with *Yorkshire Observer*, 1935, *passim*. The newspaper ran a series of profiles on those persons it considered the leading business men of the West Riding.
[2] C. H. Spiers, 'The Leather Industry', *JC*, March 1935.
[3] Conversations with P. Stanley Briggs, Esq., of the Procter Laboratory, Leeds University. Mr Briggs had considerable experience both as a businessman in the leather industry and as a lecturer in the department since 1923. Since this conversation he has become more widely famous as the inventor of waterproof leather. *Daily Telegraph*, 12 August 1970.
[4] Sir Herbert Austin, 'Youth's Prospects', *JC*, November 1930.
[5] Sir Percival Perry, 'Youth's Prospects', *JC*, July–August 1931.
[6] The Earl of Birkenhead, *The Prof. in Two Worlds*, p. 93.
[7] *Report of H.M. Inspectors on Technical Education for the Automobile Engineering Industry* (HMSO, 1923).

for example, Leyland, Daimler, and Hillman before 1930. Bristol did more than most to provide graduates for the motor car industry,[1] Professor Morgan being Vice-President and then President of the Institute of Automobile Engineers in the 1920s. Perhaps the most significant cracking of the ice was the changed policy of Rolls Royce. 'For many years,' they noted, 'training in these works beyond the trade apprenticeships level was a coveted privilege open to only a few who were required to pay a heavy premium.' But by the end of the 1930s they were taking graduates without premium, paying them a salary and offering the Henry Royce Fellowship for post-graduate university research.[2] The first Liverpool engineering graduate went to Rolls Royce in 1937,[3] and Mr Harry Grylls, the late technical director of Rolls Royce, joined the firm from Trinity College, Cambridge, in 1930.[4]

It would be difficult, however, to argue that the under-use of graduates in these three industries reflected adversely on their performance. Vehicles, the most conspicuously and deliberately disengaged of the industries, had one of the best growth records of the whole of the inter-war years with a 66 per cent increase in output between 1929 and 1937, second only to electrical engineering in its expansion. Leather, whose neglect was less justifiable, had an above average growth performance with 34 per cent, and textiles only slightly below average with 27 per cent. Nor can we see in the latter two any fault attributable to low standards. English natural tanned leather and English worsteds and cottons had an unequalled reputation for quality, indeed the criticism of the leather industry was not against this but its unwillingness to adopt the cheap artificial

[1] MS. Minutes and Reports of University of Bristol Faculty of Engineering 1919–37. The Bristol output of graduates to the motor industry was:

1920–1	Bentley, Cubitt's at Aylesbury, Long Ashton Motor Company, Wolseley
1921–2	Blackburn Motor Company, Wolseley
1922–3	Rolls Royce, Whiting's at Bath
1923–4	Douglas Motors, Leyland, Sunbeam, Wolseley
1924–5	Douglas Motors
1925–6	Rolls Royce
1927–8	Rolls Royce
1933–4	Riley
1936–7	Rolls Royce

[2] *JC*, March 1938.
[3] *Journal of the University of Liverpool Engineering Society*. It may illustrate the slow and limited reception of university engineers into the motor car industry to indicate their reception from the 383 engineers produced by Liverpool of whose careers we have record.

1922	Daracq	1935	Leyland
1925	Daimler	1937	Leyland
1926	Daimler	1937	Rolls Royce
1930	Daimler	1938	Armstrong Siddeley

[4] *Daily Telegraph*, 24 July 1969, on the late Mr Harry Grylls.

substitute methods of the Germans. We certainly cannot argue that the relative disengagement of these industries resulted in poor quality or poor growth performance.

Next—and we may consider this more serious—was the other kind of disengagement, where the universities did not produce sufficient of certain types of industrial skill. Some industries were chronically deficient in graduates while others were caught short in buoyant times, often as a result of severe contractions in the supply of their specialist labour in preceding depressions. In the first category of the chronically under-supplied were the chemical engineers, the metallurgists, the geologists, and oil engineers. While chemistry courses were very common, chemical engineering was a late comer, notably from 1923 at University College and also Imperial College, London. What was really needed by industry was the chemist who could convert laboratory processes into large-scale manufacture, and this shortage was a major bottleneck for most of the 1920s.[1] Throughout the period the total output of men with honours degrees in chemistry was 4,167 between 1926 and 1939, whereas that for applied chemistry was only 300. The reasons for this persistent lag in spite of industry's demands were probably twofold. First, students feared that chemical engineering would give them far less job security than pure chemistry since with the latter they had school-teaching to fall back on. Second, universities hard pressed for finance were understandably chary of starting very expensive departments which experience showed few students would wish to enter.[2] Thus the real interests of industry in this field were not served as well as they might have been.

The metallurgy problem persisted throughout the inter-war years. After the war, large numbers of metallurgists had been produced by the universities but with the post-war slump the output had fallen. By 1927 it was far too low,[3] down to about fifteen a year, and in 1931, too, the output was regarded as definitely less than could be absorbed within industry.[4] If there was a shortage of metallurgists even in the depression it was not surprising that the shortage became acute in the recovery of the 1930s. By 1937 and 1938 their supply was regarded as being dangerously low. Professor R. S. Hutton of Cambridge noted that an anomalous imbalance had arisen here *vis-à-vis* the chemical industry. 'The metal industries in short employ five times as many workers as the chemical industries and have an output valued at

---

[1] E. C. Williams, 'Chemical Engineering as a Career', *JC*, November and December 1926. The author was the Professor of the Ramsay Laboratories, University College, London. W. E. Gibbs, 'A Growing Demand for Chemical Engineers', *JC*, January 1929.

[2] University of Liverpool Vice-Chancellor's Report, 1922, p. 75.

[3] F. C. Thompson, 'The Supply of University Trained Metallurgists', *JC*, June 1927. The author was the Professor of Metallurgy at Manchester.

[4] F. C. Thompson, 'Good Prospects in Metallurgy', *JC*, February 1931, and 'Prospects for University Trained Metallurgists', *JC*, April 1926.

three and three quarter times that of the chemical industry. Yet the universities are training far more chemists than metallurgists.'[1] In fact in 1935-6 the ratio was 369 men taking chemistry degrees to fourteen in metallurgy. Only in 1938 did Cambridge hold its first examination in metallurgy as part of Part II of the Natural Science Tripos, and Hutton himself bemoaned this as late. Here was another weakness in the supply of graduate expertise to British industry, especially dangerous since the steel industry in 1936-7 was enjoying a boom 'unique in the history of the British iron and steel industry' under the stimulus of tariff and re-armament.[2]

The geologists and oil engineers likewise were in chronic short supply. A large demand and a shortage was noted during the 1920s in spite of the unusual activities of Birmingham University in filling this gap in training.[3] In the 1920s, for example, Anglo-Persian started taking on young English drillers to replace the Americans, Poles, and Canadians, 'almost all of whom were inefficient'. Also 1927 saw the beginning of the great Kirkuk field in Iraq.[4] Even during the depression oil engineering graduates were 'absorbed into the industry with some avidity' for the profession 'cannot find all the personnel it demands'.[5] The demand for geologists, always serious throughout these years and reflected in their unusually high salaries, became desperate by the end of the 1930s. Even Tizard, who held strong views about the overproduction of some types of scientist, admitted that as regards geologists 'we cannot supply enough'.[6] It was not that the universities did not cater for geology, but many departments were half empty. The reason for this lay fundamentally with the schools, in that the subject was not included in the syllabus for Higher School Certificate.[7] These areas of chronic shortages, which were never overcome even in depression, suggest certain deep-seated defects of a curricular nature. They were all specialisms somewhat removed from chemistry and physics, and they raised the dilemma of the degree of specialism and generalism desirable both at school and university levels. One could argue that it would have been better

---

[1] 'More Students wanted for the Profession of Metallurgist', *JC*, June 1937, and R. S. Hutton, 'The Training and Employment of Metallurgists', *JC*, May 1938.
[2] *Britain in Recovery* (British Association, 1937), 'The Iron and Steel Industry', p. 370.
[3] A. W. Nash, 'Openings for Young Men in the Petroleum Industry', *JC*, April 1930.
[4] Henry Longhurst, *Adventure in Oil, the Story of British Petroleum* (London, 1959), pp. 70 and 147.
[5] A. E. Dunstan, 'The Technologist in the Petroleum Industry', *JC*, November 1932.
[6] H. T. Tizard, 'Geologists for Mining', *JC*, July–August 1936.
[7] Vice-Chancellor's Report, University of Liverpool, 1939, p. 58. Liverpool was a good example of a university trying to meet the geology gap but hampered by the paucity of entrants from schools.

if schools had accepted a shade more specialism in their sixth form curriculum to the degree of accepting geology, for example, as a sixth form subject. At the university level the reverse may have been the fault; that chemistry courses were too specialized and did not admit of sufficient introduction of tangential subjects like chemical engineering and metallurgy at an early stage in the degree. This would have made possible some kind of Part II specialization in these branches at the finals honours level. The late introduction of metallurgy in this manner at Cambridge in 1938, for example, is indicative of a too tardy recognition of the problem for the health of industry. Imperial College likewise revised its chemistry syllabus in 1937 to allow of more specialization in the later parts of the course.

As well as areas of chronic shortage there were also others where shortages were created by unexpected expansions of certain types of careers. In this category fell mechanical engineering, marine engineering, and mining, a trio relating to the older industries as our earlier trio tended to relate to the 'new' ones. The position with mechanical engineering was little short of astonishing. In the early and mid 1920s this had been an amply supplied subject and one much taken up by ex-servicemen. But at the end of the 1920s the extraordinary situation shown in Table 26 arose. At a stroke, mechanical engineering changed

TABLE 26 *Honours degrees awarded*

	Engineering general	Electrical engineering	Mechanical engineering
1927/8	115	42	123
1928/9	200	51	226
1929/30	196	44	36

overnight from being the most popular branch of engineering to a minority branch, as men preferred more general engineering degrees. That this was not merely some artificial change in accounting but was a real situation was reflected in the immediate concern that by 1929 the supply of mechanical engineers was 'reaching a level which gives cause for alarm among the leaders of the profession'.[1] And the numerical relationship between mechanical engineers and engineers in general remained roughly the same throughout the rest of the period. It is more surprising that this drastic trend received no explanation. Possibly it may have been due to the end of the working of the ex-servicemen through the system, or to a belief that mechanical engineering, as the traditional form relating to the basic industries, would be more vulnerable in slump than newer forms like

[1] 'Mechanical Engineering, the Need for More Entrants', *JC*, March 1929.

electrical engineering. In 1936 it was still being noted that men were going into the new branches of aero- and electrical engineering to the neglect of the mechanical, and that there was an excess of demand for mechanical engineers.[1] Ironically, since this shortage was partly caused by a shift to electrical engineering there arose fears in the later 1930s that there was an actual overproduction of electrical engineers matching an underproduction of mechanicals.[2] Here was a case where career choice in trying to be shrewd in avoiding depression seemed to have over compensated, leaving the deserted occupation under-staffed and the newly espoused one over-supplied to the detriment of the industrial economy as a whole.

The other branch of engineering where this was markedly the case was marine engineering and shipbuilding.[3] There was scarcely an occupation and a university discipline more deserted in the 1920s. Although there were valuable scholarships tenable at universities given by leading shipbuilding firms, these were neglected. Indeed at Glasgow University the enrolments for the marine engineering course had fallen right off from seventy-six in 1921 down to eight in 1928. This also proved to be an over-reaction since the decline continued in the thirties to such an extent that by 1936 there was a shortage of marine engineers and executives noted on the Clyde, Tyne, and Tees as trade began to revive.[4] The case of coal mining was perhaps the strangest of the three. Due to natural doubts about the health of the industry in the 1920s applicants for courses declined. But ironically this led to a situation by 1929 where the demand for graduates so exceeded the supply that Armstrong College had to expand to cater for it.[5] In the recovery period of the later and mid 1930s coal mining graduates remained short[6] and Edinburgh University noted 'a great scarcity of technically trained young men in the mining industry'.[7] These then were the chief areas of disengagement. We regard those areas where the universities failed to supply sufficient graduates to

[1] 'Mechanical Engineering as a Profession', *JC*, September 1936.
[2] T. F. Wall, 'The Work of the Electrical Engineer', *JC*, April 1937, and Hugh Quigley, 'Are we training too many Electrical Engineers?' *JC*, June 1938. Quigley was the Economist to the Central Electricity Board. Wall did not believe there was overcrowding but noted it as a commonly held opinion of the time.
[3] Percy Hillhouse, 'Careers in Shipbuilding', *JC*, June 1930.
[4] 'Marine Engineering as a Career', *JC*, March 1936, and 'Occupational Trends, a Survey of Some Current Developments', *JC*, June 1937, also noted this concerning marine engineers.
[5] J. T. Whetton, 'Expanding Demand for Mining Engineers', *JC*, June 1929.
[6] F. Stuart Atkinson, 'The Mining and Petroleum Industries', *JC*, June 1937, and 'More Mining Engineers Wanted', *JC*, July–August 1938.
[7] *Careers in Mining Education* (University of Edinburgh, 1937). That Edinburgh should have brought out this advertisement in 1937 may indicate that a shortage of student recruits mirrored industry's shortage of graduate entrants.

industries demanding them as more dangerous than those areas where industries chose not to be graduate employers, achieving their success by their own methods of training and innovation.

Now that we have seen something of those areas of industry where graduate employment was active and those where it was not, we may focus on some of the problems of absorbing graduates into industry at the level of the firm.

Firstly the absorption of graduates by firms was as shown in Table 27, and a number of points emerge. Most important, although

TABLE 27   *Absorption of graduates by firms*

	Total no. of graduates going into firms	Firms employing them	Average no. per firm
Liverpool University engineers[1]			
1920s	167	78	2·14
1930s	215	82	2·62
Sheffield University graduates[2]			
1920s	62	49	1·27
1930s	67	52	1·29
Glasgow University graduates[3]			
1920s	95	60	1·58
1930s	102	69	1·48
St Andrews University graduates[4]			
1930s	75	42	1·79

[1] Calculated from lists in the *Journal of the University of Liverpool Engineering Society* for the period.
[2] Calculated from lists in *Floreamus* and *The Arrows*.
[3] Calculated from Reports of the Appointments Committee.
[4] Calculated from *Alumnus Chronicle of the University of St. Andrews*.

general employment opportunities for the graduate were widening qualitatively yet there did not seem to be a marked increase in the range of firms absorbing graduates in the 1930s compared with the 1920s. The numbers of firms prepared to take graduates did not increase commensurately with the numbers of graduates going into industry. On the contrary, there is evidence that the increase of graduates going into firms was to some extent absorbed by existing large employers actually increasing their share of employment. For example, whereas Metro-Vickers provided 13·8 per cent of the employment for Liverpool engineers in the 1920s, this rose to 17·7 per cent in the 1930s. Similarly, ici's proportion as a provider of employment for Glasgow graduates entering firms rose from 7·4 per cent in the 1920s to 10·8 per cent in the 1930s. The Liverpool engineers, being a specialist employment group, show the narrowest range of firms per graduate, but when graduates of all types are compared the Scottish universities seemed to rely on a rather narrower range of employing firms than Sheffield. This was probably due to the fact that there was no marked local demand for Scottish graduates within Scottish firms, with the exception of J. and P. Coats, such that they tended to be more reliant on large English or British firms.[1]

The absorption of the graduate called for certain adjustments and even strains within the firm in these years. In the first place, it entailed changes in premium apprenticeship. The traditional method of entry, into engineering works especially, had been to pay a large premium for pupillage, which served, with the cheap labour provided by the entrant, as payment for the higher level training received within the firm. But with the increasing use of the young graduate within the firm this nineteenth-century device, which was so suitable for a non-graduate entry, tended to decline—first, because it was patently unreasonable to expect the young engineer to pay both high university fees then a high premium and, second, because a good deal of the training had already been done by the universities. Third, the young graduate entrant was now far more use to the firm than his public school predecessor had been and, fourth, with the scarcity of mechanical engineers from the late 1920s firms were now more concerned to remove than to erect financial barriers to the qualified recruit. As a rough indicator, of the thirty-six firms studied by the *Journal of Careers* between 1926 and 1930, eight charged premiums; of the forty-one between 1931 and 1935 only two did so; and only one of the seventeen studied between 1936 and 1939 did so. Moreover, it was specifically noted that premium apprenticeship was on the decline in the good years of the late 1920s and that this had been in process for the previous twenty years.[2]

Just as the premium apprenticeship tended to decline in the inter-war years, so also firms began to consider the problem of training schemes specifically to attract graduates. This was not so easy and straight-forward a matter, especially for firms not used to taking graduates, and there were a number of misfires throughout the period, especially in the 1920s. By the mid 1930s Rowntree's took graduates as trainees for a probationary period. Tootal's, which under Harold Rostron became a highly education-conscious firm in the inter-war

[1] Edinburgh University Appointments Secretary's Report, 1935.
[2] 'Premium Apprenticeship', *JC*, October 1928.

years, received university apprentices for two-year training. From 1917 Lever's had their own staff college for training graduates, while Metro-Vickers, which was in the forefront of industrial education under Sir Arthur Fleming, ran courses in connection with Manchester University, and Reckitt's had a similar arrangement with Hull. The Gas Light and Coke Company, Morland and Impey, LNER, and LMS were also singled out as firms significant in the development of company training for the graduate, while of these only the LNER was still charging premiums.[1] And yet, in perspective, the graduate training scheme was still the mark of the advanced firm in the 1930s. For example, of 114 firms surveyed as taking Cambridge graduates in 1937–8, only twelve had training schemes and only twenty-two graduates out of 326 in the survey referred to their firms as having one.[2]

The introduction of the graduate, particularly when a firm was looking for a rapid solution to the problem of succession to high office, could lead to considerable friction within the firm. The compacting of generations caused by the introduction and promotion of young graduates, and the leapfrogging of old hands this entailed, added to the prejudice against the university man. Cadbury's, which had a considerable influx of graduates to the 1920s, was very sensitive to this problem and was at pains to point out that 'this method of filling important posts has however by no means superseded the older one of promoting able men and women from the lower ranks of the firm's employees'.[3] At the Calico Printers' Association the Manchester managers were noted for considerable prejudice against graduates, and indeed graduates were leaving because of the hostility of the staff.[4] These strains did not go unnoticed or unremarked from the university side of the link. At Liverpool the Vice-Chancellor observed in 1924 that the introduction of young graduates into the firm was 'experiencing difficulties' since those graduates appointed to positions of responsibility over the heads of those who left school five years earlier, 'are encountering grave opposition, not open but veiled. Too often by keeping back information . . . those immediately beneath them employ every opportunity to make obvious their unfitness and bring about their resignation or discharge.'[5]

The reverse problem could also arise, of a managerial structure without sufficient gradations of responsibility to bring graduates on. Boots, for example, was in this difficulty in introducing graduates

---

[1] R. W. Ferguson (ed.), *Training in Industry, a Report embodying the Results of Enquiries conducted between 1931 and 1934 by the Association for Education in Industry and Commerce* (London, 1935).
[2] *University Education and Business* (Spens), op. cit.
[3] Iolo A. Williams, *The Firm of Cadbury, 1891–1931* (London, 1931), p. 241.
[4] CAB Memoranda, 5 September 1928, 3 March 1932.
[5] Report of the Vice-Chancellor, 1924, p. 8.

without modifying the hierarchical structure. Consequently 'there seems to be nothing between them, and the managers of the department which our fellows can take en route to higher posts'.[1] This also seemed to be a difficulty in the mining industry where many companies 'have not up to the present appreciated the necessity of making positions suitable for young men to fill the gap between that of being a student and the more responsible position of manager'.[2] This was a problem shared with the motor car industry. J. B. Priestley, in a perceptive account of the Daimler works at Coventry and his conversation with an Oxford graduate there, remarked that 'these new methods of production demanded fewer and fewer intermediaries between the two or three managers and their planning department on the one side and the thousands of artisans on the other side. The technical man with his university degree was worse off than the workmen themselves.'[3] The Oxford man with whom he conversed had little chance of an opening and was poorly paid. It is not surprising that the motor car industry was not so keen on graduates.

We can obtain a broad view of the relative importance of graduates in different industries by comparing the output of graduates with certain types of qualifications with the total labour force in the industries to which those qualifications relate. In Table 28 we take a number of leading industrial classifications and present in column (b) the average of the total male labour force in those industries for 1925 and 1938. We then select those degree qualifications most likely to serve those industries and calculate the total output of male graduates for the whole period 1925–39 and present this in column (a). The third column presents column (a) as a proportion of column (b) and provides some indicator of the relative bulk of graduates within the range of industries concerned. These are then ranked in order of those where graduates are numerically most important within the labour force down to those where they are least important. It will be stressed that column (c) does *not* give the proportion of graduates in any particular industry, which is not possible; but it does give an indication of the *relative* importance of graduates between different industries. Column (d) provides an interesting confirmatory check on this ranking. In 1951 the census data made it possible to calculate what percentage of the labour force in any industry belonged to any particular social class. We present Routh's calculations of the percentage of those people who were in the highest 1A social grouping for the industries we are concerned with. We find that his ranking works out to be almost the same as ours. This indeed should not be surprising since the persons classified as

[1] CAB Memorandum, Boots, 25 February 1939.
[2] *Careers in Mining Education* (University of Edinburgh, 1937), p. 6, citing a letter from the managing director of a coal company.
[3] J. B. Priestley, *English Journey* (London, 1934), p. 74.

TABLE 28 The position of graduates in relation to the total labour force

(a) Output of male graduates 1925–39[1]		(b) Average of total male labour force in the industry for years 1925 and 1938[2]	(c) (a) as proportion of (b)	(d) Routh's ranking 1951[3]
Chemistry	4,167	Chemicals	1:37	Chemicals 3·83
Applied chemistry	300			
Oil technology	63 } 4,530			
Gas engineering	37	Gas, water, electricity supply	1:235	Gas, electricity, water 3·66
Electrical engineering	781 } 818			
Engineering general	2,581	Engineering, shipbuilding and metal trades	1:428	Engineering and shipbuilding 1·63
Mechanical engineering	746			
Marine engineering	11			
Naval architecture	30			
Electrical engineering	781 } 4,149			
Metallurgy	231	Metal manufacture	1:1,411	Metal manufacture 1·23
Glass	14	Glass trades	1:2,857	Glass ..
Leather	16	Leather and leather goods	1:3,000	Leather 0·38
Mining	201	Mining	1:5,768	Mining 0·65
Textiles	19	Textile trades	1:25,736	Textiles 0·33

[1] Calculated from UGC Returns.
[2] Estimated number of insured employees by industry, B. R. Mitchell, *Abstract of British Historical Statistics* (Cambridge, 1962), pp. 62–3.
[3] Guy Routh, *Occupation and Pay in Great Britain, 1906–60* (Cambridge, 1965), table 17, p. 39. This is the first year this distribution by social class is available.

1A in an industry in 1951 will tend to be those people who entered the industry as graduates in the 1920s and 1930s; many of the people in column (d) must in fact be substantially the same people as those in column (a) but twenty years older in their careers.

That the ranking shown by the industries in both columns is roughly similar lends confirmation to the view that this is a fairly true representation of the relative importance of graduates in different industries. In any case, all other evidence and indeed common sense is in accord with what the table suggests, that graduates were a more important element in the labour forces of the chemical, gas, and engineering industries than they were in textiles and leather. In mining they were an important element qualitatively but obviously small compared with the labour force as a whole.

It is stressed that the above ratios are national figures constructed to obtain some idea of the relative spread between industries. They are *not* in themselves proportions of graduates in the labour force. This is far more difficult to trace but one or two figures are available. In the British Dyestuffs Corporation in 1926 there were 3,000 workmen and 130 graduates.[1] Cadbury's intake ratios were one graduate to forty-eight non-graduates in 1939,[2] and an estimate for industry as a whole in the 1920s was one graduate to fifty non-graduates.[3] ICI in 1932 employed thirty graduates per 1,000 employees.[4] These give graduate percentages of 4·15, 2, 2, and 3 per cent respectively which gives some idea of the order of magnitude.

What could the firm offer the graduate in terms of employment security and salaries? Did graduate status help to protect university men from the effects of unemployment, and how sensitive were graduate entrants to industry to swings in the economy? The trends of graduate unemployment may be seen from the figures in Table 29.

Unemployment levels were probably high according to the evidence of appointments officers' reports in the early 1920s following the post-war boom. As the boom broke and the ex-servicemen came on to the market, so they experienced a rise in unemployment rates common in the country. Glasgow, Edinburgh, and Cambridge all noted difficulties in placing graduates in 1921, 1920 and 1923, 1921 and 1923 respectively. Thus, although we have no quantitative data for these years there can be no doubt that this was the common experience. When recovery was on the way, unemployment levels

---

[1] *JC*, June 1926.
[2] *JC*, February 1939.
[3] Maxwell Garnett speaking at the Congress of the Universities of the Empire, 1921, p. 206.
[4] M. J. S. Clapham of ICI speaking at 'Industry and the Universities' (Conference of Committee of Vice-Chancellors and CBI, 1965), pp. 7–12.

TABLE 29 *Percentages of Graduates enrolled with university appointment boards remaining unemployed in each year 1923–39*

	1923	1924	1925	1926	1927	1928	1929	1930	1931	1932	1933	1934	1935	1936	1937	1938	1939
Imperial College							1·99	1·3	4·15	9·5	8·3	6·7	2·75	2·5	1·2		
Exeter											1·5	4·0	2·9	0·8	1·4	2·7	
Glasgow													7·5	9·5	6·7	2·95	
Birmingham			40·2	33·9	26·6	13·4	12·8	11·9	16·5	22·4	18·8						
Birmingham technologists											20·2	10·9	9·7	7·2	2·8	4·4	1·7
Percentage of insured workers over sixteen unemployed in UK	11·6	10·9	11·2	12·7	10·6	11·2	11·0	14·6	21·5	22·5	21·3	17·7	16·4	14·3	11·3	13·3	11·7

moved sharply down in the fairly prosperous years of the later 1920s.
These years did not cause concern or investigation in the graduate
employment field, and it was possible in 1929 for the AUT sub-
committee on universities and industry to observe with gratification
that 'it would appear that the relations [of universities to industry]
are not unsatisfactory'.[1]

When depression struck it did have a fairly sharp effect on
graduate unemployment levels, and both Birmingham and Imperial
College graduates experienced peaks of unemployment in 1932,
which was also the peak in national averages, after sharp rises
in the preceding year. But in England, at least, what surprised
observers was the relative lack of harm that the depression did
to graduate employment compared with unemployment levels
in other countries. Henry Tizard, surveying the field in 1931, expressed surprise at the strength of demand for chemists (a science
vulnerable through overproduction) in spite of the depression.
Engineers, he thought, had no difficulty in getting jobs, metallurgy
was good, and there was a shortage of mining engineers.[2] This was
perhaps not so surprising. The hard core of depressed industries and
regions were those of textiles, coal, and shipbuilding, the first of
which was not a significant graduate employer, and the last two of
which had undergone a severe contraction of graduate output in
the 1920s. Tizard was not alone in his optimistic view. The UGC
observed that 'in the years immediately following the acute financial
crisis of 1931 a certain number of graduates undoubtedly found difficulty in getting posts. On the other hand, the position could hardly be
described as serious, since the majority did eventually find employment.'[3] Also the DSIR found that of ninety-two science students who
had completed courses by the end of 1929 only four were unemployed
in May 1930, and the work obtained by the other eighty-eight was
regarded as satisfactory.[4] Finally, H. J. Crawford, the well-informed
Secretary of the London Appointments Office, also agreed that 'on
the whole it is surprising how well the university trained man and
woman have weathered the depression . . .'.[5]

In order to put a little hard evidence into this general feeling of
well-being, Mrs Eleanor Rathbone made a special survey of the
problem.[6] She sent a questionnaire to 22,399 graduates, of whom
4,327 replied. She was able to tell from this how many from her sample

[1] AUT Sub-Committee on the Relationship of the Universities to Industry;
Minute, 10 October 1929.
[2] H. T. Tizard, 'Careers in Scientific Industry', *JC*, January 1931.
[3] UGC Report for the Period 1929/30–1934/35, published 1936, pp. 29–30.
[4] Cited in *Graduate Employment* (NUS, 1937).
[5] H. J. Crawford, 'The Graduate in Business, a Review and a Forecast', *JC.*,
January 1935.
[6] Eleanor Rathbone, 'Do University Graduates require Insurance against
Unemployment?', *The New University*, December 1934.

were unemployed in April 1934 and, more importantly for our study, how many suffered some unemployment since 1 April 1931. She found that of those graduates in technical work, engineering, chemistry and research, 9·9 per cent of those replying were unemployed in April 1934, and 15·9 per cent had suffered some unemployment since April 1931. Graduates in commercial, banking, secretarial, and selling work were better off; 3·8 per cent of those who replied were unemployed in 1934 and 9 per cent had suffered some unemployment since 1931. She suggested that while there was 6·5 per cent unemployment among all those who replied, the overall level may be less since those who did not reply were less likely to be out of work and concerned to make their plight known. In spite of this generally not too unfavourable picture, Mrs Rathbone recognized that there was a fair amount of under-employment of graduates as clerks and the like, and Henry Tizard similarly thought that too many graduate scientists were going into jobs better filled by people of less training.[1]

The Scottish position during the depression was rather worse.[2] T. A. Joynt obtained evidence of the employment position in late 1933 of 1,468 graduates of Edinburgh University who graduated in 1930 and 1931. Of these the following percentages were still unemployed.

	Arts hons M.A.	Arts M.A. ordinary	Pure science	Applied science
Men	5·9	14·3	33·3	16·3
Women	26·8	29·9	5·9	0

These figures ought to be fairly comparable with Mrs Rathbone's since they were taken at the same time and covered the same period. They reveal a noticeably worse position in Scotland than she found for England. The low arts M.A. figures do not, of course, relate to the high receptivity of Scottish industry for the arts graduate, but to the fact that these people are almost all absorbed by school-teaching. Much more serious was the high unemployment of Scottish scientists, and even applied scientists, in an economy that was less diversified and less science-based than that of England.

After the 1932 peak in unemployment, recovery got under way. First, it is interesting to note that the recovery of graduate employment was much more marked than for employment in general. Although the unemployment figures for Birmingham technologists in 1932 and Birmingham graduates in general in 1931 are very similar to the national averages, yet from 1934–7 the reduction of unemployment amongst the Birmingham graduates is vastly greater

[1] H. T. Tizard, 'Science at the Universities, is the Output of Graduates Excessive?', *JC*, October 1934.
[2] T. A. Joynt, 'Graduates and Employment', *University of Edinburgh Journal*, summer 1934.

than that in the country at large. From 1932–7 there was a nine-fold reduction in unemployment levels at Imperial College, eleven-fold between graduates in general and technologists at Birmingham, but only about half in the country at large. This is all the more striking because the effect of the depression had been to increase student numbers, drawing students into the universities and keeping them there, with the effect of unloading them onto the labour market in the mid 1930s. One would not have been surprised had this resulted in a lagging effect artificially prolonging high graduate unemployment rates. That this did not take place further confirms the strength of the graduate recovery. Second, the timing of recovery differed between Scotland and England, both as regards graduates and labour in general. The sharp contraction of Glasgow graduate unemployment figures came only after 1938 for graduates overall, and the Appointments Officer there noted that this was due to the increase in armaments manufacture The Scottish recovery of the later 1930s was more marked than that of England and later.[1] Third, it is interesting to note that the recession of 1938 was sufficient to have a noticeable effect on the Exeter and Birmingham figures, both of which moved up slightly in sympathy with the national trend, although the Scottish figures, with their particular circumstances, moved down.

From the point of view of the student seeking a job in industry, the years of the mid and later 1930s were clearly much better. In 1937 the National Union of Students found the situation basically satisfactory. They thought that 'in regard to employment there would seem to be relatively little difficulty for graduates ultimately to find a post, though often there is a time lag between the completion of the course and the obtaining of the post, sometimes as much as 12 months'.[2] With regard to the Welsh situation, however, there was no more concern for congratulation over their graduate employment than over the plight of their national economy as a whole. In the University of Wales, 25–30 per cent of graduates still remained unemployed a year after graduating, and 10–12 per cent still two years after graduating.[3] In the same year as the NUS survey, Dr W. M. Kotschnig came to a broadly optimistic conclusion for Britain as a whole in the light of his comparative studies on the issue. Britain could not be said to have any great problem of graduate unemployment compared with most other European countries and this was attributed to our unusually low ratio of students to population.[4] It is noteworthy that

[1] H. W. Richardson, *Economic Recovery in Britain, 1932–39* (London, 1967).
[2] *Graduate Employment, a Report of the 1937 Congress of the National Union of Students* (NUS, 1937).
[3] T. K. Rees, 'Graduate Employment in Wales', appendix D of the NUS survey, op. cit.
[4] W. M. Kotschnig, *Unemployment in the Learned Professions*, section 4. See table II, p. 17.

TABLE 30 Salary profiles of first occupations of Imperial College leavers (in £s)

	−200	200+	225+	250+	275+	300+	325+	350+	375+	400+	450+	500+	550+	600+
1920														
Chemists		1	1	2					1	3				1
Engineers	4	2	2											1
Mining engineers						1				1		1		
1930														
Chemists	2	1		6	2	2	1							1
Engineers	26	6	2	7	2	4		1			2	3		1
Mining engineers										1		2	1	
1939														
Chemists	1	2	2	8	5	3		1			1			1
Mechanical engineers	7	12		6		3	1							
Mining engineers			1	4		2	1	2		1	2	3		
Physicists		1		2							1			
Civil engineers	8	3		3										
Electrical engineers	24	8	1								1			

when Kotschnig was compiling his book he approached the Cambridge Appointments Officer, who recorded privately that Kotschnig's study would be useful for 'discounting some of the pessimism one sees expressed about the university blind alley in these times'.[1]

Such commentators and surveyors usually made some proviso that even though actual employment figures were not bad, they could not know how many students were happily or suitably placed in their occupations. Accordingly, at the end of the decade the University of Birmingham tried to probe deeper into this more subjective area of unsuitable employment.[2] It was found that in 1938, 60 per cent of Birmingham students graduating in the inter-war years were quite satisfied with their jobs and only 20 per cent actually dissatisfied. Within the dissatisfied group, 11·4 per cent felt that way because they were misemployed, that is they were doing jobs for which they were not trained or which were well below their level of training. The situation seemed worst with pure scientists, about half of whom were dissatisfied, and about a quarter of whom did not find their qualifications of use. The guild concluded that 'although nearly all graduates are in a post of some kind or other at the moment, far too many are not in the right posts'.

If graduate unemployment, with these reservations, was not so severe as people feared, what of graduate salaries? It is possible to calculate the starting salaries of Imperial College leavers for 1920, 1930 and 1939 to show the salary profiles according to subject and industrial sectors (see Table 30).[3]

It is evident that engineers were in general less well paid than chemists. This was largely due to the fact that engineers regarded the first year or so of work as still being training, and the substitute for paying pupillage was usually to accept a rather low salary. Chemists were fairly well paid, but it was evident that their position seemed to have sagged somewhat. Whereas in 1920 the median salary was £300, by 1930 it had sunk to the £250–300 bracket, which would be in line with the national trends. However, it did not recover by the late 1930s as we would expect from the rise in professional salaries from about 1935. £250–300 was quite the most usual salary at which graduates started, and one cannot see much difference throughout the whole period save this slight sag. Graduates with qualification in mining and geology were by far the best paid of all, with their salaries in 1920 ranging from £300 to £600 a year. To illustrate the different fortunes of the occupations the upper quartile for each is given.

[1] CAB Memorandum, International Student Service (under whose auspices Kotschnig was writing), 3 December 1932.
[2] Graduate Employment, a Report . . . Guild of Undergraduates of the University of Birmingham (May 1938).
[3] Calculated from lists in Appointments Office Records in Imperial College Archives.

	1920	*1930*	*1939*	
Chemist	400	300	300	
Engineer	250	250	250	mechanical
			200	civil
			200	electrical
Mining	600	550	450	

These may be compared with the starting salaries quoted in the notes of the Cambridge Appointments Officer for the period 1920–37 grouped chronologically and by industry:

		£
1920	Watford Manufacturing Company	250
1924	Medway Oil Storage Company	360–600
	Enos	156–260
	Lyons	250
1925	Metro-Vickers	150
	Sun Life	250
	BTH	175
1928	Venesta	250–300
	Yorks. Copper Works	150–250
1929	Pilkington's	400
1930	Lissen's	260
1932	Rowntree's	250
1933	MacFarlane Lang	200
	Whitbread	300
1936	J. and P. Coats	200
	Norwich Union	120
1937	W. Hollins	300
	Coca Cola	312–64

Food	250, 250, 250, 200, 300, 312–64
Electricals	150, 175, 260
Textiles	200, 300
Glass	250–300, 400

What again is remarkable is the rough similarity apart from the unrealistic Norwich Union quotation. The great electrical firms tended to be low, but the popular domestic consumption food industries which were doing well on the rising real incomes of the employed, offered a good range of competitive prospects.

How far did starting salary relate to academic performance? Was, in fact, industry efficiently taking account of the different intellectual skill levels of its graduate entrants, offering condign rewards for performance at the university, or was it just haphazardly recruiting the 'right type' by rule of thumb and instinct? This is a matter of some importance. If the universities were providing the kind of relevant education that industry needed, and if industry was aware of it, then we should expect to find industry paying some attention to university assessments of academic quality and reflecting this recognition in cash terms. If, on the other hand, what the universities were doing was irrelevant, and the firms cared little or nothing for what a graduate had learned and accordingly placed little weight on the university's assessment, then we would have no reason to expect degree performance to relate to initial starting salary. In the unique case where we have found it possible to make this test—for Imperial College chemists of the mid 1930s—we find that there was indeed a connection between degree performance and pay. The relation of performance and salary was as follows:[1]

7 first class degrees, average starting salary   £262
12 second class degrees, average starting salary £253
4 pass class degrees, average starting salary   £218

Thus we may fairly conclude that industries employing chemists, at least, did respect the education that Imperial College was providing and did place some weight on the academic performance of its entrants to the extent of reflecting this approbation in salaries.

This increasing involvement of the universities and industry in the inter-war years did not take place without provoking a strong reaction among certain elements of both staff and students who were inclined to regard the liaison with suspicion and distaste. On the student side there were various connected grounds for complaint. First, there were fears that the demands of industry were making the universities too narrowly technical in their training, to the neglect of genuine liberal education.[2] It was leading to the warping of examinations into an excessive concern for technical detail, and universities were becoming factories for turning out 'the embryo technician from the grammar school'. Moreover, for some this was merely symptomatic of the debauching of the ideals of universities by the 'ignobility and squalor' of industrial and commercial culture as industry, increasingly seen as a sinister hidden force in the 1930s came to attain 'control over all the spheres of life'.[3] Ironically, while some students stressed their revulsion from industry and the wish to disengage the universi-

---

[1] Calculated by collating 1935 examination lists for chemists with 1936–7 and 1937–8 Appointments Records in Imperial College Archives. The actual marks gained in examination and the salaries for the same individuals were traced although they were, of course, confidential at the time.
[2] For example, A. W. Coysh, 'The University and the Community', *Floreamus*, March 1928. H. G. G. Herklots, *The New Universities*, especially 'The Shadow of Industrialism', pp. 26–9. R. Nunn May, 'This Desirable Residence', *The University*, summer, 1928. W. J. Diplock, *Isis or the Future of Oxford* (London, 1929). Brian Simon, *A Student's View of the Universities*.
[3] E.g. D. M. Patch, *Blind Guides, a Student Looks at the University* (London, 1939). 'Achilles', 'The Systems', *The Ram* (Exeter University) autumn, 1939.

ties from too close contact with it, others reviled industry for being unable to provide them with careers when they graduated. As one Bangor student noted, 'it is impossible to get rid of the feeling that we have been betrayed'. It is worth noting that, unlike the situation in the 1960s, there was no evident connection between this radical, anti-industry student opinion and the tradition of student hooliganism which was non-ideological in character.

This student hostility to the closer involvement with the world of business and industry found its counterpart in a stronger, and much better expressed, opposition on the part of many prominent academics both in arts and sciences. An early warning had been sounded by Lord Rutherford when opening the Wills Physics Laboratories at Bristol University in 1927. He said that 'he would view as an unmitigated disaster the utilization of university laboratories mainly for research bearing on industry'.[1] This was hardly likely to happen with the Wills, but it was a particularly relevant comment for other parts of the university. For example, Bristol University made overtures to local industry of a character that Rutherford would have deplored. They invited local firms to finance research fellowships within the university, 'thus you might select some subject of research connected with the problems of your own business. You would have full access to the research and prior knowledge of the results obtained'.[2] This and Bristol University engineering department's extensive service work for firms was exactly the kind of thing that Rutherford was worried about. Around the same time the Vice-Chancellor of Reading gave a similar warning that using universities for utilitarian work was like cutting blocks with a razor, and those who do it 'debase and belittle and pervert the purposes for which universities stand'.[3]

However, the concentrated reaction that attracted most sustained attention came in the early 1930s. Ironically, it began with foreign professors looking at Britain from the outside. Wilhelm Dibelius, Professor of English at Berlin, pointed out the dangers, especially in the northern civic universities, where both career-making students and supporting industrialists 'conceive of science as a useful instrument in winning a large income in a short time', while it was the universities' duty to emphasize scientific study for its own sake. He concluded with a cautious warning that 'so far the dependence of the

---

[1] Lord Rutherford, 21 October 1927, reported in *Nonesuch*, November 1927, p. 127. *Nonesuch* was the Bristol University magazine but Rutherford's statement was quite widely reported.
[2] The Colston Research Society for the Promotion of Research in the University of Bristol, 1929, printing a letter to firms, 19 March 1922.
[3] W. M. Childs, *The New University of Reading, some Ideas for which it Stands* (Reading, 1926), p. 22. It is interesting to note that his concern had grown during the decade. In 1921 he wrote *Universities and their Freedom* (London, 1921) without a trace of concern for this issue.

newer universities on capitalism has not proved dangerous, but their position is hardly strong enough to be viewed with entire satisfaction'.[1] Another foreign professor, Abraham Flexner, did indeed view the situation in 1930 with a good deal less than entire satisfaction. While considering that the independence of British universities had not on the whole been subject to 'serious interference from capitalist influences', yet he was sharply critical of the development of specific technologies in the universities—Birmingham's brewing, Leed's dyeing and gas engineering, Sheffield's glass, and so forth. Flexner noted that although this was not so bad as the situation in his native United States, yet it 'is none the less deplorable . . . for it is neither liberal nor university quality'.[2] The attack gathered momentum in the same year as Harold Laski, expressing his admiration of Flexner, voiced the fear that the finance of university research by outside bodies was moulding their development irrespective of academic considerations.[3]

Increasing doubt and apprehension became crystallized in the writings of Sir Ernest Barker in 1931. Like Flexner he deplored the brewing, textiles, and commerce education developments of the previous decade. He thought that it was a 'great mistake' to blur the distinction between the university and the technical college, and feared that universities would thereby degenerate into 'handy' institutions furnishing 'even the world of business' with recruits. For Barker the ancient universities in particular had the duty of defending for the rest the 'stronghold of pure learning' and 'long time values against the demands of material progress'.[4] It is interesting to remember that only one or two years previously Barker had been Principal of King's College, London, with its important engineering element which he especially admired.[5] Was there a curious dichotomy between his former position in the 1920s and his fears of technology in the 1930s? However, to Barker's voice was soon added that of perhaps the most eminent scientist to express his doubts about industry in the thirties, Sir James Colquhoun Irvine of St Andrews, who was noted for his outstanding work on gas and drugs during the preceding war. In addressing an American audience he stated that one of the British universities' most immediate problems was how far they were justified in further opening their doors to more utilitarian

[1] Wilhelm Dibelius, *England* (London, 1930), pp. 440–2.
[2] Abraham Flexner, *Universities, American, English and German* (Oxford, 1931), pp. 250–1, 255–6.
[3] Harold Laski, 'Foundations, Universities and Research' in *The Dangers of Obedience* (New York, 1930), p. 70.
[4] Sir Ernest Barker, *Universities in Great Britain, their Position and their Problems*. This was reprinted under the same title as a chapter in W. M. Kotschnig and E. Prys (ed.), *The University in a Changing World*.
[5] Sir Ernest Barker, *Age and Youth, Memories of Three Universities* (Oxford, 1953), p. 125.

subjects. The university could not produce both the 'educated' and the 'technically trained mind', and if science were harnessed in the university too closely to the 'wheels of industry' and factory operations then that would mean the death of scientific enquiry in the universities.

In the mid 1930s, J. D. Bernal and Julian Huxley maintained a defence of the universities against certain dangers they feared from the encroachment of industry. Huxley came to the view that the demands of industry had had a damaging and warping effect on the balance of research, over-developing 'the physical and chemical sciences which help industry',[1] to the neglect of the human sciences. J. D. Bernal, Professor of Physics in London University, agreed about this imbalance caused by industry,[2] but laid even more serious charges against industry for its damage to university science. He suggested that interference was actually stifling research, and claimed that 'increasingly in this country as well as in other countries the influence of big commercial corporations and of governments closely linked to them is tending to dominate universities particularly on the scientific side'. This had led to enforced secrecy about certain lines of research performed in universities for firms who refused to allow publication. He claimed that certain biological lines were deliberately not developed for this reason, and that 'it was only last year that in Cambridge the Council of Senate turned down a proposal that all researches carried out in the University for private firms or the government should be published'.[3] This clearly was a new tack, and something even worse than even Barker or Flexner or Irvine had in mind.

This reaction of students and faculty against industry provoked a defence of industrial involvement from two very major figures of the 1930s. The majority of professors who were in favour of close links with industry did not need to articulate their views, but went on quietly working to this end. However, they did have their own advocates in the debate which on the defenders' side, like that of the attackers, was centred closely on 1930–1. Fittingly, the defence of industrial contacts came from the Vice-Chancellors of two major industrial city universities. Sir Hector Hetherington, then at Liverpool, stated quite firmly that the modern universities were fulfilling the purpose for which they were built. 'Their graduates supply the personnel . . . their professors take a large share in the fundamental scientific research on which every improvement of industrial technique is based.'[4] He frankly approved of this, and by no means

[1] Julian Huxley, *Scientific Research and Social Needs* (London, 1934), p. 264.
[2] J. D. Bernal, *The Social Function of Science* (London, 1939), pp. 39–40.
[3] J. D. Bernal, 'Universities, Science and Society', *Time and Tide University Supplement*, 22 June 1935.
[4] Sir Hector Hetherington, 'The History and Significance of the Modern Universities' in Hugh Martin (ed.), *The Life of a Modern University*, p. 19.

regarded it as something for which to apologize. Sir Charles Grant Robertson, the Vice-Chancellor of Birmingham, was even more forthright. While admitting that the universities had not solved the problem of their relations with commerce and business, he welcomed even closer links with industry, and wanted the universities to achieve these 'not by waiting for Business to come to them, but for them to go out and capture Business'. In the second edition of his book he went further. He expressed his flat disagreement with Barker's position and advocated close connections with technical colleges; nor did he fear the intrusion of technology.[1]

While the weightiest figures defending the university–industry link were arts men not themselves concerned with technology, it was scarcely surprising that one or two technology professors entered the debate to justify their actions, though much of the spade work of this justification had already been done before 1914. A. F. Barker, the Professor of Textile Industries at Leeds, tried to give some justifications before the brunt of the attack came.[2] He considered that any argument for the inclusion of industrial subjects in the university curriculum had to depend on the value of these subjects in eliciting 'response and interest'. He considered that industry provided that 'stimulus' and so justified it. Second, he argued, a concern for technological industrial problems could lead into new areas of pure science. Barker, even at so technological a university as Leeds, clearly felt somewhat on the defensive, and his first argument has a hollow ring. However, when the debate got under way after 1928, and especially with the publication of Flexner's book, W. E. S. Turner of Sheffield went over to the attack and advocated not only technology but also specific technical training for the bluntest of reasons. First, the manufacturers needed it and wanted it; and, second, it was in the students' interests that the universities teach it because conditions of in-service training with the firm varied so much that it was better to provide a standardized training at college.[3] There he left it; he was not interested in broader issues like Flexner and Barker, and in his forthright practical approach he probably voiced the opinions of his technological colleagues who merely got on with their work of

[1] Sir Charles Grant Robertson, *The British Universities* (London, 1930), pp. 61 and 65, and ibid. (London, 1944), p. 66. See also Samuel Alexander, 'The Purpose of a University', *Political Quarterly*, July–September 1931, vol. II no. 3, pp. 337–8. Bonamy Dobree, *The Universities and Regional Life* (Earl Grey Memorial Lecture, King's College, Newcastle, 1943) for another arts professor's deliberate espousing of the view that universities should serve industry.
[2] A. F. Barker, *Leaves from a Northern University* (London, 1926), 'Applied Science in the Universities'.
[3] Report of the Proceedings of the Fourth Congress of the Universities of the British Empire, 'The University Graduate in Commerce and Industry', ofessor W. E. S. Turner.

producing technical specialists, condemning their opponents not by arguing with them but by merely ignoring them.

It is worth isolating a number of features of this important clash of opinion about the connections of the universities and industry in the inter-war years. First, while the influence of industry on university research was very much a staff pre-occupation, it did not enter into the worries of students which largely focused on teaching and examinations. There was thus a slight difference in the grounds of apprehension between the generations. There is no discernible 'feeling of betrayal' phase in staff thought as there was with the students, and accordingly the teachers did not tend to drift off into a broader questioning of values or of the system. Also the concern of staff, at least expressed on any scale, seemed to come slightly later than that of the students, in the early 1930s rather than the late 1920s. It is interesting to note, too, certain features about the main faculty participants in the debate. Those suspicious of excessive industrial involvement were almost equally divided between arts and sciences—Rutherford, Irvine, Bernal, and Flexner on the one hand and Laski, Dibelius, and Ernest Barker on the other. Thus it was certainly not a simple matter of resistance to industry coming from arts men as part of some arts-versus-science controversy. Indeed, paradoxically, the academics who articulated their specific support for this connection tended to be arts men—Hetherington, Grant Robertson, Alexander, Dobree—two philosophers, a historian, and a literary critic. It is also significant that the two arts men holding vice-chancellorships should have espoused industry, and that the one science vice-chancellor in this group should have been suspicious of it. It would have been tactically very dubious ground for an arts vice-chancellor publicly to start criticizing industry and scientists, and one does not find an instance of this. Irvine probably felt that he could do so because his own record of industrial liaison was particularly good. With some of the protagonists their attitudes to industry were a part of their well-known political attitudes. Laski, Bernal, and Simon were and are well-known personalities on the left. On the other hand, it is remarkable that some of the most reactionary views came from the students, one of them an important NUS figure. Herklots's highly patronizing attitude to the civic universities and Diplock's scathing remarks about scholarship boys would have aroused a storm of protest had they been printed by senior academics.

In the last two chapters on the relationship between the universities, their graduate output and industry in the inter-war years we have seen how the increasingly scientific nature of industry and especially the rise of research within the firm, the increasing scale of organization and problems of management succession, all increased the need for the graduate in industry. Accordingly, informed opinion among business leaders came to favour them in spite of some remaining anti-university prejudice. The universities, especially in England, developed a wide range of technological subjects and specialisms to cater for most industrial needs, but in terms of their output of graduates, science and technology showed something of a fall from the early 1920s and was markedly lower in Scotland and Wales than in England. Continuing the developments prior to 1914, attempts were made to develop economic and commercial subjects, frequently in directions making them of more immediate practical relevance to industry. But by and large, in spite of some traceable change in attitude in the 1930s, industry remained sceptical of the value of such studies. The flow of talent into the universities was highly inefficient due to defects in the educational system, and industry could certainly not count on obtaining its share of the nation's highest intelligence in the form of graduates. Moreover, the universities played some part in diverting talent into the professions rather than industry. However, in spite of this, levels of graduate output to industry remained fairly high and remarkably consistent between the 1920s and 1930s, though responsive to short run swings in the general climate of business activity. Levels for England tended to be higher than those for Scotland and Wales, reflecting the different balances of arts and industrial sciences between the different countries, and the apparently greater innovative vigour of the English universities in developing new fields of study. As a specialized part of that output the PH.D.s were proving their worth and they showed a slightly higher propensity to enter industry, chiefly into the developing field of research.

The rising new industries, aircraft, canning, dyes and so forth, became avid absorbers of graduates from the beginning, and graduates also took over more traditional industries, electricity, gas, and other forms of engineering. But, on the other hand, there remained in these years important areas of disengagement, where the flow of graduates into industries was not particularly good. Less dangerously, high growth industries like motor cars arranged their labour force and training in their own way without reference to the graduate and they seemed not to be greatly damaged by this. In other more serious cases there were urgent shortages of certain skills such as metallurgists and oil geologists, which must either have retarded the growth of industries needing them or greatly raised their costs. The homogeneity of the rates of absorption of graduates between the 1920s and 1930s reflected the consistency of the levels of output to industry between the decades, but there was some evidence of the very large firms becoming relatively somewhat more important in the second decade than the first. We do not find a perhaps expected pattern of a few large firms employing in the 1920s and then their example spreading to other firms and greatly widening the range of graduate employers. The reception of the graduate created strains within the firm and many firms did not seem to have fully thought out the implications of this changed recruitment. Premium apprenticeship gradually died out and training schemes were gradually built up, though with many false starts and inefficiencies even in major far-sighted companies. There was also evidence of some conflict between generations, and different qualification levels in the firm with the advent of the young graduate and also certain failures to adjust the hierarchical structure of management to provide a planned career ladder up which this new type of labour could advance. In these years the university man was probably about 1–5 per cent of a manufacturing labour force. Chemical, gas, electricity, and engineering industries showed the greatest propensity to absorb graduates, and mining and textiles the least in proportion to their total labour forces.

The graduate was certainly in a beneficial position as regards security against unemployment. His unemployment was reduced faster and more markedly in the 1930s recovery than that of labour as a whole, and the evidence of several investigators suggested that, contrary to expectation, graduate unemployment was not a serious problem in England, though it was more so in Scotland and Wales. In terms of salaries industrial employment remained attractive, though with a slight sag in salaries through the period. Those for mining and geology engineers were among the highest, reflecting the shortage of men with these qualifications. Finally, we observed a strong groundswell of hostility emerging in the universities against this closer involvement with industry, dating specifically from the end of the 1920s after a period of high graduate recruitment to industry. The inter-war years thus saw a considerable advance in the further involvement of the universities and industry in spite of the depressed conditions of business. To a modest extent this was also true in the parallel movement of the woman graduate in business to which we should now turn.

11
The University Woman in Business and Industry Before 1939

*'Business is more and more attracting the modern
[woman] graduate, who may be found on the first rung of
the ladder assisting to sell hats at Peter Jones' or books at
Bumpus'. . . . scientific research claims a few. . .'*[1]

Thus far this study has been concerned with the universities as
producers of male graduates. As we move into the inter-war years,
however, it becomes necessary to consider a parallel movement,
that of the rise of the university education of women and particularly
the reception of these female graduates into business and industry.

The rise of women's education in the later nineteenth century and
the creation of women's colleges is a familiar theme. From the
foundation of Queen's College, Harley Street, and Bedford College,
London, in the 1840s the education of middle-class girls developed
under its own impetus. After the creation of girls' schools under the
influence of Miss Buss and Miss Beale and the Girls' Public Day
School Trust, the time was ripe in the 1870s and 1880s for allowing
girls to proceed from these schools to higher education. In the 1870s
Newnham began and the girls of Hitchen moved to Girton, while in
Oxford an association started that spawned Lady Margaret Hall and
Somerville. When in the 1880s the Victoria federation and the other
civic universities were formed, there were no bars to the entrance of
women, and the same decade saw the spread of women's colleges in
London University, women having been admitted to the London
degree from 1878. And yet these developments, though of profound
social significance, had little impact on the relations of the universities and industry before 1914. The concern for women's higher
education in its early stages arose from such pressures as Victorian
feminism and the suffragist movement, the peculiar excess of women
in the population and the concern to provide them with occupations
in various forms of teaching. Industrial considerations scarcely
entered into it and there is no trace of industrial motives behind the

[1] Eleanora Carus Wilson, *Westfield College 1882–1932*, p. 66.
314

setting up of the women's colleges. Some did receive financial help from industrialists; Girton from Sir Alfred Yarrow, Newnham from the Rathbones, Bedford from Tate and Beecham, while Holloway was founded by a patent medicine manufacturer who hoped that girls would find a wider range of occupations beyond teaching. But there is little evidence that businessmen gave this support, as they did to the civic universities, in the expectation that such education would raise a generation of women graduates useful for business and industry. Nor is there any other than the slightest evidence that university women actually went into business and industry before 1914.[1] Sir William Ashley noted in 1909 that 'the openings for women in business, though they are increasing are still so few that the difficulty of placing women graduates even of real ability in class work, might be almost insuperable'.[2] The vast majority of the early women graduates went to staff the new high schools and the local authority girls' secondary schools and indeed it would have been a disaster for the education system if they had gone into industry in any numbers at that time. The benefits to business and industry came not with these early generations but with their successors whom they themselves taught. These successors, entering higher education after about 1910, were able to move out into a widening field of non-academic employment in the inter-war years, within which business and industry was an important part. It is with this that this chapter is concerned.

To some extent the war itself stimulated the change in the employment patterns of the woman graduate. At the artisan level the exigencies of war-time production brought women into munitions engineering works in addition to their traditional work in textiles, and generally forced the economy to substitute women's labour for that of men in a whole range of activities. The war also increased the proportions of women graduates becoming involved with industrial and business matters. For example, at Somerville College, Oxford, of the 351 women whose war work occupations were known, twenty-seven or 7·7 per cent were in industrial work[3] which compares well with Girton's less than 1 per cent for the pre-war period. However the war's real importance was not in the quantitative but the qualitative change that it induced, particularly in leading to the wide acceptance of highly educated women in industrial science and industrial welfare work, both new professions which were virtually created by war and which then became part of the changing pattern of employment in the inter-war years.

[1] The statistical evidence for this is given in Table 31.
[2] Letter, Sir William Ashley to E. Agnes Purdie, 13 February 1909. Ashley Letter Books, op. cit.
[3] Somerville Students Association Report, November 1917, listing all the war work of their graduates. Evidence for Manchester and Birmingham also suggests the same.

The pressures of war rapidly broke down prejudices against the woman scientist. For example, in 1913 Ethel Sargant, an honorary fellow of Girton, organized a register of university women qualified for work of national importance during the coming war, and this was taken over by the Ministry of Labour. Consequently Margaret Meyer, the Girton director of studies in mathematics, and Newnham mathematicians found themselves working on calculations for aeroplane construction during the war.[1] Nor was this exceptional for there was a great demand for women chemists from Bangor University College for war work.[2] Similarly Sarah Marks, one of Girton's first scientists, had initially had some struggle to get herself accepted seriously in this profession, but her work on naval search-lighting became fully recognized during the war though she was probably best known for her Ayrton anti-gas fan.[3] On a larger scale, women graduates were trained for managerial and training work in the new optical glass industry[4] and as analysts.[5]

More important than the university women in science, however, was their enormous increase in industrial welfare work during the war. Prior to the war there were probably about seventy welfare workers in Britain, chiefly, if not exclusively, women and mostly in the newer female labour consumer industries. The first lady factory inspectors had been appointed from 1893 and the Workmen's Compensation Act forced firms to consider provision for first aid and accidents. Similarly, other factors such as the influence of reformer entrepreneurs like Rowntree and Cadbury, the social conscience of the 1890s, the concern for scientific efficiency in the running of large firms, and the legislation against sweating, all contributed to a climate of opinion more receptive to the woman welfare manager looking after the interests of the somewhat rough girl labour of the day. In the 1890s and 1900s Wills, Carr's and Jacob's biscuits, Robertson's jam, Colman's, and Rowntree's, among others, appointed women for this purpose and this led to the formation of the Welfare Workers' Association in 1913 to give professional unity to this new occupation for women.[6] The universities played an important role in this development, particularly by establishing university settlements which were ideal forms of training for girls

[1] Barbara Stephen, *Girton College, 1869–1932*, pp. 189, 187; Alice Gardner, *A Short History of Newnham College* (Cambridge, 1921), p. 137.
[2] Report of the Professor of Chemistry University College of North Wales, Bangor, 1917–18.
[3] Evelyn Sharp, *Hertha Ayrton, a Memoir 1854–1923* (London, 1926). She was the wife of Professor Ayrton of South Kensington, the first woman to address the Royal Society and the first woman MIEE.
[4] *OHMM*, vol. XI, pt III, Optical Munitions and Glassware, p. 18.
[5] Letter, Professor J. O. Arnold of Sheffield to Sir Joseph Thomson, 25 June 1917, expressing pleasure at the success of women trained by his department.
[6] M. M. Niven, *Personnel Management* (London, 1967).

interested in this kind of social work. A settlement in London was begun by the Cambridge women's colleges in 1887. Lady Margaret Hall had one from 1897, including in its work apprenticing and finding work for young people, and Royal Holloway had its 'Daisy Club' for factory workers. In this way the contemporary concern over poverty and the rise of social economics created a form of training in social work providing an entrée into industrial life for the fairly high born and highly educated woman. More formally, Bedford College started its hygiene course in 1895, another training ground for the future lady factory inspector, and arranged factory visits for students wishing to take up industrial welfare work.[1]

But the war itself gave a much greater impetus to this form of career, and for the first time brought the universities into active co-operation in training. The reasons for this were obvious. Not only were women working in the traditional textile industry and the newer consumer goods, but now they were by dilution replacing men in all manner of munitions engineering, formerly regarded as unsuitable for them. This in turn gave rise to problems of fatigue, lighting, and feeding and all aspects of morale and efficiency which, in the wasteful pre-war use of men, had either not arisen or been too casually disregarded. Consequently women managers were most suitable for dealing with the personal problems of women labour apart from the fact that men would have been drafted to the front. The lady welfare supervisor ceased to be regarded as the luxury of the advanced and paternalist firm for they became compulsory in all factories where explosives were used from 1916. In this same year Seebohm Rowntree, one of the pre-war pioneers of the movement, was appointed to set up the Welfare Department of the Ministry of Munitions. Consequently by the end of the war, welfare workers had risen from a mere sixty or seventy to about 1,000.

The universities now became closely involved in the birth of this new profession. It was at Leeds University that the Welfare Workers' Association reformed itself as the Central Association of Welfare Workers and this held its annual meetings at universities. But, more important, the universities engaged in the formal training of welfare workers and notable graduates were taking their place in the ranks of the profession. For example, in 1917 Professor Urwick invited Miss Agatha Harrison to join the staff of LSE. She herself was a non-graduate but had much welfare experience at Boots and the Dairycoates tin box factory and it was she at LSE who in the war years created the first nucleus of graduate students who were to be welfare officers.[2] It was also evident that women who graduated before the

[1] *Committee on Industry and Trade, 1924–7* (Balfour), Minutes of Evidence, vol. I, Q. 3554–5.

[2] Irene Harrison, *Agatha Harrison, an Impression by her Sister* (London, 1956), chapter 3.

war were becoming prominent in the movement, for example, Gladys Broughton with an M.A. from University College, London, in 1909, who became the Head Welfare Officer at the Ministry of Munitions; also Mildred Bulkley of Cheltenham Ladies College, and with a 'first' from LSE, who likewise became a welfare officer at the ministry.[1] Finally, within the firm, Miss E. G. May with an M.A. degree was appointed welfare supervisor to British Thomson Houston in 1917 and remained a celebrated success throughout the inter-war years.[2] The two former gained recognition with OBE and MBE respectively. It was clear from these three notable cases that a new career pattern was being created for the woman graduate which, even so early, was winning modest recognition from the state in the form of the new orders. But although outstanding, they were not untypical. For example, throughout the North of England, many Lancashire and Yorkshire cotton mills used to take 'enormous numbers' of social science students from the universities to staff new welfare departments during the war, partly for the normal laudable reasons but also partly to avoid paying supertax, though in the harder times of the 1920s the departments and the personnel vanished as quickly as they had arisen.[3]

That the universities were taking part in this work, though all in a somewhat individualistic manner, caused some disquiet. The Association of Welfare Workers was concerned that standards varied and that 'the universities' courses were not being used'. This attention to the role of the universities led to a Home Office conference in July 1917, which led to the setting up of the Joint University Council for Social Studies to consider the training of welfare supervisors and to co-ordinate social study departments of universities.[4] Sir William Ashley was the chairman and their view of social studies reflected his own pragmatic view of economics which was to be useful for health and welfare workers, factory inspectors, and employment exchange managers. The Association of Welfare Workers rightly felt aggrieved that the new JUCSS had paid so little attention to them though they co-operated fully with and appreciated the contribution of the universities—'the value of the work done by the universities and especially L.S.E. in helping to raise standards by providing training courses, and the encouragement of individuals like Professor Urwick, cannot be overestimated'.[5]

*   *   *

[1] London School of Economics Register of Students, 1895–1932 (London, 1934).
[2] H. A. Price-Hughes, *B.T.H. Reminiscences* (Rugby, 1946), p. 82.
[3] *University of Liverpool Society Chronicle*, June 1933, p. 3.
[4] *Social Study and Training at the University*, (Report drawn up by the Joint University Council for Social Studies 1918).
[5] M. M. Niven, op. cit., p. 65.

If it was plain that the war drew university women into industry, especially on the welfare management side, what factors still operated in peace-time to give some continuity to this flow once the peculiar pressures of the war were removed?[1] In the first place, the economic pressure was now considerable. Taxation had risen to abnormal heights during the war and never fell below four shillings in the pound throughout the inter-war years. Further, as the post-war boom gave way to depression in the 1920s, so families found themselves less prosperous, and the value of small savings accumulated before the war had already been eroded by the inflation of the war and post-war boom. The unmarried girl could not remain as a financial burden to her family and was expected to work to support herself if not to supplement the budget of the parents. This was linked also with the other major factor, namely the high risks of women remaining unmarried. For example, in 1921 there were 1·7 million young women aged between twenty and twenty-four compared with 1·3 million men aged between twenty-five and thirty. In 1921 and 1931 about a third of women aged between twenty-five and thirty-five were unmarried, partly due to the war and partly to the long-term predominance of females in the sex structure of the population. For whatever reason, more women had to make their own careers. Furthermore, there was the problem of caring for elderly parents. Although taxation made this slightly easier, there was a startling rise in longevity. There were about twice as many people aged between seventy and seventy-four in England and Wales in 1931 as there had been in 1901, and much of the burden of their support must have been falling on their unmarried daughters, hence the greater importance of her career and earning capacity. But even if a girl married it would be unusual for her husband, if of the same level of society, to be able to earn enough to support her while they were both young. This meant either postponing marriage or both husband and wife working together. In fact most women married between the ages of twenty-five and thirty-five, thus suggesting at least some years of career working. All these factors plus the experience of the war, which made it natural and fitting for women to take employment, and the freer and indeed more expensive ways of the twenties, pushed the intelligent young girl, graduate or not, into a career. But was it a career in industry and business?

Certainly the range of industrial and business opportunities for the woman graduate greatly broadened in the inter-war years. Business became more attractive to women because of the obvious intrinsic interest of many of its activities, but also because with the declining birth rate school-teaching, although secure, was not so expanding an

[1] Ray (Mrs Oliver) Strachey, *Careers and Openings for Women*. Mrs Strachey was the first Chairman of the Cambridge University Women's Appointments Board.

occupation as in the later nineteenth century. Industry and business found women useful partly because they believed that feminine attributes of sensibility and taste were qualities that were commercially relevant in such activities as stores and advertising. Moreover, as scientists they were cheaper than men and equally suitable in non-executive positions. Let us consider in turn the fields of post-war industrial welfare, engineering, advertising, stores, industrial sciences, secretarial, and accountancy work, and the reception of the woman graduate into them.

The profession of lady industrial welfare worker which we have seen starting just before and during the war continued to develop in the inter-war years despite the setback of the slump. In the immediate post-war period, there was an initial setback with the closing down of several departments started in war-time conditions, especially with the onset of depression in Lancashire textiles. In any case the depressed state of industry was inimical to the development of the movement, partly because there was little money to spare and partly because with male labour so cheap and plentiful once again there was less concern than there had been during the war to conciliate and care for it. However, the profession did continue to develop and became subject to important new influences such as the war-time development of industrial psychology which made it more scientific and moved its emphasis somewhat away from the philanthropic ideas of welfare of the 1890s. Significantly, in 1931 the Institute of Welfare Workers changed its name to that of the Institute of Labour Management, and more men began to enter what was and still remained a predominantly women's profession. This slight change of emphasis is seen in the career of one of the best known women in the field at the time, Miss Anne Shaw, M.A., of Metro-Vickers. She began as a superintendent of women at Trafford Park in 1933 and then with this new influence of industrial psychology became increasingly involved in time and motion study, becoming in turn head of time and motion for Metro-Vickers and then for the whole of AEI.[1] Women graduates like Miss Shaw and Miss May of BTH were but the best known in a profession which by 1939 was some 1,800 strong of whom 60 per cent were still women. At a less prominent level than Miss Shaw and Miss May something of the nature of training and life of women in this employment may be gained from an account by an Exeter girl graduate.[2] Nancy Daldy, after graduating from Exeter, joined the Institute of Labour Management and was placed by them in a cotton mill and then in an engineering works before taking a term's course at Loughborough College in engineering. This was followed by practical work as a hospital nurse, and

---

[1] John Dummelow, *Metropolitan Vickers Electrical Co. Ltd., 1899–1949* (Manchester, 1949).
[2] Nancy E. Daldy, 'Factory Welfare Work', *The Ram*, spring, 1932.

after this varied training and experience she went to work for a dyeing and cleaning firm, looking after staff selection, health and cleanliness, social activities, and supervising evening classes. Industrial welfare was clearly a diverse kind of occupation with a very mixed training and highly interesting for the adaptable intelligent girl graduate.

Welfare work was the development of an already existing profession, but the woman engineer was more truly a creation of the inter-war years. Although numerically less important than welfare work, engineering for women attracted a good deal of attention in these two decades, largely due to the flair for publicity of its chief advocates, notably through the exploitation of Amy Johnson's flights to the Cape and Australia and more fundamentally through the work of the various organizations of which Dame Caroline Haslett was the mainspring. During the war, Caroline Haslett, not herself a graduate, had gained unusual experience in the Cochran Boiler Company as a practical engineer, and by 1918 was manager of their London office. Immediately after the war, Lady Parsons, the wife of the turbine inventor, Sir Charles, and an engineer in her own right, formed the Women's Engineering Society of which Miss Haslett became the first secretary.[1] The formation of this organization was most apposite, for the early 1920s was a period of important new developments in the entry of women into engineering. For example, in 1920 Atlanta Ltd was formed as a company of women engineers at Loughborough, some of whom were studying for their B.SC. at the same time. In spring 1921 a Mr G. L. Ward opened his works in London specifically for women who wished to obtain pre-university workshop industrial training. Later in that year, Miss Chitty became the first woman to gain a 'first' in the Cambridge Mechanical Sciences Tripos, and at the end of the year Miss Drummond became the first woman to complete a full engineering apprenticeship of five years. In the next year, 1922, Margaret Partridge, B.SC., set up her famous lighting and heating firm in Exeter, dealing with large-scale electrical contracting—she it was who did the work for Winchester Cathedral—while in 1923 Liverpool University produced its first woman 'first' in engineering, Pearl Swan, who went to Metropolitan Vickers.[2] All these closely clustered developments in the early 1920s were important first steps in the movement.

Although the post-war depression struck, the movement received an important stimulus from the great Empire Exhibition held at Wembley in 1925, part of which was an International Conference of Women in Science, Industry and Commerce which was opened by Queen Elizabeth the Queen Mother, then the Duchess of York,

[1] Rosalind Messenger, *The Doors of Opportunity, a Biography of Dame Caroline Haslett.*
[2] *The Woman Engineer, passim,* September 1920–March 1923.

performing her first royal engagement. The speeches were quite unremarkable, but as a stage managed exposition of women's rights to be taken seriously in the engineering field it could hardly have been bettered. However, it was not all pageantry for by then there were women graduate engineers with Metro-Vickers, the Cambridge Instrument Company, Dorman Long, BTH, and the Consolidated Pneumatic Tool Company, girls ranging from the universities of Bristol, Edinburgh, Glasgow, and Liverpool.

Other significant long-term movements took place in 1925 as well as the conference. A Business and University Committee was formed to act as a link between industry, commerce, and the universities in so far as the interests of women were concerned. This was chaired by the Viscountess Rhondda, herself a director of twenty-eight companies, with Miss Haslett as secretary. Firms were supposed to write to them if they required highly qualified women, but it is difficult to believe that in those depressed times the offer was much pursued and one hears rather little of this body thereafter.[1] However, the British Federation of University Women had a Business and Industry Committee at least from 1932 which may have been a continuation.

More important was the hiving off of the Electrical Association for Women in the same year. While the Viscountess Astor was the president, the driving force was the ubiquitous Caroline Haslett as director. This idea arose in her mind from the first World Power Conference of 1924 and her realization of the implications of the spread of electricity supply for women in the home. Among its aims it was 'to encourage the study of electrical application in the curricula or educational schemes of universities . . .',[2] and this body, unlike the Business and University Committee, does seem to have been of first-rate importance. It had the backing of the British Electrical and Allied Manufacturers' Association and the Cable Makers' Association, GEC and AEI, and such individuals in the industry as Ferranti, and Colonel Crompton who was their benign landlord. Equally important, it had the firm financial backing of the Central Electricity Board. This electrical appliance movement not only freed the housewife from drudgery but it also provided a career outlet for the woman engineer. Very few women were really happy with the hard labour and grime of mechanical engineering which was in any case a difficult branch for women to enter.[3] But the light electrical field, especially

---

[1] *The Woman Engineer*, September 1925. Vera Brittain, *Women's Work in Modern England* (London, 1928), p. 37. Rosalind Messenger does not mention her sister's connection with this body, but see British Federation of University Women Report, 1932–3.

[2] 'The Women's Electrical Association', 1925 (a publicity leaflet).

[3] 'Careers and Openings for Women in Engineering, a Discussion at Southampton University College', *The Woman Engineer*, September–October 1932.

as it related to domestic matters, was more attractive and this came to be seen as their main opportunity in design, sales, publicity, and contracting.[1] It was fitting and symbolic that a decade after the award of public honours to women welfare workers the women engineers should have received similar public recognition. Caroline Haslett was made a CBE in 1931 and Amy Johnson on whom the same honour had been conferred in 1930 reflected her prestige on the Women's Engineering Society by becoming its president from 1934–1937.

By the 1920s advertising was already being noted as one of the most promising fields for women of flair and imagination.[2] Although advertising had been a marked feature of some of the new consumer industries firms of the late nineteenth century, it was in the 1920s that it became a more self-conscious profession. In 1920 an earlier body became the Incorporated Society of British Advertisers; six years later the Advertising Association of Great Britain was formed, and in 1927 the Institute of Incorporated Practitioners in Advertising.[3] In the 1920s it was still not uncommon for firms to manage their own publicity affairs, and this provided opportunities for women in appointments within the firm. For example, it was noted in the early 1920s that 'every large drapery house employs one or two advertising managers',[4] and certainly Lever's and Harrods used LSE women on advertising as staff employees. But this decade also saw the rise of the advertising agency replacing this activity as a function of the firm and making it the work of the central professional specialist. Sir Charles Higham noted that by the mid 1920s the advertising agency had achieved a new status as 'the professional adviser of the advertiser instead of merely being the paid tout of the newspapers'.[5] Consequently such firms as J. Walter Thompson, Palmer, Newbould and Company, and Sir William Crawford's arose, taking on these centralized services and in turn acting as employers of women who would previously have sought such a career in the firm. Crawford's, perhaps the leading native British firm, was started by a Glaswegian who gathered a galaxy of design and copywriting talent, including Jean Cocteau, and quickly took over the accounts of Guinness, Swan pens, and the overseas advertising for Chrysler cars. Through his poster services he similarly revolutionized bill poster advertising in Britain in the 1920s. But his major achievement was in the advertising for the Empire Marketing Board from 1926

---

[1] J. F. A. Browne, 'Co-operation between the Universities and Industry and Commerce in the Matter of Placement', *The Woman Engineer*, December 1932.
[2] Vera Brittain, op. cit., p. 40.
[3] Blanche B. Elliott, *A History of English Advertising* (London, 1952).
[4] Mary Davis, *Employment for Women*.
[5] Sir Charles Higham, *Advertising* (London, 1925), p. 66. Higham had made his name in the big government war-time advertising campaigns. See E. S. Turner, *The Shocking History of Advertising* (London, 1965), p. 170.

and its 'Buy British' campaign for which he was knighted in 1931.[1] He is particularly noted here because his was the chief firm absorbing LSE women into this profession in the 1920s and early 1930s.

Why should they want graduates for this type of work and why specifically women? An ex-Edinburgh graduate in the business in 1930, noting that more university people were going into advertising, thought that the university was a good preparation for learning 'how the world works and how people think about things'.[2] Florence Sangster, the managing director of Crawford's and a director of Poster Services, was a keen employer of women graduates, because of their 'quick handling and collating of facts'. It was also argued that since the bulk of consumer buying was done by women and so much of the advertising had to be aimed at them, then women were best fitted to devise the advertising that would most appeal to their own sex. Ironically, Miss Sangster, whose career seemed the clearest vindication of this view, did not agree with it although she noted that it was a common one among her colleagues.[3]

Women in advertising, either in firms or agencies, were concerned with the buying of space in media, in estimating the best allocation of available funds, and 'visualizing' the scope of campaigns. There was also a reciprocal career as advertising managers in those media dealing with the agencies. For example, *Time and Tide* took an LSE woman graduate for this work in the 1920s, and in the 1930s the advertising manager of *Punch* was also a woman,[4] indeed a Cambridge lady graduate went into this same office in 1936.[5] Market research arose as yet a further branch of this spreading profession in the inter-war years. This brought in women with mathematics and statistics qualifications alongside their more literary sisters, the copywriters.[6] E. Maud Woodyard, the managing director of Saward, Baker and Company, claimed that her own agency had been the first to start a really competent and comprehensive market research department in Britain using statistical analysis.[7]

---

[1] G. H. Saxon Mills, *There is a Tide, the Life and Work of Sir William Crawford, K.B.E., Embodying an Historical Study of Modern British Advertising* (London, 1954).
[2] W. D. H. McCullough, 'Scope for University Men and Women in Advertising', *JC*, February 1930.
[3] Florence Sangster, 'Advertising' in M. I. Cole (ed.), *The Road to Success* (London, 1936).
[4] E. Maud Woodyard, *Careers for Women in Advertising*, p. 7.
[5] Cambridge University Womens Appointments Board, Secretary's unpublished typescript report for 5 February 1936. It also noted another Cambridge girl graduate going into market research with Mars Bars.
[6] D. W. Hughes, *Careers for Our Daughters* (London, 1936), pp. 93–4. 'The old universities and the new . . . have contributed graduates to this calling [advertising] principally to copywriting but also to administration and market research'.
[7] E. Maud Woodyard, op. cit.

The entry into advertising could be rather haphazard for women graduates, especially in the 1920s, reflecting the uncertainty of the economic climate and also the fact that it had no clear qualifications of recruitment but was open to any comers with the nerve to push their way in. For example, Amy Johnson graduated in economics at Sheffield University and took a secretarial course before a stint in an accountant's office. This provided her with the experience to be taken on by a local Hull advertising firm as a secretary in return for being taught the trade of copywriting. Being used as a drudge, she left for London, only to fail to gain employment with Sir Charles Higham's advertising agency. After this she returned to accountancy after a grim time in a West End store.[1] Another celebrity, Miss Storm Jameson, the novelist and a Leeds graduate, also had a flirtation with advertising in the immediate post-war years. Having gained a 'first' in English she drifted into the trade and joined the Carlton Agency in Covent Garden in 1919. She became, she says, 'a skilful copywriter, admirably persuasive about face cream, admirably succinct and convincing about roofing tiles and arc welding lamps . . .'. But growing rapidly to despise the whole business, she left in the same year for publishing.[2] These episodes in the lives of university women better known for other things give some of the flavour of the insecurity, poverty, fly-by-night quality of life of women graduates who tried to break out of the well-worn path to teaching in the 1920s. It took a certain restless, abnormally enterprising spirit such as these ladies possessed to consider embarking on so hazardous a course, but even so for neither of them did it prove successful. However, by the mid 1930s the London Appointments Board was sanguine; 'women have attained success in advertising work. There are women at the head of several publicity departments of large commercial firms and of periodicals, and as directors of publicity firms. There is a Women's Advertising Club of London . . .',[3] and Miss Woodyard could claim that 'in the advertising business there is no sex prejudice in the path of a woman's recognition and progress'.

Also in the marketing field many large stores made a special point of employing graduate women, as from about 1910 to the early 1930s several of them had had to rethink their policies of managerial recruitment and training. In 1912, for example, Selfridge's began to take university graduates for managerial training.[5] In the early 1920s Lewis's likewise began to readjust to the increasing scale of their enterprise which had flourished during the war. Before 1922 the firm had depended almost entirely on the personal dominance of Louis Cohen but 'the new conditions demanded specialized

[1] Amy Johnson in *Myself when Young* (London, 1938).
[2] Storm Jameson, *Journey from the North* (London, 1969), pp. 133–9.
[3] H. J. Crawford, *Appointments and Careers for Graduates and Students*, p. 43.
[4] Reginald Pound, *Selfridge* (London, 1960), p. 94.

managerial responsibility, initiative and enterprise'.[1] Finding, however, that the old buyers did not altogether suit the new expanding and responsible roles, staff training was begun in 1926 specifically to train future heads of stores. Also each store had its welfare supervisor from 1921, and the advertising of the group was handled by their central publicity organization which grew considerably from 1922. All these changes benefited women graduates for whom Lewis's were an important outlet of employment. Peter Jones were also pioneers in experimenting with university women in the retail trade though their managing director came to believe as a result 'that a university education did not materially increase the efficiency of either men or women in business'.[2] However, Peter Jones took quite a number of LSE girls in the 1920s as did the John Lewis partnership, the latter perhaps chiefly because of the influence of Miss Hope Glen, OBE, one of the keenest advocates of university women in stores work who moved to John Lewis's after work with Peter Jones.[3] Marks and Spencer seemed to enter into this activity slightly later than many of the others and in their case it was a response to their vast expansion from 1927 to 1937.[4] For example, in 1934 a personnel department was set up and a system of training store managers started. However, in the 1930s the role of the educated woman within Marks and Spencer was changing from management to buying and welfare, largely because men were regarded as more suitable for the control of the vast 'superstores' that Simon Marks was developing from the 1920s. Among other multiple shops J. Lyons also tried employing university women for a nine months' training course,[5] and Harrods and Bourne and Hollingsworth were likewise important graduate women employers. All the stores we have mentioned were used as outlets at various times by Oxford, Cambridge, and LSE for their women graduates. It was also some indication of the increasing professionalism of this type of career that Gladys Burlton, a Westfield College graduate, was able to set up her own agency for training women like herself in modern methods of salesmanship.[6]

Within the field of scientific manufacturing industry, women began to play an important part in the inter-war years. There were, among several, Dr Frances Heywood who was responsible for all chemical and physical testing for the Monotype Corporation,[7] Dr

[1] Asa Briggs, *Friends of the People* (London, 1955), pp. 147–9.
[2] *British Federation of University Women Newssheet and Review*, May 1931, 'University Women in Business'.
[3] E. Hope Glen, 'Retail Buying in Stores' in M. I. Cole, op. cit.
[4] Goronwy Rees, *St. Michael, a History of Marks and Spencer* (London, 1969), p. 91.
[5] Ray Strachey, op. cit., p. 172.
[6] Eleanora Carus Wilson, op. cit., p. 66.
[7] D. W. Hughes, op. cit., p. 223. Also 'A Woman in Metallurgy', *The Woman Engineer*, December 1927.

Hamer of Ilford's and Dr Dorothy Jordan Lloyd, the Director of research of the British Leather Manufacturers' Research Association. Women were also prominent in other research associations or Civil Service research establishments.[1] There were six women in the Building Research Station, two in fuel research, and one in heating and ventilation, and there was even a leading woman authority on aerodynamics at Farnborough. Indeed, much of women's industrial research was for public establishments of this kind rather than for the firm itself. However, a number of firms with research establishments did take women scientists especially in the light consumer fields such as foods, pharmaceuticals, textiles, and photography. Some of the more prominent were Lyons, United Dairies, cws, Boots, Lever's, May and Baker, Chivers, Glaxo, Fuller's, Peek Frean, Robertson's, Schweppes, Kodak, and Burroughs Wellcome. Lyons, for example, had a large staff of graduate chemists, four of whom at the end of the 1920s were women; indeed 'an old Cheltenham girl does jams, honeys, golden syrups and sugars'.[2] In perspective there were about 200 women members of the Institute of Chemistry by the mid 1930s, most of whom must have been in industry.

There is also evidence that what one would think of as being women's traditional crafts were also becoming scientific degree subjects in the inter-war years. For example, Bristol and London awarded degrees in domestic science with obvious implications for dietetics and the catering trades.[3] The King's College of Household and Domestic Science (now Queen Elizabeth College) had been incorporated into the University of London from 1908 as the leading centre for this form of women's higher education, producing women relevant for the hotel and mass catering trades as well as for the food processing firms.[4] With the application of chemistry and biochemistry to the food trades, this traditional women's activity became a highly qualified professional career with United Dairies, Chivers, and Robertson's among others taking women graduates. Rather surprisingly, laundry management does not seem to have been regarded as a graduate activity in spite of its being a field of chemical application and calling for the control of a female labour force, though the linen manager of the Savoy Hotel was a woman graduate. On the other hand, interior decorating did become a university subject with University College, London, running a specialized course in this; there was clearly an expanding field in the décor of

[1] 'Prospects of Employment for Women Science Graduates—Industrial Research Laboratories', *JC*, May 1938.
[2] Elsie Lang, *British Women in the Twentieth Century* (London, 1929), p. 261.
[3] D. W. Hughes, op. cit., p. 99.
[4] Helen Sillitoe, *A History of the Teaching of Domestic Science Subjects* (London, 1933). J. F. C. Hearnshaw, *Centenary History of King's College, London, 1828–1928*, appendix I.

hotels and the plushier cinemas of the 1930s. In all these ways the woman scientist either at the higher levels of research or in more homely fields of domestic science technology found a wide range of new occupations open to her which had scarcely existed before the war.

In industry and business generally secretarial work was coming to be regarded as suitable for women with degrees. It was noted that employers had formerly been suspicious of university women as 'superior in the offensive sense, and to be sadly unadaptable', but 'it is now an extra qualification for secretarial work to have a degree'.[1] However, there was a national variation in this for Scottish women graduates found it extremely difficult to get responsible secretarial work with prospects within Scotland itself, whereas there was plenty of demand for such people in London and the South East.[2] However, London University was sceptical whether this was even the case in England—'the Board has reason to believe that many women graduates who take up secretarial work fail to secure posts which can be regarded as satisfactory for an educated woman'[3]—although it agreed that large numbers of graduates did take up such training. On the other hand, for graduates like Amy Johnson, with no wish to teach, a short secretarial course proved a stepping stone into advertising and accountancy although she detested both and was well paid in neither. Accountancy itself was changing in important ways from the 1920s. The Sex Disqualification Act of 1919 opened up chartered accountancy and the legal profession to women; consequently by 1931 there were 119 women accountants. Within accountancy as a whole, cost accountancy was a branch of special relevance to manufacturing industry and this was 'slowly opening to women' by the late 1930s. Indeed, by 1936 'the chief cost accountants in three or four firms of considerable size in London and the provinces are women'.[4]

It has been evident, then, that especially since the war there was a considerable expansion of types of occupations absorbing women graduates into business and industry.

We may now consider the actual proportions of women graduates going into business and industry in the inter-war years compared with the pre-1914 period. This is indicated on Table 31.

It was quite clear that entry into business and industry before the war was generally negligible apart from the specific example of LSE,

[1] Ray Strachey, op. cit., p. 178. Ethel Phesey in 'The Woman Student and Her Career', *The University*, Easter 1928, stressed this also.
[2] Typescript report of Queen Margaret College, 1929–30 (University of Glasgow Archives), and W. T. Baxter, 'Careers for Graduates, Prospects Offered by University Training', *The Scotsman*, 15 and 16 October 1936.
[3] University of London Appointments Board Report, 1938–9.
[4] D. W. Hughes, op. cit., p. 88.

whose figures in any case reach forward into the 1920s. The inter-war years did see an advance on this formerly negative position although the great majority of women graduates still went into teaching before and after 1914. The median percentage for all the inter-war figures is 7 per cent, and it is interesting to note that this median 7 per cent is in general accord with the most comprehensive figures, those for the Cambridge colleges. Thus we can be clear that there was a rise in the inter-war years compared with the pre-war years though it was a modest one and in some places fitful. Second, there is some evidence that within the inter-war years there was a very slight rise from the 1920s to the 1930s; again the Cambridge figures show this as do the overall London figures. Taking all the figures on the chart, the median for the 1920s is 6 and that for the 1930s is 9. It is a slight rise, as we may expect, but the thirties were not strikingly better than the twenties in this regard. There was a greater difference between the 1920s and the pre-war decades than between the 1930s and the 1920s. Third, the bulk of women went into firms in non-technical capacities, to stores, advertising, and librarianship, and even on the research side they went to research associations rather than directly to firms. The woman production manager, in spite of all the other changes, was a rarity. Fourth, there is an interesting negative point about the relationship between social class and entry into industry. It might have been a common-sense expectation that girls of high social class might have been unwilling to enter industry and business especially since their brothers at contemporary Oxford and Cambridge preferred the professions more markedly than men from the English civic universities. However, this is far from clear. The high social prestige women's colleges—Girton, Newnham, Royal Holloway, and St Andrews—all show proportions of women entering business life which are more consistently high than most of the others. Indeed, employers in stores, advertising, and the like may well have preferred the qualities that these graduate women of good background could bring to the firm.

Next we may consider how these women graduates fared as regards salaries and unemployment in the inter-war years. It may be expected that women graduates would be paid less than men, partly because they were more numerous and partly because some were likely to marry and would not need to accept a self-supporting wage. Consequently we might also expect unemployment to be a slightly less urgent problem with women graduates than with men.

In the first place, it is indisputable that women graduates' salaries were lower than those of men. Some of the clearest evidence for this comes from Birmingham University where a survey of graduates taken in 1938 was able to measure salaries by subject and sex for graduates who had left at various times throughout the inter-war

TABLE 31   *Changing percentage proportions of entry into business and industry of women graduates*

Institution	Period	%	Period	%	Period	%	Period	%	Period	%	Period	%
Girton[1]	1870–1910	1	1920	X	1925	7·5	1932	7·35	1935	10·1	1938	9·4
Newnham[2]			1920	3·6	1925	7·6	1932	4·5	1935	12·2	1938	9·2
Imperial College[3]							1933–1939	35·5				
London School of Economics[4]	1902–20	13	1920–32	16·4								
Royal Holloway[5]	pre-1914	2·6	1917–21	4	1922–6	6·5	1927–31	5·1	1932–5	5		
London University[6]					1930–1	13·7	1931–2	11·9	1932–3	16·5	1933–4	19·9
									1934–5	18·6	1935–6	21·7
Manchester[7]	1896–1900	X					1932–5 2·6 (chemists)					
Liverpool[8]	pre-1914	X	1919–25	28·6	1926–30	X						
Birmingham[9]	pre-1914	X	1919–25	3·9	1925–31	3·6						
Newcastle[10]	pre-1914	X	1919–24	13·3	1925–9	X	1930–4	6·6	1935–8	X		

	pre-1914	1919–24	1921–5	1925–9	1926–30	1929–38	1930–4	1931–9	1935–6	1935–9	1936–7
Leeds	X										
Sheffield[12]	X		10		6·2			2·1			
Durham[13]						X					
Glasgow[14]									1		2·16
Aberdeen[15]	X										
St Andrews[16]	X	7		6			24			33	

(X = nil or negligible cases)

1 *Girton College Register, 1896–1946.*
2 *Newnham College Register,* vol. I, 1871–1923; vol. II, 1924–1950.
3 Unpublished typescript reports of the Imperial College Appointments Board (Imperial College Archives).
4 *The London School of Economics and Political Science Register, 1895–1932.*
5 Calendar of the Royal Holloway College, University of London, 1962/3, containing the List of Former Students.
6 University of London Appointments Board Reports, 1931–6.
7 Reports of the Manchester University Council to Court, 1896–1900. *The Physical Laboratories of the University of Manchester, a Record of 25 years* (Manchester, 1906). *Manchester University Chemical Society Magazine,* 1932–5.
8 Lists in *Liverpool Society Chronicle,* vols 1–13.
9 *University of Birmingham Register of Graduates,* 1932 ed.
10 *King's (Newcastle) Old Students Association Year Book,* 1938.
11 *Leeds University Old Students Association Year Book,* 1930–1.
12 Lists in *Floreamus,* 1918–20; *The Arrows,* 1929–37; *The Sheffield University Magazine,* 1937–9.
13 'Durham College in the University of Durham, First Appointments obtained by Students leaving during the period 1929–38' (unpublished typescript in the archives of the University of Newcastle).
14 Reports of Queen Margaret College (typescript in Glasgow University Archives).
15 Records of the Arts Class of 1895–99 (Aberdeen, 1900); Records of the Arts Class of 1909–1912/13 (Aberdeen, 1959).
16 *Alumnus Chronicle of the University of St. Andrews,* vols I–IV, nos, 1–27, 1927–40.

TABLE 32   *Salaries of Birmingham graduates (in £s)*

Date of leaving university	Pure science		Arts		Commerce	
	Men	Women	Men	Women	Men	Women
1937–8	200–250	150–250	150–250	150–200	150–200	150–200
5–10 years ago (1928–33?)	250–350	250–300	300–350	250–300	250–350	X
10–15 years ago (1923–28?)	350–400	X	300–350	300–350	350–400	X
15–20 years ago (1918–23?)	400–450	X	450–500	300–400	c. 600	X

(X = nil or negligible cases)

TABLE 33   *Starting salaries of Imperial College students in the 1930s*

Men	Women in industry	Women outside it
1sts £262 (average)		
2nds £253 (average)	Research physicists, Dufay Chromax £250	
	Assistant chemist, Lodge Plugs £234	
	British Rubber Products Research Association £230	
Pass £218 (average)	Chemist, Express Dairy Company £200	
	Paint Varnish Research Association £200	Assistant, University College £200
	British Aircraft Manufacturing Company £182	
	Chemist, Cory Company £180	City and Guilds College £175
	Librarian, BTH £156	
	Typist, Autocheques £90	

years. The figures[1] are shown in Table 32. It is evident that in most cases the women's salaries lag slightly behind the men's—usually by about fifty pounds. This evidence may also be corroborated with information from Imperial College where it is possible to compare the salaries of scientists of different sexes. We have seen earlier that the average starting salary in the 1930s for men with first class degrees was £262, for those with second class degrees £253, and for pass degree men £218. In the light of this we can now compare, in Table 33, women's starting salaries from the college both in industry and outside it. Women's industrial salaries compared well with academic ones, as we may expect, and the research posts for women in industry seemed quite well paid. However, it is evident again that the women were paid somewhat less than men and the bottom four firms of the centre column were certainly benefiting from women's scientific knowledge more cheaply than if they had employed men.[2]

TABLE 34   *Proportion of graduates unemployed in Glasgow*[1]

| | Men | | Women | |
	No.	%	No.	%
1935/6	63:650	9·5	55:313	17·6
1936/7	39:585	6·7	7:232	3·0
1937/8	17:576	3·0	11:220	5·0

[1] Typescript reports of Glasgow University Appointments Board (in the Board Offices) and Queen Margaret College, reports to the board (in the university archives).

If women graduates were cheaper than men did they accordingly face less of an unemployment problem than male graduates? In the labour force as a whole women of all social classes tended to be less unemployed than males, not so much because they displaced males as that many of the newer industries, unlike the heavy basic industries, tended to absorb women's labour.[3] Comparative evidence can be gleaned for Glasgow, Edinburgh, and London as shown in Tables 34, 35, and 36.

[1] Graduate Employment, a Report . . . of the Guild of Undergraduates of the University of Birmingham, May 1938. (Where there are gaps the numbers involved were too few to classify.) Since the survey listed its categories in terms of five, ten, fifteen, and twenty years ago—presumably before 1938—it is not clear if there is some overlap between the first and last years of the categories. However, this does not affect the general point.
[2] Calculated from various typescripts of the Imperial College Appointments Board for the 1930s, in the college archives. This confidential and personal information was not published.
[3] H. W. Singer, *Unemployment and the Unemployed* (London, 1940), p. 18.

TABLE 35   *Proportion of graduates unemployed in Edinburgh*[1]

	Men					Women				
	Pure science No. %		Applied science No. %		Art hons. MA No. %	Pure science No. %		Applied science No. %		Arts hon. MA No. %
1929/30	9:26	34·6	5:26	19·2	4:51 7·8	0:9		0:2		10:49 20·4
1930/1	6:19	31·6	5:35	14·3	2:50 4·0	1:8	12·5	0:1		16:48 33·3
1933			8:132 (6·1%) all subjects					40:187 (21·4%) all subjects		

[1] Annual Reports of the Employments Secretary, Edinburgh University. T. A. Joynt, 'Graduates and Employment', *University of Edinburgh Journal*, 1934, pp. 242–6.

TABLE 36   *Proportion of graduates unemployed in London*[1]

	Imperial College No. %		University Appointments Board (Women)[2] No. %	
1930/31	49:1180	4·2	105:643	16·6
1932/3	101:1222	8·3	162:786	20·6
1933/4	77:1142	6·7	283:981	28·8

[1] Calculated from a chart in the papers of Imperial College Appointments Board in the college archives.
[2] Calculated from University of London Appointments Board Reports.

These are graduate unemployed as a proportion of total graduates for that year or graduates on the register of the appointments board. These are not figures of unemployment comparable with national figures—they are certainly not comparable between universities for the same years—but they should be comparable for the same subjects in the same university between sexes. Although we are not inclined to lay as much weight on these figures as on the salary figures, certain points emerge. For Glasgow there is no clear evidence that women were less subject to unemployment than men. Indeed the evidence is slightly the other way. At Edinburgh, women scientists seemed to have better employment opportunities than men scientists, clearly a reflection of the slight salary differentials seen above, but on the other hand women arts graduates had vastly greater difficulties in getting work than male arts graduates. In the London case we are comparing all sorts of women with male scientists and in that case the women experienced significantly more unemployment.

In spite of the limitations of the evidence we can be fairly confident that although women graduates were paid less than men in both arts and sciences they only seemed to gain an advantage in reduced unemployment on the science side. On the arts side the differences in costs were not such as to induce employers generally to prefer women. Otherwise men still had the advantage.

Some protagonists in the movement for getting closer links between the woman graduate and industry were disappointed that they had not achieved more success than they did. Mrs Strachey, who knew more about the matter than most, complained to the Cambridge Appointments Board,[1]

> no progress has been made. No women were recruited directly
> for executive situations. The few who achieved such positions
> have started as shorthand typists. A university degree is still a
> disadvantage in business. From time to time a big man like
> Lord Trent or Mr Cadbury has agreed to try university
> women, but nothing has happened as the matter has been
> shelved by hostile subordinates.

This was rather excessively gloomy, but in spite of the advances we have considered a number of barriers still impeded the entry and progress of women graduates in industry. First, production management as opposed to research work in factories was more physically arduous as a full-time peace-time occupation than most women were prepared to tolerate. The career of the first woman student of metallurgy at Birmingham University is suggestive. She intended to enter her father's firm and qualified accordingly but then, finding life in the works too physically taxing, she moved to academic life.[2] There were some notable women managers in the inter-war years— Mrs Gaskin, the Chairman of Batchelors' Peas; Mrs Greaves, the first woman member of the Institution of Quarry Managers; Mrs Piggott of Manfield shoes; and the wife of Major Douglas—of Social Credit fame—who was a shipyard manager in her own right. But even for women scientists, who were a minority anyway, school-teaching still seemed a more suitably feminine occupation, or research which was at least a stage removed in the firm from the physical and social unpleasantness of the works. Second, firms often put up barriers that would deter even women graduates

---

[1] MS. Minute Book of the Committee Appointed to consider the Cambridge University Womens Appointments Board, 15 July 1938. See also Mrs Strachey's speech in Report of the Proceedings of the Fifth Quinquennial Congress of the Universities of the British Empire, 1936: 'Careers for University Students'.

[2] C. M. Shaw Scott, 'Women's Contribution to Metallurgy', *The Woman Engineer*, June 1926.

who were keen to join them. The reasons were partly legal. In the first place, women were not allowed to work at night in engineering works, which meant that they could not fit into a shift system and firms were unwilling to accommodate such inflexible labour. The Women's Engineering Society fought a long and eventually successful battle over this from 1928 to 1934 as the leading factor preventing women obtaining apprentice training in industry. Further, if women were employed as apprentices then they had to have a woman supervisor. This meant that it was difficult for sympathetic firms to take merely one or two women; they committed themselves to take a sufficiently large number to make it worth employing a female supervisor, knowing that the whole team could not fit into shift work anyway.[1] Most firms were reasonably unwilling to do this. Both these factors made it difficult for women to get vital pre- and post-graduate practical experience in works. There could also be blunt prejudice against women engineers at the universities as well as in industry. At King's College, London, for example, there was uproar when it was rumoured in 1932 that women students in engineering would enter the college and a delegation was sent from the students to the professorial board against it. The professor, Ernest Wilson, concluded the matter by declaring that 'there is no such thing as a woman engineer'. Accordingly no women were allowed into King's to study engineering.[2]

We have noted that women tended to go into research, but even here there were barriers imposed by some firms, depending in many cases on whether they regarded research work as a preliminary to production management. For example, earlier we cited some firms that took women graduates for their research laboratories, but on the other hand there is a much more surprising list of firms which deliberately did not or did so only with great reluctance. These included Crosse and Blackwell, Fry's, Cadbury's, Virol, Heinz, Brown and Polson, Nestlé, Jacob's, Courtauld's, and Reckitt's—all of whom might be regarded as producing largely for women buyers.[3] The reasons for this resistance were partly the unwillingness of firms to accept wastage through marriage, but also their unwillingness to take women into research who could not be transferred to plant control. This was certainly the case with ICI which did not favour research women for this reason, and also much of the pharmaceutical industry.[4] Hence women graduate research scientists' preference for DSIR group research. The crux of the question was

[1] Joan Beale, 'Women in . . . Electrical Engineering', *JC*, May 1935. Miss Beale had an engineering degree from University College, London.
[2] W. O. Skeat, *King's College, London, Engineering Society, 1847–1957* (London, 1957), p. 56.
[3] 'Prospects of Employment for Women Science Graduates', *JC*, May 1938.
[4] D. W. Hughes, op. cit., p. 208.

simply that most firms did not regard most women as suitable for executive positions controlling gangs of men considerably older, rougher, and less well educated than themselves.[1] Very few women ever wanted to put themselves in this position anyway and the firms made sure that most of the rest never got the opportunity.

Finally, one of the main bars to women entering business and industrial life was the motivation of the women themselves. In considering these various barriers raised by industry against women graduates we rather assume that a large proportion of women wished to seek such careers in the first place, but this itself would be fallacious, for much of the resistance came from themselves. In a preference survey taken among Glasgow University women in 1938[2] in the first term of their final year it was found that fourteen actually preferred teaching, three the Civil Service, two journalism and one each library, secretarial, and research posts. Not one chose business or industry as a preferred employment.

We have been considering a socially important if quantitatively modest advance. Before the First World War business motivations played no discernible part in the women's higher education movement and in spite of the important demographic and financial pressures moving educated girls into careers, the universities were not providing women graduates for industry. During the war itself the nascent profession of industrial welfare worker became extremely important and the woman industrial scientist also emerged, though to a lesser extent. In the inter-war years the changing of the industrial structure away from the predominance of the basic heavy industries gave rise to a variety of attractive light and intelligent jobs that many graduate women took up—welfare work, advertising, stores, secretarial work, cost accountancy, and scientific research in consumer goods firms or with Research Associations. Accordingly there was an increase in women graduates going into business from negligible proportions to a level of which around 7 per cent would not be an unfair rough indication. This was still marginal to the vast bulk of women graduates who still went into school-teaching. However, women were attractive to employers, partly for their qualities of taste which were commercially relevant in consumer goods selling and marketing, but also because they were somewhat cheaper than their male counterparts. However, except in science this margin of cheapness did not seem to give women graduates any marked advantage over men in avoiding unemployment in these years. This was probably because there were still deep-rooted inconveniences in employing women who were not regarded yet as suitable for executive roles even when they were

[1] 'Executive Women in the Engineering Industry, a Debate', *The Woman Engineer*, March 1934. (Hugh Quigley simply asserted that they were not suitable, but annoyingly refused to explain his reasons.)
[2] Report of Glasgow University Appointments Board, 1938–9.

scientifically qualified. All these factors caused some staunch advocates of the movement to feel that even by the end of the inter-war years it had been only a moderate success.

And yet was too much attention paid to the graduate as the spearhead of the widening of women's employment? Some of the most original and distinctively feminine careers created by women in the inter-war years were in non-graduate fields—Barbara Colvin in landscape design, Susie Cooper in the art of chinaware, Dorothy Wilding in photography, while even Elizabeth Scott, who designed the Shakespeare Memorial Theatre at Stratford in the thirties, was a non-graduate. These growing points in the changing career opportunities of the inter-war years lay outside the universities which for the majority of its women members were too often a firm if constricting road leading too easily back to the traditional occupation of teaching. On the other hand, we should not under-rate this period for the developing relationship of the woman graduate and industry. While the attempt to get a satisfactory *rapprochement* is still a problem today, yet to have made the initial moves away from the totally negative position of the pre-1914 era reflects well on the insight and imagination of those involved in moving the girl graduate in this direction. For it needed enlightened employers like F. J. Marquis, Simon Marks, and William Crawford to pull the girl into the firm as well as energetic feminists like Caroline Haslett and Mrs Strachey to push her thither. Their complementary efforts amid depression and the admitted inertia of the mass of girls themselves are among the many changes for good in those maligned decades.

12
War and Post-war
1939-59

*'The part which the universities thus played in the national
struggle for survival did not pass unnoticed by the public mind;
and there has emerged from the war a new and sustained
public interest in the universities and a strong realization of the
unique contribution which they have to offer to the national
wellbeing, whether in peace or war.'*[1]

With the outbreak of hostilities in September 1939 arrangements for
the use of the universities and their personnel in war industry were
devised to avoid the chaotic waste and delay experienced in the early
stages of the 1914–18 war. First, the eighteen-to-nineteen age group
was not immediately called up though in September 1939 the age of
obligation for military service was reduced to eighteen. In practice
the government was not calling up men before their twentieth
birthday, so that most students were able to complete two years'
study and also to take important examinations even after the age
of twenty.[2] Until roughly the end of 1940 'the universities and
colleges continued to function in a remarkably normal fashion'.[3]
In January 1941, while the call up of eighteen-year-olds was deferred,
those aged nineteen were brought into the forces. However, boys at
school who were going on to the universities and technical colleges
studying science and engineering were also allowed to continue to
their finals. Joint recruiting boards had been set up at each of the
universities at the start of the war and these dealt with the deferment
problems of scientists. However, by October 1942 the restrictions on
arts students had so tightened as to remove virtually any deferment
at all. Thus a flow of young trained scientists and technologists
through the universities was maintained and this was to be vital for
war-time science and industry.[4]

[1] *University Development from 1935 to 1948*, Report of the *UGC*, 1948, p. 6.
[2] C. M. Bowra, 'Conditions at Oxford in Wartime', *Oxford*, spring 1940.
[3] H. C. Dent, *Education in Transition, a Sociological Study of the Impact of
War on English Education, 1939–42* (London, 1944), p. 140.
[4] H. M. D. Parker, *Manpower, a Study in Wartime Policy and Administration*,
pp. 319–22.

Second, following the Munich crisis, a central register was formed of men holding higher education and scientific qualifications, with the Royal Society, the Institutes of Physics and Chemistry, and notable industrial research departments registering or circularizing their members. Likewise students graduating in special subjects were referred to the central register after being interviewed by their respective joint recruiting boards which 'provisionally allocated them to the Services, Government Departments or industry'. In spite of this, some critics still thought that the bringing of the university scientists into play was not as rapid as it might have been. The Vice-Chancellor of Durham, for example, complained in January 1940 that the rich stock of second line university scientific specialists was not being used and he called for 'clearer directions to the Universities in the future as to the lines upon which war research and training for such research should proceed'.[1] Sir Harry Melville also deplored that 'during the last War there was far too long a delay in bringing the government scientists and the university scientists into effective contact'.[2]

Third, steps were taken to move some colleges in dangerous areas to less vulnerable parts of the country. Plans for the evacuation of parts of London University were worked out after Munich and University College, for example, dispersed to Aberystwyth, Bangor, Cardiff, Swansea, Sheffield, Oxford, and Cambridge.[3] In this case it was most opportune as the college was devastated by air raids the following year[4] and indeed suffered more damage than all the other British universities put together. King's College moved to Bristol and its own buildings in the Strand were heavily damaged in October 1940 and May 1941. The metallurgy department of Imperial College moved to Swansea.

Major changes frequently took place within universities as outside bodies took over laboratories and as university scientists were redeployed into government and industrial scientific work. For example, the RAE Farnborough took over the Singer Laboratories at Exeter University and the Ministry of Aircraft Production used part of the buildings as drawing offices.[5] The Swansea chemistry department was likewise taken over by a section of the Armaments Research Department,[6] who also used the engineering department at Nottingham, while Boots occupied one of the chemistry laboratories in the same university. Finally, the Admiralty Signals School at

[1] Eustace Percy, 'The University in Wartime', *Durham University Journal*, January 1940.
[2] Home Universities Conference, 1955. Speech by Prof. H. W. Melville, p. 63.
[3] University College London Report, February 1939—February 1940.
[4] Ibid., February 1940–February 1941.
[5] John Murray, *The War and the College*.
[6] 'University College, Swansea', *JRIC*, 1955.

Portsmouth was relocated in the Wills Physics Laboratories at Bristol University. As outside government and industrial bodies came into the universities, so conversely university staff were redeployed into government and industry according to their specialisms. The movement of Edinburgh University scientists into outside activities provides an illustrative example of this.[1]

Chemists: Ministry of Supply (2), North British Rayon, Babcock and Wilcox, ICI (2), unspecified work on gas and drugs (2).

Engineers: Telecommunications Research Association at Malvern, Metro-Vickers.

Physicists: Chalk River, Air Ministry, Admiralty (3).

It was evident that most university scientists in this case went into government science work though much of it was inevitably of industrial application, with about one-third going into firms within industry. The university scientist totally penetrated those areas of government where science was involved. From Lord Cherwell of the Clarendon acting as adviser to Churchill; Tizard, Rector of Imperial College, advising Beaverbrook at the Ministry of Aircraft Production; Professors Bernal and Zuckerman advising Lord Mountbatten; down through the 'F.R.S. Regime' at the Armaments Research Department to the drafting of the youngest B.SC. by the joint recruiting boards, the university scientist was becoming a vital figure in the conduct of the war. Moreover, his withdrawal from the university and involvement with government and industry in urgent practical problems gave him a new width of vision. Conversely, the new close involvement of industry and industrial scientists with university men and facilities made possible a hitherto unprecedented rapidity of technical change in several areas of the war effort.

The two most striking areas of advance due to university and industry co-operation leading to war-time developments of considerable future industrial significance were radar and atomic energy. Watson Watt had begun the work at Slough from the mid 1930s that was to lead to radar, and with the approach of war from 1938 Professor Cockcroft and his team at the Cavendish were initiated into the secrets of the system at Bawdsey. The connection between the Cavendish and the Bawdsey Research Station grew closer in the spring of 1939, and during the following summer it became evident that a wider range of scientists would have to be brought in from the universities. In the long vacation of 1939 Cockcroft accordingly contacted physicists in a number of universities to acquaint them

[1] *Handbook of the Departments in the University of Edinburgh related to Industry*, 1949, gives career sketches of the members of scientific departments and their war-time activity.

with radar, its problems and implications for the coming war.[1] In addition to Cambridge, the other chief university centres used for this work were Oxford, Birmingham, and Bristol. After the outbreak of war, Professor Lindemann of the Clarendon became Churchill's scientific adviser and he naturally suggested that his own laboratory should play an important part in this work. The heart of the problem was the generation of shorter and shorter wavelengths for radio-location purposes. The work of the Clarendon 'was therefore the design and early development of suitable valves and methods for receiving and transmitting waves of ever smaller length', partly to prevent jamming and also to increase the effectiveness of smaller equipment needed to be housed in aeroplanes and ships. When they started work the smallest wavelength at which sets could be designed was 50 cm. but they were able to reduce this to 3 cm. by the end of the war. Also they devised means of using the same aerial for both transmitting and receiving and of preventing receiving systems being damaged by strong signals being sent during the transmission of an impulse.[2]

The third major university working on the problem was Birmingham under Professor Marcus Oliphant. They were concerned not only with creating very short waves but also with the problem of transmitting them at very great power. Whereas only a few watts were possible in 1939, as a result of the Birmingham work the resonant cavity magnetron ultra short wave centimetric transmitting valve was developed, capable of giving pulses of hundreds of kilowatts though no bigger than a child's fist.[3] Bristol was a fourth centre, a Bristol team having been brought in by Cockcroft, and it was in the Wills Laboratories at the university that the klystron valve was developed by the Admiralty Signal Establishment who were stationed there.[4] A good deal of this work in the universities was done with the collaboration of firms in the electrical industry who developed the products. In particular U-boat detection radar was the joint work of Cockcroft at the High Voltage Laboratory in Cambridge, and Pye's. The cavity magnetron was developed with GEC and BTH[5] at Wembley and Rugby, the klystron valve with GEC and EMI, and the metadyne for gun control depended on the collaboration of Professor Dannatt from Birmingham and Metro-Vickers.[6]

---

[1] On these developments generally see M. M. Postan, D. Hay. and J. D. Scott, *The Design and Development of Weapons*. Also Ronald W. Clark, *The Rise of the Boffins*.
[2] T. C. Keeley, 'Physics at Oxford during the War—I Radar', *The Oxford Magazine*, 16 May 1946.
[3] J. G. Crowther and R. Whiddington, *Science at War*, p. 35.
[4] Letter, 14 February 1961, Professor Tyndall to Mr Butterfield (Bristol University Archives, DM 363/82) on Bristol University in war-time. Also article on Professor Skinner in *New Society*, 14 November 1957.
[5] H. A. Price Hughes, *B.T.H. Reminiscences* (BTH, 1946), p. 94.
[6] J. Dummelow, *Metropolitan Vickers, 1899–1949* (Manchester, 1949), p. 172.

This close involvement of university departments and leading electrical firms did much to bring a more satisfactory liaison between the universities and the electrical industry than had existed before the war.

With the development of radar so there arose an acute shortage of wireless personnel which the universities were called upon to remedy. Under Lord Hankey's committee a special radio syllabus was devised which university students of physics and mathematics were encouraged to take. Early in the summer of 1941, state bursaries were provided for scientists at universities with the full costs of fees and residence being met for boys and girls studying radio, engineering, and chemistry, while in September the age of the applicants was lowered to seventeen; 'thus there has come into being a new type of undergraduate; the young scientist whose future services are already earmarked by the State'.[1] The universities absorbed this influx of scientists—2,000 bursaries were announced in October 1941—by the device of the shortened war degree courses of two years three months and the addition of a fourth term to the academic year. Accordingly many university physics departments, especially in the university colleges—Nottingham, Leicester, and Southampton, for example— where research of first-rate war importance was not otherwise taking place, were used for this vital training as well as for other technical training in fitting and turning for the services. At Birkbeck College, similarly, where the head of department, Professor J. D. Bernal, was away on high level advisory work, the laboratory was used for radio teaching and this became a part of the B.Sc. for the duration of the war.[2]

As in radar so also in atomic energy there was an intimate association of university and industrial scientists in war technology which was to create a new industry in the years of peace.[3] The development of atomic physics had been the special preserve of the universities from the early work of J. J. Thomson and Rutherford at the Cavendish. So advanced in character was this work that it was virtually confined to the universities, unlike many areas of electrical science, for example, where expertise lay as much in industrial research laboratories. Physicists had become aware early in 1939 of the possibility of the fission of uranium and after the outbreak of war work on this was developed by Professor G. P. Thomson of Imperial College and Professor Marcus Oliphant of Birmingham. Two refugee scientists, Rudolf Peierls and O. R. Frisch, then also at

[1] H. C. Dent, op. cit., p. 143.
[2] E. H. Warmington, *A History of Birkbeck College, University of London, during the Second World War, 1939–1945* (London, 1954), p. 83.
[3] Margaret Gowing, *Britain and Atomic Energy, 1939–45*. Ronald W. Clark, *The Birth of the Bomb*. F. S. Simon, 'Physics at Oxford during the War— II Atomic Energy', *The Oxford Magazine*, 13 June 1946.

Birmingham University, worked out the critical size of a future bomb, its effects and methods of detonation, and under Thomson the MAUD Committee was established to consider the development of such a weapon. The Maud Committee then farmed out problems to select universities and began to bring in industrial scientists.

The main university groups involved were the Cavendish under Cockcroft and Bragg, Francis Simon's group at Oxford, Rudolf Peierls at Birmingham, and Sir James Chadwick with Otto Frisch at Liverpool. These latter also controlled the Bristol University Wills Laboratory physicists while much of the chemistry was the responsibility of Professor Norman Haworth, also at Birmingham. It was through the work of this last group that industrial firms were brought into collaboration in the project, with Haworth preparing the uranium required by ICI. From 1941 it was decided to build the bomb, and accordingly the Maud Committee activities were turned over to the deliberately misleadingly named 'Tube Alloys', headed by Sir Wallace Ackers of ICI, bringing a yet closer industrial involvement. The work of the various groupings was fairly clearly divided. Sir James Chadwick, the discoverer of the neutron, controlled the Liverpool and Cavendish teams working on 'cross sections' or the estimation of how many nuclear fissions would take place with fast neutrons bombarding nuclei of uranium. The mathematical and theoretical work on bomb assembly and performance was done by Peierls at Birmingham, while at Oxford the Clarendon dealt with the problem of the production of enriched uranium 235 by gaseous diffusion. It was in this area that the close connections between university and industrial contributions were most clearly seen. The problem was to separate out pure uranium 235 by pumping a gaseous compound of uranium through hundreds of stages of membranes and filters, causing the lighter atoms to pass through more quickly than the heavier with the emerging gas being successively 'enriched'. In the search for means of constructing the very fine mesh of the filters ICI Metals at Witton were called in and ICI's Kynoch Press and thence printing firms—Lund Humphries and the Sun Engraving Company of Watford—familiar with problems of the photo-reproduction of very fine dots. The actual plant itself was built by Metro-Vickers. This area of the project saw one of the widest interconnections of varied industrial personnel of the war, and Simon subsequently reflected that this close experience of working with industrial firms would be a long run asset for the universities concerned, notably for Oxford not hitherto conspicuous for this kind of liaison.

However, there were those who felt a certain unease about the university-industry linkages in Tube Alloys. Margaret Gowing has noted, 'the work was unhappily poised between the stages of university research and full industrial development'. The ICI men wanted work to be more concentrated under a single director and feared its diffusion, while the university men wished for the opposite and, remembering the days of Maud and academic control, feared that this would be displaced by the control of industrialists. By this stage of the war, however, the close mixing of industrial and university scientists was more normal. The team that went to Berkeley in 1944 comprised academics like Oliphant but also industrial research men from BTH, ICI, and Metro-Vickers working in harmony.

The civil industrial atomic energy of the post-war period took its roots specifically from the work of British scientists at Chalk River in Canada under Cockcroft, and it was meetings of Cockcroft (Cambridge), Chadwick (Liverpool), Oliphant (Birmingham), Massey (London), and Skinner (Bristol) in Washington that clarified ideas on what was to become Harwell, and which Cockcroft, on Chadwick's recommendation, returned from Chalk River to administer. The concern for atomic energy originated by the universities thus led to very considerable university and industrial collaboration during the war in the production of the bomb as a weapon, and the activities of the leading British university scientists in the later stages of the war led directly to the origins of a new peace-time industry.

Certain university departments dealt with more specialized problems stemming from their own fortes. Southampton's expertise in aero and other engines was called upon to devise means of water recovery for vehicles in the desert.[1] At the other extreme, in Cambridge, Max Perutz's experience with glaciology enabled him to solve for Lord Mountbatten the problem of the icing of ships in Arctic waters and the devising of a snow fighting machine that became the 'Weazel'.[2] In the development of materials the Manchester faculty of technology, renowned for its excellence in textile and paper research before the war, became important in the design and testing of fabrics for webbing, parachutes, barrage balloons, and camouflage.[3] Sheffield University's experience with steels was used in the devising of refractories for steel melting furnaces with the loss of supplies from Europe.[4] They also worked on steel forgings and the fragmentation of the steel of shell casings to increase their lethal effectiveness, while their earlier war-time development of glass technology was of further value in devising glass for aeroplanes to

[1] 'Investigations and Experimental Developments made for the various fighting services in the War period', unpublished private memorandum by Wing Commander Professor Cave-Brown-Cave. Cave-Brown-Cave became the Director of Camouflage. Many of these experiments were carried out at Southampton by Mr Leech but with the professor's advice.
[2] David Lampe, *Pyke, the Unknown Genius* (London, 1959).
[3] *Manchester Municipal College of Technology Jubilee, 1902–52* (Manchester, 1952), pp. 18–20.
[4] University of Sheffield, Record of War Work, 1939–45. (Sheffield University Library, PAM 378.4274).

withstand severe cold, impact, and bullets. The obvious chemical problems came in for their due share of university attention. Sheffield University became the centre for a research team under the Ministry of Supply working on the improvement of the consistency of the amatol used in the filling factories and the development of more powerful mixtures of RDX and TNT. In drugs Imperial College focused on the production of penicillin and the synthesizing of vitamin A, while the chemical technology department in the same college dealt with methane as an alternative fuel, incendiary bombs, flash bombs for photography, and rocket fuels.[1]

More original, and possibly more important in its implications for future industry than these predictable concerns with devising gadgets and improving materials, was the development of the techniques of operational research.[2] This arose from the use of radar with anti-aircraft guns. University scientists, under Professor Blackett of Imperial College, were formed into a team to maintain and service the systems, and from this starting point 'Blackett's Circus', as it was called, went on to make studies on the calculation of rounds fired per hit and the scientific grouping of guns to achieve maximum effect. Statistical techniques came to be applicable to such problems as the optimum size and shape of convoys to reduce loss through submarines, and the timetabling (by an Aberdeen University geneticist) of coastal command planes to double their patrolling capacity. Scientific study was made of the effects of weapons and blast with such accuracy that Professor J. D. Bernal was able, uncannily, to calculate and forecast the effects of a 500-bomber raid on Coventry before it actually took place. These techniques developed to deal with specific war-time military problems, then became developed in peace-time to be applicable as techniques of industrial management.

A number of points emerge from the foregoing consideration of the universities and war-time science and industry. First, in some ways the Second World War was not so striking a watershed as the first. In the First World War, scandalous neglect of the universities had given way to spectacular and varied proofs of the value of university science to twentieth-century warfare. By the outbreak of the 1939–45 war these lessons had already been well learned and few supposed that the war could have been waged without the universities which, it was assumed, would do their bit. Hence the pre-existence of the central register from 1938, Cockcroft's activities in the long vacation of 1939, and the various schemes about call up and deferment. It was the First World War which proved that modern warfare

---

[1] Typescript 'History of the Chemistry Department of Imperial College' (in the college archives). Typescript 'Report by Sir Alfred Egerton on the Work of the Department of Chemical Technology during the War' (in the college archives).
[2] J. G. Crowther and R. Whiddington, op. cit., 'Operational Research'.

was impossible without university science; by the second this was already assumed and catered for.[1] Second, the long-term beneficial effects of the war stemming from university-industrial activity were immense. The significance of radar and atomic energy need not be restressed; that of operational research has been referred to. In less obvious fields the work of Imperial College on methane, though little valued at the time, greatly developed the technology of liquefaction in which Britain had hitherto been backward, and the same college's work on synthetic rubber led to much fundamental research in acetylenic compounds and laid the foundations of the British school of acetylene chemistry. These were university contributions, but in perspective it will be borne in mind that whole areas of scientific industrial advance during the war, notably in aeroplane design and especially the jet engine, were not particularly the products of university activity.

Third, it was evident that very close links were established during the war between university scientists and firms, notably with GEC BTH, ICI, EMI, and Metro-Vickers in the radar and atomic energy fields. These links seemed especially important with the laboratories of the great electrical firms which had emerged in the inter-war years as major centres of innovating science in their own right. The war brought these and the university departments of physics into close touch, whereas they had been criticized for being too distant from each other in the 1930s.[2] The fusion also allayed some suspicions that Cavendish physics was having a baleful effect on British university physics in the inter-war years by turning it away from practical industrial technology. When the war came with its all too pressing practical problems, it was quite evident that Cockcroft, Oliphant, Chadwick, and the other heirs and creators of the Cavendish tradition were able with remarkable fluency to move between the practical and theoretical problems of radar and atomic energy. Many scientists indeed were involved at different parts of the war with both projects.

Fourth, the demands of war and the relative responses to them gave some indicator of the relative strengths of British universities compared with the First World War and the nineteenth century. The Second World War was a war of physics (atomic energy, radar, wireless) as the First World War had been one of chemistry (drugs, dyes, glass explosives), and there seemed to be fewer centres of excellence in the former than in the latter. In particular, Cambridge now showed itself

[1] For example, *Science in War* (Penguin Special, 1940) by Professor Zuckerman and others urging the greater employment of science in the war effort but properly reticent on the main developments already under way.
[2] *Report on the Extension of Scientific Research in Manchester University particularly in Relation to the Industries of its Area* considered that the war had brought an initiate liaison of university departments and firms in the electrical field which had been formerly lacking.

as the premier university in Britain as was becoming evident in the inter-war years. Also, perhaps more strikingly, Oxford, the rightful object of contempt for its neglect of science before 1920, had emerged during the war as playing a very major role indeed in physical science. Birmingham was the leading civic university, continuing its great war-time tradition of 1914–18, and Bristol with its Wills Laboratory was playing a much more important role than would have been predictable in 1918.

By contrast the other major civic universities—Manchester, Leeds, Sheffied, Newcastle—seem relatively less important in the second war than the first though performing valuable services in their own traditional areas if without any striking major new advances. By even sharper contrast, the Scottish and Welsh universities figure scarcely at all in the major developments of radar and atomic energy. This close focusing of major advanced war science on very few universities—Oxford, Cambridge, Birmingham, Bristol, Liverpool (London having been largely dispersed elsewhere)—was probably due to a number of factors peculiar to that war. The need for secrecy argued in favour of restricting centres of activity—official university records like reports and printed senate minutes, for example, are vastly more reticent in the Second World War than the first, and, quite properly, yield virtually no information. The need for constant collaboration between teams of researchers also argued for having the teams in reasonable proximity, especially with the difficulties of war-time travel. This itself would strongly militate against having such centres of research in Scotland and Wales, or indeed north of Birmingham (Liverpool being the exception because of the location there of Sir James Chadwick's cyclotron). Apart from these factors there was also the personal one that Max Born, Tait Professor of Natural Philosophy at Edinburgh and an authority on atomic physics, chose not to be involved in the work for the atomic bomb on moral grounds. Ironically, the physicist from Edinburgh who did take part, Klaus Fuchs, was a celebrated disaster. For these reasons the major activities of the war science effort seemed to be borne by fewer universities in the second than in the first war, and by English universities rather than by those elsewhere in Britain.

As the war began to draw towards a close, various bodies started to consider again the future relations between industry and the universities in peace-time. A private conference at Nuffield College in 1942 deplored that more students had not gone into industry before the war and asserted that 'in our view industry has the right to claim a higher proportion of the best men from the universities than it has been getting in the past'.[1] The Association of Scientific Workers also

[1] *Industry and Education, a Statement* (Nuffield College, 1943). This was the result of a conference at Oxford in September 1942, including Sir Lawrence

welcomed the closer links between university and industrial laboratories that the war had brought, and the extended introduction of
applied technical science into university work.[1] More formally there
was a concern to create machinery to link the industrial and university worlds with proposals for joint conferences of the Conference
of Management Associations and university staffs through the AUT.
Ironically, the managers added that the universities would have to
convene such meetings 'since they were the sellers and had to convince
industry that they had the men industry wanted', a view looking
backwards to the 1930s and bearing no relation to the real situation as
it developed in the 1940s and 1950s.[2]

Apart from these general if laudable sentiments for even closer
relations between the universities and industry, the later years of the
war saw a more urgent and precise concern about the quantity and
supply of graduates for future manpower needs. Lord Percy's
committee of 1945 considered 'that the annual intake into industries
of the country of men trained by universities and technical colleges
has been, and still is, insufficient both in quantity and quality'.[3] Industry was not getting its fair share of high national ability, partly
because the industrialists did not know how to make their wants
known to universities. As a corrective they proposed regional advisory
councils to organize closer consultation and links between industry
and universities, and they called for more management-type education
to be included within science degrees. Very specifically they stressed
that the pre-war output of engineers was too low at 700 a year, and
that the war-time post-1943 annual degree output of engineers of
3,000 would have to be maintained in peace-time and not cut back.
The Barlow committee of the following year took an even more urgent view of the problem. They considered that there were about
60,000 qualified scientists in Britain at that time but that the demand
would increase such that 70,000 would be needed by 1950 and 90,000
by 1955. They called on the universities to double their output of
scientists from 2,500 to 5,000 a year to achieve this, for if expansion
were limited to existing rates then there would be a shortfall of
scientists of the order of 26,000 by 1955. Barlow considered this
expansion perfectly possible in the light of the fact that only 2 per

Bragg, Walter Citrine, Henry Tizard, A. P. M. Fleming, G. D. H. Cole, and
others.
[1] *Science in the Universities, Report to the UGC*, Association of Scientific
Workers, Oxford, March 1944.
[2] Confederation of Management Associations, Universities Sub-committee,
31 May 1945 (AUT File 107).
[3] *Higher Technological Education*, Report of a Special Committee (Percy)
(HMSO, 1945). Percy himself considered that his main task as Rector of King's
College, Newcastle, was 'to meet the postwar demand for an expanded
production of scientists and technologists'. Lord Eustace Percy, *Some
Memories*, p. 209.

cent of the population ever got to university whereas 5 per cent of the population had an intelligence as great as the upper half of existing university students. The new educational reforms of the 1944 Act indeed made this possibility of expansion more feasible, since by making intelligence rather than fee-paying the criterion for entry to the grammar school, more of the working-class could be expected to win grammar school places and thence to move to university. Barlow accordingly recommended a considerable expansion of existing universities and the foundation of a new one to cope with this pressing post-war problem.[1]

Apart from these major official reports all manner of other interested bodies made their own proposals for expansion. *The Economist* called for a raising of the student population from 50,000 to 100,000 by 1960 and to 150,000 by 1975, partly on the grounds of our need for scientists.[2] The NUT wanted a quadrupling in ten to twenty years and the AUT a 50 per cent increase.[3] The Confederation of Management Associations wanted 200,000 graduates in industry on the assumption that 2·5 per cent of the industrial labour force should be university men.[4] The FBI also welcomed the trend for expansion though without quantifying their demands.[5] Following Percy and Barlow, the official body assessing scientific manpower needs was the Technical Personnel Committee with its various subcommittees dealing with specific sciences. They calculated that an annual output of 870 physicists a year would be needed compared with the 750 then produced, envisaging considerable expansion of demand from rubber, electricals, and textiles.[6] The chemical engineers feared that without expansion the existing university supply would meet only 85 per cent of the demand, with a deficiency of 200 a year.[7] It was curious to some, in the light of this, that when Sir Walter Moberly wrote his widely discussed book on *The Crisis in the University* he should have in mind moral and philosophical matters and he was

[1] 1945 XIV *Scientific Manpower* (Barlow), Cmd. 6824.
[2] 'University Prospect', *The Economist*, 9, 16 and 23 February 1946.
[3] Bruce Truscott, *Redbrick and these Vital Days* (London, 1945), p. 38.
[4] Report of a Joint Conference of the Confederation of Management Associations and AUT, 23 February 1946, in AUT archives, 'Meetings with other Bodies'. Mr G. Cheliotti of GEC made this estimate and considered the existing numbers of graduates in industry only a 'small fraction' of 200,000.
[5] *The Education and Training of Technologists*, Report of a Study Group set up by the FBI Industrial Research and Education Committees, 1949.
[6] *Present and Future Supply and Demand for Persons with Professiona Qualifications in Physics* (HMSO, 1949).
[7] *Present and Future Supply . . . Chemical Engineering* (HMSO, 1950). Many unpublished background papers of these committees are to be found in Professor Tyndall's papers in Bristol University Archives, D.M. 363. The most powerful industrial evidence for expansion came from Sir Ewart Smith of ICI: 'The Relation between the output of Technical Staff and Industrial Development', Memorandum, 29 December 1949.

scarcely concerned with technological manpower at all. Over this he was roundly attacked by Lord Simon for whom the real crisis was not philosophical but economic; the failure of the universities to produce enough manpower usable in a starved and expanding industry.[1]

The response of the universities to these new demands for expansion was impressive if never quite adequate. The Barlow report recommendation of a doubling of scientists and technologists in ten years was achieved in five, and numbers of students rose successively through the 1940s and 1950s with a temporary recession as the post-war bulge of ex-servicemen passed through.[2]

TABLE 37   *University expansion*

	Undergraduates	Advanced students	Total	First year entrants
1938–9	46,908	3,094	50,002	15,153
1946–7	64,960	3,492	68,452	22,545
1949–50	78,064	7,357	85,421	24,331
1954–5	69,493	12,212	81,705	22,463
1960–1	89,863	17,836	107,699	29,510

The initial expansion of the 1940s was clearly due to the return of men after the war, but after a slight pause the upward movement continued with the 'trend' to staying on in the sixth form in the 1950s providing the dynamic behind expansion even before the post-war birth 'bulge' reached the universities. This expansion was underlain not only by the expansion of existing, especially civic, universities, but also by the rise to full university status and expansion of several university colleges. Nottingham obtained its charter in 1948, Southampton in 1952, Hull in 1954, Exeter in 1955, Leicester in 1957, while the University College of North Staffordshire opened in 1950 and became Keele University in 1962. The 1950s, rather in risk of being overshadowed in university history by the more spectacular decade that was to follow, was a flowering of newly chartered universities hitherto paralleled only by the 1900s.

From the point of view of industry, what was as important as the overall expansion of the university population was the change in the balance within it. While the proportion of arts and social studies students remained fairly constant throughout the post-war period, the

[1] Sir Walter Moberly, *The Crisis in the University* (London, 1949), for Simon's rejoinder see George F. Kneller, *Higher Learning in Britain*, p. 180.
[2] *University Development*, Reports of the UGC, 1935–48; 1947–52; 1952–57; 1957–62.

TABLE 38   *Full-time students by faculties (percentage of total)*

	1938–9	1949–50	1953–4	1957–8	1961–2
Arts and social	44·7	43·6	43·0	43·1	43·0
Pure science	15·3	19·8	21·1	22·7	25·4
Applied science	10·6	12·8	12·4	14·5	15·2

pure and applied scientists rose markedly in importance compared with their relative positions in the pre-war period.

The rise of the sciences in these years came not at the expense of the arts but of medicine and dentistry which became relatively much less important than they had been in the 1930s, partly under the influence of Sir Henry Willink's recommendations for a contraction in medical education in the 1950s. This swing was aided by government decisions greatly to expand science and technology at the universities, notably at Imperial College from 1953. The Manchester College of Science and Technology became independent of the LEA in 1956 on its way into being expanded into UMIST. At the school level, the Industrial Fund for the Advancement of Scientific Education in Schools was formed in 1955 to provide grants for science buildings in independent and direct grant schools, while the glamour associated in the public mind with developments in atomic energy and jet aircraft in the 1950s all fed the swing to science in schools and universities in that decade.

However creditable the expansion and the swing to science were in these post-war years they did not keep pace with the consistently heavy demand of industry for university scientists.[1] With the economy running at nearly full employment, in planned contrast to the 1930s, there was scarcely a recession to touch the graduate until the end of the 1950s. Consequently, demand for the traditional industrial scientists, the chemists, and engineers both electrical and mechanical, remained considerably in excess of supply and even at an 'insatiable level' through the late 1940s to the middle 1950s.[2] From about 1955, however, new demands were added to traditional ones. First, a number of universities noted in the mid 1950s that industry was beginning to discover the mathematician as an expert useful for economic analysis and statistics, and also for operational research which belatedly

[1] This paragraph is based on the Reports of the Appointments Boards of Cambridge, Sheffield, and Durham. The last two were not printed but I am grateful to Mr E. A. Ovens of Sheffield, and Mr J. K. Hudson of Durham for allowing me to use their private typescripts.
[2] The Anglo-American Council on Productivity, *Report on Universities and Industry*, November 1951, noted 'British industrialists require more qualified engineers than they can recruit at present time' and considered this a major discrepancy between ourselves and the Americans.

seemed to be filtering into business techniques following its developments during the war. This aggravated the problems of the schools
in trying to recruit mathematics teachers at the time of the 'bulge'
and became one of the roots of the swing from science that was to
cause such concern in the 1960s. Also in the mid 1950s, the aircraft
and atomic energy industries were proving highly attractive as
graduate absorbers, partly because they entailed indefinite deferment
from National Service for their entrants. The lighter electronic side
also came to displace heavy electricals as the chief area taking graduates in electrical engineering, and in all these fields—atomic energy,
aircraft, and electronics—the physicist and mathematician was
coming into his own in the 1950s as the graduate chemist in industry
had done in the previous generation.

This intense demand for graduates up to 1957 forced industry
into a variety of policies in order to attract them in this sellers'
market. In the late 1940s, for instance, there was a spate of conferences
run by the FBI both nationally and regionally on the problem of the
graduate in industry, there were the joint meetings of the AUT and
the CMA, the Oxford Conference of the Industrial Welfare Society,
the Home Universities' Conference, and so forth. Scarcely before had
such an intensive and repetitive concern been shown about this
problem as in the late 1940s and early 1950s. More practically,
training schemes began to burgeon, and in the continued intensive
competition for graduates there was a considerable rethinking of
these in the mid 1950s to improve their quality and attractiveness.
For example, twenty-six of forty-three firms investigated by PEP in
1957 had training schemes and most of these had been introduced or
revised since 1945.[1] Also, as a precursor to the training scheme,
vacation courses began, at Cambridge for example from 1953, with
a view to giving second-year undergraduates some experience of
industry to influence favourably their future choice of career. The
FBI regions were important in organizing these, and by 1954 some
300 British firms were arranging vacation courses for 2,000 students.[2]
Yet in its insatiable search for talent, industry was reaching even
further back than undergraduates—to such an extent that by 1956
firms were selecting promising schoolboys and financing their
university careers in order to secure their recruitment on graduation.
Around 1954 and 1955 there were important rises in industrial
starting salaries to remove the discrepancy between those in industry
and teaching.[3] For example, in 1949 16 per cent of University College,

[1] PEP, *Graduates in Industry* (London, 1957), p. 135.
[2] *Industry and the Graduate* (FBI, 1954), p. 22.
[3] PEP, *Graduate Employment, a Sample Survey* (London, 1956), p. 149. When
comparative salaries were tested for the same sample in 1954, industrial
salaries were then clearly above teaching salaries for people at the same stage
of their career.

London, engineers had been dissatisfied with their salaries and 27 per cent of scientists.[1] But by the mid 1950s, under pressure of demand from industry, industrial salaries had risen. In the Manchester survey,[2] the most favoured industrial occupations for graduates starting work between 1949 and 1954, and their highest and lowest (presumably starting) salaries were:

Industrial branch	Number entering	Highest/lowest salary (£s)
Chemicals	46	1,750/530
Textiles	29	2,000/700
Electricals	29	1,300/525
Civil engineering	25	1,000/500

This was some improvement on the £421 and £530 average salaries for London engineers and scientists respectively in 1949. Finally, between 1945 and 1954, six new university appointments boards were created, thus further helping the flow of graduates into industry.[3]

All these developments, training schemes, vacation courses, conferences, and salary rises were the responses of industry to the situation of the shortage of scientific and technical graduates at a time of acute and chronic demand. These blandishments raised the graduate intake into industry to probably its highest level thus far. PEP noted in the 1950s that 'industry has become, and that only recently, the largest single user of university men' and 'the universities now send more men into industry than into any other walk of life',[4] indicating that of nearly 7,000 graduates of 1950, 37·8 per cent went into industrial occupations.[5] Similarly, of Cambridge male graduates of 1952 and 1953, 32 per cent were in industry in 1961, nor had there been any significant change in proportions between the first occupations entered by these graduates in the 1950s and the occupations they held in 1961. By this time 57 per cent of engineers, 41 per cent of scientists and mathematicians, 37 per cent of lawyers, and 30 per cent of economics and other arts graduates were going into industry and commerce as a career. Within this industrial group 31·2 per cent were engaged on research, 23 per cent on sales and advertising, and 17 per cent on production.[6] It was a powerful indicator of the leading position that industry had come to assume in the employment pattern of graduates by the 1950s.

This fervent courtship of the graduate by industry and his response,

[1] University College London Union, a Report on the Employment Survey, 1949.
[2] University of Manchester Quinquennial Survey of Graduate Appointments, 1949–54.
[3] Lord Heyworth, *University Appointments Boards* (UGC, HMSO, 1964).
[4] PEP *Graduates in Industry*, op. cit., pp. 43 and 71.
[5] PEP *Graduate Employment*, op. cit., p. 59.
[6] Christine Craig, *The Employment of Cambridge Graduates*.

which had dominated the 1940s and 1950s, paused in the late 1950s. In 1957–8 the long phase of war and post-war boom came to an end as the ardour of industry was for the first time cooled, and the graduate found himself faced with a mild recession. There were cutbacks in investment; changes in government defence policy caused a retrenchment in the aircraft industry, halting the demand for graduates which had risen since the mid 1950s; and a hardening in the demand for graduates in engineering and technology was evident. 'The continuing expansion of university departments of science and technology, the virtual ending of National Service for graduates and the extension of technological training within industry' were all pointed to as factors contributing to this slight climacteric. Also the Dip. Tech. was proving more of a success than was expected and some firms in electrical engineering preferred to expand this type of training rather than take graduates. The Sheffield Appointments Officer bade a valediction to the passing era of panic recruitment and stockpiling of graduates of the post-war decade. There were now 'signs', he noted, 'that graduate recruitment may be entering upon a more realistic phase'.

This urgent demand of industry for the graduate and the shortage of scientists prompted a greater attention in the 1950s to the potentialities of the arts graduate. Apart from the shortage of scientists as a motive, there was the example of the Civil Service with its long tradition of using high quality arts men for administration. Also, a strong body of opinion that liked to stress the importance of 'character' and 'breadth of vision' as opposed to specific technical qualifications was far from averse to the arts man who was supposed to possess these 'rounded' qualities that outweighed his lack of expertise.[1] Just after the war it was somewhat grudgingly conceded that there may be openings for arts graduates in industry in personnel and library work.[2] In practice the movement of arts graduates into industry was more buoyant in the 1950s than would have been thought possible just after the war. By the late 1950s the arts graduates were being referred to as an élite among managers, many of them still young and having entered management in the early 1950s with high earnings though they did not tend to move between firms.[3] The Acton Society Trust Survey on the problem likewise found a marked increase of firms taking arts graduates between 1946 and 1952, with peak years 1954 to 1956 for the usual reasons of shortage of technologists, but coupled with the view that higher qualities of leadership and a sense of personal relationships were found among students of

[1] *Report of the Conference on Industry and the Universities*, FBI, 1949. Session IV on the Arts Graduate gives a spectrum of views.
[2] Percy Dunsheath, *The Graduate in Industry*, pp. 249–53.
[3] R. V. Clements, *Managers, a Study of their Careers in Industry* (London, 1958), p. 143.

arts.[1] It was, however, somewhat disturbing that what firms most valued in the arts graduate was his 'ability to fit in' and what they least desired was the ability to work hard and show an inquiring mind. It may be thought there was some marked divergence here between the ideals of the universities who produced the graduates and the firms who were to employ them.

Accompanying this reception of the arts graduate, there was a confused but important difference of opinion on what industrialists required of graduates which ran through various FBI and other conferences of the period.[2] On the one hand were those who stressed 'character' and sporting ability and who tended to play down and even denigrate academic excellence and specific qualifications, notably from time to time Sir Ronald Weeks, Sir Humphrey Gale, and Sir Robert Wood. At its worst this view led to a kind of anti-intellectualism that took bizarre turns, as when Sir Ronald Weeks suggested that 'studiousness' was 'the real danger which faces the universities'. This attitude provoked the exasperated response of one Oxford tutor who pleaded 'we cannot put on courses on running the rugger club'. These views did not go unchallenged in the early 1950s when during the conferences we find more industrialists prepared to state frankly that they required men of very high intellectual ability who were thoroughly expert in their own field, notably Sir Frederick Handley Page, Sir Ewart Smith of ICI, and Sir Edward Herbert of Hollins. By 1955, Professor Cox of Leeds, looking back on past debates, considered that the 'emphasis on personal qualities could undoubtedly be exaggerated' and he felt that it had unnecessarily led to the exclusion of men of first-class scientific ability that industry could ill do without. This debate and the confusion it gave rise to in people's minds as to what industry really wanted had wider implications. The older 'broad' view may have been useful in preparing the minds of some industrialists to accept the non-qualified arts man, but it may also have had a damaging effect in blunting the urgency to produce academically excellent, specifically qualified technologists that all since Percy and Barlow had been calling for.

Perhaps surprisingly in the light of the greater attention paid by industry to arts graduates in these years, there was virtually no advance in the reception of women graduates into industry. Immediately after the war a common theme emerging from letters concerning

[1] Audrey Collin, Anthony M. Rees, and John Utting, *The Arts Graduate in Industry*.
[2] Conference of the Universities of Great Britain and Northern Ireland, *University Graduates in Commerce and Industry*, 1948; *Report of the Conference on Industry and the Universities*, FBI, 1949; *Report of the Conference on Industry, the Universities and the Technical Colleges*, FBI, 1950; *Report on the Conference on Industry and the Universities*, FBI, Nottingham, 1952; *Report of the Universities and Industry Conference*, FBI, Ashorne Hill, 1952; *The Education and Training of Graduate Staff for Industrial Research*, FBI, 1955.

graduate women is the frequent attempts of women teachers to move into industry, to 'personnel' and 'commerce'. At Liverpool, for example, five women teachers of whom there is record attempted to do this, without success.[1] The expanding area of women graduates' employment was not industry but the Civil Service. For example, whereas in the early 1930s fourteen women went into teaching in proportion to one into business, Judith Hubback found that in the 1940s and 1950s the proportion of women graduates going into business was non-existent and unchanging in spite of the fact that 5 per cent of her women actually intended to go into business.[2] That a good deal of resistance came from potential employers was made clear in the following year by a survey made for the Manchester region.[3] Of seventy-three firms only six employed women scientists, and most of those were large firms of 4,000+ employees, although this was a time of acute shortage of qualified scientists and technologists. Even if women got into industry they could rarely expect to rise into middle management, and whereas women gained some acceptance in research and personnel they were not regarded as suitable for production management, engineering, or senior executive work. But in any case if girls at school studied science they vastly preferred to use it in medicine; 'there is little enthusiasm among them for science based careers and almost none for science based careers in industry', accordingly 'so far women have not gained so much as a toe hold on the South Col in the industrial world'.[4] Employers suspected early marriage and early leaving, and the limited competence and flexibility of women in industry. The women themselves were resistant to science, especially in a decade when mathematics teaching was at a low ebb. Teaching offered good starting salaries and a greater geographical flexibility of employment, both important considerations for women expecting to marry early. All these served to perpetuate the problem of the disengagement of women graduates from industry in spite of the new conditions of full employment and the shortages of scientific manpower.

If industry in its desperate search for manpower was turning to the arts graduate but neglecting women, a third area which might have been exploited more to meet the shortage was the Scottish graduate. We have noted that after their greatest days in the nineteenth century, the Scottish universities seemed to be somewhat more disengaged from industry than their English counterparts. This still

[1] Files of the Liverpool University Appointments Office for the 1940s. I am grateful to Miss Barbara Johnstone for permission to use these letters.
[2] Judith Hubback, *Wives who went to College*, p. 46.
[3] Women in Engineering, Report by a Committee . . . to enquire into the Employment of Women Scientists and Technologists in the Engineering Industry in the Manchester Area (Manchester, 1958).
[4] Nancy Seear, Veronica Roberts, and John Brock, *A Career for Women in Industry?*, pp. 44 and 93.

seemed to be so judging from their placements even in the boom times of the late 1940s and 1950s. Scottish graduates, for example, made a particularly poor showing in getting into major British industrial enterprises.[1] Whereas Scottish students as a proportion of those in Britain was 18·6 per cent, yet from the end of the war to 1955 they had been securing only 3 per cent of the graduate entry places into the National Coal Board, 6 per cent in ICI, 9 per cent in Lever Brothers, 6 per cent in Cadbury's, and 8 per cent in 'a leading motor company'. It was suggested that this was due to the skimped nature of Scottish student life and its lack of residences, industrial employers having a decided preference for residential universities. This may have been so but it seems an area of graduate talent less justifiably neglected than the women.

Industry not only drew closer to the universities in its search for manpower but it became more closely involved with the finance of universities and specifically in the finance of university research. While it is never possible to isolate benefactions from industry precisely, it was noteworthy that during the 1950s there was an extraordinary rise in benefactions to universities, doubling from £12 million in 1952–7 to £24 million in 1957–63. This betokened, the UGC suggested, considerable confidence in universities on the part of 'foundations, firms and individuals'.[2] Coming through whatever form, the roots of the bulk of this finance must have lain in industry. More directly the same period also saw an even more remarkable rise in payments for research by outside bodies as a source of university finance. This rose

1956–7   £2·6 million—6·5 per cent of university finance
1961–2   £8·2 million—11·1 per cent of university finance

which was quite the largest rise of any source of university income. For some this rise was timely but at the same time was to be regarded warily. In a survey taken before this marked expansion it was found that 'the direct contacts between industry and university research are on a small scale, the resulting research projects engaging something like 20 per cent of the resources of the scientific and technological departments or perhaps 5 per cent of the whole resources of the universities.'[3] Also about 20 to 25 per cent of teachers in scientific and technological departments were doing work for industrial bodies outside the university, with more consultancy at Oxford and Cam-

[1] J. P. Macintosh, 'Why our Graduates Fail', *The Scotsman*, 20 and 21 November 1956. Macintosh's point about residence was later amply confirmed by the UGC. 'Industry as the employer has every opportunity to judge the value of residence and has given the clearest proof of its belief in residence', *University Development, 1952–7*, p. 29.
[2] UGC *University Development, 1957–62*, p. 54.
[3] V. E. Cosslett, *The Relations between Scientific Research in the Universities and Industrial Research, a Report on Conditions in Great Britain*, pp. 27–8.

bridge and more routine testing in Scottish universities. Although Dr Cosslett considered this to be on a 'small scale', it seemed to be in accord with his own norms that not more than a quarter of the activity of a department should be for outside bodies. Others, notably Professor Mott, had no fears and welcomed yet further expansion of the involvement of industrial support in university research and the latter's orientation towards industry.[1] Not only did firms give more money for university research, but there was strong evidence that they were establishing good contacts with their regional university and coming to rely on it rather than on other bodies as the source of their science. The Manchester survey found that no less than 40 per cent of the 225 firms surveyed had active links with a university or technical college, the great bulk consulting Manchester University.[2] Frequently these close links between the university and industrialists had been based on working friendships originating in war-time committees, and this survey concluded that whatever were other defects of firms' attitudes to science their relations with universities was 'much wider and closer . . . than could have been generally expected'.

The post-war years were thus characterized by an urgent recognition of the need to expand the supply of scientists and technologists whose importance had been yet further enhanced by the activities of war-time science. The demands of industry proved insatiable, not only for the traditional technologies but also increasingly for the physical sciences whose new potentialities were revealed by the war. In spite of the marked expansion of the universities and the notable increase in the proportion of science and technology students, the universities were unable to keep pace with industry. This led to various devices to publicize industry and to attract the graduate as well as higher salaries and a turning to the arts graduate to fill in the gap, though not a further employment of women. Apart from their greedy absorption of graduates which reached new peaks, industry also in the mid 1950s very greatly increased its private finance of universities and even more strikingly its finance of research, while the connections between industry and the universities in the research field were good. Such was the period of consistent and steady improvement in many fields of industry–university relations that preceded the following watershed decade of more turbulent change in the 1960s.

[1] *The Financing of Research in Universities by Outside Bodies*, Home Universities Conference, 1955, Professor Neville Mott, p. 77.
[2] *Industry and Science, a Study of their Relationship in the Greater Manchester Area* (Manchester, 1954).

13
The Sixties

'A university should measure its success just as much by the number of millionaires as by the number of Nobel Prize winners which it produces.'[1]

'there is no doubt that it would be valuable if the universities collectively made a further deliberate effort to gear a larger part of their "output" to the economic and industrial needs of the nation.'[2]

The 1960s were the most marked watershed in the history of British universities since the rise of the civic colleges in the 1870s and 1880s. Under various pressures a powerful expansion took place and urgent measures sought to link the universities and industry even closer than they had ever been before. All this, and less happy events, brought an unprecedented attention, both public and scholarly, to matters of higher education in this decade.

The real factors behind the need for university expansion and a rebalancing of their activities more in favour of science and technology were manifold. First, there was the already manifest phenomenon of the 'trend' to staying on in the sixth form. The number of boys and girls in sixth forms rose between 1947 and 1958 from 32,000 to 53,000, an increase of 66 per cent. This did not simply reflect a rise in the number of children, for births and the birth-rate fell in the early 1930s and remained roughly constant for the rest of the decade. Rather it represented a real tendency to staying on at school with 40 per cent of an age group of fourteen in 1954 going into the sixth form as seventeen-year-olds in 1957. This in itself was a sharp rise within the decade from a comparative figure of 32·8 per cent for 1950.[3] This trend to staying on was one of the dynamic features be-

[1] H.R.H. Prince Philip at his installation as Chancellor of the University of Salford, 16 June 1967.
[2] *University Development*, UGC *Report on Years, 1962–7*, Cmnd. 3820, appendix XII, p. 221.
[3] *Fifteen to eighteen, Report of the Central Advisory Council for Education* (Crowther), 1959, pp. 226–7.

360

hind the creditable expansion of higher education in the 1950s even before the advent of the birth bulge.

Second, to the trend was added the bulge of those children born in the aftermath of the war who were due to come of age to enter the universities in the late 1960s. It was estimated that the population of eighteen-year-olds would rise from 533,000 in 1959 to a peak of 812,000 in 1965, with 1964–7 being the most difficult years of the bulge.[1] With the operation of the trend and the beginning of the bulge from 1960, a situation was arising in the early 1960s whereby there was an increase in the percentage of an age group obtaining qualifications to enter universities but with no commensurate expansion of places to receive them. In 1961, 6·9 per cent of the university entrance age group had the entrance qualifications, but only 4 per cent actually got in. If this situation were to continue, Robbins estimated that there would be a shortfall between planned and required places of 25,000 by 1967 unless further expansion occurred.[2]

Third, it was hoped by Robbins and others that an expansion of facilities would partly rectify the considerable imbalance in chances of obtaining university places that existed between the social classes. Of children of higher professional parents born in 1940, a third went on to degree level higher education, but only 1 per cent of children of semi- and unskilled workers did so.[3] Although some sociologists were fairly content that the operation of the 1944 Education Act and the abolition of fees was bringing working-class children into the grammar school in about the right proportions,[4] yet the imbalance of opportunity seemed to persist most flagrantly at the university level. Accordingly, higher education came to be regarded as a right for those with the intelligence to benefit from it rather than as a reward for which to compete. This was reflected administratively in the grant changes of 1962 which abolished the competitive state and local authority scholarship system and placed on the local authorities the obligation to finance any qualified student who gained a university place. It was hoped that removal of barriers and the expansion of provision would dredge up more wasted talent from the working class.

Fourth, not only were there demographic and social gaps to be

---

[1] *The Age Group Bulge and its Possible Effects on University Policy*, Home Universities Conference, 1955.
[2] *Higher Education* (Robbins) (henceforth cited as Robbins), Cmnd. 2154, 1963, p. 260.
[3] Robbins, p. 50. A. Little and J. Westergaard, 'The Trend of Class Differentials in Educational Opportunity in England and Wales', *British Journal of Sociology*, 1964, suggested that 14½ per cent of children of professional and managerial fathers born in the late 1930s reached university and only ½ per cent of children of semi-skilled and unskilled fathers.
[4] J. E. Floud, A. H. Halsey and F. M. Martin, *Social Class and Educational Opportunity* (London, 1956).

closed at home, but also others in which we lagged behind advanced nations abroad. In Britain in 1958–9 only 4·5 per cent of an age group went into higher education of degree standard compared with 7 per cent in France, 10 per cent in Sweden, 5 per cent in the USSR, and 20 per cent in the USA. On the other hand, since 2·4 per cent of an age group in Britain obtained degrees in science, engineering, or agriculture, this compared well with the 2 per cent of France, Germany, and Sweden. Our output was comparatively better than our intake, largely due to lower rates of wastage attendant on higher standards of selection in Britain. However, there were two areas where we were more distinctly backward. In 1959, first degrees in technology in Britain as a proportion of first degrees in science and technology were only 36 per cent compared with 65 in Canada, 48 in France, 68 in Germany, 49 in the USA and so forth.[1] A rebalancing was needed within science and technology in favour of technology.[2] A rebalancing was also needed between the levels of degrees, so Robbins considered, though this was to be a matter of debate later. Whereas, for example, out of an age group of 100,000 in the USA, 2,300 went on to postgraduate work of whom 500 gained PH.D., in Britain only 500 went on and 200 gained doctorates. Robbins considered that there was much more room for the sub-doctorate post-graduate course in Britain to add on that extra specialist expertise after a broadly based first degree. Hence the initially vigorous movement to create fourth year M.A. courses which have since proved somewhat abortive for lack of finance.

Fifth, there also seemed to be some connections between higher education and economic growth that justified expansion. Since 1945, Britain had experienced relatively slow growth of the Gross Domestic Product of 2·5 per cent per annum compared with Germany's 7·6 and France's 4·6. Britain's was in fact the lowest in Europe. Our 2·4 per cent per annum growth rate for productivity was also the second lowest in Europe.[3] It can be pointed out such comparisons were necessarily vitiated by the destruction of the war and the lower levels from which other European countries began their recoveries. It was also observed that although our growth rates appeared low in comparison with Europe in an unusual period of recovery, yet they were quite normal compared with our own historical experience of growth back to 1900. Yet whatever the qualifications and the realities of the matter, the belief in our laggard slow growth and the need to rectify it became an element in the faith invested in the expansion of

[1] Robbins, p. 127.
[2] Sir Willis Jackson, in *Scientific, Technological and Technical Manpower* (Fawley Foundation Lecture, 1963), demonstrated and deplored the over predominance of basic science as opposed to technological specialisms in Imperial College entrants.
[3] M. M. Postan, *An Economic History of Western Europe, 1945–64* (London, 1967), pp. 12, 17.

higher education at that time. This was one of the implicit assumptions in the Robbins report itself. While denying the possibility of measuring net social gain or of estimating aggregate manpower needs of industry, they considered that there must be a relation between the stock of education and the productivity of industry, and that even though exact rates of return could never be calculated yet external economies must accrue however unquantifiable they may be.[1] The PEP report of 1960 also called for an expansion of scientific education as one of the ways out of slow post-war growth.[2] Firmer data on the connection between high growth rates and levels of higher education in Europe were presented by Michael Kaser in 1963 which gave some plausibility to such views. Comparing percentage per annum growth of Gross National Product and numbers of university students per 1,000 primary students, Kaser found the following relationships for various dates in the 1950s: Japan 7% 48; Germany 11% 41; Sweden 5% 17; Italy 5% 35; France 5% 28. And then at the bottom of the league for growth and next to the bottom for university students came England and Wales 2% 20.[3] Kaser was careful to point out that he was drawing no conclusions about the contribution of higher education to economic growth, indeed the sequence of cause and effect may have been the reverse. But it was not totally naïve at that time for advocates of expansion to believe that one of the contributory ways for Britain to raise her levels of growth to those of her major competitors was for her to raise her levels of higher education to their levels also.

Whatever reservations economists may have felt about the possibility of quantifying such assumptions, British industry itself was clear that it would benefit from the expansion of higher education. Looking back over the scramble for science graduates in the 1940s and 1950s, they were well aware that the universities had not kept pace with the demands of industry and they hoped that an expansion would rectify this by raising university entrance from 4 to 7 per cent of school leavers, providing a 'more prolonged period of broadly based education'.[4] It was noted that 'there is a tremendous amount of goodwill in industry towards these amazing proposals for the development of higher education'.[5]

---

[1] Robbins, pp. 71–4, and Lord Robbins, 'Recent Discussion of the Problems of Higher Education in Great Britain' in *The University in the Modern World*.
[2] PEP, *Growth in the British Economy* (London, 1960), p. 73.
[3] M. C. Kaser, 'Education and Economic Progress: Experience in Industrialized Market Economics' in E. A. G. Robinson and J. Vaizey, *The Economics of Education* (London, 1966). The conference at which this paper was presented was 1963.
[4] *Higher Education, Evidence to the Government Committee* (Robbins) by the Federation of British Industries, November 1961.
[5] *Universities and the Future Pattern of Higher Education*, Home Universities Conference, 1963: D. R. O. Thomas of the FBI.

Industry had good reason for such views, first because it was apparent that the industrial labour force was rapidly changing in ways that favoured the graduate and, second, because there was a good deal of leeway which an expansion in the number of graduates could make up. During the 1950s there was a decline in semi-skilled and unskilled manual occupations in the occupational structure of the country but a large expansion by 72 per cent in scientific, professional, and higher technical occupations requiring degree qualifications. Occupational groups 1-4 rose by 27·1 per cent and groups 5-7 fell by −0·4 per cent.[1] It was clear that were this trend to continue a further massive upward shift in the educational qualifications of the population would be needed to fill these expanding areas and the ill-educated would be even less required than before. At the level of the firm this was also strikingly true. In 1932 ICI employed thirty graduates per 1,000 employees, but by 1965 it had risen to seventy per 1,000, and by 1980 it was expected to be 150 per 1,000. There was less need for brute strength and routine dexterity and diligence; the 'ox man' and the 'ant woman' were being displaced by the graduate.[2] It was also evident that although the graduate element in management was considerably expanding, there was still ample room for yet further expansion. For example, of 102 large companies investigated in 1964 with 2,000 or more employees, 69 per cent of top managers and 58 per cent of middle managers held university degrees or qualifications of equivalent professional standing, while in another study in the early 1960s it was found that only 37 per cent of all managers in private industry had university degrees.[3] There was clearly room in the future for more graduates at these levels of industry and an expansion in the 1960s could augur nothing but good for the future.

Finally, given these real factors behind the need to expand, the time was also ripe in political terms.[4] Both political parties were highly favourable towards science and the expansion of higher education. The pre-Robbins expansion of the 1950s had been undertaken by the Conservatives under whose support for scientific research Britain had become a leading country in the generation of atomic power. On their part, Labour and notably Mr Wilson recognized the intrinsic importance of science and technology and also saw it as an issue with which to refashion a classless 'technocratic' image for the party. Most importantly, in contrast to the Conservatives, their emphasis was on science for industry rather than on the prestige 'big science' for atomic energy that had marked the achievements of the 1950s.

[1] *The Flow into Employment of Scientists, Engineers and Technologists* (Swann) (henceforth cited as Swann), Cmnd. 3760, 1968, p. 45.
[2] M. J. S. Clapham of ICI, *Industry and the Universities, Aspects of Interdependence* (Conference of Committee of Vice-Chancellors and CBI, 1965), pp. 7–12.
[3] M. M. Postan, op. cit., pp. 281–2.
[4] Norman J. Vig, *Science and Technology in British Politics.*

They had already set up their own study group on higher education under Lord Taylor which prior to Robbins had advocated considerable expansion. Thus the developments of the sixties came about under an administration already strongly committed politically to science and education as one of its main interests.

The expansion of the universities accordingly took place throughout the 1960s.[1]

	1961/2	1967/8
Undergraduates taking first degrees	89,219	164,653
Post-graduates	19,362	35,019
Total of all students	113,143	200,121

The Robbins report had called for 197,000 students by 1967/8 and this target was more than reached. It entailed a rise in the universities' current expenditure as a share of the GNP from 0·30 per cent in 1961/2 to 0·49 per cent in 1966/7[2] at which latter date the total direct cost of the universities stood at £198 million per annum excluding maintenance grants.[3] In social terms university entrants as a percentage of their age group rose from 3·8 in 1957 to 6·3 per cent in 1967.[4] Not only was there this impressive doubling of students within the 1960s, but from the point of view of industry there were healthy swings in the balance of studies (see Table 39).

TABLE 39   *Percentage of students by field of study*

	Undergraduates		Post-graduates	
	1961–2	1966–7	1961–2	1966–7
Arts	30·9	24·1	36·2	32
Social	11·3	19·5	9·8	14·9
Pure science	24·6	23·1	29·1	28·3
Applied science	15·2	20·6	15·5	18·2

There was clearly a swing towards even more applied science, contributed to by the creation of the technological universities. Within the non-science subjects the social studies were rising to prominence and near parity with the pure arts which may have had some beneficial implications for industry, but the overall arts plus social studies proportion of 42·2 per cent was just about the same as it ever had been since before the war. In spite of the stress being laid on

[1] *University Development* UGC *Reports on the Years* 1962–7, and UGC *Annual Survey*, 1967–8.
[2] Richard Layard, John King, and Claus Moser, *The Impact of Robbins*, p. 88.
[3] G. Brosan (ed.), *Patterns and Policies in Higher Education*, p. 39.
[4] Richard Layard, *et al.*, op. cit., p. 24.

science and technology and the advent of the technological universities, the relative position of the arts within the universities remained undiminished. If the build up and balance of types of students revealed certain encouraging features for industry, so too did the swing in the employment of graduates towards industry and commerce during the decade. The proportions rose as shown in Table 40.[1]

TABLE 40   *Percentage of first degree graduates going into industry and commerce*

	Arts and social			Pure science	Applied science	Pure and applied	Total
	Men	Women	Total	Men	Men	Women	
1962	18	5	14	25	54	15	34
1963	17	4	13	23	52	14	32
1964	16	4	11	25	51	16	33

	Arts		Social		Total	Pure science		Applied science		Total
	M	W	M	W		M	W	M	W	
1965	12·7	3·2	21·7	8·8	11·9	27·8	19·0	52·1	20·0	34·6
1966	12·3	3·3	21·5	6·6	11·8	29·0	18·6	54·5	30·8	37·5
1967	13·6	4·2	21·6	8·2	13·2	28·9	20·4	52·1	29·7	36·8

This table deals with industry and commerce as a proportion of all activities taken up by first degree graduates. A large proportion, of course, did not take up any occupation at all but proceeded to teacher training. A slight rise was evident in going into industry by scientists though not particularly by the arts graduates. Table 41 indicates the proportion going into industry of all those taking up their first employment on graduating (thus excluding those going on to further training and hence presumably a large proportion of teachers).

Of those occupations adopted immediately on graduation, industry was already the pre-eminent career by the early 1960s, and this rose in relative importance quite markedly throughout the decade, for women even more than for men. Graduates with higher degrees show a similar trend (see Table 42).

Whereas there were no arts or social men or women with higher degrees going into industry in 1963, by the end of the decade there had been a marked rise in this non-scientific sector especially in men

[1] Calculated from UGC *First Employment of University Graduates*, 1961–2 and following years.

TABLE 41   *Percentage of first degree graduates taking up first employment at home in industry and commerce*

	Men	Women	Total
1962	64·9	22·1	56·4
1963	63·5	21·4	54·4
1964	67·9	25·0	58·2
1965	69·2	26·4	58·9
1966	72·3	27·3	62·7
1967	70·2	32·2	62·2
1968	71·3	33·0	62·6
1969	73·5	41·0	66·1

TABLE 42   *Percentage of graduates with higher degrees taking up first employment in industry and commerce*

	Arts		Social		Pure science Men	Men Applied science	Women Pure and applied	
	Men	Women	Men	Women	Men			
1963	—	—	—	—	28·9	56·6	9·9	
1964	—	—	6	—	24·8	53·7	11·4	
							Pure	Applied
1965	2	—	10·7	11·1	24·1	56·9	1·2	
1966	3·1	—	20·3	—	27·6	61·6	6·9	3
1967	2	4·3	15·3	—	35·0	56·6	12·9	35·3
					Pure and applied		Pure and applied	
1968	1·5	3·2	31·6	9·3	46·5		17·5	
1969	5·5	0·8	32·1	8·2	53·5		24·1	

with degrees in social studies, presumably chiefly economics. The other noteworthy rises were those of male pure scientists and, as with first degrees, of women scientists. In general the trend towards taking up careers in industry and commerce was a healthy one as far as industry was concerned, but the weak area was the relative lack of change in the proportion of first degree arts graduates taking up such careers. Almost all other categories of both sexes otherwise showed a tendency to go into industry more than they had formerly done.

This expansion of students and to some extent this greater inclination towards industry was achieved not only by the continued development of existing universities but by the creation of new ones. In 1956 certain leading technical colleges were designated as colleges of advanced technology to concentrate on advanced work including the diplomas of honours degree standard to be awarded by the National Council for Academic Awards. In 1965 these CATS were raised to the status of universities. Eight of them in England— Battersea (University of Surrey), Aston, Bradford, Bristol (University of Bath), Brunel, Loughborough, Northampton (City University), Salford—were granted charters while Chelsea became part of the University of London. In Scotland Heriot-Watt became an independent university and in Wales the Cardiff CAT became part of the University of Wales as the University of Wales Institute of Science and Technology (UWIST). These former CATs, which had been on a direct grant from the Ministry of Education from 1962, came under the UGC as universities from 1965. Apart from the technological universities created out of older institutions specifically geared to industry, a range of 'new' universities was built at Sussex, York, Canterbury, Lancaster, East Anglia, and Warwick. They were unique among modern foundations in that they served no period of tutelage to a parent university, but were allowed the privilege of devising their own courses and granting their own degrees from the beginning. In Scotland, Strathclyde, the former Royal College of Science and Technology in Glasgow, was chartered in 1964, Dundee became at last separated from St Andrews as an independent university in 1967, and in the same year Stirling, the only genuinely new Scottish university and the only one in Britain resulting from the Robbins report, received its charter. In Northern Ireland the university at Coleraine was started on the recommendation of the Lockwood committee.

As the CATS moved to become universities, so in 1966 a further group of technical colleges, initially twenty-seven and ultimately thirty, were designated as Polytechnics to concentrate on advanced work and prepare students for degrees through the London external degree and the National Council for Academic Awards. This in itself has raised certain doubts and fears that the Polytechnics, especially if they engage in considerable research to raise their status, will diffuse both research effort and resources for higher education to the detriment of the newer universities. Their presence, valuable to industry and a matter of considerable local pride in many towns, perpetuates the binary system whereby part of the higher education of the country operates independently under the UGC with another part under the local authorities. The government finally called a halt to these important new changes by announcing in February 1965 that no new universities were to be authorized for the next ten years. Let us now turn to consider the relevance and contributions of the new and the technological universities to British industry in the 1960s.

While the old civic universities and the new technological ones naturally orientated much of their work towards industry, this was less evidently the case with the newly created foundations of the sixties, many of which were situated in towns and areas not noted for industrial activity. At Sussex, in many ways the leader of the movement and the first, there was little indication that service to industry was a prominent consideration in the minds of the early shapers of the institution.[1] Sussex did establish a school of applied science and is prominent in operational research. Otherwise the chief value of Sussex in those years was not so much its direct service to industry as its rethinking of what Professor Briggs has called the 'new map of learning', the breaking down of traditional divisions between subjects and the concern to find cross connections between science and social studies that have influenced thinking in most of the newer universities. Perhaps most important of all the spectacular success of Sussex cast a certain reflected prestige on the new universities movement generally in the mid 1960s. It gave a certain *élan* and even glamour to a development that could easily have been doomed by public scepticism or indifference to the painful slow growth of, say, a Hull or a Keele in their earliest days. The University of East Anglia was similarly rooted in a region not noted for industry and its chief connections have been with food science, agriculture, and fisheries. The John Innes Institute, the Food Research Institute, and the research department of the British Sugar Corporation being grouped about the campus, while its biology school has close connection with Lowestoft fisheries research.[2] York also in the 1960s showed little signs of close involvement with industry though its fortes included social and economic research and they received substantial sums from ICI and Dorman Long for their endowment.[3] At Kent there was virtually no trace of important connections with industry though they developed electronics as a specialism.[4]

These four new universities were somewhat disengaged from industry. But rather more involved were those of Essex, Lancaster, and Warwick. At Essex, the Vice-Chancellor, in a manner unusual among heads of the new non-technological universities, stated clearly his intention for close relations with industry: 'universities . . . should work much more closely with industry', and 'we hope to provide the

[1] Sir John Fulton, *Experiment in Higher Education*. David Daiches, *The Idea of a New University: an Experiment in Sussex*, notably the articles by Asa Briggs, R. Blin Stoyle, and W. G. Stone. 'Sussex' by Sir John Fulton in Murray Ross, *New Universities in the Modern World*. *New Universities*, a contribution by Sir John Fulton to Home Universities Conference, 1960.

[2] Frank Thistlethwaite, 'The University of East Anglia' in Murray Ross, op. cit. Michael Sanderson, 'Research in the School of Biological Sciences', *University of East Anglia Bulletin*, April 1967, for a review of the main activities and linkages of this school which was intended as a special strength of the university.

[3] Vice-Chancellor's Reports, University of York, 1963/4–1968/9. Lord James, 'The University of York' in Murray Ross, op. cit.

[4] Reports of the Vice-Chancellor, University of Kent at Canterbury, 1966–70.

kind of man we believe industry needs from universities, scientists keen to apply their knowledge to industrial problems'.[1] Since biology was to be developed at the University of East Anglia, the chosen forte for Essex was the physical sciences to provide 'a firm base for the student of electronics and other branches of engineering which are the leading industries of Essex'.[2] Their electrical engineering began under a professor who had been the former chief scientist for Plessey-UK and an authority on transistors, while the GPO gave the university £100,000 for a chair of telecommunications. Close contacts were maintained with Plessey, Marconi, GEC, and the Bell Telephone Laboratories in the United States. A second most important area linking the university with industry was its polymer work with their 'Polymer Meeting Points' building strong ties with industry, notably Dunlop and Ilford.[3]

Lancaster is a particularly interesting case in this second batch.[4] It was not placed in an especially thriving area industrially, unlike Essex and Warwick. Yet it has transcended its environment to establish all manner of enterprising links with industry in ways that were not self-evidently dictated by the industrial conditions of its immediate region. Their strength in this regard lay not so much in technology as in their new developments of what in the inter-war years would have been regarded as 'commerce'. They began with a chair in marketing, given by the Institute of Marketing and the first in Britain. This undertook project work for industrial firms, and by the end of the sixties had formed its own consultancy firm, Lumina Ltd. ICI gave a chair of systems engineering and to this was added the Wolfson Chair of Financial Control and a chair of commercial systems studies, and in 1969 a chair of behaviour in organizations. They noted that 'a considerable number of staff are recruited from industry and commerce' and all these various chairs and specialisms formed a Lancaster School of Business and Organizational Studies which 'undertook much practical contract work for industry'. Moreover the vice-chancellor played an important part in 'Enterprise Lancaster', a project for bringing new science based industries into the town and offering them the facilities of the university.[5] As an instance of forging links with industry, in spite of a not particularly favourable environment, Lancaster's was one of the most striking achievements among the new universities.

However, perhaps the most involved of all was Warwick.[6] No

[1] Albert E. Sloman, *A University in the Making*.
[2] W. Boyd Alexander, 'England's New Seven' in John Lawlor (ed.), *The New University*.
[3] Reports of the Vice-Chancellor, University of Essex, 1965-9.
[4] Reports of the Vice-Chancellor, University of Lancaster, 1965-9.
[5] Harold Perkin, *New Universities in the United Kingdom*.
[6] Reports of the Vice Chancellor, University of Warwick, 1965-9. The quotations are from the 1965-6 Report. See also E. P. Thompson, *Warwick*

other new university made such firm statements in its early days about 'our determination to have a close relationship with industry and commerce' and regarding 'research collaboration with industry as an essential part of our programme'. Indeed, being placed in a more industrial region than any other of the new universities and having Lord Rootes as their first chancellor it was right that they should see this as the chief direction of their future service. Accordingly an important part of their work was of this character. The Institute of Directors financed a chair of business studies, Pressed Steel Fisher one of industrial relations, Barclay's one of management information systems, and these together with other interests in economics and computing formed the core of a Centre for Industrial and Business Studies, a leading centre for management education. With this also went a concentration on engineering in connection with Decca, Bristol Siddeley, Mullard's, and others. Work was done with English Electric and Alfred Herbert's on the application of glass and ceramics in engineering, and methods for automating the testing of internal combustion engines and machine tools were developed, of clear relevance to the local industries of Coventry and the Midlands. Moreover, the Midlands Computer Consortium, a group of Midlands civil engineers, set up a unit in the university to advance the application of computers to structural design. The university was also unusual in including research in the automobile industry among its engineering interests.[1] None of the other new universities achieved such close and fruitful links with industry across the range of arts and sciences and this special position, desired by some and regarded with suspicion by others, was a root of the disturbances there in 1970.

It was evident that most of the new universities were not specially committed to industry, and that much of the involvement of those who were lay not so much in science and technology as in various branches of social studies/economics/management education. As one observer has remarked, 'it is a paradox that whereas the talk of politicians was the need for technologists and applied scientists the new universities devoted so much of their resources to the arts and social sciences'.[2] There were hard practical reasons why this had to be so. Partly it was a response to the Dainton 'swing' in sixth form preferences to those subjects.[3] Also it was a hard fact that unit costs per student place were lower in the social studies than in any other

---

University Ltd, chapter I, 'The Business University', for an indication of the close involvement of industry in the foundation and running of the university.

[1] Reports, op. cit., *passim*.
[2] Michael Beloff, *The Plateglass Universities*, p. 39.
[3] The swing towards arts and social studies and away from science and technology in the subject preferences of sixth formers in the 1960s. This was highlighted by the Dainton report which is discussed later.

branch of study and that they had the highest staff-student ratio of any except education.[1] The HUC Conference of 1955 had already spotted the dilemma. To achieve expansion on this scale without astronomic costs, the arts and social studies would have to be encouraged rather than technology. It would not be possible to absorb such an expansion if it came on the science side; on the other hand it would not be easy to absorb into employment the graduate products of such an expansion if they were not on the science side.[2] The new universities accordingly had certain characteristics of disengagement from industry by the end of the 1960s. For example, 29 per cent of their science departments had no contact with industry, much closer to Oxbridge and Scottish levels than to those of traditional civic universities. Also, they had the lowest proportion of research students, 20 per cent, wishing to take their PH.D. in conjunction with industry.[3] The rise of the new universities is a movement of great significance that will prove to shed considerable social benefits in future years, but we need not, at the standpoint of the end of the 1960s, exaggerate their importance for industry. However, this is not a serious defect, nor is Beloff's 'paradox' a real one, for the particular problem of relations with industry was more than amply dealt with by the parallel movement of the creation of the technological universities.

In 1965 the CATs came under the UGC as fully fledged technological universities considerably more committed by their historical traditions to the direct service of industry than any other form of British university. Most of them had begun as nineteenth-century technical colleges in industrial cities or in parts of London, and their survival had long depended on their usefulness in industrial training for local needs. With their new status as universities they brought to higher education a directness of approach and a frank and unapologetic closeness of alignment with industry well reflected in the Duke of Edinburgh's comment at Salford cited at the head of this chapter. They were prepared to teach sandwich courses with students partly in industry and partly in the university. They dealt with specifically technological subjects of direct application that had scarcely been considered proper scientific university subjects before. They were concerned not only with pure research—of which there was almost too much in British science—but the solution of practical problems that had to be made to work and also to make a profit. All laid a heavy stress on the basic sciences and branches of engineering, though each had some special fortes in which they could be of special service to areas of British industry. Loughborough, for example, taking advantage of its

[1] *University Development*, UGC *Report on the Years, 1962–7*, p. 43.
[2] Home Universities Conference, 1955.
[3] *Industry, Science and the Universities, Report of a Working Party on Universities and Industrial Research to the Universities and Industry Joint Committee.* (Docksey) (henceforth cited as Docksey), July 1970, pp. 81, 100.

proximity to Derby, had close relations with Rolls Royce, having combined research projects with the firm in auto engineering while the firm had established an industrial readership. The college prided itself on its arrangements for the PH.D., having reduced residential qualifications to a minimum so that the bulk of time and work could be carried out in industry, creating advanced students 'whose attitudes are industrial rather than academic'. The university also ran its own consultancy firm, Loughborough Consultants Ltd.[1] The new University of Surrey was particularly celebrated for its work in the civil engineering of structures, taking part in the designing of a hangar for the Boeing 747 for BOAC, in work for the Victoria underground and the noted Terrapin prefabricated buildings. It was also a rare example of university level studies in catering, hotel management, and tourism supported by Forte's and doing work for Marks and Spencer.[2] In this it filled in some gaps in a major British industry capable of scientific treatment from the biochemical, nutritional, and management economics sides that had been largely neglected by the universities.

The City University was important in civil engineering associated with fluids and in advising on the Morecambe Bay barrage. It was also prominent in aeronautics, claiming that its air transport engineering in conjunction with BEA and BOAC was unique.[3] Bradford University noted that 'we are as committed as ever, indeed more so than before to close interaction with industry', and this found expression in three main areas. They naturally related themselves to the textile industries of the West Riding, forming a Material and Fibres Research Centre, while its important Management Centre dealt specifically with production managers for the textile industry. Second, it claimed to be the largest school of chemical engineering in Western Europe and, third, it showed a consciousness unusual even among the technological universities in the late sixties of the need for education for the Common Market with its foreign language students working in industry abroad and its technology students spending vacation courses in European industry.[4] The University of Bath was the old Merchant Venturers Technical College of Bristol and subsequently the University of Bristol faculty of engineering. As this migrated to Bath, so engineering remained its forte, especially aero engineering in connection with BAC and Bristol Siddeley.[5] Salford, with its Centre for Transport Studies, 'probably has more people actively engaged in transport studies than any other university in the country', and

---

[1] Vice-Chancellor's Reports, Loughborough University of Technology, 1967/8–1968/9.
[2] Reports of the Vice-Chancellor, University of Surrey, 1966–7, 1967–8.
[3] Reports of the Vice-Chancellor, City University, 1966–7–1968/9.
[4] Vice-Chancellor's Reports, University of Bradford, 1967–69.
[5] Gerald Walters (ed), *A Technological University, an Experiment in Bath.*

their civil engineering department worked on traffic and car journey problems. Salford was also in the forefront of problems on the mixing and transport of paints and plastics and also in tribology, the science of lubrication and friction.[1] Across the city its neighbour, UMIST (the University of Manchester Institute of Science and Technology), was created out of the old Manchester College of Science and Technology, dealing with textile chemistry, with a special chair of marketing supported by Viyella, and special studies in paper and machine tools.[2]

In Scotland the two technological universities created in the 1960s were Heriot-Watt in Edinburgh and Strathclyde in Glasgow. Both were ancient institutions, the latter being the first British technical college, dating from 1796, and the former dating from 1822 as a school of art. Both had been affiliated to the older universities of their respective cities before Strathclyde received its charter in 1964 and Heriot-Watt in 1966. Heriot-Watt, while hiving off its technological specialism in printing, retained and developed others that fitted in with 'its declared policy to strengthen and extend its many links with industry'. In 1967 they set up their Low Cost Automation Centre, the first in any university in the UK. They continued their work on brewing and distilling as a major centre for education and research for these important Edinburgh and Highland industries, while Unilink was established as their industrial liaison division.[3] Strathclyde was not created a university as part of the upgrading of the CATs but had long enjoyed a special status under the UGC. As it had been the first and the archetype of the British technical colleges, so now it became an archetype and perhaps the most powerful of the new technological universities. Although the Robbins notion of the SISTER (Special Institute for Scientific and Technological Education and Research) had been rejected as unduly invidious, the chartering of Strathclyde in 1964 was intended to build it up as a powerhouse of expertise and training for British industry analogous to Imperial College, its younger English counterpart. Accordingly, the range and depth of its links are among the most impressive of any university in Britain. Their fibre science serves the local textile industry, notably carpets, their water resources work in civil engineering is 'well known internationally', their bio-engineering department worked on the development of the artificial kidney. Their electrical engineering staff worked closely with Reyrolle on high voltage measurement and had substantial research contracts with Hoover. On the management side they had the largest department of economics in Britain, and with their school of Business Administration they formed a division of the Scottish

---

[1] University of Salford, Vice-Chancellor's Reports, 1965/7–1968/9.
[2] Newscuttings Books of UMIST (Manchester Central Library), *passim*.
[3] Annual Reports Heriot-Watt University, 1966/7–1968/9, and newscuttings of Heriot-Watt i n Edinburgh Central Library.

Business School. Of especial importance their Centre for Industrial Innovation was opened in 1969 as one of eight university based centres supported by the Ministry of Technology, while it also ran other specialized connections, the Institute of Advanced Machine Tool and Control Technology, also with Mintech, and the Scottish Hotel School.[1]

The Scottish technological universities had a more markedly beneficial rebalancing effect on the Scottish universities generally than the English ones did in England. We have noted before that since the First World War the Scottish universities were more disengaged from industry than the English. This chiefly stemmed not only from the relatively weak state of Scottish industry but also from the relative neglect of industrial science in the older Scottish universities. For example, in the early 1960s, whereas a normal proportion of science and technology students at Cambridge and English civic universities was around 50 per cent, in the Scottish universities it was commonly 36 per cent, with Edinburgh even lower at 27.[2] Strathclyde's proportion, on the other hand, was 92 per cent and was a welcome and overdue redressing of the imbalance. Second, while one of the problems of the Scottish economy was its lack of new industries, both these new universities spoke positively of their aims to create new science based industries in the Lowlands. Heriot-Watt claimed to create a 'Route 128 phenomenon' around its new campus —a reference to the clustering of scientific industry around MIT in the United States whence their new principal had just come. Strathclyde also looked to its Centre for Industrial Innovation to help create new scientific industry for the Scottish economy. The nearest analogy in the English foundations was Lancaster's avowed aim to revivify its own region.

And yet in spite of this brave show and very considerable real achievement there were certain unsatisfactory elements about the technological universities for which they were not to blame. First, they were not always attracting students sufficient in either quantity or quality. For example, in 1969 more than 1,500 university places were not filled and these were chiefly in science and engineering.[3] The experiences of even the high prestige UMIST were indicative. In 1964 only 80 per cent of their places were filled, which Sir John Cockcroft attributed to the poor image of technology in schools. In 1965 they expected 100 students for machine tool studies but obtained only twenty-five. In 1966 they could not muster enough students for their paper course and empty places still remained in 1967 although this was in the peak of the bulge.[4] Such institutions, especially with

[1] Annual Reports, University of Strathclyde, 1966/7–1968/9.
[2] *Observer*, 4 November 1962.
[3] *Daily Telegraph*, 30 January 1970, reviewing UCCA *Seventh Report*.
[4] UMIST Newscuttings, op. cit., *passim*, for many references of this kind.

their specialized technology courses, were obviously suffering from the swing against science and technology while the sixth formers' preference for science was channelling itself into the expanding orthodox science courses in traditional universities. This problem was also associated with another that caused some bad feeling in the later 1960s. The Vice-Chancellor of Salford, for example, deplored that the rate of increase of his non-recurrent grant was severely cut back to 1–2 per cent from 1968/9 to 1971/2, whereas that of an unspecified arts based university was moving ahead at 5–6 per cent per annum.[1] There was a wider serious issue, as he pointed out:

> accepting the national economic situation has called for restrictions, it does not seem sensible to foresake those institutions whose output of graduates is almost totally in science, engineering and technology. To allow the mutable preferences of sixth formers to determine those areas of higher education in which the nation will invest its resources is an abrogation of responsibility which will only encourage a greater swing away from science and technology than the present one.

One does not have to be placed in the position of that Vice-Chancellor to consider that there may have been a case in the late 1960s for flying in the face of the Dainton swing and giving extraordinary special privileges and financial help to the technological universities, even at the expense of failing to achieve an aggregate growth of student numbers by not providing places for all the arts and social studies students who might have wished to attend. There was a clash here between higher education for technology and industry and expansion as an act of social justice in which the latter predominated.

The third cause for unease related specifically to Scotland. In spite of the powerful new presence of Strathclyde as an industry-serving university, there were disturbing signs that Scottish industry was relatively unreceptive to science. For example, most of the work done at the National Engineering Laboratory at East Kilbride was for English firms, only 9 per cent being for Scottish firms which were largely apathetic.[2] Also Heriot-Watt's plans for a multi-access computer to be used by firms around Edinburgh failed since only nine firms showed any interest.[3] Third it was found in the fibre section at Strathclyde that the finance of research projects came chiefly from outside Scotland, whereas Scottish firms were more interested in the more limited routine testing services that the department could provide.[4] This reflects not only a certain discredit on Scottish indus-

---

[1] Report of the Vice-Chancellor, University of Salford, 1967/8.
[2] *Evening Dispatch*, 17 January 1963.
[3] *The Scotsman*, 11 February 1966.
[4] Annual Report, University of Strathclyde, 1966/7.

try but also on the older universities which had evidently not educated it to a higher degree of scientific awareness. It may be that Strathclyde with its outgoing and somewhat entrepreneurial manner may in the future go some way to rectifying this.

As well as the creation of new universities and technological universities there was a third area of innovation in the sixties which to some extent cut across both, namely the concern to form business schools. The development of scientific and technological education still left an acute awareness that we had nothing to match the higher business education of the United States, notably that of the Harvard Business School. It then became an aim to create one or two such institutions in Britain that could hope to match the qualities of that great exemplar. The serious modern revival of this form of industrial management education in universities began with a US government grant of 9 million dollars in 1953 to promote productivity in UK industry. Part of this, on the advice of the UGC, went into education and part of this into a readership in industrial management at Cambridge. The Leverhulme Trust provided temporary openings in industry for lecturers to help produce the hybrid academic with management experience who was needed for such management education and whose non-existence seriously vitiated the development of the movement.[1] Lord Franks recommended that two schools should be established, associated with existing universities, one jointly with LSE and Imperial College and a second associated with Manchester University dealing with both post-graduate and post-experience courses. Such courses would cover 'operational research, linear programming, resource allocation and strategic and business planning, decision theory and its applications and the use and application of computer techniques'.[2]

Following on this recommendation, the UGC, in conjunction with the Foundation for Management Education formed under Sir Keith Joseph to raise money from industry, established the two national business schools at London and Manchester in 1965 as was suggested. As well as these major centres it will also be borne in mind that the UGC was supporting management education at a number of other universities, notably Lancaster and Warwick, which from their inception had been developing clusters of professorships giving them a powerful basis for such studies. The UGC considered that the enthusiasm with which management education was taken up by the universities in the 1960s was 'an outstanding example of the universities' responsiveness to national needs'.[3] 'Management' became somewhat fashionable at the time, with many centres trying to jump on the

[1] *University Development*, UGC *Report for the Years, 1952–7*, pp. 57–8.
[2] Lord Franks, *British Business Schools* (British Institute of Management, 1963).
[3] *University Development*, UGC *Report for the Years, 1962–7*.

bandwagon and being urged to do so.[1] The dangers of spreading too little talent too widely were obviated by Franks's realistic policy of concentration. However, in the tide of enthusiasm and the obvious readiness of industry to provide the money, the UGC and the foundation considered in the late 1960s that a new appeal could be mounted in 1969 to finance two more; a Scottish business school with the co-operation of Strathclyde, Glasgow, and Edinburgh, and another in the Midlands linking the activities of Birmingham, Aston, Warwick, and Bradford. Although the joint partnership of the UGC and the foundation was due to finish in 1972, so successful did it prove that it was decided to continue it through the 1970s.[2] And yet inevitably criticism followed the first flush of enthusiasm. Business schools and courses were criticized for providing courses so general as to be of no use to students in any particular industry, a fault Warwick shrewdly sought to overcome by dealing specifically with newspapers and engineering.[3] More damning was the fact that it was quite evident by the early 1970s that standards of entrance to such courses were too low, and consequently they were taking and graduating students totally lacking in management potential while too few of the teachers, using American literature, had any practical knowledge of British business conditions and problems.[4]

While these developments were taking place in the formation of new institutions, the sixties also saw a remarkable and unprecedented creation of administrative arrangements as linking mechanisms binding the universities and industry more formally and closely together than ever before. First, the CBI and the Committee of Vice-Chancellors held an important conference in 1965 and this resulted in the creation of a Joint Committee on the Relations of Industry and the Universities. Second, the UGC itself became more positively involved in effecting co-operation between the universities and industry from 1967 when a sub-committee on university–industry collaboration was established to advise the UGC on proposals from the universities entailing work for industry. The UGC then gave 'pump priming assistance' to universities for specific schemes to promote closer links between the university concerned and industry. Accordingly support was given in this way to projects like Lancaster's bridging courses from university to industry, Bath's Fluid Power Centre, and Stirling's new departure in technological economics. But probably the most important effect was the creation of a third mechanism, the financing of industrial liaison posts in universities,

---

[1] Lord Butler, *The Responsibilities of Education, the Professions, Industry, the Universities and Government* (London, 1968).
[2] *Annual Survey*, 1968–9.
[3] *The Times*, 3 August 1970, 'Business School for Specialists'.
[4] *Daily Telegraph*, 2 July 1971, 'Need to Raise Quality of Business Graduates', citing Report of the Council of Industry for Management Education.

eight departments or officers being created or helped in the first two years. Thus specialist officers were established in universities with the special duty of seeking out industrial contacts and indicating to firms how best their university could help them.[1] Fourth, the SRC introduced Science and Industry Awards for students spending twelve months in industry after graduating and Co-operative Awards in Pure Science (CAPS) for students working on projects agreed between industry and the universities. There were also 'Swann Awards' for students who were part of a multidisciplinary team working in collaboration with an industrial company. Fifth, there were created six university based industrial units supported by the Ministry of Technology specifically to act as powerhouses to surrounding industry, to take on research contracts and to stimulate innovation in industry. The Centre for Industrial Innovation at Strathclyde opened in 1969 was a leading example.

All these developments, the contributions of the new and technological universities, the business schools and the administrative linking devices, lay behind the closer involvement of the universities and industry in the 1960s, but there were two countervailing trends which caused much concern at the time: first, the 'swing' away from science in the preference of school leavers and, second, the notorious 'brain drain'. Whereas there was a steady increase in the proportion of A levels gained in mathematics and science up to 1960 (64·54%), from that date into the 1960s there was a marked falling off and a swing in preferences to the arts and to a greater extent to the social sciences, notably economics.[2] Whereas from the point of view of the industrialist the attraction to economics of former potential arts students may have been regarded as desirable, the attraction to economics of potential scientists and technologists was a switch of more questionable value. This had another sinister effect. Whereas the proportion of candidates for university entrance who were accepted remained fairly constant between 1965 and 1969, such was the fall in the chemistry candidates coming forward that their acceptance ratio rose sharply from 63 per cent to 82 per cent, which may indicate a deterioration in the standards of those accepted. Dainton pointed out that the young needed to be convinced that a far better managerial training was science and engineering first, then followed by economics. The

---

[1] There were industrial liaison officers at Liverpool, UMIST, Nottingham, Sheffield, Lancaster, Edinburgh, Surrey, and Belfast, most dating from 1965. There were also ILOs supported by Mintech at UMIST, UWIST, Aston, Bath, Brunel, City, Heriot-Watt, Strathclyde, and Surrey. The first historical reference I find to this activity was Edinburgh University's Industrial Liaison Committee dating from 1947. In the second half of the sixties it became a familiar feature of industrially orientated universities.

[2] *Enquiry into the Flow of Candidates in Science and Technology into Higher Education* (Dainton), interim, 1966, Cmnd. 2893; final, 1968, Cmnd. 3541.

report called for more 'breadth, humanity' in science courses, and improvement in science teaching, the continuation of mathematics teaching for all school children until leaving, and the retention of compulsory science and mathematics for all sixth formers. But at root they had to admit that science required intellectual rigour, and 'most young people are now able to choose apparently less rigorous alternatives'. It was a frank observation on some aspects of curricular change and fashion in the sixties from which industry stood to lose.

The second dangerous factor working contrary to trends that would otherwise have been beneficial to industry, was a serious drift abroad of scientists and technologists in the 1960s.[1] Attention was drawn to the fact that by 1966 23 per cent of the new supply of scientists created three years earlier were leaving the country and, even worse, 42 per cent of the engineers and the technologists. In the latter case this was nearly a doubling of the loss since the beginning of the decade. The working party considered 'we cannot afford to be complacent about a situation where engineers equal in number to two in every five of the new annual supply choose to work abroad often in the competing industries of foreign nations. . . .' To the loss of what was spent on their education and what they could have contributed to British industry was added the damage that they could also do to the country by working for our competitors. Industry was urged to stem the flood by higher salaries and by ceasing to give the impression that it was not interested in first-class scientists, while the universities were urged to direct their scientific education more towards industry and to change the prevalent notion that academic research was the only respectable end of such education.

This increased involvement with business and industry, especially in the later part of the decade, did not take place without a revival in a more virulent and intellectually more considered form of that anti-industry, anti-capitalist sentiment we saw developing in universities in the 1930s. Consequently, while the student of the 1940s and 1950s had been relatively quiescent, 'student unrest' became a recurrent problem in many universities in the late sixties. After the trouble at LSE in 1967[2] and the revolt of the Paris students in 1968, anti-capitalist sentiments became a clear and well publicized element in the student revolt movement. For the socialist student the universities were the educational expressions of a repressive capitalist system in which they fulfilled two main roles. They inevitably provided the science with which industrial capitalism sustained itself, training experts to extract even more surplus value out of the working classes through the devising of new technology and management

[1] *The Brain Drain, Report of the Working Party on Migration* (Jones), Cmnd. 3417, 1967.
[2] See Harry Kidd, *The Trouble at L.S.E., 1966–67.*

techniques. They also, through the transmission of culture, acted as 'maintaining the general ideological control of the ruling class' over the student body. Many graduates as teachers and social workers would then go on to exert this control to maintain an orderly society in which capitalism could flourish. What the Socialists wished to impress upon students was the necessity of replacing industrial capitalism, not with the state capitalism of the USSR, nor the abolition of industry itself and a return to neo-agrarianism, but with workers' control of industry in a workers' state. Their appeal they considered especially potent to the new generation of graduates because they, unlike their predecessors in times when a university education was a more élite preserve, would be placed in relatively lowly positions in industrial and other occupations. Accordingly they had more solidarity of interest with the working-class who had long experienced this situation than with a ruling class very few could ever hope to enter. Moreover, their lack of power in university matters merely foreshadowed their future lack of power in the wider society outside if they did not seize it for themselves.[1]

Such were the views of higher education being widely publicized by organs like *International Socialism* and the *New Left Review* in the late sixties and gaining some acceptance within the student body. What seemed to lend some plausibility to these opinions in some quarters was the affair at Warwick in 1970 when student discontent was able to find a very direct target in 'industry' and 'the capitalist system'.[2] As we have seen this was the new foundation most closely involved with industry, and the issue here was the apparent interference of one local industrialist and member of the council in checking on the (left wing) political activities of two members of staff. That the industrialist was right to be wary of and to investigate activities that could have had a potentially damaging effect on the business for which he was responsible was clear. But that he should seek to act against these individuals through the university of which both he and they were members seemed to some more open to question and lent weight to suspicions of excessive industrial influence on the university. However, this event focused most sharply the conflict between the Left and the close connections between the universities and industry. It led not only to a variety of sit-ins elsewhere in search of 'political files', but also to the formation of a Council for Academic Freedom and Democracy later in the year to resist a situation in which academics 'cannot prevent their work being dictated by the

[1] C. Harman, D. Clark, and others, *Education, Capitalism and the Student Revolt* (International Socialist Publication, 1968), pp. 16, 50. Alexander Cockburn and Robin Blackburn, *Student Power* (London, 1969), pp. 8, 10, 41, and 78. I am grateful to my colleague, Mr Gerald Crompton, for explanatory conversation on these matters.
[2] E. P. Thompson, op. cit.

needs of government, industry or commerce'.[1] Much student unrest is superficially about issues that have little or nothing to do with industry or capitalism—the moral tutelage role of the university, examinations, 'relevant' curricula, and so forth. And yet whatever the ostensible grievances that can raise a large proportion of the student body to militant action, these can be exploited by smaller groups with a broader ideological perspective who can expect to recruit other students to such wider views through more immediately trivial issues. Most universities have small bodies of activist students organized in Socialist Societies, branches of International Socialism, or Spartacist groups which 'are in revolt against the whole structure of industrial society, capitalist and communist alike'.[2] To say that, such groups of student opinion are hostile to industrial capitalism, or indeed to the whole of industry as it is organized in Britain today, is a risible understatement; they would wish to do away with the whole Christian/monarchist/private property/parliamentary fabric of British society of which it is a part.

Apart from these anti-industry views of the Left, what was more important was the attitude towards industry of the mass of students who were potential entrants. There was general agreement that industry had a poor image among students. At Oxford in the early 1960s very few students showed any interest in taking up this career. 'Industry . . . failed to captivate the imaginations of Oxford students,' though attitudes were more receptive in Manchester.[3] Attitudes to going into industry also related to social class, students of professional and senior managerial background preferred the professions, while industrial management was more the goal of sons of foremen and manual workers.[4] Another survey, after showing the low prestige of technology among sixth formers, went on to demonstrate the unwilling attitudes towards industry among scientists in five universities. Although half the scientists studied intended to do research they were highly resistant to research in industry which they considered 'unknown and unfriendly territory'.[5] Part of the trouble lay with industry and its bad sense of self publicity. A survey of attitudes in 1970 found that most students had a 'sadly misconceived' picture of industry and its 'cut throat business ethics' and, importantly, they totally underestimated the nature of the financial rewards industrial careers could give.[6] However, although such

[1] Leaflet, 'If You Think', for the formation of the CAFD, 1970.
[2] Sir Eric Ashby cited in Vice-Chancellor's Report, City University, 1967/8.
[3] Ferdynand Zweig, *The Student in the Age of Anxiety* (London, 1963), pp. 36-7.
[4] Peter Marris, *The Experience of Higher Education* (London, 1964), p. 159.
[5] Donald Hutchings, *The Science Undergraduate; a Study of Science Students at Five English Universities.*
[6] *The Times*, 3 August 1970, citing a survey by *Business Management*. See also Docksey, op. cit., p. 61, for criticism of the poor image students held of industry.

surveys taken at one point of time painted a gloomy picture, there was some evidence that with the build up of science and technology in the universities and the swing to industrial careers indicated by the UGC, there was also an underlying shift of attitudes among students more in favour of industry. It was found that when students were asked at various times throughout the decade their attitudes to various occupations, then the preference for industry rose steadily. On a 20-point scale industry scored 9 in 1964, 12 in 1968 and 13 in 1969, and its overall position in the range of choice of careers rose from sixth to third. This was in accord with similar rises in attractiveness of advertising, accountancy, and consultancy and a decline in interest in academic and military careers.[1] It was evident that this trend in preference as well as the actual increase in output to industry were contemporary with and far more important than the parallel disturbances of anti-capitalist unrest which attracted a disproportionate amount of attention at the time, but which clearly had no effect in deflecting the swing to industry.

Although more scientists were being produced and more were going into industry, there were doubts about the suitability of university scientific education for industry, some aspects of which evoked considerable attack, and defence, in the sixties. The chief criticism of undergraduate courses in science was of their narrowness and excessive specialization. As one report noted, 'many indications exist that the extent of specialization that is normal in British universities is possibly superfluous, and the opinion has also been expressed that it may even be inimical to the subsequent performance of graduates'.[2] This high degree of specialization, it is argued, is particularly inappropriate because such is the pace and nature of technical change that specialized knowledge acquired at university rapidly becomes obsolete. Also, with this change more occupations are created which are not specific to any particular discipline and which can be performed by personnel coming from different specialist backgrounds. Equally importantly, the very area where specialist knowledge was most needed, in research, was actually declining as a proportion of the scientific workforce in British industry from 44 per cent to 37 per cent between 1956 and 1965. Moreover, the American balance was towards a more general first degree in science with the specialism coming only at post-graduate level rather than earlier as in Britain. The same point was echoed by the Docksey report which found that too many university science departments were based

[1] David Willings, 'Careers Guidance, Luxury or Necessity?' I am grateful to Mr Willings for sending me a copy of his paper. It received some attention in the *Daily Telegraph*, 21 July 1970.
[2] M. C. McCarthy, *The Employment of Highly Specialised Graduates, a Comparative Study in the U.K. and the U.S.A.*

on single disciplines 'whereas much industrial research and development is multidisciplinary . . .'[1] In particular they suggested that industry wanted its scientists to have a wider knowledge of technological economics rather than specialized science, a development Stirling University was taking up. That industry preferred a more general education for its scientists came to be a widely held belief at this time. But it did receive something of a check from the most detailed study, that done for the chemical industry, which found that although the view was prevalent elsewhere, employers in this industry really preferred to recruit specialist trained chemistry graduates and there was no evidence of their wanting a more generally educated product.[2]

A second area of criticism was particularly concerned with engineering. Here the fear was that since more potential engineers were going to university and consequently to a more theoretical education, it was necessary to build back into the engineer's training some practical experience of working in commercial conditions. University laboratory work in this was too often unhelpful and irrelevant. Thus it was proposed to initiate 'matching section' periods of one to two years post-graduate training in manufacturing engineering, and 'design and manufacture group projects' run jointly by industry and universities and colleges to reshape the practically orientated but scientific engineering graduate for industry.[3] Such 'Bosworth courses' were started at Southampton University in semiconductors and at Edinburgh in microelectronics.

A third area where the products of the universities did not match industries' needs was in the arts. Whereas some areas of industry seemed to want the more generally educated scientist in the 1960s, it did not welcome a similar broadening in its arts graduates.[4] Two contradictory trends in preferences were discerned, that for scientists with a multidisciplinary education and that for arts men with a vocational specialism, notably economics. It was a fallacy of the time to suppose that as industry wanted a broader science education so also it desired a broader arts and social studies programme, mixing economics with sociology, literature, history, and so forth as was to become common especially in the new universities. Whereas we have noted earlier a turning to the arts graduate by industry in the 1950s partly due to the shortage of technologists, yet in the 1960s there was considerable evidence that industry was becoming suspicious of the arts man and of diluting technological studies with arts sub-

[1] Docksey, op. cit., p. 116.
[2] Royal Institute of Chemistry, *Report of the Committee of Enquiry into the Relationship between University Courses in Chemistry and the Needs of Industry* (Eaborn), p. 4.
[3] *Education and Training Requirements for the Electrical and Mechanical Manufacturing Industries* (Bosworth).
[4] Durham University Appointments Board Report, 1962/3.

jects. Dainton preferred a first degree in engineering or science rather than economics for the potential entrant to industry. *The Times* was critical of Swann, suggesting that industry did not want scientists with a broad smattering of social studies.[1] Eaborn suggested that the chemists wanted no dilution of specialist chemistry with arts subjects. Most particularly, G. S. Bosworth considered that the recruiting of too many arts and social studies graduates into industry 'can have serious risks for the future. It can result in too few science based business managers being produced and it can also blunt the need to recruit more good calibre technologists in all aspects of manufacturing'.[2] If industry in the late 1960s and early 1970s is making it clear that it prefers science and technology based managers, the recent massive expansion of the social studies, ostensibly for industrial purposes, may prove a mismatch. As the Robbins fourth year M.A. failed to develop for lack of finance, then many general courses were unable to give their graduates that extra year of specialism to which the first degree was intended as a broad introduction. Accordingly, some early generations of arts students were graduates whose mixed subject arts degrees were of somewhat limited value in employment terms. Curricular change has in many cases taken account of the lack of the M.A. to tighten up the degree of specialism in the B.A.

Fourth, there were criticisms that university activity did not lead sufficiently or directly into industrial production. For example, it was a matter of concern that the vast bulk of graduates in industry went into and preferred research rather than production management. Seventy-five per cent of physicists in industry were in research and development and only 3 per cent in general management,[3] while 30·3 per cent of all graduates in science and technology took jobs in research and development and only 6 per cent in management.[4] Bosworth especially wanted more graduates to go straight into manufacturing for this was where four-fifths of industrial investment lay and where graduate expertise was needed, as much if not more than in R and D. This lack of carry-over directly into production was also criticized in relation to the work of the scientific staff even at Imperial College which should have been in the forefront of such liaison.[5] Here it was found that although about thirty commercially exploitable ideas were generated in the college a year, and although about 70

---

[1] *The Times*, 25 September 1968, cited Richard Layard, *et al.*, op. cit., p. 52.
[2] *Graduate Training in Manufacturing Technology* (Bosworth Report II), p. 9.
[3] The Institute of Physics and the Physical Society, *Report of the Working Party on Industry and the Physics, Ph.D.*, an Interim Report, p. 15.
[4] *Graduate Training in Manufacturing Technology* (Bosworth), p. 7. Bosworth's figures were a percentage of all occupations entered, those of the working party were for graduates in physics entering industry.
[5] B. E. Launder and G. A. Webster, *University Research and the Considerations Affecting its Commercial Exploitation, a Survey of Six Departments at Imperial College, January 1969.* (Technical Development Capital Ltd., 1969).

per cent of their originators took some steps to act further on them, yet they did not come to fruition as they ought to have done. The National Research and Development Corporation was not proving a totally satisfactory means of developing such ideas into production nor were the staff well informed about the raising of private venture capital. But, most importantly, the staff originating the ideas were not found to be strongly motivated to exploit their ideas commercially, nor did they believe that any success of this nature would have any relevance for their future career prospects. If this were so at Imperial College it was likely to be even more the case at most other universities, with the possible exception of the new ex-CATs. It was at one with the ethos transmitted by the staff to their students that research itself was the goal and that production, being regarded as of less intrinsic interest, could be left to others.

Finally, whatever the reservations voiced by industry and others about the first degree, it was the scientific PH.D. that came in for the most criticism. As the Swann report noted, 'the view is widely held in industry that the PH.D. training . . . is at best irrelevant to industry and at its worst turns graduates permanently away from industry'.[1] The Swann committee, while not wholly agreeing with industrial criticisms, considered that the PH.D. did need rethinking. It was quite evident that such was the expansion of post-graduate education in science that twice as many 'doctors' would be produced as would be needed in research posts outside industry. Given this situation, there was a strong case for creating post-graduate courses that would be shorter and would have a more applied and vocational content and orientation in the expectation that such students would go into industry. The universities were advised to 'consider drastic action to bring within its scope other forms of post-graduate training more closely orientated to the requirements of industry'. Accordingly industry ought to become more associated with the planning of such courses, and more latitude ought to be allowed for students already in industry to be able to pursue higher degrees while still remaining in industry. Many technological universities prided themselves on their arrangements for this and the Science Research Council was increasing its awards to applicants for higher degrees with industrial experience through the Industrial Studentship and Fellowship schemes.

The most astringent critics of post-graduate work for potential industrial entrants pointed out that industry did not really want PH.D.s in any case and did not value such a qualification more than a one-year post-graduate diploma: 'industry clearly considers that the two years of extra experience and employment are as valuable as two years of research at a university'.[2] Any assumptions that it was

---

[1] Swann, p. 61.
[2] Ernest Rudd and Stephen Hatch, *Graduate Study and After*, p. 137 and *passim*.

necessary to expand three-year post-graduate education for the benefit of industry were proving completely unfounded, for there was a
'dissonance between graduate education and careers conducive to
economic growth'. Other attacks on the supposed excessive numbers
of scientific PH.D.s, the narrowness of their education and research
projects, and the need for many of them to be given some alternative
form of post-graduate education more orientated towards industry,
came variously at this time from Lord Blackett P.R.S. and Sir Brian
Flowers, the Chairman of the SRC, whose grant policy was seeking to
give effect to this.[1] As with some aspects of the first degree a dissenting voice came from the Eaborn committee on the chemical industry.
They found, contrary to Swann, that there was no evidence that the
PH.D. was diverting students from industry. They found the proportion of PH.D. students working on problems of industrial application
to be about 30 per cent, representing 'a much greater degree of industrial involvement in university chemical research than is generally
appreciated', and they even considered the numbers of PH.D.s not
greatly excessive and about right for the mid 1970s.

Lest this foregoing consideration of criticisms should give an
unduly adverse perspective of the relations of the universities and
industry at the end of the 1960s, it is worth recalling the findings of
the Docksey report which, like the Eaborn report, presented a somewhat comforting view of the state of progress at the end of the
decade. In many ways there were healthy signs. Only 9 per cent of
companies of 5,000+ employees had no contact with universities,
86 per cent of all companies were in favour of close collaboration
with universities, 81 per cent of firms using university consultants
found them useful and effective, forty-three out of sixty universities
and colleges had specifically close links with industry and only five
out of the sixty had no such contacts and no good reason for not
having them. Docksey concluded that they simply could not sub-
stantiate a number of harsh criticisms often made about the university-industry connection. Eaborn likewise found that there was no
serious dissatisfaction at all in firms in the chemical industry concerning the links with universities or their graduates. It is worth
stressing the findings of these two leading reports of 1970 because,
while it is always easier to cause a stir with accusations of a scandal-
ously bad situation in need of reform, such considered statements of
satisfaction tend too easily to be either discounted as improbable or
ignored as unexceptional. That they could be made in 1970 is
important to us as a landmark in that progressive drawing together
of the universities and industry it has been the purpose of this study
to examine.

[1] Lord Blackett in *Daily Telegraph*, 3 December 1970. Sir Brian Flowers
speaking at the University of East Anglia, 25 March 1969, and also *Daily
Telegraph*, 19 May 1971.

The sixties seemed to end on a melancholy note in contrast to the buoyant optimism of the earlier part of the decade. It was evident that not only had the expansion of higher education had no effect on our growth rate, but that the situation had deteriorated.[1]

Percentage growth GDP:

1960	1961	1962	1963	1964	1965	1966	1967	1968	1969	1970
4·9	3·56	0·97	3·87	5·34	2·67	2·0	1·86	3·21	1·65	1·52

Industrial production:

1960	1961	1962	1963	1964	1965	1966	1967	1968	1969	1970
7·02	1·3	1·03	3·41	8·3	3·14	1·34	0·62	5·2	2·59	0·89

Inevitably it would be a matter of decades before the effects of the higher education expansion would show discernible benefits through the work of its graduates in industry. Furthermore, scarcely had this expansion of graduates taken place than the economy ran into a recession with the highest unemployment since the beginning of the war. Accordingly, by the end of 1970 6·2 per cent of arts graduates and 4·5 per cent of science graduates who had graduated that summer were still unemployed. These factors, coupled with the recurrence of disorder at a number of universities and the lowered estimation in which they were then held, led to considerable scepticism of the value of further expansion. Calls were also made for a return to the education of a scholarly élite rather than the pursuance of policies that would give a broadly based three years' full-time higher education for all who demanded it.[2] At the root of this malaise occasioned by rapid expansion were disagreements and confusions concerning the role of higher education. Indeed its close involvement with industry had contributed to bring about this malaise just as it rendered impossible a return to the scholarly élitism called for in some quarters. With a consideration of these matters and the theme as a whole we should now conclude.

[1] Calculated from *National Institute Economic Review*, May 1971.
[2] Lord Todd in his introductory address to the British Association at Durham, 1970, and, for example, Rhodes Boyson, 'Too Many Graduates?', *Daily Telegraph*, 15 June 1971.

Conclusion

This study has tried to show that various pressures arose in the nineteenth century which induced the universities and industry to turn towards each other. The fear of French and then German competition, the increasingly scientific nature of innovation, the emergence of the large firm and the rise of special skills like accountancy all created a need for the graduate in industry. Oxford and Cambridge were not suited to supply this need though the latter reformed and removed some of the institutional barriers impeding the scientific education of the secular potential businessman. The origin of the appointments boards in both universities created an important new device for a closer linking of the universities and industry which others soon copied. Because of the defects of the ancient universities, new civic universities in the North and Midlands arose, directly financed by industry and business and frequently owing their existence to them. Accordingly all developed industrial specialisms in their research and teaching which served local and national industry, while a large proportion of their graduates, unlike those of the ancient universities, went into industrial careers. Parallel with these technological developments there were later moves from the 1890s to develop economics as a suitable university training for businessmen in which Cambridge, Birmingham, and LSE took a lead that others followed.

The Welsh and Scottish traditions underwent a somewhat different experience. The Welsh university colleges arose largely as an expression of Welsh national culture. They received little support from industry, save that of south Lancashire, their studies had little industrial relevance and their output to Welsh industry was slight. They presented a pathological example of a university movement largely disengaged from industry and greatly weakened thereby. The Scottish case was more complicated. Their problem was to modify an old university system based on assumptions of giving a rather general mixed arts and science education to large numbers of students destined for the ministry and teaching. Increasing scientific education and increasing permitted specialism seemed to them the way to adjust to the demands of industry. At the same time, in their research, Scottish professors in engineering, electrical physics, and shipbuilding

389

presented an example of close involvement in industry that was a model to the English professoriate.

The First World War was seen as a very important phase in this development in that it presented a number of challenging problems in the field of drugs, explosives, aeronautics, and so forth which university personnel tackled with striking and well publicized success. Moreover, at that time the universities were almost unique in containing the scientists with the ability to handle such problems. The war also created a 'cult' of science and brought direct government sponsorship of it. Moreover, the pressures of war-time and the collaboration of university personnel with firms brought formal contacts between the universities and industry on a greater scale than had existed hitherto. The war also showed the worth of women graduates in industry as welfare officers, and also had the effect of turning many servicemen's thoughts to higher education and future careers in science and technology after the war.

In the inter-war years, in spite of depression, the progressive connection of the universities and industry continued in several areas. The rise of research within the firm, especially in the 1920s, created a new and most important entrée for the graduate into the firm. Also the increase of 'functionalism' in management and problems of management succession created by war-time losses inclined more firms to turn to the graduate. Many of the 'new' industries by their scientific nature required men with a higher scientific education, while for the non-scientific graduate new developments in economics and commercial education created new courses in industrial administration. For women, still forced into careers by their excess in the population, new fields opened in advertising, stores, welfare management, and light electrical engineering which brought the woman graduate into industry virtually for the first time.

It was no surprise that in the Second World War the universities should have been at the very heart of the war-time science for the production of radar and the atomic bomb, both in close contact with industry. After the war and up to the late 1950s, the graduate was never so much in demand from industry, as not only the traditional chemist and physicist but also the mathematician was avidly absorbed into the firm. The arts graduate, too, was turned to more than before to fill in the gaps of industry's needs which even the contemporary urgent concern about increasing technological manpower had failed fully to meet. In this situation, and faced with the coming to university age of children born in the immediate post-war years, the country embarked on a major expansion of the universities, creating 'new' ones whose involvement with industry tended not to be great, and upgrading former colleges of technology into 'technological' universities the basis of whose existence was their connection with industry.

The increasing involvement of the universities with industry is perhaps the most important single development in the history of the British universities over the last hundred years. It will be stressed, however, that it is far from the only important connection. Indeed, such parallel themes as the connection of the universities with agriculture, with medicine, with teacher training, or the Civil Service would well merit thorough investigation which is not the purpose of this study to pursue. While this is not a study of the whole history of British universities in general but of one vital theme in their modern development, we believe this connection to have been of special importance. It has created a situation in which it would be virtually impossible for a university to return purely to that liberal education envisaged by Mill and Newman, to studies, in Newman's words 'independent of sequel' and not 'informed by any end'. To engage totally in such studies would almost inevitably entail cutting off such an institution from industrial support and the precedents for that in the last hundred years have been almost uniformly gloomy—Cambridge before the 1890s, Dundee after the 1890s, and the Welsh colleges before 1914. It has frequently been stressed how essential industrial support has been for the vitality, health, and very existence of the universities. This has not only been so most obviously at the financial level, but because the testing of their research and of their graduate products in subsequent work situations has given a beneficially astringent effect to studies, which those without practical application cannot have. Also the requirements of industry have opened up a whole range of new subjects and cross connections which would not necessarily have come about without those demands—the chemistry of glass, the mathematics of flight, the biology of the food fishes, for example. Finally, the favourable regard of the local business community, as in Birmingham, Liverpool, or Manchester, has provided a climate powerfully conducive to the healthy growth of universities as its lack elsewhere has retarded it.

Reciprocally, if the industrial and business connection has been vital for the universities so has it been for industry. This has been so through the original knowledge that the universities have provided of which ample evidence has been given in this study. Much of the expertise for the electrical industry before the 1920s came from the universities, while others like fisheries, canning, mining, marine engineering, leather, dyes, and so forth have been highly dependent on university work for their developing science. Indeed, universities virtually created many of them. It is the exceptions like motor car engineering and cotton textiles which stand out as unusual in owing little to the universities. This reliance was probably relatively greater before the 1920s than after. Then, with the rise of research laboratories within the firm, the universities became merely one of a

number of agencies producing new industrial science, and in the case
of dyes and electricals, for example, the chief locus of innovation
moved from the university to the firm. But for most others the
university, with the research association and the firm laboratory,
remained a major fount of new ideas. Second, even where the
universities were not innovating, their consultancy services often had
a widespread and profound effect in improving the scientific efficiency
of firms even in routine matters, as was seen, for example, in Roscoe's
advisory work in chemistry from Manchester University and Arnold's
in metallurgy from Sheffield. Third, and most obvious, the universities have been increasingly suppliers of personnel with as much as
one-third of their output going into these fields. In the nineteenth
century it was the chemist and the engineer, and then successively
with a widening range of occupations, the economist, welfare worker,
physicist, and latterly the mathematician and the arts graduate.
Indeed, in those areas where from time to time the universities have
conspicuously failed to produce certain types of labour—metallurgists, geologists, and mechanical engineers in the thirties, for example
—then industry was loud to complain of the serious deleterious
effects this lack of supply was having.

This close and progressive enmeshment of industrial considerations in the very fabric of British universities that has taken place
over the last hundred years has posed a number of problems and
dilemmas for the present and the future. First, there is the conflict
of criteria about the optimum size of the university population. On
the one hand is the belief that the numbers of students ought to be
related to and even restricted by the demands of society, including
industry, for their future services as graduates. The obvious drawbacks of this approach are that it is extremely difficult to forecast
with precision future demand for certain types of labour, partly
because of the difficulty of predicting future economic performance
and partly because of the impossibility of foretelling technical
change. Thus predictions about future requirements of types of
skills may be as awry as those about amounts of skill. If this criterion
is a dubious one—and we have seen various examples of shortfalls
and overproductions in the past—then the other is to base estimates
of proposed university populations on numbers of people qualified
and willing to attend a university, rather than on estimates of their
subsequent job prospects. Indeed, much of the expansion of the
1960s was argued in terms of social justice for qualified school
leavers as much as on the need for technical manpower. The activities
of the 'new' universities are largely catering for the former considerations rather than the latter. This distinction is an important one
here because after a period of rapid expansion the early 1970s began
with a period of recession and fears of graduate unemployment
which led easily to arguments about 'overexpansion'. The point

we would wish to stress is that a too close consideration of supposed immediate industrial needs in response to temporary and fluctuating circumstances could lead to the acceptance of criteria about university numbers not only socially unjust, but also against the best interests of industry itself, which can have no wish to return to the scramble for graduates in short supply that characterized the late 1940s and 1950s. The concept that young people who are so qualified may attend a university as a right is an important innovation and it would be retrograde if the close involvement universities have with industry should cause it to be abandoned in favour of criteria based on manpower planning, were these latter more restrictive.

The second dilemma posed by the involvement of the universities and industry is the nature of the education to be provided. We have seen ample evidence of the power of industrial needs to change and amplify the content of university teaching, and these effects have generally been beneficial and enriching for the universities. But on the other hand, two kinds of conflicts may arise over the content of education where the interests of industry may not be those of the university as a centre of excellence in scholarship. The first of these centres around the problem of specialism and generalism. To say that industry has preferred more or less specialization would be too crude. Historically it has sometimes called for more and sometimes less. For example, the changes in the Scottish universities' curricula were a move towards specialism for the benefit of industry as were the demands for specialist geology and metallurgy in the inter-war years. But, conversely, at other times it has been in the interests of industry to require a widening of the context of certain subjects. This was so with the widening of the Mathematical Tripos in the 1900s to include applied subjects, the creation of chemical engineering out of two specialisms in the 1920s, and the placing of economics in successively wider contexts to produce commerce courses in the 1900s and industrial administration programmes in the 1930s. It is frequently argued that such is the pace of technical change that any science or technology studied by students so rapidly becomes obsolete that there is consequently little point in studying anything to much degree of specialist depth. This lends weight to arguments in favour of broadly based multidisciplinary general degrees which would purport to give a certain 'flexibility' to cope with future change. Were this to become widely followed, and especially if science degrees were much diluted with arts, the dangers of producing graduates having a broad smattering of most things in general and mentally equipped for nothing in particular would be considerable. This is not an English tradition, but the nearest approach was the old Scottish unreformed university education which even in the nineteenth century became increasingly unsuitable as an education for an industrial society, and which could only survive because almost all its science professors had had a supplementary education at Cambridge in mathematics, the stronghold of specialized high excellence. We have noted that the Eaborn report made an unfashionable stand against this generalist approach on behalf of chemical education and the chemical industry. If industry came to believe that a lower level general education best served its purpose there may be a conflict of duty presented to the universities who would prefer to continue teaching at the highest level, holding out to the student the possibility of achieving excellence and depth of grasp in some coherent, if limited, area of scholarship.

The second potential area of conflict of interest about the whole content of education is that over the type of student required by industry. Here there is a long standing clash between the demands of scholarship and notions of a wider 'rounded' non-academic education. At Oxford and Cambridge in the nineteenth century there were plenty of men whose purpose in being there was not learning but the social and sporting life; indeed this disturbed several witnesses to the Royal Commissions on the two universities in the 1850s. However, the evidence of the early appointments officers of the two universities suggested that before 1914 firms were taking graduates with the highest degrees they could get. They certainly took academic attainment into account and believed it relevant as a predictor of ability and future success. Evidence from Imperial College for the 1930s also suggests the same. In the inter-war years, however, there arose the concept of the 'right type', the paragon of appointments office and industrial literature, who represented a balanced ideal of academic work, sport, travel, and so forth. This in itself was admirable, but by the late 1940s some industrial opinion seemed to have toppled over to an extreme. In particular some of the comments at contemporary FBI conferences denigrating academic excellence and condemning 'studiousness' as a danger to the universities strongly suggested that the ideals of businessmen and the ideals to which universities ought to cling had sharply diverged. The humorous retort, 'we cannot put on courses on running the rugger club', well characterized the fatuousness of some of the statements to which it was reacting. Similarly the Acton Society Trust found that 'ability to fit in' was far more highly valued by firms than intellectual curiosity and originality of thought as a characteristic of its graduate recruits. This divergence of values between the universities and industry is a serious point. It may well be that for many students the essentially academic education of universities would be a less suitable training for business than some kind of mixed educational-cum-adventure, outward bound, initiative-testing kind of post-school experience. The Army is very properly making a strong case in its advertising for short service commissions in arguing their future value for potential industrial entrants. It might have been a bold stroke if instead of financing one or two of the new universities, the government had experimented with a form of residential college providing this kind of initiative training but without any pretensions to undertake academic work to a high level. This would be preferable to a situation in which universities take on more and more non-academic and non-intellectual functions to which their students divert increasing amounts of time, knowing well that industry has less interest in the class of their degree than in their other activities. If there is a divergence of values between the scholar and the business man, universities should make quite clear both to students and to industry which values they are primarily concerned to foster.

Occasionally we have noted in the past instances of industrial interference in university affairs or clashes between university and industrial interests—as with the restrictions on Arnold's publishing, Pope's interference in economics at Bristol, Webb's resignation, the clash of Mackay and Alsop and Brunner at Liverpool, and the Warwick incident. And yet in spite of the considerable stir such suspicions about business raised in the 1930s, we do not regard them as truly deep and serious threats to the university system. More dangerous than these surface scandals is the insidious assumption that the activity of universities ought to be, and can be, measured in terms of some rate of return on expenditure. Such assumptions are understandably attendant upon the great increase in public expenditure on higher education in the 1960s and owe much to the contemporary rise of the economics of education as a study. But at the root is the close relation that the universities and industry now bear towards each other. It would be deplorable if these three factors, all good in themselves, created an attitude of mind in which the only education that was valued was that which apparently gave this measurable return and which served the economy in a quantifiable manner. The most crude form of this attitude was seen in some remarkable attacks on the Open University in the summer of 1971 on the grounds that it had not been able to show such a return. This may be the most adverse effect of the whole movement of the *rapprochement* of the universities and industry if it coarsens the public view of the purposes of education to a crudely measurable vocationalism. This drifting change should be seen in its historical context.

Before the drawing together of the universities and industry, we have seen that attitudes to the functions of universities were dominated by the old liberal anti-vocational education ideal. It has been one of the virtues of this drawing together greatly to enrich university activity and to widen its scope beyond the narrowness of curriculum envisaged by the liberal education ideal. This created universities with a healthy mixture of vocational and liberal education as the civic universities espoused the pure arts—which they were obliged to do to gain entrance to Victoria and to become chartered universities—and as Oxford and Cambridge improved their sciences and accepted technology. It would be an undesirable reversal if this balance of liberal and vocational education were then tilted to the other extreme in which only vocational and chiefly industrial subjects capable of yielding a measurable return became regarded as worthwhile objects of university study. There are certain rapidly developing areas of higher education where such justifications are manifestly absent. In particular the Open University, dealing with the middle-aged, ought to have no need to justify itself on such grounds. The same is true of the education of women. Some of the chief beneficiaries of the expansion of the 1960s have been middle-class girls and they are precisely the people who find it most difficult to obtain employment on graduating and who with early marriage are least likely to remain long in any employment they eventually obtain. But to recognize this is in no way to invalidate the extending of higher education to the second-chance middle-aged or to girls, the beneficial effects of which in social and personal terms are likely to prove great though totally outside the realms of calculation. Whereas before the engagement with industry too much university education was of a consumption rather than a productive character, there is a danger with the close involvement of the universities and industry of swinging to an equally unbalanced opposite extreme of denying the validity of consumption education, of the widening and disciplining of the mind for its own sake, and seeking to test such education by the criteria of 'investment' in 'human capital'. This is one of the risks attendant upon greatly increased public expenditure in a higher education system whose recent tradition has been so closely geared to industry.

At the beginning of the period with which this study deals university men were chiefly destined for the learned professions. Throughout the period we have been concerned with, they have filtered increasingly into a widening range of industrial and business employments in the circumstances we have considered. For the future, with continued expansion, graduates will continue to filter into a whole range of occupations in which they have not formerly been greatly involved—into junior and infant teaching, the police, secretarial posts, the management of cinemas, grocery stores, and football clubs and all manner of occupations calling for the absorption and ordering of information and the taking of decisions and initiative. Although graduate status will lose slightly whatever 'special' character it bestowed on its holder in the 1900s or the 1930s, yet it would be wrong to regard such future occupational change as a 'waste' of graduates or as evidence of 'overexpansion'. The small minority with the self-igniting desire for scholarship will continue to be stimulated by university life as before. The bulk of the rest, merely as intelligent and moderately hard working as their predecessors ever were, will transmit at least something of university values a little more widely in a society that can only benefit from them.

The universities have been able to retain those values and standards whilst absorbing the stimulus and adapting to the needs of industry over the last hundred years. To continue to do so in the face of further democratization presents the next immediate challenge from which, compared with their response to industrial involvement, they have rather less to fear but rather less to gain.

Select Bibliography

The items listed are a selection of those found especially valuable in the writing of this study. Works of general economic and industrial history are not normally included. Very full bibliographies of the literature on university education will be found in:

Cordeaux, E. H., and Merry, D. H., *A Bibliography of Printed Works relating to the University of Oxford* (Oxford, 1968).

Powell, John, *Universities and University Education: a Select Bibliography* (National Foundation for Educational Research in England and Wales, London, 1966).

Silver, Harold and Teague, S. John, *The History of British Universities 1800–1969, excluding Oxford and Cambridge, a Bibliography* (Research into Higher Education Monographs, London, 1970).

Unpublished materials

University of Aberdeen Library

Notes on Natural Philosophy Lectures by Professor David Thomson, 1870–1.

Association of University Teachers

Files on Graduate Employment: the Universities and Industry: Meetings with other Bodies.

University College of North Wales, Bangor, Library

Belmont Papers, 67 (iii), Letters, 1883.
Lloyd Papers, 231, 'The University College of North Wales'.

University of Birmingham Library

MS. Register of Students, Faculties of Arts and Science, 1892–4.
Joseph Chamberlain Papers, JC 12/1/1/1–34.
Letter Books of the Dean of the Faculty of Science, 1904–19.
Minute Books of Sir William Ashley's Commerce Seminar, 1902–8.
Letter Books of the Dean of the Faculty of Commerce, University of Birmingham, 1907–12 and 1913–20.
Sir William Ashley's Papers on the War Work of Birmingham University Staff.
Interview Forms, Higher Education for Ex-Servicemen.
University of Birmingham Appointments Board Reports, 1932–9.

Bristol University Archives

J. W. Arrowsmith, Letters, DM. 219.
Professor A. M. Tyndall's Papers, DM. 362, 363.
Minute Book of Bristol University Faculty of Engineering, 1909–22, DM. 236.
Autobiography of M. W. Travers, DM. 389.
Notes on the History of the Department of Economics, University of Bristol, DM. 219.

Archives of Bristol University Engineering Department

File 17, 'War Work', 1919.
Correspondence, G. H. Pope and Professor J. Wertheimer, 1911.

Cambridge University Archives

Papers of Sir George Darwin, 1897–1904.
28.1. (Economics).
28.6. (Mathematical Tripos).
28.6. (1) (Mathematical Tripos).
28.9. (Natural Sciences Tripos).
28.17. (Mechanical Sciences Tripos).
39.11. (Professor of Chemistry).
39.17.2. (Professor of Geology).
39.20. (Jacksonian Professor of Natural Philosophy).
39.23. (Mineralogy).
39.26. (Professor of Political Economy).
39.34. (Mechanism and Engineering).
39.34.1. (Engineering Studies).
39.54. (Aeronautical Engineering).
48. (Appointments Association).
128. (Mining Engineering).

Cambridge University Appointments Board

Confidential typescript memoranda of Cambridge University Appointments Board on interviews with and visits to firms, 4 vols, 1919–39.
Minute Books and Reports of Cambridge University Womens' Appointments Board, 1930–9.

Marshall Library, Cambridge

Alfred Marshall's Papers.

University of Durham Library

Thorp MSS.

Durham University Appointments Board Offices, Durham

Durham University Appointments Board Reports, 1957–66.

Edinburgh University Library

Lyon Playfair's Chemistry Lectures, 1858–69.
Archibald Geikie's Lectures on Geology, 1871–2.
P. G. Tait's Lectures on Natural Philosophy, 1881–2.
A. Crum Brown's Chemistry Lectures, 1884.
Sir John Smith Flett's Memoirs of Student Days at Edinburgh, 1886–94.
Papers of Charles Sarolea and Professor Bernard Pares, 1916.

Edinburgh University Appointments Board Offices

Annual Reports of Edinburgh University Appointments Secretary, 1923–38.

Glasgow University Library

J. McCallum, Notes on Natural Philosophy, 1880.
Principal G. G. Ramsay's Papers.

Department of Natural Philosophy, University of Glasgow

Letters of Lord Kelvin.

Glasgow University Archives

Items 4776, 4600, 4781. UBE 17553. F/NCB/F 5705, 5608, 17560, 5927, 6061.
Reports of Queen Margaret College, Glasgow Appointments Committee 1921–38.

Glasgow University Appointments Board Offices

Reports of Glasgow University Appointments Board, 1921–39.

Leeds University Appointments Board Offices

Leeds University Appointments Board Register.

University of Liverpool, Registrar's Department

Collection of Papers and Letters on War Work, Liverpool University
Various Papers, 'Misc. Histories I, II'.

Imperial College Archives, London

Technical Optics, 1912–18, File 131.
Zaharoff Chair of Aviation, 1918, 1919–23, File 1120.
Aeronautics Committee, 1909–13, 1925–34, Files 1921, 1928.
Minutes and Reports of Imperial College Appointments Board, 1912–13, 1920–39.
Typescript histories of the Departments of Chemistry, Physics, Chemical Engineering, Mathematics, Civil Engineering, Geology, and Metallurgy.

University College, London, Library

Ernest George Coker, Engineering at University College, London, 1925.

Manchester University Library

Letter Books of Sir Henry Roscoe 1878–83, MSS. CH R108.
Sir Henry Roscoe's Lecture Notes, 1857–8, MSS. CH R106.
Sir Sydney Chapman, Some Memories and Reflections, MSS. EH C.91.

Manchester Central Library

Reports of Manchester University Appointments Board, 1935–50.

University of Newcastle Archives

Durham Colleges in the University of Durham, First Appointments obtained by students leaving during the period 1929–39.
King's College, Newcastle upon Tyne, Posts Obtained by Students after leaving College during the past ten or twelve years, 1928–39.

Department of Engineering, University of Newcastle

Record Cards of Engineering Students, Newcastle University, 1920–45.

Bodleian Library, Oxford

F. B. Hunt and C. E. Escritt, Historical Notes on the Oxford University Appointments Committee, 1951, 2632.c.17.

University of St Andrews Library

Papers of J. D. Forbes.
Papers of Sir D'Arcy Wentworth Thompson,
Draft typescripts for a Biographical Register of Alumni, St Andrews (compiled by and in the possession of Mr R. N. Smart).

Sheffield University Library

Letter Books of Professor O. Arnold, Metallurgical Department, Sheffield University, 1904–18.

University of Sheffield Appointments Office

Reports of the Appointments Officer, University of Sheffield, 1946–62.

Southampton University Library

Papers of K. H. Vickers, Principal of University College, Southampton, 1922–47.
Memoranda on Investigations and Experimental Developments made between 1934–9.
Investigations and Experimental Developments made for the various fighting services during the war period. Memoranda by Professor Cave-Brown-Cave.

Newspaper cuttings collections

Dundee University
Edinburgh University (in Edinburgn City Library)
Exeter University
Heriot-Watt (in Edinburgh City Library)
Imperial College, London
Leeds University
Leeds University Textile Department
Liverpool University (in the university and the City Library)
UMIST (in Manchester City Library)

Registers and calendars

Records of the Arts Classes, University of Aberdeen, 1866–70; 1876–80, 1886–90; 1895–9; 1909–1912/13 (Aberdeen 1905, 1907, 1924, 1900, 1959).

Roll of Graduates of the University of Aberdeen 1901–25 with Supplement 1860–1910, (ed.) Theodore Watt (Aberdeen, 1935).

The Balliol College Register 1833–1933 (Oxford, 1934).

University of Birmingham Register of Graduates (1932).

University of Birmingham Register of Old Mining Students (1938).

Brasenose College Register 1509–1909 (Oxford, 1909).

The Daubeny Laboratory Register 1904–1915 (ed.) R. T. Gunther (Oxford, 1916).

Register of Exeter College, Oxford, 1891–1921 (ed.) A. B. How (Oxford, 1928).

Girton College Register 1869–1946 (Cambridge, 1946).

Roll of Graduates of the University of Glasgow 1727–1897 (Glasgow, 1898).

A Register of the Alumni of Keble College, Oxford, 1870–1925 (Oxford, 1927).

Leeds University Old Students Association Year Book (1930–1).

The London School of Economics and Political Science Register 1895–1932 (London, 1934).

The Victoria University of Manchester, Register of Graduates up to 1 July 1908 (Manchester, 1908).

Merton College Register 1900–1964 (Oxford, 1964).

Newnham College Register: vol. I, 1871–1923; vol. II, 1924–1950 (privately printed, Cambridge 1963).

Calendar of the Royal Holloway College (1962–3).

Reports

Government and UGC

1852 XXII *Report of Her Majesty's Commissioners . . . Universities and Colleges of Oxford.*

1852–3 XLIV *Report of Her Majesty's Commissioners . . . University and Colleges of Cambridge.*

1863 XLVI *Minutes of Evidence taken before the Durham University Commissioners.*

1871 XXIV, C. 318; 1872 XXV, C. 536; 1873 XXVIII, C. 868; 1874 XXII, C. 884, 958, 1087; 1875 XXVIII, C. 1279, 1297, 1298, 1363, *Reports of the Royal Commission on Scientific Instruction and the Advancement of Science* (Devonshire).

1878 XXXII–XXXIV *Report of the Royal Commissioners appointed to inquire into the Universities of Scotland*, C. 1935, 1935–I, 1935–II, 1935–III.

1881 XXXIII *Report of the Committee . . . Intermediate and Higher Education in Wales and Monmouthshire* (Aberdare), C. 3047, 3047–I.

1884 XXIX, C. 3981; 1884 XXXI, C. 3981-II; *Report of the Royal Commission on Technical Instruction* (Samuelson).

1886 XXIII *Third Report of the Royal Commission on Trade and Industry*, C. 4797, 4893.

1889 XXXIX *Report of the Royal Commissioners . . . Higher Education in London* (Selborne), C. 5709, 5709–I.

1894 XXXIV *Report of the Commissioners . . . University of London* (Cowper), C. 7425, 7425–I.

1898 XXIV *Special Reports on Educational Subjects*, 'The London School of Economics and Political Science' by W. A. S. Hewins, C. 8743.

1900 XXV *General Report of the Commissioners under the Universities (Scotland) Act 1889*, Cd. 276.

1909 XIX *Report of the Committee on the University of Wales and its Constituent Colleges* (Raleigh), Cd. 4571, 4572.

1910 XXIII, Cd. 5165, 5166; 1911 XX, Cd. 5527, 5528, 5910, 5911; 1913 XL, Cd. 6717, 6718; *Royal Commission on the University of London* (Haldane).

1910 LXXII; 1912–13 XXII, Cd. 6140 *Reports of the Advisory Committee on Grants to University Colleges.*

1900 XX, Cd. 331–1914–16 XIX, Cd. 8137, 8138 *Reports from Universities and University Colleges to the Board of Education.*

1913 XVIII, Cd, 6739, 6740; 1914 XVI, Cd. 7338, 7339, 7340; 1914–16 XI, Cd. 7748, 7749, 7832, 8130; *Royal Commission on the Civil Service.*

1916 VIII, Cd. 8274; 1917–18 XI, Cd. 8594, 1918 IX, Cd. 9045; 1919 XXI, Cmd. 165; 1920 XV, Cmd. 722 *Reports of the Board of Education 1914/15–1918/19.*

1916 VIII, Cd. 8336; 1917–18 XI, Cd. 8718; 1918 IX, Cd. 9144; 1919 XXIX, Cmd. 320; *Reports of the Committee of the Privy Council for Scientific and Industrial Research 1915/16, 1917/18, 1918, 1919.*

1917–18 XII, Cd. 8500, 8507, 8698, 8699; 1918 XIV, Cd. 8991, 8993, *Royal Commission on University Education in Wales* (Haldane).

1918 IX *Natural Science in Education, the Report of the Committee on the Position of Natural Science in the Educational System of Great Britain* (Sir Joseph Thomson), Cd. 9011.

1918 IX *Report of the Committee . . . Position of Modern Languages in the Educational System of Great Britain* (Sir Stanley Leathes), Cd. 9036.

1919 XXXIII *British Air Effort during the War*, Cmd. 100.

1920 IX *Report of the Air Ministry Committee on Education and Research in Aeronautics* (Glazebrook), Cmd. 554.

Official History of the Ministry of Munitions, vols IX–XII, HMSO, London, 1922.

1922 X *Report of the Royal Commission on Oxford and Cambridge Universities*, Cmd. 1588.

Reports of the University Grants Committee 1925, 1930, 1936 and *Annual Returns 1920–1939*.

Report of the Committee on Industry and Trade, 'Factors in Industrial and Commercial Efficiency' (Balfour), 1927.

Final Report of the Committee on Education for Salesmanship (Goodenough) HMSO, London, 1931.

1934–5 VIII *Royal Commission on the University of Durham*, Cmd. 4815.

Higher Technological Education (Percy), 1945.

1945–6 XIV *Scientific Manpower* (Barlow) Cmd. 6824.

1945–6 XIV *Report of the Committee on the Provision for Social and Economic Research* (Clapham), Cmd. 6868.

University Development from 1935 to 1948. Report of the UGC, 1948.

University Development, UGC *Report on the Years, 1947–52*, Cmd. 8875, 1953; *1952–7*, Cmnd. 534, 1958; *1957–62*, Cmnd. 2267, 1963; *1962–7*, Cmnd. 3820, 1968; *Annual Survey 1967–8*, Cmnd. 3914, 1969; *Annual Survey 1968–9*, Cmnd. 4261, 1970.

The First Employment of University Graduates, UGC, 1962–9.

Higher Education (Robbins), Cmnd. 2154, 1963.

University Appointments Boards (Heyworth), UGC, 1964.

Enquiry into the Flow of Candidates in Science and Technology into Higher Education (Dainton), Interim Cmnd. 2893, 1966; Final Cmnd. 3541, 1968.

Education and Training Requirements for the Electrical and Mechanical Manufacturing Industries (Bosworth), HMSO, 1966.

The Brain Drain, Report of the Working Party on Migration (Jones), Cmnd. 3417, 1967.

The Flow into Employment of Scientists, Engineers and Technologists (Swann), Cmnd. 3760, 1968.

Graduate Training in Manufacturing Technology (Bosworth), HMSO, 1970.

University bodies

Reports of the University College of Wales, Aberystwyth, 1880–1900.

Quinquennial Report of the University College of Wales, Aberystwyth, 1908–13.

Report of Zoological Department of the University College of Wales, Aberystwyth: Fisheries in Cardigan Bay, 1913.

Minutes of Court, University College of North Wales, Bangor, 17, 18 April, 24 October 1900.

Principal's Review of the Work and Growth of the College, University College of North Wales, Bangor, 1905.

Reports of Heads of Departments, University College of North Wales, Bangor, 1904–18.

Reports on the Work of the Mining Research Laboratory, University of Birmingham, 1921–35.

Reports of the Work of the Department of Oil Engineering and Refining, University of Birmingham, 1926–8.

Graduate Employment, a Report . . . of the Guild of Undergraduates of the University of Birmingham, May 1938.

Reports of the University of Bradford, 1967–9.

Reports of the Cambridge University Appointments Board, 1899–1967.

University Education and Business, Report by a Committee appointed by the Cambridge University Appointments Board (Cambridge, 1946).

Reports of the Principal, University College of South Wales and Monmouthshire, Cardiff, 1897–1939.

Reports of the Principal, Dundee University College, 1883–1915.

Reports of Durham College of Science and Armstrong College, 1895–1918.

Reports of the Department of Economics, Armstrong College, Durham, 1912–14.

The University of Durham Department of Science, Record for the Period 1924–34.

Reports of Armstrong College Standing Committee for Research, Durham, 1927–37.

Reports of Heriot-Watt University, Edinburgh, 1966–8.

Reports of the University of Essex, 1964–6.

Annual Reports of the University College of the South West of England, Exeter, 1922–38.

Report of the Faculty of Arts . . . instituting a new group of Economic and Political Science, University of Glasgow, 1897.

Minutes of the University of Glasgow General Council, 1901–11.

Reports of the University of Kent, 1966–70.

Reports of the University of Lancaster, 1965–9.

Report of the Committee appointed to investigate . . . the best means to be adopted for the establishment of a Yorkshire College of Science (Leeds, 1872).

Yorkshire College of Science, Leeds, Report of the Inauguration, 1875.

Annual Reports of Leeds University, 1914–18.

Reports of the Department of Leather Industries, University of Leeds, 1903–35.

Reports of the Department of Textile Industries, University of Leeds, 1888–91, 1903–13.

Report of the Livesey Professor, Department of Coal Gas and Fuel Industries, University of Leeds, 1912–13.

Leeds University Appointments Board, Report on the First Ten Years Work of the Board, 1931.

Liverpool University Annual Reports, 1922–39.

Annual Reports of Imperial College, London, 1908–19.

Annual Reports of King's College, London, 1880–1913, 1928–39.

Annual Reports of University College, London, 1880–1918, 1931–45.

University College, London, Committee Minutes, 1915–18.

University College, London, Union, a Report on the Employment Survey, 1949.

University of London Appointments Board, Reports and Minutes, 1909–14, 1931–39.

Reports of the City University, (London) 1966–8.

Reports of Loughborough University, 1967–9.

Reports of Council, University of Manchester, 1891–1913.

Report on the War Work of the Manchester Municipal College of Technology, 1920.

Report on the Extension of Scientific Research in Manchester University, particularly in Relation to the Industries of its Area (Manchester, 1944).

University of Manchester, Quinquennial Survey of Graduates' Appointments 1949–54.

Women in Engineering: Report by a Committee . . . Manchester College of Science and Technology (Manchester, 1958).

Reports of the Committee for Economics, Oxford, 1904–14.

Reports of the Engineering and Mining Subjects Committee, Oxford University, 1905–12.

Report of a Committee on the Proposed Degree in Economics, Oxford, 1915.

Report of Somerville College (Oxford) Students Association, 1917.

Reports of Oxford University Appointments Committee, 1906–14, 1920–39.

Reports of the University of Salford, 1965–8.

Reports to the Steel Research Committee, University of Sheffield, 1907–10.

Reports . . . Mining and Fuel Technology, University of Sheffield, 1928–37.

Reports of the Research Department for the Cold Working of Steel, University of Sheffield, 1932–6.

Reports of Southampton University College, 1901–45.

Reports of the University of Strathclyde 1966–8.

Reports of Surrey University, 1966–8.

Reports of the Appointments Board, University of Wales, 1914–15, 1923–38.

Reports of the University of Warwick, 1965–8.

Reports of the University of York, 1963–8.

Other bodies (issued in London, unless otherwise indicated)

Anglo-American Council on Productivity, *Report on Universities and Industry*, 1951.

Association of British Chambers of Commerce, *Report on the Commercial Employment of Students with Degrees in Commerce*, January 1939.

Association for Education in Industry and Commerce, *Report on Education for Higher Positions in Commerce*, October 1929.

Association for Education in Industry and Commerce, *Report on Education for Management*, May 1928.

Association for Education in Industry and Commerce, *Young Men in Industry and Commerce, Report of the Conference at Liverpool*, 1930.

Association for Education in Industry and Commerce, *Training in Industry, a Report* . . . (ed.) R. W. Ferguson, 1935.

Association of Scientific Workers, *Science in the Universities; Report to the UGC* (Oxford, 1944).

British Association for the Advancement of Science, *Report on Methods of Economic Training in this and other Countries*, 1894.

British Business Schools, a Report by Rt. Hon. Lord Franks (British Institute of Management, 1963).

British Federation of University Women, *Annual Reports*, 1930–9.

Committee of Vice-Chancellors . . . and the CBI, *Industry and the Universities, aspects of Interdependence*, 1965.

Committee of Vice-Chancellors and Principals of the UK, *Report on the Quinquennium 1962–7*, 1967.

Conference of the Universities of Great Britain and Northern Ireland, *University Graduates in Commerce and Industry*, 1948.

Conference of the Universities of the United Kingdom, *Relations between the Universities and Industry*, 1962.

Congresses of the Universities of the British Empire, *Reports of the Proceedings*: 1912, 1921, 1926, 1931, 1936.

Cosslett, V. E., *The Relations between Scientific Research in the Universities and Industrial Research, a Report on Conditions in Great Britain* (AUT, 1955).

FBI, *The Education and Training of Graduate Staff for Industrial Research*, 1955.

FBI, *Report of the Conference on Industry and the Universities*, 1949.

FBI, *Report of the Nottingham Conference on Industry and the Universities*, 1953.

FBI, *Report of the Oxford Conference on Industry, the Universities and the Technical Colleges*, 1950.

FBI, *Report of the Universities and Industry Conference*, 1953.

Home Universities Conference, *The Financing of Research in Universities by Outside Bodies*, 1955.

Home Universities Conference, *New Universities*, 1960.

Institute of Physics and the Physical Society, *Report of Working Party on Industry and the Physics Ph.D.: an Interim Report*, 1969.

Joint University Council for Social Studies, *Social Study and Training at the Universities*, a Report, 1918.

Launder, B. E. and Webster, G. E., *University Research and the Considerations affecting its Commercial Exploitation, a Survey of Six Departments at Imperial College*, January 1969 (Technical Development Capital Ltd, 1969).

LCC Technical Education Board, *Report of the Special Subcommittee on Commercial Education*, 1899.

LCC Technical Education Board, *Report of the Special Subcommittee on the Application of Science to Industry*, 1902.

Manchester Joint Research Council, *Industry and Science, a study . . .* (Manchester, 1954).

National Union of Students, *Graduate Employment*, a Report of the 1937 Congress, 1937.

Neglect of Science Conference, *Report of the Proceedings*, 1916.

Royal Institute of Chemistry, *Report of the Committee of Enquiry into the Relationship between University Courses in Chemistry and the Needs of Industry* (Eaborn), 1970.

Report of an Inquiry into the Relationship of Technical Education to other forms of Education and to Industry and Commerce (Lord Emmott) (Association of Teachers in Technical Institutions, 1927).

Industry, Science and Universities, Report of a Working Party . . . to the Universities and Industry Joint Committee (Docksey) (Confederation of British Industry, 1970).

Biography and memoir

Allen, B. M., *William Garnett, a Memoir* (Cambridge, 1933).

Amery, Julian, *Life of Joseph Chamberlain*, vol. IV (London, 1951).

Armstrong, Henry E., *James Dewar, 1842–1923* (London, 1924).

Ashley, Anne, *William James Ashley: a Life* (London, 1932).

Atlay, J. B., *Sir Henry Wentworth Acland, Bart., a Memoir* (London, 1903).

Bates, L. F., *Sir Alfred Ewing, a Pioneer in Physics and Engineering* (London, 1946).

Birkenhead, Earl of, *The Prof. in Two Worlds* (London, 1961).

Birks, J. B., *Rutherford at Manchester* (London, 1962).

Brodetsky, Selig, *Memoirs* (London, 1960).

Bunce, J. T., *Josiah Mason, a Biography* (London, 1890).

Campbell, L., and Garnett, William, *The Life of James Clerk Maxwell* (London, 1882).

Clark, Ronald W., *Tizard* (London, 1965).

Constable, Thomas, *Memoir of Lewis D. B. Gordon* (Edinburgh, 1877).

Davies, W. E., *Sir Hugh Owen, his Life and Work* (London, 1885).

Draper, W. H., *Sir Nathan Bodington* (London, 1912).

Ewing, A. W., *The Man of Room 40, the Life of Sir Alfred Ewing* (London, 1939).

Fleming, Sir Ambrose, *Memoirs of a Scientific Life* (London, 1934).

Gibson, A. H., *Osborne Reynolds and his Work in Hydraulics and Hydrodynamics* (London, 1946).

Haldane, R. B., *An Autobiography* (London, 1929).

Heilbron, Sir Ian, *The Life and Work of George Gerald Henderson* (London, 1947).

Henderson, Sir James, *MacQuorn Rankine* (Glasgow, 1932).

Henriques, Robert, *Sir Robert Waley Cohen* (London, 1966).

Hodgson, Stuart, *Ramsay Muir, an Autobiography and Some Essays* (London, 1943).

Jenkin, Fleeming, *The Papers of Fleeming Jenkin*. 2 vols incl. 'Memoir' by R. L. Stevenson (London, 1887).

Jones, K. V., *Life of John Viriamu Jones* (London, 1915).

Knott, C. G., *The Life and Scientific Work of Peter Guthrie Tait* (Cambridge, 1911).

Larmor, Joseph, (ed.), *Memoir and Correspondence of the late Sir George Gabriel Stokes* (Cambridge, 1907).

Lloyd, Sir John, *Sir Harry Reichel 1856–1931* (Cardiff, 1934).

Lodge, Sir Oliver, *Past Years, an Autobiography* (London, 1931).

Marshall, Mary Paley, *What I Remember* (Cambridge, 1947).

Messenger, Rosalind, *The Doors of Opportunity, a biography of Dame Caroline Haslett* (London, 1967).

Owen, H. I. and Owen, H. I., *Sir Isambard Owen, a Biography* (Caernarvon, 1963).

Percy, Lord Eustace, *Some Memories* (London, 1958).

Pigou, A. C. (ed.), *Memorials of Alfred Marshall* (London, 1925).

Rankine, W. J. MacQuorn, *Miscellaneous Scientific Papers*, incl. 'Memoir' by P. G. Tait (London, 1881).

Redmayne, Sir Richard, *Men, Mines and Memories* (London, 1942).

Roscoe, Sir Henry, *The Life and Experiences of Sir Henry Enfield Roscoe* (London, 1906).
Strutt, R. J., *John William Strutt, Third Baron Rayleigh* (London, 1924).
Stuart, James, *Reminiscences* (London, 1912).
Thompson, Silvanus P., *The Life of William Thomson, Baron Kelvin of Largs*, 2 vols (London, 1910).
Thompson, Ruth D'Arcy, *D'Arcy Wentworth Thompson, the Scholar Naturalist, 1860–1948* (Oxford, 1958).
Thomson, Sir Joseph J. *Recollections and Reflections* (London, 1936).
Tilden, Sir William, *Sir William Ramsay, KCB, FRS* (London, 1918).
Williams, David, *Thomas Francis Roberts 1860–1919* (Cardiff, 1961).
Wilson, J. A., *Memoir of George Wilson* (Edinburgh, 1860).

Books, pamphlets, etc.

'John Adamson', *Birmingham University and Commerce* (private circulation, 1901) (copy in Birmingham University Library).
Alsop, James W., *A New University* (Liverpool, 1903).
Anderson, C. A. and Schnaper, Miriam, *School and Society in England, Social Backgrounds of Oxford and Cambridge Students* (Annals of American Research, Public Affairs Press, Washington, 1952).
Anderson, P. J., *Studies in the History and Development of the University of Aberdeen* (Aberdeen, 1906).
Armytage, W. H. G., *Civic Universities* (London, 1965).
Ashby, Sir Eric, *Technology and the Academics* (London, 1959).
Ashley, William J. *Commercial Education* (London, 1926).
Ashley, William J., *The Faculty of Commerce in the University of Birmingham, its Purpose and Programme* (Birmingham, 1902).
Barker, Sir Ernest, *Universities in Great Britain, their Position and their Problems* (London, 1931).
Bellot, H. Hale, *University College, London, 1826–1926* (London, 1929).
Beloff, Michael, *The Plateglass Universities* (London, 1968).
Beveridge, Janet, *An Epic of Clare Market, Birth and Early Days of the London School of Economics* (London, 1960).
Beveridge, Lord, *The London School of Economics and its Problems, 1919–1937* (London, 1960).
Bill, E. G. W. and Mason, J. F. A., *Christ Church and Reform 1850–1867* (Oxford, 1970).
Bowen, E. J., and Hartley, H., *Chemistry at Oxford* (Cambridge, 1966).
Bowie, James A., *Education for Business Management* (Oxford, 1930).
Brittain, Vera, *The Women at Oxford* (London, 1960).
Brosan G., (ed.), *Patterns and Policies in Higher Education* (London, 1971).
Brown, E. J., *The Private Donor in the History of the University of Leeds* (Leeds, 1953).
Brown, J. C., *The First Page of the History of University College, Liverpool* (Liverpool, 1892).
Bullock, James Malcolm, *A History of the University of Aberdeen, 1495–1895* (London, 1895).
Burns, C. Delisle, *A Short History of Birkbeck College* (London, 1924).
Bury, Patrick, *Corpus Christi College, Cambridge, A History 1822–1952* (Cambridge, 1952).

Caine, Sir Sydney, *The History of the Foundation of the London School of Economics and Political Science* (London, 1963).

The Campden Research Station (Bristol, 1937) (copy in Bristol University Library).

Cant, R. G., *The University of St. Andrews, a Short History* (Edinburgh, 1946).

Carnelley, Thomas, *Introductory Lecture on the Occasion of the Opening of the New Dye House and Technical Museum of the Chemical Department of University College Dundee* (Aberdeen, 1889).

Carnelley, Thomas, *The True Place of Chemistry in the University Curriculum* (Aberdeen, 1889).

Carus Wilson, Eleanora, *Westfield College 1882–1932* (London, 1932).

A History of the Cavendish Laboratory 1871–1910 (London, 1910).

Chapman, A. W., *The Story of a Modern University: the History of the University of Sheffield* (Oxford, 1955).

Charlton, H. B., *Portrait of a University, 1851–1951* (Manchester, 1951).

Childs, W. M., *Making a University, an Account of the University Movement at Reading* (London, 1933).

Clark, Ronald W., *The Birth of the Bomb* (London, 1961).

Clark, Ronald W., *The Rise of the Boffins* (London, 1962).

Clement, A. G., and Robertson, R. H. S., *Scotland's Scientific Heritage* (Edinburgh, 1961).

Collin, Audrey, Rees, Anthony, M., and Utting, John, *The Arts Graduate in Industry* (Acton Society Trust, London, 1962).

The Colston Research Society for the Promotion of Research in the University of Bristol (1929) (copy in Bristol University Library).

Cottle, Basil, and Sherborne, J. W., *The Life of a University* (Bristol, 1959).

Coutts, James, *A History of the University of Glasgow* (Glasgow, 1909).

Craig, Christine, *The Employment of Cambridge Graduates* (Cambridge, 1963).

Crawford, H. J., *Appointments and Careers for Graduates and Students* (University of London Appointments Board, London, 1934).

Crosskey, Henry W., 'A Plea for a Midland University' (reprinted from *Proceedings of the Birmingham Philosophical Society*, 10 February 1889) (copy in Birmingham University Library).

Crowther, J. C. and Whiddington, R., *Science at War* (DSIR, HMSO, London, 1947).

Daiches, David, *The Idea of a New University: an Experiment in Sussex* (London, 1964).

Darroch, Alexander, *The Place and Function of the Scottish Universities in our Educational System* (Edinburgh, 1905).

Davie, G. E., *The Democratic Intellect: Scotland and her Universities in the Nineteenth Century* (Edinburgh, 1961).

Davies, W. C. and Jones, W. L., *The University of Wales* (London, 1905).

Davis, H. W. C., *A History of Balliol College, Oxford* (Oxford, 1963).

Davis, Mary, Employment for Women (University of Wales Appointments Board, Cardiff, *c.* 1923).

Dent, H. C., *Education in Transition* (London, 1944).

Dent, H. C., *Universities in Transition* (London, 1961).

Dumbell, S., *The University of Liverpool 1903–53* (Liverpool, 1953).

Dunsheath, Percy, *The Graduate in Industry* (London, 1947).

Dyer, Henry, *A Modern University, with Special Reference to the Require-ments of Science* (Perth, 1889).

Ellis, T. I., *The Development of Higher Education in Wales* (Wrexham, 1935).

Ellis, T. I. (ed.), *Thomas Charles Edwards' Letters* (National Library of Wales, Journal Supplement, series III, no. 3, 1952).

Evans, D. Emrys, *The University of Wales, a Historical Sketch* (Cardiff, 1953).

Fiddes, Edward, *Chapters in the History of Owens College and of Man-chester University, 1851–1914* (Manchester, 1937).

Findlay, Alexander, *The Teaching of Chemistry in the Universities of Aberdeen* (Aberdeen, 1935).

Findlay, Alexander, *The Training of Chemists a National Duty* (n.d., c. 1916) (copy in University College, Aberystwyth, Library).

Firth, Sir Charles, *Modern Languages at Oxford, 1724–1929* (London, 1929).

Fisher, H. A. L., *The Place of the University in National Life* (Oxford, 1919).

Flexner, Abraham, *Universities: American, English, German* (London, 1931).

Fowler, J. T., *Durham University. Earlier Foundations and Present Colleges* (London, 1904).

Fulton, Sir John, *Experiment in Higher Education* (London, 1965).

Gallie, W. B., *A New University: A. D. Lindsay and the Keele Experiment* (London, 1960).

Gatty, William, *The Gatty Marine Laboratory . . . in the University of St. Andrews* (Dundee, 1896).

Giles, C. W. Scott, *Sidney Sussex College, a Short History* (Cambridge 1951).

Glazebrook, Sir Richard, *Science and Industry, the Place of Cambridge in any Scheme for their Combination* (Cambridge, 1917).

Godwin, George, *Queen Mary College, an Adventure in Education* (London, 1939).

Gotch, Francis, 'Bristol and West of England University' (reprinted from *Bristol Times and Mirror*, 2 October 1907) (copy in Bristol University Library).

Gowing, Margaret, *Britain and Atomic Energy, 1939–45* (London, 1964).

Graduate Employment (PEP, London, 1956).

Graduates in Industry (PEP, London, 1957).

Gray, A. F. and Brittain, F., *A History of Jesus College, Cambridge* (London, 1960).

Gunther, R. T., *A History of the Daubeny Laboratory, Magdalen College, Oxford* (Oxford, 1904).

Haldane, R. B., *A University for the West of England* (an address to the Bristol University College Colston Society, 5 February 1902) (copy in Bristol University Library).

Haldane, R. B., *Universities and National Life* (London, 1910).

Hamilton, M. A., *Newnham, an Informal Biography* (London, 1936).

The Hartley Institution and its Proposed Extension as a Local University College (Southampton, 1887).

Hartog, P. J., *The Owens College, Manchester* (Manchester, 1900).

Hearnshaw, J. F. C., *The Centenary History of King's College, London, 1828–1928* (London, 1929).

Herkless, W. R., *Scottish University Reform* (Glasgow, 1884).

Herklots, H. G. G., *The New Universities* (London, 1928).

Hetherington, Sir Hector, *The University College at Exeter, 1920–25* (Exeter, 1963).

Hilken, T. J. N., *Engineering at Cambridge University, 1783–1965* (Cambridge, 1967).

Hodgkin, R. H., *Six Centuries of an Oxford College* (Oxford, 1949).

Horn, D. B., *A Short History of the University of Edinburgh 1556–1889* (Edinburgh, 1967).

Hubback, Judith, *Wives who Went to College* (London, 1957).

Hughes, Thomas, *Tom Brown at Oxford* (London, 1869).

Hutchings, Donald, *The Science Undergraduate: a Study of Science Students at Five English Universities* (Oxford, 1967).

Hutchison, T. W., *A Review of Economic Doctrines 1870–1929* (Oxford, 1953).

Huxley, T. H., *Collected Essays*, vol. III, *Science and Education* (London, 1902).

Industry and Education, a Statement (Nuffield College, Oxford 1943); (copy in AUT Office file 107).

Irvine, Sir James C., *The Chair of Chemistry in the United College of St. Salvator and St. Leonard* (Edinburgh, 1941).

James, Edmund J., *The Education of Businessmen in Europe, a Report to the American Bankers Association* (New York, 1893).

Jenkin, C. F., *Engineering Science, an Inaugural Lecture* (Oxford, 1908).

Jones, J. Viriamu, *Prifysgol Cymru* (Cardiff, 1896).

Kearney, Hugh, *Scholars and Gentlemen, Universities and Society in Pre-Industrial Britain 1500–1700* (London, 1970).

Kent, Andrew, *An Eighteenth Century Lectureship in Chemistry* (Glasgow, 1950).

Kidd, Harry, *The Trouble at L.S.E., 1966–67*, (Oxford, 1969).

Kneller, George F., *Higher Learning in Britain* (Cambridge and Berkeley, 1955).

Knight, W., *Early Chapters in the History of the University of St. Andrews and Dundee* (Dundee, 1902).

Kotschnig, W. M., *Unemployment in the Learned Professions* (Oxford, 1937).

Kotschnig, W. M. and Prys, E., *The University in a Changing World* (Oxford, 1932).

Lane, A. G., *The History of Armstrong College* (Newcastle on Tyne, 1907).

Lapworth, Charles, *The Mason College and Technical Education* (Birmingham, 1884).

Lawlor, John (ed.), *The New University* (London, 1968).

Layard, Richard, King, John and Moser, Claus, *The Impact of Robbins* (London, 1969).

Lees Smith, H. B., A Chair of Commerce in Connection with the University of Bristol, an Address (1909) (copy in Bristol University Library).

Logan, Sir Douglas, *Haldane and the University of London* (London, 1960).

McCarthy, M. C., *The Employment of Highly Specialised Graduates, a*

Comparative Study in the U.K. and the U.S.A. (Science Policy Studies no. 3, HMSO, London, 1968).

MacGregor, J. G., *Research in the Scottish Universities* (Edinburgh, 1901).

Mackay, D. I., *Geographical Mobility and the Brain Drain* (London, 1969).

Mackay, J. M., *A New University* (Liverpool, 1914).

Mackay, R. J., (ed.), *Business and Science, Collected Papers to the Department of Industrial Co-operation at the Centenary Meeting of the British Association* (London, 1931).

Mackie, J. D., *The University of Glasgow 1451–1951* (Glasgow, 1954).

McPherson, R. G., *Theory of Higher Education in Nineteenth Century England* (University of Georgia Monographs, no. 4, 1959).

Mallett, C. E., *A History of the University of Oxford*, vol. III, *Modern Oxford* (London, 1927).

Manchester Municipal College of Technology Jubilee 1902–52 (Manchester, 1952).

Marshall, Alfred, *The New Cambridge Curriculum in Economics . . . its Purpose and Plan* (London, 1903).

Marshall, Alfred, A Plea for the Creation of a Curriculum in Economics and Associated Branches of Political Science (1902) (Cambridge University Library, Cam. c. 902.5).

Martin, Hugh, *The Life of a Modern University* (London, 1930).

Meelboom, J. A., *Commercial Education, a Review and Some Criticisms* (London, 1899).

Melville, Sir Harry, *The Department of Scientific and Industrial Research* (London, 1962).

Mill, J. S., *Inaugural Address delivered to the University of St. Andrews* (London, 1867).

Miller, Edward, *Portrait of a College, a History of the College of St. John the Evangelist in Cambridge* (Cambridge, 1961).

A Miscellany Presented to John Macdonald Mackay (Liverpool, 1914).

Morgan, Alexander, *Scottish University Studies* (Oxford, 1933).

Morgan, I. (ed.), *The College by the Sea* (Students Representative Council and the College Council, Aberystwyth, 1928).

Muir, Ramsay, *The Plea for a Liverpool University* (Liverpool, 1901).

Muir, Ramsay, *The University of Liverpool: Its Present State* (Liverpool, 1907).

Murray, David, *Memories of the Old College of Glasgow* (Glasgow, 1927).

Murray, John, *The War and the College* (Exeter, 1943).

Musgrave, P. W., *Technical Change, the Labour Force and Education* (Oxford, 1967).

Neilson, J. B., *Fortuna Domus* (Glasgow, 1952).

Newman, J. H., *Discourses on the Scope and Nature of University Education* (Dublin, 1852).

Nicholas, Thomas, *Middle and High Schools and a University for Wales* (London, 1863).

The North Wales College, History of the College Movement . . . and the Claims of Bangor (Bangor, 1883).

Nuffield College, the Problem Facing British Universities (Oxford, 1948).

Nussey, G. H. and Nussey, A., *A Technical Institution for Leeds and District* (Leeds, 1867).

The Obligation of Universities to the Social Order (New York University Press, New York, 1933).

Owen, Sir Isambard, *The Significance of a University* (Bristol, 1909).

The Owens College, Substance of the Report . . . on the General Character and Plan of the College (Manchester, 1850).

Parker, H. M. D. *Manpower, a Study in Wartime Policy and Administration*, Official History of the Second World War (HMSO, London, 1957).

Parry, H. Lloyd, *History of the Royal Albert Memorial University College, Exeter* (1911 ?) (copy in Exeter University Library).

Patterson, A. Temple, *The University of Southampton* (Southampton, 1962).

Penson, T. H., *A Plea for Greater Recognition of Economics at Oxford* (1920) (in Bodleian Library, GA Oxon b 141 (133)).

Percival, J., *The Connection of the Universities and the Great Towns* (London, 1873).

Percival, J., *Firth College and its Future Work* (Sheffield, 1882) (copy in Sheffield City Library).

Perkin, Harold, *Key Profession: the History of the Association of University Teachers* (London, 1969).

Perkin, Harold, *New Universities in the United Kingdom* (OECD, 1969).

Photoelasticity at University College London . . . the Work of E. G. Coker and L. N. G. Filon 1909–1937 (London, 1959).

The Physical Laboratories of the University of Manchester, a Record of 25 Years Work (Manchester, 1906).

Postan, M. M., Hay, D. and Scott, J. D. *The Design and Development of Weapons*, Official History of the Second World War (HMSO, London, 1964).

Powell, M. J., *Royal Holloway College, 1887–1937* (London?, 1937?).

Poynting, J. H., *University Training in our Provincial Colleges* (Birmingham, 1883) (copy in Birmingham University Library).

Price, L. L., *The Present Position of Economic Study in Oxford* (1902) (copy in Bodleian Library, GA Oxon c. 104 (159)).

Pryme, George, *A Syllabus of a Course of Lectures on the Principles of Political Economy* (Cambridge, 1859, 4th ed.).

Purdie, T., *The Relations of Science to University Teaching in Scotland* (St Andrews, 1885).

Rashdall, Rev. H., *The Universities of Europe in the Middle Ages*, vol. II, pt. II (Oxford, 1895).

Redmayne, R. A. S., *The Mining Department of the University of Birmingham* (London, 1905).

Roach, J. P. C., 'The University of Cambridge', *Victoria County History o, Cambridgeshire*, vol. III (Oxford, 1959).

Robbins, Lord, *The University in the Modern World* (London, 1966).

Roberts, H. A., *Careers for University Men* (Cambridge, 1914).

Robertson, Sir Charles Grant, *The British Universities* (London, 1930, 1944).

Ross, Murray, *New Universities in the Modern World* (London, 1966).

Rothblatt, Sheldon, *The Revolt of the Dons, Cambridge and Society in Victorian England* (London, 1968).

The Royal Charter of the Imperial College of Science and Technology Jubilee 1907–57 (London, 1957).

Rudd, Ernest and Hatch, Stephen, *Graduate Study and After* (London, 1968).

Seear, Nancy, Roberts, Veronica and Brock, John, *A Career for Women in Industry?* (London, 1964).

Seeley, J. R., *A Midland University* (Birmingham, 1887).

Seward, A. C. (ed.), *Science and the Nation, Essays by Cambridge Graduates* (Cambridge, 1917).

Shadwell, Arthur, *Industrial Efficiency, a Comparative Study of Industrial Life in England, Germany and America* (London, 1906).

Shimmin, A. N., *The University of Leeds, the First Half Century* (Cambridge, 1954).

Sidgwick, Henry, *The Scope and Method of Economic Science, an Address to the Economic Science and Statistics Section of the British Association at Aberdeen* (London, 1885).

Sidgwick, N. V., *The Chemistry Department, University College Dundee 1883–1950* (Dundee, 1950).

Simmons, Jack, *New University* (Leicester, 1958).

Simon, Brian, *A Student's View of the Universities* (London, 1943).

Simpson, W. Douglas, *The Fusion of 1860 . . . a History of the United University of Aberdeen 1860–1960* (Edinburgh, 1963).

Sloman, Albert E., *A University in the Making* (London, 1964).

Smith, B. M. D., *Education for Management, its Conception and Implementation in the Faculty of Commerce at Birmingham* (University of Birmingham Faculty of Commerce Occasional Paper no. 5, 1965).

Smithells, Arthur, *From a Modern University* (Oxford, 1921).

Sparrow, John, *Mark Pattison and the Idea of a University* (Cambridge, 1967).

Spencer, Herbert, 'What Knowledge is of Most Worth?' (1859), reprinted in F. A. Cavenagh, *Spencer on Education* (Cambridge, 1932).

Stephen, Barbara, *Girton College, 1869–1932* (Cambridge, 1933).

Strachey, Ray, *Careers and Openings for Women* (London, 1935).

Taylor, Frank H., *The Need of Educated Men in Industrial Affairs* (1911) (copy in Cambridge University Library, Cam. c. 911. 5.).

Thompson, E. P., *Warwick University Ltd.* (London, 1970).

Thompson, Joseph, *The Owens College, its Foundation and Growth* (Manchester, 1886).

Travers, Morris W., *A Contribution to the Study of the University Problem setting forth the need for the Establishment of a University in Bristol* (Bristol, 1906).

Trow, A. H., *Inaugural Address* (Cardiff, 1919).

Trow, A. H. and Brown, D. J. A., *The University College of South Wales and Monmouthshire 1883–1933, a Short History of the College* (Cardiff, 1933).

Turner, A. Logan, *History of the University of Edinburgh 1883–1933* (Edinburgh, 1933).

University College and the University of Liverpool 1882–1907, a brief record of Work and Progress (Liverpool, 1907).

University College, London, Centenary Addresses (London, 1927).

University College of Wales, Aberystwyth, an Outline History 1872–1947 (Cardiff, 1947).

The University of Birmingham and the Study of Metals (c. 1920) (copy in Birmingham University Library).

University of Bristol and the National Fruit and Cider Institute (1935) (copy in Bristol University Library).

The University of Glasgow, its Position and Wants (Glasgow, 1900).

The University of Liverpool 1903–1928, a brief record of Work and Progress (Liverpool, 1928).

Vig, Norman J., *Science and Technology in British Politics* (Oxford, 1968).

Vincent, E. W., and Hinton, P., *The University of Birmingham, its History and Significance* (Birmingham, 1947).

Walters, Gerald, *A Technological University, an Experiment in Bath* (Bath, 1966).

Ward, W. R., *Victorian Oxford* (London, 1965).

Webb, Sidney, *London Education* (London, 1904).

Whiting, C. E., *The University of Durham, 1832–1932* (London, 1932).

Williams, B. T., *The Desirableness of a University for Wales* (London and Carmarthen, 1853).

Williams, E. C., *The Aims and Future Work of the Ramsay Memorial Laboratory of Chemical Engineering* (1924) (copy in University College, London, Library).

Wilson, George, *The Industrial Museum of Scotland in its Relation to Commercial Enterprise* (Edinburgh, 1858).

Winstanley, D. A., *Early Victorian Cambridge* (Cambridge, 1940, 1955).

Winstanley, D. A., *Later Victorian Cambridge* (Cambridge, 1947).

Wood, A. C., *A History of the University College, Nottingham, 1881–1948,* (Oxford, 1953).

Woodyard, E. Maud *Careers for Women in Advertising* (London, 1932).

The Yorkshire College, Leeds (London, 1895) (reprinted from *The Record of Technical and Secondary Education* Oct., 1895) (copy in Leeds City Library).

Articles and journals

Anderson, C. Arnold, 'The Social Composition of University Student Bodies, the Recruitment of Nineteenth Century Elites in Four Nations: an Historical Case Study', *The Year Book of Education* (London, 1959).

Ashley, William, 'The Enlargement of Economics', *Economic Journal,* 1908.

Biographical Memoirs of Fellows of the Royal Society (Royal Society, London) A. M. Tyndall, 1962, Vol. 8, pp. 159–64; Morris William Travers, 1963, Vol. 9, pp. 301–11; W. S. Turner, 1964, Vol. 10, pp. 325–32; Thomas Percy Hilditch, 1966, Vol. 12 pp. 259–75.

Blair, R., 'The Relation of Science to Industry and Commerce', *Nature.* 15 September 1910.

'Business Careers for Undergraduates', *Oxford Magazine*, January 1930.

Cardwell, D. S. L., 'The Development of Scientific Research in Modern Universities: a Comparative Study of Motives and Opportunities', in A. C. Crombie (ed.), *Scientific Change* (London, 1963).

Clark, G. N. 'Social Studies at Oxford', *The American Oxonian*, July 1934.

Clayton, R. H., 'Training Leaders for Industry' *Memoirs and Proceedings of the Manchester Literary and Philosophical Society*, vol. LXXXII, 1937–8.

Coats, A. W., 'Alfred Marshall and the Early Development of the London School of Economics, Some Unpublished Letters', *Economica*, vol. 34, November 1967.

Coats, A. W., 'J. E. Symes, Henry George and Academic Freedom in Nottingham during the 1880's', *Renaissance and Modern Studies*, vol. VII, 1963.

Coats, A. W., 'The Origins and Early Development of the Royal Economic Society', *Economic Journal*, June 1968.

Coats, A. W., 'Sociological Aspects of British Economic Thought 1880–1930', *Journal of Political Economy*, October 1967.

Coats, A. W., 'The Social Composition of the Royal Economic Society and the Beginnings of the British Economics "Profession" 1890–1915', *British Journal of Sociology*, March 1970.

Cormack, J. D., 'Technical Education in the University of London', *Engineering*, 31 October 1902.

Dale, Sir Alfred, 'Liverpool University's Contribution to Victory', *Liverpool Courier*, 23 September 1919.

Gillespie, Charles C. 'English Ideas of the University in the Nineteenth Century', in Margaret Clapp (ed.), *The Modern University* (Cornell University Press, 1950).

Glass, D. V. and Gray, J. L., 'Opportunity and the Older Universities' in Lancelot Hogben (ed.), *Political Arithmetic* (London, 1938).

Greenwood, Major, 'The Social Distribution of University Education', *Journal of the Royal Statistical Society*, vol. CII, 1939.

Greenwood, Major, 'University Education: its Recent History and Function', *Journal of the Royal Statistical Society*, vol. XCVIII, 1935.

Hall, R. L., 'Economics in Oxford', *Oxford Magazine*, 27 January 1938.

Hayek, F. A., 'The London School of Economics 1895–1945', *Economica*, vol. XIII, 1946.

Heathcote, Henry L., 'The University Training of Industrial Chemists', *Journal of the Society of the Chemical Industry*, 27 February 1909.

Hewins, W. A. S., 'The Teaching of Economics', *Journal of the Society of Arts*, 4 December 1896.

Irvine, J. C., 'The Work of St. Andrews University Chemical Laboratory during the War', *The Citizen*, 19 February 1921.

Jenkins, Hester and Jones, D. Caradog, 'Social Class of Cambridge University Alumni of the Eighteenth and Nineteenth Centuries', *British Journal of Sociology*, vol. I, 1950.

Joynt, T. A., 'Graduates and Employment', *University of Edinburgh Journal*, Summer 1934.

Knox, T. M., 'Graduates in Business', *Oxford Magazine*, January 1938.

Lodge, Sir Oliver, 'A Modern University', *Nature*, 21 and 28 June 1900.

Louis, Henry, Presidential Address, *Journal of the Society of the Chemical Industry*, vol. XXXVIII, no. 14, July 1919.

Masson, Irvine, 'University Training and Business Posts', *Durham University Journal*, March 1935.

'The Organisation of University Education in the Metropolis', *The Times*, 4 and 8 June 1901.

Perry, John, 'Oxford and Science', *Nature*, 21 December 1903.

'Physics in Oxford during the War: I. Radar', by T. C. Keeley; II. 'Atomic Energy', by F. S. Simon, *Oxford Magazine*, 16 May and 13 June 1946.

Rashdall, H., 'The Functions of a University in a Commercial Centre', *Economic Review*, January 1902.

Roach, J. P. C., 'Victorian Universities and the National Intelligensia' *Victorian Studies*, December 1959.

Roberts, H. A., 'Education in Science as a Preparation for Industrial Work', *Journal of the Royal Society of Arts*, 1 March 1912.

Sanderson, Michael, 'The Universities and Industry in England 1919–1939', *Yorkshire Bulletin of Economic and Social Research*, May 1969.

Sanderson, Michael, 'Research and the Firm in British Industry 1919–1939', *Science Studies*, April 1972.

Sanderson, Michael, 'The University of London and Industrial Progress 1880–1914', *Journal of Contemporary History*, April 1972.

'Science for War, the Work of the Modern Universities', *The Times*, 9 February 1916.

Scott, W. R., 'Report of the Special Committee on University Training in Industrial Administration', *Monthly Journal of the Glasgow Chamber of Commerce and Manufacture*, March 1929.

Shipley, A. E. and Roberts, H. A., 'A Plea for Cambridge', *Quarterly Review*, April 1906.

Stallybrass, W. T. S., 'Oxford in 1914–18', *Oxford*, Winter 1939.

Taylor, F. Sherwood, 'The Teaching of Science at Oxford in the Nineteenth Century', *Annals of Science*, vol. 8, no. 1, March 1952.

Turner, W. E. S., 'The Department of Glass Technology: its Foundation and Work since 1915', *Transactions of the Society of Glass Technology*, vol. XXI, 1937.

'University Prospect' *Economist*, 9, 16, and 23 February 1946.

Watson, Sir David Milne, 'University Men in Commerce and Industry', *Oxford*, Winter 1934.

Floreamus (University of Sheffield).

Glasgow University Magazine.

The Gryphon (Leeds).

Hartley and Southampton University College Magazine.

The Journal of Careers.

Journal of the Royal Institute of Chemistry articles on University Chemistry Departments: 1953, vol. 77, Leeds, Cambridge, Edinburgh, Aberdeen, St Andrews, Glasgow; 1954, vol. 78, Birmingham; 1955, vol. 79, Reading, Swansea, Cardiff, Bedford College, Leicester, Oxford; 1956, vol. 80, Aberystwyth.

Journal of the University of Manchester.

The King's Engineer (King's College, London).

Manchester University Chemical Society Magazine.

Manchester University Magazine.

Newssheet and Review of the British Federation of University Women.

Nonesuch (University of Bristol).

The Northerner (University of Newcastle).

Omnibus (UCNW, Bangor).

Owens College Union Magazine.

Oxford.

The Ram (Exeter University).

St. Andrews Alumnus Chronicle.

The Serpent (Manchester University).

The Student (Edinburgh University).
Time and Tide University Supplements April–October 1935.
The University (National Union of Students).
The University Bulletin (Association of University Teachers).
The University of Liverpool Engineering Society Journal.
University of Liverpool Society Chronicle.
Wessex (Southampton University).
Wessex News (Southampton University).
The Woman Engineer.

Index